CONTENTS

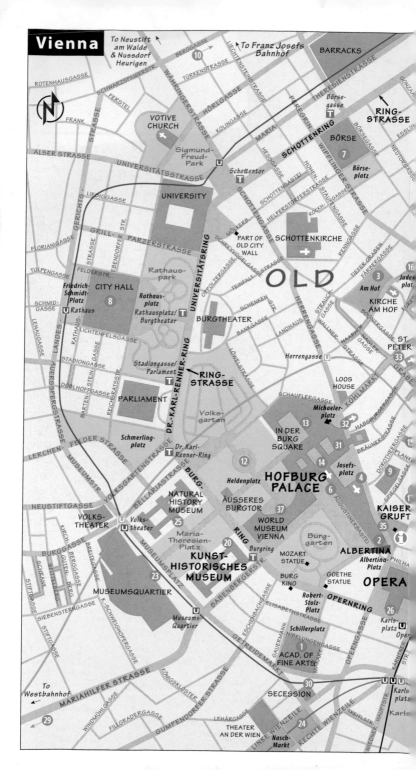

Vienna

To Neustift am Walde & Nussdorf Heurigen

To Franz Josefs Bahnhof

BARRACKS

BEKGGASSE

TÜRKENSTRASSE

10

LIECHTENSTEINSTRASSE

THERESIENGASSE

GONZA

BERGGASSE

ROTENHAUSGASSE

SCHWARZSPANIERSTR

WÄHRINGERSTRASSE

HÖRLGASSE

PFERGRIN

Börse-gasse

RING-STRASSE

BÖRSE

BÖRSEGASSE

ESSLIN

FRANK.

FERSTEL

STRASSE

VOTIVE CHURCH

KOLINGASSE

MARIA

SCHOTTENRING

7

Börse-platz

NEUTORGASSE

ALSER STRASSE

UNIVERSITÄTSSTRASSE

Sigmund-Freud-Park

HESSGASSE

WIPPLINGERSTRASSE

HOHEN-STAUFENGASSE

Schottentor

SCHOTTENRING

SCHOTTENGASSE

HELFERSTORFERSTRASSE

RÖCKH.

SCHOTTENGASSE

UNIVERSITY

PART OF OLD CITY WALL

SCHOTTENKIRCHE

KENIGGASSE

GRILL-PARZERSTRASSE

LIEBIGGASSE

SCHREYVOGELGASSE

MÖLKER-BASTEI

STAUFENGASSE

OLD

TIEFER GRABEN

FÄRBERGASSE

16

Juden-plat

FLORIANIGASSE

GERICHTS-

STRASSE

FELDERSTR

EBENDORFER STR

UNIVERSITÄTSRING

OPPOLZERGASSE

TEINFALT-STR.

STRAUCH-GASSE

3

Am Hof

TULPENGASSE

5TER-STR

CITY HALL

8

Rathaus-park

Rathaus-platz

SCHENKEN-STR.

WALLNER-

KIRCHE AM HOF

BÖGNERGASSE

HAARHOF

NAGLER-GASSE

ST. PETER

SCHMID-GASSE

Friedrich-Schmidt-Platz

U Rathaus

Rathausplatz/Burgtheater

HEKRENGASSE

LANDHAUSGASSE

33

LENAUGASSE

LICHTENFELSGASSE

BURGTHEATER

Herrengasse U

STRAUCH-

KOHLMARKT

GRAB

LANDES-

RATHAUS-

GASSE

LÖWELSTRASSE

LOOS HOUSE

STADIONGASSE

Stadiongasse/Parlament

DR.-KARL-RENNER-RING

BANKGASSE

SCHAUFLERGASSE

Michaeler-platz

32

HABSBURGERGASSE

DÖBLHOFFGASSE

BARTEN-

STEIN-

GASSE

REICHSRATSSTR

PARLIAMENT

RING-STRASSE

Volks-garten

13

IN DER BURG SQUARE

31

BRÄUNERSTRASSE

AUERSPERGSTRASSE

Schmerling-platz

BELLARIASTRASSE

Dr. Karl-Renner-Ring

12

Heldenplatz

14

6

HOFBURG PALACE

Josefs-platz

4

9

DOROTHERGASSE

PLANK.

SPIEGELGASSE

L

FELDER-

STRASSE

LERCHEN-

MUSEUMSTR

VOLKSGARTENSTRASSE

BURG-

NATURAL HISTORY MUSEUM

25

ÄUSSERES BURGTOR

37

WORLD MUSEUM VIENNA

AUGUSTINERBASTEI

KAISER GRUFT

35

NEUSTIFTGASSE

VOLKS-THEATER

U Volks-theater

RING

Maria-Theresien-Platz

Burg-garten

ALBERTINA

Albertina-Platz

2

i

PHILHA

BURGGASSE

KIRCH.

BREITEG.

GUTEN.

BERG.

20

Burgring

MOZART STATUE

GOETHE STATUE

OPERA

KUNST-HISTORISCHES MUSEUM

MUSEUMSPLATZ

23

BABENBERGERSTR.

BURG KINO

Robert-Stolz-Platz

OPERNRING

26

SCHRANK.

STIFTGASSE

SIEBENSTERNGASSE

K.-SCHWEIGHOFERGASSE

MUSEUMSQUARTIER

U Museums-Quartier

ESCHENBACHGASSE

GAUERMANN

NIBELUNGENGASSE

Schillerplatz

OPERNGASSE

Karls-platz

U Oper

KÄRNTNER STR.

ELISABETHSTRASSE

1

ACAD. OF FINE ARTS

30

SECESSION

U U U

Karls-platz

To Westbahnhof

MARIAHILFER STRASSE

WINDMÜHLGASSE

KÖNIGSKLOSTER.

GETREIDEMARKT

LEHÁRGASSE

LINKE WIENZEILE

24

Nasch-Markt

RECHTE WIENZEILE

WIEDNER-HAUPTSTR.

TREITLSTR.

Karls

29

FILLGRADERGASSE

GUMPENDORFER STRASSE

THEATER AN DER WIEN

N

Rick Steves®

VIENNA
SALZBURG & TIROL

MOZART

SIGHTS

1. Academy of Fine Arts (temp. closed)
2. Albertina Museum
3. Am Hof Square
4. Augustinian Church & State Hall
5. To Belvedere Palace & Mus. of Military History
6. Butterfly House
7. Börse (Stock Exchange)
8. City Hall
9. Dorotheum Auction House
10. To Freud Museum
11. Haus der Musik
12. Heldenplatz
13. Hofburg Imperial Apartments
14. Hofburg Treasury & Boys' Choir Chapel
15. Jewish Museum Dorotheergasse
16. Jewish Museum Judenplatz
17. Kaisergruft (Crypt)
18. To Karlskirche
19. To Kunst Haus Wien & Hundertwasserhaus
20. Kunsthistorisches Museum
21. Mozarthaus Vienna Museum
22. Museum of Applied Art (MAK)
23. MuseumsQuartier
24. Naschmarkt
25. Natural History Museum
26. Opera
27. Plague Column
28. To Prater Park
29. To Schönbrunn Palace & Imperial Furniture Collection
30. Secession Building
31. Spanish Riding School
32. St. Michael's Church Crypt
33. St. Peter's Church
34. St. Stephen's Cathedral
35. Theatermuseum (Acad. of Fine Arts)
36. Wien Ticket Pavilion
37. World Museum Vienna

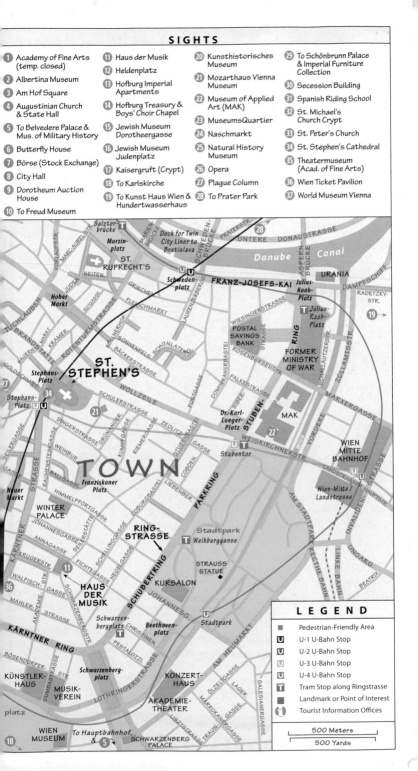

LEGEND

- Pedestrian-Friendly Area
- U-1 U-Bahn Stop
- U-2 U-Bahn Stop
- U-3 U-Bahn Stop
- U-4 U-Bahn Stop
- T Tram Stop along Ringstrasse
- Landmark or Point of Interest
- Tourist Information Offices

500 Meters
500 Yards

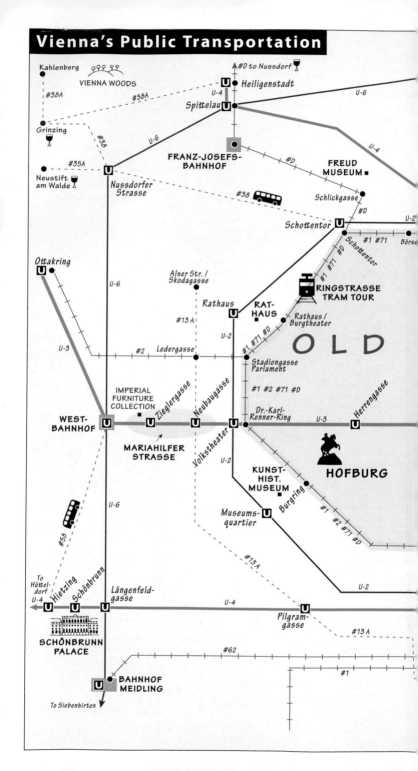

Vienna's Public Transportation

Kahlenberg

VIENNA WOODS

#38A

#35A

Grinzing

#35A

Neustift
am Walde

#35B

Nussdorfer
Strasse

#38

#D to Nussdorf

Heiligenstadt

U-4

Spittelau

U-6

FRANZ-JOSEFS-
BAHNHOF

#D

U-6

FREUD
MUSEUM

Schlickgasse

#D

Schottentor

U-2

#1 #71

Börse

Ottakring

U-6

Alser Str. /
Skodagasse

Rathaus

RAT-
HAUS

Rathaus /
Burgtheater

Schottentor

RINGSTRASSE
TRAM TOUR

O L D

#13 A

U-2

#2 Ledergasse

#1 #71 #D

U-3

Stadiongasse
Parlament

IMPERIAL
FURNITURE
COLLECTION

Zieglergasse

Neubaugasse

#1 #2 #71 #D

WEST-
BAHNHOF

MARIAHILFER
STRASSE

Volkstheater

Dr.-Karl-
Renner-Ring

U-3

Herrengasse

U-2

KUNST-
HIST.
MUSEUM

HOFBURG

#5B

U-6

Museums-
quartier

Burgring

#1 #2 #71 #D

To
Hüttel-
dorf
U-4

Hietzing

Schönbrunn

Längenfeld-
gasse

U-4

Pilgram-
gasse

SCHÖNBRUNN
PALACE

#13 A

U-2

#62

BAHNHOF
MEIDLING

#1

To Siebenhirten

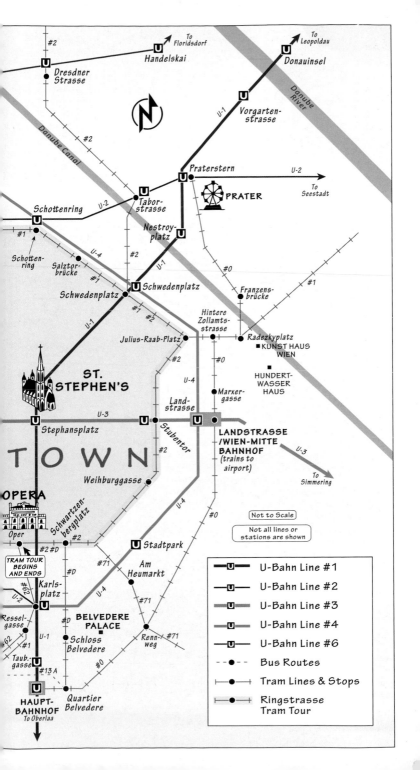

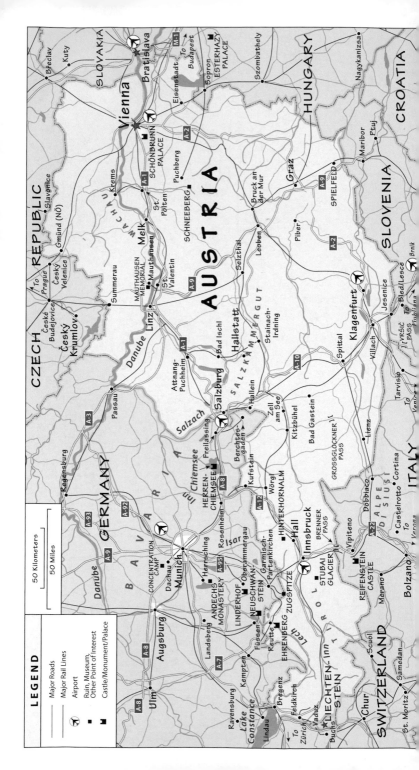

Rick Steves®

VIENNA
SALZBURG & TIROL

Welcome to Rick Steves' Europe

Travel is intensified living—maximum thrills per minute and one of the last great sources of legal adventure. Travel is freedom. It's recess, and we need it.

I discovered a passion for European travel as a teen and have been sharing it ever since—through my tours, public television and radio shows, and travel guidebooks. Over the years, I've taught millions of travelers how to best enjoy Europe's blockbuster sights—and experience "Back Door" discoveries that most tourists miss.

This book offers you a balanced mix of Vienna's elegant big-city sights and its easy-to-reach side trips, both within Austria and beyond. It's selective: Rather than listing dozens of Viennese cafés, I recommend only the best ones. And it's in-depth: My self-guided museum tours and city walks provide insight into Vienna's vibrant history and today's living, breathing culture.

I advocate traveling simply and smartly. Take advantage of my money- and time-saving tips on sightseeing, transportation, and more. Try local, characteristic alternatives to expensive hotels and restaurants. In many ways, spending more money only builds a thicker wall between you and what you traveled so far to see.

We visit Austria to experience it—to become temporary locals. Thoughtful travel engages us with the world, as we learn to appreciate other cultures and new ways to measure quality of life.

Judging by the positive feedback I receive from readers, this book will help you enjoy a fun, affordable, and rewarding vacation—whether it's your first trip or your tenth.

Gute Reise! Happy travels!

Rick Steves

INTRODUCTION

Austria offers alpine scenery, world-class museums, cobbled quaintness, and Wiener schnitzel. Unlike Germany, its industrious neighbor to the northwest, Austria is content to bask in its good living and opulent past as the former head of one of Europe's grandest empires. Austrians are relaxed, gregarious people who love the outdoors as much as a good cup of coffee in a café.

This book focuses on Vienna and all of its cultural offerings, as well as the Danube Valley, Salzburg, Hallstatt (the gem of the Salzkammergut Lake District), and the mountainous Tirol region, including its southern portion over the border in Italy. We also duck into Germany (Berchtesgaden and Bavarian sights) and Slovakia (Bratislava).

I'll give you all the information and opinions necessary to wring the maximum value out of your limited time and money. If you plan two weeks or less in Austria and have a normal appetite for information, this book is all you need.

Experiencing Europe's culture, people, and natural wonders economically and hassle-free has been my goal over decades of traveling, tour guiding, and travel writing. With this new edition, I pass on to you the lessons I've learned.

The destinations covered in this book are balanced to include a comfortable mix of cities and villages, mountaintop hikes and medieval castles, sleepy river cruises and sky-high gondola rides. While you'll find the predictable biggies (such as Mozart's house and the Vienna State Opera), I've also mixed in a healthy dose of Back Door intimacy (thrilling mountain luges, a beer with monks, and the newly exciting capital of Slovakia—just an hour from Vienna).

The best is, of course, only my opinion. But after spending much of my adult life exploring and researching Europe, I've de-

Vienna, Salzburg & Tirol: Best Two-Week Trip by Train

Day	Plan	Sleep in
1	Fly into Vienna	Vienna
2	Vienna	Vienna
3	Vienna	Vienna
4	Vienna	Vienna (or Melk if biking or cruising Danube on Day 5)
5	Danube Valley (Melk to Krems and back)	Melk
6	To Salzburg via Mauthausen	Salzburg
7	Salzburg	Salzburg
8	Salzburg	Salzburg
9	To Hallstatt*	Hallstatt
10	Hallstatt and surroundings	Hallstatt
11	To Innsbruck	Innsbruck
12	Innsbruck; to Bavarian Alps**	Füssen or Reutte
13	Bavarian Alps and castles**	Füssen or Reutte
14	Travel on or fly home from Munich	

*For more cultural thrills at the expense of some alpine ones, you could give Bratislava two nights and a day rather than idyllic—but very touristy—Hallstatt.

**For days 12-13, you can head north to the Bavarian Alps (as outlined above) or turn south, to Italy's Dolomite peaks (home base in Bolzano or Castelrotto, and fly out from Milan or Venice).

With More Time: Depending on your interests, you could easily spend several more days in Vienna (for museums, the music scene, and going to cafés and wine gardens) and a couple more days in Salzburg (for the music scene, nearby sights, day-

veloped a sixth sense for what travelers enjoy. The places featured in this book will fit travel dreams you didn't even know you had.

Planning Your Trip

This section will help you get started on planning your trip—with advice on trip costs, when to go, and what you should know before you take off.

TRIP COSTS

Five components make up your trip costs: airfare to Europe, transportation in Europe, room and board, sightseeing and entertainment, and shopping and miscellany.

Airfare to Europe: A basic round-trip flight from the US to

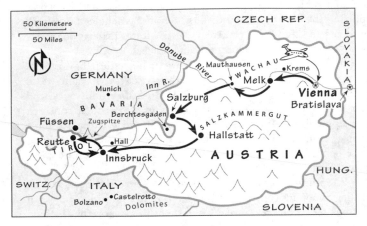

tripping to Berchtesgaden). Surprising and quirky Bratislava is worth considering for two nights and an entire day. The countryside of southern Bavaria, western Tirol, and the Italian Dolomites are great places to linger and explore (consider a few days of car rental).

With a Car: Pick up your car when you leave Vienna. After Melk (in the Danube Valley), drive to Hallstatt, with a stop at Mauthausen en route. After Hallstatt, head to Salzburg. From Salzburg, you can drive (via Berchtesgaden, if you're interested) through southern Bavaria en route to Füssen or Reutte. Then drive eastward through Tirol's Inn Valley via Innsbruck to the Dolomites just south, then return to Innsbruck to drop off your car.

Vienna can cost, on average, about $1,000-2,000 total, depending on where you fly from and when (cheaper in winter). Consider saving time and money by flying into one city and out of another; for instance, into Vienna and out of Munich. Overall, Kayak.com is the best place to start searching for flights on a combination of mainstream and budget carriers.

Transportation in Europe: For a two-week whirlwind trip of this book's destinations by public transportation, allow $300 per person. If you plan to rent a car, allow at least $250 per week, not including tolls, gas, and supplemental insurance. If you need the car for three weeks or more, leasing can save you money on insurance and taxes.

A short flight can be cheaper than the train (check www.skyscanner.com for intra-European flights).

INTRODUCTION

Room and Board: You can manage comfortably in Austria on $125 a day per person for room and board (less in small towns, more in big cities). This allows $15 for lunch, $25 for dinner, $5 for beer and *Eis* (ice cream), and $80 for lodging (based on two people splitting the cost of a $160 double room that includes breakfast). Students and tightwads can enjoy Austria for as little as $65 a day ($35 per hostel bed, $30 for meals and snacks).

Sightseeing and Entertainment: In big cities, figure $10-20 per major sight (Vienna's Kunsthistorisches Museum—$15, Mozart's Residence in Salzburg—$11), $6-8 for minor ones, and $25-50 for splurge experiences (such as walking tours, concerts, and alpine lifts). An overall average of $30 a day works for most people. Don't skimp here. After all, this category is the driving force behind your trip—you came to sightsee, enjoy, and experience Austria.

Shopping and Miscellany: Figure $5 per coffee, beer, and ice cream. Shopping can vary in cost from nearly nothing to a small fortune. Good budget travelers find that this category has little to do with assembling a trip full of lifelong memories.

SIGHTSEEING PRIORITIES

So much to see, so little time. How to choose? Depending on the length of your trip, and taking geographic proximity into account, these are my recommended priorities:

3 days:	Vienna
5 days, add:	Salzburg
7 days, add:	Hallstatt
10 days, add:	Danube Valley, Bavaria, and western Tirol
14 days, add:	Innsbruck, Dolomites, Bratislava
16 days, add:	More time in Vienna

This includes nearly everything on my "Best Two-Week Trip." If you don't have time to see it all, prioritize according to your interests. The "Vienna, Salzburg & Tirol at a Glance" sidebar can help you decide where to go.

WHEN TO GO

The "tourist season" runs roughly from May through September. Summer has its advantages: best weather, snow-free alpine trails, very long days (light until after 21:00), and the busiest schedule of tourist fun. Summer visitors should note, however, that three Viennese institutions—the Boys' Choir, State Opera, and Spanish Riding School with its Lipizzaner stallions—cease performances in July and August. Salzburg is fun, festive, and crowded from mid-July through August when it hosts the famous Salzburg Festival, one of many music festivals held throughout the year.

Travel during "shoulder season" (spring and fall) is easier and can be a bit less expensive. Shoulder-season travelers usually enjoy smaller crowds, decent weather, the full range of sights and tourist fun spots, and the ability to grab a room almost whenever and wherever they like—often at a flexible price. In spring, watch out for a string of public holidays, which can limit sightseeing hours (but can also mean special festivities). In fall, fun harvest and wine festivals enliven many towns and villages, while forests and vineyards display beautiful fiery colors.

Winter travelers find concert seasons in full swing, with absolutely no crowds, but some accommodations and sights are either closed or run on a limited schedule. The weather can be cold and dreary, and nightfall draws the shades on sightseeing well before dinnertime. But dustings of snow turn Austrian towns and landscapes into a wonderland. December offers the chance to wander through traditional Christmas markets, and Vienna lights up (and fills up) over New Year's Eve (a.k.a. Silvester), when it hosts one of Europe's biggest year-end celebrations.

For more information, see the climate chart in the appendix.

BEFORE YOU GO

You'll have a smoother trip if you tackle a few things ahead of time. For more information on these topics, see the Practicalities chapter (and www.ricksteves.com, which has helpful travel tips and talks).

Make sure your passport is valid. If it's due to expire within six months of your ticketed date of return, you need to renew it. Allow up to six weeks to renew or get a passport (www.travel.state. gov).

Arrange your transportation. Book your international flights. Figure out your transportation options: It's worth thinking about buying train tickets online in advance, getting a rail pass, renting a car, or booking cheap European flights. (You can wing it once you're there, but it may cost more.) Drivers: Consider bringing an International Driving Permit along with your license (sold at AAA offices in the US, www.aaa.com).

Book rooms well in advance if you'll be traveling during peak season (May-Sept) or any major holidays or festivals.

Make reservations or buy tickets ahead for major sights. Note that in Vienna and Salzburg (especially during its festival), major **musical events** can be sold out far in advance. In summer, avoid long waits by reserving ahead (a day or two is enough) for your **Schönbrunn Palace** visit. Planning ahead of time will guarantee you a seat to see the **Lipizzaner stallions, Vienna Boys' Choir,** and performances at the **Vienna State Opera**—though I prefer cheap, on-the-spot experiences (such as same-day standing-room tickets for the opera).

Vienna, Salzburg & Tirol at a Glance

Vienna and Nearby

▲▲▲**Vienna** Austria's regal capital city, rich with swirling architecture and world-class museums; impressive Habsburg sights (Schönbrunn Palace, in-city royal apartments, treasury, crypt, and Lipizzaner stallions); massive St. Stephen's Cathedral; and a grand classical-music tradition, from the renowned Vienna State Opera to the famous Boys' Choir.

▲**Danube Valley** Romantic, bikeable valley west of Vienna, dotted with ruined castles, adorable villages and vineyards, and highlighted by the beautiful "Wachau" stretch between Melk (with its glorious abbey) and the riverside town of Krems. Farther west is the powerful Mauthausen concentration-camp memorial.

▲▲**Bratislava, Slovakia** Once-depressed communist town, now a thriving capital city, less than an hour from Vienna and bursting with colorfully restored buildings; a quirky traffic-free old town; and a people-friendly Danube riverfront area.

Salzburg and the Salzkammergut

▲▲▲**Salzburg** Musical mecca for fans of Mozart and *The Sound of Music,* offering a dramatic castle, Baroque churches, near-nightly concerts, and an old town full of winding lanes; plus nearby Berchtesgaden (in Germany), soaked in alpine scenery and Nazi history.

▲▲**Hallstatt and the Salzkammergut** Scenic lake district, home to the pristine—if touristy—village of Hallstatt, with its medieval town center, fun salt mine, plentiful hiking opportunities, and placid swan-filled lake.

Tirol

▲**Innsbruck** Distinctive capital of Austria's panhandle Tirol region and mountain-sports mecca known for its ski jump, plus little neighboring Hall, with a quaint old town.

▲▲▲**Bavarian Alps** This Alps-straddling region boasts the fairytale castles of Neuschwanstein, Hohenschwangau, and Linderhof; inviting villages such as the Austrian retreat of Reutte and German towns of Füssen and Oberammergau; the towering Zugspitze and its high-altitude lifts; and hiking, luge, and other mountain activities.

▲▲**The Dolomites** Italy's rugged rooftop in the South Tirol region, featuring the Alpe di Siusi (alpine meadows laced with lifts and hiking trails), Austrian-feeling Castelrotto (charming village), and Italian-flavored Bolzano (home of Ötzi the Iceman).

∩ Stick This Guidebook in Your Ear!

My free Rick Steves Audio Europe app makes it easy to download my audio tours of many of Europe's top attractions and listen to them offline during your travels. In this book, these include Vienna's Ringstrasse Tram Tour, Vienna City Walk, and St. Stephen's Cathedral Tour, as well as Salzburg's Town Walk. Sights covered by my audio tours are marked in this book with this symbol: ∩. The app also offers insightful travel interviews from my public radio show with experts from Austria and around the globe. It's all free! You can download the app via Apple's App Store, Google Play, or Amazon's Appstore. For more information, see www.ricksteves.com/audioeurope.

To avoid peak-season ticket-buying lines (and ensure an entry spot) at **Neuschwanstein Castle** (in Bavaria), reserve tickets ahead.

Hire guides in advance. If you plan to hire a local guide, reserve ahead by email. Popular guides can get booked up.

Consider travel insurance. Compare the cost of the insurance to the amount of your potential loss. Check whether your existing insurance (health, homeowners, or renters) covers you and your possessions overseas.

Call your bank. Alert your bank that you'll be using your debit and credit cards in Europe. Ask about transaction fees, and get the PIN number for your credit card. You don't need to bring euros for your trip; you can withdraw euros from cash machines in Europe.

Use your smartphone smartly. Sign up for an international service plan to reduce your costs, or rely on Wi-Fi in Europe instead. Download any apps you'll want on the road, such as maps, translation, transit schedules, and Rick Steves Audio Europe (see sidebar).

Pack light. You'll walk with your luggage more than you think. Bring a single carry-on bag and a daypack. Use the packing checklist in the appendix as a guide.

Travel Smart

If you have a positive attitude, equip yourself with good information (this book), and expect to travel smart, you will.

Read—and reread—this book. To have an "A" trip, be an "A" student. Note opening hours of sights, closed days, crowd-beating tips, and whether reservations are required or advisable. Check the latest at www.ricksteves.com/update.

Be your own tour guide. As you travel, get up-to-date info on sights, reserve tickets and tours, reconfirm hotels and travel arrangements, and check transit connections. Visit local tourist information offices (TIs). Upon arrival in a new town, lay the groundwork for a smooth departure; confirm the train, bus, or road you'll take when you leave.

Outsmart thieves. Pickpockets abound in crowded places where tourists congregate. Treat commotions as smokescreens for theft. Keep your cash, credit cards, and passport secure in a money belt tucked under your clothes; carry only a day's spending money in your front pocket. Don't set valuable items down on counters or café tabletops, where they can be quickly stolen or easily forgotten.

Minimize potential loss. Keep expensive gear to a minimum. Bring photocopies or take photos of important documents (passport and cards) to aid in replacement if they're lost or stolen. Back up photos and files frequently.

Guard your time and energy. Taking a taxi can be a good value if it saves you a long wait for a cheap bus or an exhausting walk across town. To avoid long lines, follow my crowd-beating tips, such as making advance reservations, or sightseeing early or late (see the Entertainment in Vienna chapter for a list of sights open late).

Be flexible. Even if you have a well-planned itinerary, expect changes, strikes, closures, sore feet, bad weather, and so on. Your Plan B could turn out to be even better.

Attempt the language. Many Austrians and Germans—especially in the tourist trade and in cities—speak English, but if you learn some German, even just a few phrases, you'll get more smiles and make more friends. Practice the survival phrases near the end of this book, and even better, bring a phrase book.

Connect with the culture. Interacting with locals carbonates your experience. Enjoy the friendliness of the Austrian people. Ask questions; most locals are happy to point you in their idea of the right direction. Set up your own quest for the best Baroque building, Sacher torte, wine garden, or whatever. When an opportunity pops up, make it a habit to say "yes."

Austria...here you come!

AUSTRIA

During the grand old Habsburg days, Austria was Europe's most powerful empire. Its royalty built a giant kingdom (*Österreich* means "Eastern Realm") of more than 50 million people by making love, not war—having lots of children and marrying them into the other royal houses of Europe.

Of course, when you start a world war (WWI) and lose, you lose your vast empire. Today, this small, landlocked country clings to its elegant past more than any other nation in Europe. The waltz is still the rage. Music has long been a key part of Austria's heritage. The giants of classical music—Haydn, Mozart, Beethoven—were born here or moved here to write and perform their masterpieces. Music lovers flock to Salzburg every summer to attend its famous festival. But traditional folk music is also part of the Austrian soul. The world's best-loved Christmas carol, "Silent Night," was written by Austrians with just a guitar for accompaniment. Don't be surprised if you hear yodeling for someone's birthday—try joining in.

Austrians are very sociable—it's important to greet people in the breakfast room and those you pass on the streets or meet in shops. The Austrian version of "Hi" is a cheerful *"Grüss Gott"* (for more on the language, see "Hurdling the Language Barrier" in the Practicalities chapter and "German Survival Phrases for Austria" in the appendix).

While Austria has gained notoriety for electing racist right-wingers, that attitude does not prevail everywhere. Large parts of the country may be conservative, but its capital city, Vienna, is extremely liberal. In fact, for 80 years (except for the Nazi occupation), Vienna has had a socialist government with progressive, people-oriented programs. After the fall of the Soviet Union, the leading political party changed its name to "Social Democrat"... but its people-oriented agenda is still the same. When the Aus-

Austria Almanac

Official Name: Republik Österreich ("Eastern Realm"), or simply Österreich.

Population: Of Austria's 8.7 million people, 91 percent are ethnic Austrians; 4 percent are from the former Yugoslavia. Three out of four Austrians are Catholic; about one in 20 is Muslim. German is the dominant language (though there are a few Slovene- and Hungarian-speaking villages in border areas).

Latitude and Longitude: 47°N and 13°E. The latitude is the same as Minnesota or Washington state.

Area: With 32,400 square miles, Austria is similar in size to South Carolina.

Geography: The northeast is flat and well-populated; the less-populated southwest is mountainous, with the Alps rising up to the 12,450-foot Grossglockner peak. The 1,770-mile-long Danube River meanders west-to-east through the upper part of the country, passing through Vienna.

Biggest Cities: One in five Austrians lives in the capital of Vienna (1.8 million in the city; 2.6 million in the greater metropolitan area). Other cities include Graz (population 280,000), Linz (203,000), and Salzburg (152,000).

Economy: Austria borders eight other European countries and is well-integrated into the EU economy. The Gross Domestic Product is $390 billion (similar to that of Massachusetts). Its per-capita GDP of $44,700 is among Europe's highest. One of its biggest moneymakers is tourism. Austria produces wood, paper products (nearly half the land is forested)...and Red Bull Energy Drink. The country's aging population increasingly collects social security—a situation that will strain the national budget in years to come.

Government: Austria has been officially neutral since 1955, and its citizens take a dim view of European unity. Like much of Europe, Austria has seen right-leaning parties make substantial gains in recent elections—particularly the nationalist Freedom Party. The federal president, Alexander Van der Bellen, is a member of the Green Party and held off Freedom Party candidate Norbert Hofer in a 2016 election, but the current chancellor, Sebastian Kurz of the center-right Austrian People's Party, has formed a coalition with the Freedom Party. At 31, he became Austria's youngest-ever chancellor and the youngest head of government in the world when he was sworn in in 2017—an event that drew thousands of protestors to Vienna's Hofburg Palace. Austria is the only EU nation with a minimum voting age of 16.

Flag: Three horizontal bands of red, white, and red.

The Average Austrian: A typical Austrian is 43 years old, has 1.4 children, and will live to 81. He or she inhabits a 900-square-foot home, and spends time with a circle of close friends. Chances is someone in that circle is a smoker—Austrians are among the highest consumers of cigarettes in Europe.

trian drag-queen actor Conchita Wurst won the Eurovision song contest in 2014, many saw it as a vote of confidence for tolerance and openness.

While Vienna sits in the flat Danube Valley, much of Austria's character is found in its mountains. Austrians excel in mountain climbing and winter sports such as alpine skiing. Innsbruck has twice been the site of the Winter Olympics. When watching ski races, it's never hard to find fans celebrating with red-and-white flags at the finish line—Austria has won more Olympic medals in alpine skiing than any other country.

Austria lost a piece of its mountains after World War I, when Tirol was divided between Austria and Italy. Many residents of Italy's South Tirol still speak German, and it's the first language in some of their schools. Though there was bitterness at the time of the division, today, with no border guards and a shared currency, you can hardly tell you're in a different country.

While Austrians talked about unity with Germany long before Hitler ever said *"Anschluss,"* they cherish their distinct cultural and historical traditions. They speak German, but are not Germans—just as Canadians are not Americans. Austria is mellow and relaxed compared to Deutschland. *Gemütlichkeit* is the word most often used to describe this special Austrian cozy-and-easy approach to life. It's good living—whether engulfed in mountain beauty or bathed in lavish high culture. People stroll as if every day were Sunday, topping things off with a cheerful visit to a coffee or pastry shop.

It must be nice to be past your prime—no longer troubled by being powerful, able to kick back and enjoy the good life, Austrian style: long vacations, long lifespans, wonderful pastries, and pristine nature.

VIENNA

Wien

ORIENTATION TO VIENNA

Vienna is the capital of Austria, the cradle of classical music, the home of the rich Habsburg heritage, and one of the world's most livable cities. The city center is skyscraper-free, pedestrian-friendly, dotted with quiet parks, and traversed by electric trams. Many buildings still reflect 18th- and 19th-century elegance, when the city was at the forefront of the arts and sciences. Compared with most modern European urban centers, the pace of life is slow.

For much of its 2,500-year history, Vienna (*Wien* in German—pronounced "veen") was on the frontier of civilized Europe. Located on the south bank of the Danube, it was threatened by Germanic barbarians (in Roman times), marauding Magyars (today's Hungarians, 10th century), Mongol hordes (13th century), Ottoman Turks (the sieges of 1529 and 1683), and encroachment by the Soviet Union after World War II.

The Habsburg dynasty ruled their great empire from Vienna, setting the stage for its position as an enduring cultural capital. Among the Habsburgs, Holy Roman Empress Maria Theresa in the late 1700s was famous for having 16 children and cleverly marrying many of them into royal families around Europe to expand the family's reach.

Vienna reached its peak in the 19th century, when it was on par with London and Paris in size and importance. Emerging as a cultural powerhouse, it was home to groundbreaking composers (Beethoven, Mozart, Brahms, Strauss), scientists (Doppler, Boltzmann), philosophers (Freud, Husserl, Schlick, Gödel, Steiner), architects (Wagner, Loos), and painters (Klimt, Schiele, Kokoschka). By the turn of the 20th century, Vienna was one of the world's most populous cities and sat on the cusp between stuffy Old World monarchism and subversive modern trends.

After the turmoil of the two world wars and the loss of Aus-

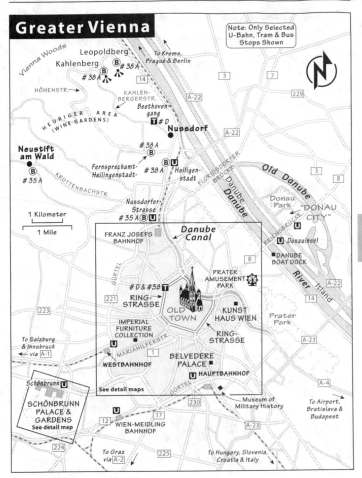

Greater Vienna

Note: Only Selected U-Bahn, Tram & Bus Stops Shown

ORIENTATION

tria's empire, Vienna has settled down into a somewhat sleepy, pleasant place where culture is still king. Classical music is everywhere. People nurse a pastry and coffee over the daily paper at small cafés. It's a city of world-class museums, big and small. Anyone with an interest in painting, music, architecture, beautiful objects, or Sacher torte with whipped cream will feel right at home.

VIENNA: A VERBAL MAP

Vienna sits between the Vienna Woods (Wienerwald) and the Danube River (Donau). To the southeast is industrial sprawl. The Alps, which arc across Europe from Marseille, end at Vienna's wooded hills, providing a popular playground for walking and sipping new wine. This greenery's momentum carries on into the city.

ORIENTATION

Vienna Past and Present

The capital of the once-grand Habsburg Empire, Vienna is a head without a body. It was from Vienna that the Habsburgs started and lost World War I and, with it, the empire's far-flung holdings. Culturally, historically, and touristically, this city is the sum of its illustrious past, ranking right up there with Paris, London, and Rome.

Vienna has stood for centuries as the easternmost city of the West. In Roman times, it was Vindobona, on the Danube facing the barbarians. In the Middle Ages, Vienna was Europe's bastion against the Ottomans—a Christian breakwater against the rising tide of Islam (armies of up to 200,000 were repelled in 1529 and 1683). During this period, as the Ottomans dreamed of conquering what they called "the big apple" for their sultan, Vienna lived with a constant fear of invasion (and for a time the Habsburg court ruled from safer Prague). Of all of Vienna's great palaces, none was built until after 1683, when the Turkish threat was finally over.

The Habsburgs, who ruled their enormous empire from 1273 to 1918, shaped Vienna into the city we see today. Some ad agency has convinced Vienna to make Elisabeth, wife of Emperor Franz Josef—with her narcissism and struggles with royal life—the darling of the local tourist scene. You'll see images of "Sisi" (SEE-see) all over town. But stay focused on the Habsburgs who mattered: Maria Theresa (ruled 1740-1780, see sidebar in the Sights chapter) and her great-great-grandson Franz Josef (ruled 1848-1916, see sidebar in the Hofburg Imperial Apartments Tour chapter).

In the wake of Napoleon's power grab—and ultimate defeat—the 1814-1815 Congress of Vienna reconfigured the political landscape of 19th-century Europe so that no one country would be too strong. Over the next 100 years, Vienna enjoyed its violin-

More than half of Vienna is parkland, filled with ponds, gardens, trees, and statue-maker memories of Austria's glory days.

Think of the city map as a target with concentric circles: The bull's-eye is St. Stephen's Cathedral, the towering spired church south of the Danube. Surrounding that is the old town, bound tightly by the circular road known as the Ringstrasse, marking what used to be the city wall. The Gürtel, a broader, later ring road, contains the rest of downtown. Outside the Gürtel lies the uninteresting sprawl of modern Vienna.

Addresses start with the *Bezirk* (district) number, followed by the street and building number. For example, the address "7, Lindengasse 4" is in the seventh district, #4 on Lindengasse. The Ringstrasse (a.k.a. the Ring) circles the first district. The Gürtel contains districts two through nine. Any address higher than the ninth *Bezirk* is far from the center.

filled belle époque, giving us our romantic image of the city: fine wine, chocolates, cafés, waltzes, and the good life.

In 1900, Vienna's 2.2 million inhabitants made it the world's fifth-largest city—after New York, London, Paris, and Berlin. The empire itself encompassed more than 50 million people, of whom only 12 million spoke German as their mother tongue. Emigration from the provinces to Vienna was common, and a true Viennese person today is a Habsburg cocktail, with ancestors from the distant corners of the old empire: not just from the Czech Republic, Slovakia, and Hungary, but also Slovenia, Serbia, Croatia, Bosnia, Italy, Transylvania, Ukraine, and Poland.

While Vienna's old walls had held out would-be invaders (including the Ottomans), they were no match for WWII bombs, which destroyed nearly a quarter of the city's buildings. Vienna received more postwar Marshall Plan money than German cities did, as the US considered it a bulwark against western expansion by the USSR. In modern times, neutral Austria extended deep into the USSR's Warsaw Pact buffer zone, but after an uneasy Cold War experience, the city emerged in remarkably good shape.

Today, Vienna is not an outpost, but rather the center of a dynamic area that includes Brno, Bratislava, and Budapest. The university students you'll see were born after the formation of the European Union and think nothing of zipping across borders for lunch.

Vienna's population has dropped to 1.8 million, with dogs being the preferred "child" and the average Austrian woman having only 1.4 children. Vienna, once the capital of a far-flung realm, now feels oversized for Austria's 8.7 million residents—but its reduced political weight makes it easier to enjoy the Habsburg grandness and elegance that it has never lost.

ORIENTATION

Much of Vienna's sightseeing—and most of my recommended restaurants—are located in the old town (the first district, inside the Ringstrasse). Walking across this circular area takes about 30 minutes. St. Stephen's Cathedral sits in the center, at the intersection of the two main (pedestrian-only) streets: Kärntner Strasse and the Graben.

Several sights sit along, or just beyond, the Ringstrasse: To the southwest are the Hofburg and related Habsburg sights, as well as the Kunsthistorisches Museum; to the south is a cluster of intriguing sights near Karlsplatz; to the southeast is Belvedere Palace. A branch of the Danube River borders the Ring to the north.

As a tourist, concern yourself only with this compact old center. When you do, sprawling Vienna becomes easily manageable.

PLANNING YOUR TIME

For a big city, Vienna is pleasant and laid-back. Packed with sights, it's worth two days and two nights on even the speediest trip. If you have more time, Vienna can easily fill it; art and music lovers in particular won't regret adding a third, fourth, or even more days.

If you're visiting Vienna as part of a longer European trip, you could sleep on the train on your way in and out—Berlin, Kraków, Venice, Rome, and Frankfurt are each a handy night-train journey away.

Palace Choices: The Hofburg and Schönbrunn are both world-class palaces, but seeing both is redundant if your time or money is limited. If you're rushed and can fit in only one palace, make it the Hofburg. It comes with the popular Sisi Museum, is adjacent to perhaps Europe's best collection of crown jewels, and is right in the town center, making for an easy visit. With more time, a visit to Schönbrunn—set outside town amid a grand and regal garden—is also a great experience. (For efficient sightseeing, drivers should note that Schönbrunn Palace is conveniently on the way out of town toward Salzburg.)

Vienna in One to Four Days

Below is a suggested itinerary for how to spend your daytime sightseeing hours. The best options for **evenings** are taking in a concert, opera, or other musical event; enjoying a leisurely dinner (and people-watching) in the stately old town; heading out to the *Heuriger* wine pubs in the foothills of the Vienna Woods; or touring the Haus der Musik interactive music museum (open nightly until 22:00). Plan your evenings based on the schedule of musical events. If you've downloaded my audio tours (see "Rick Steves Audio Europe" sidebar in the Introduction), both the Vienna City Walk and Ringstrasse Tram Tour work wonderfully in the evening. Whenever you need a break, linger in a classic Viennese café.

Day 1

9:00	Circle the Ringstrasse by tram (following my self-guided tram tour).
10:30	Drop by the TI for planning and ticket needs.
11:00	Tour the Vienna State Opera (schedule varies, confirm at TI).
14:00	Follow my Vienna City Walk, including the Kaisergruft visit and St. Stephen's Cathedral Tour (nave closes at 16:30, or 17:30 July-Aug).
18:00	Dinner and romantic stroll in the old center.

Day 2

9:00	Browse the colorful Naschmarkt.
11:00	Tour the Kunsthistorisches Museum.

14:00   Tour the Hofburg Palace Imperial Apartments and Treasury.

Day 3

8:00   Tour Schönbrunn Palace to enjoy the imperial apartments and grounds (or reserve in advance for a later time).

14:00   Visit Belvedere Palace, with its fine Viennese art and great city views.

Day 4

10:00   Enjoy (depending on your interest) the engaging Karlsplatz sights (Karlskirche, the Secession) or the Natural History Museum.

14:00   Do some shopping along Mariahilfer Strasse, or rent a bike and head out to the modern Donau City "downtown" sector, Danube Island (for fun people-watching), and Prater Park (with its amusement park).

With More Time...

Vienna itself can easily fill a longer visit. But a day trip can be more rewarding than spending extra time in town. For rustic pastoral beauty, head for Melk and the Danube Valley; for an offbeat detour into the Slavic world, hit the Slovak capital of Bratislava.

Overview

TOURIST INFORMATION

Vienna's main TI is a block behind the Vienna State Opera at Albertinaplatz (daily 9:00-19:00, includes theater box office, tel. 01/211-140, www.vienna.info). It's a rare example of a TI in Europe that is really a service (possible because tourists pay for it with a hotel tax). There are also TIs at the airport (daily 7:00-22:00) and the train station (daily 9:00-19:00).

The box office at the main TI sells tickets to all the touristy concerts. You'll get the same price here as you would at the venues or from the goofy sales people on the street—the advantage here is that they have all the options, you can review them with a knowledgeable sales person, and you can study the various venues (from glorious to boring), which can determine your experience. They also sell discount train and intercity bus tickets.

Look for the monthly program of concerts (called *Wien-Programm*, see below), the annual city guide (called *Vienna Journal*), and two good brochures: *Walks in Vienna* and *Architecture from Art Nouveau to the Present*. Ask about their program of guided walks (€16 each), and consider buying a Vienna Pass, which includes entry to many sights and lets you skip some lines (see the Sights

ORIENTATION

ORIENTATION

Daily Reminder

Sunday: All recommended sights and most tourist shops are open, but department stores and other shops are closed, including the Naschmarkt open-air market and the Dorotheum auction house. Most churches have restricted hours for sightseers, and there are no tours of the crypt at St. Michael's Church. The Spanish Riding School's Lipizzaner stallions usually perform at 11:00 (no performances mid-June-mid-Aug).

Monday: Most of the major sights are open (such as St. Stephen's Cathedral, Vienna State Opera, Hofburg Imperial Apartments and Treasury, Schönbrunn Palace, and Belvedere Palace), but many sights are closed, including the Secession, Imperial Furniture Collection, Museum of Applied Art (MAK), and the Otto Wagner exhibit at Karlsplatz. The Kunsthistorisches Museum is closed except in summer.

Tuesday: All sights are open, except the Hofburg Treasury, Natural History Museum, and the Academy of Fine Arts (while temporarily located at the Theatermuseum). The Leopold Museum (at the MuseumsQuartier) is closed except in summer. The Museum of Applied Arts (MAK) is cheaper after 18:00 and stays open until 22:00.

Wednesday: All sights (except the World Museum Vienna) are open. The Albertina and Natural History Museum stay open until 21:00.

Thursday: All sights are open. The Kunsthistorisches and MuseumsQuartier museums (Leopold and Modern Art) stay open until 21:00. The Museum of Modern Art is cheaper after 18:00.

Friday: All sights are open. The Belvedere Palace, World Museum Vienna, and Albertina Museum stay open until 21:00.

Saturday: All sights are open, except the Jewish Museum Vienna (both locations). The Spanish Riding School's Lipizzaner stallions usually perform at 11:00 (no performances mid-June-mid-Aug). The Third Man Museum is open only today (14:00-18:00).

in Vienna chapter). Ask also about the *Vienna from A to Z* booklet (which identifies historic spots marked with a set of flags throughout town).

Wien-Programm: This essential monthly entertainment guide lists all sorts of events, including music, theater, walks, expositions, and museum exhibits, including schedules for the Spanish Riding School, Vienna Boys' Choir, and Vienna State Opera (noting which performances are projected on the big screen outside the opera house). Note the table of contents and key for abbreviations on the inside cover, which helps make this dense booklet useful even for English speakers.

ARRIVAL IN VIENNA

For a comprehensive rundown on Vienna's various train stations and its airport, as well as tips on arriving or departing by car or boat, see the Vienna Connections chapter.

HELPFUL HINTS

Music Sightseeing Priorities: Be wary of Vienna's various music sights. Many "homes of composers" are pretty disappointing. My advice to music lovers is to take in a concert, tour the Vienna State Opera or snare cheap standing-room tickets to see a performance there, enjoy the Haus der Musik, or scour the wonderful Collection of Ancient Musical Instruments in the World Museum Vienna. If in town on a Sunday, don't miss the glorious music at the Augustinian Church Mass (see page 40). For tips on the many ways to hear free music in Vienna, see the Entertainment in Vienna chapter.

Sightseeing Strategies: If you plan to do a lot of sightseeing, consider buying the Vienna Pass or one of the combo-tickets (see the Sights in Vienna chapter). The Vienna Pass is pricey, so do the math and consider whether you'll need to use public transportation. In summer and on good-weather weekends, it's smart to make a timed-entry reservation for the Schönbrunn Palace.

Skip This: The highly advertised Time Travel Vienna (just off the Graben on Habsburgergasse) promises "history, fun, and action." In reality, it's €20 and 50 minutes wasted in a tacky succession of amusement-park history vignettes with much of the information in German only.

Wi-Fi: You'll find free hotspots ("Wien.at Public WLAN") around town, including at the TI, Hauptbahnhof, and Stephansplatz.

Useful App: ∩ For free audio versions of some of the self-guided tours in this book (Vienna City Walk, St. Stephen's Cathedral, Ringstrasse Tram Tour), get the **Rick Steves Audio Europe** app (for details, see the Introduction chapter).

English Bookstore: Stop by the woody and cool **Shakespeare & Co.,** in the historic and atmospheric Ruprechtsviertel district near the Danube Canal (Mon-Sat 9:00-21:00, closed Sun, north of Hoher Markt at Sterngasse 2, tel. 01/535-5053, www.shakespeare.co.at). See the "Vienna's City Center" map on page 33.

Keeping Up with the News: Yes, your phone has all the news—but you can also read it for free, in print, in Vienna's marvelous coffeehouses. It's much classier.

Laundry: For economic and efficient laundry service, head to **Kaiser Putzerei Laundry** near the opera house. It's full-service only—drop off in the morning, pay per kilo, and pick up in the

ORIENTATION

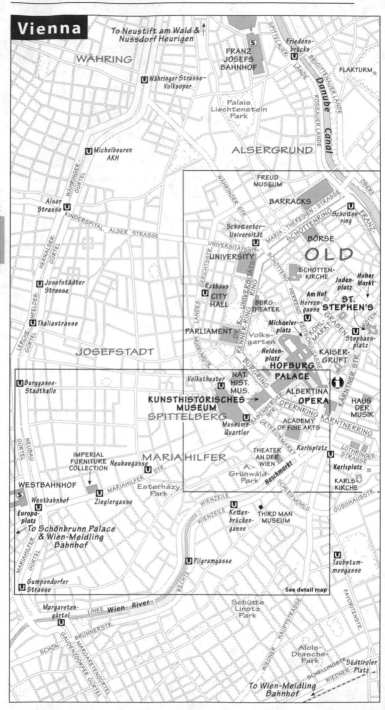

Vienna

To Neustift am Wald & Nussdorf Heurigen

WÄHRING

FRANZ JOSEFS BAHNHOF Ⓢ

Friedens-brücke

SPITTELAUER LÄNDE

BRIGITTENAUER LÄNDE

FLAKTURM

Ⓤ Währinger Strasse-Volksoper

Palais Liechtenstein Park

Danube Canal

ROSSAUER LÄNDE

ALSERGRUND

Ⓤ Michelbeuren AKH

FREUD MUSEUM

OBERE

BARRACKS

WÄHRINGER STR.

MARIA-THERESIEN-STRASSE

SCHOTTENRING

Schottenring Ⓤ

Ⓤ Alser Strasse

KINDERSPITAL ALSER STRASSE

WÄHRINGER GÜRTEL

Schottentor-Universität

UNIVERSITÄTSSTR.

BÖRSE

OLD

FRANZ

Ⓤ Josefstädter Strasse

HERNALSER GÜRTEL

UNFELDER-GÜRTEL

UNIVERSITY

GERICHTSG.

LANDES

UNIVERSITÄTS-RING

SCHOTTENG.

SCHOTTEN-KIRCHE

HERREN

Am Hof

Judenplatz

Hoher Markt

Ⓤ Thaliastrasse

Ⓤ Rathaus CITY HALL

BURG-THEATER

Herren-gasse

ST. STEPHEN'S

LERCHEN-GÜRTEL

JOSEFSTADT

DR. KARL-RENNER-RING

MÖLKER-

PARLIAMENT

Michaeler-platz

KOHL-MARKT

GRABEN

Stephans-platz Ⓤ

KÄRNTEN STR.

Ⓤ Burggasse-Stadthalle

NEUBAU GÜRTEL

Volks-garten

MUSEUMSTR.

Heldenplatz

HOFBURG PALACE

KAISER-GRUFT

Volkstheater

NAT. HIST. MUS.

BURGRING

ALBERTINA

HAUS DER MUSIK

ⓘ

KUNSTHISTORISCHES MUSEUM →

BABENBERGER STR.

OPERA

OPERNRING

KÄRNTNERRING

SPITTELBERG

GETREIDEMARKT

ACADEMY OF FINE ARTS

Karlsplatz

LOTHRINGER-STRASSE

Museums-Quartier

Ⓤ Karlsplatz

IMPERIAL FURNITURE COLLECTION

Neubaugasse

Ⓤ 6TR.

MARIAHILFER

THEATER AN DER WIEN

KARLS-KIRCHE

GUSSHAUSSTR.

WESTBAHNHOF Ⓢ

Ⓤ Westbahnhof

Zieglergasse

MARIAHILFER STR.

Esterházy Park

A: Grünwald-Park

Nachmarkt

SCHLEIFMÜHLG.

Europa-platz

MARIAHILFER GÜRTEL

WIENZEILE

WIENZEILE

Ketten-brücken-gasse Ⓤ

THIRD MAN MUSEUM

◆ To Schönbrunn Palace & Wien-Meidling Bahnhof

RECHTE

Ⓤ Taubstummengasse

FAVORITENSTR.

Ⓤ Gumpendorfer Strasse

Ⓤ Pilgramgasse

See detail map

Margaretengürtel Ⓤ

LINKE Wien River

Schütte Linotz Park

SCHÖNBRUNNER GÜRTEL

GAUDENZDORFER GÜRTEL

BRUNNERSTR.

WIEDNER HAUPTSTRASSE

Alois-Drasche-Park

SCHELLINGGASSE

WIEDNER STR.

Südtiroler Platz

To Wien-Meidling Bahnhof →

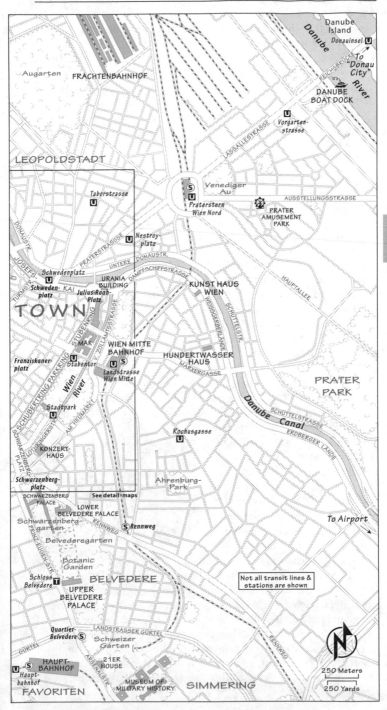

ORIENTATION

Danube Island
Donauinsel

To "Donau City"

Danube River

DANUBE BOAT DOCK

FRACHTENBAHNHOF

Augarten

LEOPOLDSTADT

Taborstrasse

Schwedenplatz
Schweden-platz

Nestroy-platz

URANIA BUILDING

Julius-Raab-Platz

TOWN

Franziskaner-platz

Stubentor

WIEN MITTE BAHNHOF

Landstrasse Wien Mitte

Stadtpark

KONZERT-HAUS

Schwarzenberg-platz

SCHWARZENBERG PALACE

LOWER BELVEDERE PALACE

Schwarzenberg-garten

Belvederegarten

Botanic Garden

Schloss Belvedere

UPPER BELVEDERE PALACE

BELVEDERE

Quartier-Belvedere

HAUPT-BAHNHOF

Hauptbahnhof

FAVORITEN

Schweizer Garten

21ER HOUSE

MUSEUM OF MILITARY HISTORY

SIMMERING

Venediger Au

Praterstern Wien Nord

Vorgarten-strasse

AUSSTELLUNGSSTRASSE

PRATER AMUSEMENT PARK

KUNST HAUS WIEN

HUNDERTWASSER HAUS

Rochusgasse

Ahrenburg-Park

Rennweg

Danube Canal

PRATER PARK

To Airport

See detail maps

Not all transit lines & stations are shown

250 Meters
250 Yards

afternoon (Mon-Fri 7:30-18:00, next to recommended Hotel zur Wiener Staatsoper at Krugerstrasse 9, tel. 01/512-4356).

Travel Agency: Conveniently located on Stephansplatz, **Ruefa** sells tickets for flights, trains, and boats to Bratislava. They'll waive the €8 service charge for train and boat tickets for my readers (Mon-Fri 9:00-18:30, closed Sat-Sun, Stephansplatz 10, tel. 01/513-4524, Gertrude and Sandra speak English).

Drinking Water: The Viennese are proud of their perfectly drinkable tap water from alpine springs. You'll spot locals refilling their little bottles at fountains all over town. In response to—and anticipation of—global warming, the city has installed shiny public water fountains with signs reminding people to stay hydrated (one is on the Graben at the corner of Spiegelgasse). Most restaurants serve *Leitungswasser* (tap water), though some charge a nominal fee (about €0.50) for the service.

GETTING AROUND VIENNA
By Public Transportation

Take full advantage of Vienna's efficient transit system, operated by **Wiener Linien,** which includes trams, buses, U-Bahn (subway), and S-Bahn (faster suburban) trains. It's fast, clean, and easy to navigate. The free Vienna city map, available at TIs and hotels, includes a small schematic transit map, but the Wiener Linien Info & Ticket offices (in major U-Bahn stations) have a simpler one.

I generally stick to the tram to zip around the Ring (trams #1, #2, #71, #D, and #O) and take the U-Bahn to outlying sights, hotels, and Vienna's train stations (see color transit map at the beginning of this book). There are five color-coded U-Bahn lines: U-1 red, U-2 purple, U-3 orange, U-4 green, and U-6 brown. If you see a bus number that starts with *N* (such as #N38), it's a night bus, which operates after other public transit stops running. Transit info: tel. 01/790-9100, www.wienerlinien.at.

Tickets and Passes: Trams, buses, and the U-Bahn and S-Bahn all use the same tickets. Except on days spent entirely within the Ring, buying a single- or multiday pass is usually a good investment (and pays off if you take at least four trips). Many people find that once they have a pass, they end up using the system more.

Buy tickets from vending machines (easy and in English), ticket offices in stations, or at tobacco shops. Most trams have ticket machines (single tickets only), but some only take coins, so it's best to purchase tickets ahead of time. You cannot purchase tickets on buses.

You have lots of choices:

- Single tickets (€2.40, €2.60 on tram, good for one journey with necessary transfers)
- 24-hour transit pass (€8)
- 48-hour transit pass (€14.10)
- 72-hour transit pass (€17.10)
- 7-day transit pass (*Wochenkarte*, €17.10—the catch is that the pass runs from Monday to Monday, so you may get less than seven days of use)
- 8-day "Climate Ticket" (*Acht-Tage-Klimakarte*, €40.80, can be shared—for example, four people for two days each). With a per-person cost of €5.10/day (compared to €8/day for a 24-hour pass), this can be a real saver for groups, but you must stay together.

Transit Tips: To get your bearings on buses, trams, the U-Bahn, and the S-Bahn, you'll want to know the end-of-the-line stop in the direction you're heading. For example, if you're in the city center at Stephansplatz and you want to take the U-Bahn to the main train station (Hauptbahnhof), you'd take U-1 going in the direction "Oberlaa."

You must stamp your ticket at the barriers in U-Bahn and S-Bahn stations, and in the machines on trams and buses (stamp multiple-use passes only the first time you board). When purchasing tickets from vending machines, you can choose to have them validated before being printed. There are no formal checks, but you may see random stops; cheaters pay a stiff fine (about €100), plus the cost of the ticket.

On trams, stop announcements are voice-only and easy to miss—carry a map. Rookies miss stops because they fail to open the door. Push buttons, pull latches—do whatever it takes.

Before you exit a U-Bahn station, study the wall-mounted street map and choose the right exit to save lots of walking.

Cute little electric buses wind through the tangled old center (from Schottentor to Stubentor). Bus #1A is best for a joyride—hop on and see where it takes you.

By Taxi, Uber, or Private Driver

Vienna's comfortable, civilized, and easy-to-flag-down **taxis** start at €3.80 (higher rates at night). You'll pay about €10 to go from the opera house to the Hauptbahnhof. Pay only what's on the meter—the only legitimate surcharges are for calling a cab (€3) or for riding to the airport (€13).

If you like Uber, the ride service (and your app) works in Vienna just like it does at home.

Consider the luxury of having your own **car and driver.** Johann (a.k.a. John) Lichtl is a gentle, honest, English-speaking cabbie who can take up to four passengers in his car (€25/hour for 2 hours or more, €27 to or from airport, mobile 0676-670-6750). Consider a custom-tailored city driving tour (2 hours), a day trip to the Danube Valley (€160; see Danube Valley chapter), or a visit to the Mauthausen Memorial with a little Danube sightseeing en route (€240).

By Bike

With more than 600 miles of bike lanes (and a powerful Green Party), Vienna is a great city on two wheels. Consider using a rental bike for the duration of your visit (Pedal Power is the best option, see listing on next page); you'll go anywhere in town faster than a taxi can take you. Biking (carefully) through Vienna's many traffic-free spaces is no problem. And bikes ride the U-Bahn for free (but aren't allowed during weekday rush hours).

The bike path along the Ring is wonderfully entertaining (in fact, my Ringstrasse Tram Tour works even better by bike than by tram, especially if you use my audio tour)—you'll enjoy the shady parklike ambience of the boulevard while rolling by many of the city's top sights.

Besides the Ring, your best sightseeing by bike is along the Danube Canal, across Danube Island, and out to the modern Donau City business district (for more on biking on Danube Island and to Donau City, see page 79). These routes are easy to follow on the free tourist city map available from the TI (some routes can also be downloaded from the TI website). Red-colored pavement is the usual marking for bike lanes, but some bike lanes are marked just with white lines.

Borrowing a Free/Cheap Bike: Citybike Wien lets you borrow bikes from public racks all over town (toll tel. 0810-500-500, www.citybikewien.at). The three-speed bikes are heavy and clunky (with solid tires to discourage thieves)—and come with a basket, built-in lock, and ads on the side—but they're per-fect for a short, practical joyride in the center (such as around the Ringstrasse).

The system is easy to use. Bikes are locked into more than 100 stalls scattered through the city center. To borrow one, register your credit card at the terminal at any rack, create a password (save it for future rentals), then unlock a bike (you can also register online at www.citybikewien.at). First-time registration is €1 (only one bike per credit card—couples must use two different cards). Since the bikes are designed for short-term use, it costs more per hour the longer you keep it (first hour—free, second hour—€1, third hour—€2, €4/hour after that). When you're done, drop off your bike at any stall (being sure it's solidly locked back in the rack).

Renting a Higher-Quality Bike: If you want to ride beyond the town center—or you simply want a better set of wheels—rent from **Pedal Power** (€6/hour, €19/4 hours, €30/24 hours, RS%—10 percent with this book, daily May-Sept 9:00-18:00, shorter hours April and Oct, rental office near the opera house, a block beyond the Ring, at Bösendorferstrasse 5, see the "Vienna's City Center" map in the next chapter, tel. 01/729-7234, www.pedalpower.at). For €16 extra they'll deliver a bike to your hotel and pick it up when you're done. They also organize bike tours (described later).

Tours in Vienna

🎧 To sightsee on your own, download my free audio tours that illuminate some of Vienna's top sights and neighborhoods, including my Vienna City Walk and tours of St. Stephen's Cathedral and the Ringstrasse (all produced from the chapters in this book). The city walk and tram tour of the Ringstrasse start at the opera house and work nicely in the evening as well as during the day. The cathedral tour can be spliced into the city walk for efficiency (for more on these audio tours, see the sidebar in the Introduction chapter). Once downloaded, you can listen to these offline.

ON FOOT
TI's "Walks in Vienna" Program
The TI's *Walks in Vienna* brochure lists more than a dozen walks given in English, all for €16. Their basic 1.5-hour "Vienna at First Glance" introductory walk is offered daily throughout the summer (leaves at 14:00 from in front of the main TI, just behind the opera house, in English and German, just show up, tel. 01/774-8901, www.wienguide.at).

Good Vienna Tours
This company (one of several offering such walks) offers a "pay what you like" 2.5-hour, English-only walk through the city center. While my Vienna City Walk is much more succinct, this can be an entertaining ramble with a local telling stories of the city. (Unlike other countries offering "free" walks, Austria requires that such guides are trained and licensed.) Just show up (pay what you think it's worth at the end—no coins, paper only, daily departures at 10:00 and 14:00, also at 17:00 July-Aug, maximum 35 people, meet

ORIENTATION

at fountain at tip of Albertina across from TI, mobile 0664/554-4315, www.goodviennatours.eu).

ON WHEELS
Consider a bus tour, bike tour, or even one by horse-and-buggy.

Red Bus Panorama City Tours
This one-hour, big-bus tour loops around the city, hitting the highlights with recorded narration. Along with the Ringstrasse, it also zips through Prater Park, over the Danube for a glimpse of the city's Danube Island playground, and into the Donau City skyscraper zone (€17, buses leave from Albertinaplatz, buy ticket from salesperson at the curb, opposite the TI behind the opera house; daily at 11:30, 14:30, and 17:30; tel. 01/512-4030, www.redbuscitytours.at).

Hop-On, Hop-Off Bus Tours
Two companies (Big Bus—red, Vienna Sightseeing—yellow) offer a complicated and busy program of hop-on, hop-off bus tours. Both offer 24-, 48-, and 72-hour tickets, including a circular bus route (with departures every 10-15 minutes) and options to add river cruises and walking tours. Prices start at around €30 for 24 hours. You'll see booths at major stops (including the opera house for Vienna Sightseeing and Albertinaplatz for Big Bus) with flyers and staff that lay out all the options. While the ride can be scenic, gets you from sight to sight conveniently, and offers a stress-free overview, the recorded narration is almost worthless and cluttered with instructions, warnings, and cross-promotions. If you're adept at public transit, a good walker, and can read this guidebook, these hop-on, hop-off tours are not a good value.

Vienna Ring Tram Tour
This yellow, made-for-tourists streetcar runs clockwise along the entire Ringstrasse (€9 for 30-minute loop, 2/hour 10:00-17:30, recorded narration, www.wienerlinien.at). The 25-minute tour starts every half-hour at Schwedenplatz. At each stop, you'll see a sign for this tram tour (look for *VRT Ring-Rund Sightseeing*). The schedule notes the next departure time.

To save money, follow my self-guided tour using city trams that circle the Ring. You'll need to make one transfer, but the trams run frequently and you'll sit alongside real *Wiener*s (□ see Ringstrasse Tram Tour chapter).

Pedal Power
Tours cover the central district in three hours and go twice daily from May to September (€36/tour includes bike, €20 extra to keep bike for the day, RS%—10 percent with this book, English tours depart at 10:00 just beyond the Ring near the opera house at

Bösendorferstrasse 5, tel. 01/729-7234, www.pedalpower.at). They also rent bikes (see "Getting Around Vienna," earlier).

Horse-and-Buggy Tour

These traditional 19th-century horse-and-buggies, called *Fiaker*, take rich romantics on clip-clop tours lasting 20 minutes (Old Town—€55), 40 minutes (Old Town and the Ring—€80), or one hour (all the above, but more thorough—€110). Before the advent of cars, one-horse versions of these served as Vienna's taxis. You can share the ride and cost with up to four people (some may allow five). Because it's a kind of guided tour, talk to a few drivers before choosing a carriage, and pick someone who's fun and speaks English (tel. 01/401-060).

LOCAL GUIDES

Vienna becomes particularly vivid and meaningful with the help of a private guide. I've enjoyed working with these guides; any of them can set you up with another good guide if they are already booked.

Quality Conventional Guides: Lisa Zeiler is a good story-teller with years of guiding experience (€160/2-3 hours, mobile 0699-1203-7550, lisa.zeiler@gmx.at). **Adrienn Bartek-Rhomberg** offers themed walks in the city as well as Schönbrunn Palace tours (€160/3 hours, €300/full day on foot, €280 "Panorama City Tour"—a 4-hour minibus and walking tour for up to six people, mobile 0650-826-6965, www.experience-vienna.at, office@experience-vienna.at).

Philosopher Guides: Wolfgang Höfler, a generalist with a knack for having psychoanalytical fun with history, enjoys the big changes of the 19th and 20th centuries. He'll take you around on foot or by bike (€160/2 hours, €50 for each additional hour, bike tours—€160/3 hours, mobile 0676-304-4940, www.vienna-aktivtours.com, office@vienna-aktivtours.com). **Gerhard Strass-gschwandtner,** who runs the Third Man Museum, is passionate about history in all its marvelous complexity (€160/2 hours, mobile 0676-475-7818, www.special-vienna.com, gerhard@special-vienna.com).

SIGHTS IN VIENNA

Vienna has a dizzying number of sights and museums, which cover the city's rich culture and vivid history through everything from paintings to music to furniture to prancing horses. Just perusing the list on your TI-issued Vienna city map can be overwhelming. To get you started, I've selected the sights that are most essential, rewarding, and user-friendly, and arranged them by neighborhood for handy sightseeing.

When you see a 📖 in a listing, it means the sight is covered in greater detail in my Vienna City Walk or one of my self-guided tours. A 🎧 means the walk or tour is also available as a free audio tour (via my Rick Steves Audio Europe app—see the Introduction chapter).

For more tips on sightseeing, see the Practicalities chapter.

SIGHTSEEING PASSES AND COMBO-TICKETS

Avid sightseers should consider a pass or combo-ticket, but do the math first. Add up the cost of all the sights you think you'll see, then consider whether you'd like to use the hop-on, hop-off bus to get around (included with the Vienna Pass). If you prefer to walk or take public transportation, you may be better off with one or more of the combo-tickets described below.

Note that those under 19 get in free to state-run museums and sights.

Passes: The **Vienna Pass** includes free entry to the city's top 60 sights and unlimited access to Vienna Sightseeing's hop-on, hop-off tour buses (€59/1 day, €89/2 days, €119/3 days; purchase at TIs and several other locations around town—check at www.viennapass.com). It also lets you skip lines at some sights, but not at the Schönbrunn Palace where lines are the most frustrating. You have to be really busy to make this pass pay for itself.

The much-promoted **Vienna Card** (www.wienkarte.at) is not worth the mental overhead for most travelers.

Combo-Tickets: Some sights offer tickets that cover several venues at a single price; buy these at any participating sight, then skip ticket-buying lines at your next sight.

The €34 **Sisi Ticket** covers the Hofburg Imperial Apartments (with its Sisi Museum and Silver Collection—must be seen the same day), Schönbrunn Palace's Grand Tour, and the Imperial Furniture Collection. At Schönbrunn, the ticket lets you enter the palace immediately, without a reserved entry time. Buy your Sisi Ticket in advance online (www.schoenbrunn.at) or at the Imperial Furniture Collection where lines are shortest.

If you're seeing the **Hofburg Treasury** (royal regalia and crown jewels) and the **Kunsthistorisches** (world-class art collection), the €20 combo-ticket is well worth it.

The **Haus der Musik** (mod museum with interactive exhibits) has a combo deal with **Mozarthaus Vienna** (exhibits and artifacts about the great composer) for €18—saving a few euros for music lovers (though the Mozarthaus will likely disappoint all but the most die-hard Mozart fans).

HOFBURG PALACE AND RELATED SIGHTS

The imposing Imperial Palace, with 640 years of architecture, art, and history, demands your attention. This first Habsburg residence grew with the family empire from the 13th century until 1913, when the last "new wing" opened. The winter residence of the Habsburg rulers until 1918, the Hofburg is still home to the Austrian president's office, 5,000 government workers, and several important museums.

Planning Your Time: Don't get confused by the Hofburg's myriad courtyards and many museums. Focus on three sights: the Imperial Apartments, the Treasury, and the museums at World Museum Vienna. With more time, consider the Hofburg's many other sights, covering various facets of the imperial lifestyle: Watch the famous Lipizzaner stallions prance at the Spanish Riding School; visit the Augustinian Church, which holds the Habsburgs' hearts—in more ways than one (it was the site of royal weddings, and the actual Habsburg hearts are in its crypt); peruse the Habsburgs' book collection at the Austrian National Library; stroll through the inviting imperial-turned-public Burggarten park; or ogle the great Habsburg art collection at the Albertina Museum.

Eating at the Hofburg: Down the tunnel between the In der Burg courtyard and Heldenplatz is the tiny but handy **$ Hofburg Stüberl** sandwich bar—ideal for a cool, quiet sit and a drink or snack (open daily). The recommended **Soho Kantine,** off the Burg-

SIGHTS

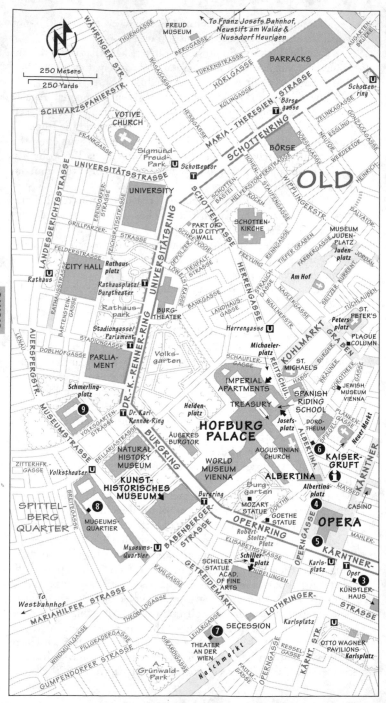

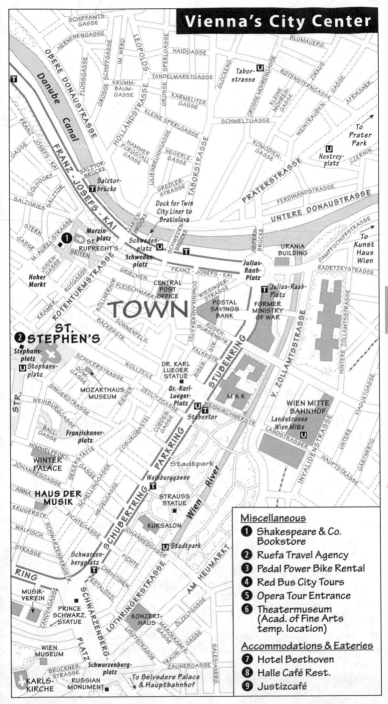

Vienna's City Center

SIGHTS

Miscellaneous

1 Shakespeare & Co. Bookstore
2 Ruefa Travel Agency
3 Pedal Power Bike Rental
4 Red Bus City Tours
5 Opera Tour Entrance
6 Theatermuseum (Acad. of Fine Arts temp. location)

Accommodations & Eateries

7 Hotel Beethoven
8 Halle Café Rest.
9 Justizcafé

garten near the butterfly house, is also a cheap and practical option (see the Eating in Vienna chapter).

▲▲▲Hofburg Imperial Apartments (Kaiserappartements)

These lavish, Versailles-type, "wish-I-were-God" royal rooms are the downtown version of the suburban Schönbrunn Palace. Palace visits are a one-way romp through three sections: a porcelain and silver collection, a museum dedicated to the enigmatic and troubled Empress Sisi, and the luxurious apartments themselves.

The Imperial Apartments are a mix of Old World luxury and modern 19th-century conveniences. Here, Emperor Franz Josef I lived and worked along with his wife Elisabeth, known as Sisi. The Sisi Museum traces the development of her legend, analyzing her fabulous but tragic life as a 19th-century Princess Diana. You'll read bits of her poetic writing, see exact copies of her now-lost jewelry, and learn about her escapes, dieting mania, and chocolate bills.

Cost and Hours: €15, includes well-done audioguide, covered by Sisi Ticket; daily 9:00-17:30, July-Aug until 18:00, last entry one hour before closing; €3 guided tours daily at 14:00; enter from under rotunda just off Michaelerplatz, through Michaelertor gate; tel. 01/533-7570, www.hofburg-wien.at.

📖 See the Hofburg Imperial Apartments Tour chapter.

▲▲▲Hofburg Treasury (Kaiserliche Schatzkammer Wien)

One of the world's most stunning collections of royal regalia, the Hofburg Treasury shows off sparkling crowns, jewels, gowns, and assorted Habsburg bling in 21 darkened rooms. The treasures, well explained by an audioguide, include the crown of the Holy Roman Emperor, Charlemagne's saber, a unicorn horn, and more precious gems than you can shake a scepter at.

Cost and Hours: €12, €20 combo-ticket with Kunsthistorisches; Wed-Mon 9:00-17:30, closed Tue; audioguide-€5 or €7/2 people, €3 guided tours daily at 16:00; from the Hofburg's central courtyard pass through the black, red, and gold gate, then follow *Schatzkammer* signs to the Schweizerhof; tel. 01/525-240, www. kaiserliche-schatzkammer.at.

📖 See the Hofburg Treasury Tour chapter.

▲▲World Museum Vienna (Welt Museum Wien)

The World Museum Vienna houses four separate collections—an armory (with a killer collection of medieval weapons), historical musical instruments, classical statuary from ancient Ephesus, and an impressive ethnographic museum. They're all part of one grand

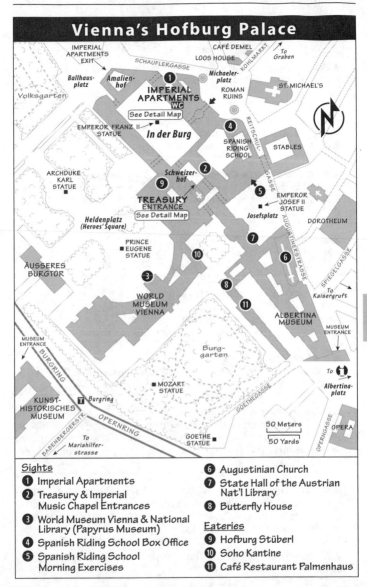

Vienna's Hofburg Palace

Sights

1. Imperial Apartments
2. Treasury & Imperial Music Chapel Entrances
3. World Museum Vienna & National Library (Papyrus Museum)
4. Spanish Riding School Box Office
5. Spanish Riding School Morning Exercises
6. Augustinian Church
7. State Hall of the Austrian Nat'l Library
8. Butterfly House

Eateries

9. Hofburg Stüberl
10. Soho Kantine
11. Café Restaurant Palmenhaus

"World Museum": They have the same entry times and are covered in one ticket. An added bonus of the World Museum is a chance to wander among the royal Habsburg halls, stairways, and painted ceilings virtually alone. You can enjoy the Hall of Columns (central courtyard, c. 1910)—the hub of the complex—for free.

Cost and Hours: €12, Thu-Tue 10:00-18:00, Fri until 21:00, closed Wed; tel. 01/534-30-5052, www.weltmuseumwien.at.

Vienna at a Glance

▲▲▲**Hofburg Imperial Apartments** Lavish main residence of the Habsburgs. **Hours:** Daily 9:00-17:30, July-Aug until 18:00. See page 34.

▲▲▲**Hofburg Treasury** The Habsburgs' collection of jewels, crowns, and other valuables—the best on the Continent. **Hours:** Wed-Mon 9:00-17:30, closed Tue. See page 34.

▲▲▲**St. Stephen's Cathedral** Enormous, historic Gothic cathedral in the center of Vienna. **Hours:** Foyer and north aisle—daily 6:00-22:00; main nave—Mon-Sat 9:00-11:30 & 13:00-16:30, Sun 13:00-16:30, July-Aug until 17:30. See page 48.

▲▲▲**Vienna State Opera** Dazzling, world-famous opera house. **Hours:** By guided tour only, July-Aug generally Mon-Sat at top of hour 10:00-15:00; fewer tours Sept-June and Sun. See page 48.

▲▲▲**Kunsthistorisches Museum** World-class exhibit of the Habsburgs' art collection, including works by Raphael, Titian, Caravaggio, Rembrandt, and Bruegel. **Hours:** Daily 10:00-18:00, Thu until 21:00, closed Mon Sept-May. See page 55.

▲▲▲**Schönbrunn Palace** Spectacular summer residence of the Habsburgs, rivaling the grandeur of Versailles. **Hours:** Daily 8:00-17:30, July-Aug until 18:30, Nov-March until 17:00. See page 77.

▲▲**World Museum Vienna** Four museums in one: uncrowded collection of armor, musical instruments, ancient Greek statues, and ethnographic treasures in the elegant halls of a Habsburg palace. **Hours:** Thu-Tue 10:00-18:00, Fri until 21:00, closed Wed. See page 34.

▲▲**Albertina Museum** Habsburg residence with state apartments, world-class collection of graphic arts and modernist classics, and first-rate special exhibits. **Hours:** Daily 10:00-18:00, Wed and Fri until 21:00. See page 43.

▲▲**Kaisergruft** Crypt for the Habsburg royalty. **Hours:** Daily 10:00-18:00. See page 44.

▲▲**Haus der Musik** Modern museum with interactive exhibits on Vienna's favorite pastime. **Hours:** Daily 10:00-22:00. See page 49.

▲▲**Natural History Museum** Big, beautiful catalog of the natural world, featuring the ancient *Venus of Willendorf*. **Hours:** Thu-Mon 9:00-18:30, Wed until 21:00, closed Tue. See page 56.

SIGHTS

▲▲**Belvedere Palace** Elegant palace of Prince Eugene of Savoy, with a collection of 19th- and 20th-century Austrian art (including Klimt). **Hours:** Daily 10:00-18:00, Fri until 21:00. See page 67.

▲**Spanish Riding School** Prancing white Lipizzaner stallions. **Hours:** Performances nearly year-round (except Jan and mid-June-mid-Aug), usually Sat-Sun at 11:00, plus training sessions generally Tue-Fri 10:00-12:00 (except July-mid-Aug). See page 39.

▲**St. Michael's Church Crypt** Final resting place of about 100 wealthy 18th-century Viennese. **Hours:** By tour Mon-Sat at 11:00 and 13:00, Nov-Easter Thu-Sat only, no tours Sun. See page 47.

▲**St. Peter's Church** Beautiful Baroque church in the old center. **Hours:** Mon-Fri 7:00-20:00, Sat-Sun 9:00-21:00. See page 51.

▲**Karlskirche** Baroque church offering the unique chance to ride an elevator up into the dome. **Hours:** Mon-Sat 9:00-18:00, Sun 12:00-19:00. See page 60.

▲**Academy of Fine Arts Painting Gallery** Small but exciting collection by 15th- to 18th-century masters, temporarily housed at the Theatermuseum. **Hours:** Wed-Mon 10:00-18:00, closed Tue. See page 61.

▲**The Secession** Art Nouveau exterior and Klimt paintings in situ. **Hours:** Tue-Sun 10:00-18:00, closed Mon. See page 62.

▲**Naschmarkt** Sprawling, lively outdoor market. **Hours:** Mon-Fri 6:00-19:30, Sat until 18:00, closed Sun, closes earlier in winter. See page 63.

▲**Museum of Military History** Huge collection of artifacts tracing the military history of the Habsburg Empire. **Hours:** Daily 9:00-17:00. See page 72.

▲**Kunst Haus Wien Museum** Modern art museum dedicated to zany local artist Hundertwasser. **Hours:** Daily 10:00-18:00. See page 73.

▲**Imperial Furniture Collection** Eclectic collection of Habsburg furniture. **Hours:** Tue-Sun 10:00-18:00, closed Mon. See page 77.

SIGHTS

Visiting the Museums: The collection is in flux and may have changed by the time you visit. Pick up a floor plan when you enter, and use the following as a guide for what you might see.

Arms and Armor Collection: Here you're welcomed by colorful mannequins of knights on horse-back. The adjoining rooms display weapons from all over the vast Habsburg Empire, including exotic Turkish suits of armor. Long after gunpowder had rendered medieval weaponry obsolete, the Habsburgs staunchly maintained the knightly code of chivalry and celebrated family events with tournaments and jousts.

Ancient Musical Instruments Collection: This exhibit shows instruments through the ages, especially the rapid evolution from harpsichord to piano. In the 19th century, Vienna was the world's musical capital. In the large entry hall, admire Beethoven's (supposed) clarinet and a strange keyboard perhaps played by Mozart. Browse around to find Leopold Mozart's violin (Room XIII) and a piano owned by Robert and Clara Schumann and later by Brahms (Room XVI).

Ephesus Museum: Here you'll see artifacts from the bustling ancient Greek, then Roman city (located on modern-day Turkey's southwest coast). One bronze statue of an athlete is a jigsaw of 234 shattered pieces meticulously put back together. Look at the scale model of the city of Ephesus; you can make out the theater, the stadium, and—in the middle of an open plain—the Temple of Artemis that is now in the museum's collection (down the stairs). The statue of Artemis from the temple, representing a fertility goddess, is draped with sexy round objects—which may have symbolized breasts, eggs, or bulls' testicles.

Ethnography Museum: This collection displays souvenirs from Habsburg expeditions around the world, all described in English, including the feather bust of a Hawaiian war god and lamps from a nearly 700-year-old mosque in Cairo.

SIGHTS

▲Spanish Riding School (Spanische Hofreitschule)

This stately 300-year-old Baroque hall at the Hofburg Palace is the home of the renowned Lipizzaner stallions. The magnificent building was an impressive expanse in its day. Built without central pillars, it offers clear views of the prancing horses under lavish chandeliers, with a grand painting of Emperor Charles VI on horseback at the head of the hall.

Lipizzaner stallions were a creation of horse-loving Habsburg Archduke Charles. Wanting to breed an intelligent and easily trainable animal, he imported Andalusian horses from his homeland of Spain, then mated them with a local line. Italian and Arabian bloodlines were later added to tweak various characteristics. The name "Lipizzaner" comes from Lipica, the Slovenian town where one of the earliest stud farms was located.

Lipizzaner stallions are known for their noble gait and Baroque profile. These regal horses have changed shape with the tenor of the times: They were bred strong and stout during wars, and frilly and slender in more cultured eras. But they're always born black, fade to gray, and turn a distinctive white in adulthood.

Seeing the Horses and Buying Tickets: The school offers three ways to see the horses—performances, morning exercises, and guided tours of the stables (check the events list on the school's **website** at www.srs.at; enter your dates under "Event Search"). You can purchase tickets online or at the **box office** (opens at 9:00, located inside the Hofburg—go through the main Hofburg entryway from Michaelerplatz, then turn left into the first passage, tel. 01/533-9031). Photos are not allowed at any events, nor are children under age 3.

To **see the horses for free,** you can just walk by the stables at any time of day when the horses are in town. From the covered passageway along Reitschulgasse, there's a big window from where you can usually see the horses poking their heads out of their stalls.

Performances: The Lipizzaner stallions put on great 80-minute performances nearly year-round. The formal emcee introduces each number in German and English as horses do their choreographed moves to jaunty recorded Viennese classical music (in 4:4 meter rather than 3:4—I guess the horses don't waltz). The pricey seats book up months in advance, but standing room is usually available the same day. With just a few rows of seats and close-up standing-room spots, there's not a bad view in the house (seats about €50-160, standing room about €25, prices vary depending on the show; Feb-mid-June and mid-Aug-Dec usually Sat-Sun at 11:00, no shows Jan and mid-June-mid-Aug).

Morning Exercises: For a less expensive, more casual experience, morning exercises with music take place on weekday mornings in the same hall and are open to the public. Don't have high

SIGHTS

Sunday-Morning Culture in Vienna

Sunday morning in Vienna can provide a cultural thrill for visitors. Three wonderful events take place within 200 yards of each other on most Sunday mornings. The Vienna Boys' Choir sings at the 9:15 Mass in the Hofburg's Imperial Music Chapel (mid-Sept-June, see the Entertainment in Vienna chapter). Without reservations, you'll stand in the lobby craning your neck to see the church service, though you can easily watch the boys on the video monitor while you listen to them live. At 11:00, choose between two other Viennese high-culture experiences: At the Hofburg's Spanish Riding School, nab a standing-room spot for the performance of the Lipizzaner stallions (see listing earlier); or, for the best church music in town, sit down in the Augustinian Church for the 11:00 Mass, with a glorious orchestra and choir leading the music (see next page).

---

expectations, as the horses often do little more than trot and warm up. Tourists line up early at Josefsplatz (the large courtyard between Michaelerplatz and Albertinaplatz), at the door marked *Spanische Hofreitschule*. But there's no need to show up when the doors open at 10:00, since tickets never really "sell out." Only the horses stay for the full two hours. As people leave, you can just prance in with no wait at all (€15, available at the door in high season—otherwise buy at visitors center on Michaelerplatz, family discounts, generally Tue-Fri 10:00-12:00, occasionally also on Mon, no exercises July-mid-Aug).

Guided Tours: One-hour guided tours in English are given almost every afternoon year-round. You'll see the Winter Riding School with its grand Baroque architecture, the Summer Riding School in a shady courtyard, and the stables (€18; tours usually daily at 13:00, 14:00, 15:00, and 16:00; reserve ahead by emailing office@srs.at or calling the box office).

▲Augustinian Church (Augustinerkirche)

Built into the Hofburg, this is the Gothic and Neo-Gothic church where the Habsburgs got married. Today, the royal hearts are in the church vault.

Cost and Hours: Free, open long hours daily; at Augustinerstrasse 3, facing Josefsplatz, with its statue of the great reform emperor, Josef II, and the royal library next door.

Visiting the Church: Process as if a bride or groom up the main aisle. In the front (above the altar on the right), notice the windows, from which royals witnessed the Mass in private. Don't miss the exquisite, pyramid-shaped memorial (by the Italian sculptor Antonio Canova) to Maria Theresa's favorite daughter, Maria Christina, with its incredibly sad, white marble procession. It's made of Carrara marble from Italy. Notice her widow, Prince Albert, with sad angel wings, leaning on a lion. Left of that is a chapel dedicated to Charles I, the last Habsburg emperor (r. 1916-1918). Pushed by present-day Habsburg royalists who worship here, Charles is beatified and on a dubious road to sainthood. (The Catholic Church requires that you perform three miracles before they'll make you a saint. Charles I's first miracle: He healed the varicose veins of a nun.) Look back at what's considered the finest pipe organ in Vienna (you'll often hear someone practicing).

Sunday Mass: The church's 11:00 Sunday Mass is a hit with music lovers. It's both a Mass and a concert, often with an orchestra accompanying the choir (acoustics are best in front). Pay by contributing to the offering plate and buying a CD afterward. Check posters by the entry or www.hochamt.at to see what's on—typically you'll hear one of Mozart's, or Haydn's many short Masses.

Viewing the Royal Hearts: The hearts of 54 Habsburg nobles are in urns in a vault off the church's Loreto Chapel (on the right beyond the Maria Christina memorial; see photo of the loaded shelves by the door). On Sunday mornings after Mass, the chapel is opened, and visitors, after listening to a 15-minute lecture in German, can peer through a tiny grate at the rows of urns. The earliest dates from 1618; the last is the heart of Franz Josef's father, who died in 1878 (€2.50, open to the public only after Sunday Mass at about 12:45).

State Hall (Prunksaal) of the Austrian National Library

The National Library's State Hall (Prunksaal) is a postcard-perfect Baroque library (entered from Josefplatz, next to the Augustinian Church, see "Vienna's Hofburg Palace" map, earlier). In this former imperial library, with a statue of Charles VI in the center, you'll find yourself whispering. The setting takes you back to 1730 and gives you the sense that, in imperial times, knowledge of the world was for the elite—and with that knowledge, the elite had power. The glorious paintings (with impressive 3-D) celebrate

high culture and the library's patron, Charles VI. More than 200,000 old books line the walls, but patrons go elsewhere to read them—the hall is just for show these days. Special exhibits fill glass cases down the nave-like main aisle with literary treasures, all well described in English.

Cost and Hours: €8, daily 10:00-18:00, Thu until 21:00, closed Mon Oct-May, tel. 01/53410, www.onb.ac.at.

Other National Library Museums: The library hosts three other minor museums (€4 combo-ticket covers all three, same hours as State Hall). Walk through the National Library's main reading room on Heldenplatz to visit the **Papyrus Museum** in the basement. This little collection tells the story of writing in Egypt from 3000 BC to AD 1000, with scant English descriptions.

A couple of blocks north of the Hofburg, in the building at Herrengasse 9 (across from the Herrengasse U-Bahn station), the library also runs the **Globe Museum** (the world's largest, with 250 terrestrial and celestial spheres) and a modest two-room museum on **Esperanto** and other planned languages.

Butterfly House (Schmetterlinghaus) in the Palace Garden (Burggarten)

The Burggarten greenbelt, once the backyard of the Hofburg and now a people's park, welcomes visitors to loiter on the grass. On nice days, it's lively with office workers enjoying a break, and the popular statue of Mozart, facing the Ringstrasse, almost seems to flirt with passersby.

The iron-and-glass pavilion (c. 1910 with playful Art Nouveau touches) now houses the recommended Café Restaurant Palmenhaus (see the Eating in Vienna chapter) and a small, fluttery butterfly exhibit. Watching the 400 free-flying butterflies is trippy any time of year, and on a chilly day, it feels great to step inside their delightfully muggy greenhouse. If you tour it, notice the butterflies hanging out on the trays with rotting slices of banana. They lick the fermented banana juice as it beads, and then just seem to hang out there in a drunken stupor... or fly giddy loop-de-loops.

Cost and Hours: €7, daily 10:00-16:45, Sat-Sun until 18:15, Nov-March daily until 15:45, tel. 01/533-8570, www.schmetterlinghaus.at.

▲▲Albertina Museum

This impressive museum has three highlights: the imposing state rooms of the former palace, noteworthy collections of classic modernist paintings and European graphic arts (sketches, etching, watercolors—especially Dürer), and excellent temporary exhibits. The building, at the southern tip of the Hofburg complex (near the opera), was the residence of Maria Theresa's favorite daughter, Maria Christina, who was allowed to marry for love rather than political strategy. Her many sisters were jealous. (Marie-Antoinette had to marry the French king...and lost her head over it.) Maria Christina's husband, Albert of Saxony, was a great collector of original drawings and prints, which he amassed to cover all the important art movements from the late Middle Ages until the early 19th century (including prized works by Dürer, Rembrandt, and Rubens). As it's Albert and Christina's gallery, it's charmingly called the "Alber-tina."

Cost and Hours: €13, daily 10:00-18:00, Wed and Fri until 21:00, helpful audioguide-€4, overlooking Albertinaplatz across from the TI and opera, tel. 01/534-830, www.albertina.at.

Visiting the Museum: After the turnstile, on the entry level you'll likely see photography exhibits. Climbing the stairs you reach the main attractions (clearly labeled)—the state rooms (*Prunkräume*) on your left on level 1, and the Batliner Collection on your right on level 2. Excellent special exhibitions (generally featuring modern art and included in your ticket) are shown on level 2 and in the basement galleries.

State Rooms (*Prunkräume*, level 1): Wander freely under chandeliers and across parquet floors through a handful of rooms of 18th-century imperial splendor, unconstrained by velvet ropes. The exhibit spaces (never crowded, well described in English, and air-conditioned) are nearly as impressive as those at Schönbrunn Palace. Many rooms are often closed for special functions, but even a few rooms give a good look at imperial Classicism—this is the only post-Rococo palace in the Habsburg realm. It's a kaleidoscope of colors, as each room's damask walls and curtains are a different rich shade of red, yellow, or green. You may see the billiard room, the tea salon, the bedrooms, and the tiny Goldkabinett, with walls plated in 23-carat gold. Most impressive is the large Hall of Muses (in pastel lavender and yellow), lined with statues of the graceful demi-goddesses (plus Apollo) who inspire the arts.

Batliner Collection (level 2): This manageable collection sweeps you quickly through modern art history, featuring minor works by major artists. Though the collection is permanent, what's on display rotates through about 100 works selected from the 300 in the archives.

Start with a room of classic Impressionism: Monet's water

SIGHTS

lilies, Degas' dancers, and Renoir's cute little girls. By 1900, the modern world was approaching, as seen in Munch's moody landscapes and (Vienna's own) Gustav Klimt's eerie femme fatales.

The next few rooms illustrate how art transitioned from Impressionism to abstraction. The Fauves (Matisse, Vlaminck, Derain) amped up the colors of Impressionism to surreal levels. Expressionists (Nolde, Kirchner) used their trademark thick paint, clashing colors, black outlines, and grotesque figures to capture the unsettled atmosphere of the WWI era. The subject matter becomes increasingly flat and two-dimensional, eventually dissolving into patterns of paint that would become purely abstract.

Another section features German, Russian, and Austrian art from between the wars. The Picasso room has canvases from various periods of his life: early Cubist experiments, portraits of the women in his life, and exuberant, colorful works from his last years on the sunny Riviera. Surrealism, paintings by Francis Bacon, and big Abstract Expressionist canvases bring art up to the cusp of the 21st century.

CHURCH CRYPTS NEAR THE HOFBURG

Two churches near the Hofburg offer starkly different looks at dearly departed Viennese: the Habsburg coffins in the Kaisergruft and the commoners' graves in St. Michael's Church.

▲▲Kaisergruft (Imperial Crypt)

Visiting the imperial remains of the Habsburg family is not as easy as you might imagine. As bodies needed to lie in state to prove to nobility that they were actually dead (in an age of "seeing is believing") the newly dead were gutted like a fish, with all the quick-to-go-bad parts removed (hearts and innards). These original organ donors left their bodies—about 150 in all—in the unassuming Kaisergruft, their hearts in the Augustinian Church (viewable Sun after Mass—see listing earlier), and their entrails in the crypt below St. Stephen's Cathedral (described later).

Cost and Hours: €7.50, daily 10:00-18:00, free map includes Habsburg family tree and a chart locating each coffin, crypt is in the Capuchin Church at Tegetthoffstrasse 2 at Neuer Markt; tel. 01/512-685-388.

Visiting the Kaisergruft: Descend into a crypt full of gray metal tombs. Start up the path, through tombs ranging from simple caskets to increasingly big monuments with elaborate metalwork ornamentation. **Josef I** (the tomb midway along on the right, with the trumpeting angel) was the Holy Roman Emperor who battled France's Louis XIV to a standstill. (Joseph's wife, Amalia, who wanted her heart to rest at her husband's feet for eternity, is in the bosom of a double-headed eagle to the right.)

Empress Maria Theresa (1717-1780) and Her Son, Emperor Josef II (1741-1790)

Maria Theresa was the only woman to officially rule the Habsburg Empire in that family's 640-year reign. She was a strong and effective empress (r. 1740-1780), but Austrians are

also quick to remember Maria Theresa as the mother of 16 children (10 survived into adulthood). Ponder the fact that the most powerful woman in Europe either was pregnant or had a newborn for most of her reign. Maria Theresa ruled after the Austrian defeat of the Ottomans, when Europe recognized Austria as a great power. (Her rival, the Prussian king, said, "When at last the Habsburgs get a great man, it's a woman.") For an abridged Habsburg family tree, see the Austria: Past & Present chapter.

Maria Theresa's reign marked the end of the feudal system and the beginning of the era of the grand state. The first of the modern rulers of the Age of Enlightenment, she was a great social reformer. During her reign, she avoided wars and expanded her empire by skillfully marrying her children into the right families. For instance, after daughter Marie-Antoinette's marriage into the French Bourbon family (to Louis XVI), a country that had been an enemy became an ally. (Unfortunately for Marie-Antoinette, Maria Theresa's timing was off.)

To stay in power during an era of revolution, Maria Theresa had to be in tune with her age. She taxed the Church and the nobility, provided six years of obligatory education to all children, and granted free health care to all in her realm. Maria Theresa also welcomed the boy genius Mozart into her court.

The empress' legacy lived on in her son, Josef II, who ruled as emperor for a decade (1780-1790). He was an even more avid reformer, building on his mother's accomplishments. An enlightened monarch, Josef mothballed the too-extravagant Schönbrunn Palace, secularized the monasteries, established religious tolerance within his realm, freed the serfs, made possible the founding of Austria's first general hospital, and promoted relatively enlightened treatment of the mentally ill. Josef was a model of practicality (for example, he banned slow-to-decompose coffins and allowed no more than six candles at funerals)—and very unpopular with other royals. But his policies succeeded in preempting the revolutionary anger of the age, largely enabling Austria to avoid the anti-monarchist turmoil that shook so much of the rest of Europe.

Karl VI (a few steps farther on the left) was Josef's little brother, best known for failing to father a male heir, but who arranged for his daughter Maria Theresa to take the throne.

You soon reach the massive pewter tomb of **Maria Theresa** under the dome, enjoying natural light. The only female Habsburg monarch, she had to be granted special dispensation to rule. Her 40-year reign was enlightened and progressive. She and her husband, **Franz I,** recline Etruscan-style atop their fancy coffin, gazing into each other's eyes as a cherub crowns them with glory. They were famously in love (though Franz was less than faithful), and their numerous children were married off to Europe's royal houses. Maria Theresa outlived her husband by 15 years, which she spent in mourning. Old and fat, she installed a special lift to transport herself down into the Kaisergruft to visit her dear, departed Franz. At the four corners of the tomb are the Habsburgs' four crowns: the Holy Roman Empire, Hungary, Bohemia, and Lombardy. At his parents' feet lies **Josef II,** the patron of Mozart and Beethoven. Compare the Rococo splendor of Maria Theresa's tomb with the simple coffin of Josef, who was known for his down-to-earth ruling style during the Age of Enlightenment.

Continuing to the right of Maria Theresa's tomb, you'll pass the tombs of **Franz II** (a.k.a. Francis I) and his son **Ferdinand I.** These two 19th-century rulers were forced to relinquish some of the Habsburg power in the face of Napoleon's armies and democratic revolutions.

Head on through the next room—created in 1960—featuring Napoleon's wife, Marie Louise, and a plaque to Franz Ferdinand (assassinated in 1914 in Sarajevo), then head down three steps to a room illustrating the Habsburgs' fading 19th-century glory. There's the appropriately austere military tomb of the long-reigning **Franz Josef** (ruled 1848 to 1916, see sidebar on page 135). Alongside is his wife, **Elisabeth**—a.k.a. Sisi (see page 128)—who always wins the "Most Flowers" award.

Their son was Crown Prince **Rudolf.** Rudolf and his teenage mistress supposedly committed suicide together in 1889 at Mayerling hunting lodge...or was it murder? It took considerable ecclesiastical hair-splitting to win Rudolf this hallowed burial spot: After examining his brain, it was determined that he was mentally disabled and therefore incapable of knowingly killing himself and his girl. In the final room (with humbler copper tombs), you reach the final Habsburgs. **Karl I** (see his bust, not a tomb), the last of the Habsburg rulers, was deposed in 1918. His sons Crown Prince **Otto** and Archduke **Karl Ludwig** are entombed near their mother, **Zita.** (They're holding a prime spot here for Karl Ludwig's wife.)

When Otto was laid to rest here in 2011, it was probably the last great Old Regime event in European history. The monarchy died hard in Austria. Today there are about 700 living Habsburg royals, mostly living in exile. When they die, they will be buried in their countries of exile, not here. Body parts and ornate tombs aside, the real legacy of the Habsburgs is the magnificence of this city. Step outside. Pan up. Watch the clouds glide by the ornate gables of Vienna.

▲St. Michael's Church Crypt (Michaelerkirche)

St. Michael's Church, which faces the Hofburg on Michaelerplatz, offers a striking contrast to the imperial crypt. Regular tours take visitors underground to see a typical church crypt, filled with the rotting wooden coffins of well-to-do commoners.

Cost and Hours: €7 for 45-minute tour, Mon-Sat at 11:00 and 13:00, no tours Sun, Nov-Easter Thu-Sat only, tours in German and English, wait at church entrance at the sign advertising the tour and pay the guide directly, mobile 0650-533-8003, www.michaelerkirche.at.

Visiting the Crypt: Climbing below the church, you'll see about a hundred 18th-century coffins and stand on three feet of debris, surrounded by niches filled with stacked lumber from decayed coffins and countless bones. You'll meet a 1769 mummy in lederhosen and a wig, along with a woman who is clutching a cross and has flowers painted on her high heels. You'll learn about death in those times, including how the wealthy—not wanting to end up in standard shallow graves—instead paid to be laid to rest below the church, and how, in 1780, Emperor Josef II ended the practice of cemetery burials in cities but allowed the rich to become the stinking rich in crypts under churches. You'll also discover why many were buried with their chins strapped shut (because when your muscles rot, your jaw falls open and you get that ghostly, skeletal look that nobody wants).

St. Michael's Church itself has an interesting history. In 1791, a few days after Mozart's death, his *Requiem* was performed here for the first time. (See the small monument just inside the door on the right.) In the rear of the nave, in a small chapel on the right, is a small memorial to Austrian victims of the Nazis at the Dachau concentration camp (a wooden cross made in 1945 at Dachau by newly freed prisoners). Just to the left of the cross is a niche with a relief of Austria's Fascist chancellor Engelbert Dollfuss, who was murdered in 1934 by Austrian Nazis for opposing union with

Germany. While he was a fascist, he was not a Nazi and not anti-Semitic.

MORE SIGHTS WITHIN THE RING

▲▲▲St. Stephen's Cathedral (Stephansdom)

This massive Gothic church with the skyscraping spire sits at the center of Vienna. Its highlights are the impressive exterior, the view from the top of the south tower, a carved pulpit, and a handful of quirky sights associated with Mozart and the Habsburg rulers.

Cost and Hours: Church foyer and north aisle—free, daily 6:00-22:00; main nave—€6 includes audioguide and guided tour (daily at 10:30); open Mon-Sat 9:00-11:30 & 13:00-16:30, Sun 13:00-16:30, July-Aug until 17:30; south and north towers, catacombs, and treasury have varying costs and hours; tel. 01/515-523-526, www.stephanskirche.at.

📖 See the St. Stephen's Cathedral Tour chapter or 🎧 download my free audio tour.

▲▲▲Vienna State Opera (Wiener Staatsoper)

The opera house, facing the Ring and near the TI, is a central point for any visitor. Vienna remains one of the world's great cities for classical music, and this building still belts out some of the finest opera, both classic and cutting-edge. While the critical reception of the building 130 years ago led the architect to commit suicide, and though it's been rebuilt since its destruction by WWII bombs, it's still a sumptuous place. The interior has a chandeliered lobby and carpeted staircases perfect for making the scene. The theater itself features five wraparound balconies, gold-and-red decor, and a bracelet-like chandelier.

Depending on your interest in opera, choose among several different ways to experience the building. You can simply admire its Neo-Renaissance charms from the outside (and maybe slip inside the lobby for a peek), or take a guided tour of the lavish interior (see next). Best of all, attend an opera performance, which can be surprisingly easy and cheap to do—and doesn't have to take up a whole evening (get details in the Entertainment in Vienna chapter).

Opera House Tours: The only way to see the opera house interior (besides attending a performance) is with a guided 45-minute tour. You'll see the opulent halls where operagoers gather at intermission, enjoying elaborate spaces with coffered ceilings, gold trim, and iron-work lamps. You'll learn about the opera's history, and have a chance to compare the old parts of the building (such as Emperor Franz Josef's ornate reception room) with the postwar reconstruction. The highlight is the 2,000-seat theater itself—where the main floor is ringed by box seating, under a huge sugar-doughnut chandelier. If it seems busy, that's because the Vienna State Opera puts on 60 different productions a year. And, with a policy of never performing the same opera on two successive nights, the stage is a hive of activity throughout the season. Your tour gives a backstage peek at the action.

Cost and Hours: €9, tours generally at the top of each hour 10:00-15:00 but schedule varies due to rehearsals and performances; more tours July-Aug (when there are no performances), fewer tours Sept-June and Sun year-round; no reservations taken, and they don't sell out—just show up at the tour entrance (southwest corner of building) 20 minutes ahead; current month's tour schedule posted online, at the door, or in the opera's *Prolog* magazine; tel. 01/514-442-606, www.wiener-staatsoper.at.

▲▲Haus der Musik

Vienna's "House of Music" is a fun and interactive experience that celebrates this hometown forte. The museum, spread over several

floors and well-described in English, is unique for its effective use of touchscreen computers and headphones to explore the physics of sound. One floor is dedicated to the heavyweight Viennese composers (Mozart, Beethoven, and company) who virtually created classical music as we know it. Really experiencing the place takes time. It's open late and is so interactive, relaxing, and fun that it can be considered an activity more than a sight—an evening of joy for music lovers.

Cost and Hours: €13, half-price after 20:00, €18 combo-ticket with Mozarthaus, daily 10:00-22:00, two blocks from the opera house at Seilerstätte 30, tel. 01/513-4850, www.hausdermusik. com. Your ticket includes a free app for added info as you visit.

Visiting the Museum: It's a one-way system; just follow the arrows on the floor. The **first floor** highlights the Vienna Philharmonic Orchestra, known the world over for their New Year's Eve concerts. (In a mini concert hall, a one-hour video—on a loop—lets you enjoy the event.) See Toscanini's baton, Mahler's cap, and well-used scores. Throw the dice to randomly "compose" a piece of music.

The **second floor** explores the physics of sound—you'll hear the world in new ways. There are "sounds of the womb," "ambience around the world," and the "Beethoven and Mozart reload" exhibit, which presents the pop music of the 18th century in contemporary terms. Wander through the "sonosphere" and marvel at the amazing acoustics. Interactive exhibits explore the nature of sound and

SIGHTS

music; I could actually hear what I thought only a piano tuner could discern. You can twist, dissect, and bend sounds to make your own musical language, merging your voice with a duck's quack or a city's traffic roar. A tube filled with pebbles demonstrates the power of sound waves...watch them bounce. The "instrumentarium" presents various tools of the trade, new and old.

The **third floor** celebrates the famous hometown boys. (With the app, you can enjoy appropriate music in each room as you stroll.) Haydn established the four-movement symphony, and pioneered the sonata-form technique of repeating a brief melody throughout a longer work (and you'll meet his parrot). Mozart was music's first charismatic rock star. See the picture of the famous performing Mozart family, with little Wolfgang and his sister at the keyboard, their father on violin, and (a portrait of) their mom behind. Beethoven (see his "square piano," a letter to his brother, and depictions of his many Vienna apartments) turned mere entertainment into serious art. His nine symphonies amped up the size of the orchestra and the emotional wattage, anticipating the powerful Romantic style. An exhibit allows you to hear what Beethoven did as he gradually lost his hearing. Schubert, who died in obscurity at 31, wrote 600 songs that are sung today and the brilliant *Unfinished Symphony*. The Strausses (father and son) created the dance craze that defines Vienna—the waltz. Mahler expanded the orchestra to its fullest range, and paved the way for atonal modernists like Schönberg, Webern, and Berg.

Before leaving, pick up a virtual baton to conduct the Vienna Philharmonic. It really works—you can go fast or slow, and bring out the section to which you direct your baton; make it through the piece, and you'll get a rousing round of applause.

▲Dorotheum Auction House (Palais Dorotheum)

For an aristocrat's flea market, drop by Austria's answer to Sotheby's. The ground floor has shops, an info desk with a schedule of upcoming auctions (Sept-June only), and a few auction items. Some pieces are available for immediate sale (marked *VKP*, for *Verkaufpreis*—"sales price"), while others are up for auction (marked *DIFF. RUF*). Labels on each item predict the auction value. Serious bidders can review what's on and even make bids via their website.

The first floor (above the mezzanine) has antique furniture and fancy knick-knacks, many brought in by people who've inherited old things and don't have room for them. The second floor has a showy antique gallery with fixed prices. Wandering through here, you feel like you're touring a museum with exhibits you can buy. Afterward, you can continue your hunt for the perfect curio on the streets around the Dorotheum, which are lined with many fine antique shops.

Cost and Hours: Free, Mon-Fri 10:00-18:00, Sat 9:00-17:00, closed Sun, classy little café on second floor, between the Graben pedestrian street and Hofburg at Dorotheergasse 17, tel. 01/51560, www.dorotheum.com.

▲St. Peter's Church (Peterskirche)

Baroque Vienna is at its best in this architectural gem, tucked away a few steps from the Graben.

Cost and Hours: Free, Mon-Fri 7:00-20:00, Sat-Sun 9:00-21:00; free organ concerts Mon-Fri at 15:00, Sat-Sun at 20:00; just off the Graben between the Plague Monument and Kohlmarkt, tel. 01/533-6433, www.peterskirche.at.

Visiting the Church: Admire the rose-and-gold, oval-shaped Baroque interior, topped with a ceiling fresco of Mary kneeling to be crowned by Jesus and the Father, while the dove of the Holy Spirit floats way up in the lantern. The church's sumptuous elements—especially the organ, altar painting, pulpit, and coat of arms (in the base of the dome) of church founder Leopold I—make St. Peter's one of the city's most beautiful and ornate churches.

To the right of the altar, a dramatic golden statue shows the martyrdom of St. John Nepomuk (c. 1340-1393). The Czech saint defied the heretical King Wenceslas, so he was tossed to his death off the Charles Bridge in Prague. In true Baroque style, we see the dramatic peak of his fall, when John has just passed the point of no return. The Virgin Mary floats overhead in a silver cloud.

But also holy was the Emperor. Looking down from above at the base of the dome is the Holy Roman Empire's double-headed eagle, with halos around each head—a reminder to all that the Emperor was indeed holy.

The present church (from 1733) stands atop earlier churches dating back to the early Middle Ages; it was built quickly and therefore consists of one pure artistic style. On either side of the nave are glass cases containing skeletons of Christian martyrs from Roman times.

Mozarthaus Vienna Museum

In September 1784, 27-year-old Wolfgang Amadeus Mozart moved into this spacious apartment with his wife, Constanze, and their week-old son Karl. For the next three years, this was the epicenter of Viennese high life. It was here that Mozart wrote *Marriage of Figaro* and *Don Giovanni* and established himself as the toast of Vienna. Today, the actual apartments are pretty boring (mostly bare rooms), but the museum does flesh out Mozart's Vienna years with paintings, videos, and a few period pieces.

Cost and Hours: €11, includes audioguide, €18 combo-ticket with Haus der Musik, daily 10:00-19:00, a block behind the cathedral, go through arcade at #5a and walk 50 yards to Domgasse 5, tel. 01/512-1791, www.mozarthausvienna.at.

Visiting the Museum: Start on the third floor, working your way down through museum displays to the actual apartment on the first floor. Exhibits set the scene: **Vienna in the 1780s,** population 50,000, was a blossoming music capital. It supported more than just the traditional church and court music. Mozart capitalized on this and profited greatly by organizing public concerts in concert halls and aristocratic homes, and he wrote crowd-pleasing pieces for the theater. Antonio Salieri, the emperor's musical director, was supposedly jealous of Mozart's God-given talent, but in reality he probably fostered the young man's career (and Mozart eventually succeeded him). Mozart joined the Freemasons, whose symbolism would appear in his opera *The Magic Flute.* Mozart loved the good life—nice clothes, gambling at cards, even peepshows—and the three years he spent in this house were his champagne years.

The second floor delves into **Mozart's Musical World.** The audioguide gives some background on his friendship with fellow-genius Haydn and his successful operas. But after 1787, the money dried up: He and Constanze moved to a cheaper place outside the city center and Wolfgang hit the road to raise money. He died just four years later at age 35 while writing his *Requiem.* His cause of death still remains a mystery.

The first-floor **apartment** consists of a half-dozen nondescript rooms, sparsely decorated with period pieces (but none of them Mozart's). See the portraits of him and Constanze, and picture them here: raising their kids, playing billiards, perhaps jamming with Haydn (though there's no evidence of that), or just gazing out the window as Mozart composed another masterpiece. Gaze out the window yourself, and appreciate that the view is relatively unchanged since Mozart's time. Unfortunately, the bare rooms themselves don't quite succeed in capturing the joie de vivre of the exuberant young genius in his prime.

Jewish Museum Vienna (Jüdisches Museum Wien)

The museum operates two buildings a 10-minute walk apart. The main museum is on Dorotheergasse (near the Hofburg), and a smaller, more archaeological exhibit is at Judenplatz, which is also the site of a Holocaust memorial (near Am Hof).

Cost and Hours: €12 ticket includes both museums; Dorotheergasse location, at #11—Sun-Fri 10:00-18:00, closed Sat, videoguide-€4; Judenplatz location, at #8—Sun-Thu 10:00-18:00, Fri until 17:00, closed Sat; tel. 01/535-0431, www.jmw.at.

Background: Jews settled in Vienna in the early Middle Ages, only to be brutally expelled in 1420 (similar events took place in other German-speaking towns). Another community formed in the 17th century, but was broken up in 1670. Even during the years when Jews were forbidden to live in Vienna, many settled in the small towns and cities of the Habsburg empire, and in the parts of Poland that the Habsburgs took over in the 1770s. In 1782, Josef II partially eased restrictions on his Jewish subjects, allowing them to own property, attend university, and even (if they paid a special tax) to live in Vienna. Still, it was not until the 1850s that the Jewish community in Vienna was allowed to build a synagogue, and it was only in 1867 that reforms allowed freedom of movement and residence for everyone in the empire.

After that, Jews moved from the small towns to Vienna in large numbers, attracted by educational and economic opportunities in the rapidly expanding and industrializing capital. Psychologist Sigmund Freud, writers Arthur Schnitzler and Stefan Zweig, and journalist Theodor Herzl were among the prominent Austrian Jews of the pre-WWI period. In 1910, almost 10 percent of Vienna's two million inhabitants were Jewish. But the officially Catholic city was a hostile, anti-Semitic environment for them, with pressure to assimilate or emigrate, especially under the Christian Socialist Karl Lueger, who was mayor from 1897 to 1910. After the Nazi annexation of Austria in 1938, Jews were once again persecuted, expelled, or forced to emigrate. Those who did not were mostly sent to their deaths in the concentration camps in Poland. After the war, only a handful returned to their homes, and today the local Jewish community numbers just a few thousand.

Visiting the Museums: The **Jewish Museum Dorotheergasse** fills a four-story downtown building with exhibits, a bookstore, and a small, reasonably priced café serving Middle Eastern fare. It documents Vienna's Jewish community from earliest times to the present.

The main part of the exhibit is on the second floor, covering

SIGHTS

the history of Vienna's Jews up to World War II; a ground-floor exhibit carries the story forward to the present day. The first floor hosts temporary exhibits, and the evocative third floor is a "visible storage" archive with stacks of Judaica and works of art that once ornamented synagogues.

The smaller, less interesting **Museum Judenplatz** was built around the scant remains of the medieval synagogue that served Vienna's 1,500 Jewish residents up until their massacre in 1420. Its main exhibit is an underground hall where you see the synagogue's foundations. The museum also has brief displays on medieval Jewish life and a well-done video re-creating the neighborhood as it looked five centuries ago.

The classy square above the ruins, called Judenplatz, is now dominated by a blocky **memorial** to the 65,000 Viennese Jews killed by the Nazis. The memorial—a library turned inside out—invokes Jewish identity as a "people of the book" and asks viewers to ponder the huge loss of culture, knowledge, and humanity that took place between 1938 and 1945.

Austrian Postal Savings Bank (Österreichische Postsparkasse)

Built between 1904 and 1912, the Postal Savings Bank was one of the key buildings in the development of modern architecture.

Today it's a pilgrimage site for architects from all over the world (for whom it's a ▲▲▲ sight), though its future is in doubt (it may have been turned into lofts by the time you visit). If it's open, hard-core Jugendstil fans may want to visit the pleasant, small museum inside, which tells the building's story through plans, photos, and news reports, and preserves the original bank-teller counters.

Cost and Hours: Free, foyer and atrium open Mon-Fri 7:00-17:30, closed Sat-Sun; museum open Mon-Fri from 10:00, closed Sat-Sun; just inside the Ringstrasse at Georg-Coch-Platz 2, tel. 059-9053-3825, www.ottowagner.com.

Background: The postal savings system was intended for working-class people, who didn't have access to the palatial banks of the 19th century—but could walk to a post office. Secessionist architect Otto Wagner believed "necessity is the master of art," and he declared that "what is impractical can never be beautiful." Everything about his design—so gray, white, and efficient—is practical. It's so clean that the service provided here feels almost sacred. This is a textbook example of form following function, and the form is beautiful.

The product of an age giddy with advancement, the building dignifies the technological and celebrates it as cultural. Study the sleek, yet elegantly modern exterior: Angles high above—made of an exciting new material, aluminum—seem to proclaim the modern age. The facade and its unadorned marble siding panels, secured by aluminum bolts, give the impression that the entire building is a safe-deposit box. The interior is similarly functionalist. The glass roof lets in light; the glass floor helps illuminate the basement. Fixtures, vents, and even the furniture fit right in—all bold, geometrical, and modern.

MUSEUM DISTRICT

In the 19th century, the Habsburgs planned to link their palace and museum buildings with a series of arches across the Ringstrasse. Although that dream was never fully realized, the awe-inspiring museums still face off across Maria-Theresien-Platz, with a monument to Maria Theresa at its center (for more on this monument, see the Vienna City Walk chapter).

▲▲▲Kunsthistorisches Museum

This exciting museum, across the Ring from the Hofburg Palace, showcases the grandeur and opulence of the Habsburgs' collected artwork in a grand building (purpose-built in 1888 to display these works). While there's little Viennese art here, you will find world-class European masterpieces galore (including canvases by Raphael, Caravaggio, Velázquez, Rubens, Vermeer, Rembrandt, and a particularly exquisite roomful of Bruegels), all well displayed on one glorious floor, plus a fine display of Egyptian, classical, and applied arts. Another highlight, filling a wing of the ground floor, is the

Habsburg "Chamber of Wonders" *(Kunstkammer),* showing off the imperial collection of exquisite fine-art objects and exotic curios (the highlight being Cellini's golden salt cellar).

Cost and Hours: €15, €20 combo-ticket with Hofburg Treasury; daily 10:00-18:00, Thu until 21:00, closed Mon Sept-May; audioguide-€5, on the Ringstrasse at Maria-Theresien-Platz, U: Volkstheater/Museumsplatz, tel. 01/525-240, www.khm.at.

📖 See the Kunsthistorisches Museum Tour chapter.

▲▲Natural History Museum (Naturhistorisches Museum)

The twin building facing the Kunsthistorisches Museum still serves the exact purpose for which it was built: to show off the Habsburgs' vast collection of plant, animal, and mineral specimens and artifacts. It's grown to become an exceptionally well-organized and enjoyable catalogue of the natural world, with 20 million objects, including moon rocks, dinosaur stuff, and the fist-sized *Venus of Willendorf* (at 25,000 years old, the world's oldest sex symbol). Even though the museum has kept its old-school charm, nearly everything on display is presented and described well enough to engage any visitor, from kids to scientifically inclined grown-ups.

Cost and Hours: €10, Thu-Mon 9:00-18:30, Wed until 21:00, closed Tue; €5 audioguide ("Top 100") isn't necessary, but can help you hit the highlights; on the Ringstrasse at Maria-Theresien-Platz, U: Volkstheater/Museumsplatz, tel. 01/521-770, www.nhm-wien. ac.at.

Visiting the Museum: For a quick visit, head first to the *Venus of Willendorf*—she's on the mezzanine level, just off Room 11 (from the entrance lobby, climb the first 12 steps, swing left, and then right towards the dinosaur skeletons). The four-inch-tall, chubby stone statuette, found in the Danube Valley in 1908, is a generic female (no face or feet) resting her hands on her ample breasts. The statue's purpose is unknown, but she may have been a symbol of fertility for our mammoth-hunting ancestors.

In Room 10 you can't miss the very lifelike Allosaurus, the most dangerous predator of the Late Jurassic period. The gigantic Diplodocus *(Diplodocus carnegii)* skeleton cast, with its long neck and tail, is named after Andrew Carnegie, who purchased the original for a museum in Pittsburgh. The turtle skeleton on the far end is the largest ever discovered.

For a more chronological visit, start with the impressive exhibit on rocks (Rooms 1-5, to the right of entrance lobby), which includes precious gemstones (emeralds, opals, and an octahedral diamond from South Africa) and one of the world's largest and oldest collections of meteorites. In Room 6, step into the dark mini theater to watch the "GaiaSphere"—an animated globe that gives a new perspective on weather, ocean currents, and human population. Rooms 7-9 cover the origins of organic life, with fossils from early microorganisms all the way to the complete skeleton of a pre-historic elephant. The timeline continues upstairs with Room 21, where you can follow hundreds of millions of years of evolution—from single cells to sea creatures, reptiles, birds, mammals, and primates. Finish with the hairless primate—man—also downstairs, in Rooms 11-14.

MuseumsQuartier

The vast grounds of the former imperial stables now corral a cut-ting-edge cultural center for contemporary arts and design. Among several impressive museums, the best are the Leopold Museum and the Museum of Modern Art. For many, the MuseumsQuartier is most enjoyable as a spot to gather in the evening for a light, fun meal, cocktails, and people-watching.

Cost and Hours: Leopold Museum—€13, open daily 10:00-18:00, Thu until 21:00, closed Tue Sept-May, audioguide-€4 or €7/2 people, tel. 01/525-700, www.leopoldmuseum.org; Museum of Modern Art—€12, €8 Thu after 18:00, open Mon 14:00-19:00, Tue-Sun 10:00-19:00, Thu until 21:00, good audioguide-€3.50, tel. 01/52500, www.mumok.at. The main entrance/visitors center is at Museumsplatz 1 (ask about combo-tickets here if visiting more than just the Leopold and Modern Art museums). U: Volksthe-ater/Museumsplatz, tel. 01/525-5881, www.mqw.at.

Visiting the MuseumsQuartier: From the Hofburg side, the main entrance (with visitors center, shop, and ticket office) leads to a big courtyard with cafés, fountains, and ever-changing "in-stallation lounge furniture," all surrounded by the quarter's various museums.

The **Leopold Museum** specializes in 20th-century Austrian modernists: Egon Schiele, Gustav Klimt, and Oskar Kokoschka, among others. Its Schiele collection is one of the largest in the world, though these works make some people uncomfortable—Schiele's nudes are *really* nude. While this is a great collection, you can see even better works from these artists in the Belvedere Palace (described later in this chapter). The museum also hosts special ex-hibits of modern Austrian art.

The **Museum of Modern Art** (Museum Moderner Kunst, a.k.a. MUMOK) is Austria's leading gallery for international modern and contemporary art. The striking lava-paneled building

Vienna with Kids

For a city known for opera, classical music, and art museums, Vienna is a surprisingly great place to take the kids. Several of the most truly Viennese experiences are either inherently kid-friendly (the Prater amusement park, horse-and-buggy rides) or come in kid-friendly form if you seek it out (opera, art museums). On Sundays, holidays, and during local summer vacations, all kids under 15 ride free on public transit; otherwise they're half-price (and kids under 6 always ride free).

Even better, anyone 18 and under gets in for free at most of the city's top museums. The TI (www.wien.info) has tons of advice on Vienna's many family-friendly activities.

Prater Park: Besides the famous red Ferris wheel and roller coasters, there are jungle gyms, pony rides, a child-size steam train, and lots more (see page 78).

Haus der Musik: The exhibits take a playful approach to music; they also host occasional children's concerts (see page 49).

Schönbrunn Palace: Families can find plenty of fun here without ever entering the palace proper. The grounds have a great maze and playground, a marionette theater, and a children's museum with kid-centric displays (kids—€7, adults—€9, consider combo-tickets with the garden features, family passes available in summer, daily 10:00-17:00, www.kaiserkinder.at). The world's oldest zoo is adjacent to the palace grounds, and older kids may also like the nearby Imperial Carriage Museum (free for kids; see the Schönbrunn Palace Tour chapter).

Natural History Museum: Dinosaurs, rocks, and lots of interactive displays that keep kids' interest (free for kids; see page 56).

Butterfly House: Free-flying butterflies in a classic Art Nouveau

is three stories tall and four stories deep, offering seven floors of far-out art that's hard for most visitors to appreciate. This state-of-the-art museum usually shows off its huge and rotating collection of works by classical 20th-century modernists (Paul Klee, Pablo Picasso, Pop artists), but check the website in advance as exhibits can change.

Rounding out the sprawling MuseumsQuartier are an architecture center, design forum, children's museum, contemporary dance space, and the **Kunsthalle Wien**—with temporary exhibits of contemporary art (www.kunsthallewien.at).

Cuisine Art: Across from the MUMOK, **$$ Halle Café**

glasshouse (kids—€5.50, see page 42).

Zoom Kindermuseum: Interactive fun for a wide range of ages, including hands-on history exhibits, art workshops, and science demonstrations—much of it available in English (free entry for kids but most activities cost €6 per child, adults—€5, reserve entry time online at least an hour ahead; Tue-Fri 8:30-16:00, Sat-Sun from 9:45, closed Mon, in the MuseumsQuartier at Museums-platz 1, www.kindermuseum.at).

Art Museums: Several of Vienna's top art museums offer clever ways to engage younger visitors (along with free admission). For example, the Upper Belvedere sends kids on an "art detective" scavenger hunt around the museum; the Kunsthistorisches Museum rents an audioguide tailored for kids.

Children's Operas: Operas, ballets, and concerts staged by the Vienna State Opera are performed at the Kinderoper, the world's only just-for-kids opera venue. Sung in German; reasonable ticket prices, performances usually around midday and about an hour long, book as far ahead as possible, just down the street from the main opera house at Walfischgasse 4, www.wiener-staatsoper.at—search for "Kinderoper".

Spanish Riding School: The morning exercises (described earlier) are low-key enough to make sense, especially because it's easy to arrive late and/or leave early (€7.50 for ages 6-18, ages 3-5 are free if they're on your lap, no kids under 3).

Donauinsel: Danube Island (described on page 79) is a great place to bike, boat, swim (in the river or at the city-run water park), or challenge the kids on a ropes course at the climbing park (www.donauinsel-kletterpark.at).

More Activities: The Stadtpark includes a good playground (see page 78). Horse-and-buggy *(Fiaker)* rides through the Old Town are a hit (see page 29). A little farther afield, there's Bogi Park's indoor play paradise (www.bogipark.at) and the Dianabad water park (www.dianabad.at).

SIGHTS

Restaurant is your best bet for food or drinks overlooking the courtyard (lunch specials, daily 10:00-24:00, Museumsplatz 1, tel. 01/523-7001).

Eating Nearby: The charming **Spittelberg** neighborhood, just beyond the MuseumsQuartier, hosts a range of pleasant eateries, including a lovely wine garden just a five-minute walk away (see page 184). If you're here on a weekday, consider a short walk to the **$ Justizcafe,** the cafeteria serving Austria's Supreme Court, which offers a fine view, great prices, average food, and a memorable lunchtime experience. Your goal is the rooftop of the Palace of Justice: Enter through the grand front door, pass through security, say "wow" to the eye-popping Historicist courtyard, head to the back of the building and ride the elevator to the fifth floor, then walk back to the front past rows of judges' chambers. You can sit inside or out on the roof, surrounded by legal beagles—go early or after the lunch rush to miss the crush (Mon-Fri 7:00-16:30, closed Sat-Sun, Schmerlingplatz 10). For location, see the "Vienna's City Center" map, earlier.

KARLSPLATZ AND NEARBY

These sights cluster around Karlsplatz, just southeast of the Ringstrasse (U: Karlsplatz). If you're walking from central Vienna, use the U-Bahn station's passageway (at the opera house) to avoid crossing busy boulevards.

Karlsplatz

This picnic-friendly square, with its Henry Moore sculpture in the pond, is the front yard of Vienna's Technical University. The gangly zone, considered just an undefined space rather than a "square," was long little more than a no-man's-land outside the city wall. The city has heroically tried to make it more inviting, and in recent years has added a playground, skateboard park, open-air summer cinema, cocktail bar (in what looks like a shipping container), and a pond meant to lend the square a beachy vibe (music festivals are hosted on a "lake stage").

The massive, domed Karlskirche and its twin spiral columns dominate the square. The small green, white, and gold pavilions that line the street across the square from the church are from the late-19th-century municipal train system *(Stadtbahn)*. One of Europe's first transit systems, this precursor to today's U-Bahn was built with a military purpose in mind: to move troops quickly in time of civil unrest—specifically, out to Schönbrunn Palace. With curvy iron frames, decorative marble slabs, and painted gold trim, these are pioneering works in the Jugendstil style, designed by the Modernist architect **Otto Wagner,** who influenced Klimt and the Secessionists (for more on this art movement, see the sidebar later in this chapter). One of the pavilions has a sweet little exhibit on Wagner that illustrates the Art Nouveau lifestyle around 1900. It also shows models for his never-built dreams and the grand expansion of Vienna (€5, Tue-Sun 10:00-18:00, closed Mon and Nov-March, near the Ringstrasse, tel. 01/5058-7478-5177, www.wienmuseum.at).

▲Karlskirche (St. Charles Church)

This "votive church" was proposed by Emperor Charles VI and dedicated to his patron saint, St. Charles Borromeo, in 1713 when an epidemic spared Vienna. The church offers some over-the-top Baroque designs, with a unique combination of columns (showing scenes from Borromeo's life, à la Trajan's Column in Rome), a classic pediment, an elliptical dome, and a terrific close-up look at its frescoes, thanks to a construction elevator that's open to the public. The entry fee is steep, but worth it if you visit the dome—but skip it if you're even slightly afraid of heights.

Cost and Hours: €8, Mon-Sat 9:00-18:00, Sun 12:00-19:00, dome elevator runs until 17:30, pick up the free info booklet, www.karlskirche.at. There are often classical music concerts performed here on period instruments (usually Thu-Sat, www.concert-vienna.info).

Visiting the Church: The dome's colorful 13,500-square-foot fresco—painted in the 1730s by Johann Michael Rottmayr—shows Signor Borromeo (in red-and-white bishop's robes) gazing up into heaven, spreading his arms wide, and pleading with Christ to spare Vienna from the plague.

After studying the frescoes from far below, ride the industrial lift, which takes you to a platform at the base of the 235-foot dome. Consider that the church was built and decorated with a scaffolding system essentially the same as this one.

At that dizzying height, you're in the clouds with cupids and angels. Many details that appear smooth and beautiful from ground level—such as gold leaf, paintings, and fake marble—look rough and sloppy up close. It's surreal to observe the 3-D figures from an unintended angle—check out Christ's leg, which looks dwarf-sized. Give yourself a minute to take it in: Faith, Hope, and Charity triumph and inspire. Borromeo lobbies heaven for relief from the plague. Meanwhile, a Protestant's Lutheran Bible is put to the torch by angels.

▲Academy of Fine Arts Painting Gallery (Akademie der Bildenden Künste Gemäldegalerie)

Vienna's art academy has a small but impressive collection of paintings, most of which is being temporarily housed at the nearby Theatermuseum while the academy is undergoing a multiyear renovation. The highlights—a triptych by the master of medieval surrealism, Hieronymus Bosch, and works by Guardi, Titian, Rubens,

Van Dyck, and other great masters—can be seen at the temporary location.

The captivating, harrowing *Last Judgment* triptych by Bosch (c. 1482, with some details added by Lucas Cranach) is the polar opposite of his most famous work, *The Garden of Earthly Delights* (in Madrid's Prado). Read the altarpiece from left to right, following the pessimistically medieval narrative about humankind's fall from God's grace: In the left panel, at the bottom, God pulls Eve from Adam's rib in the Garden of Eden. Just above that, we see a female (representing the serpent) hold out the forbidden fruit to tempt Eve. Above that, Adam and Eve are being shooed away by an angel. At the top of this panel, God sits on his cloud, evicting the fallen angels (who turn into insect-like monsters). In the middle panel, Christ holds court over the living and the dead. Notice the jarring contrast between Christ's serene expression and the grotesque scene playing out beneath him, where mutant demons slice-and-dice the damned. These disturbing images crescendo in the final (right) panel, showing an unspeakably horrific vision of hell that few artists have managed to top in the more than half-millennium since Bosch.

On your way out of the temporary exhibit, ponder how history might have been different if the academy had accepted a student who applied but was rejected twice—Adolf Hitler.

Cost and Hours: Temporary exhibit at Theatermuseum—€12, Wed-Mon 10:00-18:00, closed Tue; audioguide-€2, in the Palais Lobokowitz at Lobkowitzplatz 2, tel. 01/588-162-201, www.akbild.ac.at; Academy of Fine Arts—closed until at least 2020, when open it's three blocks from the opera house at Schillerplatz 3.

▲The Secession

This little building was created by the Vienna Secession movement, a group of nonconformist artists led by Gustav Klimt, Otto Wagner, and friends. (For more on the art movement, see the sidebar later.)

Having turned their backs on the stuffy official art academy, the Secessionists used the building to display their radical art. The stylized trees carved into the exterior walls and the building's bushy "golden cabbage" rooftop are symbolic of a cycle of renewal. Today, the Secession continues to showcase contemporary cutting-edge art, and it preserves Gustav Klimt's famous *Beethoven Frieze*.

Cost and Hours: €9.50 includes special exhibits, Tue-Sun 10:00-18:00, closed

Mon, audioguide-€3, Friedrichstrasse 12, tel. 01/587-5307, www.secession.at.

Visiting the Museum: Start in the basement with the museum's highlight—Klimt's classic *Beethoven Frieze*. A masterpiece of Viennese Art Nouveau, this 105-foot-long fresco was the multimedia centerpiece of a 1902 exhibition honoring Ludwig van Beethoven. Klimt's still-powerful work was inspired by Beethoven's *Ninth Symphony*. Klimt embellished the frieze with painted-on gold (aided by his brother, a goldsmith) and by gluing on reflective glass and mother-of-pearl for the ladies' dresses and jewelry. Working clockwise around the room, follow Klimt's story.

Left Wall: Floating female figures drift and weave and search—like we all do—for happiness. Unfortunately, their aspirations are dashed and brought to earth, leaving them kneeling and humble. They plead for help from heroes stronger than themselves—represented by the firm knight in gold, who revives their hopes and helps them carry on.

Center Wall: The women encounter many obstacles in their pursuit of happiness—the three dangerous Gorgons (naked ladies with snake hair), the gorilla-faced monster of fear, and the three seductive women of temptation. These obstacles can leave us bent over with grief (like the woman on the right), while our hopes pass by overhead.

Right Wall: But we can still find happiness through art, thanks to Lady Poetry (with the lyre) and the great hero of the arts: Beethoven. In the original 1902 exhibition, a statue of Beethoven appeared at this crucial turning point in the narrative, where the blank space is today.

Beethoven's presence inspires the yearning souls to carry on. Swept up in a column of fire, they finally reach true happiness. At the climax of the frieze, a heavenly choir serenades a naked couple embracing in ecstasy, singing the "Ode to Joy"—Friedrich Schiller's poem incorporated into the *Ninth Symphony*: "Joy, you beautiful spark of the gods...under thy gentle wings, all men shall become brothers."

The Rest of the Secession: There's a small exhibit of scale models and photos about the construction of this influential building. Don't overlook the interesting temporary exhibits (included in your ticket). A committee mounts special contemporary exhibits every three months that highlight local art happenings. They illustrate how the free spirit of Vienna's Secession survives a century after its founding.

▲Naschmarkt

In 1898, the city decided to cover up its Vienna River. The long, wide square they created was filled with a lively produce market

Jugendstil and the Vienna Secession

As Europe approached the dawn of a new (*nouveau*) century, artists began creating a truly new and free art style that left behind the stodginess of the 19th century. Though the Art Nouveau movement began in Paris and Belgium, each country gave it its own spin. In German-speaking lands, Art Nouveau was called Jugendstil (meaning "youth style").

Background

Art Nouveau was forward-looking and modern, embracing the new technology of iron and glass. But it was also a reaction against the sheer ugliness of the mass-produced, boxy, rigidly geometrical art of the Industrial Age. For inspiration, Art Nouveau artists embraced nature (which abhors a straight line) and the sinuous curves of organic plant forms. Art Nouveau street lamps twist and bend like flower stems. Ironwork fountains sprout buds that squirt water. Dining rooms are paneled with leafy garlands of carved wood. Advertising posters feature flowery typefaces and beautiful young women rendered in pure, curving lines. Art Nouveau was a total "look" that could be applied to furniture, jewelry, paintings, and even entire buildings.

Imagine being a cutting-edge artist in late-19th-century Vienna, surrounded by conformity. Take, for example, the Ringstrasse, with its Neo-Greek, Neo-Gothic, Neo-Baroque architecture. There was nothing daring or new—architects had simply redone what had already been done (Historicism). This drove Vienna's impatient young generation of artists (Gustav Klimt, Otto Wagner, Egon Schiele, Oskar Kokoschka, and company) to escape, or "secede," from all this conventionalism. They established the Secession and transcended into a world of pure beauty, hedonism, eroticism, and aesthetics.

The Secession preferred buildings that were simple and geometrically pure, decorated with a few unadulterated Art Nouveau touches. Architects, painters, and poets had no single unifying style, except a commitment to what was natural and free of tradition. The Secessionist motto was: "To each age its art, and to art its liberty."

Secession Sights

Here are some of Vienna's best Jugendstil sights (for more, grab

that still bustles most days. It's long been known as *the* place to get exotic faraway foods. In fact, locals say, "From here start the Balkans."

Hours and Location: Mon-Fri 6:00-19:30, Sat until 18:00, closed Sun, closes earlier in winter; restaurants open until 23:00; between Linke Wienzeile and Rechte Wienzeile, U: Karlsplatz.

Visiting the Naschmarkt: The stalls of the Naschmarkt

the TI's brochure, *Architecture from Art Nouveau to the Present*).

The Secession: This clean-lined building was the headquarters

of The Secession and where young artists first exhibited their "youth-style" art in 1897. It's nicknamed the "golden cabbage" for its bushy gilded rooftop (actually, those are the laurel leaves of Apollo, the God of Poetry).

Belvedere Palace: This museum's collection includes work by Klimt, who gained fame painting slender young women entwined together in florid embraces, exploring the same highly charged erotic terrain

as his contemporary, Sigmund Freud. Klimt took the decorative element of Art Nouveau to extremes (for more about the palace, see page 67).

The Anchor Clock on Hoher Markt: This mosaic-decorated clock (1911-1917) was actually an advertisement for a life insurance company. Spanning two buildings, it's full of symbolism, stretching from the butterfly on the left to the Grim Reaper on the right. The clock honors 12 great figures from Vienna's history, from Marcus Aurelius to Joseph Haydn. While each gets his own top-of-the-hour moment, all parade by at high noon in a musical act. A plaque on the left names each figure. Notice the novel way the clock marks the time.

Karlsplatz: Otto Wagner designed several structures for Vienna's subway system, including these original arched entrances (see page 60).

Austrian Postal Savings Bank: This early-20th-century building is a key example of Wagner's modern work (see page 54).

SIGHTS

(roughly, "Nibble Market") stretch along Wienzeile street, just a short stroll south of the opera house. This "Belly of Vienna" comes with two parallel lanes—one lined with fun and reasonable eateries, and the other featuring the town's top-end produce and gourmet goodies. This is where top chefs like to get their ingredients. At the gourmet vinegar stall, you can sample the vinegar as you would perfume—with a drop on your wrist (see photo). Farther from the center, the Naschmarkt becomes likably seedy, less expensive, and surrounded by sausage stands, Turkish *döner kebab* stalls, cafés, and theaters. At the market's far end is a line of buildings with fine Art Nouveau facades. Each Saturday, the Naschmarkt is infested by a huge flea market where, in olden days, locals would come to hire a monkey to pick little critters out of their hair (flea market sets up west of the Kettenbrückengasse U-Bahn station).

Picnickers can pick up their grub in the market and head over to Karlsplatz or the Burggarten. In recent years, some stalls have been taken over by hip new eateries and bars, bringing a youthful vibe and fun new tastes to the market scene.

▲Wien Museum Karlsplatz

This underappreciated city history museum walks you through the story of Vienna with well-presented artifacts and good English descriptions. It will likely be closed by the time you visit for a modern facelift and expansion project (Karlsplatz 8, tel. 01/505-8747, www.wienmuseum.at).

▲Mariahilfer Strasse Stroll

While there are more stately and elegant streets in the central district, the best opportunity to simply feel the pulse of workaday Viennese life is a little farther out, along Mariahilfer Strasse. The street has recently gone mostly pedestrian-only, and is fast becoming an attraction in itself. An easy plan is to ride the U-3 to the Zieglergasse stop, then stroll and browse your way downhill to the MuseumsQuartier U-Bahn station.

If you're interested in how Austria handles its people's appetite for marijuana, search out three interesting stops along this corridor: Bushplanet Headshop (at Esterhazygasse 32, near the Neubaugasse U-Bahn stop), Hemp Embassy Museum (next to Bushplanet Headshop—basically a display of big, sparkling marijuana plants), and Bushplanet Growshop (set back in a courtyard off Mariahilfer Strasse at #115, both Bushplanet locations open Mon-Fri 10:00-19:00, Sat until 18:00, closed Sun, www.bushplanet.at; see map on page 173).

To add some fine-art culture to your stroll, drop in at the nearby Imperial Furniture Collection, where you'll see everything from Habsburg thrones to commodes (see listing later in this chapter).

For a fine and free city view (along with reasonable eating), escalate to the top floor of the honeycombed Gerngross shopping center and find the Brandauer restaurant (at Mariahilfer Strasse #42).

Just off Mariahilfer Strasse #24 (near Capistrangasse) is a passageway (sometimes closed) leading to a chilling bit of WWII history: a Nazi flak tower built in 1944. Mighty towers like this, which housed antiaircraft guns and doubled as bomb shelters, survive in Hamburg, Berlin, and Vienna (where six still stand). This bomb shelter is connected by tunnel to today's Austrian government and still serves as a bunker of last resort.

MUSEUMS BEYOND THE RING

The following museums are located outside the Ringstrasse but inside the Gürtel, or outer ring road (see the "Vienna" map in the Orientation to Vienna chapter).

South of the Ring
▲▲Belvedere Palace (Schloss Belvedere)

This is the elegant palace of Prince Eugene of Savoy (1663-1736), the still much-appreciated conqueror of the Ottomans. Eugene, a Frenchman considered too short and too ugly to be in the service of Louis XIV, offered his services to the Habsburgs. While he was indeed short and ugly, he became the greatest military genius of his age, the savior of Austria, and the toast of Viennese society. When you conquer cities,  as Eugene did, you get really rich. With his wealth he built this palace complex. Only Eugene had the cash to compete with the Habsburgs, and from his new palace he looked down on the Hofburg—both literally and figuratively. He lived in the lower palace and entertained in the upper one, which he built to rival Schönbrunn, with a similar layout and feel.

Prince Eugene had no heirs, so the state got his property, and Emperor Josef II established the Belvedere as Austria's first great public art gallery. Today you can tour Eugene's lavish palace, see sweeping views of the gardens and the Vienna skyline, and enjoy world-class art starring Gustav Klimt, French Impressionism, and a grab bag of other 19th- and early-20th-century artists. While Vienna's other art collections show off works by masters from around Europe, this has the city's best collection of homegrown artists.

The palace complex includes the Upper Palace (world-class art collection), smaller Lower Palace (historical rooms and temporary exhibits), the 21er Haus (modern pavilion mostly filled with contemporary art), and pleasantly beautiful Baroque-style gardens

The Third Man and Vienna Pre- and Post-World War II

Released in 1949 and voted one of the greatest films of all time by the British Film Institute, *The Third Man* is still screened several times a week at Vienna's Burg Kino cinema, and has inspired one of the city's most fascinating museums.

Movie: British novelist Graham Greene wrote the screenplay for this European *noir* thriller. It takes place in post-WWII Vienna—which was then a city divided, like Berlin, among the four victorious Allies. The film is rife with intrigue, including a dramatic cemetery scene, depictions of coffeehouse culture surviving amid the rubble, and Orson Welles being chased through the sewers. This tale of a divided city afraid of falling under Soviet rule is an enjoyable two-hour experience.

You can catch *The Third Man* in Vienna at the Burg Kino (€7-9, in English; about 3 showings weekly—usually Sun afternoon, Fri evening, and Tue early evening; a block from the opera at Opernring 19, tel. 01/587-8406, www.burgkino.at).

Museum: The ▲ **Third Man Museum** (Dritte Mann Museum) is the life's work of Karin Höfler and Gerhard Strassgschwandtner. They have lovingly curated a vast collection of artifacts about the film, its popularity around the world, and postwar Vienna. *Third Man* fans will love the quirky movie artifacts, but even if you're just interested in Vienna in the pre- and postwar years, the museum is worthwhile. Displays cover the 1930s, when Austria was ripe for the *Anschluss* (annexation with Germany); the plight of 1.7 million displaced people in Austria after the war; the challenges of de-Nazification after 1945; and candid interviews with soldiers. As a bonus, the museum takes a fascinating look at moviemaking and marketing around 1950.

Don't be shy about asking for a personal tour from Gerhard or Karin (€10, RS%—€2 discount with this book, Sat only 14:00-18:00, also some guided tours on summer Wed at 14:00—confirm on website, tour lasts 80 minutes; U: Kettenbrückengasse, a long block south of the Naschmarkt at Pressgasse 25, tel. 01/586-4872, www.3mpc.net). *Third Man* fans can also arrange a private opening and tour by appointment (€120 for up to 12 people).

(free and fun to explore). For most visitors, only the Upper Palace is worth the entrance fee.

Cost and Hours: €15 for Upper Belvedere Palace only, €22 for Klimt Ticket covering Upper and Lower Palaces (and special exhibits), gardens free; daily 10:00-18:00, Fri until 21:00, grounds open until dusk; audioguide-€4 or €7/2 people; good English descriptions; entrance at Prinz-Eugen-Strasse 27, tel. 01/7955-7134, www.belvedere.at.

Eating at the Belvedere: There's a charming little sit-down café on the ground floor of the Upper Palace; in summer you can dine outdoors in the garden.

Getting There: The palace is a 15-minute walk south of the Ring. To get there from the center, catch tram #D at the opera house (direction: Hauptbahnhof). Get off at the Schloss Belvedere stop (just below the Upper Palace gate), cross the street, walk uphill one block, go through the gate (on left), and look immediately to the right for the small building with the ticket office.

Visiting the Belvedere: The two grand buildings of the Belvedere Palace are separated by a fine garden that slopes down from the Upper to Lower Palace. For our purposes, the **Upper Palace** is what matters. Go around to the front to enter. Once inside, the palace's eclectic collection is tailor-made for browsing. There are two grand floors, set around impressive middle halls, plus a third floor worth a peek. Throughout, look for small illustrations that show the rooms as they looked in Eugene's day.

The main floor displays a timeline of the Belvedere's history (on the left past the gift shop) and medieval art (on the right). From the entrance, climb the staircase to the first floor and enter a grand red-and-gold, chandeliered room.

Marble Hall: This was Prince Eugene's party room. The ceiling fresco shows Eugene (in the center, wearing blue and pink) about to be crowned with a laurel wreath for his military victories and contributions to Vienna. While it's easy to think of the palace as a museum, see it also as a monument to a military hero. It's strewn with images of war in which the adversaries wear lots of turbans, as some of Austria's adversaries were Ottoman Muslims.

Belvedere means "beautiful view," and the **view from the Marble Hall** is the most iconic of the city (it's notably captured in Canaletto's painting displayed at the Kunsthistorisches Museum). Look over the Baroque gardens, the mysterious sphinxes (which symbolized solving riddles and the finely educated mind of your host, Eugene), the Lower Palace, and the city. Left

to right, find the green dome of St. Peter's Church, the spire of St. Stephen's (where Eugene is buried, see page 106), and much nearer, the black dome of the Silesian Church. St. Stephen's spire is 400 feet tall, and no other tall buildings are allowed inside the Ringstrasse. The hills beyond—covered with vineyards—are where the Viennese love to go to sample new wine. Behind the spire you can see Kahlenberg, a high hill in the Vienna Woods, from where you can walk down to several recommended *Heurigen* (wine gardens—see the Eating in Vienna chapter). These hills are the beginnings of the Alps, which stretch from here all the way to France.

The square you're overlooking was filled with people on May 15, 1955, as city leaders stood on the balcony just in front of you and proclaimed the famous words "Austria is free"—heralding Austrian independence after the decade-long Allied occupation following World War II. The Allied powers—France, Great Britain, the US, and the Soviet Union—signed the treaty re-establishing Austria as a sovereign country right here in the Marble Hall.

Now head to the East Wing—facing the garden, to the right.

East Wing: Sumptuous paintings by **Gustav Klimt** and his contemporaries (including Monet) fill the rooms in the East Wing. You can get caught up in his fascination with the beauty and danger he saw in women. To Klimt, all art was erotic art. He painted during the turn of the 20th century, when Vienna was a splendid laboratory of hedonism. For him, Eve was the prototypical woman; her body, not the apple, provided the seduction. Frustrated by the censorship of his age, Klimt refused every form of state support. Even fully clothed, his women have a bewitching eroticism in a world full of pollen and pistils.

The famous painting *Judith* (1901) shows no biblical heroine—Klimt paints her as a high-society Viennese woman with an ostentatious dog-collar necklace. With half-closed eyes and slightly parted lips, she's dismissive...yet mysterious and bewitching. Holding the head of her biblical victim, she's the modern femme fatale.

At the far end of the East Wing you'll find what is perhaps Klimt's best-known painting, *The Kiss*, where two lovers are wrapped up in the colorful gold-and-jeweled cloak of bliss. Klimt's woman is no longer dominating, but submissive, abandoning herself to her man in a fertile field and a vast universe. In a glow emanating from a radiance of desire, the body she presses against is a self-portrait of the artist himself.

Around 1900, Austrian artists influenced by Klimt came to the fore, soaking up Symbolism, Expressionism, and other Modernist trends. Look for some **Max Oppenheimer** portraits, famous for the way they almost comically exaggerate his subjects' features to demonstrate their personality traits.

While Klimt's works are seductive and otherworldly, **Egon Schiele**'s tend to be darker and more introspective. One of Schiele's most recognizable works, *The Embrace*, shows a couple engaged in an erotically charged, rippling moment of passion. Striking a darker tone is *The Family*. This melancholy painting from 1918 is Schiele's last major painting—he and his pregnant wife died in the influenza epidemic that swept through Europe after World War I.

The Rest of the Upper Palace: The Belvedere's collection goes

Gustav Klimt (1862-1918)

Klimt, a noted womanizer, made a career painting the female form as beautiful, seductive, and dangerous. His erotic paintings scandalized official Vienna, and he was a founder of the Secessionist art group, whose members "seceded" from bourgeois constraints. He dedicated his later years to works commissioned by the liberal elite.

Klimt explored multimedia. Besides oil paints, he painted with gold leaf or applied bright objects to the canvas/panel for decorative effect. He often worked in a square-frame format. (Occasionally he and his brother, a gold engraver, made the frames as well.) There's no strong perspective in his best-known paintings; the background and foreground are merged together into a flat decorative pattern. His women are clearly drawn, emerging from the complex design. With their come-hither looks and erotic poses, they capture the overripe beauty and edgy decadence of turn-of-the-century Vienna.

through the whole range of 19th- and 20th-century art: Historicism, Romanticism, Impressionism, Realism, tired tourism, Expressionism, Art Nouveau, and early Modernism. In the West Wing of the first floor is the Belvedere's collection of Austrian Baroque art, including a fascinating corner room of grotesquely grimacing heads by **Franz Xaver Messerschmidt** (1736-1783), a quirky 18th-

century Habsburg court sculptor who left the imperial life to follow his own, somewhat deranged muse. After his promising career was cut short by mental illness, Messerschmidt relocated to Bratislava and spent the rest of his days sculpting a series of eerily lifelike "character heads" *(Kopfstücke)* whose unusual faces are contorted by extreme emotions. Strolling through this collection made my cheeks hurt. Messerschmidt served as his own model for these works, pinching himself to create a pain reaction he could replicate in stone.

The **second floor** up shows off early-19th-century paintings in the Biedermeier style. This was the period (1815-1848) when conservative elements in Central Europe clamped down on Napoleon's revolutionary ideas. The paintings here are realistic portraits, landscapes, and scenes from everyday life and from history. The style is soft-focus, hypersensitive, super-sweet, and sentimentally Romantic—the poor are happy, things are lit impossibly well, and folk life is idealized. (Then came the democratic revolutions of 1848, the invention of the camera, Realism and Impressionism...and all hell broke loose.) The final rooms display Renoir's ladies and Van Gogh's rough brushstrokes, from a time more concerned with light and native landscapes.

Lower Palace: On the opposite end of the delightfully manicured gardens (and covered by a separate ticket) is the home where

Prince Eugene actually hung his helmet. Today it contains a small stretch of three of his private apartments (relatively uninteresting compared to the sumptuous Habsburg apartments elsewhere in town). The Lower Palace also houses some generally good special exhibits, as well as the entrance to the privy garden and stables (until 12:00).

▲Museum of Military History (Heeresgeschichtliches Museum)

While much of the Habsburg Empire was built on strategic marriages rather than the spoils of war, a big part of Habsburg history is military. And this huge place, built about 1860 as an arsenal by Franz Josef, tells the story well with a thoughtful motto (apparently learned from the school of hard knocks): "Wars belong in museums."

You'll wander the wings of this vast museum nearly all alone. Its two floors hold a rich collection of artifacts and historic treasures from the times of Maria Theresa to Prince Eugene to Franz Josef. The particularly interesting 20th-century section on the ground floor includes exhibits devoted to Sarajevo in 1914 (with the car Franz Ferdinand rode in and the uniform he wore when he was assassinated), Chancellor Dollfuss and the pre-Hitler Austrian Fascist party, the *Anschluss*, and World War II.

Cost and Hours: €6, includes good audioguide, free first Sun of the month; daily 9:00-17:00, small café on site, on Arsenalstrasse, tel. 01/795-610, www.hgm.at. It's a five-minute walk from the Quartier Belvedere tram/S-Bahn stop behind the Belvedere Palace (see the "Vienna" map in the Orientation to Vienna chapter).

SIGHTS

East of the Ring
Museum of Applied Arts
(Museum für Angewandte Kunst, a.k.a. MAK)

Facing the old town from across the Ring, the MAK, as it's called, is a design museum best known for its collection of furniture and decorative art from Vienna's artistic golden age, which is show-cased in the permanent Vienna 1900 exhibit. The museum's unique gift shop also makes for a fun diversion.

Cost and Hours: €12, €5 Tue after 18:00; open Tue 10:00-22:00, Wed-Sun until 18:00, closed Mon; multimedia guide-€2, classy restaurant with pleasant garden seating, Stubenring 5—take U-Bahn or tram #2 to Stubentor, tel. 01/711-360, www.mak.at.

Visiting the Museum: Stepping into this museum is like step-ping into a grand Italian Renaissance palace, but the contents in-side tell of a different time. Fans of the graphic arts and furniture design should head to the top floor and the three-room **Vienna 1900** exhibit. The display follows local designers as they moved from Historicism through Art Nouveau and on to Modernism and Internationalism. The walls are lined with a fine collection of pe-riod posters. The "less-is-more" approach is represented by Josef Hoffman's functional chairs and desks, and a complete bedroom installation by Margaret Schütte-Lihotsky. A wooden relief of the goddess Diana, by Carl Otto Czeschka, is impressive. You'll also find nine sketches by Gustav Klimt for a frieze for a mansion in Belgium (incorporating a version of *The Kiss*). Nearby is Marga-ret MacDonald Mackintosh's *Seven Princesses,* a rare Art Nouveau frieze made for the music room of a turn-of-the-century Viennese collector.

In the basement, the **MAK Design Lab** ("MAK Design Labor" in German) is also worth seeing. It's a big, up-to-date ex-hibit that's partly conventional (you look at lots of old stuff)—but presented in a way that encourages visitors to think about the de-sign challenges of everyday life, and the use and function of the objects we employ to sit, eat, clothe ourselves, communicate, and create things.

The remaining collections (Asian, Baroque, and carpets—on the ground floor) are skippable for most.

▲Kunst Haus Wien Museum and Hundertwasserhaus

This "make yourself at home" museum and nearby apartment com-plex are a hit with lovers of modern art, mixing the work and phi-losophy of local painter/environmentalist Friedensreich Hundert-wasser (1928-2000), a.k.a. "100H_2O."

Cost and Hours: €11 for museum, €12 combo-ticket includes special exhibitions, open daily 10:00-18:00, audioguide-€3, tel. 01/712-0491, www.kunsthauswien.com.

Cuisine Art: Don't miss the leafy garden café that begs you to sit down and enjoy Hundertwasser's creation.

Getting There: It's located at Untere Weissgerberstrasse 13, near the Radetzkyplatz stop on trams #O and #1 (signs point the way). Take the U-Bahn to Landstrasse and either walk 10 minutes downhill (north) along Untere Viaduktgasse (a block east of the station), or transfer to tram #O (direction: Praterstern) and ride three stops to Radetzkyplatz.

Visiting the Museum: Stand in front of the jaunty checkerboard building that houses the Kunst Haus Wien Museum. Consider Hundertwasser's style. He was against "window racism":

Neighboring houses allow only one kind of window, but 100H$_2$O's windows are each different—and he encouraged residents in his Hundertwasserhaus (see below) to personalize them. He recognized "tree tenants" as well as human tenants. His buildings are spritzed with a forest and topped with dirt and grassy little parks—close to nature and good for the soul.

Hundertwasser's floors and sidewalks are irregular—to "stimulate the brain" (although current residents complain it just causes wobbly furniture and sprained ankles). Thus 100H$_2$O waged a one-man fight—during the 1950s and 1960s, when concrete and glass ruled—to save the human soul from the city. (Hundertwasser claimed that "straight lines are godless.")

Inside the museum, start with his interesting biography. His fun paintings are half psychedelic Jugendstil and half just kids' stuff. Notice the photographs from his 1950s days as part of Vienna's bohemian scene. Throughout the museum, keep an eye out for the fun philosophical quotes from an artist who believed, "If man is creative, he comes nearer to his creator."

Hundertwasserhaus: The Kunst Haus Wien provides by far the best look at Hundertwasser, but for an actual lived-in apartment complex by the green master, walk 10 minutes to the one-with-nature Hundertwasserhaus (at Löwengasse and Kegelgasse). This complex of 50 apartments, subsidized by the government to

Restitution of Art Stolen by Nazis

The Austrian government has worked to fairly reimburse victims of the Nazis, whose buildings, businesses, personal belongings, and art were taken after the 1938 *Anschluss* (when Germany annexed Austria).

A fund of more than $200 million was established by the Austrian government and corporations that profited through collaboration with the Nazis. Surviving locals (mostly Jews) who paid a *Reichsfluchtsteuer* ("tax for fleeing the country") were located and given some money. Former slave laborers were also tracked down and given €5,000 each.

Most significantly for sightseers, great art was restored to its rightful owners. The big news for the Vienna art world was the return of several Gustav Klimt paintings to their former owners, most notably Klimt's portrait of Adele Bloch-Bauer, which for years had been part of Vienna's Belvedere Palace collection. The painting was restored to Adele's heirs living in America, who in 2006 sold the portrait for $135 million—one of the highest prices ever paid for a painting. The Austrian government had an opportunity to buy back the portrait, but decided against it. Adele's portrait now belongs to the Neue Galerie, a New York City museum devoted to early-20th-century German and Austrian art and design. Fortunately for art viewers visiting Vienna, the most famous Klimt (*The Kiss*) remains in the Belvedere Palace.

provide affordable housing, was built in the 1980s as a breath of architectural fresh air in a city of boring, blocky apartment complexes. While not open to visitors, it's worth seeing for its fun and colorful patchwork exterior and the Hundertwasser festival of shops nearby. Don't miss the view from both streets to see the "tree tenants" and the internal winter garden that residents enjoy.

Hundertwasser detractors—of which there are many—remind visitors that $100H_2O$ was a painter, not an architect. They describe the Hundertwasserhaus as a "1950s house built in the 1980s" that was colorfully painted with no real concern for the environment, communal living, or even practical comfort. Almost all of the original inhabitants got fed up with the novelty and moved out.

North of the Ring
Sigmund Freud Museum
Freud enthusiasts (and detractors) enjoy seeing the apartment and home office of the man who fundamentally changed our understanding of the human psyche. Dr. Sigmund Freud (1856-1939), a graduate of Vienna University, established his practice here in 1891. For the next 47 years, he received troubled patients who

hoped to find peace by telling him their dreams, life traumas, and secret urges. It was here that he wrote his influential works, including the landmark *Interpretation of Dreams* (1899). The museum is narrowly focused on Freud's life. If you're looking for a critical appraisal of whether he was a cocaine-addicted charlatan or a sincere doctor groping toward an understanding of human nature, you won't find it here.

The museum may be under renovation when you visit; if it is, a temporary exhibit will be set up nearby (at Berggasse 15) with a few artifacts on display at a reduced entrance fee.

Cost and Hours: €12, includes smartphone app, daily 10:00-18:00, tiny bookshop, half-block from the Schlickgasse stop on tram #D, Berggasse 19, tel. 01/319-1596, www.freud-museum.at.

Visiting the Museum: Freud's three-room office has been turned into a permanent display on his life, while the larger apartment (where he lived with his family) is used for temporary exhibits. Freud, who was Jewish, fled Vienna for England when the Nazis came to power. He took most of his possessions with him, including the famous couch that patients reclined on (now in a London museum), so the museum doesn't really give you a feel for how he lived.

In the office entryway, you can see Freud's cane, hat, pocket flask, and a few other objects. The waiting room is the most furnished, with original furniture, his books, and his collection of primitive fertility figurines. The consulting room and study are lined with old photos and documents that trace Freud's fascinating life: a happy childhood (first in a small Moravian town, then in Vienna); medical school in the then-pioneering field of psychology; research into the ef-

fects of cocaine; a happy marriage, large family, and wholesome middle-class lifestyle; use of hypnosis as therapy; years of self-analysis and first patients in analysis; publication of controversial works on dreams and sexuality; association with other budding psychologists such as the Swiss Carl Jung; and, finally, his hard-earned recognition and worldwide fame.

West of the Ring
▲Imperial Furniture Collection (Hofmobiliendepot)

Bizarre, sensuous, eccentric, or precious, this underappreciated collection (on four fascinating floors) is your peek at the Habsburgs' furniture—from the empress' wheelchair ("to increase her fertility she was put on a rich diet and became corpulent") to the emperor's spittoon—all thoughtfully described in English. Evocative paintings help bring the furniture to life.

The Habsburgs had many palaces, but only the Hofburg was permanently furnished. The rest were done on the fly—set up and taken down by a gang of royal roadies called the "Depot of Court Movables" *(Hofmobiliendepot)*. When the monarchy was dissolved in 1918, the state of Austria took possession of the Hofmobiliendepot's inventory—165,000 items. Now this royal storehouse is open to the public in a fine and sprawling museum. Don't go here for the Jugendstil furnishings. The older Baroque, Rococo, and Biedermeier pieces are the most impressive and tied most intimately to the royals.

Cost and Hours: €9.50, includes audioguide, covered by Sisi Ticket, Tue-Sun 10:00-18:00, closed Mon, Mariahilfer Strasse 88, main entrance around the corner at Andreasgasse 7, U: Zieglergasse, tel. 01/5243-3570, www.hofmobiliendepot.at.

Tip: To avoid lines at the Schönbrunn Palace and the Hofburg Imperial Apartments, buy your Sisi Ticket here first or purchase in advance online (www.schoenbrunn.at).

Nearby: Combine a visit to this museum with a stroll down the lively shopping boulevard, Mariahilfer Strasse (described earlier).

ON VIENNA'S OUTSKIRTS
▲▲▲Schönbrunn Palace (Schloss Schönbrunn)

The Habsburgs' former summer residence, just a 10-minute subway ride from downtown Vienna, is second only to Versailles among Europe's grand palaces. Originally built in the 16th century as a small hunting lodge near a beautiful spring *(schön-brunn)*, the residence grew over the next 300 years into the palace you see today. The highlight of the vast complex's many sights is a tour of the Imperial Apartments where the Habsburg nobles lived (including Maria Theresa and her 16 children, and Franz Josef and Sisi). You can also stroll the palace gardens, visit the world's oldest zoo, and view royal transport from the 19th century at the Imperial Carriage Museum.

Visits to the palace are by timed-entry tours. Since the place can be mobbed with visitors, it's smart to make reservations in advance, or buy a Sisi Ticket online or at the Imperial Furniture Collection (described earlier).

📖 See the Schönbrunn Palace Tour chapter.

Activities in Vienna

These activities allow you to take it easy and enjoy the Viennese good life.

▲▲Cafés
A break for *Kaffee und Kuchen* (coffee and cake) in one of the city's historical cafés is a must on any Viennese visit (see my recommended cafés in the Eating in Vienna chapter; for more on Austria's sweet treats and its coffee, see the Practicalities chapter).

▲*Heuriger* Wine Gardens
Locals and tourists alike enjoy lingering in these rustic wine gardens in rural neighborhoods, easily accessible by public transportation from downtown Vienna (see the Eating in Vienna chapter).

▲Stadtpark (City Park)
Vienna's major park, along the eastern edge of the Ring, is a waltzing world of gardens, memorials to local musicians, ponds, peacocks, music in bandstands, and Viennese escaping the city. Notice the Jugendstil entrance at the Stadtpark U-Bahn station. The faux-Renaissance Kursalon hall, where Johann Strauss was the violin-toting master of waltzing ceremonies, hosts touristy concerts daily, in three-quarter time (for details, see page 199). Find the famous golden statue of Strauss with his violin (next to the Kursalon, straight in from the Weihburggasse tram stop).

▲Prater Park (Wiener Prater)
Since the 1780s, when the reformist Emperor Josef II gave his hunting grounds to the people of Vienna as a public park, this place has been Vienna's playground. For the tourist, the "Prater" is the sugary-smelling, tired, and sprawling amusement park *(Wurstelprater)*. For locals, the "Prater" is the vast, adjacent green park with its three-mile-long, tree-lined main boulevard (Hauptallee). The park still tempts visitors with its huge 220-foot-tall, famous, and lazy Ferris wheel *(Riesenrad),* fun roller coasters, bumper cars, Lilliputian railroad, and endless eateries. Especially if you're traveling with kids, this is a fun place to share the evening with thousands of Viennese and tourists.

Cost and Hours: Park is free and always open; amusement park—rides cost €2-8 and run May-Oct roughly 10:00-22:00, but often later in good weather in summer, fewer rides open in off-season; U: Praterstern, www.prater.at.

Eating at Prater Park: For a local-style family dinner, eat at

Shopping in Vienna

Traditional Austrian Clothing: If you're interested in picking up a classy felt suit or dirndl, you'll find shops all over town. Most central is the fancy **Loden-Plankl** shop, with a vast world of traditional Austrian formalwear upstairs (across from the Hofburg, at Michaelerplatz 6). The **Tostmann Trachten** shop is the ultimate for serious shopping. Frau Tostmann powered the resurgence of this style. Her place is like a shrine to traditional Austrian and folk clothing (called *Tracht*)—handmade and very expensive (Schottengasse 3A, 3-minute walk from Am Hof, tel. 01/533-5331).

Artsy Gifts: Vienna's museum shops are some of Europe's best. The design store in the Museum of Applied Arts (MAK) is a delight; the shops of the Albertina Museum, Kunsthistorisches Museum, Belvedere Palace, Kunst Haus Wien, Sigmund Freud Museum, and the MuseumsQuartier museums are also particularly good. For the best in Austrian design and handicrafts, visit Österreichische Werkstätten, a shop/gallery just south of the cathedral (Mon-Sat 10:00-18:30, closed Sun, Kärntner Strasse 6, www.oew.at).

Window Shopping: The narrow streets north and west of the cathedral are sprinkled with old-fashioned shops that seem to belong to another era, carrying a curiously narrow range of items for sale (old clocks, men's ties, gloves, and so on). Dedicated window shoppers will enjoy the Dorotheum auction house (see page 50).

$$ Schweizerhaus (good food, great Czech Budvar—the original "Budweiser"—beer, classic conviviality) at the back of the park near the green tower.

Danube Island (Donauinsel)

In the 1970s, as part of a flood protection program, the city dug a channel (the so-called "Neue Donau"—New Danube) parallel to the Danube River. With the dredged-out dirt, the engineers formed 12-mile-long Danube Island. Originally just an industrial site, it's evolved into a much-loved idyllic escape from the city (easy U-Bahn access on U-1: Donauinsel).

The skinny island provides a natural wonderland. All along the pedestrianized, grassy park, you'll find locals at play (especially recent immigrants and others who can't afford their own cabin or fancy vacation). The swimming comes tough, though, with rocky entries rather than sand. The best activity here is a bike ride. If you venture far from the crowds, you're likely to encounter nudists on inline skates.

Biking Danube Island: For a simple, breezy joyride, bike up and down the traffic-free and people-filled island. Weather permitting, you can rent a bike from **Rad und Skaterverleih** (€5/hour, €25/day, May-Aug daily 9:00-21:00, shorter hours spring and fall, closed off-season; from Donauinsel U-Bahn station—head left up U-Bahn platform following signs to *Am Hubertsdamm*, then left again once outside to pass under the Reichsbrücke (the bridge spanning the island) and go straight ahead 70 yards; tel. 01/263-5242, www.fahrradverleih.at).

Donau City (Donaustadt)

This modern part of town, just beyond Danube Island, is the sky-scraping "Manhattan" of Austria. It was laid out as a potential Vienna-Budapest expo site in the 1990s. But Austrians voted down the fair idea, and eventually the real estate became today's modern planned city: It's quiet and traffic-free, with inviting plazas and a small church dwarfed by towering places of business. The high-rise DC Tower is the tallest office building in Austria. With business, residential, and shopping zones surrounded by inviting parkland, this corner of the city is likely to grow as Vienna expands. Its centerpiece is the futuristic UNO City, one of four United Nations headquarters worldwide. While it lacks the Old World character, charm, and elegance of the rest of Vienna, Donau City may interest travelers who are into contemporary glass-and-steel architecture (U: Kaisermühlen VIC).

Biking to Donau City and Beyond: Sightseers on bikes can cross the Danube to Donau City. From the opera house, it's pretty much a straight pedal around the center via the Ringstrasse, past Prater Park, and across the river. The way is easy enough to find with the help of the basic tourist map from the TI. (Recommended local guide Wolfgang Höfler leads tours along this route, which he shared with me; see the Orientation to Vienna chapter.)

The route will take you over four stretches of water: the Danube Canal, the actual Danube, the New Danube, and the Old Danube. Along the way, you'll gain a better understanding of the massive engineering done over the years to contain and tame the river.

As you leave the city center, you'll first pedal over the Danube Canal, an arm of the river that brings river traffic into the city; then you hit the main part of the river and the man-made Danube Island (itself a part of the city's flood barriers). From the Reichsbrücke bridge over the island, survey the river's traffic. The cruise industry is booming, and Vienna's river cruise port is hosting more boats than ever. Many of them sail from here all the way to Romania and the Black Sea coast.

In the distance, across the river, are the skyscrapers of Donau City. To reach it, continue across the bridge over Danube Island and cross the New Danube. From Donau City, the bike path leads across the Old Danube (Alte Donau)—one arm of the river but now a lake, which hosts a frolicking park with all the water fun a hot-and-tired city could hope for, including lakeside cafés and boat rentals. From here you can simply retrace your route, or you can make a big circle by following the delightful bike path southeast along the Old Danube to the next bridge (Praterbrücke). This leads to the vast Prater Park, where you'll follow the breezy main boulevard (Hauptallee) back to the big Ferris wheel and ultimately to downtown.

A Walk in the Vienna Woods (Wienerwald)

For a quick side-trip into the woods and out of the city, catch the U-4 subway line to Heiligenstadt, then bus #38A to Kahlenberg, where you'll enjoy great views and a café overlooking the city. From there, it's a peaceful 45-minute downhill hike to the *Heurigen* of Nussdorf or to enjoy some new wine (see page 15). Your free TI-produced city map can be helpful...just go downhill. For an overview of this area, see the "Greater Vienna" map on page 15.

SIGHTS

VIENNA CITY WALK

Vienna, one of Europe's grandest cities of the past, is also a vibrant city of today. Here in Vienna's urban core, where old meets new, you'll get the lay of the land as you stroll between the city's three most important landmarks: the opera house, St. Stephen's Cathedral, and the Hofburg Palace. Along the way, we'll drop into some of the smaller sights that help make this city so intriguing: the poignant monuments that subtly cobble together this proud nation's often-illustrious, sometimes-tragic history; the genteel stores, cafés, and pastry shops where the Viennese continually perfect their knack for fine living; the unassuming churches where the remains of the Habsburg monarchs are entombed; and the defiantly stern architectural styles that emerged to counteract all that frilly Habsburg excess. Use this walk as a springboard for exploring this fine city—and, along the way, get an overview of Vienna's past and present.

Orientation

Length of This Walk: Allow one hour for the walk alone, and more time if you plan to stop at any major sights along the way.

When to Go: This walk works just as well in the evening as it does during the day, as long as you don't plan on touring some of the sights you'll pass.

Opera House: A visit is possible only with a 45-minute guided tour—€9.50, July-Aug generally daily at the top of each hour 10:00-15:00; Sept-June fewer tours.

Albertina Museum: €13, daily 10:00-18:00, Wed and Fri until 21:00.

Kaisergruft: €7.50, daily 10:00-18:00.

St. Stephen's Cathedral: Church foyer and north aisle—free, daily

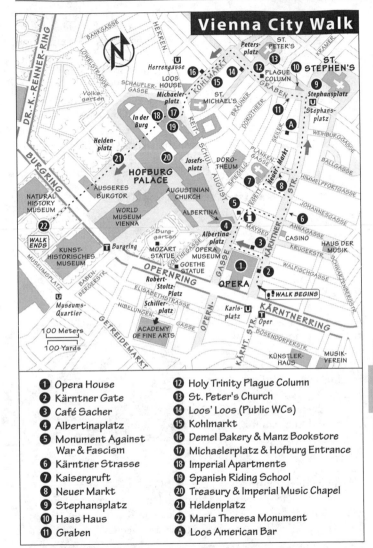

Vienna City Walk

1. Opera House
2. Kärntner Gate
3. Café Sacher
4. Albertinaplatz
5. Monument Against War & Fascism
6. Kärntner Strasse
7. Kaisergruft
8. Neuer Markt
9. Stephansplatz
10. Haas Haus
11. Graben
12. Holy Trinity Plague Column
13. St. Peter's Church
14. Loos' Loos (Public WCs)
15. Kohlmarkt
16. Demel Bakery & Manz Bookstore
17. Michaelerplatz & Hofburg Entrance
18. Imperial Apartments
19. Spanish Riding School
20. Treasury & Imperial Music Chapel
21. Heldenplatz
22. Maria Theresa Monument
A. Loos American Bar

6:00-22:00; main nave—€6 including audioguide, Mon-Sat 9:00-11:30 & 13:00-16:30, Sun 13:00-16:30, July-Aug until 17:30. The cathedral's towers, catacombs, and treasury have varying costs and hours—see the St. Stephen's Cathedral Tour chapter.

St. Peter's Church: Free; Mon-Fri 7:00-20:00, Sat-Sun 9:00-21:00; free organ concerts Mon-Fri at 15:00, Sat-Sun at 20:00.

St. Michael's Church Crypt: €7 for 45-minute tour, Mon-Sat at 11:00 and 13:00, none on Sun, Nov-Easter Thu-Sat only.

Hofburg Imperial Apartments: €15, covered by Sisi Ticket (see page 31); daily 9:00-17:30, July-Aug until 18:00, last entry one hour before closing.

Hofburg Treasury: €12, €20 combo-ticket with Kunsthistorisches Museum, Wed-Mon 9:00-17:30, closed Tue.

Tours: 🎧 Download my free Vienna City Walk audio tour. For efficiency, you can splice my St. Stephen's Cathedral audio tour (see next chapter) into this walk.

Starring: Vienna's "big three" (opera house, cathedral, palace), plus an array of sights, squares, and shops tucked between them.

The Walk Begins

• *Begin at the square outside Vienna's landmark opera house, home of the Vienna State Opera. (The entrance faces the Ringstrasse; we're starting at the busy pedestrian square that's to the right of the entrance as you're facing it.)*

❶ Opera House

If Vienna is the world capital of classical music, this building is its throne room, one of the planet's premier houses of music. It's typical of Vienna's 19th-century buildings in that it features a revival style—Neo-Renaissance—with arched windows, half-columns, and the sloping, copper mansard roof typical of French Renaissance *châteaux* (see sidebar on page 123).

Since the structure was built in 1869, almost all of the opera world's luminaries have passed through here. Its former musical directors include Gustav Mahler, Herbert von Karajan, and Richard Strauss. Luciano Pavarotti, Maria Callas, Placido Domingo, and

HECTOR BERLIOZ

*1803 LA CÔTE-SAINT-ANDRÉ
†1869 PARIS*

many other greats have sung from its stage.

In the pavement along the side of the opera house (and all along Kärntner Strasse, the bustling shopping street we'll visit shortly), you'll find star plaques forming a Hollywood-style walk of fame. These represent the stars of classical music—famous composers, singers, musicians, and conductors.

Looking up at the opera, notice the giant outdoor screen onto which some live performances are projected (as noted in the posted schedules and on the screen itself).

If you're a fan, take a guided tour of the opera (see page 48). Or consider springing for an evening performance (standing-room tickets are surprisingly cheap; see the Entertainment in Vienna chapter). Regular opera tickets are sold at various points near here: The closest ticket office is the small one just below the screen, while the main one is on the other side of the building, across the street on Operngasse. For information about other entertainment options during your visit, check in at the Wien Ticket kiosk in the booth on this square.

The opera house marks a busy intersection in Vienna, where Kärntner Strasse meets the Ring. The Karlsplatz U-Bahn station in front of the opera is an underground shopping mall with fast food, newsstands, and lots of pickpockets.

• *With your back to the Ringstrasse and the opera house on your left, face the busy pedestrian boulevard that leads into the center of town.*

❷ Kärntner Gate

Even though the center of town sits on an irregular medieval street plan, you'll notice the parallel rows of more modern, uniform buildings in front of you. These were built where the city wall once stood. The opera's lower stage is where the old moat used to be— outside the walls. This was a main gate, through which a road led to the Kärnten (Carinthia) region of southern Austria.

Notice the pedestrian signals and how they feature both gay and straight couples. Vienna's Green Party is part of the city's current ruling coalition and they like to remind the world that, while Austria's national government is more conservative (reflect-

ing the fears and concerns of rural and small-town voters), Vienna celebrates diversity.

• *Walk behind the opera and across the street toward the dark-red awning to find the famous...*

❸ Café Sacher

This is the home of the world's classiest chocolate cake, the Sacher torte: two layers of cake separated by apricot jam and covered in dark-chocolate icing, usually served with whipped cream. It was invented in a fit of improvisation in 1832 by Franz Sacher, dessert chef to Prince Metternich (the mastermind diplomat who redrew the map of post-Napoleonic Europe). The cake became world famous when the inventor's son served it next door at his hotel (you may have noticed the fancy doormen). Pop in for a peek at 19th-century elegance. Many locals complain that the cakes here have gone downhill, and many tourists are surprised by how dry they are—you really need that dollop of *Schlagobers*. Still, coffee and a slice of cake here can be €8 well invested for the history alone (daily 8:00-24:00). While the café itself is grotesquely touristy, the adjacent Sacher Stube has ambience and natives to spare (same prices, daily 10:00-24:00). For maximum elegance, sit inside.

• *Continue past Hotel Sacher. At the end of the street is a small, triangular, cobbled square adorned with memorial sculptures.*

❹ Albertinaplatz

Overlooking the square, the tan-and-white Neoclassical building marks the tip of the Hofburg Palace—the sprawling complex of buildings that was long the seat of Habsburg power (we'll end this walk at the palace's center). The balustraded terrace up top was originally part of Vienna's defensive rampart. Later, it was the balcony of Empress Maria Theresa's daughter Maria Christina, who lived at this end of the palace. Today, her home houses  the **Albertina Museum,** topped by a sleek, controversial titanium canopy (called the "diving board" by critics). The museum's plush, 19th-century state rooms are the only Neoclassical (post-Rococo) palace rooms anywhere in the Habsburg realm. And the Batliner Collection of modernist paintings (Monet to Picasso) is a delight (see page 43).

High above (just left of the "diving board"), a statue of Archduke Albrecht looks down on the city. A symbol of Habsburg oppression, he brutally suppressed popular uprisings in Vienna and Italy in the mid-1800s.

At street level is a grand fountain of Danubius, the Danube River god, flanked by six little gods. Each represents a major tributary that feeds the Danube as it flows through Austria.

The local hotdog stand to the left of Danubius (with the bunny on the rooftop, a reminder that the famous Albrecht Dürer watercolor *Hare* is in the adjacent Albertina) is known for its quality local sausages. This is the operagoers' hangout...they gather here in their fine ballgowns and tuxedos enjoying some of the best of Vienna's beloved wurst.

Albertinaplatz itself is filled with sculptures that make up the powerful, thought-provoking ❺ **Monument Against War and Fascism,** which commemorates the dark years when Austria came under Nazi rule (1938-1945).

The memorial has four parts. The split white monument, *The Gates of Violence,* remembers victims of all wars and violence.

Standing directly in front of it, you're at the gates of a concentration camp. Then, as you explore the statues, you step into a montage of wartime images: clubs and WWI gas masks, a dying woman birthing a future soldier, victims of cruel medical experimentation, and chained slave laborers sitting on a pedestal of granite cut from the infamous quarry at Mauthausen concentration camp (see page 226). The hunched-over figure on the ground behind is a Jew forced to scrub anti-Nazi graffiti off a street with a brush. Of Vienna's 200,000 Jews, more than 65,000 died in Nazi concentration camps. The sculpture with its head buried in the stone is Orpheus entering the underworld, meant to remind Austrians (and the rest of us) of the victims of Nazism...and the consequences of not keeping our governments on track. Behind that, the 1945 declaration that established Austria's second republic—and enshrined human rights—is cut into the stone.

Viewing this monument gains even more emotional impact when you realize what happened on this spot: During a WWII bombing attack, several hundred people were buried alive when the cellar they were using as shelter was demolished.

Austria was led into World War II by Germany, which annexed the country in 1938 with disturbingly little resistance, saying Austrians were wannabe Germans anyway. But Austrians are not Germans (this makes for an interesting topic of conversation with Austrians you may meet). They're quick to proudly tell you that Austria was founded in the 10th century, whereas Germany wasn't born until 1870. For seven years just before and during World War II (1938-1945), there was no Austria. In 1955, after 10 years of joint occupation by the victorious Allies, Austria regained total independence on the condition that it would be forever neutral (and never join NATO or the Warsaw Pact). To this day, Austria is outside of NATO (and Germany).

Behind the monument is **Café Tirolerhof,** a classic Viennese café. Refreshingly air-conditioned, it's full of things that time has passed by: chandeliers, marble tables, upholstered booths, waiters in tuxes, and newspapers. (For more on Vienna's cafés, see page 186.)

This square is where many of the city's walking tours and bus tours start. You may see Red Bus City Tour buses, big private tour buses, and color-coded umbrellas advertising "free" walking tours. The Vienna TI (with a handy ticket desk for concerts) also overlooks the square.

• *From the café, turn right on Führichsgasse. Walk one block until you hit...*

❻ Kärntner Strasse

This grand, traffic-free street is the people-watching delight of this in-love-with-life city. Today's Kärntner Strasse (KAYRNT-ner SHTRAH-seh) is mostly a crass commercial pedestrian mall—its famed elegant shops long gone. But locals know it's the same road Crusaders marched down as they headed off from St. Stephen's Cathedral for the Holy Land in the 12th century. Today it's full of shoppers and street musicians.

Where Führichsgasse meets Kärntner Strasse, note the old Grundemann Esterházy Palace—now a **Casino** (across the street and to your right, at #41)—once venerable, now tacky, it exemplifies the worst of the street's evolution. Turn left to head up Kärntner Strasse, going away from the opera house. As you walk along, be sure to look up, above the modern storefronts, for glimpses of the street's former glory.

Local shops can't compete with the international chains, considering the high rent here. But one venerable shop that has survived is near the end of the block, on the left at #26: **J & L Lobmeyr Crystal** ("Founded in 1823") still has its impressive brown storefront with gold trim, statues, and the Habsburg double eagle. In the market for some $400 napkin rings? Lobmeyr's your place. Inside, breathe in the classic Old World ambience as you climb up to the glass museum (free entry, closed Sun).

• *At the end of the block, turn left on Marco d'Aviano Gasse (passing the fragrant flower stall) to make a short detour to the square called Neuer Markt. Straight ahead is an orange-ish church with a triangular roof and cross, the Capuchin Church. In its basement is the...*

❼ Kaisergruft

Under the church sits the Imperial Crypt, filled with what's left of Austria's emperors, empresses, and other Habsburg royalty. For centuries, Vienna was the heart of a vast empire ruled by the Habsburg family, and here is where they lie buried in their fancy pewter coffins. You'll find all the Habsburg greats, including Maria Theresa, her son Josef II (Mozart's patron), Franz Josef, and Empress Sisi. Before moving on, consider paying your respects here (see page 44).

• *Stretching north from the Kaisergruft is the square called...*

❽ Neuer Markt

A block farther down, in the center of Neuer Markt, is the **four rivers fountain** showing Lady Providence surrounded by figures

symbolizing the rivers that flow into the Danube. The sexy statues offended Empress Maria Theresa, who actually organized "Chastity Commissions" to defend her capital city's moral standards. The modern buildings around you were built after World War II.

• *Lady Providence's one bare breast points back to Kärntner Strasse (50 yards away). Before you head back to the busy shopping street, you could stop for a sweet treat at the heavenly, recommended Kurkonditorei Oberlaa (at the far-left corner of the square).*

Leave the square and return to Kärntner Strasse, where you'll turn left. Continuing down Kärntner Strasse, you'll find lots of shops filled with merchandise proven to entice tourists. The **Gustav Klimt "exhibition"** *across the street (opposite Kupferschmiedgasse), while not an exhibition, is fun for Klimt fans. At #6 (a block farther along, on the left) is the* **Austrian Workshop** *(Österreichische Werkstätten, closed Sun). Calling itself "the right place for Austrian design," it shows off traditional, locally made gifts (with an*

VIENNA CITY WALK

elegant-yet-simple Arts and Crafts Movement sensibility) and has more exhibits upstairs.

*As you approach St. Stephen's Cathedral, you're likely to first see it as a reflection in the round-glass windows of the postmodern Haas Haus. The traditional **Aida Cafeteria** (left) is a favorite for sitting over a coffee or pastry and people-watching. Pass the U-Bahn station (which has WCs) where the street spills into Vienna's main square...*

❾ Stephansplatz

The cathedral's frilly spire looms overhead, worshippers and tourists pour inside the church, and shoppers buzz around the outside. You're at the center of Vienna.

The Gothic **St. Stephen's Cathedral** (c. 1300-1450) is known for its 450-foot south tower; its colorful, patterned roof; and its place in Viennese history. When it was built, it was a huge church for what was then a tiny town, and it helped put the fledgling city on the map.

At this point, you may want to take a break from the walk to tour the church (☐ see the St. Stephen's Cathedral Tour chapter).

Where Kärntner Strasse hits Stephansplatz, the grand, soot-covered building with red columns is the **Equitable Building** (filled with lawyers, bankers, and insurance brokers). It's a fine example of Neoclassicism from the turn of the 20th century—look up and imagine how slick Vienna must have felt in 1900.

Facing St. Stephen's is the sleek concrete-and-glass ❿ **Haas Haus,** a postmodern building by noted Austrian architect Hans Hollein (finished in 1990). The curved facade is supposed to echo the Roman fortress of Vindobona (its ruins were found near here). Although the Viennese initially protested having this stark modern tower right next to their beloved cathedral, since then, it's become a fixture of Vienna's main square. Notice how the smooth, rounded glass reflects St. Stephen's pointy architecture, providing a great photo opportunity—especially at twilight. The café and pricey restaurant on the rooftop offer a nice perch, complete with a view of Stephansplatz below—though not necessarily of the cathedral (take the elevator

up to the sixth floor, which has a glassed-in lounge; walk up one flight to reach the terrace and restaurant).

• *Exit the square with your back to the cathedral. Walk past the Haas Haus, and bear right down the street called the...*

❶ Graben

This was once a *Graben,* or ditch—originally the moat for the Roman military camp. Back during Vienna's 19th-century heyday,

more than 200,000 people were packed into the city's inner center (inside the Ringstrasse), walking on dirt streets. Today this area houses 20,000. The Graben was a busy street with three lanes of traffic until the 1970s, when the city inaugurated its new subway system and the street was turned into one of Europe's first pedestrian-only zones. Take a moment to enjoy a slow 360-degree spin tour. Absorb the scene—you're standing in an area surrounded by history, postwar rebuilding, grand architecture, fine cafés, and people enjoying life...for me, quintessential Europe.

As you stroll down the Graben from Stephansplatz, after about 50 yards, you'll reach a modern water dispenser. Vienna has suffered fiercely hot summers lately, leading the city government to install watering stations and shady benches for its citizens and visitors.

In another 50 yards, you reach Dorotheergasse, on your left, which leads (after two more long blocks) to the **Dorotheum** auction house. Consider poking your nose in here later for some fancy window shopping (see page 50). Also along this street are two recommended eateries: the sandwich shop Buffet Trześniewski—one of my favorite places for lunch—and the classic Café Hawelka.

In the middle of the Graben pedestrian zone is the extravagantly blobby ❷ **Holy Trinity plague column** *(Pestsäule).* The 60-foot pillar of clouds sprouts angels and cherubs, with the wonderfully gilded Father, Son, and Holy Ghost at the top (all protected by an anti-pigeon net).

In 1679, Vienna was hit by a massive epidemic of bubonic plague. Around 75,000 Viennese died—about a third of the city.

VIENNA CITY WALK

Adolf Loos (1870-1933)

"Decoration is a crime," wrote Adolf Loos, the turn-of-the-20th-century architect who was Vienna's answer to Frank Lloyd Wright. Foreshadowing the Modernist style of "less is more" and "form follows function," Loos stripped buildings down to their structural skeletons.

In his day, most buildings were plastered with fake Greek columns, frosted with Baroque balustrades, and studded with statues. Even the newer buildings featured flowery Art Nouveau additions. Loos' sparse, geometrical style stood out at the time—and it still does more than a century later. Loos was convinced that unnecessary ornamentation was a waste of workers' valuable time and energy, and was a symbol of an unevolved society. (He even went so far as to compare decoration on a facade with a lavatory wall smeared with excrement.) On this walk, you'll pass several examples of his work:

Loos American Bar (a half-block off Kärntner Strasse, on the left just before Stephansplatz at Kärntner Durchgang 10, see "Vienna City Walk" map): Built in 1908, the same year that Loos published his famous essay "Ornament and Crime," this tiny bar features Loos' specialties—and fine cocktails. The facade is cubical, with square columns and crossbeams (and no flowery capitals). The interior is elegant and understated, with rich marble and mirrors that appear to expand the small space. As they have little patience with gawkers, the best way to admire the interior is to sit down and order a drink.

Public WCs on Graben: These are some of the classiest bathrooms in town (see stop #14).

Manz Bookstore: The facade is a perfect cube, divided into other simple, rectangular shapes.

Loos House on Michaelerplatz: This boldly stripped-down facade (pictured above) peers defiantly across the square at the over-the-top Hofburg. Compare it with the Hofburg's ornate, Neo-Baroque look (done only a few decades earlier) to see how revolutionary Loos was (see sidebar, later).

Loos Room in the Wien Museum Karlsplatz: The architect's finely furnished living room is preserved and on display in the city's history museum on Karlsplatz (may be closed for renovation, check www.wienmuseum.at).

Emperor Leopold I dropped to his knees (something emperors never did in public) and begged God to save the city. (Find Leopold about a quarter of the way up the monument, just above the brown banner. Hint: The typical inbreeding of royal families left him with a gaping underbite.) His prayer was heard by Lady Faith (the statue below Leopold, carrying a cross). With the help of a heartless little cupid, she tosses an old naked woman—symbolizing the plague—into the abyss and saves the city. In gratitude, Leopold vowed to erect this monument, which became a model for cities throughout the empire that were ravaged by the same plague. (The three golden banners represent the core of that empire: Austria, Hungary, and Bohemia.)

• *Thirty yards past the plague monument, look down the short street to the right, which frames a Baroque church with a stately green dome.*

⓭ St. Peter's Church

Leopold I ordered this church to be built as a thank-you for surviving the 1679 plague. The church stands on the site of a much older church that may have been Vienna's first (or second) Christian church. Inside, St. Peter's shows Vienna at its Baroque best (for a description, see page 51). Note that the church offers free organ concerts (daily at 15:00, advertised at the entry).

• *Continue west on the Graben, where you'll immediately find some stairs leading underground to...*

VIENNA CITY WALK

⓮ Loos' Loos

In about 1900, a local chemical maker needed a publicity stunt to prove that his chemicals really got things clean. He purchased two wine cellars under the Graben and had them turned into classy WCs in the Modernist style (designed by Adolf Loos—see sidebar), complete with chandeliers and finely crafted mahogany. While the chandeliers are gone, the restrooms remain a relatively appealing place to do your business. (In the men's room, the 1883 urinals survive but are enjoying a peaceful retirement behind protective glass.) Locals and tourists happily pay €0.50 for a quick visit.

• *The Graben dead-ends at the aristocratic supermarket Julius Meinl am Graben (see listing on page 182). From here, you could turn right into Vienna's "golden corner," with the city's finest shops. But we'll turn left. In the distance is the big green-and-gold dome of the Hofburg, where we'll head soon. The street leading up to the Hofburg is...*

⑮ Kohlmarkt

This is Vienna's most elegant and unaffordable shopping street, lined with Cartier, Armani, Gucci, Tiffany, and the emperor's

palace at the end. Strolling Kohlmarkt, daydream about the edible window displays at ⑯ **Demel,** the ultimate Viennese chocolate shop (#14, daily 9:00-19:00). Step into the shop, where even the decor is sugary. The room is filled with Art Nouveau boxes of Empress Sisi's choco-dreams come true: *Kandierte Veilchen* (candied violet petals), *Katzenzungen* (cats' tongues), and so on. The cakes here are moist (compared with the dry Sacher tortes). The enticing window displays change monthly, reflecting current happenings in Vienna.

Wander inside. There's an impressive cancan of Vienna's most beloved cakes—displayed to tempt visitors (point to the cake you want). Farther in, you can see the bakery in action. Sit inside, with a view of the cakemaking, or outside, with the street action (upstairs is less crowded). Shops like this boast "K.u.K."—signifying that

during the Habsburgs' heyday, it was patronized by the *König und Kaiser* (king and emperor—same guy). If you happen to be looking through Demel's window at exactly 19:01, just after closing, you can witness one of the great tragedies of modern Europe: the daily dumping of its unsold cakes.

Next to Demel, the **Manz Bookstore** has a Loos-designed facade (see the "Adolf Loos" sidebar).

• *Kohlmarkt ends at the square called...*

⑰ Michaelerplatz

This square is dominated by the **Hofburg Palace.** Study the grand

Neo-Baroque facade, dating from about 1900. The four heroic giants illustrate Hercules wrestling with his great challenges (Emperor Franz Josef, who commissioned the gate, felt he could relate). The facade's Hercules statues remind mere mortals to stay in their place.

In the center of this square, a scant bit of **Roman Vienna** lies exposed just beneath street level.

Spin Tour: Do a slow, clockwise pan to get your bearings, starting (over your left shoulder as you face the Hofburg) with **St. Michael's Church,** which offers fascinating tours of its crypt (see page 47). To the right of that is the fancy **Loden-Plankl shop,** with traditional Austrian formalwear, including dirndls. Farther to the right, across Augustinerstrasse, is the wing of the palace that houses the **Spanish Riding School** and its famous white Lipizzaner stallions (see page 39). Farther down this street lies **Josefsplatz,** with the **Augustinian Church** (see page 40), and the Dorotheum auction house. At the end of the street are Albertinaplatz and the opera house (where we started this walk).

Continue your spin: Two buildings over from the Hofburg (to the right), the modern **Loos House** (now a bank) has a facade featuring a perfectly geometrical grid of square columns and windows. Compared to the Neo-Baroque facade of the Hofburg, the stern Modernism of the Loos House appears to be from an entirely different age. And yet, both of these—as well  as the Eiffel Tower and Mad Ludwig's fairy-tale Neuschwanstein Castle—were built in the same generation, roughly around 1900. In many ways, this jarring juxtaposition exemplifies the architectural turmoil of the turn of the 20th century, and represents the passing of the torch from Europe's age of divine monarchs to the modern era (see sidebar).

• *Let's take a look at where Austria's glorious history began—at the...*

Hofburg Imperial Palace

This is the complex of palaces where the Habsburg emperors lived out their lives (except in summer, when they resided at Schönbrunn Palace). Enter the Hofburg through the gate, where you immediately find yourself beneath a big rotunda (the netting is there to keep birds from perching). The doorway on the right is the entrance to the ⓭ **Imperial Apartments,** where the Habsburg emperors once lived in chandeliered elegance. Today you can tour its

Michaelerplatz:
Where New Faces Down Old

It's fascinating to think of Michaelerplatz as the architectural embodiment of a fundamental showdown that took place at the dawn of the 20th century, between the old and the new.

Emperor Franz Josef came to power during the popular revolution year of 1848 (as an 18-year-old, he was locked in his palace for safety). Once in power, he saw that the real threat to him was not from without, but from within. He dismantled the city wall and moved his army's barracks to the center of the city. But near the end of his reign, the modern world was clearly closing in.

Franz Josef's Neo-Baroque design for the Hofburg, featuring huge statues of Hercules in action at the gate, represents a desperate last stand of the absolutism of the emperor. Hercules was a favorite of emperors—a prototype of the modern ruler. The only mythical figure that was half-god, Hercules earned this half-divinity with hard labors. Like Hercules, the emperor's position was a combination of privileged birth and achievement—legitimized both by God and by his own hard work. (Blue bloods throughout Europe favored statues of Hercules for this reason.)

A few decades after Franz Josef erected his celebration of divine right, Loos responded with his starkly different house across the street. Although the Loos House might seem boring today, in its time, this anti-Historicist, anti-Art Nouveau statement was shocking. Inspired by his studies in the US (and by Frank Lloyd Wright), it was considered to be Vienna's first "modern" building, with a trapezoidal footprint that makes no attempt to hide the awkwardly shaped street corner it stands on. Windows lack the customary cornice framing the top—a "house without eyebrows."

And so, from his front door, the emperor had to look at the modern world staring him rudely in the face, sneering, "Divine power is B.S. and your time is past." The emperor was angered by the bank building's lack of decor. Loos relented only slightly by putting up the 10 flower boxes (or "moustaches") beneath the windows.

But a few flowers couldn't disguise the notion that the divine monarchy was beginning to share Vienna with new ideas. As Loos worked, Stalin, Hitler, Trotsky, and Freud were all rattling about Vienna. Women were smoking and riding bikes. It was a scary time...a time ripe with change. And, of course, by 1918, after the Great War, the Habsburgs and the rest of Europe's autocratic imperial families were history.

lavish rooms, as well as a museum about Empress Sisi, and a porcelain and silver collection (📖 see the Hofburg Imperial Apartments Tour chapter). To the left is the ticket office for the ⑲ **Spanish Riding School** (see page 39).

Continuing on, you emerge from the rotunda into the main courtyard of the Hofburg, called **In der Burg.** The Caesar-like statue is of Habsburg Emperor Franz II (1768-1835), grandson of Maria Theresa, grandfather of Franz Josef, and father-in-law of Napoleon. Behind him is a tower with three kinds of clocks (the yellow disc shows the phase of the moon tonight). To the right of Franz are the Imperial Apartments, and to the left are the offices of Austria's mostly ceremonial presi-

dent (the more powerful chancellor lives in a building just behind this courtyard).

Franz Josef faces the oldest part of the palace. The colorful red, black, and gold gateway (behind you), which used to have a drawbridge, leads over the moat and into the 13th-century Swiss Court (Schweizerhof), named for the Swiss mercenary guards once stationed there. Study the gate. Imagine the drawbridge and the chain. Notice the Habsburg coat of arms with the imperial eagle above and the Renaissance painting on the ceiling of the passageway.

As you enter the Gothic courtyard, you're passing into the historic core of the palace, the site of the first fortress, and, historically, the place of last refuge. Here you'll find the ⑳ **Treasury** (Schatzkammer; 📖 see the Hofburg Treasury Tour chapter) and the **Imperial Music Chapel** (Hofmusikkapelle, see page 195), where the Boys' Choir sings Mass. Ever since Joseph Haydn and Franz Schubert were choirboys here, visitors have gathered like groupies on Sundays to hear the famed choir sing.

Returning to the bigger In der Burg courtyard, face Franz and turn left, passing through the **tunnel,** with a few tourist shops and restaurants, to spill out into spacious ㉑ **Heldenplatz** (Heroes' Square). On the left is the impressive curved facade of the **World Museum Vienna** (formerly the New Palace). This vast wing was built in the early 1900s to be the new Habsburg living quarters (and was meant to have a matching building facing it). But in 1914,

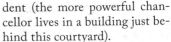

the heir to the throne, Archduke Franz Ferdinand—while waiting politely for his long-lived uncle, Emperor Franz Josef, to die—was assassinated in Sarajevo. The archduke's death sparked World War I and the eventual end of eight centuries of Habsburg rule.

The World Museum Vienna contains an eclectic collection of ethnography, weaponry, suits of armor, musical instruments, and ancient Greek statues (see page 34). The two equestrian statues depict Prince Eugene of Savoy (1663-1736), who battled the Ottoman Turks, and Archduke Charles (1771-1847), who battled Napoleon. Eugene gazes toward the far distance at the prickly spires of Vienna's City Hall.

Spin Tour: Make a slow 360-degree turn, and imagine this huge square filled with people.

In 1938, 300,000 Viennese gathered here, entirely filling vast Heroes' Square, to welcome Adolf Hitler and celebrate their annexation with Germany—the *Anschluss*. The Nazi tyrant stood on the balcony of the then New Palace and declared, "Before the face of German history, I declare my former homeland now a part of the Third Reich. One of the pearls of the Third Reich will be Vienna." He never said "Austria," a word that was now forbidden.

When pondering why the Austrians—eyes teary with joy and vigorously waving their Nazi flags—so willingly accepted Hitler's rule, it's important to remember that Austria was already a fascist nation. Austrian Chancellor Engelbert Dollfuss, though pro-Catholic, pro-Habsburg, and anti-Hitler, was a fascist dictator who silenced any left-wing opposition. Also, memories of the grand Habsburg Empire were still fresh in the collective psyche. The once vast and mighty empire of 50 million at its 19th-century peak came out of World War I a tiny landlocked land of six million that now suffered terrible unemployment. The opportunistic Hitler promised jobs along with a return to greatness—and the Austrian people gobbled it up.

Standing here, it's fascinating to consider Austrian aspirations for grandeur. In fact, the Habsburgs envisioned an ancient Rome-inspired Imperial Forum stretching from here across the Ringstrasse.

• *Walk on through the Greek-columned passageway (the Äusseres Burgtor), cross the Ringstrasse, and stand between the giant Kunsthistorisches and Natural History Museums, built in the 1880s to house the private art and scientific collections of the empire and to celebrate its culture and power. The emperor planned to tie these grand buildings and the palace together with two mighty triumphal arches spanning the Ringstrasse, connecting them into an awe-inspiring ensemble. And today, while the emperor's vision died with his empire, a huge statue of perhaps the greatest of the Habsburgs, Maria Theresa, stands in the center of it all.*

❷ Maria Theresa Monument

Vienna's biggest monument shows the empress (the empire's only female ruler) holding a scroll from her father granting the right

of a woman to inherit his throne. The statues and reliefs surrounding her speak volumes about her reign: Her four top generals sit on horseback while her four top advisers stand. Behind them, reliefs celebrate cultural leaders of her day, including little Wolfie Mozart with mentor "Papa" Joseph Haydn (with his hand on Mozart's shoulder, facing the Natural History Museum). The moral of this propaganda: that a strong military and a wise ruler are prerequisites for a thriving culture—attributes that characterized the 40-year rule of the woman who was perhaps Austria's greatest monarch.

• *Our walk is finished. You're in the heart of Viennese sightseeing. Surrounding this square are some of the city's top museums. And the Hofburg Palace itself contains many of Vienna's best sights and museums. From the opera to the Hofburg, from chocolate to churches, from St. Stephen's to Sacher tortes—Vienna waits for you.*

ST. STEPHEN'S CATHEDRAL TOUR

This massive church is the Gothic needle around which Vienna spins. According to the medieval vision of its creators, it stands like a giant jeweled reliquary, offering praise to God from the center of the city. The church and its towers, especially the 450-foot south tower, give the city its most iconic image. (Check your pockets for €0.10 coins; those minted in Austria feature the south tower.) The cathedral has survived Vienna's many wars and today symbolizes the city's spirit and love of freedom.

Orientation

Cost: It's free to enter the foyer and north aisle of the church, but it costs €6 to get into the main nave (with an included audioguide), where most of the interesting items are located. The south and north towers, catacombs, and treasury (all described later) cost extra. The €15 combo-ticket covers everything but is overkill for most visitors.

Hours: The church doors are open daily 6:00-22:00, but the main nave is open for tourists Mon-Sat 9:00-11:30 & 13:00-16:30, Sun 13:00-16:30, July-Aug until 17:30. During services, the main nave is reserved for worshippers, but you can look into the church from the back.

Information: Tel. 01/515-523-526, www.stephanskirche.at.

Tours: The tours in English are entertaining (free with €6 entry, daily at 10:30, check information board inside entry to confirm schedule). Otherwise the included audioguide is helpful.

ɠ Download my free St. Stephen's Cathedral audio tour.

Treasury: Consider riding the elevator (just inside the cathedral's entry) to the treasury. Tucked away in a loft in the oldest part of the church, it offers precious relics, dazzling church art, a

St. Stephen's Cathedral

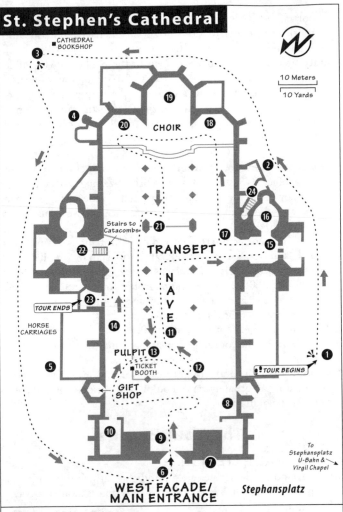

CATHEDRAL BOOKSHOP

10 Meters
10 Yards

③

④

⑳   CHOIR   ⑲   ⑱

②

㉔

⑯

Stairs to Catacombs

㉑

⑰   ⑮

TRANSEPT

㉒

N A V E

㉓   TOUR ENDS

⑭

⑪

HORSE CARRIAGES

PULPIT   ⑬

⑤   TICKET BOOTH   ⑫

GIFT SHOP

⑧

⑩   ⑨

⑦

①

! TOUR BEGINS

To Stephansplatz U-Bahn & Virgil Chapel

⑥

WEST FACADE/ MAIN ENTRANCE   Stephansplatz

ST. STEPHEN'S CATHEDRAL

① South Side View & Old Photos
② Reliefs, Memorials & Former Tombstones
③ North Tower View
④ Pulpit with Vanquished Turk
⑤ Stonemason's Hut
⑥ West Facade & Main Entrance
⑦ 05 Sign
⑧ Maria Pócs Icon
⑨ Organ & Treasury
⑩ Chapel of Prince Eugene of Savoy
⑪ Main Nave
⑫ Pillar Statues (Madonna with the Protective Mantle)
⑬ Pulpit with Self-Portrait
⑭ Similar Self-Portrait
⑮ Mozart Plaque
⑯ Mozart Baptistery
⑰ Madonna of the Servants
⑱ Tomb of Frederick III
⑲ High Altar
⑳ Wiener Neustädter Altar
㉑ Plaque of Rebuilding
㉒ Catacombs Entry
㉓ North Tower (Elevator)
㉔ South Tower (Stairs)

portrait of Rudolf IV (considered the earliest German portrait), and wonderful views down on the nave (€6, daily 9:00-16:30, July-Aug until 17:30).

Catacombs: The catacombs are open to the public only by guided tour (€6, daily 10:00-11:30 & 13:30-16:30, tours generally depart on the half-hour and are in German and English together). Just be at the stairs in the left/north transept to meet the guide—you'll pay at the end. You'll see a crypt for bishops and archbishops, and Crock-Pots of Habsburg guts filling dusty shelves.

Towers: The iconic **south tower** rewards a tough climb up a claustrophobic, 343-step staircase with dizzying views through windows near the top. You can reach it via the entrance outside the church, around the right as you face the west facade (€5, daily 9:00-17:30).

The shorter **north tower** holds the famous "Pummerin" bell, and you ascend via elevator (no stairs). But it's much lower, not as exciting, and has lesser views (€6, daily 9:00-18:30 & 19:00-21:30, entrance inside the church on the left/north side of the nave; you can access this elevator without buying a ticket for the main nave).

English Mass: Each Saturday at 19:00.

Theft Alert: All the commotion in and around the church makes it a favorite for pickpockets. Be on guard.

Starring: The cathedral's mighty exterior and evocative interior, including an ornately carved pulpit and various bits and pieces of Austrian history.

The Tour Begins

CATHEDRAL EXTERIOR

Before we go inside, let's circle around the cathedral for a look at its impressive exterior. We'll stop at several points along the way to take it all in.

❶ South Side

• *As you face the church's main entry, go to the right across the little square. From here, you can absorb the sheer magnitude of this massive church, with its skyscraping spire.*

The church we see today is the third one on this spot. A tall, black, glassy info post describes the Virgil Chapel that stood here 800 years ago. Its dank shell survives today below your feet, viewable from the nearby U-Bahn station. Today's church dates mainly from 1300 to 1450, when builders expanded on an earlier structure and added two huge towers at the end of each transept. When it was built, St. Stephen's—covering almost an acre of land—was a huge church for what was then just a modest town of 10,000. The ruler who built the church was competing with St. Vitus Cathedral, which was being built at the same time in Prague; he made sure that Vienna's grand church was bigger than Prague's. This helped convince the region's religious authorities that Vienna deserved a bishop, thus making St. Stephen's a "cathedral." Politically, this helped Vienna become a city to be reckoned with, and it soon replaced Prague as the seat of the Holy Roman Empire.

The impressive 450-foot **south tower**—capped with a golden orb and cross—took 65 years to build and was finished in 1433. The tower is a rarity among medieval churches in that it was completed before the Gothic style—and the age of faith—petered out.

Find the Turkish **cannonball** stuck in a buttress (above the low, green roof on the middle buttress, marked with the date *1683*)—a souvenir from one of several Ottoman sieges of the city.

The nave's sharply pitched **roof** stands 200 feet tall and is covered in 230,000 colorful ceramic tiles. The zigzag pattern is purely decorative, with no special symbolism.

The cathedral was heavily damaged at the end of World War II. (Near where you are standing, at the base of the tower, there may be **old photos** showing the destruc-

tion.) In 1945, Vienna was caught in the chaos between the occupying Nazis and the approaching Soviets. Allied bombs sparked fires in nearby buildings, and the embers leapt to the cathedral rooftop. The original timbered Gothic roof burned, the cathedral's huge bell crashed to the ground, and the fire raged for two days. Civic pride prompted a financial outpouring, and the roof was rebuilt to its original splendor by 1952—doubly impressive considering the bombed-out state of the impoverished country at that time. Locals who contributed to the postwar reconstruction each had a chance to "own" one tile for their donation. Inside, we'll see a plaque honoring the rebuilding of the cathedral.

The little buildings lining the church exterior are **sacristies** (utility buildings used for running the church).

• *Circle the church exterior counterclockwise, passing the **entrance to the***

south tower *(the 343-step tower climb is described at the end of this chapter)*.

Just past the tower entrance, look for the carved ❷ **reliefs and memorials** and former **tombstones** now decorating the church wall. These are a reminder that the area around the church was a graveyard until the 18th century when it was cleaned out for health concerns.

• *As you hook around behind the church, pause at the cathedral bookshop (Dombuchhandlung) at the far corner of the square.*

❸ North Tower View

This spot provides a fine, wide-angle view of the stubby north tower and the apse of the church. From this vantage point, you can see the exoskeletal fundamentals of **Gothic architecture:** buttresses shoring up a very heavy roof, allowing for large windows that could be filled with stained glass to bathe the interior in colorful light. A battalion of storm-drain gargoyles stands ready to vomit water during downpours. Colored tiles on the roof show not the two-headed eagle of Habsburg times (as on the other side), but two distinct eagles of modern times (1950): the state of Austria on the left and the city of Vienna on the right.

Just above street level, notice the marble ❹ **pulpit** under the golden starburst. Political ranting against other religions was only allowed outside the church. So, the priest would stand here, stoking public opinion against the Muslim Ottomans (or Jews or Protestants), in front of crowds far bigger than could fit into the church. Above the pulpit (in a scene from around 1700), a saint stands victoriously atop a vanquished Turk.

• *Continue circling the church, passing a line of horse carriages waiting to take tourists for a ride (€55 for 20 minutes). Watch for the blocky, modern-looking building huddled next to the side of the cathedral. This is the...*

❺ Stonemason's Hut

There's always been a stonemason's hut here, as workers must keep the church in good repair. Even today, the masonry is maintained in the traditional way—a never-ending task. Unfortunately, the local limestone used in the Middle Ages is quite porous and absorbs modern pollution. Until the 1960s, this was a very busy traffic circle, and today's acidic air still takes its toll. Each winter, when rainwater soaks into the surface and then freezes, the stone corrodes—and must be repaired. Your church entry ticket helps fund this ongoing work.

Across the street (past the horse carriages) is the **archbishop's palace,** where the head of this church still lives today (enjoying a very short commute).

• *Around the corner is the cathedral's front door. Stand at the back of the square, across from the main entrance, to take in the entire...*

❻ West Facade

The Romanesque-style main entrance includes bits of the oldest part of the church (which stood here in the 1200s). Right be-  hind you is the site of Vindobona, a Roman garrison town. Before the Romans converted to Christianity, there was a pagan temple here, and this entrance pays homage to that ancient heritage. Roman-era statues are embedded inside the facade, and the two **octagonal towers** flanking the main doorway are dubbed the "heathen towers" because they're built with a few recycled Roman stones (flipped over to hide the pagan inscriptions and expose the smooth sides).

Ten yards to the right of the main doorway, about chest high, is the symbol ❼ "O5," carved into the wall by anti-Nazi rebels (behind the Plexiglas, under the first plaque). The story goes that Hitler—who'd actually grown up in Austria—spurned his roots. When he attained power, he refused to call the country "Österreich," its native name, insisting on the Nazi term "Ostmark." Austrian patriots wrote the code "O5" to keep the true name alive: The "5" stands for the fifth letter of the alphabet (E), which often stands in for an umlaut, giving the "O" its correct pronunciation for "Österreich."

Step up to the main door. Before entering, study the details overhead. Christ—looking down from the tympanum—is triumphant over death. Flanked by angels with dramatic wings, he welcomes all. Ornate, tree-like pillars support a canopy of foliage and creatures, all full of meaning to the faithful medieval worshiper. The fine circa-1240 carvings above the door were once brightly painted. The paint was scrubbed off in the 19th century, when pure stone was more in vogue.

• *Enter the church.*

CATHEDRAL FOYER

Find a spot to peer through the gate down the immense nave—more than a football field long and nine stories tall. It's lined with clusters of slender pillars that soar upward to support the ribbed crisscross arches of the ceiling. Stylistically, the nave is Gothic with a Baroque overlay. It's a spacious, glorious venue that's often used for high-profile concerts (there's a ticket office outside the church, to the right as you face the main doorway). We'll venture down the main nave soon, but first, take some time to explore the foyer area.

To the right as you enter, in a gold-and-silver sunburst frame, is a crude Byzantine-style ❽ **Maria Pócs Icon** (Pötscher Madonna), brought here from a humble Hungarian village church. The picture of Mary and Child is said to have

wept real tears in 1697, as Central Europe was once again being threatened by the Turks. (Skeptics note it's painted on wood and the "tears" may have been resin beading up.) Prince Eugene of Savoy (described below) saved the day at the stunning Battle of Zenta in modern-day Serbia—a victory that broke the back of the Ottoman army. If you see crowds of pilgrims leaving flowers or lighting candles around the icon, they're most likely Hungarians thanking the Virgin for helping Prince Eugene drive the Ottomans out of their homeland.

Over the main doorway is the choir loft, with the 10,000-pipe ❾ **organ,** a 1960 replacement for the famous one destroyed during World War II. This organ is one of Europe's biggest, but it's currently broken and sits unused...too large to remove. Architects aren't sure whether it serves a structural purpose and adds support to the actual building.

Along the left wall is the **gift shop.** Step in to marvel at the 14th-century statuary decorating its wall—some of the finest carvings in the church.

To the left of the gift shop is the gated entrance to the ❿ **Chapel of Prince Eugene of Savoy.** Prince Eugene (1663-1736), a teenage seminary student from France, arrived in Vienna in 1683 as the city was about to be overrun by the Ottoman Turks. He volunteered for the army and helped save the city, launching a brilliant career as a military man for the Habsburgs. His specialty was conquering the Ottomans. He was well-rewarded and eventually owned six palaces in and around Vienna including the Belvedere. When he died, the grateful Austrians buried him here, under this chapel, marked by a tomb hatch in the floor.

• *Nearby is the entrance to the* ⓫ *main nave. Buy a ticket and walk to the center.*

MAIN NAVE
• *Looking down the nave, note the statues on the columns (about 30 feet above the ground).*

⓬ Pillar Statues
The nave's columns are richly populated with 77 life-size stone stat-

ues, making a saintly parade to the high altar.

Check out the first pillar on the right (directly above the black metal fence). Facing the wall is the **Madonna with the Protective Mantle,** shown giving refuge to people of all walks of life (notice the many happy people of faith tucked under her cape). Also on that same pillar, find Moses with the Ten Commandments (to the left of the Madonna, but hard to see because of the barrier). On other columns, Bible students can find their favorite characters and saints—more Madonnas, St. George (killing the dragon), St. Francis of Assisi, arrow-pierced St. Sebastian, and so on.

• *Start down the nave toward the altar. At the second pillar on the left is the...*

⓭ Pulpit
The Gothic sandstone pulpit (c. 1500) is a masterpiece carved from three separate blocks (see if you can find the seams). A spiral stairway winds up to the lectern, surrounded and supported by the four "Latin Church Fathers," who translated the Bible into Latin in the 4th century (making it more widely accessible to the faithful) and whose writings influenced early Catholic dogma. Each has a very different and very

human facial expression (from back to front): Ambrose (daydreamer), Jerome (skeptic), Gregory (explainer), and Augustine (listener).

The pulpit is as crammed with religious meaning as it is with beautifully realistic carvings. The top of the stairway's railing swarms with lizards and toads—symbols of corrupt teaching. The "Dog of the Lord" stands at the top, making sure none of those toads pollutes the sermon. Below the toads, wheels with three parts (the Trinity) roll up, while wheels with four spokes (the four seasons and four cardinal directions, symbolizing mortal life on earth) roll down.

Find the guy peeking out from under the stairs. This may be a **self-portrait of the sculptor.** In medieval times, art was done for

the glory of God, and artists worked anonymously. But this pulpit was carved as humanist Renaissance ideals were creeping in from Italy—and individual artists were becoming famous. So the artist included what may be a rare self-portrait bust in his work. He leans out from a window, sculptor's compass in hand, to observe the world and his work. The artist, long thought to be Hungarian mason Anton Pilgram, is now believed to be the Dutch sculptor Nicolaes Gerhaert van Leyden; both worked extensively on the cathedral.

About 20 paces toward the front, peering out from the left wall (about 15 feet up), is a similar ⓯ **self-portrait of the architect** in color, taken from the original organ case. He holds a compass and L-square and symbolically shoulders the heavy burden of being a master builder of this huge place.

• *Continue up the nave. We'll visit several sights at the front of the church, moving in a roughly counterclockwise direction.*

Halfway up the nave, turn right and enter the south transept. Go all the way to the doors, then look left to find the...

⓯ Mozart Plaque

A plaque on the wall honors one of Vienna's most famous citizens—Wolfgang Amadeus Mozart, who had strong ties to this cathedral (see sidebar).

Look into the adjacent chapel at the fine ⓰ **baptistery** (stone bottom, matching carved-wood top, from around 1500). This is where Mozart's children were baptized.

On the right-hand column near the entrance to the south transept, notice the fine carved black stone statue of the ⓱ **Madonna**

Mozart in St. Stephen's Cathedral

Wolfgang Amadeus Mozart (1756-1791) was married in St. Stephen's, attended Mass here, and had two of his children baptized here.

Mozart spent most of his adult life in Vienna. Born in Salzburg, Mozart was a child prodigy who toured Europe. He performed for Empress Maria Theresa's family in Vienna when he was eight. At 25, he left Salzburg in a huff (freeing himself from his domineering father) and settled in Vienna. Here he found instant fame as a concert pianist and freelance composer, writing *The Marriage of Figaro, Don Giovanni,* and *The Magic Flute.* He married Constanze Weber in St. Stephen's, and they set up house in a lavish apartment a block east of the church (now the lackluster Mozarthaus museum—see page 52). Mozart lived at the heart of Viennese society—among musicians, actors, and aristocrats. He played in a string quartet with Joseph Haydn. Mozart may have heard Haydn playing the pipe organ right here.

After his early success, Mozart fell on hard times, and the couple had to move to the suburbs. When Mozart died at 35, he was not buried at St. Stephen's, because the cemetery that once surrounded the church had been cleared out a decade earlier as an anti-plague measure. Instead, his remains were dumped into a mass grave outside town. But he was honored with a funeral service here in St. Stephen's.

of the Servants (from 1330). This remains a favorite of working people.

• *Now walk down the right aisle to the front. Dominating the chapel at the front-right corner of the church is the...*

⑱ Tomb of Frederick III

This imposing, red-marble tomb is like a big king-size-bed coffin with an effigy of Frederick lying on top (not visible—but there's a photo of the effigy on the left). The top of the tomb is decorated with his coats of arms, representing the many territories he ruled over. It's by the same Nicolaes Gerhaert van Leyden who likely sculpted the pulpit.

Frederick III (1415-1493) is considered the "father" of Vienna for turning the small village into a royal city with a cosmopolitan feel. Frederick secured a bishopric, turning the newly completed St. Stephen's church into a cathedral. The emperor's major contribution to Austria, however, was in fathering Maximilian I and

ST. STEPHEN'S CATHEDRAL

marrying him off to Mary of Burgundy, instantly making the Habsburg Empire a major player in European politics. This lavish tomb (made of marble from Salzburg) is as long-lasting as Frederick's legacy. To make sure it stayed that way, locals saved his tomb from damage during World War II by encasing it in a shell of brick.

• *Walk to the middle of the church and face the...*

⓲ High Altar

The tall, ornate, black marble altarpiece (1641, by Tobias and Johann Pock) is topped with a statue of Mary that barely fits under the towering vaults of the ceiling. It frames a large painting of the stoning of St. Stephen, painted on copper. Stephen (at the bottom), having refused to stop professing his faith, is pelted with rocks by angry pagans. As he kneels, ready to die, he gazes up to see a vision of Christ, the cross, and the angels of heaven. The stained glass behind the painting—some of the oldest in the church—creates a kaleidoscopic jeweled backdrop.

Turn 180 degrees and look back for a view of the nave (not cluttered by the many Baroque chapels added in the 17th and 18th centuries, which are hidden behind the columns from this angle). What you see here is pretty close to a pure Gothic aesthetic.

• *Ten steps to the left of the main altar is the...*

⓴ Wiener Neustädter Altar

The triptych altarpiece—the symmetrical counterpart of Frederick III's tomb—was commissioned by Frederick in 1447. Its gilded wooden statues are especially impressive.

• *Return to the high altar and walk back up the middle of the nave. When you reach the third set of pillars, look immediately to the right (on the column with the black gate attached). About 10 feet above the ground is the...*

㉑ Plaque of Rebuilding

St. Stephen's is proud to be Austria's national church. The plaque explains in German how each region contributed to the rebuilding after World War II: *Die Glocke* (the bell) was financed by the state of Upper Austria. *Das Tor* (the entrance portal) was from Steiermark, the windows from Tirol, the pews from Vorarlberg, the floor from Lower Austria, and so on.

During World War II, many of the city's top art treasures were stowed safely in cellars and salt mines—hidden by both the Nazi occupiers (to protect against war damage) and by citizens (to protect against Nazi looters). The stained-glass windows behind the high altar were meticulously dismantled and packed away. The pulpit was encased, like the tomb of Frederick III, in a shell of brick. As the war was drawing to a close, it appeared St. Stephen's would escape major damage. But as the Nazis were fleeing, the bitter Nazi commander in charge of the city ordered that the church be destroyed. Fortunately, his underlings disobeyed. Unfortunately, the church accidentally caught fire during Allied bombing shortly thereafter, and the wooden roof collapsed onto the stone vaults of the ceiling. The Tupperware-colored glass on either side of the nave dates from the 1950s.

From this spot consider the history St. Stephen's Cathedral has seen—and survived—as the towering centerpiece of this grand European capital.

• *Your cathedral tour is over. Head back toward the main entrance. Along the north side of the nave, you have two options: Tour the catacombs or ascend the north tower (both described below). Or you can head outside for the pulse-raising climb up the south tower.*

OTHER CATHEDRAL SIGHTS

• *Near the middle of the church, at the left/north transept, is the entrance to the...*

ⓩ Catacombs

The catacombs (viewable by guided tour only) hold the bodies—or at least the innards—of 72 Habsburgs, including that of Rudolf IV, the man who began building the south tower. This is where Austria's rulers were buried before the Kaisergruft was built (see page 44), and where later Habsburgs' entrails were entombed. The copper urns preserve the imperial organs in alcohol. I touched Maria Theresa's urn and it wobbled.

• *Also in the north nave, but closer to the cathedral's main door, is the entrance for the north tower (look for the* Aufzug zur Pummerin *sign).*

㉓ North Tower

The cramped north tower elevator takes you to a mediocre view and a big bell. Nicknamed "the Boomer" (Pummerin), it's old (first cast in 1711), big (nearly 10 feet across), and very heavy (21 tons). By comparison, the Liberty Bell is four feet across and weighs one ton.

It's supposedly the second-biggest bell in the world that rings by swinging. A physical symbol of victory over the Ottomans in 1683, the Pummerin was cast from cannons (and cannonballs) captured from the Ottomans when the siege of Vienna was lifted. During the WWII fire that damaged the church, the Pummerin fell to the ground and cracked. It had to be melted down and recast. These days, locals know the Pummerin as the bell that rings in the Austrian New Year. You'll see its original 1,700-pound clapper in the catacombs if you take that tour.

• *Exit the church. Make a U-turn to the left if you're up for a climb up the...*

❷❹ South Tower

The 450-foot-high south tower, once key to the city's defense as a lookout point, is still dear to Viennese hearts. (It's long been affectionately nicknamed "Steffl," Viennese for "Stevie.") No church spire in (what was) the Austro-Hungarian Empire is taller—by Habsburg decree. It offers a far better view than the north tower, but you'll earn it by hiking 343 tightly wound steps up the spiral staircase (this hike burns about one Sacher torte's worth of calories). From the top, use your city map to locate the famous sights. There are great views of the colorful church roof, the low-level Viennese skyline (major skyscrapers are regulated in the city center), and—in the distance—the Vienna Woods.

• *The oldest part of this sight is inside the nearby U-Bahn station.*

Virgil Chapel

Before today's cathedral was built, a humble Romanesque chapel (circa 1200) stood adjacent to the site. It was excavated in 1972 and is tourable today. It has a few surviving wall frescoes and a tiny museum with medieval artifacts under its 35-foot-tall arches. Access is via the Stephansplatz U-Bahn station, underground in front of the cathedral (€5 including audioguide, Tue-Sun 10:00-18:00, closed Mon).

ST. STEPHEN'S CATHEDRAL

RINGSTRASSE TRAM TOUR

In the 1860s, Emperor Franz Josef had Vienna's ingrown medieval wall torn down and replaced with a grand boulevard 190 feet wide. The road, arcing nearly three miles around the city's core, predates all the buildings that line it. Those buildings are very "Neo": Neoclassical, Neo-Gothic, and Neo-Renaissance—an approach called Historicism (see sidebar later in this chapter). One of Europe's great streets, the Ringstrasse is lined with many of Vienna's top sights.

This self-guided tram tour gives you a fun orientation and a ridiculously quick glimpse of some major sights as you glide by. Vienna's red trams (a.k.a. streetcars) circle the Ring. Most of them are sleek and modern. Neither tram #1 nor #2 makes the entire loop around the Ring, but you can see it all by making one transfer between them (at the Schwedenplatz stop). Enjoying this circular tram ride is a no-stress way to sit shoulder-to-shoulder with ordinary *Wieners* and see their city. In fact, my hope is that you'll feel like a *Wiener* yourself as you make this big loop.

If you have a transit pass (instead of a ticket), you can—and should—jump on and off as you go, seeing sights that interest you. Some of the best stops are Weihburggasse (Stadtpark), Stubentor (Museum of Applied Arts, a.k.a. MAK), Rathausplatz (City Hall and its summertime food circus), and Burgring (Kunsthistorisches Museum and Hofburg Palace).

You may find that the tram goes faster than you can read. It's best to look through this chapter ahead of time, then ride with an eye out for the various sights described here. As you go, use time spent waiting at red lights and tram stops to read the next segment to prepare for what's coming up. Better yet, listen to the audio version of this tour on my 🎧 Rick Steves Audio Europe app.

Or, to do this tour at your own pace, consider renting a **bike.** This allows you to easily stop at sights or to detour to nearby points

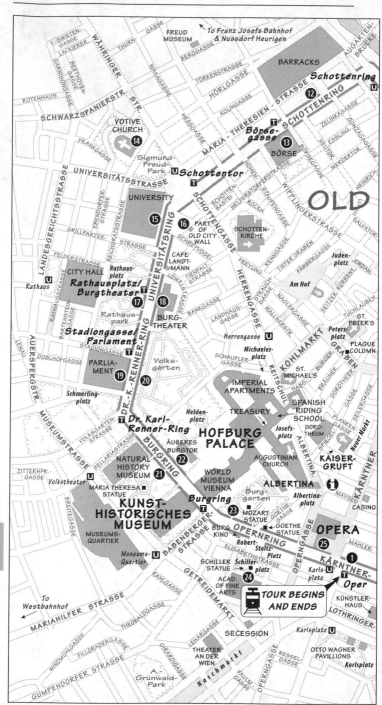

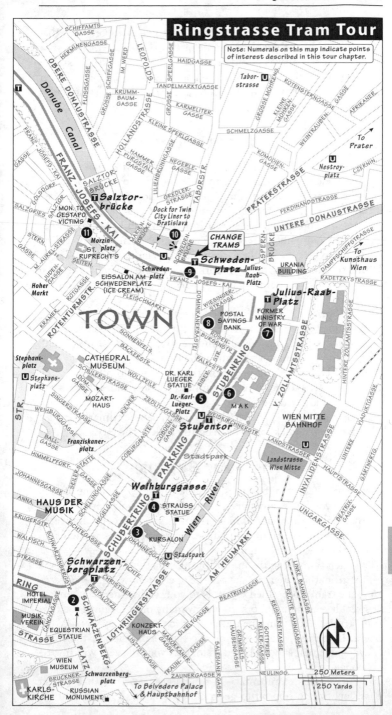

Ringstrasse Tram Tour

Note: Numerals on this map indicate points of interest described in this tour chapter.

of interest. The grassy median strip has excellent bike paths that run along almost the entire circuit of the Ring (except for a few blocks after the votive church, near the end of this tour). The City-bike Wien rental program is cheap and easy, and the Pedal Power bike rental shop is just two blocks from the opera house (for details on both, see the Orientation to Vienna chapter).

Orientation

Cost: €2.40 (one transit ticket), there's a coin-op machine on tram. A single ticket can be used to cover the whole route, including the transfer between trams (but you're not otherwise allowed to interrupt your trip). With a transit pass (€8/24 hours), you're free to hop off whenever you like, then hop back on another tram (they come along every few minutes). For more on riding Vienna's trams, see the Orientation to Vienna chapter.

When to Go: While this tour works fine in the daylight, the tram ride is also pleasant after dark, when nearly every sight on the route is well-lit.

Pricier Option: A yellow just-for-tourists streetcar circles the Ring without requiring a transfer—but it costs more and runs less frequently (€9 for one 30-minute loop, 2/hour 10:00-17:30, see the Orientation to Vienna chapter).

Tours: ∩ Download my free Ringstrasse Tram audio tour.

Length of This Tour: About 45 minutes; allow more time if you hop off along the way.

Starring: Vienna's grandest boulevard, major landmarks, and a dizzyingly quick, once-over-lightly look at the city.

The Tour Begins

To help you keep your bearings, this tour includes the name of each tram stop you'll pass and tells you which way to look along the way. Stop names are announced in German as you approach, indicated on monitors in the tram, and labeled in small letters at each stop (above the round street signs).

Catch tram #2 in the middle of the street in front of the opera house (from the underpass next to the opera, follow signs to *Opern-ring;* the tram stop, called **Oper,** is to your right when you emerge at street level, and monitors show how many minutes until the next tram arrives). You want the tram going to the right, as you face the opera. If you can, grab a seat on the right-hand side of the tram. (Few people will stay on board as long as you, so seats will invariably open up.)

Again, this commentary is ridiculously fast. With a transit pass, feel free to hop off to get a closer look at anything that intrigues you. (Another tram will come along every 5-10 minutes.) And remember: You can read ahead at each tram stop and be free to sightsee as you roll.

• *Let's go. As you leave the **Oper stop**...*

❶ Look Left

Just next to the opera house, the city's main pedestrian drag, Kärntner Strasse, leads to the zigzag-mosaic roof of **St. Stephen's Cathedral.** This tram tour makes a 360-degree circle (with a connection halfway through) around the cathedral, staying about this same distance from the great church that marks the center of Vienna.

• *Seconds later...*

❷ Look Left then Right

Along this stretch, you'll pass a string of Vienna's finest five-star hotels, including **Hotel Imperial** (on the right)—the choice of nearly every visiting big shot, from the Rolling Stones to Queen Elizabeth.

Fifty yards after the hotel (also on the right), at Schwarzenbergplatz, an **equestrian statue** honors Prince Charles Schwarzenberg, who fought Napoleon. From the end of World War II until 1955, Austria and its capital were occupied by foreign troops, including Russian forces; during that time the square was named Stalinplatz after the Soviet dictator.

In the distance beyond the prince, at the far end of the long square, look for a fountain with a big colonnade just behind it. This **Russian monument** was built in 1945 as a forced thank-you to the Soviets for liberating Austria from the Nazis. Formerly a sore point, now the monument is just ignored.

• *Coming up seconds later is the **Schwarzenbergplatz stop**. When you pass it...*

❸ Look Right

Three blocks beyond the Schwarzenbergplatz stop is the huge **Stadtpark** (City Park). This inviting green space honors many great Viennese musicians and composers with statues. At the beginning of the park, the gold-and-cream concert hall behind the trees is the **Kursalon,** opened in 1867 by the Strauss brothers, who directed many waltzes here. Touristy Strauss concerts are held in this building (for details, see the Entertainment in Vienna chapter). If the weather's nice, hop off at the next stop (Weihburggasse) for a stroll in the park.

• *Right at the **Weihburggasse** stop...*

❹ Look Right

In the park but barely visible from the tram is a gilded tribute to "Waltz King" **Johann Strauss** (squint through the park gate a few yards beyond the stop to find a statue in a white arch). He holds a violin as he did when he conducted his orchestra, whipping his fans into a three-quarter-time frenzy.

• *The next four sights pass quickly, so read about them while you're waiting at the next stop (**Stubentor**). Just after the tram sets off again...*

❺ Look Left

Centered in a public square is a bronze statue (now turned green) of **Dr. Karl Lueger,** the mayor who shaped Vienna into a modern city (see "The Birth of Modern Vienna" sidebar, later).

• *Immediately after the Lueger statue...*

❻ Look Right

The big, red-brick building across the street is the **Museum of Applied Arts** (MAK), showing furniture and design through the ages (also has good café and gift shop; see page 73).

• *A block after the museum...*

❼ Look Right

The long, white building used to be the **Austrian Ministry of War**—back when that was a major operation. Above its oval windows, you can see busts of soldiers wearing Stratego-style military helmets. Each bust shows the uniform of a different regiment and the folkloric tradition of its country within the Habsburg realm.

• *Now (quickly or it's gone)...*

❽ Look Left

Directly opposite the start of the Ministry of War (set back on a little square, in a little gap between the buildings) is the **Post-**

al Savings Bank (see page 54). Designed by Otto Wagner, it's one of the rare Secessionist buildings facing the Ring. (For more on the Secession, see the sidebar on page 64.)
• *Immediately after the **Julius-Raab-Platz stop**, the tram makes a sharp left turn. Hop off at the next stop, **Schwedenplatz**.*

❾ Get Off and Transfer
Hop off tram #2 at the Schwedenplatz stop and wait for tram #1 (heading in the same direction you've been going, and leaving from the next track, just to your left). Gelato fans may want to prolong the wait a little with a break at Eissalon am Schwedenplatz. Before venturing away from the platform, check the electronic board at the stop to see how many minutes until the next tram arrives, but don't rush; they come along every 5-10 minutes. Take your time here to enjoy the canal scenery.
• *For a good viewpoint, walk out onto a bridge or climb up the wooden stairs of the restaurant immediately opposite the tram stop.*

❿ Canal View While You Wait...
The waterway is the **Danube Canal** (a.k.a. the "Baby Danube"), one of the many small arms of the river that once made up the Danube at this location.

The rest have been gathered together in a mightier modern-day Danube, farther away. The river was engineered for stability and trade in 1873. This area was once the center of the original Roman town, Vindobona. Located on the banks of the Danube, Vindobona marked the end of the civilized world. To the north lay the barbarian (non-Latin-speaking) Germanic lands.

To the far left are the Vienna Woods in the foothills of the Alps. To the right is the Urania, Franz Josef's 1910 observatory. The embankment has become a lazy park-like people-zone with restaurant boats, swimming pools, sundecks, bars with lounge chairs for sunning, and bike paths.

The modern boat station is for the fast boat to Bratislava, the capital city of Slovakia, just over an hour away downstream.

If some of the buildings across the canal seem a bit drab, that's because in April 1945, the last month of World War II, this prime real estate was cleared by bombs. Postwar buildings were constructed on the cheap and are now being replaced by sleek, futuristic buildings.

The Birth of Modern Vienna

This tour quickly passes a statue of Dr. Karl Lueger (1844-1910), the influential mayor of Vienna during the pivotal period

around the turn of the 20th century. Although controversial for his anti-Semitic and anti-immigrant rhetoric, Lueger worked together with architect Otto Wagner (1841-1918) to shape the modern Vienna you see today. Read this information during any downtime (or before you board the tram), so you can recognize Lueger when you see him (at stop #5).

While Lueger was mayor (1897-1910), Vienna was in the midst of an incredible growth spurt: In 1850, the city had 500,000 residents; at its peak, around 1900, the population was 2.2 million—about 20 percent more than the city's current population of 1.8 million.

Emperor Franz Josef put Lueger and Wagner (the "Father of Modern Vienna") to work with a staff of 60 architects to turn the city into a capital befitting the grandiose Habsburg Empire. Consider the dramatic changes this team oversaw in a relatively short time: In the previous generation, Roman-style aqueducts still brought fresh spring water into the city from the Alps. By the 20th century, the city had modern plumbing. Thomas Edison supervised the electrical lighting of Schönbrunn Palace, and shortly after that, gas lighting brightened the entire Ringstrasse. The Danube was tamed by building solid banks, along with other flood-control projects. In the 1870s, engineers even began an artificial island that took a century to complete.

As Vienna grew and sprawled, it became decentralized, as with "city centers" all over the place. To tie it all together, the new Vienna needed a fine tram and subway system. Consequently, much of the city's subway infrastructure also dates from this era. Around town, you'll notice that some of the older U-Bahn stops are still Art Nouveau in design. Also during this time (in 1898), the horse-drawn tramline around the Ringstrasse was converted to electric power.

In so many ways, the Vienna of today was created during this brief spurt of architectural and engineering energy. Lueger himself has fallen into disrepute because of his racist politics (Hitler cited him as an inspiration in *Mein Kampf*). After decades of controversy, the part of the Ring named after Lueger in 1934 was rechristened the Universitätsring in 2012, and many would like to see his statue removed as well.

By the way, this is called Schwedenplatz ("Sweden Square") because after World War I, Vienna was overwhelmed with hungry orphans. The Swedes took several thousand in, raised them, and finally sent them home healthy and well-fed.

• *Get ready—here comes tram #1. This time, grab a seat on the left if you can. Keep an eye toward the old city center—the spire of St. Stephen's Cathedral peeks above the buildings on your left (beyond the golden arches). After three blocks, opposite the gas station...*

⓫ Look Left

You'll see the ivy-covered walls and round Romanesque arches of **St. Ruprecht's** (Ruprechtskirche), the oldest church in Vienna. It was built in the 11th century on a bit of Roman ruins.

• *Take a breather for a bit—there's not much to see until after the next stop (Schottenring).*

In the Meantime...

It's interesting to remember that the Ringstrasse replaced the mighty walls that once protected Vienna from external enemies.

Imagine the great imperial capital contained within its three-mile-long wall, most of which dated from the 16th to 18th century. As was typical of city walls, it was lined with cannons (2,200, in Vienna's case) and surrounded by a "shooting field" or "cannonball zone." This swath of land, as wide as a cannonball could fly (about 400 yards), was clear-cut so no one could approach without being targeted.

After the popular unrest and uprisings of 1848, the emperor realized the true threat against him was from inside. He rid the city of its walls in about 1860, built this boulevard and transportation infrastructure (useful for moving citizens in good times and soldiers in bad), and, as you'll see in a moment, moved his army closer at hand. Napoleon III's remodel of Paris demonstrated that wide boulevards make it impossible for revolutionaries to erect barricades to block the movement of people and supplies. That encouraged Franz Josef to implement a similarly broad street plan for his Ring. A straight stretch of boulevard may seem just stately, but for an embattled emperor, it's an easy-to-defend corridor.

Vienna's wall survived longer than those in most European capital cities because its Old Regime rulers did. When the emperor had the walls taken down, the shooting field was wide open and ripe for development. Hence, the wonderful architecture that lines the outer edge of the Ringstrasse is all from the same era (post-1860).

• *The tram leaves the canal after the **Schottenring stop** and turns left. About 100 yards after that left turn, you should...*

⓬ Look Right

Through a gap in the buildings, you'll get a glimpse of a
huge, red-brick castle—actually
high-profile **barracks** for 6,000
troops built here at the com-
mand of a nervous Emperor
Franz Josef (who found himself
on the throne as an 18-year-old
in 1848, the same year people's
revolts against autocracy were
sweeping across Europe).

• *When you pull into the Börsegasse stop...*

⓭ Look Left

The orange-and-white, Neo-Renaissance temple of money—the
Börse—is Vienna's stock exchange. The next block is lined with
banks and insurance companies—the financial district of Austria.
• *At the next stop (Schottentor)...*

⓮ Look Right

The huge, frilly, Neo-Gothic church across
the small park is a **"votive church,"** a type
of church built to fulfill a vow in thanks for
God's help—in this case, when an 1853 assassination attempt on Emperor Franz Josef
failed.

Look left and right to see the fine lines
of buildings (two blocks on the left, three on
the right) built in the free-fire zone of the
wall after 1870. This string of grand, late-
19th-century buildings stretches three miles
along the real estate freed up with the demo-
lition of the wall. What a gift to developers!
• *Just after the Schottentor stop...*

⓯ Look Right

You're looking at the main building of the **University of Vienna**
(Universität Wien). Established in 1365, the university has no
real campus, as its buildings are scattered around town. It's considered the oldest continuously operating university in the German-speaking world.
• *Immediately opposite the university...*

⓰ Look Left

A chunk of the old **city wall** is visible (behind a gilded angel).

RINGSTRASSE TRAM

Historicism

Most of the architecture along the Ring is known as "Historicism" because it's all Neo-this and Neo-that. It takes design elements from the past—Greek columns, Renaissance arches, Baroque frills—and plasters them on the facade to simulate a building from the past.

Generally, the style fits the purpose of the particular building. For example, the Neoclassical parliament building celebrates ancient Greek notions of democracy. The Neo-Gothic City Hall recalls when medieval burghers ran the city government in Gothic days. Neo-Renaissance museums, such as the Kunsthistorisches and Natural History Museums, celebrate learning. And the Neo-Baroque National Theater recalls the age when opera and theater flourished.

Beethoven lived and composed in the building just above the piece of wall.

• *As you pull into the **Rathausplatz/Burgtheater stop**, first...*

⓱ Look Right

The Neo-Gothic **City Hall** (Rathaus) flies both the flag of Austria and the flag of Europe. The square in front (Rathausplatz) is a festive site in summer, with a thriving food circus and a huge screen showing outdoor movies, operas, and concerts (July-Aug daily and nightly until late; see the Entertainment in Vienna chapter).

• *And then...*

⓲ Look Left

Immediately across the street from City Hall is the **Burgtheater,** Austria's national theater. Locals brag it's the "leading theater in the German-speaking world."

• *Just after the **Stadiongasse/Parlament stop**...*

⓳ Look Right

The Neo-Greek temple of democracy houses the **Austrian Parliament.** The lady with the golden helmet is Athena, goddess of wisdom.

• *And then swivel to...*

⑳ Look Left

Across the street from the Parliament is the imperial park called the **Volksgarten,** with a fine public rose garden.

• *The next stop is* **Dr. Karl-Renner-Ring.** *When the tram pulls away...*

㉑ Look Right

The vast building is the **Natural History Museum** (Naturhistorisches Museum), which faces its twin, the **Kunsthistorisches Museum,** containing the city's greatest collection of paintings. The **MuseumsQuartier** behind them completes the ensemble with a collection of modern art museums. A hefty statue of Empress Maria Theresa squats between the museums, facing the grand gate to the Hofburg Palace.

• *Now...*

㉒ Look Left

Opposite Maria Theresa, the arched gate (the only surviving castle gate of the old town wall) leads to the **Hofburg,** the emperor's palace. Of the five arches, the center one was used only by the emperor.

Your tour is nearly finished. Consider hopping off here to visit the Hofburg or the Kunsthistorisches Museum.

• *Fifty yards after the* **Burgring stop...**

㉓ Look Left

Until 1918, the appealing **Burggarten** was the private garden of the emperor. Today locals enjoy relaxing here, and it's also home to a famous statue of **Mozart** (pictured here; he's hiding behind the leaves).

On the right is the Burg Kino theater, which plays the movie *The Third Man* several times a week in English (see page 68).

A hundred yards farther (back on the left, just after the park), the German philosopher **Goethe** sits in a big, thought-provoking chair.

• *Now it's time to...*

㉔ Look Right

Goethe seems to be playing trivia with German poet **Schiller** across the street (in the little park set back from the street). Behind the statue of Schiller is the **Academy of Fine Arts** (described on page 61).

RINGSTRASSE TRAM

• *Get ready to...*

❷ Look Left...and Get Off

Hey, there's the **opera house** again. Jump off the tram and see the rest of the city. (To join me on a walking tour of Vienna's center, which starts here at the opera, 📖 see the Vienna City Walk chapter.)

HOFBURG IMPERIAL APARTMENTS TOUR

In this tour of the Hofburg Imperial Apartments, you'll see the lavish, Versailles-like rooms that were home to the hardworking Emperor Franz Josef I and his reclusive, eccentric empress, known as "Sisi." From here, the Habsburgs ruled their vast empire.

Franz Josef was the last of the great Habsburg monarchs, and these apartments straddle the transition from old to new. You'll see chandeliered luxury alongside office furniture and electric lights.

Franz Josef and Sisi were also a study in contrasts. Where Franz was earnest, practical, and spartan, Sisi was poetic, high-strung, and luxury-loving. Together, they lived their lives in the cocoon of the Imperial Apartments, seemingly oblivious to how the world was changing around them.

Orientation

Cost: €15, includes well-done audioguide; also covered by €34 Sisi Ticket, which includes the Schönbrunn Palace Grand Tour and the Imperial Furniture Collection (to avoid lines, buy your Sisi Ticket at the Imperial Furniture Collection or online—www.schoenbrunn.at).

Hours: Daily 9:00-17:30, July-Aug until 18:00, last entry one hour before closing.

Information: Tel. 01/533-7570, www.hofburg-wien.at.

When to Go: It can be crowded midmornings, so go either right at opening time or after 14:00.

Getting There: Enter from under the rotunda just off Michaelerplatz, through the Michaelertor gate.

Tours: Guided tours (€3) run daily at 14:00. The included audioguide brings the exhibit to life; with it and this chapter, you won't need to buy the official guidebook.

Length of This Tour: If you listen to the entire audioguide, allow 40 minutes for the porcelain and silver collection, 30 minutes for the Sisi Museum, and 40 minutes for the apartments.

OVERVIEW

The Imperial Apartments are part of the large Hofburg Palace complex (for an overview of the entire palace area, see the "Vienna's Hofburg Palace" map in the Sights in Vienna chapter). Your ticket grants you admission to three separate exhibits, which you'll visit on a one-way route. The first floor holds a collection of precious porcelain and silver knickknacks *(Silberkammer)*. You then go upstairs to the Sisi Museum, which has displays about her life. This leads into the 20 or so

rooms of the Imperial Apartments *(Kaiserappartements),* starting in Franz Josef's rooms, then heading into the dozen rooms where his wife Sisi lived.

The Tour Begins

IMPERIAL PORCELAIN AND SILVER COLLECTION
• *Your visit (and the excellent audioguide) starts on the ground floor.*

Tableware Collection
The audioguide actually manages to make the Habsburg court's vast tableware collection interesting. The cabinets are full (with the contents intact—this area was never bombed), and the displays were functional so that servants could select the proper items, as the royals would entertain up to 800 guests at a time. Browse the collection to gawk at the opulence and to take in some colorful Habsburg trivia. (Who'da thunk that the court had an official way to fold a napkin—and that the technique remains a closely guarded secret?) Still, I wouldn't bog down here, as there's much more to see upstairs.

• *Once you're through all those rooms of dishes, climb the stairs—the same staircase used by the emperors and empresses who lived here. At the top is a timeline of Sisi's life. Swipe your ticket to pass through the turnstile, consider the rare WC ("go when you can, not when you have to"), and enter the room with the...*

Sisi (1837-1898)

Empress Elisabeth—Franz Josef's beautiful wife—was the 19th-century equivalent of Princess Diana. Born on Christmas Eve and known as "Sisi" since childhood, she became an instant celebrity when she married Franz Josef at 16.

The daughter of a Bavarian duke, Sisi enjoyed an idyllic girlhood riding horses in the forests near Munich. But after marrying, she became obsessed with preserving her reputation as a beautiful empress, maintaining her Barbie-doll figure (her goal: to stay under 110 pounds), and tending to her fairy-tale, ankle-length hair. In the 1860s, she was considered one of the most beautiful women in the world. But, despite severe dieting and fanatical exercise, age—not to mention the near impossibility of adhering to such demanding standards of feminine beauty—took their toll. After turning 30, she refused to allow photographs or portraits, and was generally seen in public with a delicate fan covering her face (and bad teeth).

Complex and influential, Sisi was adored by Franz Josef, whom she respected. Although Franz Josef was supposed to have married Sisi's sister Helene (in an arranged diplomatic marriage), he fell in love with Sisi instead. It was one of the Habsburgs' few marriages for love.

Sisi had a special affinity for Hungary. She enthusiastically studied and spoke Hungarian, and her personal mission and political cause was promoting Hungary's bid for autonomy within the empire—which her husband accommodated in 1867 by dividing his empire into the "Dual Monarchy" of the Austro-Hungarian Empire. Her personal tragedy was the death of her son Rudolf, the crown prince, in an apparent suicide (an incident often dramatized as the "Mayerling Affair," named after the royal hunting lodge where it happened). Disliking Vienna and the confines of the court and eager for time out of the spotlight, Sisi traveled more and more frequently. (She spent so much time in Budapest, and with Hungarian statesman Count Andrássy, that many believe her third daughter to be the count's.)

As the years passed, the restless Sisi and her hardworking husband became estranged. In 1898, while visiting Geneva, Switzerland, she was murdered by an Italian anarchist. Sisi's beauty, bittersweet life, and tragic death helped create her larger-than-life legacy. However, her importance is often inflated by melodramatic accounts of her life. The Sisi Museum (here in the Hofburg) seeks to tell a more accurate story.

Model of the Hofburg

Survey the model. It shows the original 19th-century vision of the Habsburgs: an Austrian "Foro Romano" glorifying the imperial family, with a garden of statues surrounded by a vast and symmetrical complex reaching all the way to the imperial stables at the far end. But by this time, the era of emperors was rapidly passing; this vision would never come to fruition, and by 1918 the Habsburgs were history.

Circle to the far side to find where you're standing right now, near the Hofburg's largest dome. That dome tops the entrance to the Hofburg from Michaelerplatz.

The Hofburg was the epicenter of one of Europe's great political powers—600 years of Habsburgs lived here. The Hofburg started as a 13th-century medieval castle (near where you are right now) and expanded over the centuries to today's 240,000-square-meter (60-acre) complex, now owned by the state.

A world within a world, the Hofburg was a kind of forbidden city accessible only to the ruling elite until 1891. Stand at the center and imagine the unfinished bit filled in, and ponder the imperial greatness of the palace complex. The twin buildings just before the stables were purpose-built to be museums.

To the left of the dome (as you face the facade) is the steeple of the Augustinian Church. It was there, in 1854, that Franz Josef married 16-year-old Elisabeth of Bavaria, and their story began.
• *Now enter a darkened room at the beginning of the...*

SISI MUSEUM

Empress Elisabeth (1837-1898)—a.k.a. "Sisi" (SEE-see)—was Franz Josef's mysterious, beautiful, and narcissistic wife. This museum traces her fabulous but tragic life—and it does so with the help of her flowery poetry, which is posted for reading as you stroll through these ornate halls. She wrote thousands of pages of intimate insights into her rich—yet unhappy—life.

Sisi's Death

The exhibit starts with Sisi's sad end, showing her **death mask,** photos of her **funeral procession** (by the Hercules statues facing Michaelerplatz), and an **engraving** of a grieving Franz Josef. It was at her death that the obscure, private empress' legend began to grow.
• *Continue into the corridor.*

The Sisi Myth

Sisi was not a major public figure in her lifetime, as **newspaper clippings** of the day make clear. She was often absent from public functions, and the censored press was gagged from reporting on her eccentricities. After her death, however, her image quickly be-

Hofburg Imperial Apartments Tour

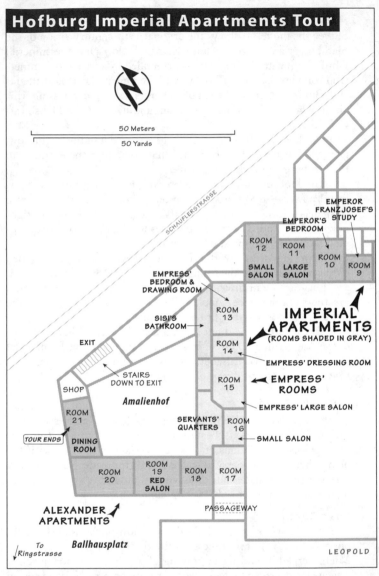

SCHAUFLERSTRASSE

EMPEROR FRANZ JOSEF'S STUDY

EMPEROR'S BEDROOM

ROOM 12 — SMALL SALON

ROOM 11 — LARGE SALON

ROOM 10

ROOM 9

EMPRESS' BEDROOM & DRAWING ROOM

SISI'S BATHROOM

ROOM 13

ROOM 14

IMPERIAL APARTMENTS (ROOMS SHADED IN GRAY)

EMPRESS' DRESSING ROOM

ROOM 15

◄ EMPRESS' ROOMS

EMPRESS' LARGE SALON

EXIT

STAIRS DOWN TO EXIT

Amalienhof

SHOP

ROOM 21

SERVANTS' QUARTERS

ROOM 16

SMALL SALON

TOUR ENDS

DINING ROOM

ROOM 20

ROOM 19 RED SALON

ROOM 18

ROOM 17

ALEXANDER APARTMENTS

PASSAGEWAY

To *Ringstrasse*

Ballhausplatz

LEOPOLD

50 Meters

50 Yards

came a commodity and began appearing on everyday items such as **candy tins** and **beer steins.**

The plaster-cast life-sized **statue** captures the one element of her persona everyone knew: her beauty. Sisi was nearly 5'8" (a head taller than her husband), had a 20-inch waist (she wore very tight corsets), and weighed only about 100 pounds. (Her waistline eventually grew...to 21 inches. That was at age 50, after giving birth to four children.) This statue, a copy of one of 30 statues that were

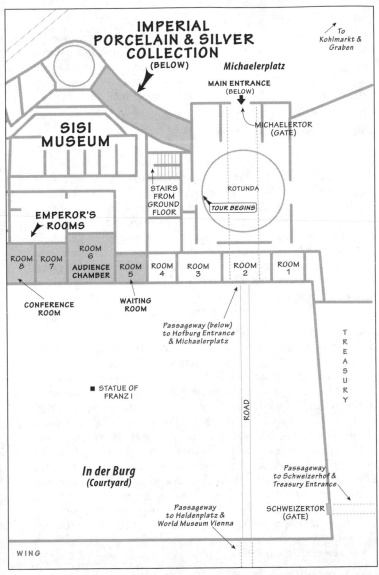

erected in her honor in European cities, shows her holding one of her trademark fans. It doesn't show off her magnificent hair, however, which reached down as far as her ankles in her youth.

Sisi-mania really got going in the 1950s with a series of **movies** based on her life (starring Romy Schneider), depicting the empress as beautiful and innocent, and either crying or singing at any given point in the films.

• *Round the corner into the next room.*

Sisi's Childhood

Sisi grew up in Bavaria, far from sophisticated city life. (See her **baby shoes** in a box and the picture of her **childhood palace.**) Franz Josef—who'd been engaged to her older sister—spied seemingly happy-go-lucky Sisi when she was 15 and fell in love. They married. At the wedding reception, Sisi burst into tears, the first sign that something was not right.

The Ballroom: Sisi at Court

In the glass display cases are replicas of her **gowns. Big portraits** of Sisi (considered the most realistic in existence) and Franz Josef show them dressed to the nines. **Jewels** (also replicas) reproduce some of the finery she wore as empress—but to her, they were her "chains." She hated official court duties and the constraints of public life, and hated being the center of attention. Sisi's mother-in-law dominated her child-rearing, her first-born died as an infant, and she complained that she couldn't sleep or eat. However, she did participate in one political cause—championing the rights of Habsburg-controlled Hungary (see her **bust** and **portrait as Queen of Hungary**).

• *Head into the next, darkened room.*

Sisi's Beauty

Sisi longed for the carefree days of her youth. She began to withdraw from public life, passing time riding horses (see **horse** statuettes and pictures) and tending obsessively to maintaining her physical beauty. In the glass case on the right wall, you'll see some of her **menus,** and a **bill from Demel.** Her **recipes** for beauty preparations included creams and lotions as well as wearing a raw-meat face mask while she slept. Sisi weighed herself obsessively on her gold-trimmed **scale** and tried all types of diets, including bouillon made with a **duck press.** (She never gave up pastries and ice cream, however.) After she turned 30, Sisi refused to appear in any portraits or photographs, preferring that only her more youthful depictions be preserved. Appreciate the **white gloves,** the **ivory fan,** and the **white nightgown** (displayed nearby)...because her life was about to turn even more dark.

• *Then enter the darkest room.*

Death of Sisi's Son

A mannequin wears a replica of Sisi's **black dress,** and nearby you'll see **black jewels** and accessories. In 1889, Sisi and Franz Josef's son, Prince Rudolf—whose life had veered into sex, drugs, and liberal politics—apparently killed his lover and himself in a suicide pact. Sisi was shattered and retreated further from public life.

• *Stroll through several more rooms.*

Escape

Sisi consoled herself with **poetry** (the museum has quotes on the walls) that expresses a longing to escape into an ideal world. As you continue through the exhibit, you'll see she also consoled herself with travel. There's a reconstruction of her **rail car**—a step above a *couchette*. A **map** shows her visits to Britain, Eastern Europe, and her favorite spot, Greece.

Final Room: Assassination

Sisi met her fate while traveling. While walking along a street in Geneva, Sisi was stalked and attacked by an Italian anarchist who despised royal oppressors and wanted notoriety for his cause. (He'd planned on assassinating a less-famous French prince that day—whom he'd been unable to track down—but quickly changed plans when word got out that Sisi was in town.) The murder weapon was a small, crude, knife-like file. It made only a small wound, but it proved fatal.

• *After the Sisi Museum, a one-way route takes you through a series of royal rooms. The first room—as if to make clear that there was more to the Habsburgs than Sisi—shows a family tree tracing the Habsburgs from 1273 (Rudolf I at upper left) to their messy WWI demise (Karl I, lower right). From here, enter the private apartments of the royal family (Franz Josef's first, then Sisi's). Much of the following commentary complements the information you'll hear in the audioguide.*

IMPERIAL APARTMENTS

These were the private apartments and public meeting rooms for the emperor and empress. Franz Josef I lived here from 1857 until his death in 1916. (He had hoped to move to new digs in the New Palace—which now houses the World Museum Vienna—but that was not finished until after his death.)

Franz Josef was the last legendary Habsburg. (For an abridged Habsburg family tree, see the Austria: Past & Present chapter.) In these rooms, he presided over defeats and liberal inroads as the world was changing and the monarchy becoming obsolete. Here he met with advisors and welcomed foreign dignitaries; hosted lavish, white-gloved balls and stuffy formal dinners; and raised his children. He slept (alone) on his austere bed while his beloved wife Sisi retreated to her own rooms. He suffered through the execution of his brother, the suicide of his son and heir, the murder of his wife, and the assassination of his nephew, Archduke Ferdinand, which sparked World War I and spelled the end of the Habsburg Monarchy.

The Emperor's Rooms
Waiting Room for the Audience Room

Every citizen had the right to meet privately with the emperor, and people traveled far to do so. While they waited nervously, they had these **three huge paintings** to stare at—propaganda art showing crowds of commoners enthusiastic about their Habsburg rulers.

The painting on the right shows an 1809 scene of Emperor Franz II (Franz Josef's grandfather) returning to Vienna, celebrating the news that Napoleon had begun his retreat.

In the central painting, Franz II makes his first public appearance to adoring crowds after recovering from a life-threatening illness (1826).

In the painting on the left, Franz II returns to Vienna (see the Karlskirche in the background) to celebrate the defeat of Napoleon. The 1815 Congress of Vienna that followed was the greatest assembly of diplomats in European history. Its goal: to establish peace by shoring up Europe's monarchies against the rise of democracy and nationalism. It worked for about a century, until a colossal war—World War I—wiped out the Habsburgs and other European royal families.

This room's **chandelier**—considered the best in the palace—is Baroque, made of Bohemian crystal. It lit things until 1891, when the palace installed electric lights.

Audience Chamber

This is the room where Franz Josef received commoners from around the empire. Imagine you've traveled for days to have your say before the emperor. You're wearing your new fancy suit—Franz Josef required that men coming before him wear a tailcoat, women a black gown with a train. You've rehearsed what you want to say. You hope your hair looks good.

Suddenly, you're face-to-face with the emp himself. (The **portrait** on the easel shows Franz Josef in 1915, when he was more than 80 years old.) Despite your efforts, you probably weren't in this room long. He'd stand at the **lectern** (far left) as the visiting commoners had their say (but for no more than two-and-a-half minutes). Standing kept things moving. You'd hear a brief response from him (quite likely the same he'd given all day), and then you'd back out of the room while bowing (also required). On the lectern is a partial **list** of 56 appointments he had on January 3, 1910 (three columns: family name, meeting topic, and *Anmerkung*—the emperor's "action log").

Conference Room

The emperor and his cabinet sat at this long Empire-style table to discuss policy. An ongoing topic was what to do with unruly

Emperor Franz Josef (1830-1916)

Franz Josef I—who ruled for 68 years (1848-1916)—was the embodiment of the Habsburg Empire as it finished its six-century-long ride. Born in 1830, Franz Josef had a stern upbringing that instilled in him a powerful sense of duty and—like so many men of power—a love of all things military.

His uncle, Ferdinand I, suffered from profound epilepsy, which prevented him from being an effective ruler. As the revolutions of 1848 rattled royal families throughout Europe, the Habsburgs forced Ferdinand to abdicate and put 18-year-old Franz Josef on the throne. Ironically, in one of his first acts as emperor, Franz Josef—whose wife would later become closely identified with Hungarian independence—put down the 1848 revolt in Hungary with bloody harshness. He spent the first part of his long reign understandably paranoid, as social discontent continued to simmer.

Franz Josef was very conservative. But worse, he wrongly believed that he was a talented military tactician, leading Austria into catastrophic battles against Italy (which was fighting for its unification and independence) in the 1860s. As his army endured severe, avoidable casualties, it became clear: Franz Josef was a disaster as a general.

Wearing his uniform to the end, Franz Josef never saw what a dinosaur his monarchy was becoming, and never thought it strange that the majority of his subjects didn't even speak German. Franz Josef had no interest in democracy and pointedly never set foot in Austria's parliament building. Like his contemporary Queen Victoria, he was a microcosm of his empire—old-fashioned and sacrosanct. His passion for low-grade paperwork earned him the nickname "Joe Bureaucrat." Mired in these petty details, he missed the big picture. In 1914, he helped start a Great War that ultimately ended the age of monarchs. The year 1918 marked the end of Europe's big royal families: Hohenzollerns (Prussia), Romanovs (Russia), and Habsburgs (Austria).

Hungary. After 1867, Franz Josef granted Hungary a measure of independence (thus creating the "Austro-Hungarian Empire"). Hungarian diplomats attended meetings here, watched over by **paintings** on the wall showing Austria's army suppressing the popular Hungarian uprising...subtle. (You can see his longtime personal servant standing by in the distant room.)

Emperor Franz Josef's Study

This room evokes how seriously the emperor took his responsibilities as the top official of a vast empire. Famously energetic, Franz Josef lived a spartan life dedicated to duty. The **desk** was originally positioned in such a way that Franz Josef could look up from his work and see the **portrait** of his lovely, long-haired, tiny-waisted Empress Elisabeth reflected in the mirror. Notice the **trompe l'oeil paintings** above each door, giving the believable illusion of marble relief. Notice also all the **family photos**—the perfect gift for the dad/uncle/hubby who has it all.

The walls between the rooms are wide enough to hide servants' corridors (the hidden door to his valet's room is in the back-left corner). The emperor lived with a personal staff of 14: "three valets, four lackeys, two doormen, two manservants, and three chambermaids."

Emperor's Bedroom

Franz Josef famously slept on this no-frills **iron bed** and used the **portable washstand** until 1880 (when the palace got running water). He typically rose before dawn and started his day in prayer, kneeling at the **prayer stool** against the far wall. After all, he was a "Divine Right" ruler. While he had a typical emperor's share of mistresses, his dresser was always well-stocked with **photos** of Sisi, even after their estrangement. An **etching** shows the empress (dressed in black after the 1889 suicide of her son)—a fine rider and avid hunter—sitting sidesaddle while jumping a hedge.

Large Salon

This red-walled room was for royal family gatherings and went unused after Sisi's death. The big, ornate **stove** in the corner was fed from behind (this remained a standard form of heating through the 19th century).

Small Salon

This room is dedicated to the memory of Franz Josef's brother (see the **portrait with the weird beard**), the Emperor Maximilian I of Mexico, who was overthrown and executed in 1867. It was also a smoking room. This was a necessity in the early 19th century, when smoking was newly fashionable for men, and was never done in the presence of women.

After the birth of their last child in 1868, Franz Josef and Sisi began to drift further apart. Left of the door is a small **button** the emperor had to buzz before entering his estranged wife's quarters. You, however, can go right in.

• *Climb three steps and enter Sisi's wing.*

Empress' Rooms
Empress' Bedroom and Drawing Room
This was Sisi's room, refurbished in the Neo-Rococo style in 1854. There's the red **carpet,** covered with oriental rugs. The room always had lots of fresh flowers. Sisi not only slept here, but also lived here—the bed was rolled in and out daily—until her death in 1898. The **desk** is where she sat and wrote her letters and sad poems.

Empress' Dressing/Exercise Room
Servants worked three hours a day on Sisi's famous hair, while she passed the time reading and learning Hungarian. She'd exercise on the **wooden structure** and on the **rings** suspended from the doorway to the left. Afterward, she'd get a massage on the red-covered **bed.** You can psychoanalyze Sisi from the **portraits and photos** she chose to hang on her walls. They're mostly her favorite dogs, her Bavarian family, and several portraits of the romantic and anti-monarchist poet Heinrich Heine. Her infatuation with the liberal Heine, whose family was Jewish, caused a stir in royal circles.

Empress' Lavatory and Bathroom
Detour into the behind-the-scenes palace. In the narrow passage-way, you'll walk by Sisi's hand-painted porcelain, dolphin-head **WC** (on the right). The big tank left of the tub warmed her towels. In the main bathroom, you'll see her huge copper tub (with the original wall coverings behind it), where servants washed her hair. Sisi was the first Habsburg to have running water in her bathroom (notice the hot and cold faucets). Beneath the carpet you're walking on is the first linoleum ever used in Vienna (c. 1880). As you leave, notice a bit of the faded original wallpaper behind protective glass.

Servants' Quarters (Bergl Rooms)
Next, enter the servants' quarters, with hand-painted **tropical scenes.** Take time to enjoy the playful details. Painted by Johann Bergl in the 1770s, these date from the reign of Maria Theresa, a century before the decor you've seen up to this point. As you leave these rooms and reenter the imperial world, look back (through an open door) to the room on the left.

Empress' Large Salon
The room is **painted** with Mediterranean escapes, the 19th-century equivalent of travel posters. Franz Josef and Sisi would—on their good days—share breakfast in this room.

Small Salon
The portrait is of **Crown Prince Rudolf,** Franz Josef's and Sisi's only son. On the morning of January 30, 1889, the 30-year-old Rudolf and a beautiful baroness were found shot dead in his hunting lodge in Mayerling. An investigation never came up with a com-

plete explanation, but Rudolf had obviously been cheating on his wife, and the affair ended in an apparent murder-suicide. The scandal shocked the empire and tainted the Habsburgs; Sisi retreated further into her fantasy world, and Franz Josef carried on stoically with a broken heart. The mysterious "Mayerling Affair" has been dramatized in numerous movies, plays, an opera, and even a ballet.

• *Leaving Sisi's wing, turn the corner into the white-and-gold rooms occupied by the czar of Russia during the 1814-1815 Congress of Vienna. Sisi and Franz Josef used the rooms for formal occasions and public functions.*

Alexander Apartments
Red Salon
The Gobelin wall hangings (one of the four is an original) were a 1776 gift from Marie-Antoinette and Louis XVI in Paris to their Viennese counterparts.

Dining Room
It's dinnertime, and Franz Josef has called his extended family together. The settings are modest...just silver. Gold was saved for formal state dinners. Next to each name card was a menu listing the chef responsible for each dish. (Talk about pressure.) While the Hofburg had tableware for 4,000, feeding 3,000 was a typical day. The cellar was stocked with 60,000 bottles of wine. The kitchen was huge—50 birds could be roasted at once on the hand-turned spits.

The emperor sat in the center of the long table. "Ladies and gentlemen" alternated in the seating. The green glasses were specifically for Rhenish wine (dry whites from the Rhine valley). Franz Josef enforced strict protocol at mealtime: No one could speak without being spoken to by the emperor, and no one could eat after he was done. While the rest of Europe was growing democracy and expanding personal freedoms, the Habsburgs preserved their ossified worldview to the bitter end.

In 1918, World War I ended, Austria was created as a modern nation-state, the Habsburgs were tossed out...and Hofburg Palace was destined to become the museum you've just toured.

• *Drop off your audioguide, zip through the shop, go down the stairs, and you're back on the street. Two quick lefts take you back to the palace square (In der Burg), where the Treasury awaits just past the black, red, and gold gate on the far side (see the next chapter).*

HOFBURG TREASURY TOUR

The Hofburg Palace's Imperial Treasury contains the best jewels on the Continent. Slip through the vault doors and reflect on the glitter of 21 rooms filled with secular and religious ornaments: scepters, swords, crowns, orbs, weighty robes, double-headed eagles, gowns, gem-studded bangles, and a unicorn horn.

There are plenty of beautiful objects here—I've highlighted those that have the most history behind them. But you could spend hours in here marveling at the riches of the bygone empire.

Use this chapter to get the lay of the land, but renting the excellent audioguide gives you a deeper explanation of these historic jewels.

Orientation

Cost: €12, €20 combo-ticket with Kunsthistorisches Museum.

Hours: Wed-Mon 9:00-17:30, closed Tue.

Information: Tel. 01/525-240, www.kaiserliche-schatzkammer.at.

Getting There: The Treasury is tucked away in the Hofburg Palace complex. From the Hofburg's central courtyard (In der Burg), pass through the black, red, and gold gate (Schweizertor), following *Schatzkammer* signs, which lead into the Schweizerhof courtyard; the Treasury entrance is in the far-right corner (see the "Vienna's Hofburg Palace" map in the Sights in Vienna chapter).

Tours: The €5 audioguide (€7/2 people) describes 100 stops—well worth it to get the most out of this dazzling collection. Guided tours (€3) leave at 16:00 daily.

Starring: The Imperial Crown and other accessories of the Holy Roman Emperors, plus many other crowns, jewels, robes, and priceless knickknacks.

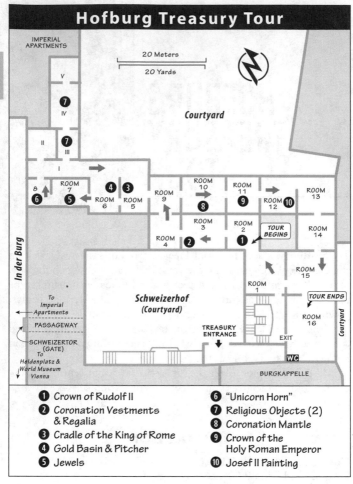

Hofburg Treasury Tour

1. Crown of Rudolf II
2. Coronation Vestments & Regalia
3. Cradle of the King of Rome
4. Gold Basin & Pitcher
5. Jewels
6. "Unicorn Horn"
7. Religious Objects (2)
8. Coronation Mantle
9. Crown of the Holy Roman Emperor
10. Josef II Painting

The Tour Begins

The Habsburgs saw themselves as the successors to the ancient Roman emperors, and they wanted crowns and royal regalia to match the pomp of the ancients. They used these precious objects for coronation ceremonies, official ribbon-cutting events, and their own personal pleasure. You'll see the prestigious crowns and accoutrements of the rulers of the Holy Roman Empire (a medieval alliance of Germanic kingdoms so named because it wanted to be considered the continuation of the Roman Empire). Other crowns belonged to Austrian dukes and kings, and some robes and paraphernalia were used by Austria's religious elite. And many costly things were created simply for the enjoyment of the wealthy Habsburgs.

• *Skip through Room 1 to where we'll begin, in Room 2. Note throughout the treasury how paintings hung in each room relate to the jewels on display.*

FROM THE FIRST HABSBURG TO NAPOLEON
Room 2
The personal ❶ **crown of Rudolf II** (1602) occupies the center of the room along with its accompanying scepter and orb; a bust of Rudolf II (1552-1612) sits nearby. The

crown's design symbolically merges a bishop's miter ("Holy"), the arch across the top of a Roman emperor's helmet ("Roman"), and the typical medieval king's crown ("Emperor"). Accompanying the crown are the matching **scepter** (made from the ivory tusk of a narwhal) and **orb** (holding four diamonds to symbolize the four corners of the world, which the emperor ruled). Orbs have been royal symbols of the world since ancient Roman times. They seem to indicate that, even in pre-Columbus days, Europe's intelligentsia assumed the world was round.

This crown was Rudolf's personal one. He wore a different crown (which we'll see later) in his official role as Holy Roman Emperor. In many dynasties, a personal crown like this was dismantled by the next ruler to custom-make his own. But Rudolf's crown was so well-crafted that it was passed down through the generations,

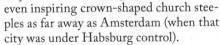

even inspiring crown-shaped church steeples as far away as Amsterdam (when that city was under Habsburg control).

Two centuries later (1806), this crown and scepter became the official regalia of Austria's rulers, as seen in the large **portrait of Franz I** (the open-legged guy behind you). Napoleon Bonaparte had just conquered Austria and dissolved the Holy Roman Empire. Franz (r. 1792-1835) was allowed to remain in power, but he had to downgrade his title from "Franz II, Holy Roman Emperor" to "Franz I, Emperor of Austria."

Rooms 3 and 4

These rooms contain some of the ❷ **corona-tion vestments and regalia** needed for the new Austrian (not Holy Roman) Emperor. There was a different one for each of the emperor's subsidiary titles, for example, King of Hungary or King of Lombardy. So many crowns and kingdoms in the Habsburgs' vast empire! Those with the white ermine collars are modeled after Napoleon's coronation robes. Sketches on the wall were done to get the royal OK. Notice in the group of four robes how Franz marked an X on his choice.

• *For more on how Napoleon had an impact on Habsburg Austria, pass through Room 9 and into...*

Room 5

Ponder the ❸ **Cradle of the King of Rome,** once occupied by Napoleon's son, who was born in 1811 and made King of Rome. The

little eagle at the foot is symbolically not yet able to fly, but glory-bound. Glory is symbolized by the star, with dad's big *N* raised high. While it's fun to think of Napoleon's baby snoozing in here, this was actually a ceremonial "throne bed" that was rarely used.

Napoleon Bonaparte (1769-1821) was a French commoner who rose to power as a charismatic general in the Revolution. While pledging allegiance to democracy, he in fact crowned himself Emperor of France and hobnobbed with Europe's royalty. When his wife Josephine could not bear him a male heir, Napoleon divorced her and married into the Habsburg family.

Portraits show Napoleon and his new bride, Marie Louise, Franz I/II's daughter (and Marie-Antoinette's great-niece). Napoleon gave her a **jewel chest** decorated with the bees of industriousness, his personal emblem. With the birth of the baby King of Rome, Napoleon and Marie Louise were poised to start a new dynasty of European rulers...but then Napoleon met his Waterloo, and the Habsburgs remained in power.

• *Exit to the left of the cradle.*

MISCELLANEOUS WONDERS
Room 6

For Divine Right kings, even child-rearing was a sacred ritual that needed elaborate regalia for public ceremonies. The 23-pound ❹ **gold basin and pitcher** were used to baptize noble children, who were dressed in the **baptismal dresses** displayed nearby.

Room 7

These ❺ **jewels** are the true "treasures," a cabinet of wonders used by Habsburgs to impress their relatives (or to hock when funds got low). The irregularly shaped, 2,680-karat **emerald** is rough-cut, as the cutter wanted to do only the minimum to avoid making a mistake and shattering the giant gem. The helmet-like, jewel-studded **crown** (left wall) was a gift from Muslim Turks supporting a Hungarian king who, as a Protestant, was a thorn in the side of the Catholic Habsburgs (who eventually toppled him).

Room 8

The eight-foot-tall, 500-year-old ❻ **"unicorn horn"** (actually a narwhal tusk), was considered to have magical healing powers bestowed from on high. This one was owned by the Holy Roman Emperor—clearly a divine monarch. The huge **agate bowl,** cut from a single piece, may have been made in ancient Roman times and eventually found its way into the collection of their successors, the Habsburgs. It was thought to be the Holy Grail when it was stolen from Constantinople.

Religious Rooms

After Room 8, you enter several rooms of ❼ **religious objects**—crucifixes, chalices, mini-altarpieces, reliquaries, and bishops' vestments. Like the medieval kings who preceded them, Habsburg rulers mixed the institutions of church and state, so these precious religious accoutrements were also part of their display of secular power.

• *Browse these rooms, then backtrack, passing by the Cradle of the King of Rome, and eventually reaching...*

REGALIA OF THE HOLY ROMAN EMPIRE
Room 10

The next few rooms contain some of the oldest and most venerated objects in the Treasury—the robes, crowns, and sacred objects of the Holy Roman Emperor.

The big red-silk and gold-thread ❽ **coronation mantle**, nearly 900 years old, was worn by Holy Roman Emperors when they received their crown. Thousands of tiny white pearls were drilled and threaded for this one garment. Notice the oriental

imagery: a palm tree in the center, flanked by lions subduing camels. The hem is written in Arabic (wishing its wearer "great wealth, gifts, and pleasure"). This robe, brought back from the East by Crusaders, gave the Germanic emperors an exotic look that recalled

great biblical kings such as Solomon. Many Holy Roman Emperors were crowned by the pope himself. That fact, plus this Eastern-looking mantle, helped put the "Holy" in Holy Roman Emperor.

Room 11

The collection's highlight is the 10th-century ❾ **crown of the Holy Roman Emperor.** It was probably made for Otto I (c. 960), the first king to call himself Holy Roman Emperor.

The Imperial Crown swirls with symbolism "proving" that the emperor was both holy and Roman: The cross on top says

the HRE ruled as Christ's representative on earth, and the jeweled arch over the top is reminiscent of the parade helmet of ancient Romans. The jewels themselves allude to the wearer's kinghood in the here and now. Imagine the impression this priceless, glittering crown must have made on the emperor's medieval subjects.

King Solomon's portrait on the crown (to the right of the cross) is Old Testament

Charlemagne (Karl der Grosse) and the Holy Roman Empire

The title "Holy Roman Emperor" conveyed three important concepts: **Holy,** meaning the emperor ruled by divine authority (not as a pagan Roman); **Roman,** indicating he was a successor to the ancient Roman Empire; and **Emperor,** meaning he ruled over many different nationalities.

Charlemagne (747-814) briefly united much of Western Europe—that is, the former Roman Empire. On Christmas Eve in the year 800, he was crowned "Roman Emperor" by the pope in St. Peter's Basilica in Rome. After Charlemagne's death, the empire split apart. His successors (who ruled only a portion of Charlemagne's empire) still wanted to envision themselves as inheritors of Charlemagne's greatness. They took to calling themselves Roman Emperors, adding the "Holy" part in the 11th century to emphasize that they ruled by divine authority.

The Holy Roman Emperorship was an elected, not necessarily hereditary, office. Traditionally, the rulers of four important provinces would gather with three powerful archbishops to pick the new ruler; these seven "kingmakers" each held the prestigious title of Elector. The practice lasted through medieval and Renaissance times to the Napoleonic Wars, with most of the emperors hailing from the Habsburg family.

At the empire's peak around 1520, it truly was great. Emperor Charles V ruled Spain in addition to the HRE, so his realm stretched from Vienna to Spain, from Holland to Sicily, and from Bohemia to Bolivia in the New World. But throughout much of its existence, the HRE consisted of little more than petty dukes, ruling a loose coalition of independent nobles. It was Voltaire who quipped that the HRE was "neither holy, nor Roman, nor an empire."

Napoleon ended the title in 1806. The last Habsburg emperors (including Franz Josef) were merely emperors of Austria.

proof that kings can be wise and good. King David (next panel) is similar proof that they can be just. The crown's eight sides represent the celestial city of Jerusalem's eight gates. The jewels on the front panel symbolize the 12 apostles.

On the forehead of the crown, notice that beneath the cross there's a pale-blue, heart-shaped sapphire. Look a little small for the prime spot? That's because this is a replacement for a long-lost opal said to have had almost mythical, magical powers.

Nearby is the 11th-century **Imperial Cross** that preceded the emperor in ceremonies. Encrusted with jewels, it had a hollow compartment (its core is wood) that carried substantial chunks thought to be from *the* cross on which Jesus was crucified and *the* Holy Lance used to pierce his side (both pieces are displayed in the same glass case). Holy Roman Emperors actually carried the lance into battle in the 10th century. Look behind the cross to see how it was a box that could be clipped open and shut, used for holding holy relics. You can see bits of the "true cross" anywhere, but this is a prime piece—with the actual nail hole.

Another case has additional objects used in the coronation ceremony: The **orb** (orbs were modeled on late-Roman ceremonial objects, then topped with the cross) and **scepter** (the one with the oak leaves), along with the sword, were carried ahead of the emperor in the procession. In earlier times, these objects were thought to have belonged to Charlemagne himself, the greatest ruler of medieval Europe, but in fact they're mostly from 300 to 400 years later (c. 1200).

Another glass case contains more objects said to belong to Charlemagne. Some of these may be authentic, since they're closer to his era. You'll see the jeweled, purse-like **reliquary of St. Stephen** and the **saber of Charlemagne**. The gold-covered **Book of the Gospels** was the Bible that emperors placed their hands on to swear the oath of office. On the wall nearby, the **tall painting** depicts Charlemagne modeling the Imperial Crown—although the crown wasn't made until a hundred years after he died.

Room 12

Now picture all this regalia used together. The ❿ **Josef II painting** shows the coronation of Maria Theresa's son as Holy

Roman Emperor in 1764. Set in a church in Frankfurt (filled with the bigwigs—literally—of the day), Josef is wearing the same crown and royal garb that you've just seen.

Emperors followed the same coronation ritual that originated in the 10th century. The new emperor would don the mantle. The entourage paraded into a church for Mass, led by the religious authorities carrying the Imperial Cross. The emperor placed his hand on the Book of the Gospels and swore his oath. Then he knelt before the three archbishop Electors, who placed the Imperial Crown on his head (sometimes he even traveled to Rome to be crowned by the pope himself). The new emperor rose, accepted the orb and scepter, and—dut dutta dah!—you had a new ruler.

• *The tour is over. Pass through Rooms 13–16 to reach the exit, browsing relics, portraits, and objects along the way.*

KUNSTHISTORISCHES MUSEUM TOUR

The Kunsthistorwhateveritis Museum—let's just say "Kunst" (koonst)—houses the family collection of Austria's luxury-loving Habsburg rulers. Their joie de vivre is reflected in this collection—some of the most beautiful, sexy, and fun art from two centuries (c. 1450-1650). At their peak of power in the 1500s, the Habsburgs ruled Austria, Germany, northern Italy, the Netherlands, and Spain—and you'll see a wide variety of art from all these places and beyond.

The building itself is worth notice—a lavish textbook example of Historicism. Despite its palatial feel, it was originally designed for the same purpose it serves today: to showcase its treasures in an inviting space while impressing visitors with the grandeur of the empire.

This chapter gives just a taste of the Kunst. Hit these highlights—mainly large canvases in the large halls—then explore the smaller side rooms for more delights.

Orientation

Cost: €15, free for those under age 19, €20 combo-ticket includes the Hofburg Treasury.

Hours: Daily 10:00-18:00, Thu until 21:00, closed Mon Sept-May.

Information: Tel. 01/525-240, www.khm.at.

Getting There: It's on the Ringstrasse at Maria-Theresien-Platz, U: Volkstheater/Museumsplatz (exit toward *Burgring*).

Tours: The excellent €5 audioguide, covering nearly 600 items, is worthwhile if you want an in-depth tour beyond the items covered in this chapter.

Services: There's a free cloakroom. The restaurant is on the first floor.

Starring: The world's best collection of Bruegel, plus Titian, Caravaggio, a Vermeer gem, and Rembrandt self-portraits.

OVERVIEW

Of the museum's many exhibits, we'll tour only the Painting Gallery (Gemäldegalerie) on the first floor. Italian-Spanish-French art is on one half of the floor, and Northern European art on the other. On our tour, we'll get a sampling of each. Note that the museum labels the

largest rooms with Roman numerals (Saal I, II, III) and the smaller rooms around the perimeter with Arabic (Rooms 1, 2, 3). The museum seems to constantly move paintings from room to room, so be flexible (and pick up the current floor-plan brochure in the lobby).

The Tour Begins

• *Climb the main staircase, featuring Antonio Canova's statue of Theseus clubbing a centaur. At the statue, turn 180 degrees and look up, across the atrium, at the small paintings decorating three arches. These exquisite works were done in the 1890s by a young Gustav Klimt when the soon-to-be-famous artist was just a decorator for hire. Bear right when you reach Theseus. At the top of the staircase (at the tempting café), make a U-turn to the left. Enter Saal I and walk right into the High Renaissance.*

ITALIAN RENAISSANCE

About the year 1500, Italy was in the midst of a 100-year renaissance, or "rebirth," of interest in the art and learning of ancient Greece and Rome. In painting, that meant that ordinary humans and Greek gods joined saints and angels as popular subjects.

Titian, *Danae* and *Ecce Homo*

In the long career of Titian the Venetian (it rhymes), he painted portraits, Christian Madonnas, and sexy Venuses with equal ease.

Titian captured Danae—a luscious nude reclining in bed—as she's about to be seduced. Zeus, the king of the gods, descends as a shower of gold to consort with her—you can almost see the human form of Zeus within the cloud. Danae is enraptured, opening her legs to receive him, while her servant tries to catch the heavenly spurt with a golden dish. Danae's rich, luminous flesh is set off by the dark servant at right and the threatening sky above. The white sheets beneath her make her glow even more. This is not just a

Kunsthistorisches Museum—First Floor

classic nude—it's a Renaissance Miss August. How could ultra-conservative Catholic emperors have tolerated such a downright pagan and erotic painting? Apparently, without a problem.

In the large canvas *Ecce Homo*, a crowd mills about, when suddenly there's a commotion. They nudge each other and start to point. Follow their gaze diagonally up the stairs to a battered figure entering way up in the corner. "Ecce Homo!" says Pilate. "Behold the man." And he presents Jesus to the mob. For us, as for the unsympathetic crowd,

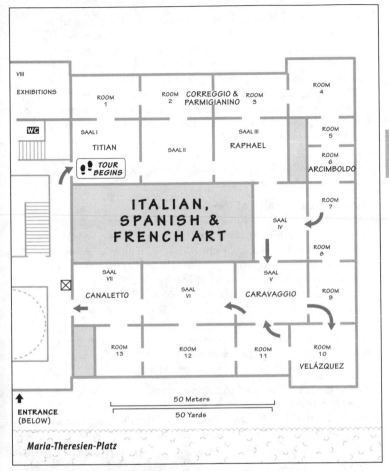

the humiliated Son of God is not the center of the scene, but almost an afterthought.

• *Continue to Saal III.*

Raphael, *Madonna of the Meadow*

Young Raphael epitomized the spirit of the High Renaissance, combining symmetry, grace, beauty, and emotion. This Madonna is a mountain of motherly love—Mary's head is the summit and her flowing robe is the base—enfolding Baby Jesus and John the Baptist. The geometric perfection,

serene landscape, and Mary's adoring face make this a masterpiece of sheer grace—but then you get smacked by an ironic fist: The cross the little tykes play with foreshadows their gruesome deaths.

• *Before moving on, be aware that the Kunst displays excellent small canvases in the smaller side rooms. For example, in Rooms 1–3, you may find* **Correggio's** Jupiter and Io, *showing Zeus seducing another female, this time disguised as a cloud.* **Parmigianino's** Self-Portrait in a Convex Mirror *depicts the artist gazing into a convex mirror and perfectly reproducing the curved reflection on a convex piece of wood. Amazing.*

Farther along, through the small rooms along the far end of this wing (and likely in Room 6), find...

Arcimboldo, Portraits of the Seasons

These four cleverly deceptive portraits by the Habsburg court painter depict the four seasons (and elements) as people. For example, take *Summer*—a.k.a. "Fruit Face." With a pickle nose, pear chin, and corn-husk ears, this guy literally is what he eats. Its grotesque weirdness makes it typical of Mannerist art.

• *Saal IV is hung with paintings from floor to ceiling to show how art was displayed in Baroque days by society's elites—just gathering lots of expensive canvases and showing off. Notice how the ceiling is stuccoed with busts and themes that relate to the art hung in this room—a reminder that the building was made specifically for its art, and the art came first. Next, move along to find Caravaggio in Saal V.*

Caravaggio, *Madonna of the Rosary* and *David with the Head of Goliath*

Caravaggio shocked the art world with brutally honest reality. Compared with Raphael's super-sweet *Madonna of the Meadow*, Caravaggio's *Madonna of the Rosary* (the biggest canvas in the room) looks perfectly ordinary, and the saints kneeling around her have dirty feet.

In *David with the Head of Goliath*, Caravaggio turns a third-degree-interrogation light on a familiar Bible story. David shoves the dripping head of the slain giant right in our noses. The painting, bled of color, is virtually a black-and-white crime-scene photo—slightly overexposed. Out of the deep darkness shine only a few crucial details. This David is not a heroic Renaissance man like Michelangelo's famous statue, but a homeless teen that Caravaggio paid to portray

God's servant. And the severed head of Goliath is none other than Caravaggio himself, an in-your-face self-portrait.

• *Move into Room 10, in the corner of the museum.*

Velázquez, Habsburg Family Portraits

When the Habsburgs ruled both Austria and Spain, cousins kept in touch through portraits of themselves and their kids. Diego Velázquez was the greatest of Spain's "photojournalist" painters—

heavily influenced by Caravaggio's realism, capturing his subjects without passing judgment, flattering, or glorifying them.

For example, watch little Margarita Habsburg grow up in three different portraits on the same wall, from age two to age nine. Margarita was destined from birth to marry her Austrian cousin, the future Emperor Leopold I. Pictures like these, sent from Spain every few years, let her pen pal/fiancé get to know her.

Also see a portrait of Margarita's little brother, *Philip Prosper,* wearing a dress. Sadly, Philip was a

sickly boy who would only live two years longer. The amulets he's wearing were intended to fend off illness. His hand rests limply on the back of the chair—above an adorable puppy who seems to be asking, "But who will play with me?"

The kids' oh-so-serious faces, regal poses, and royal trappings are contradicted by their natural precociousness. No wonder Velázquez was so popular.

Also notice that all of these kids are quite, ahem, homely. To understand why, find the portrait of their dad, Philip IV, which shows the defects of royal inbreeding: weepy eyes, no eyebrows, thin hair, an underbite, and a pointed chin (sorry, that pointy moustache doesn't hide anything).

• *Return to the main Saals and continue on, past glimpses of Baroque art, featuring large, colorful canvases showcasing over-the-top emotions and pudgy, winged babies (the surefire mark of Baroque art). In Saal VII, find paintings of the Habsburg summer palace, Schloss Schönbrunn,* *by **Canaletto**, one of which also shows the Viennese skyline in the distance.*

Exit Saal VII. Cross under the dome and through the café, then walk into the part of the museum dedicated to Northern European art, through Saal XV and into XIV and XIII for the big-canvas, bright-colored world of Baroque.

NORTHERN ART

The "Northern Renaissance," brought on by the economic boom of Dutch and Flemish trading, was more secular and Protestant than Catholic-funded Italian art. We'll see fewer Madonnas, saints, and Greek gods and more peasants, landscapes, and food. Paintings are smaller and darker, full of down-to-earth objects. Northern artists sweated the details, encouraging the patient viewer to appreciate the beauty in everyday things.

Peter Paul Rubens

Rubens' work runs the gamut, from realistic portraits to lounging nudes, Greek myths to altarpieces, from pious devotion to violent sex.

But, can we be sure it's Baroque? Ah yes, I'm sure you'll find a pudgy, winged baby somewhere, hovering in the heavens. Take the large *Ildefonso Altarpiece* (likely in Saal XIII, a rare canvas done entirely in Rubens' hand), where a glorious Mary appears—with her entourage of darling PWBs—to reward the grateful Spanish St. Ildefonso with a chasuble (priest's smock).

In Rubens' *Self-Portrait*, admire the darling of Catholic-dominated Flanders (northern Belgium) in his prime: famous, wealthy, well-traveled, the friend of kings and princes, an artist, diplomat, man about town, and—obviously—confident.

The 53-year-old Rubens married Hélène Fourment, a dimpled girl of 16 (find her portrait nearby). She pulls the fur around her ample flesh, simultaneously covering herself and exalting her charms. Rubens called this painting *The Little Fur*—and used the same name for his young bride. Hmm.

Hélène's sweet cellulite was surely an inspiration to Rubens—many of his female figures have Hélène's gentle face and dimpled proportions.

How could Rubens paint all these enormous canvases in one lifetime? He had help. He ran a busy studio with about 60 artists. Rubens generally painted a small model "cartoon" (you can see several here) from which his team of artists would paint the big canvas. He'd then amp up their work with what he called "the fury of the brush" and it was shipped out...another Rubens masterpiece. For example, the giant canvas *The Miracles of St. Ignatius of Loyola* was painted partly by assistants, guided by Rubens' sketches.

• *Pass through several rooms until you reach Room 18, with a small jewel of a canvas by Vermeer.*

Jan Vermeer

In his small canvases, the Dutch painter Jan Vermeer quiets the world down to where we can hear our own heartbeat, letting us ap-

preciate the beauty in common things.

The curtain opens and we see *The Art of Painting,* a behind-the-scenes look at Vermeer at work. He's painting a model dressed in blue, starting with her laurel-leaf headdress. The studio is its own little dollhouse world framed by a chair in the foreground and the wall in back. Then Vermeer fills this space with the few gems he wants us to focus on—the chandelier, the map, the painter's costume. Everything is lit by a crystal-clear light, letting us see these everyday items with fresh eyes.

The painting is also called *The Allegory of Painting.* The model has the laurel leaves, trumpet, and book that symbolize the muse

of history and fame. The artist—his back to the public—earnestly tries to capture fleeting fame with a small sheet of canvas.

• *In the corner room (Room 17), find dark, brooding works by...*

Rembrandt van Rijn

Rembrandt became wealthy by painting portraits of Holland's upwardly mobile businessmen, but his greatest subject was himself. In the *Large Self-Portrait* we see the hands-on-hips, defiant, open-stance determination of a man who will do what he wants, and if people don't like it, tough.

In typical Rembrandt style, most of the canvas is a dark, smudgy brown, with only the side of his face glowing from the darkness. (Remember Caravaggio? Rembrandt did.) Unfortunately, the year this was painted, Rembrandt's fortunes changed.

Looking at the *Small Self-Portrait* from 1657, consider Rembrandt's last years. His wife died, his children died young, and commissions for paintings dried up as his style veered from the popular style of the day. He had to auction off paintings to pay his debts, and he died a poor man. Rembrandt's numerous self-portraits painted from youth until old age show a man always changing—from wide-eyed youth to successful portraitist to this disillusioned, but still defiant, old man.

• *Nearby, Saal X contains the largest collection of Bruegels in captivity. Linger. If you like it, linger longer.*

Pieter Bruegel the Elder

The undisputed master of the slice-of-life village scene was Pieter Bruegel the Elder (c. 1525-1569)—think of him as the Norman Rockwell of the 16th century. His name (pronounced "BROY-gull") is sometimes spelled *Brueghel*. Don't confuse Pieter Bruegel the Elder with his sons, Pieter Brueghel the Younger and Jan Brueghel, who added luster and an "h" to the family name (and whose works are also displayed in the Kunst). Despite his many rural paintings, Bruegel was actually a cultivated urbanite who liked to wear peasants' clothing to observe country folk at play (a trans-fest-ite?). He celebrated their simple life, but he also skewered their weaknesses—not to single them out as hicks, but as universal examples of human folly. About a quarter of all known Bruegel paintings are gathered in this exciting room.

The Peasant Wedding, Bruegel's most famous work, is less about the wedding than the food. It's a farmers' feeding frenzy, as the barnful of wedding guests scramble to get their share of free eats. Two men bring in the next course, a tray of fresh porridge. The bagpiper pauses to check it out. A guy grabs bowls and passes them down the table, taking our attention with them. Everyone's going at it, including a kid in an oversized red cap who  licks the bowl with his fingers. In the middle of it all, look who's been completely forgotten—the demure bride sitting in front of the blue-green cloth. According to Flemish tradition, the bride was not allowed to speak or eat at the party, and the groom was not in attendance at all. (One thing: The guy carrying the front end of the food tray—is he stepping forward with his right leg, or with his left, or with...all three?)

Speaking of two left feet, Bruegel's *Peasant Dance* shows a celebration at the consecration of a village church. Peasants happily clog to the tune of a lone bagpiper, who wails away while his pit crew keeps him lubed with wine. Notice the overexuberant guy in the green hat on the left, who accidentally smacks his buddy in the face. As with his other peasant paintings, Bruegel captures the warts-and-all scene accurately—it's neither romanticized nor patronizing.

Find several Bruegel landscape paintings. These are part of an original series of six "calendar" paintings, depicting the seasons of the year. We see these scenes from above, emphasizing the landscape as much as the people. *Gloomy Day* opens the cycle, as winter turns to spring...slowly. The snow has melted, flooding the distant river, the trees are still leafless, and the villagers stir, cutting wood

and mending fences. We skip ahead to autumn in *The Return of the Herd*—still sunny, but winter's storms are fast approaching. Finally, in *Hunters in Snow,* it's the dead of winter, and three dog-tired hunters with their tired dogs trudge along with only a single fox to show for their efforts. As they crest the hill, the grove of bare trees opens up to a breathtaking view—they're almost home, where they can join their mates playing hockey. Birds soar like the hunters' rising spirits—emerging from winter's work and looking ahead to a new year.

The Tower of Babel, modeled after Rome's Colosseum, stretches into the clouds, towering over the village. Impressive as it looks, on closer inspection the tower is crooked—destined eventually to tumble onto the village. Even so, the king (in the foreground) demands further work.

• *For an unforgettable finale, return to the entry, taking the stairs back to the ground level. While the collection of Greek, Roman, and Egyptian antiquities is world class (stairs to the left), it's not uniquely Viennese so*

KUNSTHISTORISCHES MUSEUM

I won't cover it. What is Viennese is the Habsburg collection of treasures. Take the stairs to the right to enter the Kunstkammer.

REST OF THE KUNST

The *Kunstkammer* shows off the personal collection of *objets d'art* of the House of Habsburg. Amassed by 17 emperors over the cen-

turies, the *Kunstkammer* ("art cabinet") is a dazzling display of 2,000 ancient treasures, medieval curios, and jeweled wonders collected from the year 800 to 1891. The U-shaped gallery is laid out chronologically, beautifully lit, and thoughtfully described in English.

The highlight is at the end of the first long hall (on the left in Room XXIX): Benvenuto Cellini's famous golden salt cellar (pictured). It was pounded out of a sheet of gold in 1543 by the renowned Florentine goldsmith. Featuring gods of the sea and the earth with symbols of winds and seasons all around, it takes salting and peppering your food to Habsburg heights.

SCHÖNBRUNN PALACE TOUR

Among Europe's palaces, only Schönbrunn rivals Versailles. This former summer residence of the Habsburgs is big, with more than 300 rooms in the main building alone. But don't worry—only 40 rooms are shown to the public. Of the plethora of sights at the vast complex, the highlight is a tour of the palace's ▲▲▲ Imperial Apartments—the chandeliered rooms where the Habsburg nobles lived. You can also stroll the ▲▲ gardens, tour the Imperial Carriage Museum, and visit a handful of lesser sights nearby.

Orientation

Cost: Visits to the palace are by timed-entry tours (book in advance, see next page). The Imperial Apartments offer two tour options: The best is the 40-room **Grand Tour** (€20, 50 minutes, includes audioguide, covered by Sisi Ticket), which includes both the rooms of Franz Josef and Sisi, as well as the (more impressive) Rococo rooms of Maria Theresa. The **Imperial Tour** (€16, 35 minutes, includes audioguide) covers only the less-interesting first 22 rooms. For €3 more you can do the Grand Tour with a real guide, but since these live tours are offered only a few times a day, I wouldn't bother.

If venturing beyond the apartments, consider the **Classic Pass** combo-ticket (€24, available April-Oct only), which includes the Grand Tour, as well as the Gloriette viewing terrace, maze, orangery, and privy garden.

Hours: Imperial Apartments open daily 8:00-17:30, July-Aug until 18:30, Nov-March until 17:00; gardens generally open 6:30-20:00 but varies with season. The palace is busiest from 9:00 to 12:00, and crowds start to subside after 14:00.

Information: Tel. 01/8111-3239, www.schoenbrunn.at.

Advance Tickets Recommended: In summer and on good-weather weekends, definitely make a reservation. Otherwise you'll likely have to stand in line at the ticket desk, and then you'll probably have to wait again for your assigned entry time—which could be hours later. To get right in, book your entry time in advance online. Those with a Sisi Ticket can enter without a reserved entry time (buy your Sisi Ticket online or at the Imperial Furniture Museum—see page 31 for details).

If you don't have a reservation, come early or late in the day. You can save some time in line by using one of the ticket machines. If you have time to kill before your entry time, spend it exploring the gardens or Imperial Carriage Museum.

Getting There: Schönbrunn is an easy 10-minute subway ride from downtown Vienna. Take U-4 (which conveniently leaves from Karlsplatz) to Schönbrunn (direction: Hütteldorf) and follow signs for *Schloss Schönbrunn*. Exit bearing right, then cross the busy road and continue to the right, to the far, far end of the long yellow building. There you'll find the visitors center, where tickets are sold.

Length of This Tour: Allow at least three hours (including transit time) for your excursion to Schönbrunn Palace. The palace itself is sprawling and can be mobbed. After viewing the Imperial Apartments, wander the gardens (most of which are free). With more time and energy, pick and choose among the other sightseeing options and buy tickets as you go.

Eating at Schönbrunn: Eating options at the palace range from touristy sit-down restaurants to garden cafés. If looking for a tranquil escape, head for the **$$ Landtmann's Jausen Station** café located inside the gardens, a five-minute walk to the left of the palace (closed Oct-Feb).

Starring: Ornately decorated rooms graced by Franz Josef, Sisi, Maria Theresa, Napoleon, and Mozart—plus grand gardens.

The Tour Begins

In the 1500s, the Habsburgs built a small hunting lodge near a beautiful spring *(schön-brunn)*, and for the next three centuries, they made it their summer getaway from stuffy Vienna. The palace's exterior (late-1600s) is Baroque, but the interior was finished under Maria Theresa (mid-1700s) in let-them-eat-cake Rococo. As with the similar apartments at the Hofburg (the Habsburgs' winter home), these apartments give you a sense of the quirky, larger-than-life personalities who lived here. It's the place where matronly Maria Theresa raised her brood of 16 kids...where six-year-old Mozart played his first big gig...and where Maria Theresa's

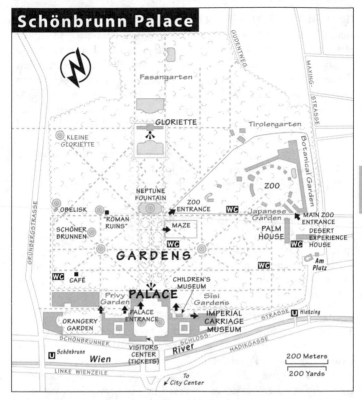

Schönbrunn Palace

Fasangarten

GUDENTWEG

MAXING-STRASSE

GLORIETTE

Tirolergarten

KLEINE GLORIETTE

Botanical Garden

NEPTUNE FOUNTAIN

ZOO

GRÜNBERGSTRASSE

OBELISK

ZOO ENTRANCE

WC

Japanese Garden

MAIN ZOO ENTRANCE

"ROMAN RUINS"

MAZE

PALM HOUSE

DESERT EXPERIENCE HOUSE

SCHÖNER BRUNNEN

WC

WC

Am Platz

G A R D E N S

WC

WC   CAFÉ

CHILDREN'S MUSEUM

PALACE

Privy Garden

Sisi Gardens

PALACE ENTRANCE

IMPERIAL CARRIAGE MUSEUM

STRASSE

Hietzing

ORANGERY GARDEN

SCHÖNBRUNNER

HADIKGASSE

Schönbrunn   Wien

VISITORS CENTER (TICKETS)

SCHLOSS- River

LINKE WIENZEILE

To City Center

200 Meters
200 Yards

SCHÖNBRUNN PALACE

great-great-grandson Franz Josef (r. 1848-1916) tried to please his self-absorbed wife Elisabeth, a.k.a. Sisi.

Your tour of the apartments, accompanied by an audio guide, follows a clearly signed one-way route. Think of the follow-ing minitour as a series of bread crumbs, leading you along while the audio guide fills in the details.

• *With your ticket in hand, approach the palace. Follow signs to the entrance gate stamped on your ticket. When your entry time arrives, don't be shy: Politely push your way through the milling crowds to get to the ticket taker. Those with a Sisi Ticket can use the Fast Lane. If you're doing the Grand Tour, keep your ticket handy as you'll need it again.*

IMPERIAL APARTMENTS

Begin in the **guards' room,** where jauntily dressed mannequins of Franz Josef's bodyguards introduce you to his luxurious world. Continue through the Billiard Room to the **Walnut Room.** Wow. Rococo-style wood paneling and gilding decorate this room where Franz Josef—a hard-working modern monarch—received official visitors. Nearby is the **study**—Franz Josef (see his mustachioed portrait) worked at this desk, sometimes joined by his beautiful, brown-haired wife Sisi (see her portrait). In the **bedchamber,** where he died barely more than a century ago, a praying stool, iron bed, and little toilet all attest to Franz Josef's spartan lifestyle (though the paintings here remind us of the grand scale of his palace).

• *As you turn the corner, you enter...*

Empress Sisi's Study and Dressing Room

See her portrait in a black dress, as well as (a reconstruction of) the spiral staircase that once led down to her apartments. The long-haired mannequin and makeup jars in the dressing room indicate how obsessive Sisi was about her looks.

• *Pass through this room to reach...*

Franz Josef's and Sisi's Bedroom

The huge wood-carved double bed suggests marital bliss, but the bed is not authentic—and as for the bliss, history suggests otherwise. Nearby is **Sisi's salon.** Though this was Sisi's reception room, the pastel paintings show her husband's distinguished ancestors—the many children of Maria Theresa (including Marie-Antoinette, immediately to the left as you enter).

Follow along to the **dining room.** The whole family ate here at the huge table; today it's set with dinnerware owned by Maria Theresa and Sisi. Next is the **children's room,** with portraits of Maria Theresa (on the easel) and some of her 11 (similar-looking) daughters. The bathroom was installed for the last Habsburg empress, Zita.

• *Turning the corner, pass through two rooms, until you reach the...*

Hall of Mirrors

In this room, six-year-old Mozart performed for Maria Theresa and her family (1762). He amazed them by playing without being able to see the keys, he jumped playfully into the empress' lap, and he even asked six-year-old Marie-Antoinette to marry him.

• *Pass through the next room, which leads to the large, breathtaking, white-and-gold...*

Great Gallery

Imagine the parties they had here: waltzers spinning across the floor, lit by chandeliers reflecting off the mirrors, beneath stunning ceiling frescoes, while enjoying views of the gardens and the Gloriette monument (described later). When WWII bombs rained on Vienna, the palace was largely spared. It took only one direct hit—crashing through this ballroom—but, thankfully, that bomb was a dud. In 1961, President Kennedy and Soviet Premier Khrushchev met here.

• *Pass through the final three rooms (pausing at a painting of Maria Theresa riding a Lipizzaner horse) until you reach the...*

Hall of Ceremonies

Wedding receptions were held here, beneath a regal portrait of Maria Theresa in a pink lace dress.

• *If you've bought the Grand Tour ticket, you can continue on. As you prepare to leave this room, look to the left of the doorway (to the right of Maria Theresa) to find a crowded painting with (supposedly) the child Mozart (behind Plexiglas, sitting next to a priest in gray). Next you'll come to...*

More Fancy Rooms

It was in the **Blue Chinese Salon,** in 1918, that the last Habsburg emperor made the decision to relinquish power, marking the end of more than six centuries of Habsburg rule. Up next, the black-lacquer **Vieux-Laque Room** was remodeled by Maria Theresa as a memorial to her beloved husband who died unexpectedly. Continue to the **Napoleon Room.** When Napoleon conquered Austria, he took over Schönbrunn and made this his bedroom. He dumped Josephine and took a Habsburg princess as his bride, and they had a son (cutely pictured holding a wreath of flowers).

• *Turn the corner through the **Porcelain Room** and enter the stunning...*

Millions Room

Admire the rosewood paneling inset with little painted scenes, and see how the mirrors reflect to infinity.

• *We're nearing the end. Pass through three (admittedly gorgeous) rooms, and turn the corner into the...*

Rich Bedchamber

This darkened room has what may have been Maria Theresa's wedding bed, where she and her husband Franz produced 16 children. Then comes their **study,** with a fitting end to this palace tour—a painting showing the happy couple who left their mark all over Schönbrunn. Maria Theresa and Franz are surrounded by their brood. Imagine these kids growing up here, riding horses, frolicking in the gardens, and preparing to marry fellow royals in order to bring peace and prosperity to the happy house of Habsburg.

PALACE GARDENS

The large, manicured grounds fill the palace's backyard, dominated by a hill-topping monument called the Gloriette. Unlike the gar-

SCHÖNBRUNN PALACE

dens of Versailles, meant to shut out the real world, Schönbrunn's park was opened to the public in 1779 while the monarchy was in full swing. It was part of Maria Theresa's reform policy, making the garden a celebration of the evolution of civilization from autocracy into real democracy.

Today it's a delightful, sprawling place to wander—especially on a sunny day. You can spend hours here, enjoying the views and the people-watching. And most of the park is free, as it has been for more than two centuries (open daily sunrise to dusk, entrance on either side of the palace). Note that a number of specialty features in the gardens charge admission but are included in the Schönbrunn passes described earlier (under "Cost").

Getting Around the Gardens: A tourist train makes the rounds all day, connecting Schönbrunn's many attractions (€8, 2/hour in peak season, none Nov-mid-March, one-hour circuit).

Visiting the Gardens: The grounds are laid out on angled, tree-lined axes that gradually incline, offering dramatic views back to the palace. The most elaborate gardens flank the palace: the **Privy Garden/Crown Prince Garden** (€4.50) and the free **Sisi Gardens.** But it's fun to just explore the expansive grounds (use the map in this book or pick one up at the palace). Highlights include several whimsical **fountains,** such as the faux "Roman ruins," the obelisk, and the Neptune Fountain (straight back from the palace). Next to the Neptune Fountain is a kid-friendly **maze** *(Irrgarten)* and playground area (€6). Other features of the garden—**Orangery** (€4.50), **Palm House** (€7), and **Desert Experience House** (€7)—are skippable for most.

If the weather is good, huff up the zigzag path above the Neptune Fountain to the **Gloriette,** a purely decorative monument celebrating an obscure Austrian military victory. To gain access to the view terraces, you can pay for a pricey drink in the café or shell out for an admission ticket (€4.50)—but views are about as good from the lawn just in front of the monument.

NEARBY SIGHTS

Schönbrunn Zoo (Tiergarten Schönbrunn)

The world's oldest zoo, next door to the palace grounds, was built in 1752 by Maria Theresa's husband for the entertainment and education of the court. He later opened it up to the public—provided that they wore proper attire. Today, it's a modern A (anteater) to Z (zebra) menagerie that's especially appealing to families.

Cost and Hours: Adults—€20, kids—€10, daily 9:00-18:30, closes earlier off-season, www.zoovienna.at.

▲Imperial Carriage Museum (Kaiserliche Wagenburg)

The Schönbrunn coach museum is a 19th-century traffic jam of 50 impressive royal carriages and sleighs. It's overpriced (but worth it if you have time to kill before your palace reservation). Highlights include silly sedan chairs, the death-black hearse carriage (used for Franz Josef in 1916, and most recently for Empress Zita in 1989), and an extravagantly gilded imperial carriage pulled by eight Cinderella horses. This was rarely used other than for the coronation of Holy Roman emperors, when it was disassembled and taken to Frankfurt for the big event (check out the huge paintings on the back wall, showing these very carriages in action). You'll also get a close look at one of Sisi's impossibly narrow-waisted gowns, and (upstairs) Sisi's "Riding Chapel," with portraits of her 25 favorite horses.

Cost and Hours: €9.50, daily 9:00-17:00, Dec-April until 16:00, audioguide-€2, 200 yards from palace, walk through right arch as you face palace, tel. 01/525-243-470, www.kaiserliche-wagenburg.at.

SCHÖNBRUNN PALACE

SLEEPING IN VIENNA

Accommodations in Vienna are plentiful and relatively cheap—a €100 double here might go for €150 in Munich and €200 in Milan. Within the Ring, you'll need to shell out over €100 for a double room with bath. But around Mariahilfer Strasse, two people can stay comfortably (though with no frills) for €75. Expect rates to spike for conventions (most frequent Sept-Oct), and to drop in November and from January to March. For some travelers, short-term, Airbnb-type rentals can be a good alternative; search for places in my recommended hotel neighborhoods.

Many of the hotels I've listed here share buildings with other businesses or residences, which can mean lots of stairs or (hopefully) an elevator. Viennese elevators and stairwells can be confusing: In most of Europe, 0 is the ground floor, and 1 is the first floor up (our "second floor"). But in Vienna, thanks to a Habsburg-legacy quirk, older buildings have at least one extra "mezzanine" floor (labeled on elevators as P, H, M, and/or A) between the ground floor and the "first" floor, so floor 1 can actually be what we'd call the second, third, or even fourth floor.

I rank accommodations from **$** budget to **$$$$** splurge. To get the best deal, contact my family-run accommodations directly by phone or email. When you book direct, the owner avoids a roughly 20 percent commission and may be able to offer you a discount. Book your accommodations well in advance if you'll be traveling during peak season or if your trip coincides with a major holiday or festival (see the appendix). For more information on rates and deals, making reservations, finding a short-term rental, and more, see the "Sleeping" section in the Practicalities chapter. And for guidance on reaching your hotel upon arrival in Vienna, see the Vienna Connections chapter.

Though the government has not yet enforced legislation to ban smoking in restaurants and bars, most hotels in Vienna are now completely nonsmoking.

WITHIN THE RING, IN THE OLD CITY CENTER

You'll pay extra to sleep in the atmospheric old center, but if you can afford it, staying here gives you the classiest Vienna experience and enables you to walk to most sights. You won't need a car, but if you are coming with one, plan ahead and ask your hotel where to park.

$$$$ Hotel am Stephansplatz is an impersonal four-star business hotel with 56 rooms. It's plush but not over-the-top, and reasonably priced for its sleek comfort and central location facing the cathedral. Every detail is modern and quality, and breakfast is superb, with a view of the city waking up around the cathedral (air-con, elevator, gym and sauna, Stephansplatz 9, U: Stephansplatz, tel. 01/534-050, www.hotelamstephansplatz.at, office@ hotelamstephansplatz.at).

$$$ Aviano Boutique Hotel is a friendly, family-run place and is the best value among my pricier listings. It has 17 rooms, all comfortable and some beautiful, with flowery carpets and other Baroque frills. It's on the third and fourth floors of a typical city-center building, but feels peaceful (breakfast extra, fans, elevator, between Neuer Markt and Kärntner Strasse at Marco d'Avianogasse 1, U: Karlsplatz or Stephansplatz, tel. 01/512-8330, www.avianoboutiquehotel.com, office@avianoboutiquehotel.at, Frau Kavka).

$$$ Hotel Pertschy, circling an old courtyard, is big and elegantly creaky. Its 56 huge rooms have chandeliers and Baroque touches. Those on the courtyard are quietest (fans, elevator, Habsburgergasse 5, U: Stephansplatz, tel. 01/534-490, www. pertschy.com, info@pertschy.com).

$$$ Hotel zur Wiener Staatsoper is quiet, with a more traditional elegance than many of my other listings. Its 22 tidy rooms come with high ceilings, chandeliers, and fancy carpets on parquet floors (fans on request, elevator, a block from the opera house at Krugerstrasse 11; U: Karlsplatz, tel. 01/513-1274, www.hotel-staatsoper.at, info@hotel-staatsoper.at, manager Ursula).

$$$ Pension Nossek offers 32 rooms with a great location on the pedestrian-only Graben...but the rooms, though decorated with lace and flowers, are worn and threadbare (air-con, elevator,

SLEEPING

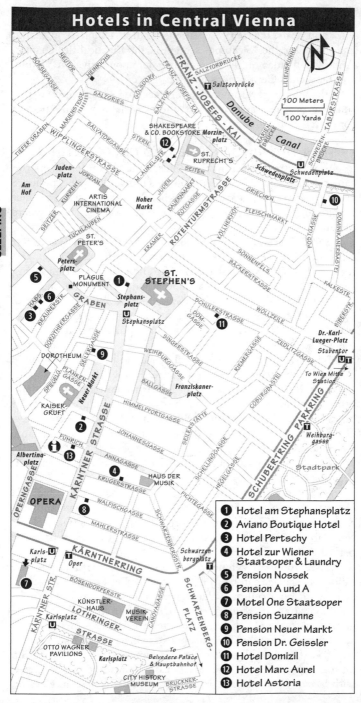

Hotels in Central Vienna

1 Hotel am Stephansplatz
2 Aviano Boutique Hotel
3 Hotel Pertschy
4 Hotel zur Wiener Staatsoper & Laundry
5 Pension Nossek
6 Pension A und A
7 Motel One Staatsoper
8 Pension Suzanne
9 Pension Neuer Markt
10 Pension Dr. Geissler
11 Hotel Domizil
12 Hotel Marc Aurel
13 Hotel Astoria

Graben 17, U: Stephansplatz, tel. 01/5337-0410, www.pension-nossek.at, reservation@pension-nossek.at).

$$$ Pension A und A, with nine rooms, offers a modern break from crusty old Vienna. This place, conveniently located just off the Graben, has a nice entryway and period elevator—but open the door and you'll find white minimalist hallways and contemporary style in the rooms (air-con, Habsburgergasse 3, U: Stephansplatz, tel. 01/890-5128, www.aunda.at, office@aunda.at).

$$ Motel One Staatsoper, part of a German chain of "budget design hotels," features sleek, smallish, modern rooms outfitted with quality materials but no frills, a 24-hour reception, funky lounge spaces, and refreshingly straightforward pricing; it's perfect for budget travelers looking for something nicer. This location—right between the opera house and Karlsplatz—has 400 rooms, including some larger options, in a smartly renovated building that's kept its Old World charm (no triples but you can slip in a child under 6 for free, breakfast extra, air-con, elevator, Elisabethstrasse 5, U: Karlsplatz, tel. 01/585-0505, www.motel-one.com, wien-staatsoper@motel-one.com).

$$ Pension Suzanne, as Baroque and doily as you'll find in this price range, is wonderfully located a few yards from the opera house. It's small and without a real lobby, but run with the class of a bigger hotel. The 26 rooms are packed with properly Viennese antique furnishings (RS%, spacious apartment for up to 6 also available, fans on request, elevator, Walfischgasse 4, U: Karlsplatz, tel. 01/513-2507, www.pension-suzanne.at, info@pension-suzanne.at, run by manager Michael).

$$ Pension Neuer Markt is perfectly central, with 37 comfy but faded pink rooms, and worn hallways with a cruise-ship ambience (in hot weather request a quiet courtyard-side room when you reserve, fans, elevator, Seilergasse 9, U: Stephansplatz, tel. 01/512-2316, www.hotelpension.at, neuermarkt@hotelpension.at).

$$ Pension Dr. Geissler, has 23 small plain-but-comfortable rooms on the eighth floor of a modern, nondescript apartment building just off Schwedenplatz, about 10 blocks northeast of St. Stephen's, near the Bratislava ferry terminal (elevator, Postgasse 14, U: Schwedenplatz—Postgasse is to the left as you face Hotel Capricorno, tel. 01/533-2803, www.hotelpension.at, dr.geissler@hotelpension.at).

NEAR NASCHMARKT

$$$ Hotel Beethoven is a smartly decorated boutique property with 47 colorful rooms and lots of attention to detail. Its comfy communal spaces and access to coffee and tea throughout the day keep it feeling like home. The location, near the Naschmarkt and overlooking the Theater an der Wien, puts you close to the action but away from the crowds and late-night noise (air-con, elevator, Sunday classical concerts, Papagenogasse 6, U: Karlsplatz, tel. 01/587-44820, www.hotel-beethoven.at, info@hotelbeethoven.at). See the map on page 32 for location.

ON OR NEAR MARIAHILFER STRASSE

Lively, pedestrianized Mariahilfer Strasse connects the Westbahnhof and the city center. The U-3 subway line runs underneath the street on its way between the Westbahnhof and St. Stephen's Cathedral, and most of these listings are within a five-minute walk of a U-Bahn stop. This vibrant, inexpensive area is filled with stores, cafés, and even a small shopping mall. It's a great neighborhood to stay in, and a glut of hotel rooms keeps prices low and competition keen. Its smaller hotels and pensions are often immigrant-run, often by well-established Hungarian families. If you're driving, your hotel may provide discounted parking at a local garage for €13-20 per day. As you'd expect, the far end of Mariahilfer Strasse (around and past the Westbahnhof) is rougher around the edges, while the section near downtown is more gentrified.

Closer to Downtown

$$$ NH Collection Wien Zentrum, part of a Spanish chain, is a stern, stylish-but-passionless business hotel on Mariahilfer Strasse. It rents 73 rooms, including a few "suites" that are ideal for families (breakfast extra, air-con, elevator, Mariahilfer Strasse 78, U: Zieglergasse, tel. 01/524-5600, www.nh-hotels.com, nhcollectionwienzentrum@nh-hotels.com).

$$ Hotel Pension Corvinus is proudly run by a hardworking Hungarian family: parents Miklós and Judith and sons Anthony and Zoltán. Its 15 comfortable rooms are bright and spacious with nice extra touches (discount if you pay cash, ask about family rooms and apartments with kitchens, air-con, elevator, Mariahilfer Strasse 57, U: Neubaugasse, tel. 01/587-7239, www.corvinus.at, hotel@corvinus.at).

$$ Hotel Kugel is run with style by hands-on owners Johannes and Christina Roller. Its 25 unique rooms, some with canopy beds, are a great value and decorated with a feminine touch (family rooms, fans, some tram noise, Siebensterngasse 43, at corner with Neubaugasse, U: Neubaugasse, tel. 01/523-3355, www.hotelkugel.at, office@hotelkugel.at).

$$ Hotel Pension Mariahilf's 12 rooms are bright and well sized (if a bit outmoded), with high ceilings. Just steps from the U-Bahn, it's especially convenient (breakfast extra, served in supermarket across the street Mon-Sat and in lobby Sun, fans, elevator, Mariahilfer Strasse 49, U: Neubaugasse, tel. 01/586-1781, www.mariahilf-hotel.at, info@mariahilf-hotel.at, friendly Babak).

$$ K&T Boardinghouse rents five modern, spacious rooms on the first floor of a quiet building a block off Mariahilfer Strasse (cash only but reserve with credit card or PayPal, 2-night minimum, no breakfast, pay air-con, Chwallagasse 2, U: Neubaugasse, mobile 0676-553-6063, www. ktboardinghouse.at, kt2@ chello.at, Tina,). From Mariahilfer Strasse, turn left at Café Ritter and walk down Schadekgasse one short block; tiny Chwallagasse is the first right.

$ Pension Kraml is a charming, 17-room place tucked away on a small street between Mariahilfer Strasse and the Naschmarkt. It's run by hardworking Stephan and feels classic, with breakfast served in the perfectly preserved family restaurant (no longer open to nonguests) that his grandmother ran in the 1950s. The rooms, which surround a pleasantly leafy courtyard, are big and quiet, with a homey, Old World ambience (family apartment available, fans, no elevator, Brauergasse 5, midway between U: Zieglergasse and Pilgramgasse, tel. 01/587-8588, www.pensionkraml.at, pension. kraml@chello.at).

$ Pension Hargita rents 28 bright and attractive rooms. While the pension is directly on bustling Mariahilfer Strasse, its windows block noise well. Don't let the dingy sign out front put you off—this spick-and-span, well-located place is a good value (breakfast extra, fans, lots of stairs and no elevator, bike parking, corner of Mariahilfer Strasse at Andreasgasse 1, right at U: Zieglergasse, tel. 01/526-1928, www.hargita.at, office@urban-hotel.at).

Near the Westbahnhof

$$ Motel One Westbahnhof, a more affordable outpost of the chain described earlier, has 441 rooms, lots of modern flair, and a vibrant lobby with plenty of inviting spaces to unwind (no triples but you can slip in a child under 6 for free, breakfast extra, air-con, attached to the Westbahnhof at Europaplatz 3, tel. 01/359-350, www.motel-one.com, wein-westbahnhof@motel-one.com).

$$ Hotel Ibis Wien Mariahilf, an impersonal high-rise hotel with American charm, is ideal for anyone tired of quaint old Europe. Its 341 cookie-cutter rooms are bright, comfortable, and modern, with all the conveniences (breakfast extra, air-con, elevator, exit Westbahnhof to the right and walk 400 yards, Mariahilfer Gürtel 22, U: Westbahnhof, tel. 01/59998, www.accorhotels.com, h0796@accor.com).

SLEEPING

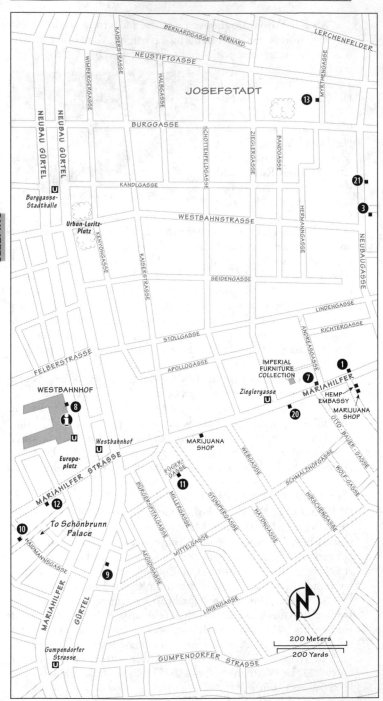

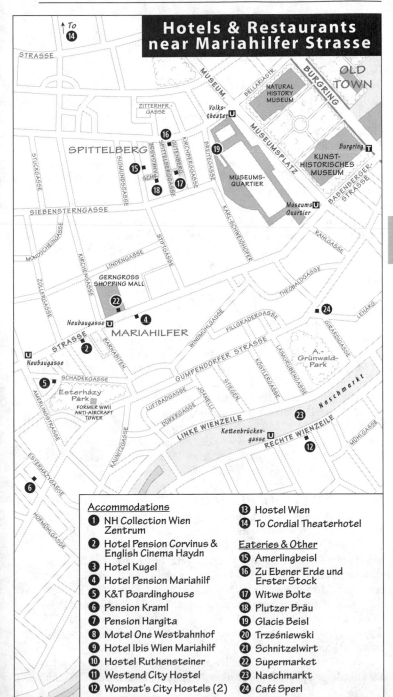

Hotels & Restaurants near Mariahilfer Strasse

SLEEPING

Accommodations

1. NH Collection Wien Zentrum
2. Hotel Pension Corvinus & English Cinema Haydn
3. Hotel Kugel
4. Hotel Pension Mariahilf
5. K&T Boardinghouse
6. Pension Kraml
7. Pension Hargita
8. Motel One Westbahnhof
9. Hotel Ibis Wien Mariahilf
10. Hostel Ruthensteiner
11. Westend City Hostel
12. Wombat's City Hostels (2)
13. Hostel Wien
14. To Cordial Theaterhotel

Eateries & Other

15. Amerlingbeisl
16. Zu Ebener Erde und Erster Stock
17. Witwe Bolte
18. Plutzer Bräu
19. Glacis Beisl
20. Trześniewski
21. Schnitzelwirt
22. Supermarket
23. Naschmarkt
24. Café Sperl

DORMS AND HOSTELS

These budget-minded options cluster near Mariahilfer Strasse and the Westbahnhof. For the first three, use the Westbahnhof U-Bahn stop.

¢ **Hostel Ruthensteiner** is your smallest and coziest option, with 100 beds in 4- to 8-bed dorms and lots of little touches (private rooms available, breakfast extra, laundry, comfy common areas with piano and guitars, bike rental, Robert-Hamerling-Gasse 24, tel. 01/893-4202, www.hostelruthensteiner.com, info@hostelruthensteiner.com). From the Westbahnhof, follow Mariahilfer Strasse away from the center to #149, and turn left on Haidmannsgasse. Go one block, then turn right.

¢ **Westend City Hostel,** just a block from the Westbahnhof and Mariahilfer Strasse, is well-run and well-located in a residential neighborhood, so it's quiet after 20:00. It has a small lounge, high-ceilinged rooms, a tiny back courtyard, and 180 beds in 4- to 12-bed dorms, each with its own bath (cash only, private rooms available, breakfast included when you book directly with the hostel, elevator, laundry, Fügergasse 3, tel. 01/597-6729, www.viennahostel.at, info@westendhostel.at).

¢ **Wombat's City Hostel** has two well-run locations—both with about 250 beds and 4 to 6 beds per room (private rooms available, bar, generous public spaces, close to the Westbahnhof at Mariahilfer Strasse 137 and near the Naschmarkt at Rechte Wienzeile 35—U: Kettenbrückengasse, tel. 01/897-2336, www.wombats-hostels.com, bookvienna@wombats.eu).

¢ **Hostel Wien** is your classic, huge, and well-run official youth hostel, with 260 beds (private rooms available, nonmembers pay €3.50 extra, always open, no curfew, coin-op laundry, Myrthengasse 7, take bus #48A from Westbahnhof, tel. 01/523-6316, www.1070vienna.at, hostel@chello.at).

MORE HOTELS IN VIENNA

If my top listings are full, here are some others to consider. Rates vary with season and demand.

Near City Hall, the **$$$ Cordial Theaterhotel** is a shiny gem of a hotel on a fun shopping street (several blocks beyond the Ring at Josefstädter Strasse 22, U: Rathaus, tel. 01/405-3648, www.cordial.at, chwien@cordial.at).

A stone's throw from Stephansplatz, **$$$ Hotel Domizil**'s 40 rooms are light, bright, and neat as a pin (Schulerstrasse 14, U: Stephansplatz or Stubentor, tel. 01/513-3199, www.hoteldomizil.at, info@hoteldomizil.at).

A few steps from Schwedenplatz, **$$$ Hotel Marc Aurel** is an affordable, plain-Jane business-class hotel with rare air-conditioning (Marc Aurel Strasse 8, U: Schwedenplatz, tel. 01/533-3640, www.hotel-marcaurel.com, info@hotel-marcaurel.com).

Just off Kärntner Strasse, **$$ Hotel Astoria** is a turn-of-the-century Old World hotel with 128 classy rooms (Kärntner Strasse 32, U: Karlsplatz, tel. 01/515-771, www.austria-trend.at/hotel-astoria, astoria@austria-trend.at).

SLEEPING

EATING IN VIENNA

The Viennese appreciate the fine points of life, and right up there with waltzing is eating. The city has many atmospheric restaurants. As you ponder the Hungarian and Bohemian influence on many menus, remember that Vienna's diverse empire may be no more, but its flavors linger. In addition to restaurants, this chapter covers two Viennese institutions: the city's café culture and its *Heuriger* wine pubs.

EATING TIPS

I rank eateries from **$** budget to **$$$$** splurge. For more advice on eating in Vienna, including details on ordering, dining, and tipping in restaurants, the types of eateries you'll encounter, and Austrian cuisine and beverages, see the "Eating" section of the Practicalities chapter. For a fun foodie guide to Vienna, see ViennaWuerstelstand.com.

Smoking in Restaurants: Although legislation has mandated a complete smoking ban in restaurants and bars, a new right-wing government has kept the ban at bay. In the meantime, some restaurants have nonsmoking sections, but expect secondhand smoke wherever you sit. Fortunately for nonsmokers, many eateries offer plenty of outdoor seating.

Local Specialty: *Tafelspitz,* a favorite of Emperor Franz Josef, is boiled beef served in a vegetable soup with bone marrow. There's a process to eating it (ask your server to explain): Your server will delicately put the beef on your plate, leaving you with the vegetable soup broth to enjoy. Fish out the bone marrow and eat it with toasted dark bread. Then tackle the boiled beef with apple horseradish sauce. The *Tafelspitz* is big and typically shared.

Cafés, Coffee, and Pastries: Vienna is known for its classic cafés—perfect places to sip some coffee and read a newspaper. A café is also a great place to try one of Vienna's famous desserts, as the city is the birthplace of the Sacher torte and a bevy of other cakes and pastry treats. For help ordering coffee and choosing among the city's favorite desserts, see the "Eating" section of the Practicalities chapter.

Heurigen: Make sure to check out a wine-garden restaurant nestled in the foothills of the Vienna Woods. At most *Heurigen,* you'll try the latest vintage wine, pick from an assortment of prepared foods, and listen to live music. For more on these, and a list of recommended places, see "*Wein* in Wien: Vienna's Wine Gardens," near the end of this chapter.

Viennese Drinks: *Gemischter Satz* is a wine that's uniquely Viennese. A blend of grapes grown and harvested together in the same vineyard, it was long considered a cheap table wine. Now it's more respected and worth trying. For a nonalcoholic and refreshing local drink, I like *Apfelsaft gespritzt* (called *Apfelschorlei* in Germany), which is apple juice mixed with soda. For a refreshing light-beer drink, go for *Radler* (half beer, half 7Up).

FINE DINING IN THE CENTER

The heart of the city offers plenty of options for a relaxing and expensive dining experience; here are some of my favorites. Reservations are always wise in the evening.

$$$ Lugeck serves the classics with a modern flair to a local "business casual" crowd with professional service but no pretense. Their slogan: "Genuine classics are always in fashion." Choose between a big, fresh, Art Deco interior, or tables on a quiet little square under a towering statue of Gutenberg. It's just a block from the recommended Zanoni & Zanoni gelato place—handy if you want a different scene for your dessert course (daily 11:30-23:00, Lugeck 4, tel. 01/512-5060, www.lugeck.com).

$$$ Artner Restaurant am Franziskanerplatz is a classy place with a smart clientele (it's a favorite of Austrian politicians). Diners enjoy the cozy interior as well as the outside seating on a quaint square. They offer a meaty and inviting modern international menu with nicely presented dishes, including gourmet hamburgers and great steaks (lunch specials, Mon-Sat 12:00-24:00, closed Sun, Franziskanerplatz 5, tel. 01/503-5034, www.artner.co.at).

EATING

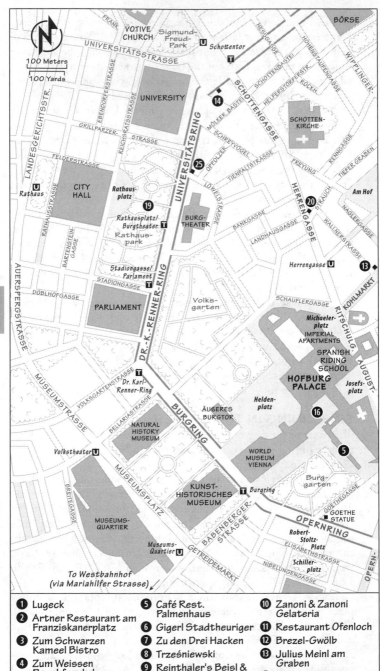

1 Lugeck	**5** Café Rest. Palmenhaus	**10** Zanoni & Zanoni Gelateria
2 Artner Restaurant am Franziskanerplatz	**6** Gigerl Stadtheuriger	**11** Restaurant Ofenloch
3 Zum Schwarzen Kameel Bistro	**7** Zu den Drei Hacken	**12** Brezel-Gwölb
4 Zum Weissen Rauchfangkehrer	**8** Trześniewski	**13** Julius Meinl am Graben
	9 Reinthaler's Beisl & Café Hawelka	**14** Yamm Vegetarian Restaurant

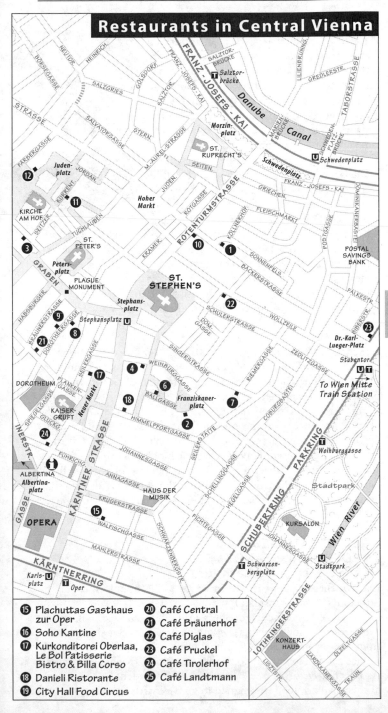

Restaurants in Central Vienna

15 Plachuttas Gasthaus zur Oper
16 Soho Kantine
17 Kurkonditorei Oberlaa, Le Bol Patisserie Bistro & Billa Corso
18 Danieli Ristorante
19 City Hall Food Circus

20 Café Central
21 Café Bräunerhof
22 Café Diglas
23 Café Pruckel
24 Café Tirolerhof
25 Café Landtmann

$$ Zum Schwarzen Kameel Bistro ("The Black Camel") has a posh, gourmet Viennese **$$$$** restaurant in the back with a thriving and more casual wine bar fronting the street. The delightfully Art Nouveau wine bar, filled with a professional local crowd enjoying small plates from the fancy restaurant kitchen, is *the* place for horseradish and thin-sliced ham (*Beinschinken mit Kren; Achtung*—the horseradish is *hot*). The kitchen is the same one they use for the fine restaurant. Eat well by ordering high on the menu; eat cheaply by sticking with the tiny open-face finger sandwiches (€1.50 each, self-serve from counter, with little pastries to assemble, too). Stand, grab a stool, find a table on the street, or sit anywhere you can (prices are the same)—it's customary to share tables. Fine Austrian wines are sold by the *Achtel* (eighth-liter glass) and listed on the board (daily 12:00-23:00, Bognergasse 5, tel. 01/533-8125).

$$$ Zum Weissen Rauchfangkehrer ("The White Chimney Sweep"), with a charming woody interior and live piano nightly, is popular for its rustic elegance and traditional cuisine (near the cathedral at Weihburggasse 4, tel. 01/512-3471).

$$$ Café Restaurant Palmenhaus overlooks the Hofburg Palace Garden. Tucked away in a green and peaceful corner two blocks behind the opera house, this is a world apart. If you want to eat modern Austrian cuisine surrounded by palm trees, this is the place. And, since it's at the edge of a huge park, it's great for families. It's an elegant, dressy, and expensive place at night, but there are moderately priced daily specials for lunch (12:00-15:00). They specialize in fresh fish with generous vegetables—options are listed on the chalkboard (daily 12:00-24:00, Jan-Feb closed Mon-Tue, extensive wine list, indoors in greenhouse or outdoors, Burggarten 1, tel. 01/533-1033).

CASUAL EATERIES AND TRADITIONAL STANDBYS
Near St. Stephen's Cathedral

Each of these eateries is within about a five-minute walk of the cathedral (U: Stephansplatz).

$ Gigerl Stadtheuriger offers a fun, near-*Heuriger* wine cellar experience without leaving the city center. You can sit and order from the menu (*Gulasch,* schnitzel, and so on) or go to the self-service counter for mostly cold cuts—just point to what looks good. As in other *Heurigen* (see "Vienna's Wine Gardens," near the end of this chapter), food is designed to go well with the wine. It's sold by the piece or weight; 100 grams *(10 dag)* is about a quarter-pound (cheese and cold meats cost about €5 per 100 grams, salads are about €2 per 100 grams; price sheet posted on wall to right of buffet line). They also have entrées, spinach strudel, quiche, *Apfelstrudel,* and, of course, casks of new and local wines. Servers take your wine order (daily 15:00-24:00, indoor/outdoor seating, behind cathedral, a block off Kärntner Strasse, just off Rauhensteingasse on Blumenstock, tel. 01/513-4431).

$$ Zu den Drei Hacken, a fun and typical *Weinstube* (wine pub), is a hit with locals for its old-fashioned specialties. In other words, if you're a carnivore looking for a nose-to-tail adventure, this is it. These are finely prepared dishes that used to be standard at home (Mon-Sat 11:00-23:00, closed Sun, indoor/outdoor seating, Singerstrasse 28, tel. 01/512-5895).

$$ Trześniewski is an institution—justly famous for its elegant open-face finger sandwiches and small beers. Started by a Polish cook who moved to Vienna, Trześniewski (chesh-NEFF-ski) has been a Vienna favorite for more than a century...and many of its regulars seem to have been here for the grand opening. Three different sandwiches and a *kleines Bier (Pfiff)* make a  fun, fast, and light €5 lunch. Point to whichever delights look tasty (or grab the English translation sheet and take time to study your 22 sandwich options). The classic favorites are *Geflügelleber* (chicken liver), *Matjes mit Zwiebel* (herring with onions), and *Speck mit Ei* (bacon and eggs). Pay for your sandwiches and a drink. Take your drink tokens to the lady on the right. Sit on the bench and scoot over to a tiny table when a spot opens up (Mon-Fri 8:30-19:30, Sat 9:00-17:00, closed Sun, 50 yards off the Graben, nearly across from Café Hawelka—see "Vienna's Café Culture," later in this chapter; Dorotheergasse 2, tel. 01/512-3291).

They have another branch at Mariahilfer Strasse 95 (near many recommended hotels—see the map in the Sleeping in Vienna chapter, Mon-Fri 8:30-19:00, Sat 9:00-18:00, closed Sun, U: Zieglergasse).

$$ Reinthaler's Beisl is another time warp that serves simple, traditional fare all day. It's handy for its location (a block off the Graben, across the street from Trześniewski) and because it's a rare restaurant in the center that's open on Sunday. Its fun, classic interior winds way back, and it also has a few tables on the quiet street

EATING

City Hall Food Circus

During the summer, scores of outdoor food stands and hundreds of picnic tables are set up in the park in front of the City Hall (Rathausplatz). Local mobs enjoy drinks and a wide range of cuisines for decent-but-not-cheap prices and classy entertainment on a big screen (see the Entertainment in Vienna chapter). The great thing here is the energy of the crowd and a feeling that you're truly eating as the Viennese do...not schnitzel and quaint traditions, but trendy "world food" with young people out having fun in a fine Vienna park (July-Aug daily from 11:00 until late, in front of City Hall on the Ringstrasse, U: Rathaus).

(use the handwritten daily menu rather than the printed English one, daily 11:00-23:00, Dorotheergasse 4, tel. 01/513-1249).

Ice Cream: *Gelateria* **Zanoni & Zanoni,** run by an Italian family for several generations, is a fun, high-energy spot mobbed by happy Viennese hungry for their €2 two-scoop cones from an extravagant ice-cream lover's menu. Just two blocks from the cathedral, with a big terrace of tables, it's a classic scene for licking and people-watching—or take it to-go and just grab a spot under the Gutenberg statue a block away (daily until 24:00, Lugeck 7, tel. 01/512-7979).

Near Am Hof Square

The streets around the square called Am Hof (U: Herrengasse) hide atmospheric medieval lanes with both indoor and outdoor eating action. The following eateries are all within a block or two of the square.

$$$ Restaurant Ofenloch serves good, traditional Viennese cuisine with formal service, both indoors and out. This delightfully intimate 300-year-old eatery has a refined yet relaxed ambience (Mon-Sat 11:00-23:00, closed Sun, Kurrentgasse 8, tel. 01/533-8844).

$$ Brezel-Gwölb, a Tolkienesque nook with tight indoor tables and outdoor dining on a quiet little square, serves simple Viennese classics in an unforgettable atmosphere. With its dark and candlelit interior and secretive-feeling outdoor seating, it's ideal for a romantic late-night glass of wine (three-course weekday lunch specials—including vegetarian option, daily 11:30-24:00; leave Am Hof on Drahtgasse, then take first left to Ledererhof 9; tel. 01/533-8811).

Gourmet Supermarket: Located right on the Graben, **Julius Meinl am Graben,** with two floors of temptations, has been famous since 1862 as a top-end delicatessen with all the gourmet fancies. Assemble a meal from the picnic fixings on the shelves. There's also a café, with light meals and great outdoor seating; a stuffy and pricey restaurant upstairs; and a takeout counter with good benches out front for people-watching while you munch (shop open Mon-Fri 8:00-19:30, Sat 9:00-18:00, closed Sun; restaurant open Mon-Sat until 24:00, closed Sun; Am Graben 19, tel. 01/532-3334).

Near the University
$$ Yamm Vegetarian Restaurant (German for "yummy") is a stylish, youthful, self-service hit with foodies for its quality vegetarian fare. Pick up a payment card and plate, serve yourself, then weigh and pay (there's plenty of friendly help). A typical plate runs about €15. They serve breakfast and have take-out options (seating inside and out, smoothies, vegan cakes, daily 8:00-22:00, Sun until 15:00, on the Ring, 100 yards from the recommended Café Landtmann, Universitätsring 10, tel. 01/532-0544).

Near the Opera
These eateries are within easy walking distance of the opera house (U: Karlsplatz).

$$$ Plachuttas Gasthaus zur Oper, a proudly Austrian place a block from the opera, has a contemporary, classy interior and inviting seating on the street. It's big, high-energy, and specializes in the local classics like *Tafelspitz* (boiled beef) and Wiener schnitzel—they actually hand out a little souvenir recipe titled "the art of the perfect Wiener schnitzel" (daily 11:00-24:00, Walfischgasse 5, tel. 01/512-2251).

$ Soho Kantine is a cave-like, government-subsidized cantina, serving the National Library staff but open to all, and offering unexciting, institutional, bargain lunches in the Hofburg. Pay for your meal—your choice of meat or vegetarian—and a drink at the bar, take your token to the kitchen, and then sit down and eat with the locals. Wednesday is schnitzel day and Friday is fish day. Facing the Burggarten's butterfly house, turn left and go 40 yards—it's hiding in a forlorn little square, through a plain door that's not signed (Mon-Fri 11:30-15:00, closed Sat-Sun and mid-July-Aug, Burggarten, mobile 0676-309-5161, Reni).

$$ Kurkonditorei Oberlaa may not have the royal and plush fame of Demel (see page 94), but this is where Viennese connoisseurs serious about the quality of their pastries go to get fat. With outdoor seating on Neuer Markt, it's particularly nice on a summer day. Upstairs has more temptations and good seating (three-course weekday lunch specials, great selection of cakes, daily 8:00-20:00, Neuer Markt 16, tel. 01/5132-9360).

$$ Le Bol Patisserie Bistro (next to Oberlaa) satisfies your need for something French. The staff speaks to you in French,

Wieners in Wien

For hard-core Viennese cuisine, drop by a *Würstelstand*. The local hot-dog stand is a fixture on city squares throughout the old center, serving a variety of hot dogs and pickled side dishes with a warm corner-meeting-place atmosphere. The *Wiener* we know is named for Vienna, but the guy who invented the weenie studied in Frankfurt. Out of nostalgia for his school years, he named his fun fast food for that city...a Frankfurter. Only in Vienna are *Wieners* called *Frankfurters*. (Got that?) When it comes to wieners, there's no pretense of being healthy. When Viennese eat at a *Würstelstand,* their friends will know it for the rest of the day by their burps.

Explore the fun menus. Be adventurous. The many varieties of hot dogs cost €3-4 each. Check out the "Best of the Wurst" sausage terms in the Practicalities chapter. Convenient stands are on Hoher Markt, the Graben, and in front of the Albertina Museum—a fun place to hang out after an opera performance as musicians and local opera buffs drop by. (By the way, the sleek modern design of the Albertina Museum stand is by famous local architect Hans Hollein, who also did the "diving board" entrance of the museum—look up.)

EATING

serving fine salads, baguette sandwiches, and fresh croissants on a small terrace or inside the cozy bistro (Mon-Sat 8:00-23:00, Sun from 9:00, Neuer Markt 14, mobile 0699-1030-1899).

$$$ Danieli Ristorante is your best classy Italian value in the Old Town. White-tablecloth dressy, but not stuffy, it has reasonable prices. Dine in their elegant, air-conditioned back room or on the street (daily 11:30-23:00, 30 yards off Kärntner Strasse opposite Neuer Markt at Himmelpfortgasse 3, tel. 01/513-7913).

Supermarket: A top-end version of the Billa supermarket chain, **Billa Corso** has three floors of food and sells hot, gourmet, ready-made meals (by weight). You're welcome to sit and enjoy whatever you've purchased inside (air-con) or out on the square. They also have a great deli selection of salads, soups, and picnic items (Mon-Fri 8:00-20:00, Sat until 19:00, Sun 10:00-18:00, Neuer Markt 17, on the corner where Seilergasse hits Neuer Markt, tel. 01/961-2133).

Spittelberg

This charming cobbled grid of traffic-free lanes is a favorite dining neighborhood for the Viennese. It's handy, set between the Muse-umsQuartier and Mariahilfer Strasse (U: Volkstheater/Museums-platz). Tables tumble down sidewalks and into breezy courtyards; the charming buildings here date mostly from the early 1800s, before the Mariahilfer Strasse neighborhood was built. It's only worth a special trip on a balmy summer evening, as it's dead in bad weather. Stroll Spittelberggasse, Schrankgasse, and Gutenberggasse, then pick your favorite. Don't miss the vine-strewn wine garden at Schrankgasse 1. To locate these restaurants, see the map in the Sleeping in Vienna chapter.

$ Amerlingbeisl is a charming, local place with a casual atmosphere both on the cobbled street and in its vine-covered courtyard. It's a great value, serving a mix of traditional Austrian and international dishes (check the board with daily specials—some vegetarian, Mon-Fri 11:30-24:00, Sat-Sun from 9:00, shorter hours in winter, Stiftgasse 8, tel. 01/526-1660).

$$$ Zu Ebener Erde und Erster Stock (loosely translated as "Downstairs, Upstairs") is a popular little restaurant with a mostly traditional Austrian menu that includes their signature *Tafelspitz* (boiled beef). Filling a cute 1750 building, it's true to its name, with two dining rooms: casual and woody downstairs (traditionally for the poor) and a fancy Biedermeier-style dining room with red-velvet chairs and violet tablecloths upstairs (where the wealthy convened). There are also a few al fresco tables along the quiet side street. Reservations are smart (seasonal specials, Mon-Fri 12:00-22:00, last seating at 20:30, closed Sat-Sun, Burggasse 13, tel. 01/523-6254, www.zu-ebener-erde-und-erster-stock.at).

$$$ Witwe Bolte is classy. The interior is tight, but its tiny square has a wonderful leafy ambience (daily 11:45-23:00, in July-Aug opens at 17:30 Mon-Fri, Gutenberggasse 13, tel. 01/523-1450).

$$ Plutzer Bräu, next door to Amerlingbeisl, feels a bit more commercial. It's a big, sprawling, impersonal brewpub serving forgettable pub grub: ribs, burgers, traditional dishes, and Czech beer (daily 10:00-24:00, Schrankgasse 4, tel. 01/526-1215).

$$ Glacis Beisl, at the top edge of the MuseumsQuartier just before Spittelberg, is popular with locals. A gravelly wine garden tucked next to a city fortification, its outdoor tables and breezy ambience are particularly appealing on a balmy evening (weekday lunch specials, reservations smart, daily 11:00-24:00, Breitegasse 4, tel. 01/526-5660, www.glacisbeisl.at).

Mariahilfer Strasse and the Naschmarkt

Mariahilfer Strasse (see map on page 172) is filled with reasonable cafés serving all types of cuisine.

$$ Trześniewski's sandwich bar is *the* place for a quick yet traditional bite. Consider the branch at Mariahilfer Strasse 95 (see the Trześniewski listing earlier in this chapter for ordering tips), or its imitators (one is at #91).

$ Schnitzelwirt is an old classic with a 1950s patina and a mixed local and tourist clientele. In this working-class place, no one finishes their schnitzel (notice the self-serve butcher paper and plastic bags for leftovers). Walking to the back, you pass the kitchen piled high with breaded cutlets waiting for the deep fryer. The schnitzels are served with a starch or salad; if you order the smallest portion, you may want to add a side dish. They also serve Austrian standards including *Szegediner Gulasch* (Mon-Sat 11:00-21:30, closed Sun, Neubaugasse 52, U: Neubaugasse, tel. 01/523-3771).

Supermarket: Look for the big **Merkur** in the basement of the Gerngross shopping mall at Mariahilfer Strasse 42 (Mon-Fri until 20:00, Sat until 18:00, closed Sun, U: Neubaugasse).

Naschmarkt: For a picnic or a trendy dinner, try the Naschmarkt, Vienna's sprawling produce market. This thriving Old World scene comes with plenty of fresh produce, cheap local-style eateries, cafés, kebab and sausage stands, and the best-value sushi in town (market open Mon-Fri 6:00-19:30, Sat until 18:00, closed Sun, closes earlier in winter; restaurants open later; U: Karlsplatz, follow *Karlsplatz* signs out of the station). Picnickers can buy supplies at the market and eat on nearby Karlsplatz (plenty of chairs facing the Karlskirche) or pop into the nearby Burggarten, behind the famous Mozart statue.

In recent years, the Naschmarkt has become fashionable for dinner (or cocktails), with an amazing variety of local and ethnic eateries to choose from. Prices are great, the produce is certainly fresh, and the dinners are as local as can be. The best plan: Stroll through the entire market to survey the options, and then pick the place that appeals. For more on the Naschmarkt, see page 63.

VIENNA'S CAFÉ CULTURE

In Vienna, the living room is down the street at the neighborhood coffeehouse. This tradition is just another example of the Viennese expertise in good living.

Each of Vienna's many long-established (and sometimes even legendary) coffeehouses has its individual character (and characters). These classic cafés can be a bit tired, with a shabby patina and famously grumpy waiters who treat you like an uninvited guest invading their living room. Yet these spaces somehow also feel welcoming, offering newspapers, pastries, sofas, quick and light workers' lunches, elegant ambience, and "take all the time you want" charm for the price of a cup of coffee. Rather than read the news on your mobile device, relax with a cup of coffee and read an actual newspaper, Vienna-style, in a café.

Café Tips: Once you claim a table or sofa in a café, make a trip to the glass display case to see the pastries of the day. The menu has all the standard offerings, but won't list the specials.

It's standard practice for your coffee to be served on a little silver tray, with a glass of tap water and perhaps a piece of chocolate on the side. For coffee-ordering lingo, see the Practicalities chapter.

Cafés in the Old Center

These are some of my favorite Viennese cafés located inside the Ring (see the "Restaurants in Central Vienna" map, earlier).

$$ Café Central is overrun with tourists. Still, it remains a classic place: lavish under Neo-Gothic columns, celebrated by 19th-century Austrian writers, and featuring live piano entertainment—schmaltzy tunes on a fine, Vienna-made Bösendorfer each evening from 17:00 to 22:00 (daily 7:30-22:00, Sun from 10:00, corner of Herrengasse and Strauchgasse, U: Herrengasse, tel. 01/533-3764).

$ Café Bräunerhof, between the Hofburg and the Graben, offers traditional ambience with few tourists and live music on weekends (Sat-Sun 15:00-18:00), along with cheap lunches on weekdays (Mon-Fri 8:00-19:30, Sat 8:00-18:00, Sun 10:00-18:00, no hot food after 15:00, Stallburggasse 2, U: Stephansplatz, tel. 01/512-3893).

$ Café Hawelka has a dark, "brooding Trotsky" atmosphere, paintings by struggling artists who couldn't pay for coffee, a saloon-wood flavor, chalkboard menu, smoked velvet couches, an international selection of newspapers, and a phone that rings for regulars. Frau Hawelka died just a couple weeks after Pope John Paul II did. Locals suspect the pontiff wanted her much-loved *Buchteln* (marmalade-filled doughnuts) in heaven. The café, which doesn't serve hot food, remains family-run (daily 8:00-24:00, just off the Graben at Dorotheergasse 6, U: Stephansplatz, tel. 01/512-8230).

Other Classics in the Old Center: All of these places are open long hours daily: **$$ Café Diglas** (good lunches, piano

Viennese Coffee:
From Ottomans to Starbucks

The story of coffee in Vienna is steeped in legend. In the 17th century, the Ottomans (invaders from the Turkish Empire) were laying siege to Vienna. A spy working for the Austrians who infiltrated the Ottoman ranks got to know the Turkish life-style...including their passion for a drug called coffee. After the Austrians persevered, the ecstatic Habsburg emperor offered the spy anything he wanted. The spy asked for the Ottomans' spilled coffee beans, which he gathered up to start the first coffee shop in town. (It's a nice story. But actually, there was already an Armenian in town running a coffeehouse.)

In the 18th century, coffee boomed as an aristocratic drink. In the 19th-century Industrial Age, people were expected to work 12-hour shifts, and coffee became a hit with the working class, too. By the 20th century, the Vienna coffee scene became so refined that old-timers remember when waiters brought a sheet with various shades of brown (like paint samples) so customers could make clear exactly how milky they wanted their coffee.

In 2003, Vienna's first Starbucks boldly opened next to the opera house—across the street from the ultimate Old World coffeehouse, the Café Sacher. The locals like the easy-chair ambience and quality of Starbucks coffee, but think it's overpriced. Viennese coffee connoisseurs aren't impressed by quantity, can't relate to flavored coffee, and think drinking out of a paper cup is really trashy. The consensus: For the same price, you can have an elegant and traditional experience in an independent, Vienna-style coffee shop instead. While the "coffee-to-go" trend has been picked up by many bakeries and other joints, the Starbucks invasion has stalled, with about half as many outlets as the 27 the Seattle-based coffee empire had planned to open.

nightly, 2 blocks behind St. Stephen's Cathedral at Wollzeile 10); **$ Café Pruckel** (at Dr.-Karl-Lueger-Platz, across from Stadtpark at Stubenring 24); **$ Café Tirolerhof** (2 blocks from the opera house, behind the TI on Tegetthoffstrasse, at Führichgasse 8); and **$ Café Landtmann** (directly across from the City Hall on the Ringstrasse at Universitätsring 4). The Landtmann is unique, as it's the only grand café built along the Ring with all the other grand buildings.

Near the Naschmarkt

$$ Café Sperl dates from 1880 and is still furnished identically to the day it opened—from the coat tree to the chairs (Mon-Sat 7:00-22:00, Sun 11:00-20:00 except closed in July-Aug, near the

Naschmarkt at Gumpendorfer Strasse 11, U: MuseumsQuartier, tel. 01/586-4158; see map in the Sleeping in Vienna chapter).

WEIN IN WIEN: VIENNA'S WINE GARDENS

The *Heuriger* (HOY-rih-gur) is unique to Vienna, dating back to the 1780s, when Emperor Josef II decreed that vintners needed no special license to serve their own wines and juices to the public in their own homes. Many families grabbed this opportunity and opened *Heurigen* (HOY-rih-gehn)—wine-garden restaurants. (The name comes from the fact that they served *heurig*—

new—wine from the most recent vintage.)

A tradition was born. Today, *Heurigen* are licensed, but do their best to maintain the old-village atmosphere, serving each fall's vintage until November 11 of the following year, when a new vintage year begins. To go with your wine, a *Heuriger* serves a variety of prepared foods that you choose from a deli counter. This is the most intimidating part of the *Heuriger* experience for tourists, but it's easily conquered—see the sidebar for tips. Some *Heurigen* compromise by offering a regular menu that you can order from. At many establishments, strolling musicians entertain—and ask for tips.

Most *Heurigen* are decorated with enormous antique presses from their vineyards. Some places even have play zones for kids. The experience is best in good weather, but you can eat indoors, too.

Hours: Most *Heurigen* open up in the afternoon (generally between 14:00 and 16:00) and close late (about 24:00), though some may stop serving food earlier (around 21:00). Some *Heurigen* may close in winter, during the grape-picking season, or just for vacation, so call or check websites if you have a specific place in mind.

Getting There: I've listed two good *Heuriger* neighborhoods on the northern outskirts of town (see the "Greater Vienna" map in the Orientation to Vienna chapter). To get here from downtown Vienna, it's best to use public transit (cheap, 30 minutes, runs late in the evening, find specific directions under each section). You can also take a 15-minute taxi ride (about €20 from the Ring).

Choosing a Place: With more than 1,700 acres of vineyards within Vienna's city limits, there are countless *Heuriger* taverns. Decide on a neighborhood, then scope out a spot that suits you. The ambience at any single *Heuriger* can change depending on that eve-

EATING

The *Heuriger* Experience

To understand how a traditional *Heuriger* works, think of a full-service deli counter at an American supermarket, with a seating section nearby. Choose from the array of prepared items and hot dishes, pay at the buffet counter, and find a table. Then order (and pay for) your wine or other drinks from the waiter who will appear at your table. (That said, many of the *Heurigen* I've listed have regular menus and table service as well.)

A quarter-liter (*Viertel,* FEER-tehl, 8 oz) glass of new wine costs about €2-3. *Most* (mohst) is lightly alcoholic grape juice—wine in its earliest stages, and usually available only in autumn. Once it gets a little more oomph, it's called *Sturm* (shtoorm), also strictly a fall drink—sometimes only during the narrow *"Sturmzeit"* window (late Sept-mid-Oct). Teetotalers can order *Traubenmost* (TROW-behn-mohst), grape juice. For more on Austrian wines, see the Practicalities chapter.

Food is generally sold by weight, often in *"10 dag"* units (that's 100 grams, or about a quarter-pound). The buffet has several sections: The core of your meal is a warm dish, generally meat (such as ham, roast beef, roast chicken, roulade, or meatloaf) carved off a big hunk. There are also warm sides *(Beilagen),* such as casseroles and sauerkraut, and a wide variety of cold salads and spreads. Rounding out the menu are bread and cheese (they'll slice it off for you).

Many *Heuriger* staff speak English, and pointing also works. Here's a menu decoder of items to look for...or to avoid (for more food terms, see the Practicalities chapter):

ning's clientele (locals, tour groups, workplace parties, birthdays). Each neighborhood I've described is a square or hub with two or three recommended spots and many other wine gardens worth considering. Wander around, then choose the *Heuriger* with the best atmosphere. Or ask a local—every Viennese will be only too glad to tell you about their favorite. (And for a near-*Heuriger* experience without leaving downtown Vienna, drop by Gigerl Stadtheuriger, described earlier in this chapter, which has the same deli-counter system as a *Heuriger,* but not the semirural atmosphere.)

Backhühner: Roasted chicken

Blutwurst or *Blunzn:* Blood sausage

Bohnen: Big white beans

Bratlfett: Gelatinous jelly made from fat drippings

Erdapfel: Potato

Fleckerl: Noodles

Fleischlaberln: Fried ground-meat patties

Kernöl: Vegetable oil

Knoblauch: Garlic

Knödl: Dumpling

Kornspitz: Whole-meal bread roll

Krapfen: Doughnut

Kren: Horseradish

Kummelbraten: Crispy roast pork with caraway

Lauch: Leek

Leberkäse: Finely ground corned beef, pork, bacon, and onions that's baked as a loaf

Liptauer: Spicy cheese spread

Presskopf: Jellied brains and innards

Roastbeef: Roast beef

Schinken: Ham

Schinkenfleckerln: Ham and noodle casserole

Schmalz: Spread made from rendered pig or goose fat

Spanferkel: Suckling pig

Speck: Fatty bacon

Specklinsen: Lentils with bacon

Stelze: Grilled knuckle of pork

Sulz: Gelatinous brick of meaty goo

Waldbauernflade: Rustic bread

Zwiebel: Onion

EATING

Neustift am Walde

This district is farthest from the city but is still easy to reach by public transit. It feels a little less touristy than other places and is the only area I list where you'll actually see the vineyards.

Getting There: Take the U-6 subway to Nussdorfer Strasse, then ride bus #35A (direction: Salmannsdorf, roughly 18 minutes, leaves from stop across the street from north side of the U-Bahn station). For Weinhof Zimmerman, get off at the Agnesgasse stop; for the other two, use the Neustift am Walde stop.

$$ Weinhof Zimmermann, a 10-minute uphill walk from

the bus stop, is my favorite. It's a sprawling farmhouse where the green tables on patios echo the terraced fields all around. While dining, you'll feel like you're actually right in the vineyard. The idyllic setting comes with rabbits in petting cages, great food, fine hillside vistas, and a coziness unmatched by the other *Heurigen* mentioned here (opens at 15:00, closed Mon, tel. 01/440-1207). From the Agnesgasse stop, hike a block uphill and turn left on Mitterwurzergasse to #20.

$$ Das Schreiberhaus Heurigen-Restaurant is a popular, family-owned place right at the bus stop. Its creaky, old-time dining rooms are papered with celebrity photos. There are 600 spaces inside and another 600 outside, music nightly after 19:00 unless it's slow, and a cobbled backyard that climbs in steps up to the vineyards. Alone among my listings, this place offers a cheap all-you-can-eat lunch buffet on weekdays until 14:00 (opens at 12:00, Rathstrasse 54, tel. 01/440-3844).

$$ Fuhrgassl Huber, which brags it's the biggest *Heuriger* in Vienna, can accommodate 1,000 people inside and just as many outside. You can lose yourself in its sprawling backyard, with vineyards streaking up the hill from terraced tables. Musicians stroll most nights after 19:00 (opens at 14:00, a few steps past Das Schreiberhaus at Neustift am Walde 68, tel. 01/440-1405, family Huber).

Nussdorf

An untouristy district, characteristic and popular with the Viennese, Nussdorf has plenty of *Heuriger* ambience. This area feels very real, with a working-class vibe, streets lined with local shops, and characteristic *Heurigen* that feel a little bit rougher around the edges.

Getting There: Take tram #D from the Ringstrasse (stops include the Opera, Hofburg/Kunsthistorisches Museum, and City Hall) to its endpoint, the Beethovengang stop (despite what it says on the front of the tram, the Nussdorf stop isn't the end—stay on for one more stop). Exit the tram, cross the tracks, go uphill 40 yards, and look for Schübel-Auer and Kierlinger on your right.

$ Schübel-Auer Heuriger is my favorite here, with a peaceful leafy garden and a rustic interior. The buffet is big and user-friendly—most dishes are labeled and the patient staff speak English (opens at 16:00, closed Sun-Mon and mid-Oct-mid-March, Kahlenberger Strasse 22, tel. 01/370-2222).

$ Heuriger Kierlinger, next door, is also good, with a particularly rollicking, woody room around its buffet and a courtyard shaded with chestnut trees (opens at 15:30, closed most of August and periodically in off-season, Kahlenberger Strasse 20, tel. 01/370-2264).

ENTERTAINMENT IN VIENNA

Vienna—the birthplace of what we call classical music—still thrives as Europe's music capital. On any given evening, you'll have your choice of opera, Strauss waltzes, Mozart chamber concerts, and lighthearted musicals. The Vienna Boys' Choir lives up to its worldwide reputation.

Besides music, you can spend an evening enjoying art, watching a classic film, or sipping Viennese wine in a village wine garden. Save some energy for Vienna after dark.

Music

As far back as the 12th century, Vienna was a mecca for musicians—both sacred and secular (troubadours). The Habsburg emperors of the 17th and 18th centuries were not only generous supporters of music, but fine musicians and composers themselves. (Maria Theresa played a mean double bass.) Composers such as Haydn, Mozart, Beethoven, Schubert, and Brahms gravitated to this music-friendly environment. They taught each other, jammed together, and spent a lot of time in Habsburg palaces. Beethoven was a famous figure, walking—lost in musical thought—through the Vienna Woods. In the city's 19th-century belle époque, "Waltz King" Johann Strauss and his brothers kept Vienna's 300 ballrooms spinning.

This musical tradition continues into modern times, leaving many prestigious Viennese institutions for today's tourists to enjoy: the Vienna State Opera, the Boys' Choir, and the great Baroque halls and churches, all busy with classical and waltz concerts. As you poke into churches and palaces, you may hear groups practicing. You're welcome to sit and listen.

ENTERTAINMENT

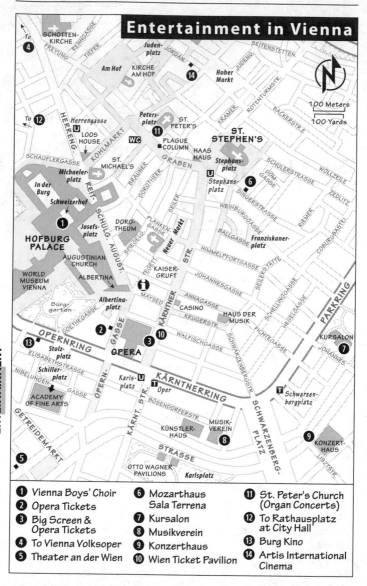

Entertainment in Vienna

1. Vienna Boys' Choir
2. Opera Tickets
3. Big Screen & Opera Tickets
4. To Vienna Volksoper
5. Theater an der Wien
6. Mozarthaus Sala Terrena
7. Kursalon
8. Musikverein
9. Konzerthaus
10. Wien Ticket Pavilion
11. St. Peter's Church (Organ Concerts)
12. To Rathausplatz at City Hall
13. Burg Kino
14. Artis International Cinema

In Vienna, it's music *con brio* from September through June, reaching a symphonic climax during the Vienna Festival each May and June. Sadly, in summer (generally July and August), the Boys' Choir, opera, and many other serious music companies are—like you—on vacation. But it's OK: Vienna hums year-round with live classical music and tickets to touristy, crowd-pleasing shows are always available.

For music lovers, Vienna is also an opportunity to make pilgrimages to the homes (now mostly small museums) of favorite composers. If you're a fan of Schubert, Brahms, Haydn, Beethoven, or Mozart, there's a sight for you. But I find these homes inconveniently located and generally underwhelming. The centrally located Haus der Musik (see the Sights in Vienna chapter) is my favorite setting for celebrating the great musicians and composers who called Vienna home.

Venues: Vienna remains the music capital of Europe, with 10,000 seats in various venues around town mostly booked with classical performances. The best-known entertainment venues are the Staatsoper (State Opera House), the Volksoper (for musicals and operettas), the Theater an der Wien (opera and other performances), the Wiener Musikverein (home of the Vienna Philharmonic Orchestra), and the Wiener Konzerthaus (various events). Schedules for these venues are listed in the monthly *Wien-Programm* (available at TI, described in the Orientation to Vienna chapter). You can also check event listings at www.viennaconcerts.com.

Buying Tickets: Most tickets run from €45 to €60 (plus a stiff booking fee when purchased in advance by phone or online, or through a box office like the one at the TI). A few venues charge as little as €30; look around if you're not set on any particular concert. While it's easy to book tickets online long in advance, spontaneity is also workable, as there are invariably people selling their extra tickets at face value or less outside the door before concert time. If you call a concert hall directly, they can advise you on the availability of (cheaper) tickets at the door. Vienna takes care of its starving artists (and tourists) by offering cheap standing-room tickets to top-notch music and opera (generally an hour before each performance).

Classical Music to Go: To bring home Beethoven, Strauss, or the Wiener Philharmonic on a top-quality CD, shop at Gramola on the Graben or EMI on Kärntner Strasse. The Arcadia shop at the Vienna State Opera is also good.

Vienna Boys' Choir (Wiener Sängerknaben)

The boys sing (from a high balcony, heard but not seen) at the 9:15 Sunday Mass from mid-September through June in the Hofburg's **Imperial Music Chapel** (Hofmusikkapelle). The entrance is at Schweizerhof; you can get there from In der Burg square or go through the tunnel from Josefsplatz.

Reserved seats must be booked in advance (€10-36; reserve by sending an email to office@hofmusikkapelle.gv.at; call 01/533-9927 for information only—they can't book tickets at this number; www.hofmusikkapelle.gv.at).

Free (and Nearly Free) Music

While there are lots of ways to spend lots of money enjoying concerts in Europe's music capital, there are also a number of free or low-cost options. Check out these venues for their live or filmed musical offerings:

Opera House: The venerable Vienna State Opera offers hundreds of nearly free standing-room spots for its performances (Sept-June) as well as showing live performances for free (spring and fall) on a giant screen outside the building. See next page.

Rathausplatz at City Hall: Filmed classical and modern concerts are shown on a massive screen in a lively atmosphere throughout the summer. See "Open Air Music-Film Series and Food Circus," later in this chapter.

St. Peter's Church: Free organ concerts are performed daily at 15:00. See page 51.

Augustinian Church at the Hofburg: A live orchestra performs during Mass each Sunday morning for worshippers. See page 40.

Imperial Music Chapel at the Hofburg: Listen to the iconic Vienna Boys' Choir live (though you won't actually see them) in the lobby of their church each Sunday morning in season. See the "Vienna Boys' Choir" listing in this chapter.

Haus der Musik: A ticket to this museum covers entry to a mini concert hall on the first floor, where video highlights of the Vienna Philharmonic's much-loved New Year's Eve concert are played in a loop on a big screen. See page 49.

ENTERTAINMENT

Much easier, standing room inside is free and open to the first 60 who line up. Even better, rather than line up early, you can simply swing by and stand in the narthex just outside, where you can hear the boys and see the Mass on a TV monitor.

The Boys' Choir also performs at the **MuTh** concert hall on Fridays at 17:30 in September and October (€40-90, Am Augartenspitz 1 in Augarten park, U: Taborstrasse, tel. 01/347-8080, www.muth.at, tickets@muth.at).

They're talented kids, but, for my taste, not worth all the commotion. Remember, many churches have great music during Sunday Mass. Just 200 yards from the Hofburg's Boys' Choir chapel, the Augustinian Church has a glorious 11:00 service each Sunday (which generally features its wonderful organ, a choir, and a small orchestra; see listing in the Sights in Vienna chapter).

Opera

Vienna State Opera (Wiener Staatsoper)

The Vienna State Opera puts on 300 performances a year, featuring the "Orchestra of the Opera" in the pit. (Any musician aspiring to join the Vienna Philharmonic Orchestra must put in two years here before even being considered.) In July and August the singers are on summer break (as government employees, they get a nice vacation). Since there are different operas nearly nightly, you'll see big trucks out back and constant action backstage—all the sets need to be switched each day. Even though the expensive seats normally sell out long in advance, the opera is perpetually in the red and subsidized by the state, so affordable seats are often available. The excellent "electronic libretto" translation screens help make the experience worthwhile for opera newbies. (Press the button to turn yours on; press again for English.)

Opera Tickets: Main-floor seats go for €120-240; bargain hunters get limited-view seats for €13-30. You can book tickets in advance online (www.wiener-staatsoper.at). In person, head to one of the opera's two box offices: on the west side of the building (across Operngasse and facing the opera house), or the smaller one just under the big screen on the east side of the opera (facing Kärntner Strasse; both offices open Mon-Fri 9:00 until two hours before each performance, Sat 9:00-12:00, closed Sun).

Standing-Room Tickets: Unless Placido Domingo is in town, it's easy to get one of 567 standing-room tickets (*Stehplätze*, €3 up top or €4 downstairs, can purchase one ticket/person). While the front doors open one hour before the show starts, a side door (middle of building, on the Operngasse side) opens 80 minutes before curtain time, giving those in the know an early grab at standing-room tickets. Just walk straight in, then head right until you see the ticket booth marked *Stehplätze*. If fewer than 567 people are in line, there's no need to line up early. If you're one of the first 160 in line, try for the €4 "Parterre" section and you'll end up dead-center at stage level, directly under the Emperor's Box. Otherwise, you can choose between the third floor *(Balkon)*, or the fourth floor *(Galerie)*, though regulars prefer these sections because each ticket holder gets a section of railing along with a digital screen to read

ENTERTAINMENT

the libretto. While most will not want to stand through the entire performance, there are some spots that offer a wall for leaning.

Dress is casual (but do your best) at the standing-room bar. Locals save their spot along the rail by tying a scarf to it. Once you've saved your spot with your scarf, you can then walk around and explore the amazing building.

Unfortunately, if you buy a ticket but show up after the performance has started, you may be forced to watch it on a closed-circuit TV instead.

Rick's Crude Tip: For me, three hours is a lot of opera. But just to see and hear Vienna's opera in action for a half-hour is a treat. And if you go, you'll get the added entertainment of seeing Vienna all dressed up. I'd buy a standing-room ticket and plan to just watch the first part of the show. Before cutting out, have a glass of champagne at the opera's most glamorous bar (on the first floor, center front).

"Live Opera on the Square": Demonstrating its commitment to bringing opera to the masses, each spring and fall the Vienna State Opera projects several performances live on a huge screen on its building, puts out chairs for the public to enjoy...and it's all free. (These projected performances are noted as *Oper Live am Platz* in the official opera schedule—posted all around the opera building; they are also listed in the *Wien-Programm* brochure and at www.wiener-staatsoper.at.)

Vienna Volksoper

For less-serious operettas and musicals, try Vienna's other opera house, located along the Gürtel, west of the city center (see *Wien-Programm* brochure or ask at TI for schedule, Währinger Strasse 78, tel. 01/5144-43670, www.volksoper.at).

Theater an der Wien

Considered the oldest theater in Vienna, this venue was designed in 1801 for Mozart operas—intimate, with just a thousand seats. It treats Vienna's music lovers to a different opera every month (except summer)—generally Mozart with a contemporary setting and modern interpretation (facing the Naschmarkt at Linke Wienzeile 6, tel. 01/58885, www.theater-wien.at).

Touristy Mozart and Strauss Concerts

If the music comes to you, it's touristy—designed for flash-in-the-pan Mozart fans. Powdered-wig orchestra performances are given almost nightly in grand traditional settings (€30-60). Pesky wigged-and-powdered Mozarts peddle tickets in the streets (earning a commission of about €10 per ticket). They rave about the quality of the musicians, but you'll get second-rate chamber orchestras, clad in historic costumes, performing the greatest hits of

ENTERTAINMENT

Mozart and Strauss. (The musicians are usually quite good—often Hungarians, Poles, and Russians working a season here to fund music studies back home—but often haven't performed much together, so aren't "tight.") These are casual, easygoing concerts with lots of tour groups attending. While there's not a Viennese person in the audience, the tourists generally enjoy the evening.

To sort through your options, check with the ticket office in the TI (same price as on the street, but with all venues to choose from). Savvy locals suggest getting the cheapest tickets, as no one seems to care if cheapskates move up to fill unsold pricier seats.

Mozarthaus Concert Venue

Of the many fine venues in Vienna, the Sala Terrena at Mozarthaus might be my favorite. Intimate chamber-music concerts with musicians in historic costume take place in a small room richly decorated in Venetian Renaissance style (€49-59, Thu-Fri and Sun at 19:30, Sat at 18:00, near St. Stephen's Cathedral at Singerstrasse 7, tel. 01/911-9077, www.mozarthaus.at). Don't confuse this with the Mozarthaus Vienna Museum on Domgasse, which also holds concerts.

Strauss and Mozart Concerts in the Kursalon

For years, Strauss and Mozart concerts have been held in the Kursalon, the hall where the "Waltz King" himself directed wild-

ly popular concerts 100 years ago (€45-69, concerts generally nightly at 20:15, Johannesgasse 33 at corner of Parkring, tram #2: Weihburggasse or U: Stadtpark, tel. 01/512-5790 to check on availability—generally no problem to reserve—or buy online at www.soundofvienna.at). Shows last two hours and are a mix of ballet, waltzes, and a 15-piece orchestra. It's touristy—tour guides holding up banners with group numbers wait out front after the show. Even so, the performance is playful, visually fun, fine quality for most, and with a tried-and-tested, crowd-pleasing format. The conductor welcomes the crowd in German (with a wink) and English; after that...it's English only.

Musicals
The Wien Ticket pavilion next to the opera house (near Kärntner Strasse) sells tickets to contemporary American and British musicals performed in German with English subtitles (€50-110). Same-day tickets are sometimes available at a discount directly from the theater from 14:00 until 18:00 (ticket pavilion open daily 10:00-19:00). Or you can reserve (full-price) tickets for the musicals by phone or online (tel. 01/58885, line answered daily 8:00-20:00, www.wien-ticket.at).

Nightlife

If powdered wigs and opera singers in Viking helmets aren't your thing, Vienna has plenty of alternatives.

The Evening Scene
Vienna is a great place to just be out and about on a balmy evening. While tourists are attracted to the historic central district and its charming, floodlit corners, locals go elsewhere. Depending on your mood and taste, you can join them. Survey and then enjoy lively scenes with bars, cafés, trendy restaurants, and theaters in these areas: **Donaukanal** (the Danube Canal, especially popular in the summer for its imported beaches); **Naschmarkt** (after the produce stalls close up, the bars and eateries bring new life to the place through the evening); **MuseumsQuartier** (surrounded by far-out museums, a young scene of bars with local students filling the courtyard); and **City Hall** (on the parklike Rathausplatz, where in summer free concerts and a food circus of eateries attract huge local crowds—described next).

Open-Air Music-Film Series and Food Circus
A convivial, free-to-everyone people scene erupts each evening in summer (July-Aug) on Rathausplatz, the welcoming park in front of City Hall (right on the Ring-strasse). Thousands of people keep a food circus of simple stalls busy. There's not a plastic cup anywhere, just real plates and glasses—Vienna wants the quality of eating to be as high as the music that's about to begin. And most stalls are outposts of local restaurants—including some of Vienna's most esteemed—

ENTERTAINMENT

Sightseeing After Dark

Every night in Vienna some sights stay open late. Here's the scoop from Monday through Sunday (for details, see listings in the Sights in Vienna chapter):

St. Stephen's Cathedral: Nightly until 22:00 (but main nave closes earlier).

Haus der Musik: Nightly until 22:00.

Museum of Applied Arts (MAK): Tue until 22:00.

Albertina Museum: Wed and Fri until 21:00.

Natural History Museum: Wed until 21:00.

Kunsthistorisches Museum: Thu until 21:00.

Leopold Museum: Thu until 21:00.

Museum of Modern Art (MUMOK): Thu until 21:00.

Belvedere Palace: Fri until 21:00.

World Museum Vienna: Fri until 21:00.

Other late-night activities include going to an opera or concert (see "Music," earlier in this chapter); a free, open-air summer music-film series outside City Hall (see previous page); or a fun outing at the Prater amusement park (see page 78). Also remember that Vienna's coffee shops and wine gardens are generally open late. Get details in the Eating in Vienna chapter.

ENTERTAINMENT

making this a fun and easy way to sample some of the city's most interesting options. About 2,000 spots on comfy benches face a 60-foot-wide screen up against the City Hall's Neo-Gothic facade. When darkness falls, an announcer explains the program, and then the music starts. The program is different every night so check the website—mostly films of opera and classical concerts, but with some jazz and R&B too (www.filmfestival-rathausplatz.at, programs generally last about 2 hours, starting when it's dark—between 21:30 in July and 20:30 in Aug).

Since 1991, the city has paid for 60 of these summer event nights each year. Why? To promote culture. Officials know that the music-film series is mostly a "meat market" where young people come to hook up. But they believe many of these people will develop a little appreciation of classical music and high culture on the side.

Balls and Waltzing

Renowned for its ball scene, Vienna boasts hundreds of balls each year, where the classic dance is the waltz. The height of ball season falls generally between December and February, when Viennese and visitors of all ages dress up and swirl to music ranging from waltzes to jazz to contemporary beats. Balls are put on by the

Vienna Philharmonic, Vienna Boys' Choir, Vienna State Opera, and others (search for events at www.events.wien.info). The glamorous **Hofburg Silvesterball** takes place on New Year's Eve at the Hofburg Palace, featuring big-name orchestras, bands, and opera singers, a sumptuous dinner, and champagne toast (www.hofburgsilvesterball.com).

Heurigen

Viennese wine gardens, called *Heurigen*, are a great way to enjoy new wine, a light meal, and a festive local atmosphere. Eat and drink in intimate taverns or leafy courtyards, surrounded by antique wine presses, friendly *Wieners*, strolling musicians, and fellow tourists. Most gardens are located on the outskirts of town—in the legendary Vienna Woods—but they're easy to reach by tram, bus, or taxi. For more on the *Heurigen*, including recommendations and transportation information, see the Eating in Vienna chapter.

English Cinema

Several great theaters offer three or four screens of English movies nightly (€6-9). **Burg Kino,** a block from the opera house, facing the Ring (see below), tapes its weekly schedule to the door—box office opens 30 minutes before each showing. **English Cinema Haydn** is near my recommended hotels on Mariahilfer Strasse (Mariahilfer Strasse 57, tel. 01/587-2262, www.haydnkino.at), and **Artis International Cinema** is right in the town center a few minutes from the cathedral (Schultergasse 5, tel. 01/535-6570).

The Third Man at Burg Kino

This movie is set in 1949 Vienna—when it was divided, like Berlin, between the four victorious Allies. Reliving the cinematic tale of a divided city about to fall under Soviet rule and rife with smuggling is an enjoyable two-hour experience while in Vienna (€7-9, in English; about 3 showings weekly—usually Sun afternoon, Fri evening, and Tue early evening; Opernring 19, tel. 01/587-8406, www.burgkino.at). For more on *The Third Man* (and the museum of the same name), see page 68.

VIENNA CONNECTIONS

This chapter covers Vienna's major train stations and its airport, and includes tips for connections to/from Vienna by car, bus, and boat.

By Train

Vienna has an impressive new Hauptbahnhof (main train station), and is consolidating most—but not all—train departures there. Be sure to confirm which station your train uses. From Vienna's two biggest stations, the handiest connection to the center is the U-Bahn (subway); line numbers are noted later. For some stations, there's also a handy tram connection. (See the "Vienna's Public Transportation" color map at the beginning of this book.)

For schedules, check Germany's excellent all-Europe timetable at www.bahn.com. The Austrian federal railway's timetable at www.oebb.at includes prices, but it's not as user-friendly as the German site—and it doesn't always remind you about discounts or special passes. For general train information in Austria, call 051-717 (to get an operator, dial 2, then 2). For information on types of trains, schedules, passes, and tickets, see the "Transportation" section in the Practicalities chapter.

WIEN HAUPTBAHNHOF

Vienna's huge central station (just a few U-Bahn stops south of downtown) has 12 pass-through tracks, shopping, and all the services you may need—including baggage lockers, a TI desk (daily 9:00-19:00), *Reisezentrum* (long hours daily), food court (some outlets open very late), restaurants (including outposts of the recommended Oberlaa pastry shop and Akakiko Sushi), ATMs, grocery stores (some open daily until late), drugstores, bookstores, mobile-phone shops, a car-rental desk (Europcar), bike-rental shop, and a post office. Most shops are open Mon-Fri until 21:00, Sat until 18:00, and (unlike in the city center) many are open on Sunday.

Getting Between the Station and Vienna: To reach the city center, including all my recommended hotels in the center, ride the U-1 for two to four stops (direction: Leopoldau) to Karlsplatz, Stephansplatz, or Schwedenplatz—from the main hall follow the red *U1* signs; ticket machines are near the escalators. You can also take tram #D (which runs along the Ring) from outside the main entrance. To reach Mariahilfer Strasse, ride U-1 three stops to Stephansplatz, then change to U-3 (direction: Ottaring), or hop on bus #13A. Tram #O runs from the station to Landstrasse and the Wien-Mitte station (for airport trains).

The private **Westbahn** train (www.westbahn.at), which connects Vienna and Salzburg, also leaves from here and offers an alternative to the state-run ÖBB trains. For purchase on short notice, Westbahn's regular fares are half those of ÖBB, with the option to buy your ticket on board at no extra charge.

When timing any train trip out of Vienna, keep in mind that the U-Bahn stop is a bit of a walk from the main train platforms—allow at least 10 minutes to get from the U-Bahn stop to your train.

WESTBAHNHOF

This station (at the west end of Mariahilfer Strasse, on the U-3 and U-6 lines) has a bright, user-friendly mall of services, shops, and eateries (including the recommended Trześniewski—near track 9—with cheap-and-elegant finger sandwiches). You'll find a ticket office (daily 6:00-20:00), travel agencies, grocery stores, ATMs, a post office, and baggage lockers (on the ground floor by the WC). The private **Westbahn** railroad (www.westbahn.at) also serves this station.

Getting Between the Station and Vienna: For the city center, follow orange signs to the U-3 (direction: Simmering). If your hotel is along Mariahilfer Strasse, your stop is on this line, but it may be simpler to walk.

FRANZ-JOSEFS-BAHNHOF

This small station (see map on page 22) in the northern part of the city serves **Krems** and other points on the **north bank of the Danube.** Connections from **Český Krumlov** in the Czech Republic sometimes arrive here, too.

Getting Between the Station and Vienna: There's no U-Bahn stop at the station, but convenient tram #D connects it to the city center. Also note that trains coming into town from this direction stop at the Spittelau station (on the U-4 and U-6 lines), one stop before they end at the Franz-Josefs-Bahnhof; consider hopping off your train at Spittelau for a handy connection to other points in Vienna. (Similarly, if you're headed out of town and you're not near the tram #D route, take the U-Bahn to Spittelau and catch your train there.)

WIEN-MITTE BAHNHOF

This smaller station, just east of the Ring, is the terminus for S-Bahn and CAT trains to the airport and sits below a busy shopping mall. Be aware that its U-Bahn station is called **"Landstrasse."** From here, take the U-3 to hotels near Stephansplatz or Mariahilfer Strasse, and the U-4 to hotels that are closer to the airport. It's also connected directly to the Hauptbahnhof by tram #O.

TRAIN CONNECTIONS

Before leaving your hotel, confirm which station your train leaves from.

From Vienna by Train to: Melk (2/hour, 1 hour, some with change in St. Pölten, some direct trains from Westbahnhof), **Krems** (at least hourly, about 1 hour), **Mauthausen** (roughly hourly, 2 hours, change in St. Valentin or Linz), **Bratislava** (2/hour, 1 hour, alternating between Bratislava's main station and Petržalka station, or try going by bus or boat; described at the end of the Bratislava chapter), **Salzburg** (3/hour, 3 hours), **Hallstatt** (at least hourly, 4 hours, last connection leaves around 15:00, change in Attnang-Puchheim), **Innsbruck** (at least hourly, 4.5 hours), **Budapest** (nearly hourly direct, 2.5 hours, more with transfers; cheaper by bus: hourly, 3 hours, www.flixbus.com), **Prague** (7/day direct, 4 hours; more with change; night train, 6 hours), **Český Krumlov** (5/day with 2 changes, 5 hours), **Munich** (7/day direct, 4 hours; otherwise about hourly, 4.5 hours, transfer in Salzburg), **Berlin** (1/day direct, 8 hours; 6/day with change at Nürnberg or Prague, 8.5 hours), **Dresden** (4/day with 1 change, 7.5 hours), **Zürich** (5/day direct, 8 hours; nearly hourly with 1-2 changes, 9 hours; night train, 9 hours), **Ljubljana** (1/day direct, 6 hours; 4/day with change in Villach, 6.5 hours), **Zagreb** (4/day, 7-9 hours, 1 direct, others with 1-3 changes), **Kraków** (3/day, 6-7 hours with 1-2 changes; night train, 8 hours), **Warsaw** (3/day, including 2 direct, 7 hours; night train, 8 hours), **Rome** (4/day, 12.5 hours, 1-3 changes; night train, 14 hours), **Venice** (2/day direct, 8 hours; 3/day with changes, 8-10 hours; night train, 11 hours), **Frankfurt** (5/day direct, 6.5 hours; night train, 9 hours).

By Bus

The main bus station is located just east of the Ring at the U-3 Erdberg stop. **Flixbus** offers dirt-cheap rates to **Salzburg, Budapest, Prague, Bratislava,** and points beyond (www.flixbus.com).

By Plane

VIENNA INTERNATIONAL AIRPORT

The airport, 12 miles from the center, is easy to reach from downtown (airport code: VIE, airport tel. 01/700-722-233, www.viennaairport.com). The arrivals hall has an array of services: TI, shops, ATMs, eateries, and a handy supermarket. Ramps lead down to the lower-level train station.

Getting Between the Airport and Central Vienna

By Train: Trains connect the airport with the Wien-Mitte Bahnhof, on the east side of the Ring (described earlier). Choose between two ways of getting to Wien-Mitte: the regular S-7 S-Bahn train (€4.20, 24 minutes), and the express CAT train (€12, 16 minutes). Both run twice an hour on the same tracks. The airport tries to steer tourists into taking the CAT train, but it's hard to justify spending almost €8 to save eight minutes of time. I'd take the S-7, unless the CAT is departing first and you're in a big hurry. Trains from downtown start running about 5:00, while the last train from the airport leaves about 23:30.

The **S-Bahn** works just fine and is plenty fast. From the arrivals hall, go down either of the big ramps, follow the red ÖBB signs, then buy a regular two-zone public transport ticket from the multilingual red ticket machines. It's easiest to just type in your final destination and let the machine do the work. The €4.20 price includes any transfers to other trams, city buses, S- and U-Bahn lines (see www.wienerlinien.at). Trains to downtown are marked "Floridsdorf." If you'll be using public transportation in Vienna a lot, consider buying a transit pass from the machines instead of a single ticket (see page 24). As these passes are only valid in Vienna's central zone, you'll need to also buy a €2.40 single ticket to cover the stretch between the airport and the limits of the inner zone.

To take the fast **CAT** (which stands for City Airport Train), follow the green signage down the ramp to your right as you come out into the arrivals hall and buy a ticket from the green machines (one-way—€12, or €14.40 to also cover the connecting link from Wien-Mitte to your final destination by public transit; round-trip ticket valid 30 days—€21, 4 tickets—€42; usually departs both airport and downtown around :08 and :38 past the hour, www.cityairporttrain.com).

CONNECTIONS

By Bus: Convenient express airport buses operated by ÖBB go to various points in Vienna: Morzinplatz/Schwedenplatz U-Bahn station (for city-center hotels, 20 minutes), Westbahnhof (for Mariahilfer Strasse hotels, 45 minutes), and Wien-Meidling Bahnhof (30 minutes). Double check your destination as you board (€8, round-trip—€13, 2/hour, buy ticket from driver, tel. 051-717 for info, www.viennaairportlines.at).

By Taxi: The 30-minute ride into town costs a fixed €36 from the several companies with desks in the arrivals hall. You can also take a taxi from the taxi rank outside; you'll pay the metered rate (plus a trivial baggage surcharge), which should come out about the same. Save by riding the cheap train/bus downtown, then taking a taxi to your destination.

Connecting the Airport and Other Cities

Direct buses serve **Bratislava** and its airport (roughly hourly, 1 hour, buses leave from platforms 7, 8, and 9; two companies: **Flixbus,** www.flixbus.com, and **Slovak Lines/Postbus,** www.slovaklines.sk; see page 261); **Budapest** (almost hourly, 3 hours, www.flixbus.com); **Prague** (4/day, 7 hours, www.studentagency.eu, also stops in **Brno**).

BRATISLAVA AIRPORT

The airport in nearby Bratislava, Slovakia—a hub for some low-cost flights—is an hour away from Vienna (see "Bratislava Connections" in the Bratislava, Slovakia chapter).

By Car

ROUTE TIPS FOR DRIVERS

Approaching Vienna: Navigating your way into Vienna is straightforward, but study your map first. Approaching Vienna on the A-1 expressway from **Melk** or **Salzburg,** it's simple: You'll pass Schönbrunn Palace before hitting the Gürtel (the city's outer ring road); turn left onto the Gürtel to reach Mariahilfer Strasse hotels, or continue on to reach hotels inside the Ringstrasse (the city's inner ring; clockwise traffic only).

If you're approaching from **Krems,** stay on A-22 as it follows the Danube, and cross the river at the fourth bridge (Reichsbrücke). At the big roundabout, take the second right onto Praterstrasse, which leads directly to the Ringstrasse. Circle around until you reach the "spoke" street you need.

From **Budapest,** get on A-4 at Nickelsdorf; from there it's a straight shot into Vienna along the Danube Canal. From the canal, turn left at the Aspernbrücke bridge and cross the canal, which puts you directly on the Ringstrasse.

In Vienna: The city has deliberately created an expensive hell for cars in the center. Don't even try to drive here. If you must bring a car into Vienna, leave it at an expensive garage (ask your hotel if it provides discounted parking).

Leaving Vienna: To leave Vienna for points west (such as the Danube Valley and Salzburg), circle the Ringstrasse clockwise until just past the Opera. Then follow the blue signs past the Westbahnhof to *Schloss Schönbrunn* (Schönbrunn Palace), which is directly on the way to the West A-1 autobahn to Linz. If you stop at the palace for a visit, leave the palace by 15:00 and you should beat rush hour.

By Boat

High-speed boats connect Vienna to the nearby Slovakian capital of Bratislava. While it's generally cheaper and faster to take the train (€16 round-trip with ÖBB Bratislava-Ticket)—and the boat is less scenic and romantic than you might imagine—some travelers enjoy the Danube riverboat experience.

The **Twin City Liner** runs 3-5 times daily from the terminal at Vienna's Schwedenplatz, where Vienna's town center hits the canal (€30-35 one-way, 1.5 hours, U: Schwedenplatz, late March-Oct only, can fill up—reservations smart, Austrian tel. 01/904-8880, www.twincityliner.com). Their main competitor, **LOD,** is a bit cheaper, but runs only twice a day at most and is less convenient—since it uses Vienna's Reichsbrücke dock on the main river, farther from the city center (€25 one-way, €44 round-trip, 1.5 hours, Handelskai 265, U: Vorgartenstrasse, tel. from Austria 00-421-2-5293-2226, www.lod.sk).

NEAR VIENNA

DANUBE VALLEY

Melk • Wachau Valley • Mauthausen Memorial

From the Black Forest in Germany to the Black Sea in Romania, the Danube flows 1,770 miles through 10 countries. Western Europe's longest river (the Rhine is only half as long), it's also the only major river flowing west to east, making it invaluable for commercial transportation. The Danube is at its romantic best just west of Vienna. Mix a cruise with a bike ride through the Danube's Wachau Valley, lined with ruined castles, beautiful abbeys (including the glorious Melk Abbey), small towns, and vineyard upon vineyard. Note that in German, Danube is *Donau* (DOH-now), as you'll see by the signs.

Much of the valley has a warm, fairy-tale glow, but a trip here isn't complete without the chilling contrast of a visit to the Mauthausen concentration camp memorial. Visiting this concentration camp, though a little difficult for nondrivers, is unforgettable and worthwhile even if you've already seen other camps.

PLANNING YOUR TIME

Allow one day to visit Melk's abbey and to cruise the Wachau Valley by boat or bike; a second day gives you time to get to Mauthausen. For drivers, it makes sense to see Mauthausen en route to (or from) Salzburg or Hallstatt. For tips on enjoying nearby riverside sights, see "Getting Around the Wachau Valley" later in this chapter.

Day Trip from Vienna: To day-trip to the Danube, catch an early train to Melk, tour its abbey, eat lunch, and take an afternoon boat trip along the river from Melk to Krems (it's easier in this direction, as you're going downstream)—or rent a bike in Melk and make the trip on two wheels instead. From Krems, catch the train back to Vienna. The Austrian railway sells a convenient Wachau Kombiticket, which includes the train trip from Vienna to Melk, entry to the Melk Abbey, a boat cruise to Krems, and the return train trip to Vienna, for €59 (a decent savings off individual tickets; buy at any Vienna train station). Groups of at least two adults can save a few more euros by buying an Einfach-Raus train ticket, or an Einfach-Raus Radticket for bicyclists (see "Transportation" in the Practicalities chapter) and taking a regional train (after 9:00 on weekdays) to Melk, then paying for the boat and the abbey separately.

The fastest train connections to Melk leave from Vienna's Hauptbahnhof and require an easy transfer en route; a few direct trains from Vienna's Westbahnhof take 10 minutes longer. From Krems, easy connections via St. Pölten return you to Vienna's Hauptbahnhof; direct trains from Krems arrive in Vienna at the small Franz-Josefs-Bahnhof (consider getting off at the previous stop, Spittelau, for better connections—on the U-4 and U-6 subway lines—to other points in Vienna).

From Vienna by Car and Driver: Johann Lichtl, based in Vienna, can take you on a day tour of the Danube Valley (see page 26).

To Hallstatt: Those heading to Hallstatt by train should avoid arriving there in the evening, when the boat stops running (see "Arrival in Hallstatt" on page 346). Plan a morning or afternoon arrival, even if that means going first to Salzburg and then doubling back to Hallstatt.

Melk

Sleepy and elegant under its huge abbey, which seems to police the Danube, the town of Melk offers a pleasant stop and is a handy springboard for the beautiful Wachau Valley.

Orientation to Melk

TOURIST INFORMATION

The TI is a block off the main square, close to the river, and has info on nearby castles, bike rentals, bike rides along the river, a list of hotels, and *Zimmer* recommendations in private homes. The TI rents an audioguide (€3/2 people, €25 deposit) and

DANUBE VALLEY

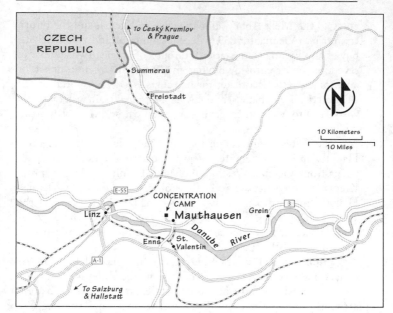

has lockers and a free WC (Mon-Sat 9:30-18:00, Sun until 15:30; April and Oct Mon-Sat 9:00-17:00, Sun 10:00-14:00; limited hours Nov-March, Kremser Strasse 5, tel. 02752/51160, www. donau.com).

ARRIVAL IN MELK

Melk is just off the A-1 autobahn that runs between Salzburg and Vienna. The town is also on the main Salzburg-Vienna train line, but only regional trains stop here; faster trains bypass the town (you'll probably transfer in Amstetten or St. Pölten).

By Train: Walk straight out of Melk's train station (lockers in station hall) and continue ahead for several blocks; at the curve, keep straight and go down the stairs, following the cobbled alley that dumps you into the center of the village. Access to Melk Abbey is up on your right (follow signs to *Stift Melk*), and the TI is to your left, a block past the square, near the river.

By Boat: Turn right as you leave the boat dock and follow the canalside bike path toward the big yellow abbey (the village is beneath its far side). In about five minutes, you'll come to a flashing light (at intersection with bridge); turn left and you're steps from the old town.

To reach the boat dock from Melk, leave the town toward the river, with the abbey on your right. Turn right when you get to the busy road and follow the canal (at the fork just before the gas station, it's quicker to jog left onto the bike path than to follow

DANUBE VALLEY

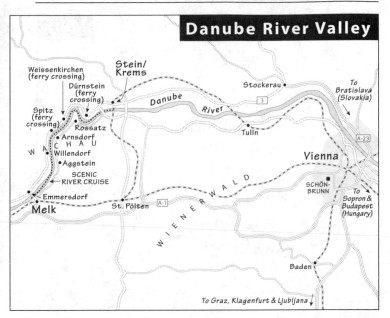

Danube River Valley

the main road). Follow signs for *Linienschifffahrt-Scheduled Trips-Wachau.*

By Car: If you're just visiting the abbey, you can park there. To park near the old town, head for the free lot just across the canal from the TI, next to Melk's open-air theater (the Wachauarena). To reach it, circle around and cross a small one-lane bridge between the boat docks and gas station, following *Wachauarena* signs.

Melk Abbey Tour

Melk's restored abbey, worth ▲▲▲ and beaming proudly over the Danube Valley, is one of Europe's great sights. Established as a fortified Benedictine abbey (Benediktinerstift) in the 11th century, it was later destroyed by fire. During an 18th-century Baroque building boom, the ruling Habsburgs commissioned architect Jakob Prandtauer to remake the abbey buildings.

The abbey church, with its 200-foot-tall dome and symmetrical towers, dominates the complex—emphasizing its sacred purpose. The gilded church, restored in 1996 to celebrate the 1,000th anniversary of the first

DANUBE VALLEY

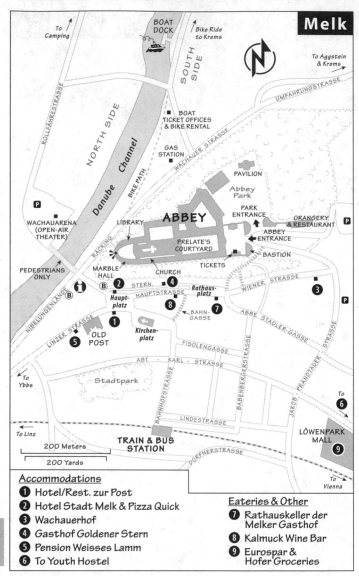

Accommodations
1 Hotel/Rest. zur Post
2 Hotel Stadt Melk & Pizza Quick
3 Wachauerhof
4 Gasthof Goldener Stern
5 Pension Weisses Lamm
6 To Youth Hostel

Eateries & Other
7 Rathauskeller der Melker Gasthof
8 Kalmuck Wine Bar
9 Eurospar & Hofer Groceries

reference to a country named Österreich (Austria), is a grand Baroque dream, a lily alone.

ORIENTATION TO THE ABBEY

Cost and Hours: €11, includes entrance to the abbey and its park and bastions; €4 for just the park and bastions; abbey—daily 9:00-17:30, April and Nov until 16:30, Dec-March by guided tour only (see next); park—May-Oct daily 9:00-18:00, closed Nov-April; free parking, tel. 02752/555-232, www.stiftmelk. at.

Tours: One-hour English tours of the abbey are offered daily (April-Oct at 10:55, 14:00, and 14:55, €13 ticket includes tour and admission). A private guide can be reserved at least one day in advance (€60 plus €11 per-person entrance fee). From Dec-March, the abbey is open only by guided tour, with departures at 11:00 and 14:00. Book guided tours in advance by calling 02752/555-232 or emailing tours@stiftmelk.at.

Eating: The **$$ Stiftrestaurant** just outside the abbey walls serves traditional Austrian food, mostly to large tour groups, on a modern terrace. There's also a snack stand in the garden pavilion.

● SELF-GUIDED TOUR

Although you can take a guided tour, it's easiest just to wander through on your own.

• *Go through the first passageway and approach the grand entry to the...*

East Facade: Imagine the abbot on the balcony greeting you as he used to greet important guests. Flanking him are statues of Peter and Paul (leaders of the apostles and patron saints of the abbey church) and the monastery's coat of arms (crossed keys). High above are the Latin words "Glory is found only in the cross" and a huge copy of the Melk Cross (one of the abbey's greatest treasures—the original is hiding in the treasury and viewable only on special occasions).

• *Pass into the main courtyard.*

Prelate's Courtyard: This is more than a museum. For 900 years, monks of St. Benedict have lived and worked here. Their task: bringing and maintaining Christianity and culture to the region. Many of the 29 monks live outside the abbey in the community and run a high school with about 900 students.

There have been low points. During the Reformation (1500s), only eight monks held down the theological fort. Napoleon made his headquarters here in 1805 and 1809. And in 1938, when Hitler annexed Austria, the monastery was squeezed into one end of the complex and nearly dissolved. But today, the institution survives—that's the point of the four modern frescoes gracing the courtyard—funded by your visit and by agriculture (historically, monasteries are big landowners).

• *In the far left-hand corner, climb the stairs to the...*

Imperial Corridor and Abbey Museum: This 640-foot-long corridor, lined with paintings of Austrian royalty, is the spine of the Abbey Museum. Duck into the first room of the museum (on the left, near beginning of hall). These rooms are filled with art

DANUBE VALLEY

treasures, an exhibit with sound-and-light effects meant to convey basic Benedictine precepts, and descriptions of the history of the Benedictines in Melk.

• *Continue through the museum—passing through the trippy mirrored room containing gold chalices and monstrances, around a beautifully preserved Northern Renaissance altarpiece, and into the room at the end, with the big rotating model of the abbey.*

Marble Hall: While the door frames are real marble, most of this large dining room/ballroom is stucco. The treasure here is

the ceiling fresco (by Tirolean Paul Troger, 1731), best appreciated from the center of the room. Notice three themes: 1) The Habsburgs liked to be portrayed as Hercules; 2) Athena, the goddess of wisdom, is included, because the Habsburgs were smart as well as strong; and 3) The Habsburgs were into art and culture. This is symbolized by angels figuratively reining in the forces of evil, darkness, and brutality. Through this wise moderation, goodness, beauty, art, and science can rule. Look up again as you leave the room to see how the columns were painted at an angle to give the illusion of a curved ceiling.

Balcony: Here you'll enjoy dramatic views of the Danube Valley, the town of Melk, and the facade of the monastery church. The huge statue above everything shows the risen Christ, cross in hand and victorious over death—the central message of the entire place.

Library: For the Benedictine monks, the library was—except for the church itself—the most important room in the abbey. Consider how much money they must have invested in its elaborate decor.

In the Middle Ages, monasteries controlled information and hoarded it in their libraries. At a time when most everyone else was illiterate, monks were Europe's educated elite and had the power to dictate what was true...and what wasn't. Students and researchers are still given access to this library and the many manuscripts housed in temperature-controlled rooms under your feet. The precious globes (one terrestrial, one celestial—with the night sky turned inside out) date from 1688 and were painstakingly researched and crafted by Franciscan monk Vincenzo Coronelli, one of the first to raise globe-making to a fine art.

The inlaid bookshelves, matching bindings, and another fine Troger fresco combine harmoniously to create a thematic counterpart to the Marble Hall. This room celebrates not wise politics, but faith. The ceiling shows a woman surrounded by groups of angels representing the four cardinal virtues (prudence, justice, faith, and recycling)—natural traits that lead to a supernatural faith. The statues flanking the doors represent the four traditional university faculties (law, medicine, philosophy, and theology).

There would be a Gutenberg Bible in this room...but the abbey sold it in 1927 (it was later donated to Yale University).

Church: The finale is the church, with its architecture, ceiling frescoes, stucco marble, grand pipe organ, and sumptuous chapels adorned with chubby cherubs. (How many can you count?) All of these elements combine in full Baroque style to make the theological point: A just battle leads to victory. The ceiling shows St. Benedict's triumphant entry into heaven (on a fancy carpet). Over the altar, below the huge papal crown, the golden saints Peter and Paul shake hands before departing for their final battles, martyrdom, and ultimate victory. And, high above, the painting in the dome shows that victory: the Holy Trinity, surrounded by saints of particular importance to Melk, happily in heaven.

OTHER ABBEY SIGHTS

Near the entrance (and exit) to the abbey, you'll find the abbey's park and bastions. The park is home to a picturesque Baroque pavilion housing some fine frescoes by Johann Wenzel Bergel and a small snack stand. The bastions offer decent views from the top terrace, and exhibits by students at the abbey's school are displayed on the second floor. Nearby, in the former orangery, is the abbey's restaurant.

Sleeping in Melk

Melk makes a fine and inexpensive overnight stop and has plentiful, usually free parking. Except during August, you shouldn't have any trouble finding a good room at a reasonable rate.

$$ Hotel zur Post is professional and well-run by the Ebner family, with 28 comfy and tidy rooms over a good restaurant. The fancy junior suites are the best, but more expensive (RS% with cash payment, family rooms, fans, elevator, free loaner bikes, sauna, free private parking, closed Jan-mid-Feb, Linzer Strasse 1, tel. 02752/52345, www.post-melk.at, info@hotelpost-melk.at).

$$ Hotel Stadt Melk has 14 bright, straightforward, smartly renovated rooms in a 17th-century building on the town's main square (RS%, fans, lots of stairs, excellent breakfast, free private parking, Hauptplatz 1, tel. 02752/524-750, www.hotelstadtmelk.at, office@hotelstadtmelk.at, Philippe and Pascal).

$$ Wachauerhof is a big, dull, traditional 72-room hotel, but it gets the job done in a good location with free private parking—try here if other options are full (lots of stairs, Wiener Strasse 30, tel. 02752/52235, www.wachauerhof-melk.at, office@wachauerhof-melk.at).

$ Gasthof Goldener Stern's 11 colorful, elegant rooms are each different, with flowers on every pillow. The pricier canopy-bed rooms are very romantic. This lively, homey place is a good value—my favorite address in town—and buzzes with guests and with the owners' creativity. It's on a narrow lane that veers up from the main square, and there's a peaceful terrace out front (family rooms, cash only, nonsmoking, free boat ticket to Spitz with 3-night stay, gluten- and lactose-free breakfasts available, call if arriving after 18:00, Sterngasse 17, tel. 02752/52214, www.sternmelk.at, goldenerstern.melk@aon.at, Regina and Kurt Schmidt).

$ Pension Weisses Lamm is low on atmosphere, but it has the cheapest beds in the center. Its 14 rooms, above a lackluster restaurant, are basic, and some are a bit dark, but all have been pleasantly renovated (cash only, nonsmoking, Linzer Strasse 7, look for namesake white lamb on sign, mobile 0664-231-5297, www.pension-weisses-lamm-melk.at, pension.weisses.lamm@hotmail.com, Kumus).

¢ Hostel: The modern, institutional youth hostel is a 10-minute walk from the train station. Go straight out from the station down Bahnhofstrasse, then turn right at the next corner onto Abt-Karl-Strasse; the hostel is just past the Löwenpark shopping mall (private rooms available, no curfew but reception closes at 21:00, closed Nov-Feb, Abt-Karl-Strasse 42, tel. 02752/52681, http://melk.noejhw.at, melk@noejhw.at).

Sleeping near Melk: If you have a car, you could stay in a nearby farm or village. The TI has a list of people renting rooms to travelers for about €30 per person, most a few miles from the center. Also consider the good guesthouse in Willendorf, a 20-minute drive from Melk (see "Towns in the Wachau Valley," later in this chapter).

Eating in Melk

$$ Gasthof Goldener Stern serves fine, inexpensive local cuisine in a relaxed, informal atmosphere (Tue-Sat 17:00-23:00, closed Sun-Mon, Sterngasse 17, tel. 02752/52214).

$$ Hotel Restaurant zur Post, classier and pricier, can be worth the few extra euros. Downstairs is a fun and atmospheric wine cellar, with both local and international wines (daily 11:30-21:30 except closed 14:00-18:00 and Mon outside high season, closed Jan-mid-Feb, courtyard and fine streetside seating with an abbey view, Linzer Strasse 1, tel. 02752/52345).

$$ Rathauskeller der Melker Gasthof takes pride in its good service and fresh ingredients. Its traditional offerings include *Tafelspitz*, goulash, and venison ragout. Eat on a busy patio or in the cozy interior (daily 10:00-23:00, Rathausplatz 13, tel. 02752/20460).

$ Kalmuck, a popular wine bar on the main street, serves inexpensive light meals and pub food and is the one place in Melk that stays lively until the wee hours (daily 10:00-late, Hauptstrasse 10, tel. 02752/517-950).

$ Pizza Quick, on the main square, has a full Italian menu and will make you a pie for €7 (daily 11:00-22:00, takeout-only later in evening, Hauptplatz 2, tel. 02752/54222).

Supermarket: Pick up picnic supplies at either the midrange **Eurospar** or the budget **Hofer,** both in the big Löwenpark mall, a 10-minute walk from downtown (Eurospar—Mon-Fri 7:00-19:00; Hofer—Mon-Fri 7:30-19:30, Abt-Karl-Strasse). Both are also open Saturday until 18:00 and closed Sunday.

Melk Connections

From Melk by Train to: Vienna's Hauptbahnhof (2/hour, 1 hour, change in St. Pölten; also some direct trains to Vienna's Westbahnhof), **Salzburg** (almost hourly, 2.5 hours, transfer in Amstetten or St. Pölten), **Mauthausen** (every 1-2 hours, 2 hours, usually 2 changes—some with significant layovers). Train info: tel. 051-717 (to get an operator, dial 2, then 2), www.oebb.at.

By **Bus to the Wachau Valley:** See the next section.

By **Car to/from the Danube Valley:** See "Route Tips for Drivers," later in this chapter.

Wachau Valley

The 24-mile stretch of the Danube between Melk and Krems is as pretty as they come—worth ▲▲. This region, called the Wachau, is blanketed with vineyards and ornamented with cute villages. Keep an eye out for wreaths of straw or greenery, hung as an invitation to come in and taste. (Don't be dismayed that the Blue Danube isn't actu-

ally blue—it's not pollution, but the result of a soft riverbed, with sediment that gets stirred up by the current in these parts.) So why do they call it "blue"? Maybe because in local slang, someone who's feeling his wine is "blue." Austrians know the region for its apricots (*Marillen* in Austrian German), which are made into the jam that fills all that Viennese Sacher torte.

GETTING AROUND THE WACHAU VALLEY

The well-run regional transit system makes it easy for visitors without a car to enjoy the valley. You have three good options for experiencing the stretch from Melk to Krems: by bike, boat, or bus.

Of these, my favorite is biking. I enjoy being untethered from a timetable while I get up-close with the valley's sights and scents. If you don't mind the limited number of sailings (and little opportunity to stop off along the way), hop a boat. If a bike or boat doesn't appeal, the easy, frequent Wachau Line bus (operated by VOR) is the way to go.

However you travel, pick up a free map from the Melk TI so you can trace the route, as well as the helpful regional bus schedule. For a very basic overview of the region, see the "Danube River Valley" map earlier in this chapter.

By Bike

From Melk to Krems: It's a three- to four-hour, gently downhill pedal to Krems. You can bike either the south or the north side of the river; I prefer the north for its interesting villages and sights (Willendorf, Spitz, and Dürnstein). If it's more important to you to have a dedicated, paved bike path the whole way, choose the more rural south side, where at worst you ride next to—but never on—the road (which has less traffic than the north side) and get a bit more time along the Danube. On both sides, you'll find plenty of vineyards and small *Gasthöfe* in the villages along the way.

You can change sides at three points—Spitz, Weissenkirchen,

and Dürnstein—where inexpensive ferries regularly carry people, bikes, and cars across the river (ferries covered by same day-pass that covers bus transit between Krems and Melk; purchase at Melk TI or pay onboard).

For a shorter bike ride that also gets you on a boat, consider taking a bike on board and cruising by boat from Melk to Spitz—a good midway point—and then biking from Spitz on to Krems (see "By Boat," later).

Bicyclists rule in this region, and you'll find all the necessary biking amenities. Bike routes are clearly marked with green *Donau-Radweg* (Danube cycling route) signs labeled with #6. You'll pass some serious bikers (or maybe they'll pass you)—the entire #6 route covers 2,270 miles and spans 10 countries. (Note: The bike-in-a-red-border signs mean "no biking.") Local TIs give out a *Donau-radweg* brochure with a helpful if basic route map.

In Melk, ask your hotel or the TI for **bike-rental** options. Some hotels rent or loan bikes. The easiest option is a small mom-and-pop shop, **Fahrrad Verleih,** next to the Melk boat ticket kiosks. Stop by their rickety shack/snack shop and pick up a bike—best to call ahead to confirm they are open (€13/day, daily April-Oct 9:00-15:00, closed off-season, another location at Spitz train station, mobile 0664-222-2070, www.wachau-touristik.at). Return your bike at the Krems boat dock or train station. Another company, **Zwölfer,** is more expensive but delivers bikes when reserved ahead (mobile 0664-606-74606).

You'll also see bike-sharing **Nextbike** stands throughout the region (including in Melk—at the train station, TI, and youth hostel—and in Krems, which makes it easy to leave the bike there and return to Melk by bus). Nextbike only works with a mobile phone, which can make it tricky for visitors. Before your trip, download the Nextbike app and register with a credit card under "Lower Austria." To borrow a bike at a stand, enter the number of the bike you want and receive a code to unlock it (€1/hour, €10/24 hours, call center supposedly open 24 hours, tel. 02742/229-901, www.nextbike.at).

Returning to Melk: You can ride a bike in both directions, but given that it's 48 miles round-trip and slightly uphill all the way back, returning via bus or train may be the better option.

One bike-friendly bus makes the trip from Krems back to Melk each day: The #WL1A (Wachau Line #1A) follows the same route as the #WL1 (see "By Bus," later in this section), but tows a bike-carrying cart with plenty of room. It leaves the Krems train station in late afternoon (as of my last visit, at 16:35)—confirm departure times at the Melk TI (bus runs daily June-late Sept, weekends only mid-April-May and late Sept-Oct, none off-season; bikes cost €2 on top of bus ticket). The #WL1A also stops in Dürn-

DANUBE VALLEY

stein, Weissenkirchen, Spitz, and Aggsbach—handy if you want to return to Melk without biking all the way to Krems.

While I like the bus ride back for the scenery it offers, cyclists who don't catch the afternoon bike-cart bus needn't panic—from Krems you can hop the **train** back to Melk, but it's more difficult (hourly, change in St. Pölten, no river views, ticket required for bike, last train at about 21:15, 1.5 hours).

In summer, a less frequent "Wachaubahn" train is designed with tourists in mind and runs along the north side of the river, connecting Krems with Emmersdorf an der Donau, the town just across the river from Melk. Bikes ride for free on this train (provided there's enough room), but the last Wachaubahn train back from Krems leaves in the late afternoon (at 16:20, as of my last visit). It's handy if you'd like a ride back even if you don't bike all the way to Krems; it makes seven scheduled stops en route—including Willendorf, Spitz, and Dürnstein (€16 one-way, €22 round-trip, 3/day, runs daily July-late Sept and on weekends April-June and late Sept-late Oct, 1 hour, regional day pass not accepted, buy ticket on board, www.wachaubahn.at). The walk from Emmersdorf to Melk is 50 minutes—don't miss the handy shuttle timed to meet the train that drops you off at the Melk train station.

If you've returned your bike in Krems, you can hop on any #WL1 bus from the train station, Stadtpark stop near TI, Krems boat dock, or any point along the way (hourly until 20:18, covered by same-day pass that covers ferries or purchase from driver).

By Boat

From Melk to Krems: For many, Danube dreams involve a boat ride on this famous waterway. It is indeed a relaxing way to take in the valley, although the limited schedule (just four boats a day in season, and two of those are only five minutes apart) makes it virtually impossible to stop off en route.

Two companies run boats along this stretch: **Brandner** (tel. 07433/259-021, www.brandner.at) and **DDSG** (tel. 01/58880, www.ddsg-blue-danube.at). They use adjacent boat docks, and charge the same amount (€25 one-way, €30 round-trip, round-trip allows stopovers, bikes ride for €2). Rail-pass holders get a 20 percent discount.

In peak season (May-Sept), boats leave from Melk daily at 11:00 (DDSG), 13:45/13:50 (Brandner/DDSG), and 16:25 (DDSG, requires change in Spitz). The trip to Krems takes 1.75

hours (but almost twice as long coming back upstream). DDSG offers a longer cruise (Sun only, July-late-Sept) that starts or ends in Vienna. In late April and October, boats go only twice a day (5 minutes apart; the 13:45/13:50 sailings). There are no boats off-season.

Getting Back to Melk: You can ride the boat in both directions, but because of the six-knot flow of the Danube, the ride back upstream takes three hours. Instead, I'd take the bus (#WL1—see next).

By Bus

From Melk to Krems: Wachau Line 1 (a.k.a. #WL1) runs nearly hourly along the north side of the river, weaving its way through cute villages and endless vineyards (hourly, one hour, €9.20 one-way between Melk and Krems; €12 day-pass makes sense if you plan to stop off en route and/or ride round-trip; day-pass sold at Melk TI). This is a fine joyride option for nonbikers who want more flexibility than the infrequent boats provide.

In Melk, catch the bus at the train station or the more central stop by the TI (Prinzlstrasse). To hop off anywhere before Krems, watch the bus's "next stop" screen, and request a stop with a push of the button (within Krems, use the second-to-last stop, Stadtpark, to avoid the walk back into the town center from the station). Ask for a regional bus schedule at the Melk TI or check online at www.vor.at.

Returning to Melk: Bus #WL1 leaves from the Krems train station, the more central Stadtpark stop near the TI, and from the boat dock. When you arrive in Melk, get off at Prinzlstrasse, which is more convenient to my recommended hotels than the station.

You can also return to Melk on bus #WL2, which leaves from the Krems train station and runs along the south side of the river. Because it runs less frequently (about every 2 hours) and takes a more rural route, I'd consider this option only if I'd already ridden the #WL1 into Krems and wanted a change of scenery (one-hour trip to Melk, same price as bus #WL1 and covered by the same day-pass).

Should you get stuck, you can always call a **taxi**—but expect fares to be exorbitant (mobile 0664-6067-4606; let them know if you need to transport a bike).

Route Tips for Drivers

With a car, you can drive from Melk to Krems on one side of the river and return on the other side. On the north side, stop at Willendorf (Venus Museum) and Dürnstein (for a glimpse at the town and perhaps a walk up to the ruined castle; use pay lots outside walls). On the south side, consider the villages of Rossatz and Rührsdorf (near Krems), which have many small *Heurigen* winery/res-taurants. Closer to Melk is the five-minute detour (signposted) up a steep, narrow road to the well-preserved ruins of Burg Aggstein, which towers over the valley with magnificent views (free overlook near parking lot, about €7/person to enter, open daily mid-March-Nov, www.ruineaggstein.at).

Towns in the Wachau Valley

Willendorf

This is known among prehistorians as the town where the oldest piece of European art was found—the well-endowed, 25,000-year-old, four-inch statuette known as the *Venus of Willendorf.* (The original is now in Vienna's Natural History Museum—see page 56.) The village is worth a visit for its two-room, smartly designed museum, the **Venusium,** which tells the figure's story and compares it with similar statues found in other parts of Europe (€2, May-Oct Tue-Sun generally 10:00-12:00 & 14:00-16:00, closed Mon and off-season, mobile 0664-7316-7471, www.willendorf.info). Above the museum, the *Zur Fundstelle* sign leads you to the point where the statue was actually found during railway construction in 1908, and you can see where the hillside has been cut away to reveal the layers of sediment deposited over the millennia.

Riverboats don't stop here, but the **#WL1** bus does (roughly hourly, 20-minute trip from Melk, 40-minute trip from Krems). It's a five-minute walk from the bus stop to the village center.

Consider eating, or even (best with a car) overnighting in Willendorf at **$ Schneider's Gasthof zur Venus,** steps from the museum. It serves **$$$** Austrian meals (restaurant closed Mon-Tue) and has six good rooms (free parking, tel. 02712/202-020, www.gasthof-zur-venus.at, schneiders@gasthof-zur-venus.at).

Dürnstein

This touristic flypaper of a town lures hordes of tour-bus and cruise-ship visitors with its traffic-free quaintness and its one claim to fame (and fortune): Richard the Lionheart was imprisoned here in 1193 on his way home from the Third Crusade. The town is a delight—almost like a Disney movie (but with stores selling over-priced ice cream and apricot jam). The ruined castle above *(Burgruine),* where Richard was kept, can be reached by a fairly steep 30-minute hike with great river views: Take Anzuggasse from the riverside promenade up to the downstream town gate, then follow *Weinbau Familie Pölz* signs up the street, which turns into a broad dirt lane lined with informative signposts, and goes all the way up to the castle. There are no services up top, so bring water. Beware:

Nonvenomous Aesculapian snakes, up to eight feet long, live in the ruin; they're harmless but best left alone.

Krems

This town is much bigger than Melk and home to a small university. Boats from Melk stop about a mile from Krems' town center (technically in the adjacent town of Stein—it's a 20-minute walk in).

To walk from the boat dock, go inland to the second roundabout, turn right on Steiner Donaulände, go under the railroad bridge, walk three blocks farther to a park, then cross through the park and turn left on Utzstrasse. The **TI** is on your right—look for the green *i* icon (mid-April-mid-Oct Mon-Fri 9:00-18:00 except Tue from 14:00, Sat 11:00-18:00, Sun 11:00-16:00; shorter hours and closed Sat-Sun mid-Oct-March, Utzstrasse 1, tel. 02732/82676, www.krems.info).

If coming on the #WL1 bus, hop off at the Stadtpark stop. To reach the TI from the stop, head left off the bus to the intersection, then left onto Utzstrasse; the TI is a half-block away on the right.

If arriving by bike, head toward the boat dock just after Stein or the train station to drop off your wheels. (Nextbike users will find their drop-off location near the TI.) Riding bikes is not permitted in the old town.

The old Krems city gate is a few doors up Utzstrasse from the TI. Stroll the large, traffic-free old town, a shopper's wonderland with a lively restaurant scene. When you're done, find Krems' rail and bus station between the old town and the river. In addition to its hourly train and bus connections to Melk (described earlier), Krems is connected by hourly trains to Vienna's Franz-Josefs-Bahnhof (1 hour) and to Vienna's Hauptbahnhof (easy change in St. Pölten, also 1 hour).

Wachau Valley Connections

For bus and train connections from Melk, see "Melk Connections," earlier in this chapter.

ROUTE TIPS FOR DRIVERS

Vienna to Hallstatt (via the Wachau Valley, Melk, and Mauthausen, 210 miles): The A-1 autobahn is the most direct route, but for better scenery leave Vienna by crossing the Danube to reach the A-22 autobahn. Head north (following *Praha/Prague* signs) to Stockerau, then take exit #30 to the S-5 highway, which leads to Krems. After Krems, take Route 3 along the river until just after Schallemmersdorf (and just before Emmersdorf), where a bridge leads across the river to Melk. In Melk, signs to *Stift Melk* lead to the Benediktinerstift (Benedictine abbey).

From Melk, it's a speedy hour to Mauthausen via the autobahn, but the curvy and scenic Route 3 along the river is worth the nausea. At Mauthausen, follow *Ehemaliges KZ-Gedenkstätte Lager* signs to the concentration camp memorial. Leaving Mauthausen, cross the Danube and follow signs to *Enns* (five minutes from Mauthausen town), and join the autobahn there (heading west). Leave the autobahn at exit #224 and follow scenic Route 145 past Gmunden to Stambach, then to road 166, which leads to Hallstatt.

For tips on going from Hallstatt to Vienna with a stop in the Wachau, see "Hallstatt Connections" on page 365.

Mauthausen Memorial

On top of one of the rolling hills flanking the Danube River, halfway between Vienna and Salzburg, stands the notorious former concentration camp at Mauthausen (MOWT-how-zehn), worth ▲▲▲. This slave-labor and death camp is the most powerful concentration-camp experience that a traveler can have in Western Europe. By visiting and putting ourselves through this emotional wringer, we heed

and respect the fervent wish of the victims—that we never forget.

The camp functioned from 1938 to 1945, initially to detain and exploit Hitler's domestic political opponents, and then (after 1943) primarily to house Jews and prisoners of war from Eastern Europe. Mauthausen also spawned a network of satellite camps (the nearby one at Gusen is also now a memorial).

Some of the Nazis' camps, such as Auschwitz in Poland, were designed to exterminate people en masse in gas chambers. At others, such as Mauthausen, inmates were essentially worked to death. In these camps, your ability to endure forced labor amounted to a stay of execution. Mauthausen is located above a granite quarry—the region has long supplied building stone to Vienna and Budapest—and the hard labor here was hacking and hauling rocks.

Among Mauthausen's most famous prisoners was Simon Wi-

DANUBE VALLEY

esenthal, who dedicated himself after the war to hunting down
Nazis and making sure they paid for their crimes. He was one of
the lucky survivors: About half of Mauthausen's 200,000 prisoners
died, mostly from starvation or exhaustion. Mauthausen was the
last concentration camp to be liberated—on May 5, 1945, a week
after Hitler's death.

Planning Your Time: Today enough of Mauthausen's buildings survive to give a gripping sense of the camp's history. You can
easily spend the whole day here. At the least, allow two hours to
visit the camp itself, or three if you watch the film at the visitors
center.

GETTING THERE

With a car, you can visit Mauthausen on the way between Salzburg
(or Hallstatt) and Vienna (or Melk), or as a day trip (easy from
Melk, doable from Hallstatt or Salzburg, a long day out from Vienna). By train, Mauthausen works best as a day trip from Salzburg
or Vienna.

By Car: From the main B-3 highway along the Danube, the
road up to the camp starts a little west of the actual town of Mauthausen. Look for and follow *KZ-Memorial* or *KZ-Mauthausen*
signs. As you arrive at the camp, bear right to reach the parking lot
(up to 4 hours free). Having a car lets you glimpse the quarry where
camp prisoners were forced to toil: Leave the main parking lot,
head down the hill to the first intersection, turn right (following
Gasthaus Kreuzmühle signs), and look for the quarry on your right
and a small unpaved parking area to your left.

By Train: Trains depart roughly hourly to Mauthausen from
Salzburg (2 hours each way, change in Linz) and Vienna (2 hours,
most from Vienna's Hauptbahnhof, change in St. Valentin or Linz).
From Melk, there are only a couple of workable connections each
day (often requiring multiple changes and lengthy layovers). It's not
impossible, but it takes longer than from Salzburg or Vienna; check
schedules carefully (www.oebb.at).

In Mauthausen, the train station is three miles from the camp,
on the other side of town. Note that there are no lockers at the station, but the memorial visitors center will store bags.

There's no bus from the station to the camp, and taxis run
about €15 (share cost with other tourists, minibus taxis available).
Call the Mauthausen-based **Taxi Brixner** (mobile 0664-462-
3699); the station attendant may call for you if you ask politely.
Arrange a return pickup with your driver, or ask the camp ticket
office to call a taxi for you when you are ready to go.

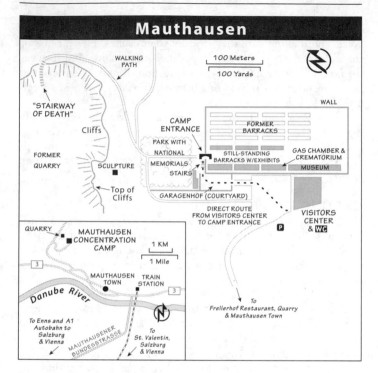

ORIENTATION TO THE MEMORIAL

Cost and Hours: Free to enter; March-Oct daily 9:00-17:30; Nov-Feb Tue-Sun until 15:45, closed Mon; last entry 45 minutes before closing.

Information: Tel. 07238/2269, www.mauthausen-memorial.org.

Tours: A worthwhile audioguide is available for €3 at the information desk (leave ID as deposit) or download the free Mauthausen Audioguide app ahead of time.

Services: The information desk has a bookstore and small lockers for daypacks. Ask information desk to store larger luggage.

Eating: Next door to the visitors center is a **café** serving drinks, snacks, and sandwiches. A **farmhouse** below the parking lot also serves meals—see "Sleeping and Eating Near the Memorial," later in this chapter.

VISITING THE MEMORIAL

The camp has two important areas for visitors. The information desk, café, and visitors center are in the **modern complex** near the parking lot. The museum is within the **camp walls.**

Stop briefly at the visitors center, especially if your arrival coincides with the start of the 45-minute film (generally screened at the top of each hour). But save a long visit in the visitors center (and perhaps the film) until after you've seen the camp itself—the most worthwhile sightseeing is inside the camp walls.

From the visitors center, circle all the way around to the camp entrance (at the left side of the building—either walk along the road, or go through the gateway, cross the aptly named Garagenhof courtyard, and climb the stairs). In the parklike area outside the camp entrance you'll find gripping **memorials** to those who perished here, erected by each home country of the camp's victims. Many yellowed photos have fresh flowers to honor loved ones who are still not forgotten.

Entering the camp brings you onto a long, open area, which was used for roll call several times a day. To either side are some original **barracks** (the others have been torn down) with exhibits. On the left, the first barracks show where records were kept and where a brothel was once opened with women from a nearby camp. The second and third barracks show inmates' housing quarters and that of "*kapos*" (prisoner functionaries) charged with maintaining order. These trustees were given special privileges and better rations, deliberately creating inequality among the prisoners. On the right, the fourth (farthest) barracks is an absorbing **museum** that presents the camp's history and shows you its crematoriums and small gas chamber.

The museum's upper floor presents the camp's history chronologically. The central aisle gives wider historical context, while displays on the left explain how the Nazi period and World War II played out in Austria and at Mauthausen specifically. Displays on the right tell the stories of Mauthausen inmates—how they came to be imprisoned here, the arbitrary rules they suffered under, and the numbers they had to wear. Exhibits include gripping artifacts and brief audio and video clips of survivors. The museum is unusual in providing biographies of many of the Nazi officers who ran the camp and detailing their postwar fates: Some committed suicide, some were sentenced to death by Allied tribunals, and others received long prison terms.

Downstairs, exhibits focus on the violence that took place here, by execution or forced labor, and testify to the camp's inhumanity.

At the end of this room, exit and walk through the **crematorium,** used to burn the bodies of those who died at Mauthausen, and a room listing the names of 81,000 inmates known to have died here. Take time to read the plaques still being sent by families of those who didn't make it. Finally you pass the small **gas chamber,** where about 3,500 inmates were killed. Afterward, you can see a few more exhibits and the camp prison in the adjoining barrack.

Back outside the camp (right in front of you as you exit), find the huge, black **menorah-like sculpture** overlooking the quarry. To your right, a rough cobbled path leads a couple hundred yards down to the **"Stairway of Death"** (inmates had a much rougher ascent before it was rebuilt in 1942). Connecting the quarry with the camp and its stone depot, the long stairway earned its name for good reason. Inmates were fed the bare minimum to continue working. If they couldn't carry slabs of rocks on their back up the stairway all day long—under the harshest of conditions and on a starvation diet—they were shot on the spot. Most died within a year of their arrival. (Toward the end of the war, the work shifted to making aircraft parts in a factory.) If the vast quarry is open, hike  down to its ground level and ponder the scene; you'll be left with a lasting and poignant impression.

Before you leave, return to the visitors center. It has computer screens with more survivor interviews, an exhibit on the camp crematorium, and a graphic 45-minute film. There are several screening rooms—ask the staff which room has the English version.

SLEEPING AND EATING NEAR THE MEMORIAL

I'd try to overnight in Vienna, Melk, or Salzburg instead of around Mauthausen. But if you're driving and have a special reason to stay near the camp, **$$ Hotel zum Goldenen Schiff,** in the town of Enns across the river (just off the autobahn, less than four miles southwest of Mauthausen), is a solid value run by the Brunner family. It has 25 comfy rooms and a quaint location right on Enns' main square (family rooms, elevator, sauna, free parking, Hauptplatz 23, tel. 07223/86086, www.hotel-brunner.at, office@hotel-brunner.at). The hotel also rents one **$$$** honeymoon double halfway up the Town Hall tower—reached by a stairway with 72 giant steps. This used to be the bell-ringer's apartment (reserve on website—and repack into a day bag).

A good option for a refreshing, peaceful meal before or after your visit to Mauthausen is the **Moststube Frellerhof,** a farmhouse 50 yards below the Mauthausen parking lot. Their specialty is apple-and-pear wine (called *Most* in this part of Austria—not the same as the Viennese *Most* made from grapes) and homemade schnapps, and they serve light, farm-fresh lunches and dinners in a fine modern dining room and shady back patio (sandwiches, limited warm food, generally May-Aug Tue-Fri 15:00-22:00, Sat-Sun from 11:00, closed Mon; same hours Sept-April but closed Mon-Wed; playground, tel. 07238/2789).

DANUBE VALLEY

BRATISLAVA, SLOVAKIA

The Slovak capital, Bratislava, is an unexpected charmer. Its old town bursts with colorfully restored facades, lively outdoor cafés, and swanky boutiques. The ramshackle industrial quarter to the east is rapidly being redeveloped into a forest of skyscrapers. The hilltop castle gleams from a recent facelift. And even the glum communist-era suburb of Petržalka has undergone a Technicolor makeover. Bratislava and Vienna have forged a new twin-city alliance for trade and commerce, making this truly the nexus of Central Europe.

It's easy to get the feeling that workaday Bratislavans—who strike some visitors as gruff—are being pulled to the cutting edge of the 21st century kicking and screaming. But many Slovaks embrace the changes and fancy themselves as the yang to Vienna's yin: If Vienna is a staid, elderly aristocrat sipping coffee, then Bratislava is a vivacious young professional jet-setting around Europe. Bratislava at night is a lively place; thanks in part to tens of thousands of university students, its youthful center thrives.

Bratislava's location—on the Danube (and the tourist circuit) smack-dab between Budapest and Vienna—makes it a convenient "on the way" destination. I admit that Bratislava used to leave me cold. But changes over the last 10-15 years have transformed it into a delightful destination. And its energy is inspiring.

PLANNING YOUR TIME

A few hours are plenty to get the gist of Bratislava. Head straight to the old town and follow my self-guided walk, finishing with one or more of the city's fine viewpoints: Ascend to the "UFO" observation deck atop the funky bridge, ride the elevator up to the Sky Bar for a peek (and maybe a drink), or hike up to the castle for the views. With more time, stroll along the Danube riverbank

Welcome to Slovakia

Sitting quietly in the very center of Central Europe, wedged between bigger and stronger nations (Hungary, Austria, the Czech Republic, and Poland), Slovakia was brutally disfigured by the communists, then overshadowed by the Czechs. But in recent years, this fledgling republic has found its wings. While the east of Slovakia is still catching up, locals brag that the region around Bratislava has the hottest economy and highest income per capita of any region in the former communist region of Europe.

With about 5.5 million people in a country of 19,000 square miles (similar to Massachusetts and New Hampshire combined), Slovakia is one of Europe's smallest nations. Recent economic reforms have caused two very different Slovakias to emerge: the modern, industrialized, flat, affluent west, centered on the capital of Bratislava; and the remote, poorer, mountainous, "backward" east, with high unemployment and traditional lifestyles.

Slovakia is ethnically diverse: In addition to the Slavic Slovaks, there are Hungarians (about 10 percent of the population, "stranded" here when Hungary lost this land after World War I) and Roma (called Gypsies in the past, also about 10 percent). Slovakia has struggled to incorporate both of these large and often-mistreated minority groups.

Slovakia has spent most of its history as someone else's backyard. For centuries, it was ruled from Budapest and known as "Upper Hungary." At other times, it was an important chunk of

to the thriving, modern Eurovea development. If you spend the evening in Bratislava, you'll find it lively with students, busy cafés, and nightlife.

Note that museums and galleries are closed on Monday.

Day-Tripping from Vienna to Bratislava

Bratislava is perfect as a stopover on the way from Vienna to Budapest. You have three transportation options: train, bus, or riverboat. It's prudent to bring your passport if visiting Bratislava for the day (though it's unlikely anyone will ask for it).

Trains connect Vienna and Bratislava easily and quickly (1 hour), leaving twice an hour from Vienna's Hauptbahnhof (main station). This is the most straightforward approach. A €16 the Habsburg Empire, ruled from neighboring Vienna. But most outsiders think first of another era: the 75 years that Slovakia was joined with the Czech Republic as the country of "Czechoslova-kia." From its start in the aftermath of World War I, this union of Czechs and Slovaks was troubled; some Slovaks chafed at being ruled from Prague, while many Czechs resented the financial burden of their poorer neighbors to the east.

After gaining their freedom during 1989's peaceful Velvet Revolution, the Czechs and Slovaks began to think of the future. The Slovaks wanted to rename the country Czecho-Slovakia (with that all-important hyphen signifying an equal partnership), and to give themselves more autonomy. The Czechs balked, relations gradually deteriorated, and Slovak nationalist candidate Vladimír Mečiar fared surprisingly well in the 1992 elections. Taking it as a sign that the two peoples wanted to part ways, politicians pushed through (in just three months) the peaceful separation of the now-independent Czech and Slovak Republics. The "Velvet Divorce" became official on January 1, 1993.

At first the Slovaks struggled. Communist rule had been particularly unkind to them, and their economy was in shambles. Visionary leaders set forth bold solutions, including a flat tax (19 percent), followed by EU membership in 2004 and adoption of the euro currency in 2009. Before long, major international corporations began to notice the same thing the Soviets had: This is a great place to build stuff, thanks to its strategic location (300 million consumers live within a day's drive), low labor costs, and a well-trained workforce. Today multiple foreign automakers have plants here, and Slovakia produces one million cars a year, making it the world's biggest car producer per capita.

Bratislava's success story is impressive. The capital region enjoys almost full employment, and seems poised to lead Slovakia into a bright future.

Bratislava-Ticket covers your round-trip train ride as well as public transportation in Bratislava (all for less than the cost of a one-way ticket). In Vienna, buy the ticket from any red ÖBB ticket machine (choosing "Bratislava" makes the option pop up). Pay careful attention to departure/arrival stations, as the Vienna connection alternates between Bratislava's two train stations, Hlavná Stanica and Petržalka. If checking your bag at the station, be sure that your return or onward connection will depart from there. The return portion of the ticket (but not the public transit benefit) is valid for four days.

The **bus** is slightly cheaper, but I'd take the train, given the good-value Bratislava-Ticket for round-trip travelers, and the absence of luggage lockers in Bratislava's bus terminals. **Flixbus** runs from Vienna's bus terminal (Erdbergstrasse 200A, U: Erd-berg) to Bratislava's convenient Most SNP bus stop beneath the SNP Bridge (€7.50 one-way, €13 round-trip, hourly, 1 hour, tel. 02/4363-7257, www.flixbus.com). **Slovak Lines/Postbus** buses connect Vienna's Hauptbahnhof with Bratislava's inconvenient official bus station (Autobusová Stanica Mlynské Nivy), about a 15-minute walk east of the old town (€5.50 one-way, 1-2/hour, 1 hour, tel. 0810-222-3336, www.slovaklines.sk). Both buses stop at the Vienna and Bratislava airports.

You can also shuttle between Vienna and Bratislava on the Danube by **riverboat**—it's relaxing, and only a little slower than the bus or train (but more expensive). (Sail with your passport, as you'll be crossing a border.) The fast **Twin City Liner** runs mod-ern catamarans between Vienna's Schwedenplatz (where Vienna's town center hits the canal) and a dock at the edge of Bratislava's old town, along Fajnorovo nábrežie (€30-35 each way, 3-5/day, late March-Oct only, 1.5 hours; reservations smart, Austrian tel. 00-43-1-904-8880, www.twincityliner.com). The competing Slovak **LOD** line connects the cities a little more cheaply (on older Rus-sian hydrofoils) but runs just twice a day and leaves from Vien-na's less-convenient Reichsbrücke dock on the main river, farther from the city center (€25 one-way, €44 round-trip, 1.5 hours, tel. 02/5293-2226, www.lod.sk).

Orientation to Bratislava

Bratislava, with 430,000 residents, is Slovakia's capital and biggest city. It has a compact, colorful old town (staré mesto), with the castle on the hill above. Most of the old town is traffic-free. This small area is surrounded by a vast construction zone, rotting residen-tial districts desperately in need of beautification, and a sprawling communist-built suburb that is seeing new life (Petržalka, across the river).

TOURIST INFORMATION

The helpful TI is at Klobučnícka 2, on Primate's Square behind the Old Town Hall (daily 9:00-19:00, Nov-April until 18:00, tel. 02/16186, www.visitbratislava.com). They also have a branch at the main train station (Hlavná Stanica; daily 9:30-18:00).

Bratislava City Card: The TI sells this card (€15/1 day, €18/2 days), which includes free transit and free or discounted admission to local sights. It's worthwhile only if you're doing the included old town walking tour (€14 without the card—see "Tours in Bratisla-va," later).

ARRIVAL IN BRATISLAVA
By Train

Trains from Vienna stop at one (but never both) of Bratislava's two train stations: Hlavná Stanica or Petržalka. Hlavná Stanica is far from welcoming, but it's walkable to some accommodations and the old town; Petržalka (in a suburban shopping area) is small, clean, and modern, but you'll have to take a bus into town. Frequent bus #93 connects the two stations in about 10 minutes. For public transit info and maps, see http://imhd.sk.

Hlavná Stanica (Main Train Station)

This decrepit station is about a half-mile north of the old town. A left-luggage desk is to your right as you exit the tracks (*úschovňa batožín;* confirm open hours for pickup). A few lockers are along track 1; more are to the left from the main hall (after the vending machines and through the door). The station also has a TI window, and there's an ATM in the main hall. A nicer, more modern waiting area is down the hallway to the left (with the tracks at your back).

Getting Downtown: From the station, it's a short bus ride or boring 15-minute walk to the town center. (**Taxis** stand by, but with rip-off prices—they'll try to charge €15 rather than the legitimate €5 drop charge for the short ride. You can try insisting on the meter, but since they're basically unregulated, it likely won't help.)

Bus #93 leaves every five minutes from the right-hand curb 50 yards in front of the station; it stops at Grassalkovich Palace, Zochova (nearest the old town), and Most SNP (the bus station under the SNP Bridge, by the river). Buy a 15-minute *základný lístok/basic* ticket from the machine for €0.70, and stamp it as you get on the bus.

To **walk** downtown, exit out the station's front door and follow the covered walkway past the bus stops. After the road bends right, take the pedestrian overpass, then head straight downhill on the busy main drag, Štefánikova. You'll pass the presidential gardens, then Grassalkovich Palace. The old town—marked by the green steeple of St. Michael's Gate (the start of my self-guided walk)—is a long block ahead of you.

Petržalka Train Station (ŽST Petržalka)

Half of the trains from Vienna arrive at this quiet, modern little train station, across the river in the modernized suburb of Petržalka. The main hall has an ATM and luggage lockers (by the door to the tracks).

Getting Downtown: Two different buses head to the old town, from opposite sides of the station. For either bus, buy a 15-minute *základný lístok/basic* ticket from the machine for €0.70,

Bratislava

Accommodations

1. Hotel Marrol's
2. Roset Boutique Hotel
3. Radisson Blu Carlton Hotel
4. To Loft Hotel & Wilson Palace
5. Aplend City Hotel Michalská
6. Penzión Virgo

Eateries & Other

7. Bratislavská Reštaurácia & Pivovar
8. Výčap u Ernőho
9. Foodstock
10. Mecheche Snack Bar
11. Urban House
12. Carnevalle, Zylinder & Café Restaurant Verne
13. Sky Bar Restaurant
14. Kaffee Mayer & Café Roland
15. Konditorei Kormüth
16. Čajovňa V Podzemí
17. Billa Supermarket

ULICA PALISÁDY

ŠTETINOVA

PANENSKÁ

LYCEJNÁ

KOZIA ULICA

PODJAVOR

KONVENTNÁ

STAROMESTSKÁ

ZOCHOVA

SVORADOVA

Zochova (B)

ZAMOCKA ULICA

BAŠTOVÁ

Fashion Courtyard

KLARISKÁ

KAPITULSKÁ

ZIDOVSKÁ

KRÁTKA

STRELECKÁ

SUMMER RIDING SCHOOL

CASTLE

←ENTRY

TOWN WALL

OLD

PREPOŠTSKÁ

STAROMESTSKÁ

VENTÚRSKA

WALK ENDS

PARLIAMENT

KNIGHTS HALL

TREASURE ROOM   TICKETS

VODNÝ

SVÄTOPLUK STATUE

ZÁM. SCHODY

OLD FOUNTAIN

ST. MARTIN'S CATHEDRAL

LUCULUS GELATO

SCHODY PRI STAREJ VODÁRNI

HOLOCAUST MEMORIAL   HANS CHRISTIAN ANDERSEN STATUE

NÁBR. ARMÁDNEHO GENERÁLA L. SVOBODU

Most SNP (Bus stop under bridge) (B)

RÁZUSOVO NÁBR.

BRATISLAVA

100 Meters
100 Yards

SNP BRIDGE

To Petržalka ↓   "UFO" OBSERVATION DECK

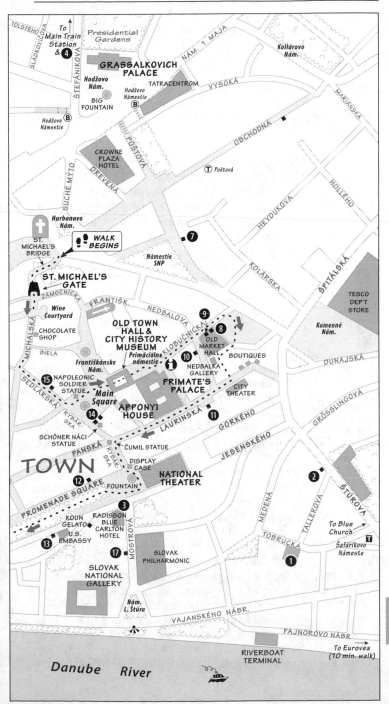

TOLSTÉHO

SLÁDKOVIČOVA

To Main Train Station & ❹

ŠTEFÁNIKOVA

Presidential Gardens

NÁM. 1. MAJA

Kollárovo Nám.

GRASSALKOVICH PALACE

Hodžovo Nám.

Hodžovo Námestie Ⓑ

TATRACENTRUM

VYSOKÁ

BIG FOUNTAIN

Hodžovo Námestie Ⓑ

MARIÁNSKA

OBCHODNÁ

POŠTOVÁ

CROWNE PLAZA HOTEL

DREVENÁ

SUCHÉ MÝTO

Ⓣ Poštová

HOLLÉHO

HEYDUKOVA

Hurbanovo Nám.

✝ ST. MICHAEL'S BRIDGE

👣 *WALK BEGINS*

Námestie SNP

❼

ŠPITÁLSKA

ST. MICHAEL'S GATE

ZÁMOČNÍCKA

FRANTIŠK.

NEDBALOVA

KOLÁRSKA

TESCO DEP'T STORE

Wine Courtyard

MICHALSKÁ

CHOCOLATE SHOP

BIELA

OLD TOWN HALL & CITY HISTORY MUSEUM

Primaciálne námestie

Františkánske Nám.

KLOBUČNÍCKA

❾

❽ OLD MARKET HALL

Kamenné Nám.

DUNAJSKÁ

SEDLÁRSKA

❿ NEDBALKA GALLERY

BOUTIQUES

❶❺ Napoleonic Soldier Statue

Main Square

PRIMATE'S PALACE

CITY THEATER

RYBÁRSKA

❶❹

APPONYI HOUSE

LAURINSKÁ

❶❶

GORKÉHO

GRÖSSLINGOVA

SCHÖNER NÁCI STATUE

PANSKÁ

RYBÁRSKA

ČUMIL STATUE

JESENSKÉHO

TOWN

DISPLAY CASE

❷

ŠTÚROVA

❶❷

FOUNTAIN

NATIONAL THEATER

PROMENADE SQUARE

❸

RADISSON BLUE CARLTON HOTEL

MEDENÁ

TALLEROVA

TOBRUCKÁ

To Blue Church

Ⓣ Šafárikovo Námeste

KOUN GELATO

MOSTOVÁ

❶❼

❶❸ U.S. EMBASSY

SLOVAK PHILHARMONIC

SLOVAK NATIONAL GALLERY

Nám. Ľ. Štúra

❶

VAJANSKÉHO NÁBR.

FAJNOROVO NÁBR

To Eurovea (10 min. walk)

BRATISLAVA

RIVERBOAT TERMINAL

Danube River

and stamp it as you board. The stop closest to the old town is Zo-chova. **Bus #80** stops closest to the station but makes more stops on the way to town: From the main hall, exit, cross the street, and turn left to find the stop (direction: Kollárova nám). **Bus #93** is more direct but a longer walk from the station: Take the long tunnel under the tracks, exit on the other side, and follow the crosswalk straight across the busy highway to find the stop (direction: Hlavná Stanica).

By Bus, Boat, or Plane

Buses from Vienna arrive at either the Most SNP stop, beneath the old town side of the SNP Bridge (a 5-minute walk to the old town) or the inconvenient official bus station (Autobusová Stanica Mlynské Nivy, about a 15-minute walk east of the old town). Riverboats use a dock a short walk downstream from the SNP Bridge, just below the old town. For more on bus and boat connections, see "Day-Tripping from Vienna to Bratislava," earlier. For information on Bratislava's airport, see "Bratislava Connections," at the end of this chapter.

HELPFUL HINTS

Money: Slovakia, like Austria, uses the euro.

Language: Many Bratislavans speak English quite well (especially young people). The Slovak language is closely related to Czech and Polish. The local word used informally for both "hi" and "bye" is easy to remember: *ahoj* (pronounced "AH-hoy," like a pirate). "Please" is *prosím* (PROH-seem), "thank you" is *ďakujem* (DYAH-koo-yehm), "good" is *dobrý* (DOH-bree), and "Cheers!" is *Na zdravie!* (nah ZDRAH-vyeh; think "nice driving").

Phone Tips: To call locally within Bratislava, dial the number without the area code. To make a long-distance call within Slovakia, start with the area code (which begins with 0). To call from Austria to Slovakia or vice versa, use the country code (421 for Slovakia, 43 for Austria) and follow the dialing instructions in the Practicalities chapter.

Taxis: Taxis come in handy here, but are poorly regulated—they can charge whatever rates they want. Any ride in the city center *should* be around €5. However, cabbies waiting at the train station and tourist spots (such as the castle) are accustomed to quoting an inflated, flat price—usually more like €10 or €15. To improve your odds, look for a taxi with a logo and telephone number prominently on the door, and insist that they use the meter. Locals call taxis rather than hailing them on the street—you can ask a hotelier or restaurant staffer to call one for you.

Supermarket: Centrally located, **Billa** is big and handy. Find it across from the Philharmonic, on Mostová street (Mon-Sat 7:00-21:00, Sun from 8:00).

Local Guidebook: For in-depth suggestions on Bratislava sightseeing, dining, and more, look for the eye-pleasing *Bratislava Active* guidebook (around €10, sold at every postcard rack).

Tours in Bratislava

Walking Tours

The TI offers a one-hour old town walking tour in English every day in summer at 14:00 (€14, free with Bratislava City Card). For €28, two people can book the same hour-long tour with the same guides as a private tour at whatever time is convenient. The TI can arrange this for you with a few hours' notice (see "Tourist Information," earlier in this chapter). This can be a great way to become friends with the city.

Local Guide

MS Agency, run by **Martin Sloboda,** offers quality guides (€130/3 hours, €160/4 hours, mobile 0905-627-265, www.bratislava-guide.sk, sloboda@msagency.sk).

Martin, a can-do entrepreneur and tireless Bratislava booster (and author of the great *Bratislava Active* guidebook described above) helped me put this chapter together. He's part of the ambitious young generation that came of age as communism fell— and whose energy and leadership are reshaping the city.

Bratislava Old Town Walk

This self-guided orientation walk circles delightfully traffic-free old Bratislava (figure 1.5 hours, not including sightseeing stops).

• *Start on the bridge about 50 yards uphill from the green copper spire of the watchtower, St. Michael's Gate (it looks like a church spire, at the top of the old town)—with the tram tracks of the ring road just beyond.*

St. Michaels Bridge

You're standing below a watchtower marking St. Michael's Gate (Michalská Brána), part of the town's medieval wall. It's capped with the Archangel Michael busy killing a dragon.

The Hungarian king gave Pressburg (as Bratislava was called back then) city status in 1291. This meant the city had permission to fortify, offer protection, and tax trade. Bratislava was at the crossroads of two medieval trade routes (the north-south "Amber Route" from the Baltics to the Mediterranean, and the east-west "Oriental Route" along the Danube). You're standing over the former dry moat, now a garden of the city library and an outdoor concert venue.

Before heading into the old town, look away from the tower. Notice the sleek-in-the-1920s Art Deco building on the right. Now a bar, when it was built in 1929 it was a supermodern department store designed to show off Bata shoes (a Czechoslovakian company that was once the largest shoe company in the world).

• *Stroll over the bridge and enter the old center. You're outside the wall, walking through a barbican—shaped like an "L" for better defense. Pause just after passing under the gate.*

St. Michael's Gate (Michalská Brána)

This is the last surviving tower of the city wall. Just below the gate, notice the "kilometer zero" plaque in the ground, marking the point from which distances in Slovakia are measured. But I wouldn't trust the distances...unless we're somehow on the equator: According to this, the North and South Poles are both 4,667 kilometers away.

• *Before you stretches...*

Michalská Street

Pretty as it is now, Bratislava's old center was a decrepit ghost town during the communist era. The communist regime believed that Bratislavans of the future would live in large, efficient apartment buildings. They saw the old town as a useless relic of the bad old days of poor plumbing, cramped living spaces, social injustice, and German domination—a view that left no room to respect, or maintain, the town's physical heritage.

For example, notice the uniform cobbles underfoot. In the 1950s, the communists sold Bratislava's original medieval cobbles to cute German towns that were rebuilding themselves in a way that preserved their elegant Old World character. Locals avoided this stripped-down, desolate corner of the city, preferring to spend time in the Petržalka suburb across the river.

With the fall of communism in 1989, the new government

began sorting out who had the rights to the old town's buildings, and returning them to their original owners. During this time, little repair or development took place (since there was no point investing in a building until ownership was clearly established). By 1998, most of the property issues were resolved. The city made the old town traffic-free, spruced up the public buildings, and encouraged private owners to restore their buildings as well.

Two decades later, the result is this delightful street, lined with inviting cafés and restaurants. Poke around to experience Bratislava's charm. Courtyards and passageways—most of them open to the public—burrow through the city's buildings. Half a block down on the left, the courtyard at #12 was once home to vintners; their former cellars are now coffee shops, massage parlors, crafts boutiques, and cigar shops. More dead-end passages with characteristic shops are across the street, at #7 and #5.

The **Cukráreň na Korze** chocolate shop (on the left, at #6) is highly regarded among locals for its delicious hot chocolate and creamy truffles. Above the shop's entrance, the **cannonball** embedded in the wall recalls Napoleon's two sieges of Bratislava (the 1809 siege was 42 days long), which caused massive suffering—even worse than during World War II (the French consumed all of the wine stocks). This is just one of several cannonballs around town. Keep an eye out for more of these reminders of one of Bratislava's darkest times.

• *Two blocks down from St. Michael's Gate, where the street changes to Ventúrska (at the signpost and big rock in the street), turn left along Sedlárska street.*

*Peek into **Konditorei Kormüth** (a few doors down on the right, at #8). Mr. Kormüth dedicated many years and lots of money to creating a 17th-century setting for his café. For €10, you can enjoy a coffee and slice of cake in this unforgettable setting while reading his story on the menu.*

Farther on, you reach the historic...

Main Square (Hlavné Námestie)

This modest square, the centerpiece of Bratislava's old town, feels too petite for a national capital. Its style is a mishmash—every building around it seems to date from a different architectural period.

The **fountain**, the most beautiful and historic in town, is a history lesson just waiting to happen. It celebrates the 1563 coronation of Maximillian II—the first Habsburg emperor to also be crowned "King of Hungary." Back then, Slovakia was part of Hungary, which was ruled from Austria. (Got that?) As a mark of respect to the locals, Austrian emperors were crowned a second time, as Hungarian kings. (The German phrase for this arrangement—*König und Kaiser*, "king and emperor," often abbreviated *"K+K"*—remains a mark of quality to this day.) I suppose if your choice as a Hungarian was to be ruled by the Ottomans or by an Austrian Habsburg, the answer was easy.

This arrangement also helps explain why Vienna and Bratislava—the present-day capitals of Austria and Slovakia—are the closest of any two capitals in Europe (you can actually see the lights of one from the other). This closeness wasn't an accident—it was for security. Long before "Slovakia" existed, Bratislava (then called Pozsony) was the capital of "rump" Hungary—what was left of Hungary after most of its territory, including the capital Buda, was conquered by the Ottomans. Bratislava was as far from the Ottoman Turks as possible, while still being in Hungary, and very well fortified. The castle crowning the hill high above the old town was the royal residence and protector of the crown jewels during this time. (For more on the complicated tricultural mix of the city—Austrian/German, Hungarian, and Slavic/Slovak—see the "City of Three Cultures" sidebar, later in this chapter.)

Standing in the middle of the main square, do a quick clockwise spin tour. (You'll need to circle around the fountain to see everything.) Begin with the bold yellow tower of the **Old Town Hall** (Stará Radnica), which dominates the square. It's Gothic at the core, but with a Baroque facade. Near the bottom of the tower, to the left of the pointed window, there's another Napoleonic cannonball embedded in the facade.

Down the street to the right of the Old Town Hall is the **Apponyi House,** the mansion of an 18th-century aristocrat that also holds the Slovak National Collection of Wine (described under "Sights in Bratislava").

Turn farther right and note the venerable cafés. The classic choice is **Kaffee Mayer,** with dark awnings and outdoor seating facing the fountain. They've been selling coffee and cakes to a genteel clientele since 1873. You can enjoy your pick-me-up in the swanky old interior or out on the square.

At the corner in front of Kaffee Mayer (you may have to walk closer to see it) is a beloved statue. The jovial chap doffing his top hat is **Schöner Náci,** who lived in Bratislava until the 1960s. This eccentric old man, a poor carpet cleaner, would dress up in his one black suit and top hat, and go strolling through the city, offering gifts to the women he fancied. (He'd often whisper *"schön"*—German for "pretty," which is how he got his nickname.) Schöner Náci now gets to spend eternity greeting visitors outside his favorite café.

Across the street, the Art Nouveau **Café Roland** is known for its 1904 Klimt-style mosaics and historic photos of the city known as Pressburg (Austrian times) or Pozsony (Hungarian times). The building was once a bank. Step inside. These days the barista stands where a different kind of bean counter once did, guarding a vault that now holds coffee.

Now walk toward the Old Town Hall. Up the little side-square to the left is a jumble of cute **mini kiosks**—sporting old-time cityscape engravings on their roofs—selling local handicrafts and knickknacks. In December, the square transforms into the city's popular and atmospheric Christmas market.

Step through the passageway leading to the Old Town Hall's gorgeously restored courtyard, with its Renaissance arcades. (The entrance to the excellent **City History Museum**—described later—is inside the courtyard.)

Continue all the way through the courtyard into **Primate's Square** (Primaciálne Námestie). The pink mansion on the right is the **Primate's Palace**—the new town hall in the old archbishop's residence—with a fine interior decorated with English tapestries (described later). At the far end of this square is the **TI**.

Continue straight ahead (with the TI on your right) down the street called Klobučnícka—**"Hatters Street."** In the Middle Ages, craftsmen gathered according to their trade, and streets were named for the craft found there. If you needed a hat, you knew where to find one.

• *Continue two blocks straight ahead to a square on your right, fronted by a fine two-story Neoclassical market hall.*

Old Market Hall (Stará Tržnica)

Built in 1910, this busy community center today hosts concerts and a Saturday market. The market hall square is a lively gathering place, too; see details on its monthly food-truck festivals under "Eating in Bratislava," later.

On the right side of the square is a stark 12-story building—the tallest in town before WWII. If it looks barren, that was the point. It's from the Bauhaus school—the rage among German architects between the world wars. The battle cries for these harbingers of modernity: "form follows function," "less is more," and "luxury does not require ornamentation." Today its ground floor is home to a dingy bingo parlor (visitors welcome).

The bombs of World War II mostly spared the old town but pulverized a nearby oil refinery and dynamite plant—targeted by Allies because they were a key part of the occupying Nazi war economy. But a few bombs went awry and hit the area just uphill from here, which accounts for all the post-1945 buildings. The concrete jungle beyond the tram tracks is modernist architecture of the 1960s communist era.

• *Find a door just to the left of the Old Market Hall facade marked* Centrál Pasáž *(press buzzer if closed). It leads through a 1920s Art Deco shopping gallery (cutting edge a century ago) to a busy pedestrian boulevard.*

Laurinská Street—Bratislava's Fashion Drag

This street is lined with fun-to-browse boutiques. In the little nook where the street bends (just to the left) are three popular, very Slovak shops: **Slowatch,** with casual clothes and bags; **Slávica,** a high-end design shop with jewelry and accessories; and **Kompot,** selling a fun variety of unique, Slovak-themed T-shirts. This is a good spot to browse for a quality, non-kitschy souvenir.

Across the street from where you entered Laurinská is the chillingly blocky facade of the communist-era **City Theater** (Mestské Divadlo). On the upper floor are Socialist Realist stained-glass windows—hard to see during the day, but illuminated at night, like a communist night light. We'll see the much fancier National Theater in a moment.

Turn right on Laurinská and stroll like a local for three long blocks—people-watching and window-shopping at more high-end shops. Soon you reach the Bratislava city seal in the cobbles (a three-towered castle with a gate half-open).

• *Just beyond that, on the left, look out or you might stumble over a bronze fellow peeking out of a manhole.*

Čumil ("the Peeper")

Čumil was the first—and is still the favorite—of the many whimsical statues that dot Bratislava's old town (such as Schöner Náci, whom we met earlier). Most date from the late 1990s, when city leaders wanted to entice locals back into the newly prettied-up and fun-loving center. There's no story behind this one—the artist simply wanted to create a playful icon and let the townspeople make up their own tales. Čumil has survived being driven over by a truck—twice—and he's still grinning.

• *Turn left at the man in the manhole and follow Rybárska to reach the long, skinny square called...*

Promenade Square (Hviezdoslavovo Námestie)

At the near end of this square is Bratislava's impressive opera house, the silver-topped **Slovak National Theater** (Slovenské Národné Divadlo). When the theater opened in the 1880s, half the shows were in German and half in Hungarian. Today, the official language is Slovak. Across the way, the opulent, beige, Neo-Baroque building is home to the Slovak Philharmonic (Slovenská Filharmónia).

Right in front of the opera house, look down into the round glass **display case** to see the foundation of the one-time Fishermen's Gate into the city. Water surrounds the base of the gate: This entire square was once a tributary of the Danube, and the Raddison Blu Carlton Hotel (long the VIP hotel in town) across the way was once a series of inns on different islands. The buildings along the old town side of the square mark where the city wall once stood. Now the square is a lively zone on balmy evenings, with several fine restaurants offering al fresco tables jammed with happy diners.

Turn right and stroll down the long square. Underfoot is a gigantic, cobbled version of Bratislava's city seal. After passing a statue of the square's namesake (Pavol Országh Hviezdoslav, a beloved Slovak poet), look for an ugly fence and barriers on the left. As usual, the US Embassy is the most heavily fortified building in the capital.

Just past the embassy is the low-profile entrance to the **Sky Bar,** an affordable rooftop restaurant with excellent views (ride the elevator to the seventh floor). The glass-roofed pavilion in the center of the square is a popular venue for summer concerts. Behind it, on the old town side of the square, is **Luculus,** where people are likely lined up outside for ice cream. (For ice cream without a line-up, you can backtrack to **Koun Gelato**—just before the US Embassy and immediately to the right of the Carlton Hotel.) On the right near the end of the park, a statue of Hans Christian Andersen is a reminder that the Danish storyteller enjoyed his visit to Bratislava, too.

• *Reaching the end of the square, you run into the barrier for a busy highway. Turn right and walk one block to find the big, black marble slab facing a modern monument.*

BRATISLAVA

City of Three Cultures:
Pressburg, Pozsony, Bratislava

Historically more of an Austrian and Hungarian city than a Slovak one, Bratislava has always been a Central European melting pot. Over the years, notable visitors, from Hans Christian Andersen to Casanova, have sung the praises of this bustling burg on the Danube.

For most of its history, Bratislava was part of the Austrian Empire and known as Press-burg, with a primarily German-speaking population. (Only the surrounding rural areas were Slovak.) The Hungarians used Pozsony (as they called it) as their capital during the century-and-a-half that Buda and Pest were occupied by Ottoman invaders.

By its turn-of-the-20th-century glory days, the city was a rich intersection of cultures—about 40 percent German, 40 percent Hungarian, and 20 percent Slovak. Shop clerks greeted customers in all three languages. It was said that the mornings belonged to the Slovaks (farmers who came into the city to sell their wares at market), the afternoons to the Hungarians (diplomats and office workers filling the cafés), and the evenings to the Austrians (wine producers who ran convivial neighborhood wine pubs where all three groups would gather). In those wine pubs, the vintner would listen to which language his customers used, then bring them a glass with the serving size expected in their home country: 0.3 liters for Hungarians, 0.25 liters for Austrians, and 0.2 liters for Slovaks (a distinction that still exists today). Jews (one-tenth of the population), and Roma (then called Gyp-

Holocaust Memorial

This was the site of Bratislava's original synagogue. You can see an etching of the building in the big slab. At the base of the memorial sculpture, look for the word "Remember" carved into the granite in Hebrew and Slovak, commemorating the 90,000 Slovak Jews who were deported to Nazi death camps. The fact that the town's main synagogue and main church (described next) were located side by side illustrates the tolerance that characterized Bratislava before Hitler. Ponder the modern statue: The open doors of an evacuated home with shadows of people who once lived there, all crowned with bullet holes and the Star of David. It evokes the fate of the more than 80,000 Slovak Jews who died in the Holocaust.

sies) rounded out the city's ethnic brew.

When the new nation of Czechoslovakia was formed from the rubble of World War I, the city shed its German and Hungarian names, and took the newly created Slavic name of Bratislava. The Slovak population was on the rise, but the city remained tricultural.

World War II changed all of that. With the dissolution of Czechoslovakia, Slovakia became an "independent" country under the thumb of the Nazis—who all but wiped out the Jewish population. At the end of the war, Czechoslovakia reunited under the USSR, and expelled the city's ethnic Germans and Hungarians in retribution for the misdeeds of Hitler and Horthy (Hungary's wartime leader).

Bratislava's urban heritage suffered terribly under the communists. The historic city's multilayered charm and delicate cultural fabric were ripped apart, then shrouded in gray. The communists were prouder of their ultramodern SNP Bridge than of the city's historic Jewish quarter—which they razed to make way for the bridge. Now the bridge and its highway slice through the center of the old town, and heavy traffic rattles the stained-glass windows of St. Martin's Cathedral. The city's Germanic heritage was also deliberately obscured.

But Bratislava's most recent chapter is one of great success. Since the fall of communism, the city has gone from gloomy victim to thriving economic center and social hub. With a healthy free market economy, it now has the chance to re-create itself as Slovakia's national capital. And its advantageous position on the Danube, a short commute from Vienna, is prompting its redevelopment as one of Europe's up-and-coming cities. Once again, the streets of Bratislava are filled with German- and Hungarian-speakers...tourists and business travelers from nearby Vienna and Budapest.

Hike up the stairs to the adjacent church. At the top of the stairs, pause to appreciate the view. Looking toward the river, you can't miss the huge **SNP Bridge** (Most SNP), the communists' pride and joy. The "SNP" is shorthand for the 1944 Slovak National Uprising against the Nazis, a common focus of communist remembrance. As with most Soviet-era landmarks in former communist countries, locals aren't crazy about this structure—not only for the questionable Starship Enterprise design, but also because of the oppressive regime it represented. However, the restaurant and observation deck up top have been renovated into a posh eatery called (appropriately enough) "UFO." You can visit it for the views, a drink, or a full meal. (For details, see the listing, later.)

While the bridge was a groundbreaking design in 1972, the freeway that runs across it messed up the city. If the highway thundering a few feet in front of this historic church's door were any closer, the off-ramp would go through the nave. In the next decade, the plan is to move the highway into a tunnel that will emerge at the bridge—returning peace to this corner of Bratislava.

• *Now turn your attention to the church towering overhead.*

St. Martin's Cathedral (Dóm Sv. Martina)

Nineteen Hungarian kings and queens were crowned in this church—more than anywhere else in Hungary. A replica of the

Hungarian crown still tops the steeple. There's relatively little to see inside the cathedral—but if it's open, duck in (Mon-Sat 9:00-11:30 & 13:00-18:00, Sun 13:30-16:30). In the fairly gloomy interior you'll find some fine carved-wood altarpieces (a Slovak specialty).

Just beyond the church is a stretch of the 15th-century **town wall.** The church was actually built into the wall, which explains its unusual north-side entry. In fact, look up to notice the fortified watchtower (with a WC drop on its left—and a security camera hanging out its hole) built into the corner of the church just above you.

• *Our walk is over. From here, you could either hike up to the* **castle** *(backtracking to the Holocaust Memorial, take the underpass beneath the highway, go up the stairs on the right marked by the* Hrad/Castle *sign, then turn left up the stepped lane marked* Zámocké Schody*), hike over the SNP Bridge (pedestrian walkway on lower level) to ride the elevator up the* **UFO viewing platform***, or head for the river and stroll downstream to the thriving and futuristic new*

*Bratislava—***Eurovea** *(all these are described under "Sights in Bratislava," later).*

Or, you could carry on as described below to end up back where you started...

Back To St. Michael's Gate

Continue the rest of the way around the church and take the grand stony staircase back down to busy Panská street. Turn left and follow Panská to the corner with Ventúrska. The **old fountain** here marks the actual cross point of the two great medieval trade routes (north-south from the Baltics to the Mediterranean, and east-west along the Danube). Head left, uphill (or north toward the Baltics, if you're an amber merchant) toward St. Michael's Gate.

Over the next few blocks, you may see the names of great **composers** on plaques marking historical buildings. Franz Liszt performed in Bratislava at age nine for local aristocrats and was discovered and sent to Vienna. Beethoven composed his *Moonlight Sonata* here. Mozart performed here at age six. Haydn conducted the orchestra here, and in the 20th century Béla Bartók called Bratislava home.

If you feel like a cup of tea along the way—or you're nervous about a nuclear attack—at #9 on the left (a long block after the fountain), climb through the thick iron door and down into **Čajovňa V Podzemí** ("The Underground Tea Room," daily 14:00-22:00 except Tue and Thu from 11:00), which fills an old bomb shelter with pillows, incense, and herby frills. A couple more blocks takes you back to where you started this walk.

Sights in Bratislava

Although Bratislava's museums are underwhelming—and you could easily have a great day here without visiting any—a few right in the old town are worth considering.

ON OR NEAR THE OLD TOWN'S MAIN SQUARE
▲Primate's Palace (Primaciálny Palác)
This tastefully restored French-Neoclassical mansion (formerly the residence of the archbishop, or "primate") dates from 1781. The religious counterpart of the castle, it filled in for Esztergom—the Hungarian religious capital—after that city was taken by the Ottomans in 1543. Even after the Ottoman defeat in the 1680s, this remained the winter residence of Hungary's archbishops. In the courtyard

gurgles a fountain with St. George slaying a three-headed dragon; the exhibits are upstairs.

Cost and Hours: €3, Tue-Sun 10:00-17:00, closed Mon, Primaciálne Námestie 1, tel. 02/5935-6394, www.bratislava.sk.

BRATISLAVA

Visiting the Museum: The palace, which now serves as the town hall, offers one fine floor of exhibits. Follow signs up the grand staircase to the ticket counter, then proceed up one more flight to the entrance lobby. From here, the Hall of Mirrors is on your left; straight ahead leads to a series of state apartments decorated with precious tapestries (on the right); and at the far end is a long picture gallery leading to the chapel.

Portraits hang in the lobby of the German-speaking royals who ruled Hungary, which ruled the Slovaks, who lived in this part of the vast Habsburg empire...history here is like a set of Russian stacking dolls. You'll see not one, but two portraits of Habsburg Empress Maria Theresa—young and old—as well as her father, Charles VI, and her son, Josef II. While Hungary was under Ottoman occupation, these Habsburg emperors came to Bratislava to also be crowned "kings of Hungary."

Hall of Mirrors: This is perhaps the most historic room in the city. In 1805, the "Peace of Pressburg" treaty was signed here—sorting out logistics after Napoleon beat the Austrians and Russians at the Battle of Austerlitz. This victory marked the peak of Napoleon's power. Today, the hall is used for concerts, city council meetings, and other important events. On the wall in the antechamber is a list of Bratislava's mayors since the 1280s.

State Rooms and Tapestries: This series of large public rooms, originally designed to impress, are now an art gallery. Distributed through several of these rooms is the museum's pride, and for many its highlight: a series of six English tapestries, illustrating the ancient Greek myth of the tragic love between Hero and Leander.

The tapestries were woven in England by Flemish weavers for the court of King Charles I (in the 1630s). They were kept in London's Hampton Court Palace until Charles was deposed and beheaded in 1649. Cromwell sold them to France to help fund his civil war, but after 1650, they disappeared...for centuries. In 1903, restorers broke through a false wall in this mansion and discovered the six tapestries, neatly folded and perfectly preserved. Nobody knows how they got here (perhaps they were squirreled away during the Napoleonic invasion, and whoever hid them didn't survive). The archbishop—who had just sold the palace to the city—cried foul and tried to claim the tapestries (valued at triple the sales price of the entire palace)...but the city said, "A deal's a deal."

Picture Gallery and Chapel: After traipsing through the grand rooms, go to the end of the main corridor and turn left down the hallway. This leads through the smaller rooms of the archbishop's private quarters, which are now a picture gallery decorated with minor Dutch, Flemish, German, and Italian paintings. At the end of this hall, a bay window looks down into the archbishop's own private chapel. When the archbishop became too ill to walk down to Mass, this window was built so he could take part in the service in his pajamas.

▲City History Museum (Mestské Múzeum)

Delving thoughtfully into Bratislava's past, this museum is rich in artifacts and well described in English and by the included audioguide. The core of the museum offers a sprawling, chronological look at local history through the 1920s, on two floors. The first floor features ecclesiastical art, including wood-carved statues. Upstairs, you'll have a chance to climb up into the Old Town Hall's tower, offering so-so views over the square, cathedral, and castle. Then you'll see more exhibits in rooms once used by the town council—courthouse, council hall, chapel, and so on. This is a fascinating look at Habsburg rule and slice-of-life Bratislava in the early 20th century. Look for the model of "Pressburg" during the age of Maria Theresa. Farther along, trilingual street signs are a reminder that historically, this was a city of three cultures and three languages (Slovak, German, Hungarian). The finale is down in the cellar: a graphic torture exhibit in the "law and order" zone, with replicas of torture equipment from the 16th through 18th centuries. At the far end of the exhibit, crouch down the passage to see three dreary and depressing cells...enough to make anybody behave.

Cost and Hours: €5, includes excellent audioguide, €6 combo-ticket with Apponyi House; open Tue-Fri 10:00-17:00, Sat-Sun 11:00-18:00, closed Mon; in the Old Town Hall—enter through courtyard, tel. 02/259-100-811, www.muzeum.bratislava.sk.

Apponyi House (Apponyiho Palác)

This nicely restored mansion of a Hungarian aristocrat is meaningless without the included audioguide (dull but informative). The museum has two parts. The cellar and ground floor feature an interesting exhibit on the vineyards of the nearby "Small Carpathian" hills, with historic presses and barrels, and a replica of an old-time wine-pub table. (If this exhibit interests you, consider a stop at the Slovak National Collection of Wine, also at Apponyi House and listed next.) Upstairs are two floors of urban apartments from old Bratislava, called the Museum of Period Rooms. The first floor up shows off the 18th-century Rococo-style rooms of the nobility—fine but not ostentatious, with ceramic stoves. The second floor up (with lower ceilings and simpler decor) illustrates 19th-century bourgeois/middle-class lifestyles, including period clothing and some Empire-style furniture.

Cost and Hours: €4, includes audioguide, €6 combo-ticket with City History Museum, Tue-Fri 10:00-17:00, Sat-Sun 11:00-18:00, closed Mon, Radničná 1, tel. 02/5920-5135, www.muzeum.bratislava.sk.

BRATISLAVA

Slovak National Collection of Wine

Run by the union of Slovak vintners, this room at the Apponyi House showcases the region's wines, 80 percent of which are white. Filling a 16th-century, brick-vaulted wine cellar, it features 100 Slovak wines that are open and eager to be tasted. Pick up the degustation list and track down what you like. An English-speaking sommelier is at your service.

Cost and Hours: Small tastings with explanations are an option, but for €23 you can taste up to 72 wines in 100 minutes... do this at the end of your sightseeing day (Tue-Fri 10:00-18:00, Sat from 11:00, closed Sun-Mon, Radničná 1, tel. 02/4552-9967, www.salonvin.sk).

▲Nedbalka Gallery of Slovak Modern Art

This sleek and modern gallery is owned by a local tech millionaire and run as a private nonprofit. Ride the elevator to the top floor and work chronologically through the permanent collection of 20th-century Slovak art in four delightful floors. The ground floor is dedicated to temporary exhibits. You'll notice glass is big in Slovakia (Chihuly is a Czech name, and Dale is well known and celebrated here). Admission includes a tablet multimedia guide and a nice coffee in the café.

Cost and Hours: €5, Tue-Sun 13:00-19:00, closed Mon, next to the Old Market Hall at Nedbalova 17, tel. 02/5441-0287, www.nedbalka.sk.

BEYOND THE OLD TOWN

Bratislava Castle and Museum
(Bratislavský Hrad a Múzeum)

The imposing Bratislava Castle, crowning Bratislava's hill, is the city's most prominent landmark. Big and iconic as it is, it's frankly dull up close—and the exhibits inside are not too exciting. Still, it's almost obligatory to head up here simply for the grand views over Bratislava and the Danube...though, if the weather's bad, you'd be forgiven for skipping it.

Cost and Hours: Castle grounds—free, museum—€10; Tue-Sun 10:00-18:00, Nov-March 9:00-17:00, closed Mon year-round, last entry one hour before closing; tel. 02/2048-3110, www.snm.sk.

Getting There: For the best walking route to the castle, see the end of the "Bratislava Old Town Walk," earlier in this chapter.

Background: When Habsburg Empress Maria Theresa took a liking to Bratislava in the 18th century, she transformed the castle from a military fortress to a royal residence suitable for holding court. She added a summer riding school (the U-shaped complex next to the castle),

an enclosed winter riding school out back, and lots more. Maria Theresa's favorite daughter, Maria Christina, lived here with her husband, Albert, when they were newlyweds. Locals nicknamed the place "little Schönbrunn," in reference to the Habsburgs' summer palace on the outskirts of Vienna.

The palace became a fortress-garrison during the Napoleonic Wars, then burned to the ground in an 1811 fire started by careless soldiers, and was left as a ruin for 150 years. An extensive rebuild, based on the original plans discovered in the Habsburg archives in 2008, has breathed new life into the castle (which is surrounded by a delightful public park).

Visiting the Castle: The best part of a visit here is the **grand view balcony** in front, overlooking the Danube, the Petržalka suburb across the river (marked by the SNP Bridge—described next), and—just below and upstream—the nondescript, boxy, white office building that houses the Slovak parliament. The castle is surrounded by gardens that are enjoyable on a nice day.

The dynamic statue in front of the castle's main entrance—with a knight waving his sword, rearing up on horseback—honors **Svätopluk** (846-894), the warrior-king who ruled over Great Moravia. His reign was the Slovaks' historical high-water mark, when its territory included parts of the present-day Czech Republic, Austria, Germany, Poland, Bulgaria, Romania, Serbia, Croatia, and Slovenia. Unfortunately, this dominance was short-lived; in the early 10th century, soon after Svätopluk's death, his kingdom was invaded by Magyars and folded into what became the Kingdom of Hungary—which Slovak lands would remain a part of for a thousand years. "Slovakia" has existed as a sovereign nation only since 1993; before that, you have to go all the way back to Svätopluk.

The castle **interior** features some modest exhibits and an opportunity to climb its tallest tower. It's overpriced and skippable, though the exhibits are gradually expanding—those with an interest in Slovak history might find it interesting. Inside, you'll pass through a modest exhibit about the restoration of the castle, then make your way up the grand, red-carpeted staircase to several floors of exhibits. On the third floor is a café (tucked amid a fun exhibit of nostalgic advertisements) and the "History of Slovakia" exhibit, which begins with the prehistoric Celts, tracks the arrival of the Slavs, and ends with the fall of Great Moravia after Svätopluk's time. Also on this floor, you can climb 87 steep, vertigo-inducing stairs to the top of the Crown Tower—the tallest part of the castle—for views over the city and the Danube basin (though the views from up top are not that much better than from down below).

▲▲SNP Bridge and UFO

Bratislava's flying-saucer-capped bridge, completed in 1972 in heavy-handed communist style, has been reclaimed by capitalists. The saucer-shaped structure called the UFO (at the Petržalka end of the bridge) is now a spruced-up café/restaurant and observation deck, allowing sweeping 360-degree views of Bratislava from about 300 feet above the Danube.

Cost and Hours: €7.50, for €2.50 more you can return for the view after dark, open daily 10:00-23:00, elevator free if you have a meal reservation or order food at the pricey restaurant, restaurant opens at 12:00, tel. 02/6252-0300, www.redmonkeygroup.com.

Getting There: Walk across the bridge from the old town (walkways cross the bridge on a level below the road; the elevator entrance is a few steps down from the downstream-side walkway).

Visiting the UFO: The **"elevator"** that takes you up is actually a funicular—you may notice you're moving at an angle. At the top,

walk up the stairs to the observation deck, passing photos of the bridge's construction.

Begin by viewing the **castle** and **old town.** The area to the right of the old town, between and beyond the skyscrapers, is a massive construction zone where the new Bratislava is taking shape.

The huge TV tower caps a forested hill beyond the old town. Below and to the left of it, the pointy monument is **Slavín,** where more than 6,800 Soviet soldiers who fought to liberate Bratislava from the Nazis are buried. Under communist rule, a nearby church was forced to take down its steeple so as not to draw attention away from the huge Soviet soldier on top of the monument.

Now turn 180 degrees and cross the platform to face **Petržalka,** a planned communist suburb that sprouted here in the 1970s. The site was once occupied by a village, and the various districts of modern Petržalka still carry their original names (which now seem ironic): "Meadows" *(Háje)*, "Woods" *(Lúky)*, and "Courtyards" *(Dvory)*. The ambitious communist planners envisioned a city laced with Venetian-style canals to help drain the marshy land, but the plans were abandoned after the harsh crackdown on the 1968 Prague Spring uprising. Without the incentives of private ownership, all they succeeded in creating was a grim and decaying sea of miserable concrete apartment *paneláky* ("panel buildings," so-called because they're made of huge prefab panels).

Today, one in six Bratislavans lives in Petržalka, and things are looking better. Like Dorothy opening the door to Oz, the formerly drab buildings have been splashed with bright new colors, and the interiors have been modernized. Far from being a slum, Petržalka is now a popular neighborhood for Bratislavan yuppies who can't yet afford to build their dream houses.

Petržalka is also a big suburban-style shopping zone (note the supermall down below). But there's still some history here. The **park** called Sad Janka Kráľa (originally, in German, Aupark)—just downriver from the bridge—was technically the first public park in Europe in the 1770s and is still a popular place for locals to relax and court.

Scanning the **horizon** beyond Petržalka, two things stick out: on the left, the old communist oil refinery (which has been fully updated and is now state-of-the-art); and on the right, a forest of modern windmills. These are just over the border, in Austria...and Bratislava is sure to grow in that direction quickly. Austria is about three miles that way, and Hungary is about six miles farther to the left.

Before you leave, consider a drink at the café. If nothing else, be sure to use the memorable WCs.

Blue Church of St. Elisabeth (Kostol Svätej Alžbety)

Just east of the old town—through a nicely manicured new park—is a fine little neighborhood of cheery, colorful Art Nouveau buildings. The main landmark here is the gentle-blue, fancifully decorated Church of St. Elisabeth—also called simply the "Little Blue Church." It's straight out of a fairy tale, with rounded edges, pretty flourishes, and vivid colors. Designed by the great Hungarian Secessionist architect Ödön Lechner, and completed in 1913, it's worth the short walk from the old town for architecture fans. While the interior is open limited hours to the public, you can often peek through the glass doors to see the similarly soft and pretty interior (Bezručova 2).

▲Eurovea and the New Bratislava

Just downstream from the old town is the modern Eurovea complex, with four layers, each a quarter-mile long: a riverside park,

luxury condos, a thriving modern shopping mall, and an office park. While it's essentially a big riverfront shopping mall, those looking for a peek at the "new Bratislava" find it worth the lovely, short riverfront stroll from the old town...which is also a chance to check out all of the moored riverboats.

Eurovea's central public space is a fountain- and statue-filled people zone between the Danube and Bratislava's new National Theater. Directly in front of the theater, the pavement is pulled back to show original Roman paving stones that were excavated here (a reminder of the city's long history as a trade crossroads). At the river end of the square, under the lion-topped pillar, a statue features General Milan Rastislav Štefánik, who represented Slovakia in a 1918 meeting in Pittsburgh and signed the "Pittsburgh Agreement"—creating the combined state of Česko-Slovensko. He's holding a bronze copy of the document as he looks out at the Danube.

The riverfront strip of Eurovea is the embryo of a huge vision for a new Bratislava. Dozens of skyscrapers are being built at once, as the city's old industrial zone (destroyed in World War II, and now destined to be the city's future tech-industry home) is one big construction site.

Exploring the old town gives you a taste of where this country has been. But wandering this riverside park, enjoying a drink in one of its chic outdoor lounges, and then browsing the thriving mall, you'll enjoy a glimpse of where Slovakia is heading.

Sleeping in Bratislava

Because Bratislava is more business city than tourist city, you'll find weekends are a little less expensive. For locations, see the "Bratislava map, earlier.

$$$ Hotel Marrol's, on a quiet urban street, is the town's most enticing splurge. Although the immediate neighborhood isn't interesting, it's just a five-minute walk from the old town, the public spaces are plush and generous, and its 53 rooms are luxurious and tastefully appointed Old World country-style. While pricey, rates drop on weekends (air-con, elevator, gorgeous lounge, Tobrucká 4, tel. 02/5778-4600, www.hotelmarrols.sk, rec@hotelmarrols.sk).

$$$ Roset Boutique Hotel, facing the ring road's tram tracks at the eastern edge of the old town (with some street noise), feels classy and upmarket. Its 28 rooms are spacious and plush (air-con, elevator, Štúrova 10, tel. 02/3217-1819, www.rosethotel.sk, reservations@rosethotel.sk).

$$$ Radisson Blu Carlton Hotel has been hosting VIPs for decades, with 170 rooms and all the big corporate trappings and expected services. It's beautifully located, facing the National Theater and Promenade Square (air-con, elevator, Hviezdoslavovo Námestie 3, tel. 02/5939-0000, www.radissonblu.com/hotel-bratislava, reservation.bratislava@radissonblu.com).

$$ Loft Hotel is an appealing midrange choice, tucked along the highway between the main train station and the old town (ask for a quieter back room facing the garden). It's professional, stylish, and trendy—with comfy leather couches in the lobby, an on-site brewpub, and a staff that prides itself on its service. Of the 121 rooms, the "standard" rooms are fine but forgettable; consider paying a bit more for a cushier, retro-industrial "superior" room (air-con, elevator, pay parking garage, Štefánikova 4, tel. 02/5751-1000, www.lofthotel.sk, reservation@lofthotel.sk). They also have 10 more-expensive, high-end rooms in the attached **Wilson Palace,** in the original building facing the main road.

$ Aplend City Hotel Michalská is a tight little hotel with a peaceful back garden tucked just inside St. Michael's Gate in the old town. The 14 rooms are comfortable, and the location—on a picturesque lane—is ideal (air-con, elevator, Baštová 4, tel. 903/998-111, www.aplendcity.com/en/hotel-michalska, michalska@aplendcity.com).

$ Penzión Virgo, on a quiet residential street an eight-minute walk from the old town, rents 12 boutique-ish rooms (breakfast extra, reserve ahead for inexpensive parking, Panenská 14, tel. 02/2092-1400, mobile 0948-350-878, www.penzionvirgo.sk, reception@penzionvirgo.sk).

Eating in Bratislava

Slovak cooking involves some Hungarian and Austrian influences, but it's closer to Czech cuisine—lots of starches and gravy, and plenty of pork, cabbage, potatoes, and dumplings. Keep an eye out for Slovakia's intensely filling national dish, *bryndzové halušky* (small potato dumplings with sheep's cheese and bits of bacon). For a fun drink and snack that locals love, try a Vinea grape soda and a sweet, crescent-shaped *Pressburger* bagel in any bar or café.

Like the Czechs, the Slovaks produce excellent beer (*pivo*, PEE-voh). The dominant brand is Zlatý Bažant ("Golden Pheasant"). Bratislava's beer halls are good places to sample Slovak beers—whether macrobrews or microbrews—and to get a hearty, affordable meal of stick-to-your-ribs pub grub. The Bratislava region also produces wines, similar to the ones that Vienna is known for. But, as nearly all is consumed locally, most outsiders don't think of Slovakia as wine country.

Bratislava is packed with inviting new eateries. In addition to heavy Slovak staples, you'll find trendy new bars and bistros, and a smattering of non-European offerings. The best plan may be to stroll the old town and keep your eyes open for the setting and cuisine that appeals to you most. Or consider the areas listed below. All are within a short walk and offer a better, more interesting dining experience than the grotesquely touristy eateries that line Michalská street and other busy streets in the old town. For locations, see the "Bratislava" map, earlier.

Traditional Beer Hall on Námestie SNP

A couple of blocks north of the old town (and named for the Slovak National Uprising), the right side of this square is dominated by the following operation.

$$ Bratislavská is a sprawling complex of eateries. The main location (door on the right) is the Bratislavská Reštaurácia. Walk through a maze of old-timey rooms, then up a flight of stairs to a huge dining hall that smells hoppy and feels happy (with the waitstaff sporting "Bar-tislava" and "Bra-tislava" T-shirts). The menu features classic Slovak dishes, and the portions are hearty and cheap. For a more intimate setting, the door to the left leads to the tight, woody Kláštorný Pivovar ("Monastery Brewery"), with a cozier ambience and the same menu. They also have tables outside on the square (daily 12:00-23:00, Námestie SNP 8, mobile 0917-927-673).

Near the Old Market Hall

While there's often nothing actually inside the Old Market Hall (which fills a city block, at the eastern edge of the old town—a 5-minute walk from the main square), it's surrounded by intriguing and trendy options. Once a month, the square in front features a "Street Food Park" with a wide variety of food trucks (worth planning around—check schedule at www.staratrznica.sk). At other times, walk around the block to survey your options (listed in order, from the front door).

$ Výčap u Ernőho is a popular, no-frills beer hall, with a row of taps up front featuring a changing selection of quality beers. If you'd like to enjoy Slovak beers with local hipsters instead of the sloppy beer-hall tourist crowd, do it here (no food, Tue-Sat 12:00-24:00, Sun from 16:00, Mon from 15:00, Námestie SNP 25, mobile 0948-360-153).

$ Foodstock is an enticing, hip, and healthy vegetarian place that advertises "good mood food." It got its start as a food truck, and now serves up a brief menu of delicious, Asian-inspired dishes and all-you-can-drink homemade iced teas in a patchouli-scented space (daily 10:00-22:00, Klobučnícka 6, mobile 0905-456-654).

$$ Mecheche Snack Bar serves tiny, fancy sandwiches as if channeling a Barcelona tapas bar (Tue-Sat 17:00-24:00, closed Sun-Mon, Nedbalova 12, mobile 0948-853-444).

$$ Urban House, behind the Old Market Hall on fashionable Laurinská street, is California-trendy with a sprawling, industrial-mod, woody-bookstore ambience, great outdoor tables, and an appealing menu. The food (burgers, pizza, and so on) is nothing special, but the scene is fun (daily 9:00-24:00, Laurinská 14, mobile 0904-001-021).

Restaurants on Promenade Square (Hviezdoslavovo Námestie)

This square is lined with restaurants, nearly all with open-feeling interior seating and mellow tables out on the square under the trees—ideal for enjoying the promenade of strollers. There's no traffic, just the sound of fountains and the breeze. A strip of three places, side-by-side, makes for easy comparison-shopping; for a view, head up to Sky Bar.

$$$ Carnevalle is a hit for its steak. Their greeting? "Nice to meat you!" Their indoors feels outdoors—a spacious, glassed-in dining hall—and their tables on the square are inviting. The tasty dishes are nicely presented by a professional waitstaff (daily 11:00-24:00, at #20, mobile 0903-123-164).

$$ Zylinder ("Top Hat") re-creates a circa-1900 atmosphere to serve classy bourgeoise cuisine that leans closer to Austrian than traditional Slovak—think sausages and schnitzels (daily 11:00-22:00, at #19, mobile 0903-123-134).

$ Café Restaurant Verne, university-owned and unburdened by the high rent of its neighbors, feels like the dive bar of the strip—with mismatched antique tables spilling out onto the cobbles. It has a cozy, lowbrow, and mellow student vibe with stick-to-your-ribs plates (pasta, goulash, salads) and drinks. You get what you pay for, but the price is right (Mon-Fri 8:00-24:00, Sat-Sun from 10:00, at #18).

Rooftop View: $$$ Sky Bar Restaurant, just past the fenced-in US Embassy, features a Thai-meets-Mediterranean menu on its seventh-floor open-roof terrace. It's a pretentious place, with local big shots dropping by and stuffy service. But the food's good and so are the views. It's smart to reserve a view table in advance to dine here—or just drop by for a pricey vodka cocktail (daily 12:00-late, Hviezdoslavovo Námestie 7, mobile 0948-109-400, www.skybar.sk).

Eurovea

This modern development facing the Danube River (a short walk downstream from the old town) has huge outdoor terraces rollicking with happy eaters. A variety of upscale and high-energy **$$-$$$ restaurants** line the swanky riverfront residential and shopping-mall complex. Options include international—French, Italian, Brazilian—as well as branches of the Czech beer-hall chain **Kolkovna** and the British pan-Asian restaurant **Wagamama.** Or you can head to the **$ food court** in the shopping mall, where you'll eat cheap. While the restaurants here are nothing special, it's a fun excuse for a stroll along the Danube promenade, and to get a peek at the emerging "new Bratislava" zone beyond the old town cobbles.

Bratislava Connections

BY TRAIN

Bratislava has two major train stations: the main station closer to the old town (Hlavná Stanica, abbreviated "Bratislava hl. st." on schedules), and Petržalka station, in the suburb across the river (for full details, see "Arrival in Bratislava," earlier). When checking schedules, pay attention to which station your train uses.

From Bratislava by Train to: Vienna (€12, 2/hour, 1 hour;

departures alternate between the two stations—half from main station usually leaving hourly at :38, half from Petržalka usually leaving hourly at :15), **Budapest** (7/day direct, 3 hours), **Sopron** (nearly hourly direct from Petržalka, 2.5 hours on RegionalExpress/REX), **Prague** (5/day direct, 4 hours). To reach other Hungarian destinations (including **Eger** and **Pécs**), it's generally easiest to change in Budapest; for Austrian destinations (such as **Salzburg** or **Innsbruck**), you'll connect through Vienna.

BY BUS
Flixbus and **Slovak Lines/Postbus** run buses that connect Bratislava to Vienna (and Vienna Airport) for about €5-8 one-way. For details, see "Day-Tripping from Vienna to Bratislava" earlier in this chapter. For airport bus connections, see "By Plane," below.

BY BOAT
Riverboats run on the Danube several times a day, connecting Bratislava to Budapest and Vienna. Conveniently, these boats dock right in front of Bratislava's old town. While they are more expensive, less frequent, and slower than the train, some travelers enjoy getting out on the Danube. For details, see "Day-Tripping from Vienna to Bratislava" earlier in this chapter.

BY PLANE
Bratislava has its own airport, but it's also convenient to fly out from the very nearby Vienna Airport (see the Connections chapter).

Bratislava Airport (Letisko Bratislava)
This airport (airport code: BTS, www.bts.aero) is six miles northeast of downtown Bratislava and also easily reached from Vienna. Budget airline Ryanair has many flights here. Some airlines market it as "Vienna-Bratislava," thanks to its proximity to both capitals. It's compact and manageable, with all the usual amenities (including ATMs).

From the Airport to Downtown Bratislava: The airport has easy **public bus** connections to Bratislava's main train station (Hlavná Stanica, €1.20, bus #61, 3-4/hour, 30 minutes). To reach the bus stop, exit straight out of the arrivals hall, cross the street, buy a ticket at the kiosk, and look for the bus stop on your right. For directions from the train station into the old town, see "Arrival in Bratislava," page 235. A **taxi** from the airport into central Bratislava should cost less than €20.

To Vienna: You can take the **Flixbus** to the Erdberg stop on

Vienna's U-3 subway line, a straight shot to Stephansplatz (€8, runs every 1-2 hours, 1 hour, www.flixbus.com) or the **Slovak Lines/Postbus** bus to Vienna's Hauptbahnhof (€10, 1-2/hour, 2 hours, www.slovaklines.sk). Bus schedules are also on the airport's website (www.bts.aero/en, under the "Transport" tab). A **taxi** from Bratislava Airport directly to Vienna costs €60-90 (depending on whether you use a cheaper Slovak or more expensive Austrian cab).

SALZBURG

& the Salzkammergut

SALZBURG

Salzburg · Berchtesgaden

Thanks to its charmingly preserved Old Town, splendid gardens, Baroque churches, and one of Europe's largest intact medieval fortresses, Salzburg feels made for tourism. As a musical mecca, the city puts on a huge annual festival, as well as constant concerts. Salzburgers are forever smiling to the tunes of Mozart and *The Sound of Music*. It's a city with class. Vagabonds visiting here wish they had nicer clothes.

In the mountains just outside Salzburg is Berchtesgaden, a German alpine town that was once a favorite of Adolf Hitler but today thrills a better class of nature lover.

PLANNING YOUR TIME

While Salzburg doesn't have blockbuster museums, the town itself is a Baroque showpiece of cobbled streets and elegant buildings—a touristy stroller's delight. If you're a fan of the movie, allow half a day for *The Sound of Music* tour, which kills a nest of sightseeing birds with one ticket (city overview, *S.O.M.* sights, and a fine drive by the lakes).

You'd probably enjoy at least two nights in Salzburg—one to swill beer in an atmospheric local garden and another to attend a concert in a Baroque hall or chapel. Seriously consider one of Salzburg's many evening musical events, even if you're not normally a music lover (some are free).

When the weather's good, take advantage of the city's proximity to alpine splendor. Bike down the river or hike across the Mönchsberg, Salzburg's mini mountain. Or consider visiting scenic Berchtesgaden, just 15 miles away, in Germany (also the site of Hitler's Eagle's Nest; see page 340).

A day trip from Salzburg to Hallstatt (the small-town highlight of the Salzkammergut Lake District) is doable by car (1.5

hours each way) but makes for a very long day by public transit (five hours round-trip). An overnight in Hallstatt is better (see the Hallstatt chapter, which includes a scenic driving tour of the Salzkammergut from Salzburg to Hallstatt).

Salzburg, Austria

Today, eight million tourists crawl Salzburg's cobbles each year. That's a lot of Mozart balls—and all that popularity has led to a glut of businesses hoping to catch the tourist dollar. Still, Salzburg is both a must and a joy.

Even without Mozart and the Von Trapps, Salzburg is steeped in history. In about AD 700, Bavaria gave Salzburg to Bishop Rupert in return for his promise to Christianize the area. For centuries, Salzburg remained an independent city-state, ruled by prince-archbishops—a cross between a king and a pope, but less powerful than either one. Salzburg's mighty fortress—looming protectively over the city—helped deter invaders.

At its peak, Salzburg controlled an area about half the size of today's Austria. Its power was funded by salt—the "white gold" of the day. It's said one barrel of salt was worth the cost of one house.

Salzburgers enjoy throwing around the names of their obscure prince-archbishops (who built various fanciful palaces and elegant squares), but only one is worth remembering: Wolf Dietrich von Raitenau (1559-1617). It was his vision of making Salzburg a mini Rome north of the Alps that gave the city an Italian flair and created much of what tourists enjoy today.

Napoleon finally put an end to Salzburg's independence in 1803 (they handed him the keys to the fortress without putting up a fight). Then, after the fall of Napoleon, Salzburg became part of Austria and was ruled by Vienna.

Thanks in part to its formidable fortress, Salzburg managed to avoid the ravages of war for 1,200 years...until World War II. Allied bombing destroyed much of the city (especially around the train station), but the historic Old Town survived.

Music lovers adore Salzburg, where you can shell out for classy performances...or are just as likely to hear musicians practicing through an open window. The city also has a beautiful setting, wrapped in alpine wonder; a stout castle with great panoramas over cut-glass peaks; a tidy—almost sterile—Old Town of interlocking squares and Baroque domes, giving it a nearly Italian feel; some engaging museums; and, overall, the most accessible taste of Austria you'll find anywhere.

SALZBURG

Orientation to Salzburg

Salzburg, a city of 150,000 (Austria's fourth largest), is divided into old and new. The Old Town (Altstadt), between the Salzach River and Salzburg's Mönchsberg mountain, holds nearly all the charm and most of the tourists. The New Town (Neustadt), across the river, has the train station, a few sights  and museums, and some good accommodations.

TOURIST INFORMATION

Salzburg has two helpful TIs (main tel. 0662/889-870, www. salzburg.info): at the **train station** (9:00-18:00, until 19:00 in summer; tel. 0662/8898-7340) and on **Mozartplatz** in the old center (daily 9:00-18:00, July-Aug often until 19:00, closed Sun in winter; tel. 0662/8898-7330).

At any TI, you can pick up a free city-center map (or purchase a map with broader coverage if biking out of town), the free bus map *(Liniennetz),* and an events guide. Inside the Mozartplatz TI is the privately run Salzburg Ticket Service counter, where you can book concert tickets.

Salzburg Card: The TIs sell the Salzburg Card, which covers all public transportation (including the Mönchsberg elevator and funicular to the fortress) and admission to all the city sights (including Hellbrunn Palace and a river cruise). The card can be a convenience and a money saver if you'll be seeing lots of sights (€28/24 hours, €37/48 hours, €43/72 hours, cheaper off-season, half-price for kids ages 6-15, www.salzburg.info). As Salzburg's major sights are pricey, busy sightseers can save plenty. Do the math on the places you want to see to evaluate whether the card makes financial sense.

ARRIVAL IN SALZBURG
By Train

The Salzburg station has tourist information, luggage lockers, a pay WC (by platform 5), and a handy Spar supermarket. Ticket counters and ticket machines for both the Austrian and German railways are off the main hall. To find the TI, follow the green-and-white information signs (the blue-and-white ones lead to a railway "InfoPoint"). Next to the train station is Forum 1, a sizable shopping mall.

Getting downtown from the station is a snap. Simply step

outside, find bus **plat-form C** (labeled *Zentrum-Altstadt*), and buy a ticket from the machine (€2 *Stundenkarte*). Buses #1, #3, #5, and #6 all do the same route into the city center before diverging. Bus #25 (from **platform B**) follows the same path

to the center and continues to Hellbrunn Palace. For most sights and Old Town hotels, get off just after the bridge (either Rathaus or Hanuschplatz, depending on the bus). For my recommended New Town hotels, get off at Makartplatz, just before the bridge.

A **taxi** from the station to most hotels is about €8.

To **walk** downtown (15 minutes), turn left as you leave the station, and walk straight down Rainerstrasse, which leads under the tracks past Mirabellplatz, turning into Dreifaltigkeitsgasse. From here, you can turn left onto Linzer Gasse for many of my recommended New Town hotels, or cross the river to the Old Town. For a slightly longer but more dramatic approach, leave the station the same way but follow the tracks to the river, turn left, and walk the riverside path toward the hilltop fortress.

By Car

Mozart never drove in Salzburg's Old Town, and neither should you. Carefully heed the *rising bollards* signs at the entrance to pedestrian zones—they mean business. (The hydraulic bollards are designed to essentially destroy the car of anyone who tries to sneak through behind a car with permission.)

The best place to park is the **park-and-ride** lot at the Alpensiedlung bus stop, near the Salzburg Süd autobahn exit. If you're coming on A-8 (for instance, from Vienna or Munich), take A-10 toward Hallein, and then take the next exit (Salzburg Süd) in the direction of Anif. Stay on the Alpenstrasse (road 150) for about 2.5 miles, following *P+R* signs, to arrive at the park-and-ride (€5/24 hours). From the parking lot, catch bus #3 or #8 into town (for ticket info, see "Getting Around Salzburg," later). Alternatively, groups of up to five people can buy a combo-ticket from the parking lot attendant, which includes the 24-hour parking fee and a 24-hour transit pass for the whole group (€14, group must stay together).

If you don't want to park-and-ride, head to the easiest, cheapest, most central parking lot: the 1,500-car Altstadtgarage, in the tunnel under the Mönchsberg (€18/day, note your slot number and which of the twin lots you're in). Your hotel may provide discounted

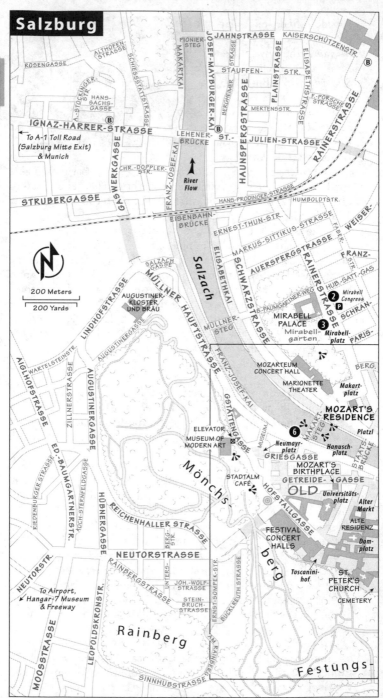

Salzburg

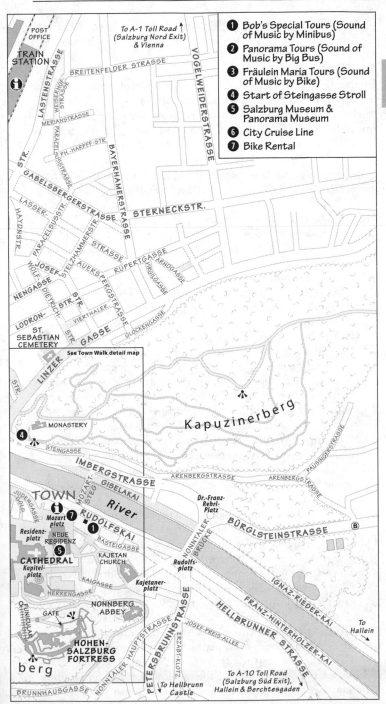

1. Bob's Special Tours (Sound of Music by Minibus)
2. Panorama Tours (Sound of Music by Big Bus)
3. Fräulein Maria Tours (Sound of Music by Bike)
4. Start of Steingasse Stroll
5. Salzburg Museum & Panorama Museum
6. City Cruise Line
7. Bike Rental

parking passes. If staying in Salzburg's New Town, the Mirabell-Congress garage makes more sense (see page 318 for directions).

By Plane

Salzburg's airport sits just behind its Mönchsberg mountain (code: SZG, tel. 0662/85800, www.salzburg-airport.com). A taxi into town runs about €15. To take a bus, cross the parking lot to the row of bus stops: Bus #10 goes to the Old Town (20 minutes); bus #2 goes to the train station, then terminates at Mirabellplatz (near several of my New Town accommodations; about 30 minutes). For either bus, buy a €2 *Stundenkarte* ticket at the machine, or pay the driver €2.60 (each bus runs every 10 minutes, less frequent on Sun).

HELPFUL HINTS

Recommendations Skewed by Kickbacks: Salzburg is addicted to the tourist dollar, and it can never get enough. Virtually all hotels are on the take when it comes to concert and tour recommendations, so take any entertainment advice with a grain of salt. If you book a concert through your hotel, you'll probably lose any discounts I've negotiated for my readers who book directly.

Festivals: The Salzburg Festival runs each year from mid-July to the end of August (for more details on this and other big annual musical events, see page 316). In mid-September, the St. Rupert's Fair (Ruperti-Kirtag), celebrating Salzburg's favorite saint, fills the sky with fireworks and Salzburg's Old Town with music and food stands (www.rupertikirtag.at). And from mid-November through Advent, Salzburg boasts a handful of Christmas markets—the biggest sprawling across Domplatz and Residenzplatz (www.christkindlmarkt.co.at), with smaller ones up at the fortress (mostly just Fri-Sun), on Mirabellplatz (daily), and elsewhere around town (www.weihnachtsmarkt-salzburg.at).

Wi-Fi: The city has free hotspots at Mirabell Gardens, Mozartplatz, and Kapitelplatz (choose *Salzburg surf!* and click *Agree*).

Laundry: A handy launderette with a few self-serve machines is at Paris-Lodron-Strasse 16, at the corner of Wolf-Dietrich-Strasse, near my recommended Linzer Gasse hotels—take bus #2, #4, or #21 to the Wolf-Dietrich-Strasse stop (self-service or same-day full-service, Mon-Fri 7:30-18:00, Sat 8:00-12:00, closed Sun, tel. 0662/876-381). If they're closed, head for **Green and Clean,** three stops from the train station on the #1 or #2 bus; board from platform D at station, get off at the Gaswerkgasse stop (daily 6:00-22:00, Ignaz-Harrer-Strasse 32, tel. 0800-102-559). See the map on page 320 for locations.

Cinema: An art-house movie theater, **Das Kino** plays films in their original language (a block off the river and Linzer Gasse on Steingasse, tel. 0662/873-100, www.daskino.at).

Market Days: Pop-up farmers markets are a fun local tradition and ideal for picking up picnic supplies or artisan trinkets. The **Grünmarkt** at Universitätsplatz in the Old Town runs Monday-Friday (7:00-19:00) and expands onto Wiener-Philharmoniker Gasse on Saturday (7:00-13:00). Around the Andräkirche and Mirabellplatz in the New Town on Thursday (5:00-13:00) is the huge **Schrannenmarkt,** Salzburg's longest running market, dating from 1906. On summer weekends, a string of craft booths with fun goodies for sale stretches along the river.

Morning Joggers: Salzburg is a great place for jogging. Within minutes you can be huffing and puffing "The hills are alive..." in green meadows outside of town. The obvious best bets in town are through the Mirabell Gardens along its riverbank pedestrian lanes.

Public Swimming Pool: The **Freibad Leopoldskron** complex, a few miles out of town and across the lake from Leopoldskron Palace (of *Sound of Music* fame), is a first-class place for a swim while surrounded by nature (and it's on the hop-on, hop-off bus route because of the palace's connection to the movie).

GETTING AROUND SALZBURG

By Bus: Most Salzburg sights I list are within the *Kernzone* (core zone) of the city's extensive bus system. I've listed prices for buying tickets from the driver; you'll pay less if you buy them ahead at a *Tabak/Trafik* shop or streetside ticket machine (these are scarce in town, but look around tram stops at major hubs—such as the main train station). Note that "09/17" tickets and one-week *Wochenkarte* passes are sold only at ticket machines or *Tabak/Trafik* shops. These are your options:

- Basic single-ride ticket *(Einzelfahrt):* €2.60 (at a machine, select *Stundenkarte)*
- Ticket for 1-2 stops in a single direction *(Kurzstrecke):* €1.30
- "09/17" ticket (valid Mon-Sat 9:00-17:00, not valid Sun or holidays): €1.50
- 24-hour ticket *(24-Stundenkarte):* €5.70
- One-week pass *(Wochenkarte,* valid 7 calendar days): €15.50— usually pays for itself if you're staying at least four days

Remember to validate your ticket by inserting it in the machine on board.

Get oriented using the free bus map *(Liniennetz),* available at the TI. Many lines converge at Hanuschplatz, on the Old Town side of the river, between the Makartsteg and Staatsbrücke bridges. To get from the Old Town to the train station, catch bus #1 from

SALZBURG

the inland side of Hanuschplatz. From the other side of the river, find the Makartplatz/Theatergasse stop and catch bus #1, #3, #5, or #6. Busy stops like Hanuschplatz and Mirabellplatz have several bus shelters; look for your bus number.

For more information, visit www.svv-info.at, call 0662/632-900 (answered 24/7), or visit the Obus transit info office downstairs from bus platform C in front of the train station (Mon-Fri 6:00-18:00, Sat 7:00-15:00, closed Sun).

By Bike: Salzburg is great fun for cyclists. **A'Velo Radladen** rents bikes in the Old Town, just outside the TI on Mozartplatz (€12/4 hours, €18/24 hours, more for electric or mountain bikes, RS%—10 percent off with this book; daily 9:30-18:00, possibly later in summer, shorter hours off-season and in bad weather; passport number for security deposit, mobile 0676-435-5950, run by George). Some of my recommended hotels and pensions also rent or loan bikes to guests.

By Funicular and Elevator: The Old Town is connected to the top of the Mönchsberg mountain (and great views) via funicular and elevator. The funicular *(Festungsbahn)* whisks you up into the imposing Hohensalzburg Fortress (included in castle admission, goes every few minutes—for details, see page 298). The elevator (Mönchsberg Aufzug) on the west side of the Old Town lifts you to the recommended Stadtalm Café, the Museum of Modern Art and its chic café, wooded paths, and more great views (see page 297 for details).

By Buggy: The horse buggies *(Fiaker)* that congregate at Residenzplatz charge €48 for a 25-minute trot around the Old Town (www.fiaker-salzburg.at).

Tours in Salzburg

IN SALZBURG
Walking Tours

Any day of the week, you can take a one-hour, informative guided walk of the Old Town without a reservation—just show up at the TI on Mozartplatz at the tour time and pay the guide (€10, daily at 12:15 and 14:00, tel. 0662/8898-7330).

To save money (and probably learn more), use this chapter's self-guided walk or ∩ download my free Salzburg Town Walk audio tour (see page 7).

Local Guides

Salzburg has many good guides. Two I have worked with and enjoyed are **Sabine Rath** (€160/2 hours, €225/4 hours, €335/8 hours, mobile 0664-201-6492, www.tourguide-salzburg.com, info@tourguide-salzburg.com) and **Anna Stellnberger** (€150/2 hours, €220/4 hours, €320/8 hours, mobile 0664-787-5177, anna. stellnberger@aon.at). Salzburg has many other guides (for a list, see www.salzburgguides.at).

Boat Tours

City Cruise Line (a.k.a. Stadt Schiff-Fahrt) runs a basic 40-minute round-trip river cruise with recorded commentary (€15, 9/day July-Aug, 6-8/day May-June and Sept, 3-4/day April and Oct, no boats Nov-March). For a longer cruise, ride to Hellbrunn (€18, €30 includes palace admission and a ride back to the Old Town on a double-decker bus—a good value; daily April-Oct at 14:00, 40 minutes one-way). Boats leave from the Old Town side of the river just downstream of the Makartsteg bridge (tel. 0662/825-858, www.salzburghighlights.at). While views can be cramped, passengers are treated to a cute finale just before docking, when the captain twirls a fun "waltz."

Hop-On, Hop-Off Bus

While most of Salzburg's top sights are concentrated in its walkable Old Town, several are scattered around the city—making a hop-on, hop-off bus tour practical here. I'd skip the sky (blue) line, which mostly hits walkable sights, and opt for the yellow line, which stretches into the outskirts (Hellbrunn Palace and several *Sound of Music* sights). Both have simple and sleepy recorded commentary (one line: €19/1 day, €23/2 days; both lines: €24/1 day, €28/2 days, RS%—10% off with this book; includes all-day transit pass for city buses, both routes run 2/hour, buy tickets and start tour at Mirabellplatz 2, tel. 0662/881-616, www.salzburg-sightseeingtours.at). To see the countryside, consider their green line, which makes a 2.5-hour loop into the Salzkammergut Lake District (€29/all day, runs 7/day).

Segway Tours

This can be an efficient, fun way to cover a lot of ground. Choose a 1.5-hour version that combines a city tour with a trip up the Mönchsberg mountain (€49), or the two-hour version that also heads into the nearby countryside (€65). Reserve ahead (3/day, daily June-Aug; Wed-Sun March-May and Sept-Oct; no tours Nov-Feb; office near recommended New Town hotels at Wolf-Dietrich-Strasse 3, tel. 0676/674-4425, www.segway-salzburg.at).

▲▲*The Sound of Music* Tours

Salzburg is the joyful setting of *The Sound of Music.* The Broadway musical and 1965 movie tell the story of a stern captain who hires a governess for his unruly children and ends up marrying her. Though the movie took plenty of Hollywood liberties (see "*The Sound of Music:* Fact and Fiction" sidebar), it's based on the actual Von Trapp family from Austria. They really did come from Salz-

SALZBURG

The Sound of Music: Fact and Fiction

Rather than visit the real-life sights from the life of Maria von Trapp and family, most tourists want to see the places where Hollywood chose to film this fanciful story. Local guides are happy not to burst any *S.O.M.* pilgrim's bubble, but keep these points in mind:

"Edelweiss": The song is not a cherished Austrian folk tune or national anthem. Like all the "Austrian" music in *S.O.M.*, it was composed for Broadway by Rodgers and Hammerstein. It was the last composition that the famed team wrote together, as Hammerstein died in 1960.

Religious Calling: *S.O.M.* implies that Maria was devoutly religious throughout her life, but Maria's foster parents raised her as a socialist and atheist. Maria discovered her religious calling while studying to be a teacher. After completing school, she entered the convent as a novitiate.

Job Description: Maria's position was not as governess to all the children, but specifically as governess and teacher for the Captain's second-oldest daughter, also called Maria, who was bedridden with rheumatic fever.

Whistling: The Captain didn't run a tight domestic ship—but he did use a whistle to call his children—each kid was trained to respond to a certain pitch.

Name Changes: Though the Von Trapp family did have seven children, the show changed all their names and even their genders. As an adult, Rupert, the eldest child, responded to the often-asked question, "Which one are you?" with "I'm Liesl!" Maria and the Captain later had three more children together.

Escape: The family didn't escape by hiking to Switzerland (which

burg. Maria really was a governess who became the captain's wife. They did sing in the Festival Hall, they did escape from the Nazis, and they ended up after the war in Vermont, where Maria passed away in 1987. The movie screens nightly at the recommended International Youth Hostel (nonguests welcome; details on page 322).

Salzburg has a number of *Sound of Music* sights—mostly locations where the movie was shot, but also some places associated with the real Von Trapps:

- Mirabell Gardens, with its arbor and Pegasus statue, where the kids sing "Do-Re-Mi."
- Festival Hall, where the real-life Von Trapps performed, and

is a five-hour drive away). Rather, they pretended to go on one of their frequent mountain hikes. With only the possessions in their backpacks, they "hiked" all the way to the station at the edge of their estate and took a train to Italy. The movie scene showing them climbing into Switzerland was filmed near Berchtesgaden, Germany...home to Hitler's Eagle's Nest, and certainly not a smart place to flee to.

Family Home: The actual Von Trapp house exists...but it's not the one in the film. The mansion in the movie is actually two different buildings—one used for the front, the other for the back. The interiors were filmed on Hollywood sets. And the much-vaunted "Sixteen Going on Seventeen" gazebo you'll see at Hellbrunn Palace was built just for the movie, then moved twice to reach its current location.

Set Shots: For the film, Boris Levin designed a reproduction of the Nonnberg Abbey courtyard so faithful to the original (down to its cobblestones and stained-glass windows) that many still believe the cloister scenes were really shot at the abbey. And no matter what you hear in Salzburg, the graveyard scene (in which the Von Trapps hide from the Nazis) was also filmed on the Fox lot.

Swindled!: In 1956, a German film producer offered Maria $9,000 cash for the rights to her book. Because it was more money than the family had seen in all their years of singing, she accepted the deal. The agent claimed that German law forbids film companies from paying royalties to foreigners (Maria had by then become a US citizen). She agreed to the contract and unknowingly signed away all film rights to her story. Later, she discovered the agent had swindled the family—no such law existed.

Restitution: Rodgers, Hammerstein, and other producers gave the Von Trapps a percentage of the royalties, even though they weren't required to—but it was a fraction of what they otherwise would have earned. But Maria wasn't bitter. She said, "The great good the film and the play are doing to individual lives is far beyond money."

where (in the movie) they sing "Edelweiss" after nervously waiting in the Toscaninihof courtyard.

- St. Peter's Cemetery, the inspiration for the scene where the family hides from Nazi guards (it was actually filmed on a Hollywood set).

- Nonnberg Abbey, where the nuns sing "How Do You Solve a Problem like Maria?"

- Leopoldskron Palace, which serves as the Von Trapps' idyllic lakeside home in the movie (though it wasn't their actual home).

- Summer Riding School's iconic arcaded stage, the setting for the Von Trapp family's final public performance in the movie.
- Hellbrunn Palace gardens, now home to the famous gazebo where Liesl, the Von Trapp's oldest daughter, sings the words, "I am sixteen going on seventeen."

There are many more sights—the horse pond, the wedding church in Mondsee, the fountain in Residenzplatz. Since they're scattered throughout greater Salzburg, taking a tour is the best way to see them efficiently.

I took a *S.O.M.* tour skeptically (as part of my research)—and enjoyed it. The bus tour version includes a quick general city tour, hits the *S.O.M.* spots, and shows you a lovely stretch of the Salzkammergut Lake District. Warning: Many think rolling through the Austrian countryside with 30 Americans singing "Doe, a deer..." is pretty schmaltzy. Locals don't understand all the commotion (many have never seen the movie). Guides are professional, but can be (understandably) jaded.

Taking a Tour: Two companies do *S.O.M.* tours by bus (Bob's and Panorama), while a third company does a bike version. It's best to reserve ahead. Note: Your hotel will be eager to call to reserve for you—to get their commission—but you won't get the discount I've negotiated.

By Minibus: Most of **Bob's Special Tours** use an eight-seat minibus (and occasionally a 16-seat bus) and therefore promote a more laid-back camaraderie with your fellow *S.O.M.* pilgrims, and waste less time loading and unloading. Online bookings close three days prior to the tour date—after that, email, call, or stop by the office to reserve (€48 for adults; RS%—€43 if you pay cash and book directly, €43 for kids 7-15 and students with ID, €38 for kids 6 and under—includes required car seat but must reserve in advance; daily at 9:00 and 14:00 year-round, tours leave from Bob's office along the river just east of Mozartplatz at Rudolfskai 38, tel. 0662/849-511, www.bobstours.com, office@bobstours.com). Nearly all of Bob's tours stop for a fun luge ride in Fuschl am See when the weather is dry (mountain bobsled—€5 extra, generally April-Oct, confirm beforehand).

By Big Bus: **Panorama Tours** uses larger buses that depart from their smart kiosk at Mirabellplatz daily at 9:15 and 14:00 year-round (€45, RS%—€5 discount for *S.O.M.* tours if you pay in cash and book by phone or in person, book by calling 0662/874-029 or 0662/883-2110, www.panoramatours.com). While they lack the personal touch of Bob's, Panorama's big buses have a higher vantage point, and the guides have a more polished (some might say *too* polished) spiel.

By Bike: **Fräulein Maria's Bicycle Tour** offers some exercise—and much better access to the in-town sights, which are skipped or

Salzburg at a Glance

▲▲▲**Salzburg Town Walk** Old Town's best sights in handy orientation walk. See page 278.

▲▲**Salzburg Cathedral** Glorious, harmonious Baroque main church of Salzburg. **Hours:** Mon-Sat 8:00-19:00, Sun from 13:00; March-April, Oct, and Dec until 18:00; Jan-Feb and Nov until 17:00. See page 282.

▲▲**Getreidegasse** Picturesque old shopping lane with characteristic wrought-iron signs. See page 290.

▲▲**Hohensalzburg Fortress** Imposing mountaintop castle, with small museums, commanding views, and concerts most evenings. **Hours:** Museums open daily May-Sept 9:00-19:00, Oct-April 9:30-17:00. See page 298.

▲▲**Salzburg Museum** Best place for city history. **Hours:** Tue-Sun 9:00-17:00, closed Mon. See page 292.

▲▲*Sound of Music* **Tours** Bus or bike through *S.O.M.* sights of Salzburg and surrounding countryside. See page 273.

▲▲**Mozart's Birthplace** House where Mozart was born in 1756, featuring his instruments and other exhibits. **Hours:** Daily July-Aug 8:30-19:00, Sept-June 9:00-17:30. See page 294.

▲▲**Hellbrunn Palace** Lavish palace on the outskirts of town featuring gardens with trick fountains. **Hours:** Daily 9:00-17:30, July-Aug until 21:00, March-April and Oct until 16:30, closed Nov-late March. See page 310.

▲**DomQuartier Museums** Prince-Archbishop Wolf Dietrich's Residenz palace, cathedral viewpoint, and religious art. **Hours:** Wed-Mon 10:00-17:00, Wed until 20:00 in July-Aug, closed Tue except in July-Aug. See page 291.

▲**Panorama Museum** Vivid peek at a panorama painting of the city in 1829. **Hours:** Daily 9:00-17:00. See page 294.

▲**Mozart's Residence** Restored house where the composer lived. **Hours:** Daily July-Aug 8:30-19:00, Sept-June 9:00-17:30. See page 306.

▲**Mönchsberg Walk** "The hills are alive" stroll right in downtown Salzburg. See page 304.

▲**Mirabell Gardens and Palace** Beautiful palace grounds and concert venue with fine views and *Sound of Music* memories. **Hours:** Gardens—always open; summer concerts in the park on Sun and Wed, and in the palace nearly nightly. See page 305.

▲**Steingasse** Historic cobbled lane with trendy pubs in a tourist-free part of old Salzburg. See page 308.

viewed from afar on the bus tours. Meet your guide (more likely a *herr* than a *fräulein*) at the Mirabell Gardens (at Mirabellplatz 4, 50 yards to the left of palace entry). The main attractions of the eight-mile pedal include the Mirabell Gardens, the horse pond, St. Peter's Cemetery, Nonnberg Abbey, Leopoldskron Palace, and, of course, the gazebo. The tour is very family-friendly, and there'll be lots of stops for goofy photo ops (€35 includes bike, €20 for kids 13-18, €15 for kids under 13, RS%—€2 discount with this book; daily April-Oct at 9:30, June-Aug also at 16:30, allow 3.5 hours, reservations required, mobile 0650-342-6297, www.mariasbicycletours. com).

BEYOND SALZBURG

Both Bob's and Panorama Tours offer day trips from Salzburg (such as Berchtesgaden/Eagle's Nest, salt mines, Hallstatt, and Salzkammergut lakes and mountains). One efficient tour worth considering is Bob's full-day *Sound of Music*/Hallstatt Tour, which first covers everything in the standard four-hour *S.O.M.* tour, then continues for a four-hour look at the scenic, lake-speckled Salzkammergut, with free time to explore charming Hallstatt (€96, RS%—€10 discount with this book, pay cash, and book directly; doesn't include entrance fees to optional Hallstatt activities such as boat ride; departs daily at 9:00; Rudolfskai 38, tel. 0662/849-511, www.bobstours.com, office@bobstours.com).

Salzburg Town Walk

I've linked the best sights in the Old Town into this handy self-guided orientation walk (rated ▲▲▲). Allow about 1.5 hours.

🎧 Download my free Salzburg Town Walk audio tour.

• *Begin at the Mozartsteg, the wrought-iron, Art Nouveau pedestrian bridge over the Salzach River.*

❶ Mozartsteg

Get your bearings: The milky-green Salzach River thunders under your feet. On the north bank is the New Town. The south side is the Old Town, dominated by a castle on a hill.

Take in the charming, well-preserved, historic core of Salzburg's Old Town. The skyline bristles with Baroque steeples and green copper domes. Salzburg has 38 Catholic churches, plus two Protestant churches and a synagogue. The biggest green dome is the cathedral, which we'll visit shortly. Overlooking it all is the castle called the Hohensalzburg Fortress. Far to the right of the fortress, find the Museum of Modern Art—a blocky modern building atop the hill. The castle-like structure behind it is a water reservoir.

The Salzach is called "salt river" not because it's salty, but be-

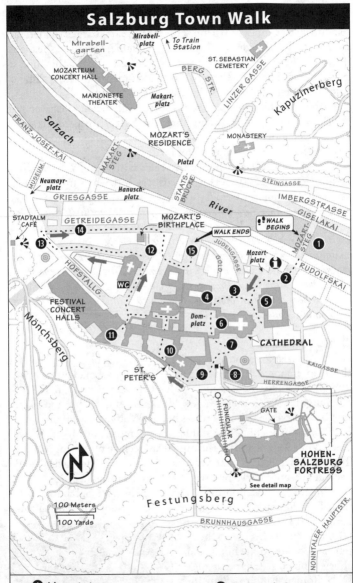

Salzburg Town Walk

1. Mozartsteg
2. Mozartplatz
3. Residenzplatz
4. Residenz
5. New Residenz & Glockenspiel
6. Salzburg Cathedral
7. Kapitelplatz
8. Waterwheel
9. St. Peter's Cemetery
10. St. Peter's Church
11. Toscaninihof
12. Universitätsplatz
13. Mönchsberg Cliff Face
14. Getreidegasse
15. Alter Markt

cause of the precious cargo it once carried. The salt mines of Hallein are just 12 miles upstream. For 2,000 years, barges carried salt from here to the wider world—to the Danube, the Black Sea, and on to the Mediterranean. As barges passed through, they had to pay a toll on their salt. The city was made great from the trading of salt *(Salz)* defended by a castle *(Burg)*—"Salz-burg."

The embankments and roads were built when the river was regulated in the 1850s. Before that, the Salzach was much wider and slower moving. Houses opposite the Old Town fronted the river with docks and "garages" for boats.

Looking upstream, notice the peak with the TV tower. This stands atop the 4,220-foot-high Gaisberg hill. The summit is a favorite destination for local nature lovers and strong bikers.

• *Now let's plunge into Salzburg's Old Town. From the bridge, walk one block toward the hill-capping castle into the Old Town. Leaving the bridge, notice Michaelstor—the remains of the 17th-century town wall (with gun holes). It was built in 1620 when Salzburg cleverly barricaded itself with a wall and neutrality to avoid the tumult of the Thirty Years' War (Catholics vs. Protestants, 1618-1648). Pass the traffic barriers (that keep this quiet town free of too much traffic) and turn right into a big square, called...*

❷ Mozartplatz

All the tourists around you probably wouldn't be here if not for the man honored by this statue—Wolfgang Amadeus Mozart. The great composer spent most of his first 25 years (1756-1781) in Salzburg. He was born just a few blocks from here. He and his father both served Salzburg's rulers before Wolfgang went on to seek his fortune in Vienna. The statue (considered a poor likeness) was erected in 1842, just after the 50th anniversary of Mozart's death. The music festival of that year planted the seed for what would become the now world-renowned Salzburg Festival.

Mozart stands atop the spot where the first Salzburgers settled. Two thousand years ago, the Romans had a salt-trading town here called Juvavum. In the year 800, Salzburg—by then Christian and home to an important abbey—joined Charlemagne's Holy Roman Empire as an independent city. The Church of St. Michael (whose yellow tower overlooks the square) dates from that time. It's Salzburg's oldest, if not biggest, church.

• *Before moving on, note the TI (which also sells concert tickets). The entrance to the Salzburg Museum is across the square (described on page*

292). *Now walk toward the cathedral and into the big square with the huge fountain.*

❸ Residenzplatz

As Salzburg's governing center, this square has long been ringed with important buildings. The cathedral borders the south side.

The Residenz—the former palace of Salzburg's rulers—is to the right (as you face the cathedral). To the left is the New Residenz, with its bell tower.

In the 1600s, this square got a makeover in the then-fashionable Italian Baroque style. The rebuilding started under energetic Prince-Archbishop Wolf Dietrich, who ruled from 1587 to 1612. Dietrich had been raised in Rome. He counted the Medicis as his cousins, and had grandiose Italian ambitions for Salzburg. Fortunately for him, the existing cathedral conveniently burned down in 1598. Dietrich set about rebuilding it as part of his grand vision to make Salzburg the "Rome of the North."

The fountain is as Italian as can be, an over-the-top version of Bernini's famous Triton Fountain in Rome. It shows Triton on top blowing his conch-shell horn. The water cascades down the basins and sprays playfully in the wind.

Notice that Salzburg's buildings are made from three distinctly different types of stone. Most common is the chunky gray conglomerate (like the cathedral's side walls) quarried from the nearby cliffs. There's also white marble (like the cathedral's towers and windows) and red marble (best seen in monuments inside buildings), both from the Alps near Berchtesgaden.

• *Turn your attention to the building on the right, the...*

❹ Residenz

This was the palace of Salzburg's powerful ruler, the prince-archbishop—that is, a ruler with both the political powers of a prince and the religious authority of an archbishop. The ornate Baroque entrance attests to the connections these rulers had with Rome. You can step inside the Residenz courtyard to get a glimpse of the impressive digs (to see the fancy interior with state rooms and an impressive collection of paintings, you must buy a DomQuartier ticket—see page 291).

Notice that the Residenz has a white-stone structure (called the Cathedral Terrace) connecting it with the cathedral. This skyway gave the prince-archbishops an easy commute to church and a chance to worship while avoiding the public.

• *At the opposite end of Residenzplatz from the Residenz is the...*

❺ New (Neue) Residenz

In the days of the prince-archbishops, this building hosted parties in its lavish rooms. These days, the New Residenz houses both the Salzburg Museum (entrance on Mozartplatz) and the Panorama Museum (entrance between the New Residenz and the cathedral; for details on both museums, see "Sights in Salzburg," later). It's also home to the Heimatwerk, a fine shop showing off local handicrafts like dirndls and locally made jelly.

The New Residenz bell tower has a famous **glockenspiel.** This 17th-century carillon has 35 bells (cast in Antwerp) and chimes daily at 7:00, 11:00, and 18:00. It also plays little tunes appropriate to the season. The mechanism is a big barrel with adjustable tabs that turns like a giant music box, pulling the right bells in the right rhythm. (Twice-weekly tours let you get up close to watch the glockenspiel action: €4, April-Oct Thu at 17:30 and Fri at 10:30, no tours Nov-March, buy ticket and meet for tour at Panorama Museum, no reservations needed—but get tickets at least a few minutes ahead as it often sells out in nice weather, ask for English handout.)

Notice the tower's ornamental top: an upside-down heart in flames surrounds the solar system, representing how God loves all of creation.

Residenzplatz sets the tone for the whole town. From here, a series of interconnecting squares—like you'll see nowhere else—make a grand procession through the Old Town. Everywhere you go, you'll see similar Italian architecture. As you walk from square to square, notice how easily you slip from noisy and commercial to peaceful and reflective.

But it wasn't always so charming and peaceful. On Residenzplatz in 1938, a huge crowd—responding to the promise of jobs and the scapegoating of immigrants and minorities—welcomed Hitler's Nazi takeover and celebrated the *Anschluss* (the "unification" of Germany and Austria).

• *Exit the square by walking under the prince-archbishop's skyway. You'll step into Domplatz (Cathedral Square). A good place to view the cathedral facade is from the far end of the square.*

❻ Salzburg Cathedral (Salzburger Dom)

Salzburg's cathedral (rated ▲▲) was one of the first Italian Baroque buildings north of the Alps. The dome stands 230 feet high,

and two domed towers flank the very Italian-esque entrance.

The church was consecrated in 1628. Experts differ on what motivated the builders. As it dates from the years of Catholic-Protestant warfare, it may have been meant to emphasize Salzburg's commitment to the Roman Catholic cause. Or it may have represented a peaceful alternative to the religious strife. Regardless, Salzburg's archbishop was the top papal official north of the Alps, and the city was the pope's northern outpost. With its rich salt production, Salzburg had enough money to stay out of the conflict and earn the nickname "The Fortified Island of Peace."

The cathedral was the center of power for the prince-archbishop in his religious role, and the government buildings surrounding it served his needs as a secular prince. But for now, it's time to visit the cathedral.

Cost and Hours: Free, donation requested, Mon-Sat 8:00-19:00, Sun from 13:00; March-April, Oct, and Dec until 18:00; Jan-Feb and Nov until 17:00; www.salzburger-dom.at. If the Jedermann theater production is under way (July and Aug), you'll find a 1,500-seat temporary theater filling the cathedral square. (And you may need to enter the cathedral through the back door.)

Visiting the Cathedral: As you approach the church, pause at the **iron gates.** The dates on the doors are milestones in the church's history. In the year 774, the first church, built in Romanesque style, was consecrated by St. Virgil (see his statue on the left), an Irish monk who became Salzburg's bishop. It was destroyed by fire in 1167, rebuilt, and then burned again in 1598. It was replaced in 1628 by the one you see today. The year 1959 marks the completion of repairs after a WWII bomb severely damaged the dome.

Because it was built in just 14 years (from 1614 to 1628), the church boasts an unusually harmonious Baroque architecture. And it's big—330 feet long, 230 feet tall—built with sturdy pillars and broad arches. When Pope John Paul II visited in 1998, some 5,000 people packed the place.

Inside, notice how you're drawn toward the light—closer to God. Imagine being part of a sacred procession, passing from the relatively dim entrance to the bright altar with its painting of Christ's resurrection, bathed in light from the dome overhead. The church never had stained glass, just clear windows to let light power the message.

Under the soaring dome, look up and admire the exceptional stucco work, by an artist from Milan. It's molded into elaborate garlands, angels, and picture frames, some of it brightly painted. You're surrounded by the tombs (and portraits) of 10 archbishops.

You're also surrounded by four organs. (Actually, five. Don't forget the biggest organ, over the entrance.) Mozart served as organist here for two years, and he composed several Masses still played today. Salzburg's prince-archbishops were great patrons of music, with a personal orchestra that played religious music in the cathedral and dinner music in the Residenz. The tradition of music continues today. Sunday Mass here can be a musical spectacle—all five organs playing, balconies filled with singers and musicians, creating glorious surround-sound. Think of the altar in Baroque terms, as the center of a stage, with sunrays serving as spotlights in this dramatic and sacred theater.

Directly under the dome, Roman-numeral plaques commemorate the visits here by Pope John Paul II in 1988 and 1998 (notice the extra *X*).

At the collection box by the back pew, black-and-white photos show the bomb damage of October 16, 1944, which left a gaping hole where the dome once was. In the first chapel on the left is a dark bronze baptismal font. It dates from 1320—a rare survivor from the medieval cathedral. The lions upon which it sits are older yet, from the 12th century...back when this part of Europe didn't really know what lions looked like. In 1756, little Wolfgang Amadeus Mozart was baptized here. For the next 25 years, this would be his home church. Amadeus, by the way, means "beloved by God."

Other Cathedral Sights: The **crypt,** with more tombs and a prayer chapel, is underwhelming (downstairs from the left transept, free). To learn more about the church, you can visit the **Cathedral Museum** as part of the DomQuartier Museums tour (see page 291). In summer, the **Cathedral Excavations Museum** (Domgrabungsmuseum, outside the church on Residenzplatz and down the stairs) shows off the church's medieval foundations and a few Roman mosaics—worthwhile only for Roman-iacs (€3, daily 9:00-17:00, closed Sept-June, www.salzburgmuseum.at).

• *As you leave the cathedral, check out the concert and Mass schedules posted near the entrance. Exiting the cathedral, turn left, heading in the direction of the distant fortress on the hill. You'll soon reach a spacious square with a golden orb.*

SALZBURG

❼ Kapitelplatz

The playful modern sculpture in the square shows a man atop a golden orb. Every year, a foundation commissions a different artist

to create a new work of public art somewhere in the city; this one's from 2007. Kapitelplatz is a pleasant square—notice the giant chessboard that often draws a crowd.

Follow the orb-man's gaze up the hill to **Hohensalzburg Fortress.** (I think he's trying to decide whether to shell out for the funicular or save money by hiking up.) Construction of the fortress began in 1077. Over the centuries, the small castle grew into a mighty, whitewashed fortress—so impressive that no army even tried attacking for over 800 years. These days, you can tour the castle grounds, visit some interior rooms and museums, and enjoy incredible views. You can walk up (Festungsgasse leads up from Kapitelplatz—follow the lane straight up from the golden ball) or, for a few euros more, take the funicular (for details, see page 297). While the castle's earliest funicular dates back to the 1500s, when animals pulled cargo up its tracks, today's funicular is electric, from 1910.

Now walk across the square to the pond surrounded by a balustrade and adorned with a Trevi fountain-like **statue of Neptune.** It looks fancy, but the pond was built as a horse bath, the 18th-century equivalent of a car wash. Notice the gold lettering above Neptune. It reads, "Leopold the Prince Built Me." But the artist added a clever twist. The inscription uses the letters "LLDVI," and so on. Those are also Roman numerals—add 'em up: L is 50, D is 500, and so on. It all adds up to 1732—the year the pond was built.

This square hosts many free events and concerts (including videos of great Salzburg Festival performances on a jumbo screen).
• *With your back to the cathedral, leave the square, exiting through the gate in the far-right corner.*

❽ Waterwheel (Wasserrad)

The waterwheel is part of a clever, still-functioning canal system built in the 12th century to bring water to Salzburg from the foothills of the Alps, 10 miles away. When the stream reached Salzburg, it was divided into five smaller canals for the citizens' use. The rushing water was harnessed to waterwheels, which powered factories. There were more than 100 watermill-powered firms as late as the 19th century. Residents also used the water to fight fires and, once a week, to flush the streets clean. Hygienic Salzburg never suffered from a plague...it's probably the only major town in

Austria with no plague monument. For more on the canal system, you might want to visit the nearby Alm River Canal exhibit (which you enter after exiting the funicular on the way down, see page 304).

This particular waterwheel (actually, it's a modern replacement) once ground grain into flour to make bread for the monks of St. Peter's Abbey. Nowadays, you can pop into the adjacent **bakery**—fragrant and traditional—and buy a fresh-baked roll for about a euro (closed Wed and Sun).

• *You've entered the borders of the former St. Peter's Abbey, a monastic complex of churches, courtyards, businesses (like the bakery), and a cemetery. Find the* Katakomben *sign and step through the wrought-iron gates into...*

❾ St. Peter's Cemetery (Petersfriedhof)

This collection of lovingly tended graves abuts the sheer rock face of the Mönchsberg (free, silence requested, daily 6:30-20:00, Oct-March until 18:00, www.stift-stpeter.at). Walk in about 50 yards past a well to a junction of lanes in the middle of the cemetery. (Stop at the round stone ball on the right—perfect for stretching that stiff back.) You're surrounded by three churches, each founded in the early Middle Ages atop a pagan Celtic holy site. The biggest church, St. Peter's, sticks its big Romanesque apse into the cemetery. Notice the fancy tombstones lining the church's wall.

The graves surrounding you are tended by descendants of the deceased. In Austria (and many other European countries), gravesites are rented, not owned. Rent bills are sent out every 10 years. If no one cares enough to make the payment, your tombstone is removed. Note the well you passed, used to fill the watering cans for the family members who keep these flowery graves so pretty.

The cemetery plays a role in *The Sound of Music.* The Captain and his large family were well known in Salzburg for their musical talents. But when Nazi Germany annexed Austria in 1938, the Von Trapps decided to flee so that the father would not be pressed into service again. In the movie, they hid here as they made their daring escape. The scene was actually filmed on a Hollywood set inspired by St. Peter's Cemetery.

Look up the cliff, which has a few buildings attached—called (not quite accurately) "catacombs." Legendary medieval hermit-monks are said to have lived in the hillside here. For a small fee, you can enter the *Katakomben* and climb lots of steps to see a few old caves, a chapel, and some fine city views (entrance at the base of the cliff, under the arcade—look for #LIV over the arch; €2, visit takes 10 minutes; daily 10:00-12:30 & 13:00-18:00, Oct-April until 17:00).

Explore the arcade at the base of the cliff with its various burial chapels. Alcove #XXI has the tomb of the cathedral architect Santino Solari—forever facing his creation. At the catacombs entry (#LIV) are two interesting tombs marked by plaques on the floor. "Marianne" is Mozart's sister, nicknamed "Nannerl." As children, Mozart and his sister performed together on grand tours of Europe's palaces. Michael Haydn was the brother of Joseph Haydn. He succeeded Mozart as church cathedral organist.

• *Exit the cemetery through the green door at the opposite end. Just outside, you enter a large courtyard anchored by...*

⓾ St. Peter's Church (Stiftskirche St. Peter)

You're standing at the birthplace of Christianity in Salzburg. St. Peter's Abbey—the monastery that surrounds this courtyard—was founded in 696, barely two centuries after the fall of Rome. The recommended Stiftskeller St. Peter restaurant in the courtyard (known these days for its Mozart Dinner Concert) brags that Charlemagne ate here in the year 803, making it (perhaps) the oldest restaurant in Europe. St. Peter's Church dates from 1147.

Cost and Hours: Free, daily 8:00-21:00, Nov-March until 19:00, www.stift-stpeter.at.

Visiting the Church: Enter the church, pausing in the atrium to admire the Romanesque **tympanum** (from 1250) over the inner doorway. Jesus sits on a rainbow, flanked by Peter and Paul. Beneath them is a stylized Tree of Life, and overhead, a Latin inscription reading, "I am the door to life, and only through me can you find eternal life."

Enter the **nave**. The once purely Romanesque interior (you may find a few surviving bits of faded 13th-century frescoes) now lies hidden under a sugary Rococo finish. It's Salzburg's only Rococo interior—all whitewashed, with highlights of pastel green, gold, and red. If it feels Bavarian, it's because it was done by Bavarian artists. The ceiling paintings feature St. Peter receiving the keys from Christ (center painting), walking on water, and joining the angels in heaven.

The monastery was founded by **St. Rupert** (c. 650-718). Find his statue at the main altar—he's the second gold statue from the left. Rupert arrived as a Christian missionary in what was then a largely pagan land. He preached the gospel, reopened the Roman salt mines, and established the city. It was he who named it "Salzburg."

Rupert's tomb is midway up the right aisle. It's adorned with a painting of him praying for his city. Beneath him is a depiction of Salzburg circa 1750 (when this was painted): one bridge, salt ships sailing the river, and angels hoisting barrels of salt to heaven.

• *Exit the courtyard at the opposite side from where you entered, through the arch under the blue-and-yellow sundial. The passageway takes you past dorms still used for student monks. At the T-intersection (where you bump into the Franciscan Church), turn right for a quick detour to appreciate another view of Domplatz.*

You're just in time for "the coronation of the Virgin Mary." The Baroque style was all about putting on a show, which is wonderfully illustrated by the **statue of Mary** (1771) that welcomes visitors in this square. As you approach her from the center of this lane, walking between the little brass rails in the cobblestones, keep an eye on the golden crown above and far behind Mary on the cathedral's facade. Just as you get to the middle arch, watch as she's crowned Queen of Heaven by the two angels on the church facade. Bravo!

Notice one more time the very Italian look of the cathedral facade: the false-front roofline; the windows flanked by classical half-columns and topped with heavy pediments; and the Baroque balustrade, decorated with garlands and masks, and studded with statues.

• *Do a U-turn and head back down Franziskanergasse. Pass beneath the archway painted with a modern Lamentation scene (1926) to enter a square called Max-Reinhardt-Platz. Pause here to admire the line of impressive Salzburg Festival concert halls ahead of you. Then turn left, through a square archway, into a small square called...*

⓫ Toscaninihof

In this small courtyard, you get a peek at the back end of the large Festival Hall complex (on your right). The Festival Hall has three theaters and seats 5,000 people (see photo on the wall). It's very busy during the Salzburg Music Festival each summer. The festival was started in the austere 1920s, after World War I, and Salzburg couldn't afford a new concert hall, so they remodeled what were once the prince-archbishop's stables and riding school.

The tunnel you see to the left leads to the actual concert hall. It's generally closed, but you might be able to look through nearby doorways and see carpenters building stage sets or hear performers practicing for an upcoming show.

The Von Trapp family performed in the Festival Hall. In the movie, this backstage courtyard is where Captain von Trapp nervously waited before walking onstage to sing "Edelweiss." Then the family slipped away to begin their escape from the Nazis.

The Toscaninihof also has the entrance to the city's huge, 1,500-space, inside-the-mountain parking lot. It originated in

1944 as the Mönchsberg air raid shelter—an underground system that offered 18,000 locals refuge from WWII bombs. The stone stairway in the courtyard leads a few flights up to a panoramic view.
• *Return to Max-Reinhardt-Platz. Continue straight along the right side of the big church, passing popular sausage stands and a public WC, then enter...*

⑫ Universitätsplatz

This square, home to the huge Baroque Kollegienkirche (University Church), also hosts Salzburg's liveliest open-air produce market (and a lot of touristy food stands). It generally runs mornings, Monday through Saturday. It's at its best early Saturday morning, when the farmers are in town. The fancy yellow facade overlooking the square marks the back end of Mozart's Birthplace, which we'll see shortly.

Find the fountain—it's about 50 yards past the church, on the right. As with public marketplaces elsewhere, it's for washing fruit and vegetables. This fountain—though modern in design—is still part of a medieval-era water system. The water plummets down a hole and on to the river. The sundial over the water hole shows both the time and the date.
• *Continue toward the end of the long, tapering square. Along the way, you'll pass several nicely arcaded medieval passageways (on the right), which lead to Salzburg's old main street, Getreidegasse. (Try weaving back and forth through some.) When you reach the traffic-control bollards, you're looking at the...*

⑬ Mönchsberg Cliff Face

Rising some 1,700 feet above you is the Mönchsberg, Salzburg's mountain. Today you see the remains of an aborted attempt in the 1600s to cut through the Mönchsberg. It proved too big a job, and when new tunneling technology arrived, that project was abandoned. The stones cut did serve as a quarry for the city's 17th-century growth spurt—the bulk of the cathedral, for example, is built of this economical and local conglomerate stone.

Early one morning in 1669, a huge landslide killed more than 200 townspeople who lived close to where the elevator is now (to the right). Since then, the cliffs have been carefully checked each spring and fall. Even today, you might see crews on the cliff, monitoring its stability.

Walk to the base of the cliff, where you'll see what was the giant horse trough for the prince-archbishops' stables. Paintings show the various breeds and temperaments of horses in the stable. Like Vienna, Salzburg had a passion for the equestrian arts.
• *Walk a block (past the toy museum—Spielzeug Museum—on your left)*

toward the river. (The elevator up the Mönchsberg is just ahead.) Opposite the church, turn right onto the long pedestrian street called...

⑩ Getreidegasse

Old Salzburg's colorful main drag, Getreidegasse (rated ▲▲) has been a center of trade since Roman times. Check out all the old wrought-iron signs that advertise what's sold inside. This was the Salzburg of prosperous medieval burghers (businessmen). These days it bustles with the tourist trade. Dating mainly from the 15th century, the buildings are tall and narrow because this was prime real estate, and there was nowhere to

build but up. Space was always tight, as the town was squeezed between the river and the mountain, and lots of land was set aside for the church. The architecture still looks much as it did in Mozart's day—though many of the buildings themselves are now inhabited by chain outlets.

Enjoy the traditional signs, and try to guess what they sold. There are signs advertising spirits, a book maker, and a horn indicating a place for the postal coach. A brewery has a star for the name of the beer, "Sternbräu." There's a window maker, a key maker, a pastry shop, a tailor, a pretzel maker, a pharmacy, a hat maker, and...ye olde hamburger shoppe, McDonald's.

On the right at #39, **Sporer** pours homemade spirits (about €4/shot, Mon-Fri 9:30-19:00, Sat 8:30-17:00, closed Sun). This has been a family-run show for a century—fun-loving, proud, and English-speaking. *Nuss* is nut, *Marille* is apricot (typical of Austria), the *Kletzen* cocktail is like a super-thick Baileys with pear, and *Edle Brande* is the stronger schnapps. The many homemade firewaters are in jugs at the end of the bar.

After noticing building #39's old doorbells—one per floor—continue down Getreidegasse. On the left at #40, **Eisgrotte** serves good ice cream. Across from Eisgrotte, a tunnel leads to the recommended **Balkan Grill** (sign reads *Bosna Grill*), the local choice for the very best wurst in town. Down the tunnel at #28 (a blacksmith shop since the 1400s), Herr Wieber, an ironworker and locksmith, welcomes the curious. Next door, McDonald's is required to keep its arches Baroque and low-key.

At Getreidegasse #9, the knot of excited tourists marks the home of Salzburg's most famous resident. Mozart was born here in 1756. It was here that he composed most of his boy-genius works. Inside you see paintings of his family, letters, and personal items (a lock of his hair, a clavichord he may have played), all trying to bring life to the Mozart story (see the description on page 294).

• *A bit farther along, at Getreidegasse #3, turn right, into the passageway. You'll walk under a whale bone (likely symbolizing the wares of an exotic import shop) and reach the Old World time-capsule café called* **Schatz Konditorei** *(worth a stop for coffee and pastry). At Schatz Konditorei, turn left through the tunnel-like passage. When you reach Sigmund-Haffner-Gasse, glance to the left (for a nice view of the city hall tower), then turn right. Walk along Sigmund-Haffner-Gasse and take your first left to reach a square called...*

⑮ Alter Markt

This is Salzburg's old marketplace. Here you'll find a sausage stand and the venerable and recommended Café Tomaselli.

• *Our walk is over. If you're up for more sightseeing, most everything's a short walk from here. The Old Town has several museums, or you can head up to the Hohensalzburg Fortress. To visit sights across the river in the New Town, cross the pedestrian bridge nearby.*

Sights in Salzburg

IN THE OLD TOWN
▲DomQuartier Museums

The interconnected museums of the DomQuartier, ringing the Domplatz, focus on religious art and the history of Salzburg's prince-archbishops. Your DomQuartier ticket admits you to a circular, indoor route through the Residenz (the ornate former palace), the cathedral (which you view from the organ loft), and a couple of adjoining buildings. For me, the highlight isn't the apartments or paintings, but the chance to walk across the gallery to the organ loft and peer into the cavernous cathedral (not permitted during Sun morning Mass, so plan accordingly).

Cost and Hours: €12, includes good audioguide, Wed-Mon 10:00-17:00, Wed until 20:00 July-Aug, closed Tue except July-Aug, last entry one hour before closing, Residenzplatz 1, tel. 0662/8042-2109, www.domquartier.at.

Visiting the DomQuartier Museums: If you enter at the Residenz (you can also enter at the cathedral), signs will guide you along the following circuit:

Once Salzburg's center of power, the **Residenz State Rooms** were the home of the prince-archbishop. Walking through these 15 chandeliered, stuccoed, tapestried, and frescoed "stately rooms" *(Prunkräume)*, you'll see elements of Renaissance, Baroque, and Classicist styles—200 years of let-them-eat-cake splendor.

The painting collection, one floor up in the **Residenz Gallery,** is strongest in Baroque paintings—not surprising in this bastion of Catholicism. The collection is always changing, but look for these highlights: Rubens' *Allegory on Charles V* shows the pope's great champion with a sword in one hand and a scepter in the other. Rembrandt's teeny-tiny *Old Woman Praying* glows, despite her wrinkled face and broken teeth (the model was probably his mother). Other highlights include Federico Barocci's intense *Self-Portrait*, Bernardo Strozzi's *Sleeping Child*, and Boucher's rosy-cheeked *Dreaming Shepherdess*. Austria is represented by F. G. Waldmüller's cheery, sun-drenched *Children at the Window*, Salzburg's own Hans Makart's honest portrait of his first wife Amalie, and lots of Romantic alpine landscapes.

In good weather, you can cross over to the cathedral the same way the prince-archbishops did—walking across their marble skyway (the **Panorama Terrace**), high above the unwashed masses. (If it's raining, you'll be sent one floor down to the indoor walkway.)

Though you don't actually tour the cathedral interior, you do glance down on the nave from high above. On this level, you can visit two small museums: the **Nordoratorium** (North Oratory) and the **Cathedral Museum,** with rich religious objects from the cathedral's long history.

Then you'll head downstairs to the **Cabinet of Curiosities** and follow the Long Gallery to the **Museum of St. Peter's Abbey**—introducing you to work and life at the abbey (which claims to be the oldest monastery north of the Alps).

▲▲Salzburg Museum

This is your best look at Salzburg's history. As the building was once the prince-archbishop's New Residence, many exhibits are in the lavish rooms where Salzburg's rulers entertained.

Cost and Hours: €8.50, €10 combo-ticket with Panorama Museum, includes heavy-but-handy high-tech audio/videoguide (ID required), Tue-Sun 9:00-17:00, closed Mon, café, on Residenzplatz, tel. 0662/620-8080, www.salzburgmuseum.at.

Visiting the Museum: The first floor and the *Kunsthalle* in the basement house temporary exhibits. But the centerpiece of the museum is the permanent **Salzburg Myth** exhibit on the second floor. You'll learn how the town's physical beauty—nestled among the Alps, near a river—attracted 19th-century Romantics who made it one of Europe's first tourist destinations, an "Alpine Arcadia." Visitors are challenged to consider how people then—as today—filtered out certain harsh realities (like poor living conditions) in favor of romanticized images of the places they visited.

Room 2.01 displays lots of gauzy landscapes of Salzburg from this era (and earlier), all remarkably recognizable. The side room holds musical instruments and plentiful audio samples, and explains how the arrival of the music festival in the 1920s spurred

Salzburg's status still more, drawing high-class visitors from across the globe. The exhibit includes strings, woodwinds, and keyboards dating back as far as the 1600s. Highlights include the enormous bassoon-like *Grossbass Pommer*, the single-stringed *tromba marina* (nicknamed "the nun's violin," its buzz resembles a trumpet), and the tiny *pochette* (pocket-sized violin).

After that prelude, several rooms address the notion of tourism in the context of city development, and the conflict of modernization versus conservation. The exhibit then focuses mostly on the glory days of the prince-archbishops (1500-1800), with displays housed in impressive ceremonial rooms. Portraits of the prince-archbishops (in Room 2.07) show them to be cultured men, with sensitive eyes and soft hands, and carrying books. But they were also powerful secular rulers of an independent state that extended far beyond today's Salzburg (see the map in Room 2.08).

Room 2.09 displays Daniel Miller's paintings of the city as seen from Kapuzinerberg and from Mönchsberg. Even though both paintings are from 1635, almost everything in them is still identifiable.

The heart of the exhibit is Room 2.11, the big, colorful hall where the Salzburg Diet (the legislature) met. The elaborate painted relief ceiling depicts heroic Romans who sacrificed for their country. Spend some time here with the grab-bag of interesting displays, including old guns, rock crystals, and coins. A portrait shows the prince-archbishop who sums up Salzburg's golden age— Wolf Dietrich von Raitenau (1559-1617). Here he is at age 28, having just assumed power. Educated, well-traveled, a military strategist, and fluent in several languages, Wolf Dietrich epitomized the kind of Renaissance man who could lead both church and state. He largely created the city we see today—the rebuilt cathedral, Residenz, Residenzplatz, and Mirabell Palace—done in the Italian Baroque style. Interactive screens describe the strict ordinances issued by this notable archbishop, including the Mandate of Religion (1588), which ordered all non-Catholics to leave the city. Today, about 95 percent of Salzburg is (nominally) Catholic, and there's only one Lutheran church.

Nearby exhibits flesh out Wolf Dietrich the man and his associates. Room 2.13 holds a portrait of the Italian architect Vincenzo Scamozzi, who contributed to the city's Baroque appearance during Wolf Dietrich's tenure. You'll also see a portrait of Salome Alt, Wolf Dietrich's mistress, a merchant's daughter which whom he shared 15 children and a retreat outside the city walls (which was later rebuilt as Mirabell Palace). This liaison prevented Wolf Dietrich's promotion to cardinal, but the couple's love never faltered. After Raitenau's death, Alt dressed as a widow for the rest of her life.

In Room 2.12, find the oldest known painted view of Salzburg (1599), and try to spot the burnt ruins of the second Romanesque church, now the site of Salzburg Cathedral.

▲Panorama Museum

Located in the New Residence, the Panorama Museum displays a wrap-around painting of the city, giving a 360-degree look at Salzburg in the year 1829.

Cost and Hours: €4 in-cludes Panorama and tempo-rary exhibits, €10 combo-ticket with Salzburg Museum, daily 9:00-17:00, Residenzplatz 9, tel. 0662/620-808-730, www.salzburgmuseum.at.

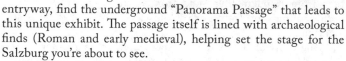

Visiting the Museum: From the Salzburg Museum entryway, find the underground "Panorama Passage" that leads to this unique exhibit. The passage itself is lined with archaeological finds (Roman and early medieval), helping set the stage for the Salzburg you're about to see.

In the early 19th century, before the advent of photography, 360-degree panorama paintings of great cities or events were popu-lar. When this one was created, the 1815 Treaty of Vienna had just divvied up post-Napoleonic Europe, and Salzburg had become part of the Habsburg realm. This photo-realistic painting served as a town portrait done at the emperor's request.

Painted by Johann Michael Sattler, the view shows the city as seen from the top of its castle. It took Sattler four years to complete (1825-29), after which the painting spent 10 years touring the great cities of Europe, showing off Salzburg's breathtaking setting. Do-nated to the city by Sattler's son in 1870, it was displayed at Mira-bell Palace until 1937 and then stored in Salzburg fortress. Today, the exquisitely restored painting, hung in a circular room, offers a fascinating look at the city as it was in the early 19th century. The river was slower and had beaches, but the Old Town looks essen-tially as it does today.

▲▲Mozart's Birthplace (Geburtshaus)

In 1747, Leopold Mozart—a musician in the prince-archbishop's band—moved into this small rental unit with his new bride. Soon they had a baby girl (Nannerl), and in 1756, a little boy was born—Wolfgang Amadeus Mozart. It was here that Mozart learned to play piano and violin, and composed his first boy-genius works. Even after the family gained fame, touring Europe's palaces and becoming the toast of Salzburg, they continued living in this rather cramped apartment.

Mozart's Salzburg

Salzburg was Mozart's home for the first 25 years of his brief, 35-year life. He was born on Getreidegasse and baptized in the cathedral. He played his first big concert, at age six, at the Residenz. He was the organist for the cathedral, conducted the prince-archbishop's orchestra, and dined at (what's now called) Café Tomaselli. It was from Salzburg that he gained Europe-wide fame, touring the continent with his talented performing family. At age 17, Mozart and his family moved into lavish digs at (today's) Mozart's Residence.

As his fame and ambitions grew, Mozart eventually left Salzburg to pursue his dreams in Vienna. His departure from Salzburg's royal court in 1781 is the stuff of legend. Mozart, full of himself, announced that he was quitting. The prince-archbishop essentially said, "You can't quit; you're fired!" and as Mozart walked out, he was literally kicked in the ass.

Mozart Sights in Salzburg: Both Mozart sights in Salzburg—the Birthplace and the Residence—are expensive and equally good. If I had to choose, I'd go with the Birthplace as the best overall introduction (though it's more crowded), and consider the Residence extra credit. If you're truly interested in Mozart and his times, buy the combo-ticket and see both.

Today this is the most popular Mozart sight in town—for fans, it's almost a pilgrimage. Shuffling through with the crowds, you'll peruse three floors of rooms displaying paintings, letters, personal items, and lots of context, all bringing life to the Mozart story.

Cost and Hours: €11, €18 combo-ticket with Mozart's Residence, daily July-Aug 8:30-19:00, Sept-June 9:00-17:30, Getreidegasse 9, tel. 0662/844-313, www.mozarteum.at. Avoid shoulder-to-shoulder crowds by visiting right when it opens or late in the day.

Visiting Mozart's Birthplace: You'll begin on the top floor in the actual apartment—five small rooms, including the kitchen and the bedroom where Mozart was born. The rooms are bare of any furnishings. Instead, you see Mozart's "square piano," detailed biographies and portraits of the famous family and some memorabilia: Mozart's childhood viola, some (possible) locks of his hair, buttons from his jacket, and a letter to his wife, whom he calls his "little rascal, pussy-pussy." Snippets of correspondence between Mozart's family members (beneath the portraits) are filled with

warmth and humor, revealing their individual personalities.

The museum portion begins with an exhibition on Mozart's life after he left Salzburg for Vienna: He jams with Haydn and wows the Viennese with electrifying concerts and new compositions. Despite his fame, Mozart fell on hard times, and died young and in debt. But, as the museum shows, his legacy lived on. Using computers, you can hear his music while following along on his handwritten scores.

Downstairs, the Mozart und Oper room examines the operas he wrote *(Don Giovanni, The Magic Flute, The Marriage of Figaro)*, with stage sets and video clips. The prize piece is an old clavichord on which Mozart supposedly composed his final work—the *Requiem*, which was played for his own funeral. (A predecessor of the more complicated piano, the clavichord's keys hit the strings with a simple teeter-totter motion that allows you to play very softly—ideal for composers living in tight apartment quarters.)

The lower-floor Wunderkind Mozart exhibit takes you on the road with the child prodigy, and gives a slice-of-life portrait of what it was like to live and travel in the 1700s (Mozart spent a third of his life journeying throughout Europe—during a time when it took 29 hours to travel just from Salzburg to Munich). The restful, oval-shaped listening room allows you to take a break from the crowds and be immersed in beautiful music and perfect acoustics.

Summer Riding School (Felsenreitschule)

Built into the mountainside, the Summer Riding School was established in 1683 by Prince-Archbishop Johann Ernst von Thun adjacent to his massive stables, now the next-door Large Festival Hall (Grosses Festspielhaus). The complex took on many uses before Austrian-American theater director Max Reinhardt took on the venue for the Salzburg Festival in 1926. While fans will recognize its iconic arcaded stage as the setting for the Von Trapp family's final public performance in *The Sound of Music*, it's worthwhile to take a guided tour of this venue to understand its architecture, artwork, and theatrical and technical feats.

Cost and Hours: Visit possible only with guided tour, €7, tours run daily at 14:00, mid-July-Aug also at 9:30 & 15:30, closed during performances or rehearsals, buy ticket at least 15 minutes in advance, departs from Salzburger Festspiele Shop (Hofstallgasse 1, www.salzburgerfestspiele.at, info@salzburgfestival.at).

Sound of Music World

This exhibition works hard to tell the story of the real Von Trapp family. The pricey "museum" has a few artifacts, an interview video with one of the Von Trapp children, and some fun photos taken of the film cast in Salzburg during filming here. The exhibit is best left to diehards, but the gift shop is fun for all.

Cost and Hours: Museum—€8, store—free to enter; daily 10:00-18:00, Getreidegasse 47—across from funicular, tel. 0662/630-860, www.soundofmusicworld.com).

ATOP THE CLIFFS ABOVE THE OLD TOWN

Atop the Mönchsberg, the mini mountain that rises behind the Old Town, is a tangle of paved walking paths with great views, a couple of cafés (one cheap, one expensive, both with million-dollar views), a modern art museum, a neighborhood of very fancy homes, and one major sight: Hohensalzburg Fortress (perched on the Festungsberg, the Mönchsberg's southern arm).

Getting There: There are three ways to get up to the cliffs: climb, take an·elevator, or ride the funicular.

The **climb** up or down is steep but quick and saves a few euros. Paths or stairs lead up from the Augustiner Bräustübl beer hall/garden, Toscaninihof (near the Salzburg Festival concert halls), and Festungsgasse (at the base of the fortress).

The Mönchsberg **elevator** *(Aufzug)* starts where Gstättengasse and Griesgasse meet, on the west side of the Old Town—look for the Museum of Modern Art entry (€2.30 one-way, €3.60 round-trip—can descend via funicular at Hohensalzburg Fortress, normally Tue-Sun 8:00-23:00, Mon until 19:00).

The **funicular** starts from Festungsgasse (just off Kapitelplatz, by the cathedral) and comes up inside the fortress complex. It's pricey—€6.50 to go up or €8 round-trip—but you can purchase a fortress ticket that includes the funicular.

If you plan to do it all, the fortress, modern art museum, and both the elevator and funicular are covered by the Salzburg Card (see under "Tourist Information," earlier). I'd do it in this order: Take the funicular to the fortress in the morning (to potentially avoid the worst crowds), take the Mönchsberg Walk over to the museum, and then take the elevator down to the Old Town. Cheapskates can see the Museum of Modern Art first, use that ticket to cover elevator and funicular rides, and then buy the "by foot" ticket to enter the fortress.

Cafés: The elevator deposits you right at the recommended Mönchsberg 32, a chic café/bar/restaurant adjacent to the modern art museum and a fine place for a drink or splurge meal. From there, it's a five-minute walk to the rustic, recommended Stadtalm Café, with wooden picnic tables and a one-with-nature allure.

Popes vs. Emperors

Salzburg was on the frontline of a medieval power struggle between the Roman Catholic Church and the Holy Roman emperors. The town's mighty Hohensalzburg Fortress—a symbol of the Church's determination to assert its power here—was built around 1077, just as the conflict was heating up.

The argument was a classic tug-of-war between papal and imperial power. The prize: the right to appoint (or "invest") church officials. Such appointments traditionally came from the Church, but in the early Middle Ages, rulers began picking bishops and abbots themselves (which Rome more or less rubber-stamped). These appointed bishops and abbots were then under considerable obligation to support their king, both spiritually and materially.

For a while, Rome put up with this turned-around system, but things came to a head under Pope Gregory VII. To remind the uppity kings of their place below God and pope, he prohibited investiture by secular ("lay") rulers in 1074. But Holy Roman Emperor Henry IV bucked the system, continuing to appoint his own church leaders and boldly renouncing Gregory VII as pope. In retaliation, Gregory excommunicated both Henry and the bishops he'd appointed.

Salzburg's Archbishop Gebhard took the pope's side against Henry. As a visible sign of ecclesiastical strength, he started construction of the massive Hohensalzburg Fortress. Henry hit back by expelling Gebhard from Salzburg in 1085. Undeterred, Gebhard spent a decade in exile mustering support for the pope and raising forces against Henry.

Gebhard eventually returned to Salzburg and resumed his position as archbishop. But the investiture back-and-forth continued until 1122, when the next pope and emperor finally reached a power-sharing accord.

▲▲Hohensalzburg Fortress (Festung)

Construction of Hohensalzburg Fortress was begun about 1077 by Archbishop Gebhard of Salzburg as a show of the Catholic Church's power (see sidebar above). Built on a rock (called Festungsberg) 400 feet above the Salzach River, the fortress was never really used. That was the idea. It was a good investment—so foreboding, nobody attacked the town for over 800 years. The city was never taken by force, but when Napoleon stopped by, Salzburg wisely surrendered. After a stint as a military barracks, the fortress was opened to the public in the 1860s by Habsburg Emperor Franz Josef. Today, it remains one of Europe's mightiest castles, dominating Salzburg's skyline and offering impressive views in both directions, cafés, and a handful of mediocre museums. It's a pleasant place to grab an ice-cream cone and wander the whitewashed maze of buildings while soaking up some medieval ambience.

Cost: Don't get bogged down in the many ticket variations; the basic choices are whether to walk or ride the funicular up, and whether you want to add on the finest rooms. Most visitors avoid the short but steep walk by opting for the one-minute trip on the funicular *(Festungsbahn)*.

The **"basic" ticket** (€12.20 by funicular, €9.40 by foot) covers most castle sights: a brief audioguide tour of a small historical exhibit and a tower-top view (signed as *A*); a variety of museums, including the modern Fortress Museum and the military-oriented Rainer Regiment museums (B); and the Marionette Exhibit.

The **"all-inclusive" ticket** (€15.20 by funicular—cheaper online and before 10:00, €11.70 by foot) covers everything in the "basic" ticket plus a brief visit to the well-presented Regency Rooms (signed as *C*). Even with a "basic" ticket, you can pay €3.50 at the door to enter the Regency Rooms (worth seeing but skippable if your time is short).

Hours: The museums are open daily 9:00-19:00, Oct-April 9:30-17:00.

Information: Tel. 0662/8424-3011, www.salzburg-burgen.at.

Avoiding Crowds: Avoid waits for the funicular ascent with the Salzburg Card (which lets you skip to the head of the line) or by walking up. In summer, there can be long waits to start the audioguide tour (only 60 people are admitted at a time). To avoid ticket-line queues, buy your ticket online before you visit. To avoid crowds in general, visit early in the morning or late in the day.

Concerts: The fortress serves as a venue for evening concerts (the Festungskonzerte), which are held in the old banquet rooms on the upper floor of the palace museum. Concerts take place 300 nights a year and

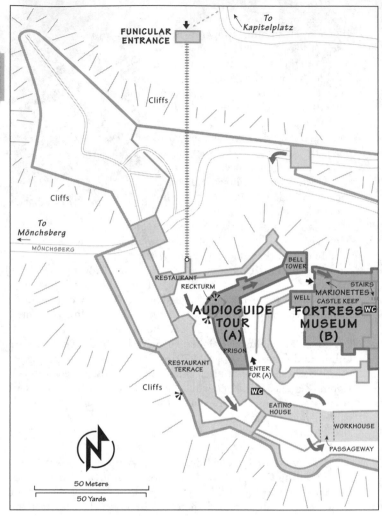

FUNICULAR
ENTRANCE

To
Kapitelplatz

Cliffs

Cliffs

To
Mönchsberg

MÖNCHSBERG

RESTAURANT

RECKTURM

BELL
TOWER

WELL

STAIRS
MARIONETTES
CASTLE KEEP

FORTRESS
MUSEUM
(B)

WC

AUDIOGUIDE
TOUR
(A)

PRISON

RESTAURANT
TERRACE

Cliffs

ENTER
FOR (A)

WC

EATING
HOUSE

WORKHOUSE

PASSAGEWAY

50 Meters

50 Yards

are a good way to see the fortress without crowds. For concert details, see page 315.

Eating: The **$$ cafés** (see photo, pervious page) to either side of the upper funicular station are a great place to linger while taking in the jaw-dropping view (daily 11:30-22:00, food served until about 20:30, closed Jan-Feb).

◒ Self-Guided Tour: The fortress is an eight-acre complex of some 50 buildings, with multiple courtyards and multiple rings of protective walls.

• *At the top of the funicular, turn right, head to the panoramic terrace, and bask in the* **view** *toward the Alps. Continue up through the for-*

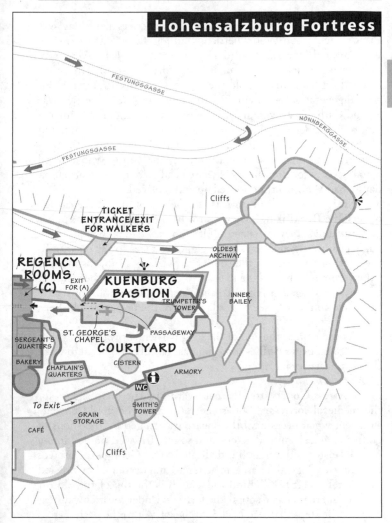

Hohensalzburg Fortress

FESTUNGSGASSE

FESTUNGSGASSE

NONNBERGGASSE

Cliffs

TICKET ENTRANCE/EXIT FOR WALKERS

OLDEST ARCHWAY

REGENCY ROOMS (C)

EXIT FOR (A)

KUENBURG BASTION

TRUMPETER'S TOWER

INNER BAILEY

ST. GEORGE'S CHAPEL

PASSAGEWAY

SERGEANT'S QUARTERS

COURTYARD

BAKERY

CHAPLAIN'S QUARTERS

CISTERN

ARMORY

WC

To Exit

GRAIN STORAGE

SMITH'S TOWER

CAFÉ

Cliffs

tress gates—two defensive rings for double protection. Emerging into the light, go left (uphill) to find the entrance to the...

Audioguide Tour (A): The audioguide leads you through a few (mostly bare) rooms. The **Stable Block** highlights 17 prince-archbishops and displays models showing the fortress' growth, starting in 1460. The last model (1810) shows it at its peak. The fortress was never taken by force, but it did make a negotiated surrender with Napoleon, and never saw action again.

The tour then takes you to the base of the **prison tower,** with a room dedicated to the art of "enhanced interrogation" (to use American military jargon)—filled with tools of that gruesome trade. One of the most esteemed prisoners held here was Prince-Archbishop Wolf Dietrich, who lost favor with the pope, was captured by a Bavarian duke, and spent his last seven years in Hohensalzburg. It's a complicated story—basically, the pope counted on Salzburg to hold the line against the Protestants for several generations following the Reformation. Wolf Dietrich was a good Catholic, as were most Salzburgers. But the town's important businessmen and the region's salt miners were Protestant, and for Salzburg's financial good, Wolf Dietrich dealt with them in a tolerant and pragmatic way. Eventually the pope—who allowed zero tolerance for Protestants in those heady Counter-Reformation days—had Wolf Dietrich locked up and replaced.

Next, climb a spiral staircase to the top of one of the castle's towers, the **Reckturm.** Jockey your way to the railing at the upper platform and survey the scene. (If it's too crowded up here, you can enjoy nearly-as-good views from bigger terraces lower down.) To the north is the city. To the south are Salzburg's suburbs in a flat valley, from which rises the majestic 6,000-foot Untersberg massif of the Berchtesgaden Alps. To the east, you can look down into the castle complex to see the palace where the prince-archbishops lived.

As you exit, at the end of the long battlement walkway, pause at the **"Salzburger Bull"**—a mechanical barrel organ used to wake the citizens every morning.

• *Exit the tour into the...*

Fortress Courtyard: The courtyard was the main square for the medieval fortress' 1,000-some residents, who could be self-sufficient when necessary. The square was ringed by the shops of craftsmen, blacksmiths, bakers, and so on. The well dipped into a rain-fed cistern. The church is dedicated to St. George, the protector of horses (logical for an army church) and decorated by fine red marble reliefs (1512). Behind the church is the top of the old lift (still in use) that helped supply the fortress. Under the archway next to it are the steps that lead back into the city, or to the paths across the Mönchsberg.

• *Just downhill from the chapel, find an opening in the wall that leads to a balcony with a view of Salzburg.*

Kuenburg Bastion: Survey Salzburg from here and think about fortifying an important city by using nature. The fortress sits atop a ridgeline with sheer cliffs on three sides, giving it a huge defensive advantage. Meanwhile, the town of Salzburg sits between the natural

defenses of the Salzach River and the ridge. (The ridgeline consists of the Mönchsberg, the cliffs to the left, and Festungsberg, the little mountain you're on.) The fortress itself has three concentric rings of defense: the original keep in the center (where the museums we're about to visit are located), the vast whitewashed walls (near you), and still more beefed-up fortifications (on the hillside below you, added against an expected Ottoman invasion). With all these defenses, the city only required a few more touches: The New Town across the river needed a bit of a wall arcing from the river to its hill. Back then, only one bridge crossed the Salzach into town, and it had a fortified gate. Cradled amid the security of its defenses—both natural and man-made—independent Salzburg thrived for nearly a thousand years.

• *Back in the main courtyard, with the chapel on your right, head uphill through the stone gate and go straight ahead up the stairs. At the very top of the long staircase is the entrance to the...*

Fortress Museum (Festungsmuseum, B): The first part of this extensive museum covers the history of the fortress, including a great town model and smaller models illustrating how the castle was constructed, and military artifacts. Follow the one-way route, exploring the exhibits on this floor, then head one floor up.

• *At this level, you have the chance to enter the...*

Regency Rooms (C): These recently restored rooms are the most beautiful in the palace, with richly painted and gilded woodwork. You'll begin by viewing a fun seven-minute video presentation/puppet show setting the historical context for when the prince-archbishop built these rooms around the year 1500—the High Middle Ages. Then you'll see the Golden Hall, where evening concerts are held, and the Royal Apartment, consisting of two rooms—one with a colorfully painted tile stove in the corner, and the other featuring a toilet with a several-hundred-foot drop.

• *You'll loop right back to where you started. From here, you can proceed into...*

More Museums: The rest of this floor belongs to the **Rainer Regiments Museum,** dedicated to the Salzburg soldiers who fought mountain-to-mountain on the Italian front during World War I. Heading downstairs, you'll find the second part of the **Fortress Museum,** with a 16th-century kitchen, torture devices (including a chastity belt), a creatively displayed collection of pikes and swords, carved-wood furniture, and a fine collection of everyday decorative arts (dishes).

• *Exiting the museums and gift shop, turn left up the passage, head back down the long staircase, then hook a U-turn at the bottom to find the...*

Marionette Exhibit: Marionette shows are a Salzburg tradition (think of the "Lonely Goatherd" scene in *The Sound of Music*). Two fun rooms show off various puppets and scenery backdrops.

Videos show glimpses of the Marionette Theater performances of Mozart classics (see page 316).

• *Our tour is over. To* **walk**—*either down to Salzburg or across the Mönchsberg (see "Mönchsberg Walk," next)—you can take any trail downhill. Eventually you'll pass through the ticket checkpoint and come to a T-intersection. Head right (downhill) to return to the Old Town (following* Altstadt *signs); or turn left (uphill), and go under the funicular tracks to make your way across Mönchsberg (following* Museum der Moderne *signs).*

To reach the **funicular**, *backtrack to the station between the two cafés. At the bottom of the lift, spend a minute or two at the fine little* **Alm River Canal Exhibit**, *which focuses on how the river powered the city before steam took over.*

▲Mönchsberg Walk

The paved, wooded walking path along the narrow ridgeline between the Mönchsberg elevator and the fortress is less than a mile long and makes for a great quiet and shady, 30-minute hike. There's some up and down, but the total elevation gain is about equal in either direction.

Frequent signposts direct you between all the key points, so it's hard to get lost. (*Festung Hohensalzburg* and *Museum der Moderne Salzburg* refer to the fortress and elevator ends of the mountain, respectively; the spots where you can go down the stairs into town are signed *Altstadt*.) Along the way, you'll see stunning views of Salzburg, rustic homes, a few unique little castle-like homes to ogle, a modern art museum (and occasional modern art sculptures in yards), a couple places to eat or enjoy a scenic drink, the sheer cliff face with its layers of sediment, and parts of the medieval wall. You can also pause to read information plaques about Salzburg's first settlers and the quarrying of the cliffs. At one point, the route forks to either a paved road or a footpath. Either works, as they converge later on.

The recommended Augustiner Bräustübl beer hall/garden is 10 minutes downhill past the Museum of Modern Art (follow signs for *Mülln;* see description on page 330).

Museum of Modern Art (Museum der Moderne Salzburg)

This stark concrete-and-glass exhibition space features artworks from the 19th and 20th centuries to the present day, with a particular emphasis on photography and graphic arts. It's located right at the top of the Mönchsberg elevator. Next to the museum is the "Sky Space," a cylindrical stone tower intended to let you contemplate the sky.

Cost and Hours: €13.30, includes round-trip elevator between Old Town and Mönchsberg—descent via funicular allowed,

Tue-Sun 10:00-18:00, Wed until 20:00, closed Mon except during festival, tel. 0662/842-220-351, www.museumdermoderne.at.

IN THE NEW TOWN, NORTH OF THE RIVER

The following sights are across the river from the Old Town. I've connected them with walking instructions (to trace the route, see map on page 279).

• *Begin at the Makartsteg pedestrian bridge, where you can enjoy the...*

Salzach River View

Scan the cityscape and notice all the churches. Salzburg has 40 of them, justifying its nickname as the "Rome of the North." The

grand buildings just across the bridge (with their elegant promenades and cafés) were built on reclaimed land in the late 19th century. Find the five streams gushing into the river. These date from the 13th century, when the river was split into five canals running through the town to power its mills. Facing upstream, the Hotel Stein (just left of next bridge) has a popular roof-terrace restaurant (see "Seven Senses Rooftop Terrace," later). Also upstream on the left, between here and the next bridge, is the recommended Café Bazar (a fine place for a drink with a view). Downstream, high overhead on the left, atop the Mönchsberg, notice the Museum of Modern Art (with a view restaurant) and a faux castle (actually a water reservoir). The Romanesque bell tower with the green copper dome in the distance is the Augustine church, site of the best beer hall in town (the recommended Augustiner Bräustübl).

• *Cross the bridge, walk two blocks inland, and take a left past the heroic statues into...*

▲Mirabell Gardens and Palace (Mirabellgarten und Schloss)

These bubbly gardens, laid out in 1730 for the prince-archbishop, have been open to the public since 1850 (thanks to Emperor Franz Josef, who was rattled by the popular revolutions of 1848). The gardens are free and open until dusk. The palace is open only as a concert venue (explained

later). The statues and the arbor (far left) were featured in *The Sound of Music.*

Walk through the gardens toward the palace and find the statue of the horse (on the river side of the palace). Look back, enjoy the garden/cathedral/castle view, and imagine how the prince-archbishop must have reveled in a vista that reminded him of all his secular and religious power.

The rearing **Pegasus statue** is the site of a famous *Sound of Music* scene where the kids all danced before lining up on the stairs with Maria (30 yards farther along). The steps lead to a small mound in the park (made of rubble from a former theater). Notice that Pegasus is missing what locals call "his best part." (They claim it made the prince feel less impressive, so he had it removed.)

Nearest the horse, stairs lead between two lions to a pair of tough gnomes welcoming you to Salzburg's **Dwarf Park.** Cross the elevated walk (noticing the city's fortified walls) to meet whimsical marble statues modeled after a dozen dwarfs who served in the court of the prince-archbishop in the 17th century.

There's plenty of **music** here, both in the park and in the palace. A brass band plays free park concerts (May-Aug Sun at 10:30 and Wed at 20:30). To properly enjoy the lavish Mirabell Palace—once the prince-archbishop's summer palace and now the seat of the mayor—get a ticket to a Schlosskonzerte (my favorite venue for a classical concert—see page 315).

• *Backtrack out of the park the way you came in, into the park-like square called Makartplatz (with the big-domed church at the top of the square). Across the square—opposite the big and bright Hotel Bristol—you'll find...*

▲Mozart's Residence (Wohnhaus)

In the fall of 1773, when Wolfgang was 17—and his family was flush with money from years of touring—the Mozarts moved here from their cramped apartment on Getreidegasse. Aimed toward the Mozart connoisseur, the exhibits feature original Mozart family instruments, a good introductory video, and includes an informative audioguide. The building itself, bombed in World War II, is a reconstruction.

MOZART'S WOHNHAUS

Cost and Hours: €11 includes informative audioguide, €18 combo-ticket with Mozart's Birthplace, daily July-Aug 8:30-19:00, Sept-June 9:00-17:30, Makartplatz 8, tel. 0662/8742-2740, www.mozarteum.at.

Visiting Mozart's Residence: The exhibit—seven rooms on one floor—starts in the main hall, which was used by the Mozarts to entertain Salzburg's high society. Consider spending time with the good introductory video in this room. Here, you can see Mozart's pianoforte from 1782, as well as his violin. The family portrait on the wall (from around 1780) shows Mozart with his sister Nannerl at the piano, their father on violin, and their mother—who'd died two years earlier in Paris. You'll also see three circular targets high on the wall, and—in the glass case nearby—the air rifle that Mozart and his family used to shoot at them.

Room 2 trumpets the successes the Mozart family enjoyed while living here: portraits of Salzburg bigwigs they hung out with, letters from Mozart bragging about his musical successes, and the publication of Leopold's treatise on playing violin.

Room 3 is dedicated to father Leopold—*Kapellmeister* of the prince—a member of the archbishop's orchestra, musician, and composer in his own right. Was Leopold a loving nurturer of young Wolfgang or an exploiting Svengali?

Room 4 stars "Nannerl" (Maria Anna), Mozart's sister, who was five years older. Though both were child prodigies, playing four-hand showpieces for Europe's crowned heads, Nannerl went on to lead a stable life as a wife and mother.

Room 5 boasts letters and music books from the nearby Mozarteum library. Room 6 describes the "cult of Mozart" and the use of his image in advertising, and Room 7 displays many portraits of Mozart (some authentic, some not), all a testament to his long legacy. By the time Mozart was 25, he'd grown tired of his father, this house, and Salzburg, and he went on to Vienna—to more triumphs, but ultimately, a sad end. You'll also learn about his son, Franz Xaver, and about Mozarteum—the organization dedicated to the "advancement of music" in Salzburg.

Nearby: Tucked inside the shop (near the WCs) is the free Mozart Sound and Film Collection, an archive of audio recordings, historic concerts on video, documentaries, and even the film *Amadeus*. Music aficionados and those with at least 30 minutes to spare will find this intriguing (Mon-Tue and Fri 9:00-13:00, Wed-Thu 13:00-17:00, closed Sat-Sun).

• *Leaving the museum, hook left around the corner and walk a few short blocks back to the main bridge (Staatsbrücke), where you'll find the Platzl, a square once used as a hay market. Pause to enjoy the kid-pleasing little fountain. Look up handsome Linzer Gasse, with its attractive small shops (we'll go there later). Just past the fountain (with your back to the river), Steingasse leads darkly to the right.*

▲Steingasse Stroll

Heading up dim, narrow Steingasse, you get a rare glimpse of medieval Salzburg. It's not the Church's Salzburg of grand squares and Baroque facades, but the people's Salzburg, of cramped quarters and humble cobbled lanes. Inviting cocktail bars along here come alive at night (see "Steingasse Pub Crawl" on page 332).

Stop at #9 (which sticks out into the lane) and look across the river into the Old Town; the city's original bridge once connected Salzburg's two halves right here. According to town lore, this building is where Joseph Mohr, who wrote the words to "Silent Night," was born—poor and illegitimate—in 1792. The popular Christmas carol was composed and first sung just outside Salzburg, in the village of Oberndorf, in 1818. Stairs lead from near here up to a 17th-century Capuchin monastery.

On the next corner, the wall is gouged out. This scar was left even after the building was restored, to serve as a reminder of the American GI who tried to get a tank down this road during a visit to the town brothel—two blocks farther up Steingasse. Within steps of here is the art cinema (showing movies in their original language, schedule in window) and three recommended bars (described on page 332).

Go deeper. At #19 (on the left), find the carvings on the old door. Some say these are notices from beggars to the begging community (more numerous after post-Reformation religious wars, which forced many people out of their homes and towns)—a kind of "hobo code" indicating whether the residents would give or not. Trace the wires of the old-fashioned doorbells to the highest floors.

Farther on, you step through the old fortified gate (at #20) and find a commanding Salzburg view across the river. Under the fortress and to the left, notice the red dome marking Nonnberg Abbey, with the oldest nunnery in the German-speaking world (established in 712). The real Maria, who inspired *The Sound of Music*, taught in this nunnery's school. In 1927, she and Captain von Trapp were married in the abbey's church. He was 47. She was 22.

From here, look back above the arch you just passed through, and up at part of the town's medieval fortification. The coat of arms on the arch is of the prince-archbishop who paid Bavaria a huge ransom to stay out of the Thirty Years' War (smart move). He then built this fortification (in 1634) in anticipation of rampaging armies from both sides.

Today, this street is for making love, not war. The Maison de Plaisir (a few doors down on the right, at #24) has for centuries been a Salzburg brothel. But the climax of this walk is more touristic.

• *For a grand view, head back to the Platzl and the bridge, enter the*

Hotel Stein (left corner, overlooking the river), and ride the elevator to the...

Seven Senses Rooftop Terrace

This **$$$** restaurant-terrace offers one of the best views in town. Hidden from the tourist crush, it's a trendy, professional, local scene. You can discreetly peek at the view, enjoy a drink or meal, or come back later to gaze into the eyes of your travel partner as you sip a nightcap (reservations smart for outdoor seating, indoor dining also offered, food served daily until 22:00, tel. 0662/877-277, www.7-senses.at).

• *Back at the Platzl and the bridge, you can head straight up...*

Linzer Gasse

The old road leading out of Salzburg toward Linz (and, beyond that, Vienna) is refreshingly traffic-free after 11:00. It's lined with good hotels, shops, and eateries, and is a delight to stroll. It feels almost like an unglitzy Getreidegasse. Just above Steingasse, at #14, is the gateway leading up to Kapuzinerberg (described later).

• *Higher up on Linzer Gasse you'll reach the...*

▲St. Sebastian Cemetery

This wonderfully evocative cemetery dates from around 1600, when, after picking up modern ideas while studying in Rome, Prince-Archbishop Wolf Dietrich emptied the cathedral square of its tombs and established this more modern (and Italian-feeling) place of burial. When he had it moved, people didn't like it. To help popularize it, he had his own mausoleum built as its centerpiece.

Cost and Hours: Free, daily 9:00-18:00, Nov-March until 16:00, entry at Linzer Gasse 43 in summer; in winter go through the arch at #37 and around the building to the doorway under the blue seal.

Visiting the Cemetery: Wander through this quiet oasis. While regular citizens are buried in the middle, the arcade is lined with the fine tombs of fine families. Stroll the entire square, enjoying the art of the dead. Mozart is buried in Vienna, his mom's in Paris, and his sister is in Salzburg's Old Town (St. Peter's)—but Wolfgang's wife Constanze ("Constantia") and his father, Leopold, are buried here (from the black iron gate entrance on Linzer Gasse, walk 19 paces and look left). Continue straight past the Mozart tomb to the circular building that is Wolf Dietrich's mausoleum (English description at door).

• *If you're ready for a bite, the cemetery is within a few steps of several good eateries (see page 331). For a grand finale to your New Town explorations, head back down Linzer Gasse to #14 and the trailhead up to...*

Kapuzinerberg City View

Kapuzinerberg, a small park-like mountain, rises from the river opposite Salzburg's castle. From Linzer Gasse 14, a lane and steps lead past 12 Stations of the Cross to a Capuchin monastery (the mountain's namesake) and a commanding city viewpoint. Once an alp used for grazing animals by the town's farmers, today Kapuzinerberg is a peaceful escape with trails and a beer garden at its far end (at the little Franziskischlössl castle). To get to the scenic viewpoint over the river and across from the castle, follow the shorter loop, circling right (find the viewpoint on the left, just before the trail descends to Steingasse and the river).

NEAR SALZBURG

The following sights and activities take you just outside Salzburg for easy side-trips.

▲▲Hellbrunn Palace and Gardens

In about 1610, Prince-Archbishop Markus Sittikus decided he needed a lavish palace with a vast and ornate garden purely for plea-

sure (I imagine after meditating on stewardship and Christ-like values). He built this summer palace and hunting lodge, and just loved inviting his VIP guests from throughout Europe to have some fun with his trick fountains. Today, Hellbrunn is a popular side-trip. While the formal garden may be one of the oldest in Europe (with a gazebo made famous by *The Sound of Music*), it's nothing special. The real draws here are those amazing fountains and the surprisingly engaging exhibits inside the palace. Perhaps most of all, Hellbrunn provides an ideal excuse to get out of the city.

Cost and Hours: €12.50 ticket includes fountain tour and palace audioguide, daily 9:00-17:30, July-Aug until 21:00—but tours after 18:00 don't include the palace interior, March-April and Oct until 16:30, these are last-tour times, closed Nov-late March, tel. 0662/820-3720, www.hellbrunn.at.

Getting There: Hellbrunn is nearly four miles south of Salzburg. Take **bus #25** from the train station or the Rathaus stop by

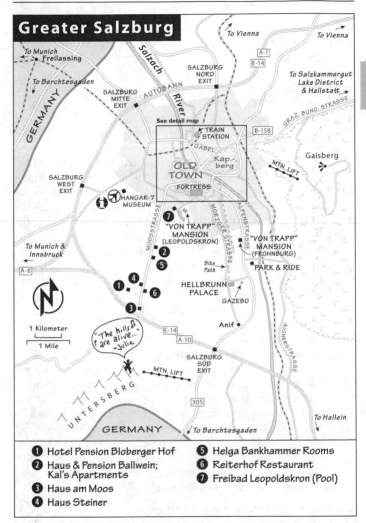

Greater Salzburg

To Vienna

To Vienna

To Munich
Freilassing

To Berchtesgaden

GERMANY

Salzach River

AUTOBAHN

SALZBURG
NORD
EXIT

A-1
E-14

To Salzkammergut
Lake District
& Hallstatt

GRAZ. BUND. STRASSE

SALZBURG
MITTE
EXIT

See detail map

TRAIN
STATION

B-158

GABEL

Gaisberg

OLD
TOWN

Kap.-
berg

MTN. LIFT

SALZBURG
WEST
EXIT

FORTRESS

HANGAR-7
MUSEUM

MOOSSTRASSE

MORZGER STRASSE

ALPENSTRASSE

7

"VON TRAPP"
MANSION
(LEOPOLDSKRON)

"VON TRAPP"
MANSION
(FROHNBURG)

To Munich &
Innsbruck

A-8

2

5

Bike
Path

PARK & RIDE

4

HELLBRUNN
PALACE

1

6

3

GAZEBO

Anif

AIGNERSTRASSE

1 Kilometer

1 Mile

♪ "The hills
are alive..."
—Julie

E-14

A-10

SALZBURG
SÜD
EXIT

MTN. LIFT

UNTERSBERG

305

To Hallein

GERMANY

To Berchtesgaden

1 Hotel Pension Bloberger Hof

2 Haus & Pension Ballwein;
Kal's Apartments

3 Haus am Moos

4 Haus Steiner

5 Helga Bankhammer Rooms

6 Reiterhof Restaurant

7 Freibad Leopoldskron (Pool)

the Staatsbrücke bridge, and get off at the Schloss Hellbrunn stop (2-3/hour, 20 minutes). Or, in good weather, the trip out to Hellbrunn is a delightful 30-minute **bike** excursion (see "Riverside or Meadow Bike Ride," later, and ask for a map when you rent your bike).

Visiting the Palace: Upon arrival, buy your **fountain tour** ticket and get a tour time (generally on the half-hour—if there's a wait until your fountain tour starts, you can see the palace first). The 40-minute English/German tours take you laughing and scrambling through a series of amazing 17th-century garden settings with lots of splashy fun and a guide who seems almost sadistic in the joy he has in soaking his group. (Hint: When you see a wet place, cover your camera.) You'll see ponds, grottoes, canals, fountains, and lots of little mechanical figures—all of them (quite remarkably) powered by 17th-century hydraulic engineering.

After the fountain tour you're free to wander the delightful **garden** and see the **gazebo** made famous by the song "Sixteen Going on Seventeen" from *The Sound of Music* (from the palace, head up the long, yellow-walled gravel road, then look right for *Sound-of-Music Pavilion* signs).

The **palace** was built in a style inspired by the Venetian architect Palladio, who was particularly popular around 1600, and it quickly became a cultural destination (enjoy the sounds of shrieking, fountain-taunted tourists below). This was the era when the aristocratic ritual was to go hunting in the morning (hence the wildlife-themed decor) and enjoy an opera in the evening. The first opera north of the Alps, imported from Italy, was performed here. The decor is Mannerist (between Renaissance and Baroque), with faux antiquities and lots of surprising moments—intentional irregularities were in vogue after the strict logic, balance, and Greek-inspired symmetry of the Renaissance.

Today, those old rooms are filled with modern, creative exhibits that help put the palace into historical context: the emerging Age of Reason, when man was determined to conquer nature (such as harnessing hydropower to soak visiting VIPs). The eclectic exhibit includes palace models and architectural drawings, a statue of Sittikus at age three (when the dream of soaking visitors was just a twinkle in his demented little eye), a stuffed unicorn, a frescoed ballroom (where you can sit on a giant turntable for a very lazy tour), and a good exhibit on how all those fountains work—including an original pipe made out of a hollowed-out larchwood log. You'll also see a wrap-around animated film reenacting the wild Carnival celebrations of Salzburg circa 1618.

▲▲Riverside or Meadow Bike Ride

The Salzach River has smooth, flat, and scenic bike lanes along each side (thanks to medieval tow paths—cargo boats would float downstream and be dragged back up by horses). On a sunny day, I can think of no more shout-worthy escape from the city. Rent a bike for an hour, pedal all the way up one side of the river to the outskirts, cross over, and pedal back. Even a quickie ride across town is a great Salzburg experience. In the evening, the riverbanks are a world of floodlit spires. For bike-rental information, see page 272.

For a longer trip, consider the pristine, meadow-filled farm-country path along Hellbrunner Allee. It's an easy four-mile ride with a worthy destination—Hellbrunn Palace (see previous listing):

From the middle of town, head along the river on Rudolfskai, with the river on your left and the fortress on your right. After passing the last bridge at the edge of the Old Town (Nonntaler Brücke), cut inland along Petersbrunnstrasse until you reach the university and Akademiestrasse. Beyond it find the start of Freisaalweg, which becomes the delightful Hellbrunner Allee bike path...which leads directly to the palace (paralleling Morzgerstrasse; see map on page 311). To make the trip a loop, you can come back along the river: Head out on Fürstenweg (past the *S.O.M.* gazebo), and follow it—carefully crossing highway 150—until you hit the river just south of the Hellbrunner Bridge. From here, you can turn left and follow the riverside path three miles back into town.

For a nine-mile ride, continue from Hellbrunn on to Hallein (where you can tour a salt mine—see next listing). If heading to Hallein directly from Salzburg, head out from the north bank of the river—the New Town side—which is more scenic.

▲Hallein Salt Mine (Salzwelten)

Of the many different salt-mine excursions from Salzburg, this one (in Bad Dürrnberg, just below the town of Hallein, 12 miles south of Salzburg) is a good choice. Wearing white overalls and sliding down sleek wooden chutes, you'll cross underground from Austria into Germany while learning about the old-time salt-mining process. The tour entails lots of time on your  feet as you walk from cavern to cavern, learning the history of the mine by watching a series of video skits with an actor channeling Prince-Archbishop Wolf Dietrich. The visit also includes a "Celtic Village" open-air museum.

Cost and Hours: €21, allow 2 hours for the visit, daily 9:00-17:00, Nov-mid-March 10:00-15:00, these are last-tour times, closed Jan, English-speaking guides—but let your linguistic needs be known loud and clear, tel. 06132/200-8511, www.salzwelten.at.

Getting There: Ride the train to Hallein (3/hour, about 20 minutes), where you can catch Postbus #41 to the salt mines in Bad Dürrnberg (runs hourly, 10 minutes). To save a few euros, buy the "ÖBB Plus" ticket, which includes the round-trip bus ride from the Hallein station and admission to the salt mine (€23.90).

Hangar-7

This hangar at the Salzburg airport (across the runways from the terminal) houses the car and aircraft collection of Dietrich Ma-

teschitz, the flamboyant founder of the Red Bull energy-drink empire. Under the hangar's modern steel-and-glass dome are 20 or so glittering planes, helicopters, and racecars, plus three eateries designed to brandish the Red Bull "culture." For gearheads, this rates ▲▲▲; for anyone else, it's a worthwhile curiosity if you have a little extra time on your way into or out of town. Mateschitz (now in his 70s) remains Salzburg's big personality: He has a mansion at the edge of town, sponsors the local "Red Bull" soccer and hockey teams, owns several chic Salzburg eateries and cocktail bars, and employs thousands of mostly good-looking Salzburgers. He seems much like the energy drink that made him rich and powerful—a high-energy, anything's-possible cultural Terminator.

Cost and Hours: Free, daily 9:00-22:00, bus #10 from Hanuschplatz to the Pressezentrum/Kuglhof stop—don't get off at the airport terminal, Wilhelm-Spazier-Strasse 7a, tel. 0662/2197, www.hangar-7.com.

Eating: Two floors up, the **$$$ Mayday Bar** has light meals and an experimental menu; in good weather, they close the bar and open an outdoor grill restaurant with similar prices. On the first floor, you'll probably want to skip the **$$$$ Ikarus Restaurant** (with a €180 fixed-price meal). By the entrance is the **$$ Carpe Diem** café.

Music in Salzburg

Music lovers come to Salzburg in late July and August for the Salzburg Festival, but there are also smaller, less expensive festivals at other times. And all year long, you can enjoy pleasant, if touristy concerts held in historic venues around town—or a musical Mass on Sunday morning. Pick up the events calendar brochure at the TI (free, bimonthly) or check www.salzburg.info (under "Events," click on "Classical Music"). I've never planned in advance, and I've enjoyed great concerts with every visit.

DAILY MUSICAL EVENTS

The following concerts are mostly geared to tourists and can have a crank-'em-out feel, but they still provide good value, especially outside festival times. Or consider Salzburg's much-loved marionette theater, with nearly daily performances.

Concerts at Hohensalzburg Fortress (Festungskonzerte)

Nearly nightly concerts—Mozart's greatest hits for beginners—are held in the "prince's chamber" of the fortress atop the hill, featuring small chamber groups (assigned seat in first six rows—€44, open seating farther back—€36, funicular ride included if you come within an hour of the concert; at 20:00 or 20:30; doors open 30 minutes early, can combine with three-course dinner beforehand, reserve at tel. 0662/825-858 or via www.salzburghighlights. at, pick up tickets at the door). The medieval-feeling chamber has windows overlooking the city, and the concert gives you a chance to enjoy the grand city view and a stroll through the castle courtyard. Purists may object to hearing Baroque music in an incongruously Gothic space.

Concerts at the Mirabell Palace (Schlosskonzerte)

The nearly nightly chamber music concerts at the Mirabell Palace are performed in the lavishly Baroque Marble Hall. They come with more sophisticated programs and better musicians than the fortress concerts...and Baroque music flying around a Baroque hall is a happy bird in the right cage (assigned seat in first five rows—€38, open seating farther back—€32; RS%—10 percent discount, use code "RICK10"; usually at 20:00 but check flier for times, doors open one hour ahead, tel. 0662/828-695, www.salzburg-palace-concerts.com).

Mozart Dinner Concert

The elegant Stiftskeller St. Peter restaurant (see page 328) offers a traditional candlelit meal with Mozart's greatest hits performed by a string quintet and singers in historic costumes gavotting among the tables. In this elegant Baroque setting, tourists clap between movements and get three courses of food (from Mozart-era recipes) mixed with three 20-minute courses of crowd-pleasing music—structured much as such evenings were in Baroque-era times (€63, RS%—use code "RICK9" to receive €9 discount; music starts nightly at 19:30, fewer nights in Feb, arrive 30 minutes before that, dress is "smart casual," to reserve email office@skg.co.at or call 0662/828-695, www.mozart-dinner-concert-salzburg.com).

Residenzkonzerte

On most afternoons, you can catch a 45-minute concert of 16th-century music ("from Baroque through Mozart") played on Renaissance instruments at the Residenz (€22, discount with Salzburg Card or DomQuartier ticket, daily at 15:00 for harpsichord and 17:00 for harpsichord and violin, tickets available 30 minutes before performance, mobile 0664-423-5645, www.agenturorpheus.at).

Marionette Theater

Spellbinding marionettes star in these operas performed to recorded music. A troupe of 10 puppeteers—actors themselves—brings to life the artfully created puppets at the end of their five-foot strings. The 180 performances a year alternate between *The Sound of Music* and various German-language operas (with handy superscripts in English). While the 300-plus-seat venue is forgettable, the art of the marionettes enchants adults and children alike. For a sneak preview, check out the videos on their website.

Cost and Hours: €20-37, kids—€15, June-Aug and Oct nearly nightly at 19:30 plus matinees on some days, fewer shows off-season, near Mozart's Residence at Schwarzstrasse 24, tel. 0662/872-406, www.marionetten.at.

WEEKLY MUSICAL EVENTS

Mozart Piano Sonatas (Klaviersonaten)

These short (45-minute) and fairly inexpensive weekend concerts in St. Peter's Abbey are ideal for families (€22, €11 for kids, €55 for a family of four, almost every Fri and Sat at 19:00 year-round, in the abbey's Romanesque Hall—a.k.a. Romanischer Saal, enter from inner courtyard 20 yards left of St. Peter's Church, mobile 0664-423-5645, www.agenturorpheus.at).

Free Brass Band Concerts

Traditional brass bands play in the Mirabell Gardens on Sundays and Wednesdays (May-Aug Sun at 10:30 and Wed at 20:30, may be canceled in bad weather).

Music at Sunday Mass

Each Sunday morning, three great churches offer a Mass, generally with glorious music. The **Salzburg Cathedral** is likely your best bet for fine music to worship by. The 10:00 service generally features a Mass written by a well-known composer performed by choir, organist, or other musicians. The worship service is often followed at 11:30 by a free organ concert (music program at www.kirchen.net/dommusik). Nearby (just outside Domplatz, with the pointy green spire), the **Franciscan Church** is the locals' choice and is enthusiastic about its musical Masses (at 9:00, www.franziskanerkirche-salzburg.at—click on "Programm"). **St. Peter's Church** sometimes has music (often at 10:15, www.stift-stpeter.at—click on "Kirchenmusik," then "Jahresprogramm").

ANNUAL MUSIC FESTIVALS

Salzburg Festival (Salzburger Festspiele)

Each summer, from mid-July to the end of August, Salzburg hosts its famous Salzburg Festival, founded in 1920 to employ Vienna's musicians in the summer. This fun and festive time is crowded—as

SALZBURG

many as 200,000 tickets are sold to festival events annually—but there are usually plenty of beds (except for a few August weekends). Events are pricey (€50-430) and take place primarily in three big halls: the Opera and Orchestra venues in the Festival House, and the Landestheater, where German-language plays are performed. The schedule is announced in November, tickets go on sale in January, and most seats are sold out by March. But many "go to the Salzburg Festival" by seeing smaller, nonfestival events that occur during the same weeks. For these unofficial events, same-day tickets are normally available—ask at the TI for details. For specifics on the festival schedule and tickets, visit www.salzburgfestival.at.

Music lovers in town during the festival who don't have tickets (or money) can still enjoy **Festival Nights,** a free series of videos of previous year's festival performances, projected on a big screen on Kapitelplatz (behind the cathedral). It's a fun scene, with plenty of folding chairs and a food circus of temporary eateries. For info and schedules, go to www.salzburg.info and search for "Festival Nights."

Other Annual Musical Festivals

The Salzburg Festival stages a week of Baroque concerts over the **Whitsunday** holiday weekend in early June (a school holiday in Austria and Bavaria). Offerings and prices are similar to those in July and August (www.salzburgerfestspiele.at/whitsun).

Mozart Week (Mozartwoche) is a high-quality, more affordable option held each year in late January. Run by the Mozarteum Foundation, it features up to three daily performances of works by both the great composer and his contemporaries (www.mozarteum.at; click on "Mozart Week" for details). Then comes the **Easter Music Festival** (Osterfestspiele), with reasonably priced concerts and operas (www.osterfestspiele-salzburg.at). The series of concerts and plays held during late October's **Culture Days** (Kulturtage) are also designed to give locals a chance to take in some high culture at a low price. And in late October, **Jazz & the City** offers free concerts scattered throughout dozens of venues in the city (www.salzburgjazz.com).

Sleeping in Salzburg

Peak season is May through October, with rates rising significantly during the summer music festival, during the four Advent weeks leading up to Christmas (when street markets are at full blast), and around Easter. Many of my Salzburg listings will let you skip breakfast to save about €10 per person—if you don't need a big breakfast, ask about this option.

IN THE NEW TOWN, NORTH OF THE RIVER
Near Linzer Gasse

These listings cluster around Linzer Gasse, a lively pedestrian shopping street a 15-minute walk or quick bus ride from the train station (for directions, see "Arrival in Salzburg") and a 10-minute walk to the Old Town. If you're coming from the Old Town, cross the main bridge (Staatsbrücke), and Linzer Gasse is straight ahead. If driving, exit the highway at Salzburg-Nord, follow Vogelweiderstrasse straight to its end, and turn right. Parking is easy at the nearby Mirabell-Congress garage (€18/day, your hotel may be able to get you a €1-2 discount, Mirabellplatz).

$$$$ Altstadthotel Wolf-Dietrich, around the corner from Linzer Gasse on pedestrian-only Wolf-Dietrich-Strasse, has 40 well-located, tastefully plush rooms (10 overlook St. Sebastian Cemetery; some are in an annex across the street). Prices include a huge breakfast spread (RS%, family rooms, nonsmoking, elevator, annex rooms have air-con, pool with loaner swimsuits, sauna, Wolf-Dietrich-Strasse 7, tel. 0662/871-275, www.salzburg-hotel.at, office@wolf-dietrich.at).

$$ Cityhotel Trumer Stube, well-located three blocks from the river just off Linzer Gasse, is a cozy, well-run, welcoming home base with 20 comfortable and attractive rooms (family rooms, in-room smartphones for free calls and navigation during your stay, nonsmoking, elevator, look for the flower boxes at Bergstrasse 6, tel. 0662/874-776, www.trumer-stube.at, info@trumer-stube.at, Vivienne).

$$ Gästehaus im Priesterseminar Salzburg occupies part of the Salzburg Seminary, where two floors have been turned into a comfortable, superbly located hotel with 60 high-ceilinged rooms. Each room has a Bible and a cross (and no TV), but guests are not required to be in a contemplative frame of mind. There's also a little guests' chapel, which looks down into the big church where Mozart used to play the organ. This is a rare place that doesn't charge extra during the Salzburg Festival—but for those dates you have to book by phone or email (family rooms, bike rental, elevator, communal kitchen, laundry facilities, reception closes at 20:00—arrange ahead if arriving later; Dreifaltigkeitsgasse 14, tel. 0662/8774-9510, www.gaestehaus-priesterseminar-salzburg.at, gaestehaus@priesterseminar.kirchen.net).

$$ Hotel Krone 1512, about five blocks from the river, offers 23 decent, simply furnished rooms in a building that dates to medieval times. Back-facing rooms are quieter than the streetside ones (earplugs smart as nearby church bells ring from 7:00-22:00). Cheapskates can save by requesting the nearly windowless "student" double. Stay awhile in their pleasant cliffside garden (RS%, email reservation for discount, higher discounts if paying cash, family rooms, elevator, Linzer Gasse 48, tel. 0662/872-300, www. krone1512.at, hotel@krone1512.at, run by Ukrainian-Austrian-Canadian Niko).

$$ Hotel Schwarzes Rössl is a university dorm that becomes a student-run hotel for the months of July, August, and September. The location couldn't be handier, and its 56 rooms, while a bit spartan, are comfortable (family rooms, cheaper rooms with shared bath, no breakfast, just off Linzer Gasse at Priesterhausgasse 6, July-Sept tel. 0662/874-426, otherwise tel. 1401-7655, www. academiahotels.at, salzburg@academiahotels.at).

$ Institute St. Sebastian is in a somewhat sterile but clean historic building next to St. Sebastian Cemetery. From October through June, it houses students but also rents 60 beds for travelers. From July through September, the students are gone, and they rent all 118 beds (including 20 twin rooms) to travelers. The building has spacious public areas, a roof garden, a piano, and some of the best rooms and dorm beds in town for the money. The immaculate doubles come with modern baths and head-to-toe twin beds (family rooms, cheaper rooms with shared bath, nonsmoking, elevator, self-service laundry, pay parking—request when you reserve; reception closes at 18:00; Linzer Gasse 41—enter through arch at #37, tel. 0662/871-386, www.st-sebastian-salzburg.at, office@st-sebastian-salzburg.at). Students like the ¢ dorms.

On Rupertgasse

These two well-run hotels are about five blocks farther from the river on Rupertgasse—a breeze for drivers, but with more street noise than the places on Linzer Gasse. They're good values if you don't mind being a 15- to 20-minute walk or quick bus ride from the Old Town or paying extra for breakfast. From the station, take bus #2 to the Bayerhammerstrasse stop; from Hanuschplatz, take #4 to Grillparzerstrasse.

$$ Hotel Jedermann is tastefully quirky and stylishly minimalist, with an artsy painted-concrete ambience (look for the owner's street-art mural), a backyard garden, and 30 rooms (family rooms, nonsmoking, elevator, pay parking, Rupertgasse 25, tel. 0662/873-2410, www.hotel-jedermann.com, office@hotel-jedermann.com, Herr und Frau Gmachl).

$$ Bergland Hotel is charming, classy, and a great value, renting 18 comfortable rooms with an oddly stylish leather-wicker-beach theme (breakfast extra, elevator, free parking if you book direct, Rupertgasse 15, tel. 0662/872-318, www.berglandhotel.at, office@berglandhotel.at, Kuhn family).

SALZBURG

Salzburg Hotels

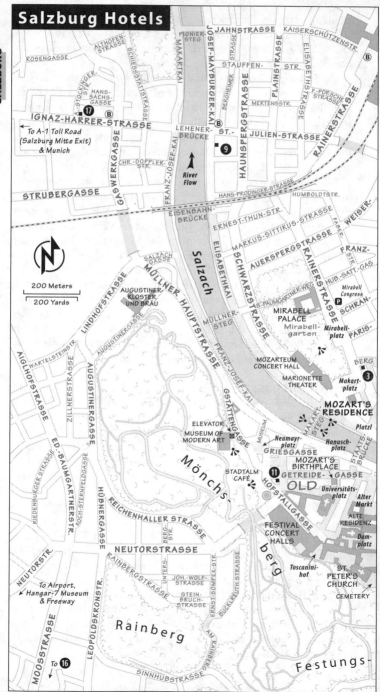

ROSENGASSE

ALTHOFEN-STRASSE

SCHIESSSTATTSTRASSE

STOCKINGER STR.

HANS-SACHS-GASSE

17 B

IGNAZ-HARRER-STRASSE

← To A-1 Toll Road
(Salzburg Mitte Exit)
& Munich

CHR.-DOPPLER-STR.

GASWERKGASSE

FRANZ-JOSEF-KAI

STRUBERGASSE

PIONIER-STEG

MAKARTKAI

JOSEF-MAYBURGER-KAI

JAHNSTRASSE   KAISERSCHÜTZENSTR.

STAUFFEN-

BERGHEIMER STRASSE

PLAINSTRASSE

ELISABETHSTRASSE

F.-PORSCHE-STRASSE

RAINERSTRASSE

B

B

LEHENER-BRÜCKE

ST.-

9

HAUNSPERGSTRASSE

JULIEN-STRASSE

MERTENSSTR.

↑ River Flow

EISENBAHN-BRÜCKE

HANS-PRODINGER-STRASSE   HUMBOLDTSTR.

ERNEST-THUN-STR.

MARKUS-SITTIKUS-STRASSE

AUERSPERGSTRASSE

FABER STR.

WEIBER

RAINERSTRASSE

FRANZ-STR.

HUB.-SATT.-GAS.

SCHWARZSTRASSE

ELISABETHKAI

SALZACH-GASSE

MÜLLNER HAUPTSTRASSE

Salzach

B.-PAUMGARTNER-WEG

Mirabell Congress

P

SCHRAN-

MIRABELL PALACE

Mirabell-platz   PARIS-

Mirabell-garten

N

200 Meters
200 Yards

LINDHOFSTRASSE

AUGUSTINER-KLOSTER UND BRÄU

AUGUSTINERGASSE

MÜLLNER-STEG

FRANZ-JOSEF-KAI

MOZARTEUM CONCERT HALL

MARIONETTE THEATER

BERG.

Makart-platz

3

WARTELSTEINSTR.

AIGLHOFSTRASSE

ZILLNERSTRASSE

AUGUSTINERGASSE

Mönchs-

GSTÄTTENGASSE

MUSEUM

ELEVATOR

MUSEUM OF MODERN ART

MOZART'S RESIDENCE

Platzl

MAKART-STEG

Neumayr-platz

Hanusch-platz

STAATS-BRÜCKE

ED.-BAUMGARTNERSTR.

RIEDENBURGER STRASSE

KOCH-STERNFELDGASSE

HÜBNERGASSE

REICHENHALLER STRASSE

BERG-STR.

STADTALM CAFÉ

GRIESGASSE

MOZART'S BIRTHPLACE

GETREIDE-GASSE

11

HOFSTALLGASSE

OLD

Universitäts-platz

Alter Markt

ALTE RESIDENZ

Dom-platz

NEUTORSTR.

← To Airport,
Hangar-7 Museum
& Freeway

NEUTORSTRASSE

LEOPOLDSKRONSTR.

RAINBERGSTRASSE

UNTERS-

JOH.-WOLF-STRASSE

STEIN-BRUCH-STRASSE

ERNST-SOMPEK-STR.

BUCKLREUTH STRASSE

AM BRÜNNL

berg

FESTIVAL CONCERT HALLS

Toscanini-hof

ST. PETER'S CHURCH

CEMETERY

Rainberg

MOOSSTRASSE

To **16**

SINNHUBSTRASSE

Festungs-

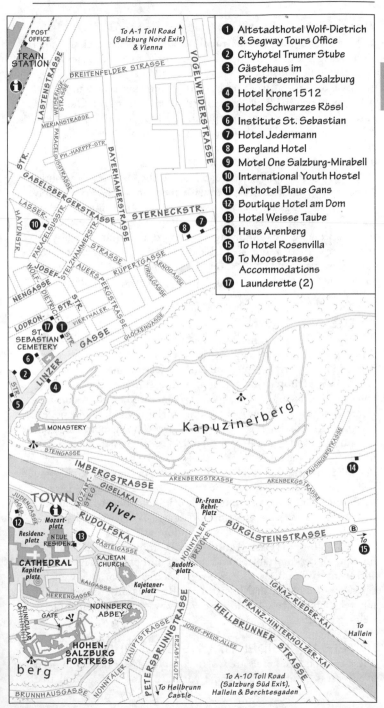

1 Altstadthotel Wolf-Dietrich & Segway Tours Office
2 Cityhotel Trumer Stube
3 Gästehaus im Priesterseminar Salzburg
4 Hotel Krone 1512
5 Hotel Schwarzes Rössl
6 Institute St. Sebastian
7 Hotel Jedermann
8 Bergland Hotel
9 Motel One Salzburg-Mirabell
10 International Youth Hostel
11 Arthotel Blaue Gans
12 Boutique Hotel am Dom
13 Hotel Weisse Taube
14 Haus Arenberg
15 To Hotel Rosenvilla
16 To Moosstrasse Accommodations
17 Launderette (2)

Near the Train Station

$ Motel One Salzburg-Mirabell is an inexpensive chain hotel right along the river. Its 119 cookie-cutter rooms are small, but the staff is helpful, the decor is fun, and the lounge is inviting. It's six blocks (or a two-stop bus ride) from the train station, and a 15-minute riverside walk or short bus ride from the Old Town (breakfast extra, elevator, pay parking, Elisabethkai 58, bus #1 or #2 from platform D at station to St.-Julien-Strasse—use underpass to cross road safely, tel. 0662/885-200, www.motel-one.com, salzburg-mirabell@motel-one.com).

¢ **International Youth Hostel,** a.k.a. the "Yo-Ho," is a youthful, easygoing backpacker haven with cheap meals, lockers, a lively bar, and showings of *The Sound of Music* every evening at 20:00 (nonguests are welcome) with a pre-show happy hour at the bar. They welcome guests of any age—if you don't mind the noisy atmosphere (private rooms available, family rooms, breakfast extra, no curfew, laundry facilities, 6 blocks from station toward Linzer Gasse and 6 blocks from river at Paracelsusstrasse 9, tel. 0662/879-649, www.yoho.at, yoho@yoho.at).

IN THE OLD TOWN

These pricier hotels are nicely located in the heart of the Old Town. Although cars are restricted in this area, your hotel will give you instructions for driving in to unload and for parking.

$$$$ Arthotel Blaue Gans, at the start of Getreidegasse, comes with class and polish. Its 35 spacious and bright rooms mix minimalist modernity with old beams and bare wood. While pricey, it's worth considering if you can score a deal (family rooms, air-con, elevator, Getreidegasse 41, tel. 0662/842-491, www.blauegans.at, office@blauegans.at).

$$$ Boutique Hotel am Dom, on the narrow Goldgasse pedestrian street, offers 15 chic, upscale, boldly decorated (read: borderline gaudy) rooms, some with original wood-beam ceilings (family rooms, air-con, elevator, Goldgasse 17, tel. 0662/842-765, www.hotelamdom.at, office@hotelamdom.at).

$$$ Hotel Weisse Taube has 31 rooms—some straightforward and comfortable, some modern and chic—all in a quiet, 14th-century building with a cozy breakfast room. It's well located about a block off Mozartplatz (RS%, family rooms, elevator, tel. 0662/842-404, Kaigasse 9, www.weissetaube.at, hotel@weissetaube.at).

HOTELS IN RESIDENTIAL NEIGHBORHOODS

These two modern hotels are worth considering for drivers in need of no-stress comfort. They come with a bit more space and free parking, but are a longish walk or bus ride to the Old Town. Get detailed driving instructions from your hosts.

$$$ Haus Arenberg rents 13 big, breezy rooms—most with generous balconies—in a modern, ranch-style mansion with a quiet garden. Though in a tony neighborhood with Porsches lining the narrow hillside lanes, it's relaxed and unpretentious. Figure a 15-minute downhill walk to the center of town (along atmospheric Steingasse) and 20 minutes back up, or take bus #6, #7, or #10 to the Volksgarten stop and hike five minutes uphill (family room, no elevator, library, electric bike rental, Blumensteinstrasse 8, tel. 0662/640-097, www.arenberg-salzburg.at, info@arenberg-salzburg.at, Leobacher family).

$$$ Hotel Rosenvilla, simpler and farther out than Haus Arenberg, offers 15 col-
orful rooms surrounded
by a leafy garden, around
the corner from a stop for
the bus into town (fam-
ily room, no elevator,
Höfelgasse 4—take bus
#7 from Hanuschplatz
to the Finanzamt stop,
tel. 0662/621-765, www.
rosenvilla.com, hotel@rosenvilla.com, Stefanie).

PENSIONS ON MOOSSTRASSE

Tucked behind Salzburg's mountain, Moosstrasse was laid out a century ago through reclaimed marshland that was meant for farms, some of which are still there. But now the street is also lined with great-value pensions that offer a roomy, comfortable alternative to pricey in-town hotels. Each one comes with free parking, farm-fresh scents, mountains in the distance, and a good breakfast (extra charge at Haus Steiner). With easy and frequent buses zipping into town in 15 minutes, the seemingly remote location shouldn't keep you away. Some places charge about 10 percent extra for one-night stays. For locations, see the map on page 320.

Handy **bus** #21 connects Moosstrasse to the center frequently (Mon-Fri 4/hour until 19:00, Sat 4/hour until 17:00, evenings and Sun 2/hour, last bus leaves downtown around 23:00). To get to these pensions from the train station, take any bus heading toward the center to Makartplatz, where you'll change to #21. If you're coming from the Old Town, catch bus #21 from Hanuschplatz, just downstream of the Staatsbrücke bridge, by the Fisch Krieg Restaurant. When traveling to your pension, the bus stops only when requested—so press the button as soon as you hear your stop announced.

If you're **driving** from the center, go through the tunnel, continue straight on Neutorstrasse, and take the fourth left onto Moosstrasse. From the autobahn, exit at *Süd* and head in the direction of *Grodig*.

$$ Hotel Pension Bloberger Hof, the most hotelesque of these options, is comfortable and friendly, with a peaceful location and 20 farmer-plush, good-value rooms—including some bigger and pricier rooms (RS%, some rooms with balcony, family rooms, family apartment with kitchen, dinner for guests available Mon-Sat 18:00-21:00, nonsmoking, elevator, free loaner bikes, free airport pickup if staying 3 nights, Hammerauer Strasse 4, bus stop: Hammerauer Strasse then head left, tel. 0662/830-227, www.blobergerhof.at, office@blobergerhof.at, Inge and daughter Sylvia).

$ Haus Ballwein offers 11 cozy, charming, and fresh rooms in a delightful, family-friendly farmhouse. Some rooms have balconies with intoxicating views (family rooms, 2-bedroom apartment for up to 5 people, cash only, farm-fresh breakfasts amid hanging teapot collection, nonsmoking, 2 free loaner bikes, Moosstrasse 69a, bus stop: Gsengerweg then cross street, tel. 0662/824-029, www.haus-ballwein.at, haus.ballwein@gmx.net, Frau Ballwein). The 11 rooms at **$$ Pension Ballwein,** across the yard—run by Frau Ballwein's son and his wife—are more polished and modern, and cost more. But the place is also fresh and roomy, and each room has a balcony (family rooms, nonsmoking, elevator, free loaner bikes, mobile 0664-222-5396, www.pension-ballwein.at, pension-ballwein@a1.net, Simon and Daniela). Frau Ballwein's daughter has four modern and slick apartments—called **$ Kal's Apartments**—just a few doors up the street (no breakfast, Moosstrasse 63b, mobile 0650-552-1116, www.kalssalzburg.at, office@kalssalzburg.at, Brigitte).

$ Haus am Moos has nine older rooms—with less rustic wood and more classy antiques—in a relaxed country atmosphere. It comes with a garden, swimming pool, breakfast buffet with mountain views, and a tiny private chapel (family rooms, nonsmoking, Moosstrasse 186a, bus stop: Lehrbauhof then head right, tel. 0662/824-921, www.ammoos.at, ammoos186a@yahoo.de, Strasser family).

$ Haus Steiner's six rooms—some with great views—are straightforward and quiet, with older modern furnishings; there's a minimum two-night stay (breakfast extra, family rooms, nonsmoking, Moosstrasse 156c, bus stop: Hammerauer Strasse then head right, tel. 0662/830-031, www.haussteiner.com, info@haussteiner.com, Rosemarie Steiner).

$ Helga Bankhammer rents four inexpensive, nondescript rooms in a farmhouse, with a real dairy farm out back (cheaper rooms with shared bath, nonsmoking, pay laundry, Moosstrasse 77, bus stop: Marienbad then cross street and turn right, tel. 0662/830-067, www.haus-bankhammer.at, bankhammer@aon.at).

Eating on Moosstrasse: $$ Reiterhof, by the Hammerauer Strasse bus stop, is a popular restaurant near these listings. They have a cozy, woody dining room that looks down into a horse-training area (Wed-Sat dinner only, Sun lunch and dinner, closed Mon-Tue, Moosstrasse 151, tel. 0662/8250).

Eating in Salzburg

Many of the restaurants and cafés listed below are open longer hours and extra days during the Salzburg Festival. On the flip side, when business is slow, eateries may close early—no matter what hours they post.

On menus, look for a local dessert specialty called *Salzburger Nockerl*. This soufflé is made to resemble mountain peaks—including a snowy dusting of powdered sugar on top. Sometimes served with raspberry sauce, this rich dessert is designed to share.

IN THE OLD TOWN
Restaurants in the Center

$$ Gasthaus zum Wilder Mann is a good bet in bad weather for traditional dishes. For a quick lunch, get the *Bauernschmaus,* a mountain of dumplings, kraut, and peasant's meats. Notice the century-old flood photos on the wall. While they have a few outdoor tables, the atmosphere is all indoors, and the menu is more geared to cold weather (kitchen open Mon-Sat 11:00-21:00, closed Sun, 2 minutes from Mozart's Birthplace, Getreidegasse 20 or Griesgasse 17, tel. 0662/841-787, www.wildermann.co.at; Robert, Kurt, and Reinhold.

$$ St. Paul Stubm Beer Garden is tucked away under the fortress with a decidedly untouristy atmosphere. The food is better than at beer halls, and a young, bohemian-chic clientele fills its two troll-like rooms and its idyllic tree-shaded garden. *Kasnock'n* is a tasty dish of *Spätzle* with cheese served in an iron pan—hearty enough for two. Reservations are smart (Mon-Sat 17:00-22:00, open later for drinks only, closed Sun, Herrengasse 16, tel. 0662/843-220, www.paul-stube.at, Bernard).

$$ Zirkelwirt serves Austrian standards (schnitzel, goulash, *Spätzle* with kraut) and big salads in an updated *Gasthaus* dining room and exotic plant-screened terrace. Just a block off Mozart-platz, it's a world away from the tourism of the Old Town (daily 11:30-22:00, Pfeifergasse 14, tel. 0662/842-796).

$$ Café Tomaselli (with its Kiosk annex and terrace seating diagonally across the way) has long been Salzburg's top place for lingering and people-watching. Tomaselli serves light meals and

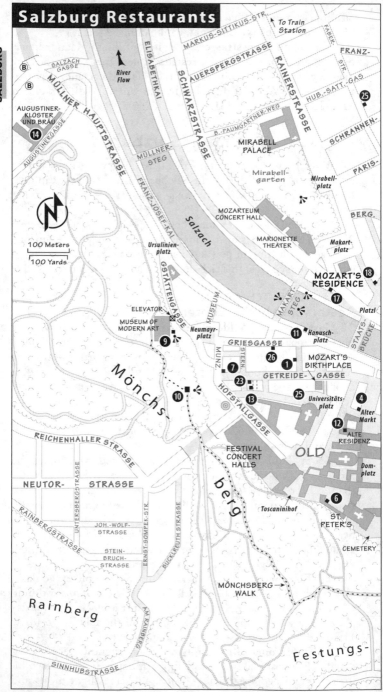

Salzburg Restaurants

SALZBURG

To Train Station

MARKUS-SITTIKUS-STR.

FRANZ-

FABER-STR.

AUERSPERGSTRASSE

RAINERSTRASSE

SCHWARZSTRASSE

HUB.-SATT-GAS.

SCHRANNEN-

PARIS-

25

ELISABETHKAI

SALZACH GASSE

B

B

MÜLLNER HAUPTSTRASSE

River Flow

AUGUSTINER-KLOSTER UND BRÄU

14

AUGUSTINERGASSE

MÜLLNER-STEG

FRANZ-JOSEF-KAI

B.-PAUMGARTNER-WEG

MIRABELL PALACE

Mirabell-garten

Mirabell-platz

BERG.

MOZARTEUM CONCERT HALL

MARIONETTE THEATER

Makart-platz

Salzach

Ursulinen-platz

GSTÄTTENGASSE

100 Meters

100 Yards

N

ELEVATOR

MUSEUM OF MODERN ART

9

MUSEUM

Neumayr-platz

Mönchs-

10

MUNZ.

STERN.

HOFSTALLGASSE

7

23

26

GRIESGASSE

13

MAKART-STEG

MOZART'S RESIDENCE

18

17

Platzl

STAATS-BRÜCKE

11

Hanusch-platz

1

MOZART'S BIRTHPLACE

GETREIDE-

GASSE

25

Universitäts-platz

4

Alter Markt

12

ALTE RESIDENZ

OLD

REICHENHALLER STRASSE

NEUTOR-

STRASSE

RAINBERGSTRASSE

UNTERSBERGSTRASSE

ERNST-SOMPEK-STR.

JOH.-WOLF-STRASSE

STEIN-BRUCH-STRASSE

BÜCKLREUTH STRASSE

-berg

FESTIVAL CONCERT HALLS

Toscaninihof

Dom-platz

6

ST. PETER'S

CEMETERY

Rainberg

AM RAINBERG

MÖNCHSBERG WALK

SINNHUBSTRASSE

Festungs-

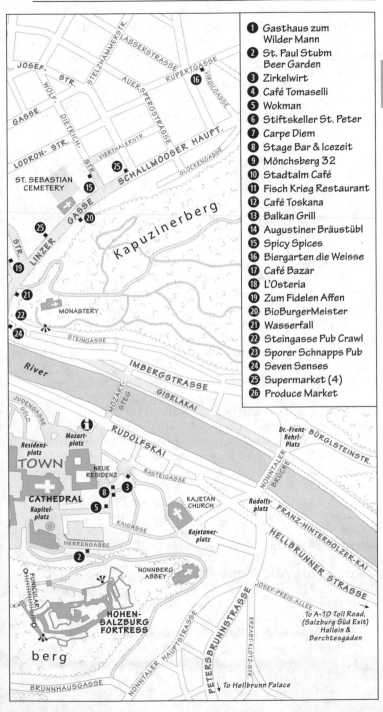

1. Gasthaus zum Wilder Mann
2. St. Paul Stubm Beer Garden
3. Zirkelwirt
4. Café Tomaselli
5. Wokman
6. Stiftskeller St. Peter
7. Carpe Diem
8. Stage Bar & Icezeit
9. Mönchsberg 32
10. Stadtalm Café
11. Fisch Krieg Restaurant
12. Café Toskana
13. Balkan Grill
14. Augustiner Bräustübl
15. Spicy Spices
16. Biergarten die Weisse
17. Café Bazar
18. L'Osteria
19. Zum Fidelen Affen
20. BioBurgerMeister
21. Wasserfall
22. Steingasse Pub Crawl
23. Sporer Schnapps Pub
24. Seven Senses
25. Supermarket (4)
26. Produce Market

lots of drinks, keeps long hours, and has fine seating on the square, a view terrace upstairs, and indoor tables. Despite its fancy wood paneling, 19th-century portraits, and chandeliers, it's surprisingly low-key (Mon-Sat 7:00-19:00, Sun from 8:00, Aug until 21:00, Alter Markt 9, tel. 0662/844-488).

$ Wokman, fragrant with fresh cilantro, is where the Nguyen family dishes up Vietnamese noodle soups and other Asian standards in a six-table restaurant a long block from the cathedral (eat in or take out, daily 11:30-21:00, closed Sun and weekday afternoons in winter, Kapitelgasse 11, mobile 0660-257-5588).

$$$$ Stiftskeller St. Peter has been in business for more than 1,000 years—it was mentioned in the biography of Charlemagne. These days it's classy and high-end touristy, serving uninspired traditional Austrian cuisine with indoor/outdoor seating (daily 11:30-22:00 or later, next to St. Peter's Church at foot of Mönchsberg, tel. 0662/841-268, www.stpeter.at). They host the recommended Mozart Dinner Concert described on page 315.

$$$$ Carpe Diem is a project by Red Bull tycoon Dietrich Mateschitz. Salzburg's beautiful people, fueled by Red Bull, present themselves here in the chic ground-floor **café** and trendy "lifestyle bar" (smoking allowed), which serves quality cocktails and fine finger food in cones (daily 8:30-23:00). Upstairs is an expensive, nonsmoking **restaurant** boasting a Michelin star (Mon-Sat 12:00-14:00 & 18:30-22:00, closed Sun, Getreidegasse 50, tel. 0662/848-800, www.carpediemfinestfingerfood.com).

Modern, Eclectic Cuisine in Kaiviertel

An oasis of contemporary, international restaurants and shops is tucked just behind the Salzburg Museum in the Kaiviertel quarter (around the intersection of Kaigasse and Chiemseegasse). Among the offerings is Polish, Irish, Vietnamese, and Mexican cuisine, as well as organic coffee. For cocktails, pizza, and snacks try **Stage Bar,** which hosts live music nightly (Tue-Sat 19:00-late, closed Sun-Mon, Chiemseegasse 3, mobile 0650-453-0547). Popular **Icezeit** serves ice cream in exotic flavors and has vegan options (Chiemseegasse 1).

On the Cliffs Above the Old Town

Riding the Mönchsberg elevator from the west end of the Old Town up to the clifftop deposits you near two very different eateries, but each has commanding city views.

$$$$ Mönchsberg 32 is a sleek, modern café/bar/restaurant overlooking Salzburg from the top of the Mönchsberg elevator. Even if you're not hiking anywhere, this makes for a great place to enjoy a €5 coffee and the view. Or settle in for a pricey but high-quality meal (weekday lunch specials, Tue-Sun 9:00-24:00, closed

Mon, popular breakfasts served until 12:00, buy a one-way elevator ticket—they give customers a free pass to descend, tel. 0662/841-000, www.m32.at).

$$ Stadtalm Café sits high above the Old Town on the edge of the cliff, with good traditional food and great views. Nearby are the remnants of the old city wall. If hiking across the Mönchsberg, make this a stop (cliff-side garden seating or cozy-mountain-hut indoor seating, generally Mon-Sat 11:30-23:00 or later, Sun until 18:00; closes earlier off-season, 5 minutes from top of Mönchsberg elevator, also reachable by stairs from Toscaninihof, Mönchsberg 19C, tel. 0662/841-729, Peter).

Eating Cheaply in the Old Town

$ Fisch Krieg Restaurant, on the river where the fishermen used to sell their catch, is a great value, serving fast, fresh, and inexpensive fish. Get your fishwich to go, or order from the affordable eat-in menu to enjoy the casual dining room—where trees grow through the ceiling—and the great riverside seating (Mon-Fri 8:30-18:30, Sat until 13:00, closed Sun, Hanuschplatz 4, tel. 0662/843-732).

$ Café Toskana is the university lunch canteen, very basic but fast and cheap—with drab indoor seating and a great courtyard for good weather. Choose between two daily soup and main-course specials (vegetarian options available, open Mon-Fri but also Sat in summer, closed Sun, generally 8:30-17:00, hot meals served 11:30-13:30 only, behind the Residenz, in the courtyard opposite Sigmund-Haffner-Gasse 16, tel. 0662/8044-6909).

$ Sausage stands *(Würstelstände)* serve the town's favorite "fast food." The best stands (like those on Universitätsplatz) use the same boiling water all day, which gives the weenies more flavor. For a list of helpful terms, see page 556. **$ Balkan Grill,** run by chatty Frau Ebner, has been a Salzburg institution since 1950, selling just one type of spicy sausage—*Bosna*—with your choice of toppings (choose one of the numbered options; takeout only, steady and sturdy local crowd, Mon-Sat 11:00-19:00, Sun 14:00-19:00, hours vary with demand, Jan-Feb closed Sun, hiding down the tunnel at Getreidegasse 33 across from Eisgrotte).

Picnics: Picnickers will appreciate the well-stocked **Billa supermarket** at Griesgasse 19a, across from the Hanuschplatz bus stop (Mon-Fri 7:40-20:00, Sat until 18:00, Sun 11:00-15:00).

SALZBURG

AWAY FROM THE CENTER

$$ Augustiner Bräustübl, a huge 1,000-seat beer garden within a monk-run brewery in the Kloster Mülln, is rustic and raw. When it's cool outside, enjoy a historic indoor setting in any of several beer-sloshed and smoke-stained halls (one of which is still for smokers). On busy nights, it's like a Munich beer hall with no music but the volume turned up. On balmy evenings, it's like a Renoir painting outdoors under chestnut trees—but with beer

breath and cigarette smoke. Local students mix with tourists eating hearty slabs of grilled meat with their fingers, while children frolic on the playground kegs. For your beer: Pick up a half-liter or full-liter mug, pay the lady (*Schank* means self-serve price, *Bedienung* is the price with waiter service), wash your mug, give Mr. Keg your receipt and empty mug, and you will be made happy. Waiters only bring beer; for food, go up the stairs, grab a tray, and assemble your meal from the deli counters (or, as long as you buy a drink, you can bring in a picnic—many do). Classic pretzels from the bakery and spiraled, salty radishes make great beer even better. Locals agree that the hot food here is not as good as the beer. Stick with the freshly cooked meat dishes: I made the mistake of choosing schnitzel, which was reheated in the microwave. For dessert—after a visit to the strudel kiosk—enjoy the incomparable floodlit view of old Salzburg from the nearby Müllnersteg pedestrian bridge and a riverside stroll home (daily 15:00-23:00, Augustinergasse 4, tel. 0662/431-246).

Getting There: It's about a 15-minute walk along the river (with the river on your right) from the Old Town side of the Staatsbrücke bridge. After passing the Müllnersteg pedestrian bridge, just after Café am Kai, follow the stairs up to a busy street, and cross it. From here, either continue up more stairs into the trees and around the small church (for a scenic approach to the monastery), or stick to the sidewalk as it curves around to Augustinergasse. Either way, your goal is the huge yellow building. Don't be fooled by second-rate gardens serving the same beer nearby. You can also take a bus from Hanuschplatz (#4, #7, #21, #24, #27, or #28) two stops to the Landeskrankenhaus stop, right in front of the beer garden. Or you can walk down from Mönchsberg (follow signs for *Mülln;* see "Mönchsberg Walk" on page 304).

NORTH OF THE RIVER
Restaurants near Linzer Gasse Hotels

$$ Spicy Spices is a trippy vegetarian-Indian restaurant where Suresh Syal (a.k.a. "Mr. Spicy") serves tasty curry and rice, samosas, organic salads, soups, and fresh juices. It's a *namaste* kind of place where everything's organic, and most items are vegan (Mon-Fri 11:00-21:00, Sat 11:30-21:00, closed Sun, Wolf-Dietrich-Strasse 1, tel. 0662/870-712).

$$ Biergarten die Weisse, close to the hotels on Rupertgasse and away from the tourists, is a longtime hit with the natives. If a beer hall can be happening, this one—modern yet with antlers—is it. Their famously good beer is made right there; favorites include fizzy wheat beer (Die Weisse Original) as well as seasonal beers (ask what's on offer). Enjoy the beer with their good, cheap, traditional food in the great garden setting or in the wide variety of indoor rooms—sports bar, young and noisy, or older and more elegant (Mon-Sat 10:00-24:00, closed Sun, Rupertgasse 10, bus #2 to Bayerhamerstrasse or #4 to Grillparzerstrasse, tel. 0662/872-246).

$$ Café Bazar overlooks the river between the Mirabell Gardens and the Staatsbrücke bridge. Its interior is as close as you'll get to a Vienna coffee house in Salzburg. While service is hit-or-miss, their outdoor terrace is a venerable spot for a classy drink with an Old Town and castle view (Mon-Sat 7:30-19:30, Sun 9:00-18:00, July-Aug daily until 23:00 or later, Schwarzstrasse 3, tel. 0662/874-278).

$$ L'Osteria, a local standby for Italian, has a fun energy, a youthful interior, and plenty of outside tables. It's a hit with locals for its pizza and weekly specials, and is one of the livelier hangouts for after-hours drinks when most of the town is closed (daily 11:00-24:00, Dreifaltigkeitsgasse 10, tel. 0662/8706-5810).

$$ Zum Fidelen Affen ("The Funky Monkey") is a reliable neighborhood eatery serving mostly traditional Austrian dishes and a few international items (pastas, big salads). The wood interior is cozy, but the big draw is the outdoor seating, which sprawls through an inviting people zone (Mon-Sat 17:00-24:00, closed Sun, Priesterhausgasse 8, tel. 0662/877-361).

$ BioBurgerMeister is a hip, crowded, order-at-the-counter place specializing in tasty American-style burgers and fries (including veggie and vegan burgers). The indoor seating is cramped—barely more than stools—but the outdoor tables on the street are pleasant (daily 11:00-22:00, across from the big church at Linzer Gasse 54, tel. 0662/265-101).

$$$$ Wasserfall is a splurge right on Linzer Gasse, serving a mostly Italian menu of pastas, meat, and fish. The sophisticated, dressy interior has an actual waterfall trickling underfoot. This is also where Salzburgers come to celebrate special occasions (Tue-Sat 17:30-24:00, closed Sun-Mon and July-mid-Aug, reservations smart, Linzer Gasse 10, tel. 0662/873-331, www.restaurant-wasserfall.at).

Groceries: The **Spar supermarket** has multiple locations around the New Town (Mon-Sat generally 7:30-18:00, closed Sun). The bustling morning **Grünmarkt produce market** (closed Sun) on Universitätsplatz, behind Mozart's Birthplace, is fun but expensive.

Steingasse Pub Crawl

For a fun post-concert activity, drop in on a couple of atmospheric bars at the Linzer Gasse end of Steingasse (described on page 308). These dark bars, filled with well-dressed Salzburgers lazily smoking cigarettes and talking philosophy as laidback tunes play, are all within about 100 yards of each other (all open until the wee hours). Most don't serve food, but **$ Reyna,** a convenient four-table pizzeria and *döner kebab* shop (at #3), stays open late.

Pepe Cocktail Bar, with Mexican decor and Latin music, serves cocktails and nachos (Wed-Sat 19:00 until late, closed Sun-Tue, live DJs on Sat, Steingasse 3, tel. 0662/873-662).

Saiten Sprung wins the "Best Atmosphere" award. The door is kept closed to keep out the crude and rowdy. Just ring the bell and enter its hellish interior—lots of stone and red decor, with mountains of melted wax beneath age-old candlesticks and an ambience of classic '70s and '80s music. Stelios, who speaks English with Greek charm, serves cocktails and fine wine, though no food (Tue-Sat 21:00-late, closed Sun-Mon except in Dec, Steingasse 11, tel. 0662/881-377).

Fridrich, two doors down, is an intimate little place under an 11th-century vault, with lots of mirrors and a silver ceiling fan. Bernd Fridrich is famous for his martinis and passionate about Austrian wines, and has a tattered collection of vinyl that keeps the 1970s alive. Their Yolanda cocktail (grapefruit and vodka) is a favorite. He and his partner Ferdinand serve little dishes designed to complement the focus on socializing and drinking, though their €16 "little bit of everything dish" can be a meal for two (Thu-Tue from 18:00, closed Wed except during festivals and Dec, Steingasse 15, tel. 0662/876-218).

Salzburg Connections

BY TRAIN

Salzburg's train station, located so close to the German border, is covered not just by Austrian rail passes, but German ones as well—including the Regional Day Ticket for Bavaria (see page 405).

Deutsche Bahn (German Railway) ticket machines at the Salzburg train station make it easy to buy tickets to German destinations. Austrian train info: Tel. 051-717 (to get an operator, dial 2, then 2), from German phone call 00-43-51-717, www.oebb.at. German train info: Tel. 0180-699-6633, from Austrian phone call 00-49-180-599-6633, www.bahn.com.

From Salzburg by Train to: Füssen (roughly hourly, 4 hours on fast trains, 5 hours on slow trains—included with Regional Day Ticket for Bavaria, change in Munich and sometimes in Kaufbeuren or Buchloe), **Reutte** (roughly hourly, 5 hours, change in Augsburg and Kempten, or in Munich and Garmisch), **Nürnberg** (hourly with change in Munich, 3 hours), **Hallstatt** (every 30-90 minutes, 50 minutes to Attnang-Puchheim, short wait, then 1.5 hours to Hallstatt; also works well by bus—see below), **Innsbruck** (hourly, 2 hours), **Vienna** (3/hour, 3 hours), **Melk** (almost hourly, 2.5 hours, transfer in Amstetten), **Munich** (2/hour, 1.5 hours on fast trains, 2 hours on slower trains—included with Regional Day Ticket for Bavaria), **Frankfurt** (4/day direct, 6 hours), **Ljubljana** (3/day, 4.5 hours, some with change in Villach), **Prague** (3/day, 5.5 hours with change in Linz; 7 hours with change in Landshut or Vienna), **Venice** (5/day, 7 hours, change in Innsbruck or Villach, short night train option).

BY BUS

To reach **Berchtesgaden,** bus #840 is easier than the train (for details see next page).

The bus trip to **Hallstatt** via Bad Ischl is cheaper, more scenic (with views of the Wolfgangsee), and only slightly slower than the train via Attnang-Puchheim—but the bus trip isn't covered by rail passes (bus #150 to Bad Ischl—Mon-Fri nearly hourly, fewer on Sat-Sun, 1.5 hours, leaves from platform F outside Salzburg train station, also stops at Mirabellplatz and Hofwirt, tel. 0810-222-333, www.postbus.at; at Bad Ischl station, change to the train—20-minute ride to Hallstatt, then ride the boat across the lake—or continue by bus #542/543 to the Lahn section of Hallstatt with a change in Gosaumühle).

ROUTE TIPS FOR DRIVERS

To drive on expressways in Austria, you need a **toll sticker** called a *Vignette* (€9/10 days, buy at the border, gas stations, car-rental agencies, or *Tabak* shops). You can skip the sticker if you stay off toll roads.

From Salzburg to Innsbruck: To leave town driving west, go through the Mönchsberg tunnel and follow blue *A-1* signs for Munich. It's 1.5 hours from Salzburg to Innsbruck.

From Salzburg to Hallstatt: See page 367 for a 1.5-hour sce-

SALZBURG

nic driving route between these two towns through the Salzkammergut (longer with stops).

From Germany to Salzburg: To avoid the A-1 toll road between the German border and Salzburg, you can exit the A-8 autobahn at Bad Reichenall while you're still in Germany, take B-20, and then B-21, which becomes B-1 as it crosses the border (this adds about 10 minutes to the drive).

Berchtesgaden, Germany

This alpine ski region, in a finger of German territory that pokes south into Austria, is famous for its fjord-like lake and its mountaintop Nazi retreat. Long before its association with Hitler, Berchtesgaden (BERKH-tehsgah-dehn) was one of the classic Romantic corners of Germany. In fact, Hitler's propagandists capitalized on the Führer's love of this region to establish the notion that the native Austrian was "truly" German at heart.

Today, the Berchtesgaden area still exerts a powerful pull on visitors. World War II buffs come here to see a top-notch documentation center, the remains of the Nazis' elaborate last-ditch bunkers, and Hitler's mountain retreat. For nature lovers, the pristine alpine setting is perfect for cruising up the romantic Königssee to get in touch with the soul of Bavarian Romanticism—or for a hike along a secluded gorge to a high waterfall. And if you have yet to do a salt-mine tour, Berchtesgaden has a good one.

Remote little Berchtesgaden can be inundated with Germans during peak season, when you may find yourself in a traffic jam of tourists. Plan your time carefully to avoid getting stuck in lines and crowds (more tips later).

GETTING THERE

From Salzburg: Berchtesgaden is 15 miles from Salzburg, and easily connected by bus #840 (runs about hourly Mon-Fri from 8:15, 6-8/day Sat-Sun from 9:15, usually at :15 past each hour, 50 minutes, buy tickets from driver, *Tageskarte* day pass covers your round trip plus local buses in Berchtesgaden—except special bus #849 up to the Eagle's Nest; check schedules at www.svv-info.at). While bus #840 originates in front of Salzburg's main train station, for many travelers it's easiest to catch it at Mirabellplatz (near many recommended New Town hotels) or in Salzburg's Old Town (on Rudolfskai, near Mozartplatz). The last bus #840 back to Salzburg from Berchtesgaden departs at 18:15 (on weekends, this bus requires an easy change at the border; the 17:15 departure is direct).

In a pinch, you can also take the train between Salzburg and Berchtesgaden (via Freilassing)—but it takes twice as long and isn't as scenic.

PLANNING YOUR TIME

Berchtesgaden's sights are excellent, but especially packed during the busy summer months of June through September (sunny weekends attract huge crowds).

If your priority is the Nazi sites, plan your day around David and Christine Harper's half-day tour (see "Tours in Berchtesgaden," later). For a leisurely pace, take the bus at 10:15 or 11:15, poke around a bit, and meet the tour at the TI at 13:15. The tour ends in time for the last bus back at 18:15.

To squeeze in more sights, leave Salzburg on the 8:15 bus (Mon-Fri) and head directly for the salt mines, Königssee (boat trip), or the Almbach Gorge (hiking; closed in winter); as long as you're at any of these sights by 9:00 or 9:30, you should avoid the worst of the crowds and still make it to the 13:15 Nazi sites tour in time. (This is trickier on weekends, when the first bus is at 9:15—expect a longer wait at sights.) Bus #840 stops at both the salt mines and the gorge on the way into town; to reach Königssee, you'll have to change buses at the Berchtesgaden station. (Doing more than one of these in addition to the tour is not realistic unless you have a car.)

Note that the Eagle's Nest is open mid-May to mid-October (confirm at www.kehlsteinhaus.de). Even if it's closed, it's still worthwhile to tour the excellent documentation center and visit the area's other sights.

Orientation to Berchtesgaden

Most of the area's major sights are just outside the small town of Berchtesgaden (pop. 7,500). The hub of activity is the train station and bus terminal, which face a huge roundabout that spans the confluence of two rivers; the TI and parking lots are across the roundabout from the station. From here, buses fan out to the various outlying sights: To the north (along

the road to Salzburg) are the salt mine and the Almbach Gorge; in the foothills to the east is Obersalzberg, with the documentation center and the remains of some Hitler-era bunkers; high on the adjacent mountaintop to the east (called Kehlstein in German) is the Eagle's Nest; and to the south is the long, skinny Königssee, which cuts deep into alpine peaks. The old center of Berchtesgaden, bypassed by most tourists, is up the hill behind the station (use the underground passage below the train tracks and cross the parking lot to reach a footpath to the old center).

Remember, you're in Germany. To call a Berchtesgaden phone number from an Austrian phone, dial 00-49 and then the number (dropping the initial zero).

ARRIVAL IN BERCHTESGADEN

By Bus: Berchtesgaden's central bus terminal (ZOB) is just in front of the train station, which is where you'll find baggage lockers (along the train platform), free WCs (near the Burger King), a few basic eateries, and history (specifically, its vintage 1937 Nazi architecture and the murals in the main hall). The oversized station was built to accommodate (and intimidate) the hordes of Hitler fans who flocked here in hopes of seeing the Führer. The building next to the station, just beyond the round tower, was Hitler's own V.I.P. reception area.

By Car: Drivers follow signs for *P-Zentrum-i*, which lead you to the main roundabout at the station. You can park free for 30 minutes in front of the TI (marked with a red *i*). For a longer stay, use the lot across the street (free, 2-hour limit but rarely enforced) or the pay Salinenplatz lot by the train station. All the outlying sights have their own parking.

TOURIST INFORMATION

The TI is across the roundabout from the train station, in the yellow building with green shutters (Mon-Fri 8:30-18:00, Sat 9:00-17:00, Sun 9:00-15:00; shorter hours and closed Sun Oct-mid-May; German tel. 08652/656-6070, www.berchtesgaden.com). You may want to pick up the local-bus schedule *(Fahrplan)*.

GETTING AROUND BERCHTESGADEN

All buses (except #849) leave from the train station, run about hourly, and are covered by the *Tageskarte* from Salzburg. Check timetables at www.rvo-bus.de, or call German tel. 08652/94480.

Bus **#840** connects Berchtesgaden to Salzburg, also stopping at the salt mine (Salzbergwerk stop, 7 minutes from Berchtesgaden) and the Almbach Gorge (Kugelmühle stop, 12 minutes)—allowing you to hop off at either sight on your way into or out of town. For more on this bus, see "Getting There," earlier.

Buses **#837** and **#848** also go to the salt mine.

Bus **#838** goes to the Obersalzberg Documentation Center and Bunker (Obersalzberg stop, 12 minutes).

Bus **#841** goes to the Königssee (Königssee stop, 9 minutes).

Bus **#849** is the only way to reach the Eagle's Nest, connecting from the Obersalzberg Documentation Center (for details, see the "Eagle's Nest" listing, later).

In a pinch, **taxis** are standing by at the train station (figure €8 to the salt mine, €12 to the Königssee, or €14 to Obersalzberg).

Tours in Berchtesgaden

Eagle's Nest Historical Tours

Since 1990, David and Christine Harper—who rightly consider this visit more an educational opportunity than simple sightseeing—have organized thoughtful tours of the Hitler-related sites near Berchtesgaden. Their bus tours, usually led by native English speakers, depart from the TI. Tours start by driving through the remains of the Nazis' Obersalzberg complex, then visit the bunkers underneath the documentation center, and end with a guided visit to the Eagle's Nest (€55/person, RS%—€3 discount with this book, includes admissions, daily at 13:15 mid-May–late Oct, 4 hours, 30 people maximum, reservations strongly recommended, private tours available, German tel. 08652/64971, www.eagles-nest-tours.com). Near the beginning or end of the season, tours are canceled if it's snowing at the Eagle's Nest.

David and Christine also do half-day private tours, which are more flexible and tailored to your interests (€250 for up to 4 people, €300 for up to 8 people); they also do great *Sound of Music* tours to Salzburg that begin in Berchtesgaden.

Bus Tours from Salzburg

While Salzburg-based tour companies (including Bob's Special Tours, www.bobstours.com, and Panorama tours, www.panoramatours.com) offer half- and full-day tours to Berchtesgaden, I don't recommend them except as a last resort. They take you to (but not into) the sights described here—meaning that you pay the tour price for the same transport that you can buy yourself for about €10 from Salzburg. Even on the full-day tours, you cannot see both the Eagle's Nest and the Obersalzberg Documentation Center—you must choose one. Instead, take David and Christine Harper's tour, or visit the documentation center and Eagle's Nest on your own by bus.

Sights near Berchtesgaden

NAZI SITES

Early in his career as a wannabe tyrant, Adolf Hitler had a radical friend who liked to vacation in Berchtesgaden, and through him Hitler came to know and love this dramatic corner of Bavaria. Berchtesgaden's part-Bavarian, part-Austrian character held a special appeal to the Austrian-German Hitler. In the 1920s, just out of prison, he checked into an alpine hotel in Obersalzberg, three miles uphill from Berchtesgaden, to finish work on his memoir and Nazi primer,  *Mein Kampf.* Because it was here that he claimed to be inspired and laid out his vision, some call Obersalzberg the "cradle of the Third Reich."

In the 1930s, after becoming the German Chancellor, Hitler chose Obersalzberg as the place to build his mountain retreat, a supersized alpine farmhouse called the Berghof—the Nazis' answer to Camp David. His handlers crafted Hitler's image here—surrounded by nature, gently receiving alpine flowers from adoring little children, lounging around with farmers in lederhosen...no modern arms industry, no big-time industrialists, no ugly extermination camps. In reality, Obersalzberg was home to much more than Hitler's alpine chalet. It was a huge compound of 80 buildings—fenced off from the public after 1936, and connected by extensive bunkers—where the major decisions leading up to World War II were hatched. Hitler himself spent about a third of his time at the Berghof, hosted world leaders in the compound, and later had it prepared for his last stand.

Some mistakenly call the entire area "Hitler's Eagle's Nest." That name actually belongs only to the Kehlsteinhaus, a small mountaintop chalet on a 6,000-foot peak that juts up two miles south of Obersalzberg. (A visiting diplomat humorously dubbed it the "Eagle's Nest," and the name stuck.) In April 1945, Britain's Royal Air Force bombed the Obersalzberg compound nearly flat, but missed the difficult-to-target Eagle's Nest entirely. Before the Allies turned the site over to the German government in 1952, they blew up most of what had survived the bombing, wanting to leave nothing to attract future neo-Nazi pilgrims. The most extensive surviving remains are of the Nazis' bunker system, intended as a last resort for the regime as the Allies closed in. In the 1990s, a museum—the Obersalzberg Documentation Center—was built on top of one of the bunkers.

▲▲▲Obersalzberg Documentation Center and Bunker

With a fine museum and the chance to walk through a network of bunkers (all that survives from Hitler's original Berghof complex),

this site provides an informative and sobering look at Nazi history.

Cost and Hours: €3 covers both museum and bunker; daily 9:00-17:00; Nov-March Tue-Sun 10:00-15:00, closed Mon; last entry one hour before closing, allow 1.5 hours for visit, essential €2 audioguide, German tel. 08652/947-960, www.obersalzberg.de.

Getting There: Hop on bus #838 from Berchtesgaden's train station (Obersalzberg stop, then a 5-minute walk). Drivers follow signs for *Obersalzberg* and *Kehlstein*, then park for free at the documentation center (lot P1 is near the Eagle's Nest bus stop, while P2 is closer to the museum and bunker).

Visiting the Museum and Bunker: From the parking lot or bus stop, walk down past the big restaurant to reach the entrance.

The small but well-presented **museum** has few actual artifacts but does a fine job of explaining the history of the site, and offers a concise and powerful overview of Nazi history. If you're visiting other documentation centers on your trip (in Nürnberg or Berlin, for example), this is a rerun. If not, it's well worth your time. There's very little English, so rent the audioguide and follow the one-way route.

First head upstairs, with exhibits about this notorious site, including the propagandists based here who cultivated a gauzy cult of personality around their mountain-loving Führer. (A subtitled 28-minute film gives eyewitness accounts of the Berghof during Hitler's heyday.) Head back down to the main floor for a look at the Nazi state and their crimes: profiles of 15 key players, from Himmler to Goebbels to Göring; the *Volksgemeinschaft* propaganda that convinced everyday Germans of their ethnic purity; and methods of terror, from the SS to concentration camps. A children's book is filled with anti-Semitic stereotypes, and a map of the concentration camp network illustrates how all roads led to Auschwitz.

Head downstairs. On your way to the bunkers, you'll pass a series of exhibits on World War II, demonstrating how this place was Hitler's "second center of power" after Berlin.

Finally, you enter the vast and complex **Platterhof bunker system.** Construction began in 1943, after the Battle of Stalingrad ended the Nazi aura of invincibility. This is a professionally engineered underground town, which held meeting rooms, offices, archives for the government, and lavish living quarters for Hitler—all connected by four miles of tunnels cut through solid rock by slave labor. You can't visit all of it, and what you can see was stripped and looted bare after the war. (Look for graffiti from French soldiers, Italian forced laborers, and American GIs.) But enough is left that you can wander among the concrete and marvel at megalomania gone mad.

▲▲▲Eagle's Nest (Kehlsteinhaus)

In 1939, the Kehlsteinhaus chalet was given to the Führer for his 50th birthday. While a fortune was spent building this perch and the road up to it, Hitler, who was afraid of heights, visited only 14 times. Hitler's mistress, Eva Braun, though, liked to hike up to the Eagle's Nest to sunbathe.

Today, the chalet that Hitler ignored is basically a three-room, reasonably priced restaurant with a scenic terrace, 100 yards below the summit of a mountain. You could say it's like any alpine hiking hut, just more massively built. On a nice day, the views are magnificent (but it's often fogged in). Bring a jacket, and go early or late in the day to avoid crowds in summer.

From the upper bus stop, a finely crafted tunnel leads to the original polished-brass elevator, which takes you the last 400 feet up to the Eagle's Nest. Wander into the fancy back dining room (the best preserved from Hitler's time), where you can see the once-sleek marble fireplace chipped up by souvenir-seeking troops in 1945.

Cost and Hours: Free, generally open mid-May–late Oct, snowfall sometimes forces a later opening or earlier closing—dates listed at www.kehlsteinhaus.de.

Getting There: The only way to reach the Eagle's Nest—even if you have your own car—is by specially equipped bus #849, which leaves from the documentation center and climbs steeply up the one-way, private road—Germany's highest (every 25 minutes, 15-minute ride, €16.60 round-trip, *Tageskarte* day passes not valid, look for *Kehlstein Busabfahrt* signs, buy ticket from bus depot window, last bus up 16:00, last bus down 16:50, free parking at documentation center).

OTHER SIGHTS NEAR BERCHTESGADEN
▲Salt Mines (Salzbergwerk Berchtesgaden)
At the Berchtesgaden salt mines, you put on traditional miners' outfits, get on funny little trains, and zip deep into the mountain. On the 1.5-hour tour (which includes time to get into and back out of your miner's gear), you'll cruise subterranean lakes; slide speedily down two long, slick, wooden banisters; and learn how locals mined salt so long ago. Tours are in German, but English speakers get audioguides.

Cost and Hours: €17—book online to see available tour times and avoid waiting in line, daily 9:00-17:00, Nov-April 11:00-15:00—these are last-entry times, German tel. 08652/600-20, www.salzbergwerk.de.

Getting There: Reach the mines from Berchtesgaden with a 20-minute walk along the river or a quick bus ride (#837, #840, or #848—see "Getting around Berchtesgaden," earlier). If you have extra time, you can take the interesting 35-minute walking route from the station to the mines through Berchtesgaden's Old Town.

Drivers look for the *Salzbergwerk* and *P* signs at the northern edge of town (on the Salzburg road). Park in the pay lot, then walk five minutes to the mine (follow signs through the pedestrian underpass and over the river).

▲Königssee

Three miles south of Berchtesgaden, the idyllic Königssee stretches like a fjord through pristine mountain scenery to the dramatically

situated Church of St. Bartholomä and beyond. This is a stunner on a nice day (less so when it's socked in). If you plan to sail the Königssee, allow at least two hours round-trip to St. Bartholomä and three hours round-trip to Salet.

Getting There: Bus #841 goes from the Berchtesgaden train station to Königssee. Walkers can take the scenically woodsy, reasonably flat 1.5-hour walk (well-signed). From the pay parking lot and bus stop (with WCs, ATMs, and a TI), a brick path leads five minutes downhill to the lakeshore

through a thicket of souvenir stores selling marmot-fat ointment, quartz chunks, carved birdhouses, lederhosen, dirndls, and "superpretzels."

Boat Trips: The big draw at Königssee is the scenic boat trips. Most visitors simply go as far as St. Bartholomä, poke around the

church there, eat some smoked fish, then take the boat back (35 minutes each way, €15 round-trip). You can stay on the boat 15 minutes longer to Salet, which is less crowded and offers a fine 15-minute hike to the smaller lake called Obersee (€18.50 round-trip). Boats, going at a sedate Bavarian speed, are filled

with Germans chuckling at the captain's commentary. For the best view, sit on the right going out, and on the left heading back. At a rock cliff midway through the journey, your captain stops, and the first mate pulls out a trumpet to demonstrate the fine echo. Boats leave with demand; you'll get a departure time when you buy your ticket (generally 2-4/hour, first boat around 8:30, last boat back between 18:00 and 19:00 depending on season—ask at ticket desk, runs late April-mid-Oct, no boats off-season, German tel. 08652/96360, www.seenschifffahrt.de). Boats fill up in nice weather (especially in July-Aug between 10:00 and 11:00). Later in the day, return boats (especially from St. Bartholomä) can be packed; if you're rushing to get back to town, keep an eye on queues for the return boats.

St. Bartholomä: The remote, red-onion-domed Church of St. Bartholomä sits on a little peninsula (once also the home of a monastery, then a hunting lodge of the Bavarian royal family). It's surrounded by a fine beer garden, rustic fishermen's pub, and inviting lakeside trails. The family next to St. Bartholomä's lives in the middle of this national park and has a license to fish—so very fresh, caught-and-smoked-today trout is the lunchtime favorite. (Look for the *Fischerei*, where you can get a filet on a baguette to go.) For a heartier meal, there's also an outpost of the Hofbräuhaus. Just up from the boat-dock area is a cluster of houses with a national park center (small German-only exhibit). Here you can get advice for hikes, which are well-signposted. The Eiskappelle "glacier" is about 1.25 hours one-way; for an easier hike, go only partway, to the river called Eisgraben. Or follow the easy 30-minute *St. Bartholomä-Rundweg* loop along the lakeshore.

Almbach Gorge (Almbachklamm)

This short, popular hike is a good option for nature lovers who come to see Berchtesgaden's Nazi sites, then want to fill up the rest of the day hiking along a stream-filled gorge. Though not a world-class attraction, it is an enjoyable way to spend two or three hours. Most visitors do it as roughly a four-mile round-trip, though you can go farther if you wish.

Getting There: Take bus #840 to the Kugelmühle stop (12 minutes toward Salzburg from Berchtesgaden) and check the next bus times—two hours between buses is enough for a quick visit, three hours for a leisurely one. Walk five minutes along Kugelmühlweg (following the *Almbachklamm* signs) to the trailhead. Drivers simply turn off the Salzburg road at *Almbachklamm* signs and turn left along Kugelmühlweg to reach the free parking lot.

Visiting the Gorge: First you'll see the **$$ Gasthaus zur Kugelmühle,** which serves meals and drinks in a pleasant setting (cash only, daily 11:30-19:30, German tel. 08650/461, www.gasthaus-kugelmuehle.de). In front of the restaurant is an old wooden apparatus for shaping marble blocks into round toy spheres (hence the name—*Kugel* means ball, *Mühle* means mill).

Just beyond is a gate where you pay €3 to enter the gorge; pick up a map and get hiking advice here (daily May-Oct 8:00-18:00; gorge closed in winter). A rushing stream cascades through the gorge, which the trail crosses and recrosses on numbered steel bridges. The trail is well maintained and exciting, and accessible to anyone who is reasonably fit, sure-footed, and wearing sturdy shoes. It's not recommended for young children because the path has some steep, unguarded drop-offs. Expect some narrow and slippery parts. The high Sulzer waterfall by bridge #19 is a traditional turnaround point. The walk there and back can be done in two hours at a good clip, but allowing three hours makes for a more pleasant visit. To gain some altitude, on the way back, at bridge #17, hike up to the Mesnerwirt Chapel.

HALLSTATT & THE SALZKAMMERGUT

Commune with nature in the Salzkammergut, Austria's Lake District. "The hills are alive," and you're surrounded by the loveliness that has turned on everyone from Emperor Franz Josef to Julie Andrews. This is *Sound of Music* country. Idyllic and majestic, but not rugged, it's a gentle land of lakes, forested mountains, and storybook villages, rich in hiking opportunities and inexpensive lodging. Settle down in the postcard-pretty, lake-cuddling town of Hallstatt (HAHL-shtaht). While there are plenty of lakes and charming villages in the Salzkammergut, Hallstatt is really the only one that matters.

Lovable Hallstatt is a tiny town bullied onto a ledge between a selfish mountain and a swan-ruled lake, the Hallstätter See, with a waterfall ripping furiously through its middle. It can be toured on foot in about 15 minutes. Salt veins in the mountain rock drew people here centuries before Christ. The symbol of Hallstatt, which you'll see all over town, consists of two adjacent spirals—a design based on jewelry found in Bronze Age Celtic graves high in the nearby mountains.

The big draws of Hallstatt are its village and its lakeside setting. Come here to relax, nibble, wander, and paddle. The lake is famous for its good fishing and pure water. If you want to do some sightseeing, dip into the endearing town museum, ride the funicular for grand lake views and a salt-mine tour, or side-trip to the nearby town of Obertraun to catch the cable car up to even higher views and ice caves. While tourist crowds can trample much of Hallstatt's charm on sunny summer weekends, the place somehow retains its unique appeal—and it's almost dead in the off-season.

PLANNING YOUR TIME

Hallstatt serves as a relaxing break between Vienna and Salzburg. One night and a few hours to browse are all you'll need to fall in love. If you want time to hike, tour the salt mine or ice caves, or just slow down, you should give it two nights and a day.

Orientation to Hallstatt

Hallstatt (pop. about 800) has two parts: the tightly packed medieval town center (which locals call the Markt) and the newer, more car-friendly Lahn, a few minutes' walk to the south. A lakeside promenade connects the old center to the Lahn. The tiny "main" boat dock (a.k.a. Market Dock), where boats from the train station arrive, is in the old center of town. Another boat dock is in the Lahn, next to Hallstatt's TI and grocery store.

TOURIST INFORMATION

At the helpful TI, in the Lahn by the boat dock and bus stop, Michelle and Hannah can explain hikes and excursions and sort through your transit options (daily May-Oct 8:30-18:00; Nov-April Mon-Fri until 17:00, closed Sat-Sun; Seestrasse 99, tel. 05950/9530, www.dachstein-salzkammergut.at, hallstatt@dachstein-salzkammergut.at).

On Mondays and Saturdays, the TI offers 1.5-hour **walking tours** of the town at 16:30, conducted in both English and German (€8, free for guests staying in a local hotel, April-Nov only). They can also arrange private tours (€120), or you can rent an audioguide to explore (€5, €50 deposit).

ARRIVAL IN HALLSTATT

By Train: If you're coming on the main train line that runs between Salzburg and Vienna, you'll change trains at Attnang-Puchheim to get to Hallstatt (you won't see Hallstatt on the schedules, but any train to Ebensee and Bad Ischl will stop at Hallstatt). Day-trippers can use the coin-op lockers at the Attnang-Puchheim station (follow signs for Schliessfächer, in the lower level near the Reisezentrum). Note: Connections can be tight—check the TV monitor.

Hallstatt's train station is a wide spot on the tracks across the lake from town. *Stefanie* (a boat) meets you at the station and glides scenically across the lake to the old town center (€2.50, meets each train until 18:50, www.hallstattschifffahrt.at). If you arrive after it stops running, you'll have to get off in Obertraun and take a taxi to Hallstatt (€15). The last departing boat-train connection leaves Hallstatt at 18:15, and the first boat goes in the morning at 6:50 (Sun at 8:10 in summer, 8:45 off-season).

Once in Hallstatt, you're steps away from the hotels in the old center and a 15-minute walk from accommodations (and the TI) in the Lahn.

By Bus: Hallstatt's bus stop is easy to miss. It's in front of the boat dock ticket kiosk and next door to the TI in the Lahn. It takes 10 minutes to walk from the bus stop into the old center along the lakeside path.

By Car: The main road skirts the old center via a long tunnel above the town; you'll emerge in the Lahn. If you're staying at one of my recommended accommodations in the Lahn, you can park right at the hotel—all have free parking.

Only locals with a special permit are allowed to drive inside the old town. As you approach town, electronic signs direct you to available parking. If you are staying at a hotel in the old town, follow signs to lot P1 (€13/day, reserved for hotel guests). Choose "Hotelticket" at the gate when you enter and hang onto your ticket—you'll need it when you leave. To reach your hotel, go to the Hotel-Shuttle Info-Point in the lot, tell the attendant (or the intercom) where you're staying, and hop on the free shuttle, which will drop you at or near your hotel. You can also use this shuttle when you depart; ask your hotelier for details. When you leave the lot, pay at the machine.

Day-trippers should head to lot P2, which is closer to the old town center (€9.50/3-12 hours; not served by hotel shuttle). If full, they may send you to the overflow P3 lot on the road to Obertraun (same price as P2).

For more parking tips, see www.hallstatt.net/parking-in-hallstatt/cars.

HELPFUL HINTS

Baggage Storage: If you're changing trains in Attnang-Puchheim you can use the lockers at that station. In Hallstatt, you can leave bags at the funicular station while visiting the salt mine and viewpoint (free, see "Sights in Hallstatt," later).

Laundry: The old town's "general store," the **Gemischtwarenhandlung am See,** has a pricey coin-operated washer and dryer (daily 9:00-18:00, across from the Protestant church, mobile 0664-917-9001). The staff of the **campground** in the Lahn will wash and dry your clothes (drop off daily May-Sept 9:00-12:00, pick up in afternoon or next morning, closed off-season, Lahnstrasse 200, tel. 06134/83220).

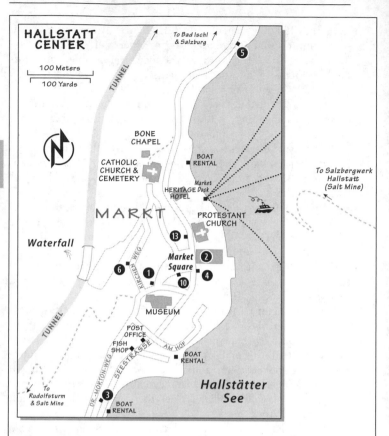

HALLSTATT CENTER

100 Meters
100 Yards

To Bad Ischl & Salzburg

TUNNEL

BONE CHAPEL

CATHOLIC CHURCH & CEMETERY

BOAT RENTAL

Market Dock

HERITAGE HOTEL

MARKT

PROTESTANT CHURCH

Waterfall

KIRCHEN WEG

Market Square

To Salzbergwerk Hallstatt (Salt Mine)

MUSEUM

TUNNEL

POST OFFICE

FISH SHOP

SEESTRASSE

AM HOF

DR.-MORTON-WEG

BOAT RENTAL

To Rudolfsturm & Salt Mine

Hallstätter See

BOAT RENTAL

HALLSTATT (side tab)

ECHERNTAL

ECHERNTALWEG

To Waldbachstrub Waterfall

1 Gasthof Zauner
2 Seehotel Rest. Grüner Baum
3 Bräugasthof Hallstatt & Rest.
4 Gasthof Simony & Rest. Am See
5 Pension Sarstein
6 Gasthaus zur Mühle Hostel
7 Pension Grüner Anger
8 Herta Höll Rooms
9 Haus Trausner
10 Marktbeisl zur Ruth Pub
11 Maik's Heisse Hütte
12 Campground (Laundry Service)
13 Grocery & Launderette
14 Grocery

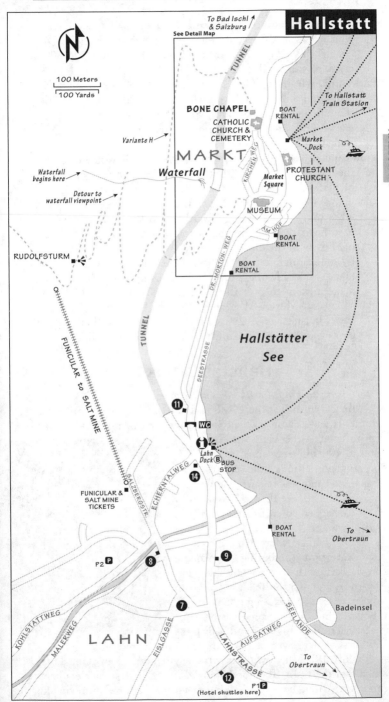

HALLSTATT

Local Guide: Cristiana Campanile is a Hallstatt-based guide who works in town and around the neighboring Lake District (€180/4 hours, €276/full day, mobile 0664-206-5083, cristiana.campanile@gmx.at).

Parks and Swimming: Green and peaceful lakeside parks line the south end of Lake Hallstatt. If you walk 15 minutes south of the old center to the Lahn, you'll find a grassy public park, playground, and swimming area (Badestrand) with the fun Badeinsel play-island.

Views and Fewer Tourists: The best high-altitude vantage point is the "Skywalk" viewpoint at the Rudolfsturm (top of the funicular). The steep, 45-minute hike down from there is also grand. Closer to town, you'll find more postcard views and fewer tourists by heading toward the north end of the village, past the market dock where the road curves and opens up (best light early in the day) or from the little park by the TI in the Lahn (best light late in the day). While most visitors stroll the touristy lakeside drag between the old and new parts of town, make a point to take the more higgledy-piggledy high lane called Dr.-Morton-Weg at least once. And, for a great view over Hallstatt, hike above Dr.-Morton-Weg on Hallberg as far as you like, or climb any path leading up the hill.

Hallstatt Walk

· *This short, self-guided walk starts at the dock.*

Boat Landing: There was a Hallstatt before there was a Rome. In fact, because of the importance of salt mining here, an entire epoch—the Hallstatt Era, from 800 to 400 BC—is named for this important spot. Through the centuries, salt was traded and people came and went by boat. You'll still see the traditional Fuhr boats, designed to carry heavy loads in shallow water.

Tiny Hallstatt has two big churches: **Protestant** (bordering the square on the left, with a grassy lakeside playground) and **Catholic** (towering up above, with its fascinating bone chapel). Its faded St. Christopher—patron saint of travelers, with his cane and baby Jesus on his shoulder—watched over those sailing in and out.

Until 1875, the town was extremely remote...then came a real road and the train. The good ship *Stefanie* shuttles travelers back and forth from here to the Hallstatt train station, immediately across the lake. The *Boote* sign advertises boat rentals. By the way, *Schmuck* is not an insult. It means "jewelry" in German.

Look down the shore at the huge homes. Several families lived in each of these houses back when Hallstatt's population was

about double its present 800. Today, the population continues to shrink, and many of these generally underused houses rent rooms to visitors.

Hallstatt gets about three months of snow each winter, but the lake hasn't frozen over since 1981. See any swans? They've patrolled the lake like they own it since the 1860s, when Emperor Franz Josef and Empress Sisi—the Princess Diana of her day (see page 128)—made this region their annual holiday retreat. Sisi loved swans, so locals made sure she'd see them here. During this period, the Romantics discovered Hallstatt, many top painters worked here, and the town got its first hotel.

Local divers discovered that the lake also served as Hallstatt's garbage can. For centuries, if something was kaputt, locals would just toss it into the lake. In 1945, Nazi medals decorating German and Austrian war heroes suddenly became dangerous to own. At the end of World War II, throughout the former Third Reich, hard-earned medals floated down to lonely lake beds, including Hallstatt's.

Walking away from the lake, look right and notice the one-lane road out of town (below the church). Until 1966, when a bigger tunnel was built above Hallstatt, all the traffic crept single-file right through the town.

• *Now, walk over the town's stream, and pop into the...*

Protestant Church: The Catholic Counter-Reformation was very strong in Austria, but pockets of Protestantism survived, especially in mining towns like Hallstatt. In 1860, Emperor Franz Josef finally allowed non-Catholic Christians to build churches. Before that, they were allowed to worship only in low-key "houses of prayer." In 1863, Hallstatt's miners pooled their humble resources and built this fine church. Step inside (free and often open). It's very plain, emphasizing the pulpit and organ

The Chinese Have a Crush on Hallstatt

Hallstatt is famous in China, and it seems to be on every Chinese tourist's bucket list. For some reason, this little alpine town is a huge hit with Asian travelers, who storm it daily. Most are day-trippers from Salzburg, and many come here for wedding portraits. Hallstatt is so popular, in fact, that in China a high-end Western-style real estate development even showcases a faux Austrian Alps centerpiece called Hallstatt II—a fake little stage set replicating the real town's facades (the main square and the Protestant church on the lake). The soundtrack for Hallstatt II? "The Sound of Music" on an endless loop.

rather than fancy art and saints. Check out the portraits: Martin Luther (left of altar), the town in about 1865 with its new church (left wall), and a century of pastors (back wall).

• *Continue past the church or take a little detour to the Catholic church and bone chapel, described later under "Sights in Hallstatt." The detour goes straight ahead past the Gemischtwarenhandlung am See (supermarket and laundry) and up the little lane on the right, following the signs marked* Kath. Kirche.

Market Square (Marktplatz): In 1750, a fire leveled this part of town. The buildings you see now are all late-18th-century structures built of stone rather than flammable wood. The three big buildings on the left are government-subsidized housing (mostly for seniors and people with health problems). Along the right side of the square, take a close look at the two-dimensional, up-against-the-wall pear tree (it likes the sun-warmed wall). The statue in the center features the Holy Trinity and was donated by a rich salt-mining family when the village was spared by the plague.

• *Continue a block past Gasthof Simony. Stop at the first corner. Look up.*

Because 20th-century Hallstatt was of no industrial importance, it was untouched by World War II. But once upon a time, its salt was worth defending. High above, barely peeking out of the trees, is **Rudolfsturm** (Rudolf's Tower). Originally a 13th-century watchtower protecting the salt mines, and later the mansion of a salt-mine boss, it's now a restaurant with a great view. (You can see the sharply angled viewing platform sticking out.) A zigzag trail connects the town with Rudolfsturm and the salt mines just beyond. The big, white houses by the Muhlbach waterfall were water-powered mills that once ground Hallstatt's grain. (If you hike up a few blocks, you'll see the river raging through town and a few quaint storybook lanes.)

• *Within a few steps are several fun shops: The "Schnaps and Holz" (wood) shop is run by Johannes who serves samples and sells little glasses of the local firewater, and works wonders in his woodshop. A nearby ceramics shop has local handmade work inspired by ancient excavations.*

From here (just before the Gemeindeamt or City Hall), face the lake and jog right down the tiny lane marked Am Hof, which leads through an intimate bit of domestic town architecture, boathouses, maybe a couple of swans, and lots of firewood (since Habsburg times, many families have rights to free wood from the nearby forest). The lane circles back to the main drag and the...

Museum Square: Climb a few steps into the museum's front yard to see a statue (on the left) and some wooden stairs (on the right). The **statue** recalls the mine manager who excavated prehistoric graves in about 1850. Much of the Schmuck sold locally is inspired by the jewelry found in the area's Bronze Age tombs.

The memorial **wooden stairs** in front of the museum are a copy of those found in Hallstatt's prehistoric mine. The original stairs, which you can see in person at the end of the salt-mine tour, are more than 3,000 years old. For thousands of years, people have been harvesting salt—precious for preserving meat—from this mountain. A brine spring sprung here, attracting Bronze Age people in about 1600 BC. At first, miners used the "dry" technique: They'd dig tunnels into the mountain, hack out big chunks of salt-rock (70 percent salt), and haul them out in leather backpacks. Later, they wised up and simply dissolved the salt in water to create a brine, flowed it out of the mountain in wooden pipes, and then boiled off the water to distill the salt. In fact, from 1595 until well into the 20th century, a 25-mile wooden pipeline carried salt brine from Hallstatt to Ebensee; finally, they replaced the last stretch of wood with plastic piping. For a look at early salt-mining implements and the town's story, visit the Hallstatt Museum (described later).

Back at street level, notice the Dachstein Sport Shop. During a renovation project, the builders dug down and hit objects spanning from prehistoric times to the 19th century, including a Celtic and ancient Roman settlement. Peek through the glass pavement on the covered porch to see where the Roman street level was. If the shop is open, pop in and climb downstairs (on the near right as you enter) to see an **archaeological excavation exhibit** with Stone Age pottery shards, part of a Roman bathhouse, and the remains of a Habsburg residence. In prehistoric times, people lived near the mines. Romans were the first Hallstatt lakeside settlers.

Continue out of the square with the water on your left. Just past the post office is the **Fischerei,** which provides the town with its cherished fresh lake fish. The county allows two commercial fishermen on the lake. They spread their nets each morning and sell their catch here to town restaurants, or to any locals cooking up a special dinner.

• *Continue along the lane. You could follow this promenade all the way to the Lahn at the far end of town. But let's go the often-overlooked scenic route: Take the first right (after the bank) and head up a few stairs to the street called...*

Dr.-Morton-Weg: Notice that the house at #26A dates from 1597. This stone structure stopped the fire of 1750 from spreading further and is painted red in remembrance. Modern houses are required to be built of stone or brick. Turn left and follow the lane past more old houses. Until 1890, this was the town's main drag, and the lake lapped at the lower doors of these houses. Therefore, many main entrances were via the attic, from this level. Enjoy this back-street view of town. Just after the arch, near #133, check out the old tools hanging from the oldest house in Hallstatt. From here, enjoy the lake view, then climb down the stairs and look back up at the striking traditional architecture (the fine woodwork on the left was rebuilt after a fire; parts of the old house on the right date to medieval times).

• *Your tour of the town is finished. Within a few minutes' walk from here are boat rentals, the town museum, and the base of the funicular (up to great views and a salt-mine tour).*

Sights in Hallstatt

▲▲Catholic Church and Bone Chapel

Hallstatt's Catholic church overlooks the town from above. The lovely church has twin altars. The one on the left was made by town artists in 1897. The one on the right is more historic—dedicated in 1515 to Mary, who's flanked by St. Barbara (on right, patron of miners) and St. Catherine (on left, patron of foresters—a lot of wood was needed to fortify the many miles of tunnels, and to boil the brine to distill the salt). Historically, miners and salt traders sat on the right

and townsfolk on the left. Note the VIP boxes in front on the left (for the mayor and town council) and on the right (for bosses of the mine).

Behind the church, in the well-tended graveyard (with each little plot lovingly cared for like a tiny garden), is the 12th-century

Chapel of St. Michael (even older than the church). Its bone chapel—or charnel house (Beinhaus)—contains more than 600 skulls. Each has been carefully decorated and marked with the deceased's name and date of death. (Skulls with dark, thick garlands are oldest—18th century; those with flowers are more recent—19th century.) Space was so limited in this cemetery that bones had only 12 peaceful, buried years here before making way for the freshly dead. Many of the

dug-up bones and skulls ended up in this chapel. They stopped this practice in the 1960s, about the same time the Catholic Church began permitting cremation. But one woman (who died in 1983) managed to sneak her skull in later (under the cross, with the gold tooth). The skulls on the books are those of priests. Notice the families stacked together for eternity: Steiner. Kierchschlager. Heuschober. Binder. It's a poignant—and eerily tangible—chronicle of a little community.

Cost and Hours: Free to enter church, bone chapel—€1.50, daily May-Sept 10:00-18:00, Oct until 16:00, shorter hours in winter, free English flier, tel. 06134/8279.

Getting There: From near the main boat dock, walk straight up the little lane (to the right of the "general store" Gemischtwarenhandlung am See), turn right at the *Kath. Kirche* signs, and climb up the covered wooden stairway.

▲▲Hallstatt Museum

This high-quality museum—well-presented and anchored by lots of actual artifacts—tells the story of Hallstatt, providing a solid background for all you'll see here. It focuses on the Hallstatt Era (800-400 BC), when this village was the salt-mining hub of a culture that spread from France to the Balkans. Back then, Celtic tribes dug for precious salt, and Hallstatt was, as its name means, the "place of salt." The highlight of the museum is the countless number of artifacts excavated from prehistoric gravesites around the mine. The museum also offers a 10-minute 3-D introductory movie and 26 displays, including ones on the Celts and Romans, the region's flora and fauna, local artists (like locally born modern sculptor Georg Zauner), and the surge in Hallstatt tourism during the Romantic Age. Everything is labeled in English, and the ring binders have translations of the longer texts.

Cost and Hours: €10; May-Sept daily 10:00-18:00; April and

Oct until 16:00; Nov-March Wed-Sun 11:00-15:00, closed Mon-Tue; Seestrasse 56, tel. 06134/8280, www.museum-hallstatt.at.

▲▲Lake Trips

For a quick **boat ride,** you can take the *Stefanie* across the lake and back for €5. It stops at the tiny Hallstatt train station for 30 minutes (note return time in the boat's window), giving you time to walk to a hanging bridge (ask the captain to point you to the Hängebrücke—HENG-eh-brick-eh—a 10-minute lakeside stroll to the left). For a longer tour, take a round-trip ride to Obertraun (€10, 4-5/day June-Sept only, 50 minutes) or Steeg (€13, 3/day mid-July-Aug only, 1.25 hours); check the posted schedule or www.hallstattschifffahrt.at for departure times.

Even better, **rent your own electric boat.** It's cheap, fun, easy, and safe, as motorized boats are outlawed on the lake, and these boats can't go very fast (they have two speeds: slow and stop). A half-hour rental is enough to do a scenic little loop just offshore from town; when split among a few people, it's cheaper than any of the boat rides listed above. I can think of no more enjoyable cheap thrill on a sunny day in Hallstatt. Two outfits rent electric boats. **Schwarzmayr** has one location next to the main boat dock, just beyond the jewelry (Schmuck) shop and another 75 yards past Bräugasthof (daily 10:00-18:00, mobile 0664-141-1675), and **Schifffahrt Hallstättersee Hemetsberger** rents from near Gasthof Simony as well as by the Lahn boat dock (daily until 19:00, tel. 06134/8228). Both have similar rates (€15/30 minutes, €20/hour for 500-watt boat; no rentals off-season or when windy). Both places also rent rowboats and paddleboats, and Schwarzmayr has stand-up paddleboards.

Another company, **Navia,** runs flat-bottom boats *(Fuhre)* reminiscent of Hallstatt's glory days when such boats transported salt to the rest of the world. Boats leave 100 yards from the TI and run to Obertraun four times a day, with more in high-season (€7 one-way, €12 round-trip; daily in good weather; April-Oct, mobile 0650-617-7165, www.navia.at).

▲▲Salt-Mine Tour and Rudolfsturm Viewpoint

Hallstatt claims to have the oldest salt mine in the world. Along with two others in the area, this one is still active, producing 1.1 million tons of salt each year (mostly used for road salt, though you can also buy souvenir shakers of table salt). Best of all, it comes with a fun funicular ride to the Rudolfsturm "Skywalk" Viewpoint, with stunning panoramas over the town and lake. Allow about three hours total for the round-trip funicular ride, viewpoint visit, and 1.5-hour salt-mine tour.

While visiting a salt mine is almost obligatory when you're in this part of Austria, one is plenty. Other options are in Hallein (see

page 313) and Berchtesgaden
(page 341). But Hallstatt's is
a good choice, as it's the easiest to reach and well worth
the time—especially on a
rainy day.

Cost: €30 for mine and
round-trip funicular, €22 for
mine tour only (you must
hike up), €9 one-way/€16 round-trip for funicular only; buy all
tickets at funicular station; no children under 4; skip the €2.50 audioguide, which simply recites posted English information plaques
scattered around the mountaintop.

Hours: Daily 9:00-16:00, Oct-early Dec & March until
14:00—these are last ascent times to make it for the day's final
tour, closed mid-Dec-early March; funicular runs at least 4/hour
and in summer, goes until 18:00 (even though the salt mine closes
earlier); arrive early or late to avoid summer crowds—especially on
rainy days; tel. 06132/200-2400, www.salzwelten.at.

Dress Warmly: Be sure to dress for the constant 47-degree
temperature in the mine.

Getting There: The funicular starts in the Lahn, close to the
bus stop, Lahn boat dock, and P2 parking lot. At the base of the
funicular, notice the train tracks leading to the Erbstollen tunnel
entrance. This lowest of the salt tunnels goes many miles into the
mountain, where a shaft connects it to the tunnels you'll see on the
tour. Today, the salty brine from these tunnels flows 25 miles to the
huge modern salt works (next to the highway) at Ebensee.

Visiting the Viewpoint and Salt Mine: Ride the funicular up
the mountain to 2,750 feet. From the top station, take the glass
elevator even higher, to a walkway that leads to the café and viewpoint in one direction, and the trailhead to the mine in the other.
If you have time before your mine tour, head to the **$$ Rudolfs-
turm café**, with affordable food, drinks, and a million-dollar view.
Just below, jutting out over the lake, is the **"Skywalk" viewpoint.**
Hallstatt's rooftops are below your toes, and Obertraun (with the
Dachstein cable car) fills the little valley at the far end of the lake.

From the viewpoint and fu-
nicular station, go across the walk-
way to reach the trailhead. From
here, it's a 15-minute, mostly level
walk to the start of the tour (past
excavation sites of many prehis-
toric tombs and a glass case with
2,500-year-old bones—but there's
little to actually see).

Salt-mine tours start every 20-30 minutes, but give yourself time to check your bag, put on miners' clothes, take silly photos of your travel partner, and explore a little museum explaining the lives of salt miners. Finally you'll meet your guide and hike 200 yards higher to a long tunnel that was dug in 1719. Tours should always be in English and German...if unsure, ask. (The many videos are half-heartedly subtitled in English.)

Inside the mountain, you'll follow your guide through several caverns, featuring high-concept audio-visual presentations (including a laser show on a glassy subterranean lake). Along the way, you'll find out how, starting 250 million years ago, ocean salt wound up in the Austrian Alps, and about mining techniques over the last 7,000 years. The highlight for most is sliding down two banisters; the second one is the longest in Europe (213 feet) and ends with a flash for a souvenir photo that clocks your speed (see how you did compared to the rest of your group).

The grand finale is the "Bronze Age Cinema," where you'll learn about—and then see—the oldest wooden staircase in Europe (and likely the world). Find out how the 26-foot-long, incredibly rickety staircase was discovered, excavated, studied in Vienna (where it was carbon-dated to 1108 BC), and finally reinstalled here. Animated figures projected on the staircase show how people dressed and worked in Bronze Age times.

At the end of the tour, you'll board a little miners' train and duck your way through narrow tunnels as you zip back out of the mountain.

Hiking Back Down to Hallstatt: If you skip the funicular down, the steep and scenic 45-minute hike back into town is (with strong knees) a joy. Find the well-tended gravel path below the skybridge that connects the funicular station with the Rudolfsturm café and viewpoint. You'll tackle extremely steep and sharp switchbacks as you gradually descend toward town. Along the path, panels teach about salt-mining history. Partway down, you'll pass the (closed) entrance to the Franz Josef mine tunnel; notice that recently retired miners have hung their hardhats here (*letzte Grubenfahrt* means "last descent"). Farther down, watch for the short detour to Terrasse-Mühlbachschlucht, which leads to a metal walkway over the waterfall that tumbles out of the cliffs toward Hallstatt. Farther along on the main path, notice the heavy-duty metal nets that protect the village from rockslides. At the fork, turn left toward Variante H. Cross back over the waterfall, then follow this gravel road, keeping an eye out on the right for the switchback steps that lead down into the Catholic church's graveyard.

▲Local Hikes

Mountain lovers, hikers, and spelunkers who use Hallstatt as their home base keep busy for days (ask the TI for ideas). You can hike up and down—or, easier, take the funicular up and hike down—to the Rudolfsturm café and viewpoint and salt mine (described earlier).

To get farther out of town, a good, short, and easy walk is the two-hour round-trip up the Echern Valley to the Waldbachstrub waterfall and back: Follow signs to the salt mines, then follow the little wooden signs marked *Echerntalweg*. With a car, consider hiking around nearby Altaussee (flat, 3-hour hike) or along Grundlsee to Toplitzsee. Regular buses connect Hallstatt with Gosausee for a pleasant hour-long walk around that lake. The TI can also recommend a great two-day hike with an overnight in a nearby mountain hut.

Biking

The best two bike rides run up the Echern Valley (nearly the same route as the hike listed above) and around the lake (ride the *Stefanie* shuttle across the lake and then enjoy the bike path around to the right via Obertraun and back to Hallstatt). There's no public bike rental in Hallstatt, but some hotels have loaner bikes for guests; if you're desperate, you can rent a bike in nearby Obertraun (at the Dormio Resort Obertraun, mobile 06131-222-3330).

NEAR HALLSTATT
▲▲Dachstein Mountain Cable Car and Caves

A few miles up the lake beyond Hall-statt, a cable car glides to the high, barren Dachstein mountain plateau, crowned by the tallest mountain in the Salzkammergut (9,800 feet). Along the way, you can hop off to tour two different caves: the refreshingly chilly Giant Ice Caves and the less-impressive Mammoth Caves.

The mighty gondola rises in three stages. The first segment stops at **Schönbergalm** (4,500 feet); this stop has limited views, but it's where you find the two caves. The second segment climbs to the summit of **Krippenstein** (6,600 feet), with the best views. And the third segment descends to **Gjaidalm** (5,800 feet), where several hikes begin.

For most, the best plan is to tour the Giant Ice Caves from Schönbergalm, then head up to Krippenstein for easy hikes to great views. (For a quick high-country experience, Krippenstein is better

Hallstatt Salt Mine or Dachstein Ice Caves?

With limited time, doing both Hallstatt's salt mine and Dachstein's ice caves is redundant, time-consuming, and expensive. Choose one.

The Hallstatt salt-mine experience is best for most. It's cheaper and much easier (no bus connections required); the lake views are arguably better than the ones at Dachstein; and the salt mine itself has more to do, historically and culturally, with this region (whereas the ice caves are basically a geological fluke).

However, the Dachstein experience has its pros and cons. It's a fun excuse to take a bus or drive along the lakeshore to another town. The cable car gains far more altitude than Hallstatt's funicular, taking you above the clouds (and, often, into snow), with views that are almost too high (though you get a sweeping panorama of snowcapped peaks, Hallstatt is reduced to just a lakeside speck). The ice caves themselves—with massive formations in gigantic caverns—are more dramatic than Hallstatt's salt mines, which are focused on the exhibits and the fun banister slides. But the ice caves require more exertion: It's a steep hike up from the cable car to the caves, and the tour itself is more demanding than the one at the salt mines.

You can't go wrong with either. But for my money, the advantage goes to Hallstatt Salt Mine.

than Gjaidalm.) To do both the caves and hikes at Krippenstein, allow five hours total, round-trip, from the valley station; if you're doing just one of these, allow 2.5 hours round-trip.

Cost: The variety of ticket options can be confusing—survey them carefully before you book. For most people, the best choice is the €44 "Dachstein Salzkammergut" ticket, covering the cable-car up to Krippenstein and the Giant Ice Caves. With less time, pick one: just the caves (€35, includes lift only as far as Schönbergalm) or just Krippenstein and back ("Panorama Ticket," €31). For other variations, see the list at the ticket desk, or check www.dachstein-salzkammergut.com (tel. 050/140).

Hours: The cable car runs May-Oct (does not stop at Gjaidalm May-mid-June). The first cable car leaves at 8:40, and it goes every 15 minutes, with the last one down from Krippenstein at 17:00 and from Schönbergalm at 17:10 (30 minutes later mid-June; 2 hours later July-mid-Sept). If touring the ice caves, you'll need to leave the valley station by 15:00 (or 16:30 in peak season; the ticket seller can advise you)—if you'll be arriving later than that, don't bother.

Services: All lift stations have eateries and free Wi-Fi.

Getting There: To drive to the valley station, drive along the main road south of Hallstatt about three miles; just before reaching the village of Obertraun, turn right up a side road for a mile, following the *Dachstein* signs. For location, see the "Salzkammergut" map later in this chapter.

Without a car, the handiest and cheapest option is bus #543 (€2, 7-9/day, 15 minutes, leaves from bus stop in the Lahn, drops you directly at cable-car station). Romantics could take the boat to Obertraun (€7, 4-5/day June-Sept only, 30 minutes)—but it's a 40-minute hike from there to the lift station. A taxi between Hallstatt and the cable-car station runs about €18 each way. Or you can walk about an hour along the lakefront.

Visiting the Caves at Schönbergalm: At the first cable-car stop, Schönbergalm, you'll find two caves and a small museum about them. If choosing between the two, the Giant Ice Caves are much more interesting than the Mammoth Caves.

Discovered in 1910, the **Giant Ice Caves** (Riesen-Eishöhle) are viewable via 50-minute, half-mile guided tours in German and

English (at the lift station, report to the ticket window to get your tour time). It's a steep 10-minute hike from the station up to the cave entry, along a paved path with switchbacks. Allow time to pause for breath (you're nearly a mile up).

Guides lead groups on this hike through an eerie, icy, subterranean world, passing limestone caverns the size of subway stations. Carved by rushing water, the caverns are named for scenes from Wagner's operas—the favorite of the mountaineers who first came here. If you're nervous, note that the iron oxide covering the ceiling takes 5,000 years to form. Things are very stable. The temperature is just around freezing, and although the many steps help keep you warm, aim to dress as the guides do, in a jacket and hat.

In the clearing just past the station is a free little **museum**—in a local-style wood cabin designed to support 200 tons of snow—with exhibits about the caves (mostly in German only; save it for the way back).

While huge and well-promoted, the **Mammoth Caves** (Mammuthöhle), also at the Schönbergalm cable-car stop, are much less interesting than the ice caves and—for most—not worth the time. Of the 30-mile limestone labyrinth excavated so far, you'll walk a half-mile (1 hour tour, 10-minute hike from lift station to cave entrance).

Hiking at Krippenstein: From the second lift station, Krippenstein, you can hike about 30 minutes to its "five fingers" view-point, with metal walkways that extend out from the mountain (not for the faint of heart). A different 30-minute hike leads to the "Dachstein Shark" viewing platform. And all around, you get 360-degree views of the surrounding mountains and a good look at the scrubby, limestone, karstic landscape (which absorbs, through its many cracks, the rainfall that ultimately carves all those caves).

Returning to Hallstatt: The last bus from the cable-car station back to Hallstatt leaves around 18:00.

Nightlife in Hallstatt

Locals would laugh at the thought. But if you want some action after dinner, you do have a few options. The **Gasthaus zur Mühle** youth hostel serves pizza in its smoky restaurant; later, when drinks replace food, it's the favored hangout of rustic, chain-smoking locals (open late, closed Tue and Nov, run by Ferdinand, described later). Or, for your late-night drink, savor the Market Square from the trendy little pub called **Marktbeisl zur Ruth,** where locals congregate with soft music, a good selection of drinks, two small rooms, and tables on the square (daily 11:00-late, tel. 06134/20017).

Sleeping in Hallstatt

Prices are highest May through October; mid-July and August can be tight (early August is worst). Hallstatt is not the place to splurge—some of the best rooms are in Gästezimmer, just as nice and modern as rooms in bigger hotels, at half the cost. In summer, a double bed in a private home costs about €60 with breakfast. It's hard for single travelers to get an advance reservation for a one-night stay (try calling the TI for help). Prices include breakfast, lots of stairs, and a silent night. *"Zimmer mit Aussicht?"* (TSIM-mer mit OWS-zeekt) means "Room with view?"—worth asking for. Like some businesses in town, the cheaper places don't take credit cards.

As most rooms here are in old buildings with well-cared-for wooden interiors, dripping laundry is a no-no at Hallstatt pensions. Be especially considerate when hanging laundry over anything but tile—when in doubt, ask your host about using their clothesline.

Remember, if you are **arriving by car** and have a reservation for a place in the old town, head directly to parking lot P1, where you'll catch a shuttle to your hotel (see "Arrival in Hallstatt," earlier in this chapter).

IN THE OLD CENTER

$$$$ Gasthof Zauner has been in the Zauner family since 1893. The 12 pricey, pine-flavored rooms near the inland end of Market Square are decorated with sturdy alpine-inspired furniture (sealed not with lacquer but with beeswax, to let the wood breathe out its calming scent). In the evenings, lederhosen-clad Herr Zauner recounts tales of local mountaineering lore, including his own impressive ascents (fans, elevator, Marktplatz 51, tel. 06134/8246, www.seewirt-zauner.at, info@seewirt-zauner.at).

$$$$ Seehotel Grüner Baum owns perhaps the town's best location—fronting Market Square and overlooking the lake in back (the second-floor lakeview balcony rooms are the best but more expensive). The owner, Monika, moved here from Vienna and renovated this stately—but still a bit creaky—old hotel with urban taste. Its 30 rooms have classy furnishings and new hardwood floors (RS%, family rooms, fans, elevator, free spa with sauna and steam bath, Marktplatz 104, tel. 06134/82630, www.gruenerbaum.cc, contact@gruenerbaum.cc).

$$$ Bräugasthof Hallstatt is like a museum filled with antique furniture and ancient family portraits. This former brewery, now a bustling restaurant, rents eight cozy, creaky upstairs rooms. It's run by Verena, who grew up in this house and also runs the Gasthof Simony. All of the rooms face the lake, and five have gorgeous little lakeview balconies (along lake at Seestrasse 120, tel. 06134/8221, www.brauhaus-lobisser.com, info@brauhaus-lobisser.com, Lobisser family).

$$$ Gasthof Simony is on the square, with a lake view, balconies, creaky wood floors, and 14 rooms with antique furniture and modern accents. While it suffers from absentee management, the location and the lakefront garden for swimming are enticing (cash only, cheaper rooms with shared bath, big family rooms, Wolfengasse 105, tel. 06134/8221, www.gasthof-simony.at, info@gasthof-simony.at).

$$ Pension Sarstein is a big, flower-bedecked house right on the water away from the old center bustle. Its four renovated rooms and three apartments are a great value, and all have lakeview balconies. You can swim from its plush and inviting lakeside garden (cheaper rooms with shared bath, family rooms, cleaning fee for apartments, Wi-Fi in lobby, loaner bikes, closed Nov-mid-April, 200 yards past the main boat dock at Gosaumühlstrasse 83, tel. 06134/8217, find its listing at www.hallstatt.net, pension.sarstein@aon.at, helpful Isabelle and Klaus Fischer).

Hostel: Located below the waterfall and along the gushing town stream, **¢-$ Gasthaus zur Mühle Jugendherberge** has 46 beds along with private rooms (breakfast extra, closed Nov, reception closed Tue Sept-mid-May—arrange in advance if arriving on Tue, Kirchenweg 36, tel. 06134/8318, www.hallstatturlaub.at, toeroe-f@hallstatturlaub.at, Ferdinand Törö). The smoky restaurant here (with a small garden annex, popular for its pizza and beer) is active late into the evening (see "Nightlife in Hallstatt," earlier).

IN THE LAHN

$$ Pension Grüner Anger, near the bus station and base of the funicular, is practical and modern. It's big and quiet, with 11 characterless but well-tended rooms and no creaks or squeaks. There are mountain views, but none of the lake (nonsmoking, self-service pay laundry, free loaner bikes, Lahn 10, tel. 06134/8397, www.anger.hallstatt.net, anger@ aon.at, Sulzbacher family). If arriving by train, have the boat captain call Herr Sulzbacher,

who will pick you up (only from 14:00-19:00) at the dock for €2 per person.

Two good **Gästezimmer** are just past the bus stop/parking lot and over the bridge. **$$ Herta Höll** rents a room and two surprisingly modern and spacious apartments with full kitchen on the ground floor of a nondescript riverside house (cash only, just before the funicular station at Salzbergstrasse 45, tel. 06134/8531, frank.hoell@aon.at). **$ Haus Trausner** has three clean, bright, new-feeling rooms adjacent to the Trausner family home (2-night minimum for reservations, cash only, breakfast in garden or your room, Lahnstrasse 27, tel. 06134/8710, trausner1@aon.at, charming Maria Trausner makes you want to settle right in). For both places, find listings at www.hallstatt.net.

Eating in Hallstatt

In this town, when someone is happy to see you, they'll often say, "Can I cook you a fish?" While everyone cooks the typical Austrian fare, fish is your best bet here. *Reinanke* (whitefish) is caught wild out of Lake Hallstatt and served the same day. *Saibling* (lake trout) is also tasty and costs less. You can enjoy good food inexpensively, with delightful lakeside settings. Restaurants in Hallstatt tend to have unreliable hours and close early even during peak season, so don't wait too long to get dinner. Most of the eateries listed here are run by recommended hotels.

$$ Restaurant Bräugasthof, on the edge of the old center, is a bustling restaurant with moody waitstaff and good food. The indoor dining room is cozy in cool weather. On a balmy evening, its great lakeside tables offer the best ambience in town—you can feed the swans while your trout is being cooked (daily 11:30-22:00, Seestrasse 120, tel. 06134/20673).

$$$ Hotel Grüner Baum feels upscale, with a more creative seasonal menu and polished service at tables overlooking the lake, inside and out (daily 12:00-22:00, until 21:00 off-season, at bottom of Market Square, tel. 06134/8263).

$$ Gasthof Simony's Restaurant am See, next door, has a simple menu and a hidden terrace with rickety tables and gorgeous lake views (daily 11:30-20:00, closed Nov & Feb-March, tel. 06134/8231).

Two Snack Stands: The snack stand on the harbor square next to the Protestant church specializes in chicken and *döner kebab* (with tables and fine lakeside picnic options nearby, daily 11:00-late). **Maik's Heisse Hütte** ("Hot Hut") in the Lahn (across from the TI) serves hamburgers and hot dogs (11:00-18:00, closed Fri).

Groceries: There's a small **Spar** supermarket across from the Protestant church and another in the Lahn across from the bus stop (Mon-Fri 7:30-18:50, Sat from 8:00, shorter hours off-season and Sun).

Hallstatt Connections

BY TRAIN

Most travelers leaving Hallstatt are going to Salzburg or Vienna. In either case, you need to catch the shuttle boat (€2.50, departs

15 minutes before every train) to the little Hallstatt train station across the lake, and then ride 1.5 hours to **Attnang-Puchheim** (trains depart every 30-90 minutes from about 7:00 to 18:00). Trains are synchronized, so after a short wait in Attnang-Puchheim, you'll catch your onward connection to **Salzburg** (50 minutes) or **Vienna** (2.5 hours; allow 4 hours total). The Hallstatt station has a ticket machine, or you can buy tickets online. In town, your hotel or the TI can help

you find schedule information. Train info: Tel. 051-717 (to get an operator, dial 2, then 2), www.oebb.at.

BY BUS

The bus ride from Hallstatt to **Salzburg** is cheaper and more scenic than the train, and only slightly slower. You can still start off from Hallstatt by rail, taking the boat across the lake to the station and then the train toward Attnang-Puchheim—but get off after about 20 minutes in Bad Ischl, where you catch bus #150 to Salzburg (€15-20, Mon-Fri nearly hourly, fewer on Sat-Sun, 1.5 hours, www.postbus.at). Alternatively, you can reach Bad Ischl on bus #542/543 from the Hallstatt bus stop (6-8/day, easy change in Gosaumühle) and then catch bus #150 to Salzburg. The Hallstatt TI has a schedule. In Salzburg, bus #150 stops at Hofwirt and Mirabellplatz (convenient to Linzergasse hotels) before ending at the main train station.

BY CAR
Route Tips for Drivers

Hallstatt to Vienna, via Mauthausen, Melk, and Wachau Valley (210 miles): Leave Hallstatt early. Follow the scenic Route 145 through Gmunden to the autobahn and head east. After Linz, take exit #155 at Enns, and follow the signs for *Mauthausen* (5 miles from the freeway). Go through Mauthausen town and follow the *Ehemaliges KZ-Gedenkstätte Lager* signs. When leaving Mauthausen for Melk, enjoy the riverside drive along scenic Route 3 (or take the autobahn if you're in a hurry or prone to carsickness). At Melk, signs to *Stift Melk* lead to the abbey. Other Melk signs lead into the town.

From Melk (get a Vienna map at the TI), cross the river again (signs to *Donaubrücke*) and stay on Route 3. After Krems, the riverside route (now the S-5) hits the autobahn (A-22), and you'll barrel right into Vienna's traffic. (See page 207 of the Vienna Connections chapter for details.)

Vice Versa: For tips on doing the above trip in reverse (Vienna to Wachau to Mauthausen to Hallstatt), see "Wachau Valley Connections" on page 225.

From Salzburg: For tips on driving here from Salzburg, see the next section.

Salzkammergut Drive

SALZBURG TO HALLSTATT

This 45-mile scenic driving route from Salzburg to Hallstatt includes worthwhile viewpoints and fine Salzkammergut scenery. Without stops, it takes about 1.5 hours. But give yourself time to pull over, enjoy the views, and go for a luge ride. The optional Mondsee detour is worth the extra hour—especially for *Sound of Music* fans who'd like to see "the wedding church." To avoid tolls and maximize scenery, stick to the most direct route (B-158).

From Salzburg to St. Gilgen

Leave Salzburg on B-158 toward St. Gilgen. About nine miles later, after passing through the town of Hof bei Salzburg, you'll enjoy fine views (on the left) of the first of the Salzkammergut lakes: **Fuschlsee.** You'll curl along the top of the lake, then head down along the lakeside. As you reach the end of the lake and the village of Fuschl, watch on the right for the **Red Bull Headquarters**—a glassy complex unmarked except for the herd of giant bronze bulls charging into the artificial lake. Dietrich Mateschitz founded Red Bull in the 1980s. Today the energy drink magnate is Austria's richest man (net worth: more than €20 billion) and employs 10,000 people—many of them in this building. Mateschitz owns several sports teams (ice hockey, car racing, and multiple soccer teams) and collects airplanes, race cars, and other expensive vehicles—you can see his collection at Hangar-7 near Salzburg's airport (see page 313).

Just after the Red Bull HQ, on the right, you'll see yellow signs for Sommerrodelbahn—a **summer luge ride.** You can pull off here for the lesser (and shorter) of the two luge rides along this route (1,970 feet, €5/ride, open May-Oct daily 10:00-18:00, closed in bad weather, tel. 06226/8452, www.rodelbahnen.at)—but a better one is coming up later.

After Fuschl, you'll crest a little saddle between lakes. Keep an eye out on the right (it comes up quickly) for a pullout near a restaurant offering a grand view over the **Wolfgangsee.** Pull over

and enjoy the view (plus you'll find toilets and picnic tables). On the left is the peak called Schafberg—accessible by a long, slow cogwheel train (featured in *The Sound of Music*) from the town of St. Wolfgang to the cliff-capping Hotel Schafbergspitze, faintly visible in clear weather. Below and

on the right is the town of St. Gilgen—which we'll pass through soon—with a cable car up to the other side of the lake.

Continuing along the road, coast down into the main round-about of **St. Gilgen** (with a giant TI kiosk—handy for regional information). At this roundabout, you could turn off for Mondsee (on Route 154); this detour, described next, adds about an hour (30 minutes of driving, plus 30 minutes to see the town and church). Otherwise, continue through the roundabout to stay on B-158, and skip down to the "From St. Gilgen to Hallstatt" section.

Mondsee Detour

Following Route 154, you'll drive north and soon reach the shore of **Mondsee** ("Moon Lake," named for its crescent shape). As the

road swings left along the lakefront, keep an eye on the left for the jagged peak called **Drachenwand** ("Dragon Wall")—which looks frightful from across the lake when lit up by a full moon.

Finally you'll reach the little town of **Mondsee,** which feels made-to-order for *Sound of Music* pilgrims. Here you'll find the Basilica of St. Michael—better known as "the wedding church," where Fräulein Maria married Baron von Trapp. Built in Romanesque style in the eighth century, St. Michael's

was refurbished in bubbly Baroque for its millennial celebration in the mid-1700s. Renovated again since then, today it's beautiful inside and out. In front of the church is a pleasant little pedestrian zone jammed with al fresco cafés (for an Apfelstrudel), tacky gift shops, benches, and playful fountains.

From Mondsee, backtrack to St. Gilgen on the Wolfgangsee (or, if you want to cut the Salzkammergut circuit short, it's easy to hop on the A-1 expressway from here and head back to Salzburg or on to Vienna).

From St. Gilgen to Hallstatt

After your Mondsee detour—or if you choose to skip it—stay on B-158, which curves through St. Gilgen along the Wolfgangsee's south shore. This main road crosses under the cable car, and then—after you exit town—passes many fine viewpoints and pullouts along the lake. A good bike-and-walking path follows the road and lakeshore.

Nearing the end of the lake, after the village of Abersee, keep an eye on the right for the *Riesenrutschbahnen* sign—marking the

best **luge ride** in the area. At 4,265 feet long and with grand lake views, this luge is one of the region's top rides (€7/ride, figure 20 minutes for the ride up and down, open May-Oct daily 10:00-18:00, closed in bad weather, tel. 06137/7085, www.rodelbahnen.at). Grab a folding go-cart, set it on the track, then sit backward as the ski lift slowly drags you up the hill. At the top, you'll take one of two tracks (each equally as fast) and scream down the winding metal course. It's easy: Push the stick to go, pull to stop, take your hands off your stick and you get hurt. For more details, see "Luge Lesson" on page 467.

After the luge, the road continues through the village of Strobl, then through a valley. Soon you'll reach the large spa resort of **Bad Ischl.** On your way through town, the highway tunnels beneath the Kaiservilla—a favorite retreat for Emperor Franz Josef to get away for a relaxing soak (and handy if you need a Habsburg history fix, www.kaiservilla.at). It was here that the emperor signed the declaration of war that kicked off World War I.

Exiting the tunnel, be ready to turn off for Route 145: At the fork, stay in the right lane, marked for Graz. (Hallstatt appears on most, but not all, signs—when in doubt, follow *Goisern*.) From here on out, you'll follow mountain rivers as the scenery crescendos. After Bad Goisern, the road forks—turn off on B-166 and follow Hallstatt signs.

Soon you'll be driving along the shore of the fjord-like **Hall-stättersee.** When you approach Hallstatt, you'll be swallowed up by a tunnel that bypasses the town center, and start to see signs for the parking lots: P1 for hotel guests, P2 for others. Emerging in the Lahn area, follow signs to your preferred lot. Welcome to Hallstatt.

TIROL

INNSBRUCK

Innsbruck, the proud capital of Tirol, is famous as a ski resort and a hiking haven. The setting is impressive—lined up along the fast-flowing Inn River, with dramatic peaks towering on both sides. Even so, some compare Innsbruck's sights to the music and architecture of Salzburg and Vienna, and write it off as stale strudel. But you're not here for music or architecture—you're here for the mountains. Make a point to get beyond Innsbruck's touristy patina, and you'll discover a pleasant high-alpine city with an appealing old town and a youthful verve that's absent in Austria's more staid cities. And Innsbruck has just enough of a Habsburg connection (thanks to the 16th-century Emperor Maximilian I, who loved the Tirolean Alps) to give it real class. It even has its very own Hofburg and Sacher Café.

The old town, with the famous copper-tiled Golden Roof, is fun to explore. The museums are well presented; the cleverly coordinated lifts make it easy to ascend high into the mountains; the hotels and restaurants in the old core ooze rustic character; and a lively student buzz and healthy outdoorsiness combine to give Innsbruck a special appeal. Although touristy, Innsbruck hustles to please those tourists, with both good-weather and rainy-day options. In this crossroads city—where, since the creation of an ancient Roman road, passing traders have sought lodging and entertainment—the natives seem to have a sense of hospitality deep in their bones.

PLANNING YOUR TIME

Most travelers view the Inn Valley as "pass-through" territory—between Salzburg to the east, the Italian Dolomites to the south, Bavaria and Munich to the north, and Switzerland to the west. If you have only a few hours, Innsbruck warrants a stretch-your-legs

The Tirol Region

The mountainous Tirol region—in Austria's western panhandle—is a winter sports mecca known for its alpine panoramas. In the region's capital, Innsbruck, the Golden Roof glitters and a mountain peak is in every view. Just up the valley, neighboring Hall is also charming, with fewer crowds. This region makes a fine stop for those en route from Germany to Italy, or from Vienna to Switzerland.

Today's Tirol is a fraction of its original size. Controlled by the Habsburgs from the mid-14th to the early 20th century, this realm was chopped up when Austria lost World War I. The southern Tirol became part of Italy, where Mussolini and other rulers worked hard to Italianize the strongly Germanic culture (see page 479). For a look at this part of the Tirol—what Austrians call the Südtirol—head to Italy's Dolomites (see the Italian Dolomites chapter). The northern fringe of Tirol—still part of Austria—contains the mountain resort town of Reutte, providing easy access to Bavaria's fairy-tale castles across the border in Germany (see the Bavarian Alps chapter). If you're day-tripping across borders, bring your passport (though you aren't likely to be asked for it).

INNSBRUCK

stroll (follow my self-guided walk, which takes a couple of hours). With a day, add a museum visit, or, better yet, head into the mountains—but allow at least 2.5 hours round-trip for this. Innsbruck deserves an overnight (or two), which allows more time for sightseeing, scenic drives and strolls, and mountain lifts. The town of Hall, with its preserved old town core, is a pleasant side-trip from Innsbruck—or it can be a practical, somewhat cheaper small-town overnight alternative that's good for drivers (covered at the end of this chapter).

Orientation to Innsbruck

Innsbruck—Austria's fourth-biggest city—has about 130,000 inhabitants (and 30,000 students). Most recommended sights, hotels, and restaurants are in the compact, traffic-free medieval center, tucked along the Inn River. Directly south of the old town, the broad Maria-Theresien-Strasse leads through an upscale neighborhood of 18th- and 19th-century buildings, bounded by the train station to the east. Suburbs climb up the foothills to the north and south. Orient yourself with the mountains called Nordkette, a chain of the Karwendel Alps to the north.

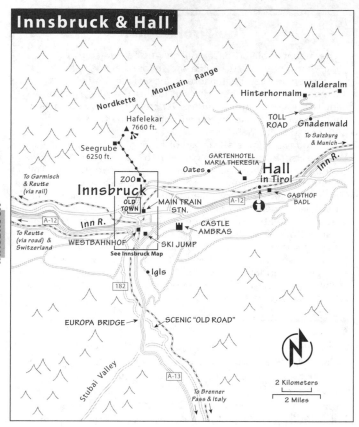

TOURIST INFORMATION

Innsbruck's main TI is at the edge of the **old town** (Mon-Sat 9:00-18:00, Sun 10:00-16:30; Burggraben 3, facing the inner ring road three blocks in front of Golden Roof, tel. 0512/5356, www. innsbruck.info). There's also a TI kiosk at the **train station** (July-Aug Mon-Sat 9:00-17:00; Sept-June Mon-Sat 10:00-15:00, closed Sun).

Innsbruck Card: The €43 Innsbruck Card includes 24 hours of free local transport as far as Hall, access to the nearby mountain lifts, the town walking tour (described later), and entry to most of the attractions I've listed. The card pays for itself if you ride the lifts to the top of the Hafelekar and back and see one major sight. It may save money if you visit many sights and connect them with the bus or Sightseer minibus—do the math. In Innsbruck, the card is sold at the TI and most participating sights. The card also covers Hall's Mint Museum (but not the Mint Tower) and is available

from Hall's TI. There are also versions valid for 48 and 72 hours
(€50 and €59).

   Welcome Card: Some hotels offer the free Innsbruck Welcome Card, which provides discounts on sightseeing and public
transport. Travelers staying three days or more also get discounts
on cable cars. Check www.innsbruck.info for more details (search
for "Welcome Card").

   Walking Tours: The TI offers a great 1.25-hour **city walk** of
Innsbruck (€13, free with Innsbruck Card, daily at 14:00). To hire
your own guide, book through Per Pedes and request **Julia Stau-
hal,** who does well-informed, engaging tours of town (price on
request, mobile 0664-433-9419, www.perpedes-tirol.at, office@
perpedes-tirol.at).

INNSBRUCK

ARRIVAL IN INNSBRUCK

By Train: Some trains stop at Innsbruck's Westbahnhof, but stay
on the train until you reach the main train station (Hauptbahnhof). Austria's second-biggest station, it has lockers, a large supermarket, a bookstore, a TI, and a *Reisezentrum* where you can get
rail information and tickets. Local buses stop out front.

   From the station, it's a 10-minute walk to the old town center. As you exit, walk to the right end of the square in front of
the station. Turn left on Brixner Strasse, and follow it past the
fountain at Bozner Platz, where it turns into Meraner Strasse. Go
straight until it dead-ends into Maria-Theresien-Strasse, then turn
right and head 300 yards into the old town. You'll pass the TI on
Burggraben (on your right), and then Hotel Weisses Kreuz and the
Golden Roof.

   By Car: The handiest (but most expensive) parking is the
City Garage at the Congress Center, right in the center of town
(€1.10/30 minutes, €14/day). This works well if you're taking the
nearby mountain cable car—ask for validation for free parking
until 18:00. The **OlympiaWorld park-and-ride,** near the stadiums
behind the train station, is another alternative (€14/day, includes
free public transport in town for 5 people).

   By Plane: The handy #F bus carries you from the airport to
central points around the city (4/hour). Buy tickets from machines
outside the station or from the driver (more expensive).

HELPFUL HINTS

Laundry: There are several self-service **Bubblepoint** launderettes
   near my recommended hotels (Mon-Fri 8:00-21:00, Sat-Sun
   until 20:00, at Brixner Strasse 1 near the train station, longer
   hours at Innstrasse 11 just across the river from old town, tel.
   0512/565-0075, www.bubblepoint.com).
Bike Rental: Find a range of choices at **Die Börse** bike shop, from

INNSBRUCK

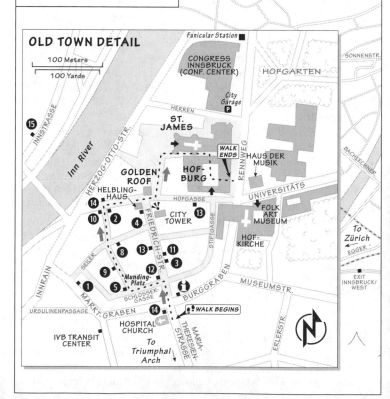

Innsbruck

Accommodations

1 Hotel Maximilian
2 Hotel Goldener Adler
3 Hotel Weisses Kreuz
4 Hotel/Rest. Weinhaus Happ
5 Nepomuk's Hostel & Café Munding
6 Ibis Innsbruck Hauptbahnhof
7 Pension Stoi

Eateries & Other

8 Die Wilderin
9 Weisses Rössl
10 Mamma Mia
11 Reformstark Martin Veg. Deli
12 Der Bäcker Ruetz
13 Tomasseli Gelato (2)
14 Groceries (3)
15 Launderettes (2)
16 Bike Rental

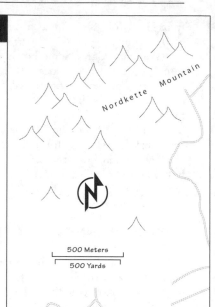

Nordkette Mountain

500 Meters
500 Yards

OLD TOWN DETAIL

100 Meters
100 Yards

Funicular Station

CONGRESS INNSBRUCK (CONF. CENTER)

HOFGARTEN

SONNENSTR.

City Garage

HERREN

ST. JAMES

WALK ENDS

HAUS DER MUSIK

BACHLECHNER

GOLDEN ROOF

HOF-BURG

RENNWEG

Inn River

HERZOG-OTTO-STR.

HELBLING-HAUS

HOFGASSE

UNIVERSITÄTS-

INNSTRASSE

CITY TOWER

STIFTGASSE

FOLK ART MUSEUM

To Zürich

EGGER

HOF-KIRCHE

EXIT INNSBRUCK/ WEST

SEILER

Munding-Platz

BURGGRABEN

MUSEUMSTR.

INNRAIN

SCHLOSSER-GASSE

MARKT-GRABEN

URSULINENPASSAGE

WALK BEGINS

MARIA-THERESIEN-STRASSE

ERLERSTR.

IVB TRANSIT CENTER

HOSPITAL CHURCH

To Triumphal Arch

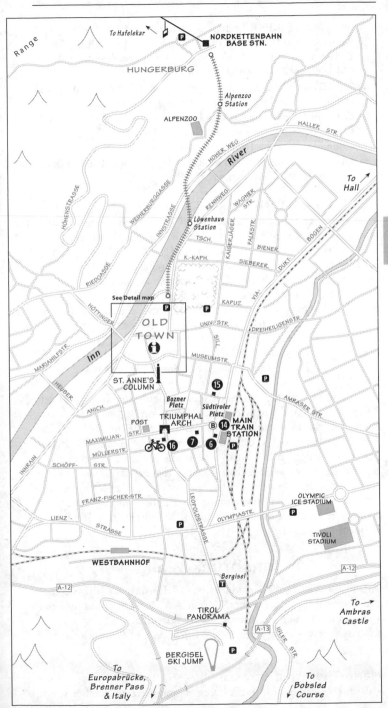

city cruisers (€16/8 hours) to mountain bikes (€24/8 hours; Mon-Sat 9:00-18:00, shorter hours on Sun, closed during bad weather; in the back courtyard at Leopoldstrasse 4, tel. 0512/581-742, www.dieboerse.at).

Guided Hikes: Hikers meet in front of Congress Innsbruck (and the lift station) late May-late Oct daily at 8:45; each day, it's a different hike in the surrounding mountains and valleys (only for people who are overnighting locally and bring the Welcome Card—see "Tourist Information," earlier; bring lunch and water; boots, rucksack, and transport included or offered at reduced price; confirm with TI).

GETTING AROUND INNSBRUCK

You won't need public transportation if you're sticking to Innsbruck's compact medieval center and the Hafelekar lift, but you'll take **trams** or **buses** to the museums and ski jump at Bergisel, Ambras Castle, and Hall. Tickets can be purchased at machines, tobacco shops, the TI, and the IVB office mentioned below.

A single ticket within Innsbruck costs €2.40 (€3 from the driver); a day pass is €5.60. You can also buy a discounted pack of eight rides for €14.60 (or €20.60 from the driver). Tickets to Hall cost more, and there's a confusing array of family and group tickets. Sort out your options at the IVB office (*Kundencenter*), near the old town (Mon-Fri 7:30-18:00, closed Sat-Sun, Stainerstrasse 2, www.ivb.at).

The made-for-tourists **Sightseer** minibus (also known as bus #TS) loops around town, connecting the key sights. Buy tickets at the TI, the IVB office, or from the driver (€16/24-hour pass, covered by Innsbruck Card, no single-ride tickets). Your Sightseer ticket also covers other buses and trams within Innsbruck. The Sightseer is pricey—more than double a regular day pass on public transit—and runs less frequently, but some find it more convenient (minimal headphone commentary in English, departs every 40 minutes from stops throughout town, May-Sept 9:55-18:40, less frequent off-season).

Innsbruck Walk

This self-guided walk introduces you to Innsbruck's historic core and connects its major sights. Worth ▲▲, it takes about an hour and a half, not counting time spent in museums.

• *Begin across the street from the TI, at the head of the pedestrianized shopping street called...*

Maria-Theresien-Strasse

This fine, Baroque-era, traffic-free shopping street stretches south

A Wedding, a Funeral, and an Arch

Europe is littered with Roman-style arches celebrating heroic victories or events of national importance. But few are as poignant as Innsbruck's Triumphal Arch: Intended to celebrate a wedding, it ended up also memorializing a funeral.

The happy: Maria Theresa's son Leopold II, archduke of Tuscany, married a Spanish princess here in Innsbruck in 1765. (Maria Theresa had 16 kids, and was expert at marrying them off to VIPs around Europe to shore up her dynasty's influence—see the sidebar on page 45.) The city spent an entire year getting ready for the big event—as if hosting an Olympics or World Cup. Old buildings were torn down, moats were filled in, and the city was modernized in anticipation of the nuptials. As the wedding day approached, Maria Theresa and her husband Franz arrived in Innsbruck for two weeks of festivities. But then tragedy struck: Franz partied a little too hard and died of a heart attack (prompting Maria Theresa to wear black for the rest of her life). The south-facing side of the arch—what you see as you approach the city center—shows the interlocked rings of the newlywed couple. But the flip side, visible as you leave town, features mournful statuary.

from the medieval center. It's named for Maria Theresa, the powerful 18th-century Habsburg empress who left her mark here in Innsbruck (as in much of her realm). Face away from the old town and take a quick visual tour of this street.

On the right, the pink Baroque church is known as the **Hospital Church** (Spitalskirche). The busy road behind you—still called the Graben (ditch)—marks the site of the moat and city wall in the olden days. It was smart to keep the hospital outside the walled town to reduce the spread of disease.

Farther along, in the middle of Maria-Theresien-Strasse, **St. Anne's Column** (Annasäule) marks the middle of the old marketplace. This was erected in the 18th century by townspeople thankful that their army had defeated an invading Bavarian army and saved the town (it's the same idea as the plague columns throughout Central Europe).

Just beyond the column, on the right, is the **Rathaus Galerien**—the former City Hall, now a sprawling shopping mall.

We're about to do a 180 and head into the old town. But if you went the other way on Maria-

Theresien-Strasse—past St. Anne's Column—in a couple of blocks you'd run into a **Triumphal Arch** with an interesting backstory (see the sidebar). Now face the old town and enjoy the classic view of Innsbruck: arcaded shopping street, twinkling Golden Roof, and a Nordkette backdrop looming high above. Notice the heavy-duty avalanche protection that stripes the slopes above town.

• *Cross the busy street, and pause at the start of the...*

Herzog-Friedrich-Strasse Pedestrian Zone

You're now within Innsbruck's old town. Facing back the way you came, look up to the right (under the little arch) to see a painting labeled *Vor-Stadttor 1765*—commemorating what was the city tower, before it was torn down for the wedding of Leopold II. Bricks from this tower were used to build the Triumphal Arch described earlier.

This part of town dates from well before the Habsburgs, however. The street you're on now, thriving with commerce today, was even more so in ancient Roman times when it was part of the **Via Claudia Augusta.** Laid out in 15 BC, this trade route over the Brenner Pass connected Italy to Germany. Innsbruck is named for the place where a bridge *(Brücke)* allowed the Via Claudia Augusta to cross the Inn River.

Look to the far end of the street, where the Golden Roof glitters. The arcades—common in Tirol—offer shelter from both sun and snow.

On the right, at #39, peek into the sleek showroom of the **Swarovski Crystal shop.** A century and a half ago, the Swarovski family moved from Bohemia (in the Czech lands) to the Inn Valley, seeking ample wood and water for their glassworks. Today they're a crystal empire with high-end shops all over the world (they also have a visitors center at their Crystal Worlds headquarters in the nearby town of Wattens).

• *From here, you could walk straight to the Golden Roof in under a minute. But instead, let's take a more scenic (and less tourist-clogged) route through...*

Innsbruck's Back Streets

Head down Schlossergasse (under the arch, across from Swarovski). After one block, you'll hit the square called **Mundingplatz.** On it, you'll find the classic Café Munding (daily 8:00-20:00), with decadent pastries. On the wall, notice the huge painting of St. Christopher, the patron saint of travelers—fitting for this historic crossroads town. Just to the right is another, smaller painting—a Madonna and Child, inspired by the locally beloved piece inside St. James' Cathedral (see "Sights in Innsbruck," later).

Facing the café, turn right and wander down Kiebachgasse, noticing the typical **Innsbruck architecture.** While Café Munding itself has had a frilly Baroque makeover, most of the houses along here have clean Gothic lines. Notice that the rooflines come to a V, funneling rain and snowmelt into exterior gutters and downspouts. Each simple house front hides a long, skinny townhouse and a spacious interior courtyard. These spaces, along with the characteristic arcades that line major shopping streets, help protect locals from the volatile alpine climate. Also notice the stout buttresses holding everything firmly in place; Tirol has suffered some devastating earthquakes.

Kiebachgasse opens up into a little zone locals call the "**Square of the Four Animals**"—look for the horse, lion, eagle, and stag (hint: one is on a weathervane).

Continue straight one more block, to the intersection with Herzog-Friedrich-Strasse. Several recommended restaurants face this picturesque intersection. Immediately on your right, duck under the arcade of the recommended **Hotel Goldener Adler,** which dates from 1390, and peruse the list of illustrious customers, chiseled into a stone plaque (Maximilian, Mozart, Goethe...). Peek in the window to the right of that plaque to see the sumptuous interior. At the far-back wall, notice the shimmering golden mosaics honoring four great Tiroleans who defended their land against Bavaria during Napoleon's time (see the Tirol Panorama listing under "Sights in Innsbruck," later).

• *Speaking of shimmering: You've been patient, and now it's time to see the most famous gold in Austria. Turn right along Herzog-Friedrich-Strasse and window-shop your way one block to the...*

Golden Roof (Goldenes Dachl)

Emperor Maximilian I (see sidebar) adored Innsbruck. And so he adorned his residence here with a balcony topped with 2,657 gilded copper tiles. The Golden Roof (1494) offered Maximilian an impressive spot from which to view his medieval spectacles. But he also enjoyed people-watching (and being seen) from here.

Examine the symbolism of the roof: Just below the balcony is a relief panel of Maximilian facing his two wives (Bianca Maria Sforza—with the golden apple—and Mary of Burgundy). To the right is another panel of Maximilian, flanked by his jester and his key adviser. Acrobatic dancers are a reminder that this balcony was designed for watching spectacles. Just below are frescoes of knights waving the

INNSBRUCK

Emperor Maximilian I (1459-1519)

Holy Roman Emperor Maximilian I—a contemporary of England's King Henry VIII—lived in the waning days of the Middle Ages, on the cusp of the Renaissance. Maximilian had one foot in the modern world and fancied himself a multifaceted "Hans of all trades" (though reportedly, a master of none). And yet, at the same time, he clung to the last romantic fantasies of the Middle Ages—he was the last Habsburg who personally led his troops into battle. (To see where he fits in among other Habsburgs, see the family tree in the Austria: Past & Present chapter.) Much of what you see in today's Innsbruck, including the Golden Roof, dates from Maximilian's time.

During the Habsburgs' peak in the 17th and 18th centuries, Vienna became their leading city. But during Maximilian's time, two centuries earlier, the focus was on Italy. He took the "Roman" part of "Holy Roman Emperor" very seriously. This made Innsbruck—the capital of Tirol (a region with a foothold in the Italian world)—extremely important. The visionary emperor hoped that once all of Italy was his, Innsbruck would become the permanent capital of his empire. In reality, he was unlucky at war and ran up huge debts.

Maximilian also loved being close to the Alps, where he could hike and hunt to his heart's content. He once said, "Tirol is like a warm coat: If you put your hand in the pocket, you always find something."

Maximilian's first wife, Mary of Burgundy, came from a land of stout stone homes. This inspired him to replace the firetrap wooden buildings of Innsbruck with fine stone townhouses—most of which still stand.

Maximilian and Mary were happy together...but only for a short time, as the queen died in a hunting accident after only five years of marriage. Forever obsessed with Italy, Maximilian remarried Princess Bianca Maria Sforza of Milan. But his heart just wasn't in it. He even sent a proxy to the ceremony (where Leonardo da Vinci was the wedding planner). He wound up with a gigantic dowry (equivalent to 200 years' tax for the entire city of Vienna), a fancy Golden Roof in Innsbruck (built to commemorate the wedding)...and a loveless marriage.

But Max and Mary's offspring went on to reshape Europe, and the world. Their grandson was Holy Roman Emperor Charles V, who was also King Charles I of Spain. He ruled over Spain and its far-flung colonies during its Golden Age—an empire that stretched from Holland to Sicily, and from Bohemia to Bolivia. Though Maximilian I had aspirations as a war hero, as with most Habsburgs, his biggest victory came with a trip to the altar.

banners of the Holy Roman Empire (black eagle) and Tirol (red eagle). Under that (beneath the windows), the row of heraldic crests identifies with more specificity the many realms Maximilian had ties to, including the Holy Roman Empire, Austria (red and white stripes), Burgundy (lions holding a complex pastiche with fleur-de-lis), and the Sforza family (a snake; also the insignia of Milan-based Alfa Romeo). To learn more, visit the little Golden Roof Museum upstairs (see "Sights in Innsbruck," later).

Turn around and look up the wide pedestrian street, enjoying the same views that Maximilian did—with one modern addition: the futuristic Bergisel ski jump, which, from this angle, is aptly nicknamed "The Cobra."

On your right, notice the over-the-top Rococo facade of the **Helblinghaus**—a rare case of an Innsbruck town house that, rather than keeping its original, stoic Gothic facade, was dressed up later. (Most locals were hardworking merchants with little money for fancy renovations; VIPs lived in frilly countryside villas.) Locals call this style *Kucherbäcker*—"cake decorator."

Next door to that house—on the wall of the green building at #12—notice the painted **jousting figures,** illustrating Maximilian's favorite spectator sport.

On the left side of the street is the bulbous **city tower** *(Stadtturm),* with a stout stone base that wears a curvy 17th-century Renaissance cap (which replaced the original steeple that tumbled away during an earthquake). This was the old town watchtower; a prison was on the second floor. Today, visitors can climb the 148 steps for a great view (€4, daily 10:00-20:00, Oct-May until 17:00).

Several doors down from the city tower—at #31, next to the McDonald's—is the historic **Hotel Weisses Kreuz.** It's built on Roman foundations, but has "only" been hosting guests for the last 500 years. The white cross *(weisses Kreuz)* is the symbol of the Order of Malta—knights who opened up guesthouses for Holy Land-bound pilgrims during the Crusades. In 1769, a 13-year-old Wolfgang Amadeus Mozart and his father stayed here on their way to Italy. A generation later, this hotel was one of the centers of resistance against Napoleon, and later still, against the Nazis (giving shelter to Jewish refugees). When American soldiers moved in from Italy, they made the hotel their headquarters. Today, it's still a functioning—and recommended—hotel.

• *Go straight up the little street called Pfarrgasse, just to the right of the Golden Roof. In one block, you'll hit Domplatz, with* **St. James' Cathedral.** *While dull on the outside, its interior is lavishly decorated, free to visit, and well worth a look (tour it now, or come back after the walk). Try to be here at 12:15, when the carillon plays.*

As you face the cathedral, take the little street around its right side. Turn right through the gate into the courtyard of the...

Hofburg

The Habsburgs had three palaces called "Hofburg"—in Vienna, in Prague, and right here. (This one's relatively tiny, with "just" 400 rooms, compared to the 2,600 rooms in Vienna's.) For the 1765 wedding of her son (see "A Wedding, a Funeral, and an Arch," earlier), Maria Theresa completely remodeled the complex in her preferred "Viennese Rococo" style, calling it "My little Schloss Schönbrunn in the Alps." The room where Maria Theresa's husband died became the chapel of a convent of nuns who were dedicated to praying 24/7 in his memory. If you tour the interior, you can peek in; you might still see a sister praying for Franz's soul.

• *Exit the door on the left side of the courtyard. You'll end up at a busy urban street called Rennweg. Across the street is a new cultural institution and concert venue called the **House of Music**.*

*Our walk is over, but several attractions are a short stroll away. To the left, you're one block from the base station of the slick, futuristic network of people movers, funiculars, and cable cars that gradually take you thousands of feet above Innsbruck's rooftops to the **Hafelekar mountaintop**. To the right, just past the Hofburg, you'll find the entrance to the **Museum of Tirolean Folk Art** and the **Hofkirche**. Or you can return to the Golden Roof for its museum or tour St. James' Cathedral. All of these options are described in the next section.*

Sights in Innsbruck

Three worthwhile sights—the Museum of Tirolean Folk Art, the Hofkirche, and the Tirol Panorama (as well as several lesser museums)—are covered by a single €11 combo-ticket. This is the only ticket sold for the folk art museum, so if you're going there, you'll get the other sights for free.

IN THE OLD TOWN

Most of these sights are connected by my self-guided "Innsbruck Walk," earlier.

Golden Roof Museum (Museum Goldenes Dachl)

This modest museum inside the Golden Roof building tells the story of Innsbruck in the time of Maximilian I. It includes exhibits about the roof and its construction, a good 15-minute film about Max and his roof, and a little balcony that lets you enjoy the same view the emperor did. There are few actual artifacts, but the exhibit is informative and well-presented.

Cost and Hours: €4.80, includes audioguide; daily 10:00-17:00, closed Nov and Mon in off-season; enter directly under the Golden Roof at Herzog-Friedrich-Strasse 15 and walk up to the first floor, tel. 0512/5360-1441.

▲▲St. James' Cathedral (Dom zu St. Jakob)

Innsbruck's cathedral is plain on the outside, but the interior is a lavish High Baroque pastry: pink and frilly, with lots of gold and optical illusions.

Cost and Hours: Free; Mon-Sat 10:15-19:30, Sun from 12:30, Nov-April until 18:30, Domplatz 6, tel. 0512/583-902, www.dibk.at.

Visiting the Cathedral: Viewing the drab **facade,** you'd never guess that the church interior is slathered in Baroque illusions. But there is one clue: On the top row of (round) windows, note that only the middle one is real—the other two are painted on, to force a sense of symmetry.

At the very top of the central facade (between the towers), notice the equestrian statue honoring **St. James** (Sankt Jakob in German, or Santiago in Spanish). Innsbruck is a crossroads town, located not only on the ancient Via Claudia Augusta, but also on the medieval Camino de Santiago (Way of St. James) pilgrimage route—which runs from here all the way to Santiago de Compostela, in northwest Spain.

Step inside. The church dates from the early 18th century, when Baroque was all the rage. Looking up, notice that the three **"domes"** over the nave are an illusion—painted onto a flat surface. Walk up the nave. Those illustrations, meant to be viewed from the back, become increasingly distorted as you move toward the front.

The frilly, gilded high altar contains one of Lucas Cranach's best-known Madonna and Childs, dubbed the *Mariahilf.* Even though Cranach was a close friend of Martin Luther—the firebrand behind Protestantism, which the Habsburgs fought bitterly in a Counter-Reformation—everyone seems to agree that this is a particularly fine depiction of Mary. Locals love that she's not shown as a crowned deity, but as an everyday mother. You'll see replicas of the *Mariahilf* around town.

For **more Baroque illusions,** stand in front of the main altar and look up into the church's one real dome. Just below the dome, flanking the clock, are figures with details that break the frame, reaching from the art world into the real world. On the right, St. Luke the Evangelist writes on a scroll, which curls down over the arch. This curl is real—sculpted from stucco. But on the left, where St. John's eagle stretches its wing over the edge of the arch, the wingtip is painted on—as is its shadow, to complete the illusion.

Also just below the dome, the two glassed-in **galleries** were attached by a walkway to the Hofburg next door, allowing royals to attend Mass without having to mingle with their subjects.

In the left transept, you'll see the elaborate altar covering the **tomb of Prince Maximilian** (not *the* Maximilian, but a later prince who ruled Tirol from 1602-1618). The canopy is supported by finely

cast bronze pillars, covered in vines, bugs, birds, and other crit-
ters. Up top, a lance-wielding St. George watches over a kneeling
Prince Max. (You'll see more dynamic statues like this one at the
Hofkirche.)

On your way back up the nave (toward the main door), look
just above the organ at the only actual round window (even though
you can see three round "windows" at this level from the outside).
Above this window and on the left, look for Lucifer being thrown
out of heaven—and out of the painting itself. It's yet another Baroque illusion in this church that specializes in them.

Hofburg (Imperial Palace)

This 18th-century Baroque palace, completely rebuilt in 1765 by
Maria Theresa and full of her family portraits, is only worth a visit
if you aren't going to the much bigger and better palaces in Vienna.
The lone advantage is that, unlike the more famous Habsburg palaces, you'll have this one virtually to yourself. You get to see the
empress' reception rooms, her private apartment, and a few rooms
of exhibits.

Cost and Hours: €9, includes 1.5-hour audioguide, daily
9:00-17:00, tel. 0512/587-186, www.hofburg-innsbruck.at.

Nearby: Should you need a Sacher torte fix, opposite the Hofburg entrance you'll find the local outpost of the venerable Viennese institution, **$$$$ Café Sacher** (daily 8:30-late).

▲Museum of Tirolean Folk Art
(Tiroler Volkskunstmuseum)

This big museum offers the best look anywhere at traditional Tirolean lifestyles. Fascinating exhibits range from wedding dresses
and gaily painted cribs to maternity clothes and babies' trousers.
You'll also see several rustic Tirolean buildings.

Cost and Hours: €11, includes admission to Hofkirche and
Tirol Panorama, open daily 9:00-17:00, Universitätsstrasse 2, tel.
0512/5948-9510, www.tiroler-landesmuseen.at.

Visiting the Museum: English explanations are limited. At
the entrance, leave your ID to borrow the worthwhile audioguide—scan the barcode near most exhibits or utilize the Helpful
Highlights tour (45 minutes).

Just past Lucifer, on the ground floor, is a fine collection of
Nativity scenes. The first floor up has exhibits on everyday items
(cookware, furniture, tools) and celebrations of Christian feast
days (the dates are on the floor). The highlight, on the first and
second floors, is the carefully reconstructed interiors of several Tirolean parlors with their small windows, wood paneling, and finely
crafted furniture. The second floor also covers traditional Tirolean
costumes (which differ from valley to valley, and from village to
village); rites of passage; and supernatural beliefs, all tied to the

uncertainty of life and the fear of death. You can also peek into the interior of the adjacent Hofkirche.

▲▲Hofkirche (Court Church)

Emperor Maximilian I liked Innsbruck so much, he wanted to be buried here—surrounded by 28 larger-than-life cast-bronze statues of his ancestors, relatives, in-laws...and  his favorite heroes of the dying Middle Ages (such as King Arthur). The church interior is worth a visit to stroll among the statues, which stand like giant chess pieces on the black-and-white-checkerboard marble floor, and to ponder one of Europe's most elaborate funerary monuments.

Cost and Hours: €7, includes audioguide, good €2 book (available at museum entrance) is a "Who's Who" of the statues; covered by combo-ticket with Museum of Tirolean Folk Art and Tirol Panorama; Mon-Sat 9:00-17:00, Sun from 12:30; Universitätsstrasse 2—enter through museum, www.tiroler-landesmuseen.at.

Visiting the Church: Start your visit with a trippy multimedia show about the life of Emperor Maximillian I—look for it in the far corner of the courtyard. Just inside the church entrance you'll find the marble-carved tomb of the locally beloved soldier Andreas Hofer, who rallied the Tiroleans to fight against—and defeat—Napoleon (commemorated by the Tirol Panorama, described later).

That's Maximilian himself, kneeling on top of the huge sarcophagus. Sadly, the real Max isn't inside. By the time he died, Maximilian (and his 400-person entourage) had become notorious for running up debts—so his supporters weren't allowed to bring his body here.

Don't miss King Arthur (as you face the altar, he's the fifth from the front on the right, next to the heavy-metal dude) and Mary of Burgundy, Maximilian's first—and favorite—wife (third from the front on the left). Some of these sculptures, including that of König Artur, were designed by German Renaissance painter Albrecht Dürer.

IN THE NEARBY MOUNTAINS

A popular mountain-sports center and host of the 1964 and 1976 Winter Olympics, Innsbruck is surrounded by 150 mountain lifts, 1,250 miles of trails, and 250 hikers' huts. The sheer sheet of rock that stretches, east to west, across Innsbruck's valley is called the

Nordkette—the "Northern Chain" of the Alps. And the *Nordkettenbahn* (described next) makes it remarkably easy to gain some altitude.

▲▲▲Nordkettenbahn up to Hafelekar

Right from the center of town, a series of three lifts—collectively called the *Nordkettenbahn*—whisk you above the tree line to the ridge perched thousands of feet directly above the Golden Roof. This is the fastest and easiest way to get your Tirolean mountain high. It's not cheap, but on a clear day, the trip is worth every euro. Allow at least 2.5 hours round-trip to the top and back, including time for the short hike up to the summit.

Cost and Hours: Funicular—€9 round-trip, €15 combo-ticket with Alpenzoo, prices slightly higher in winter, runs every 15 minutes Mon-Fri 7:15-19:15, Sat-Sun 8:00-19:15. Cable cars and funicular—€34.50 round-trip from Innsbruck, €29.30 from Hungerburg; last lift down from Hafelekar at 17:00, from Seegrube at 17:30, both run every 15 minutes. If you're going all the way to the top, it makes sense to get the Innsbruck Card for €43, which covers your trip, the Alpenzoo (described next), and much more; see "Tourist Information," earlier in this chapter. Cable-car tickets and Alpenzoo combo-tickets (but not funicular tickets) include free parking until 18:00 in the underground Congress garage. Tel. 0512/293-344, www.nordkette.com.

Ascending the Mountain: The **Hungerburgbahn funicular** leaves from the *Star Trek*-esque station (designed by Dame Zaha Hadid, the Iraqi-born British architect who also did the ski-jump stadium) located outside Congress Innsbruck (the conference center right behind the Hofburg). From here, the futuristic people-mover stops at the Löwenhaus and Alpenzoo stations before reaching the Hungerburg hillside viewpoint.

From the **Hungerburg** viewpoint (with a little cable-car museum), walk a few steps to catch the first of two cable cars that lead up into the mountains. The first one gets you to the **Seegrube** perch; you'll change there for the highest station, Hafelekar. All three stations have **$$** self-serve cafeterias.

Once up at **Hafelekar,** if you've lucked out on weather, you'll see Innsbruck stretching across the valley to the Bergisel ski jump and, just to its right, the graceful Europa Bridge that leads up the

Brenner Pass to Italy, beyond the peaks. Looking down the valley to the left, see if you can spot the town of Hall and its Mint Tower. For that "climb every mountain" feeling, hike the 10-minute trail up to the Hafelekar peak (7,657 feet, no hiking boots needed)—as you face Innsbruck, you'll see it on your left, marked by a little cross. From there, even higher views of Innsbruck are accompanied by sweeping, cut-glass panoramas over the back side of the mountain. At a minimum, walk the short path behind the lift station to peer over the ridge into the Karwendel Alps, jutting up between you and the German border. Take time to relax and soak in the view before returning to earth.

Serious hikers can choose from a range of longer hiking/walking options (well-explained in lift brochures), while hard-core mountain bikers will thrill at the steep trails—some of Europe's toughest (see "Helpful Hints," earlier, for bike-rental information).

▲Alpenzoo

This zoo is one of Innsbruck's most popular attractions (understandable when the competition is the Golden Roof). It's compact and well-designed, nestled into

the steep natural contours of the mountainside. There's almost no English, but it's fun to learn the German words for the animals and watch European children at play. Navigate by the animal outlines on the map to find the various beasts that hide out in the Alps, including wolves, chamois, marmots, and at least one gigantic vulture.

Cost and Hours: €11, €15 combo-ticket with Hungerburgbahn funicular, daily 9:00-18:00, Nov-March until 17:00, Weiherburggasse 37, tel. 0512/292-323, www.alpenzoo.at.

Getting There: The easiest way up is with the funicular (described earlier). It's OK to stop off on a round-trip ticket to Hungerburg to see the zoo, then continue up or down (follow signs 5 minutes from Alpenzoo station to the zoo itself). Or you could take the local #W bus, or just walk (following *Fussweg Alpenzoo* signs from the river).

Olympic Bobsled

For those who envy Olympic bobsled teams whooshing down curvy chutes (who doesn't?), Innsbruck offers the chance to try an actual Olympic course. In the summer, you'll ride with a pilot and three others down the 4,000-foot-long course in a sled-on-wheels; in the winter it's the real thing on ice.

Cost and Hours: Summer—€30, July-Aug only, Wed-Fri at 16:00; winter—€30, Jan-March only; in both seasons call ahead, no kids under 12, tel. 05275/51220, mobile 0664-202-4797, www.knauseder-event.at—select "Events," then *"Gästebob"* or *"Sommerbob."*

Getting There: From the city center, take bus #J from Marktgraben (near Maria-Theresien-Strasse and the TI) to the Olympia express stop (2/hour, 25 minutes)—it's a short walk along Römerstrasse to the building with the silver *Zielhaus* sign. Drivers coming from the A-12 autobahn should take the Innsbruck Mitte exit, and follow signs to *Igls* and then to *Olympia Bobbahn*.

OUTER INNSBRUCK

These sights are within a tram or bus ride of the old town.

▲Slap-Dancing (Tiroler Abend)

The Gundolf family offers an entertaining evening of slap-dancing and yodeling nightly at 20:30 from April through October (€30 includes a drink with 2-hour show, dinner—€19 extra, pick-up/drop-off service—€6, tickets and info at TI or your hotel; located far from the center at Gasthaus Sandwirt, Reichenauerstrasse 151, near Jugendherberge stop of bus #O; reservations tel. 0512/263-263, www.tirolerabend.info). The city puts on free outdoor concerts almost daily during peak season. Check the TI website for more details (www.innsbruck.info).

Ambras Castle (Schloss Ambras)

Just southeast of town is the Renaissance palace Archduke Ferdinand II (1529-1595) renovated for his wife (it was originally a medieval castle). The castle is skippable for most, but worth considering for Habsburg nuts or drivers who'd like an easy castle experience. Its extensive grounds are replete with manicured gardens, a 17th-century fake waterfall, and resident peacocks. Visit the fine armory and the archduke's assortment of the beautiful and bizarre—ranging from stuffed sharks and crocodiles, to ancient Portuguese frocks, to exquisite *objets d'art*. The beautiful Spanish Hall (built 1569-1572) is clearly the prize of the whole complex. Its intricate wooden ceiling and 27 life-size portraits of Tirolean princes make this a popular venue for classical music concerts.

Cost and Hours: €10, discounted to €7 Dec-March (when portrait gallery is closed), open daily 10:00-17:00, closed Nov, audioguide-€3, Schlossstrasse 20, tel. 01/525-244-802, www.schlossambras-innsbruck.at.

Getting There: Drivers find it just off the expressway, overlooking Innsbruck (exit at Innsbruck-Mitte, follow *Schloss Ambras* signs at the roundabout, free parking). By public transportation, you have three choices: Go direct on the Sightseer; ride bus #4134

(2/hour, 10 minutes) from the train station to the entrance gate of the grounds, then walk five minutes; or take tram #3 to the last stop and walk 15 minutes.

▲Ski Jump Stadium (Bergisel)

The ski jump here was used for the 1964 and 1976 Olympics. The original ramp (which wasn't up to modern standards) was torn down and rebuilt from scratch in 2002. The jump is interesting and the views over the city are superb, but for mountain thrills, you're better off riding up to the ridge on the other side of the valley (see "Nordkettenbahn up to Hafelekar," earlier).

INNSBRUCK

Cost and Hours: €9.50 whether you take funicular or not, €14 combo-ticket with Tirol Panorama; daily June-Oct 9:00-18:00; Dec-May Wed-Mon 10:00-17:00, closed Tue and most of Nov; funicular back down runs until 15 minutes after closing, Bergiselweg 3, tel. 0512/589-259, www.bergisel.info.

Getting There: Drivers find it just off the Brenner Pass road on the south side of town (take the Innsbruck Süd exit and follow signs to *Bergisel;* €3 to park). Using public transportation, it's an easy tram ride from the center (tram #1 to the Bergisel stop, 6/hour) and then a 10-minute uphill walk following *Bergisel* signs; near the top of the woodsy path, bear left past the wooden pavilions for the Tirol Panorama (described next), or continue uphill for the ski jump. You can avoid most of the walk by taking the pricier Sightseer bus, which drops you near the Tirol Panorama.

Picnic Spot: Park at the end of the road near the Andreas Hofer Memorial, and climb to the empty, grassy stands for a picnic.

Visiting the Jump: For the best view of the jump itself, go to the right just after you pass through the ticket gate and climb the steps (following *Olympisches Feuer* signs) to the Olympic rings and the two dishes that held the Olympic flame. (The third dish was for the 2012 Winter Youth Olympics.) The plaques here honor Dorothy Hamill, Franz Klammer, and a host of others who brought home the gold. Other plaques around the sight explain the daredevil sport itself.

To get to the top of the ski jump, you can zip up in a funicular (2-minute ride), or walk up the 455 steps. At the top, an elevator takes you up the tower to great views from an outdoor viewing platform. One level below, a **$$$** panoramic restaurant serves drinks and meals. Near the restaurant, find the launch chute where jumpers sit to psych themselves up. As you ride the funicular down alongside the jump, imagine yourself speeding down the 320-foot-long ramp, then flying into the air (jumpers reach 55 miles per hour in just four seconds)...gulp. Note the cemetery, thoughtfully placed just below the jump.

▲▲Tirol Panorama

This worthwhile museum, right by the ski jump, houses a giant panoramic painting created in 1896 to memorialize Tirol's 1809 victory over Napoleon's forces. Other exhibits trace the political and military history of Tirol. Be sure to pick up the free audioguide; although long-winded, it's essential for understanding the mostly German-captioned exhibits.

Cost and Hours: €8, covered by €11 combo-ticket with Museum of Tirolean Folk Art and Hofkirche, €14 combo-ticket with ski jump; Wed-Mon 9:00-17:00, July-Aug Thu until 19:00, closed Tue; mandatory bag check with €1 deposit, Bergisel 1 (for directions, see ski jump listing, earlier), tel. 0512/5948-9611, www. tiroler-landesmuseen.at.

Visiting the Museum: The first exhibit is the *Cyclorama*, a huge 360-degree painting of the defeat of Napoleon's forces at the hands of a ragtag Tirolean army right here at Bergisel. Napoleon had given Tirol to Bavaria, and Bavarian troops had occupied Innsbruck. But the local army managed to surprise and rout them, attacking early Sunday morning on a holiday weekend. This painting puts you right in the middle of the battle, where the audioguide explains everything in painstaking detail. Similarly to Salzburg's panorama painting (described on page 294), the piece toured Europe more than a century ago, giving the wider world a view of Innsbruck's mountain setting (though compared to Salzburg's, this panorama is bigger, more beautifully displayed, and more epic, with 3-D elements in the foreground).

The next part of the museum (in an underground passageway) is a good general exhibit on Tirolean culture and politics. Through the passageway is the adjacent and included **Kaiserjäger Museum,** dedicated to the Tirolean regiment in the Habsburg army, and in particular their sacrifices during World War I. Military-history buffs will be in their groove here, but most others will find it skippable—except for the room dedicated to Andreas Hofer, the leader of the 1809 uprising (he's the guy with the beard, and you get to see his sword). Alas, the Bavarians retook Innsbruck a few months later. Hofer was captured and executed, but remains Tirol's great hero.

NEAR INNSBRUCK
To venture out of Innsbruck, consider the following alpine adventure or a day trip to the charming town of Hall—a 20-minute drive and easily reached by public transportation (see the end of this chapter).

▲▲Alpine Side Trip by Car to Hinterhornalm
In Gnadenwald, a village sandwiched between Hall and its Alps, pay a €5 toll, pick up a brochure, then corkscrew your way up the mountain. Marveling at the crazy amount of energy put into such a remote road project, you'll finally end up at the rustic Hinterhornalm restaurant (generally daily mid-May-Oct 10:00-18:00, open later in summer—but entirely weather-dependent and often closed, closed Nov-mid-May, mobile 0664-211-2745). Hinterhornalm is a hang-gliding springboard. On good days, it's a butterfly nest. From there, it's a level 20-minute walk to Walderalm, a cluster of three dairy farms with 70 cows that share their meadow with the clouds. The cows ramble along ridge-top lanes surrounded by cut-glass peaks. The ladies of the farms serve soup, sandwiches, and drinks (very fresh milk in the afternoon) on rough plank tables. Below you spreads the Inn Valley and, in the distance, tourist-filled Innsbruck.

Sleeping in Innsbruck

Prices are highest from May through September and in December.

IN THE OLD TOWN
$$$$ Hotel Maximilian, with its back to the old town and facing a busy street, is Innsbruck's splurge option for those who value contemporary over cozy—with 46 rooms, peekaboo-glass bathroom walls, and all the comforts (family rooms, air-con, elevator, Marktgraben 7, tel. 0512/59967, www.hotel-maximilian.com).

$$$$ Hotel Goldener Adler is an Innsbruck classic, hosting guests since 1390. Today its 39 rooms are traditional with modern touches, and just down the street from the Golden Roof (family rooms, air-con, elevator, Herzog-Friedrich-Strasse 6, tel. 0512/571-111, www.goldeneradler.com, office@goldeneradler.com, Hackl family).

$$$ Hotel Weisses Kreuz, 50 yards in front of the Golden Roof, has been housing visitors for almost 600 years (see "Innsbruck Walk," earlier)—ask where Mozart slept on his visit here in 1769. While its common spaces still have an old-inn feel—with an airy atrium stairway, antique Tirolean furniture, and big wood beams—its 40 comfortable rooms are a decent value for the location (cheaper rooms with shared bath or small windows, nonsmoking, fans, elevator, great breakfast, pay parking—reserve ahead, Herzog-Friedrich-Strasse 31, tel. 0512/594-790, www.weisseskreuz.at, hotel@weisseskreuz.at).

$$ Hotel Weinhaus Happ is a solid midrange option: dated but comfortable, well-located, and reasonably priced. Most of its nine rooms face the pedestrian zone and Golden Roof (family rooms, elevator, call if arriving after 20:00, Herzog-Friedrich-Strasse 14, tel. 0512/582-980, www.weinhaus-happ.at, office@weinhaus-happ.at, Furtner family).

¢ Nepomuk's offers lots of character and 18 backpacker beds in two big well-worn, well-located apartments above Café Munding, a venerable pastry shop in the old town. It's a mix of dorm beds and simple **$** doubles with shared bathrooms and kitchen facilities. The reception and breakfast are in the café. They only accept reservations by telephone (cash only, nonsmoking, Kiebachgasse 16, tel. 0512/584-118, mobile 0664-787-9197, www.nepomuks.at).

NEAR THE TRAIN STATION

This area is practical for train travelers, but feels far from the cobbles of the old town.

$$ Ibis Innsbruck Hauptbahnhof lacks character but has 75 predictable, acceptably priced rooms directly in front of the train station. Reach the hotel through the underground passageway (by the luggage lockers), or exit the station's main doors and look for the logo (breakfast extra, nonsmoking, air-con, elevator, pay parking, Sterzinger Strasse 1, tel. 0512/570-3000, www.ibishotel.com, h5174@accor.com).

$ Pension Stoi rents 18 inexpensive, basic rooms 200 yards from the train station and a 10-minute walk from the old town center. The entranceway and oddly located reception are a bit off-putting, but the rooms are fine. Otto offers a friendly welcome and lots of local foodie tips (cheaper rooms with shared bath, family rooms, no breakfast, four free parking spaces—no guarantees but ask when you book, reception open daily 8:00-21:00; from station head down Salurnerstrasse, take first left on Adamgasse, then watch for signs in the courtyard on the right, Salurnerstrasse 7; tel. 0512/585-434, www.pensionstoi.at, pensionstoi@aon.at).

Eating in Innsbruck

$$$ Die Wilderin ("The Huntress"), a block and a half from the Golden Roof, is a foodie find, unassumingly tucked in the old town (book ahead). It's a small dinner-only eatery, with a big bar, tables on two levels, a trendy but unsnooty vibe, and a commitment to serving only dishes made with locally sourced ingredients: farm-to-table and nose-to-tail, with a mix of traditional Austrian and modern international influences. They'll explain the German-only menu (Tue-Sun 17:00-24:00, closed Mon, Seilergasse 5, tel. 0512/562-728, www.diewilderin.at).

$$$ Weisses Rössl, in the old town, satisfies culinary adventurers with traditional Tirolean treats such as oven-roasted liver and calf's head. Fear not: Schnitzels and steaks abound, or try the tasty *Grillteller* (an assortment of grilled meats) or *Hauspfand'l—*meat, potatoes, and veggies served up in a cast-iron skillet (Mon-Sat 11:45-15:00 & 18:00-22:00, closed Sun, restaurant upstairs at Kiebachgasse 8, tel. 0512/583-057).

$$ Weinhaus Happ offers standards like Wiener schnitzel, but also game, fish, and salads, in a labyrinth of cozy, traditional *Stuben.* You can order smaller, lower-priced portions of most dishes (daily 11:30-22:00, on the left as you face the Golden Roof at Herzog-Friedrich-Strasse 14, tel. 0512/582-980).

$ Mamma Mia, a cheaper escape from traditional fare, dishes up hearty portions of pizza and pasta. They have indoor and outdoor seating, or you can get it to go (daily 10:30-24:00, Kiebachgasse 2, tel. 0512/562-902).

$ Reformstark Martin Vegetarian Deli, hidden inside a health-food store, is where vegetarians can eat in or take away tasty organic meals (weekday lunch specials, Mon-Fri 8:30-18:30, Sat until 17:00, closed Sun, Herzog-Friedrich-Strasse 29, tel. 0512/565-099).

$ Der Bäcker Ruetz, part of a local bakery chain, serves quality sandwiches, pretzels, and pastries right along the main pedestrian drag (daily 7:00-18:30, Herzog-Friedrich-Strasse 36, tel. 0512/587-445).

Gelato: Locals and tourists flock to **Tomasseli,** with branches around town (including old town locations at Hofgasse 5 and Herzog-Friedrich-Strasse 30).

Supermarkets: Right in the train station, **MPreis** is large and has long hours. There's also a small MPreis in the old town and a handy **Spar** by the TI.

Innsbruck Connections

BY PUBLIC TRANSPORTATION

From Innsbruck by Train to: Salzburg (hourly, 2 hours), **Vienna** (at least hourly, 4.5 hours), **Reutte** (every 2 hours, 2.5 hours, change in Garmisch), **Füssen,** Germany (3/day, 4 hours, fastest via train to Reutte and then bus #4258/#74 to Füssen, last easy connection leaves Innsbruck around 14:30), **Munich** (every 2 hours, 2 hours), **Zürich** (every 2 hours, 3.5 hours), **Bolzano,** Italy (hourly, 2.5 hours, some regional connections change in Brennero), **Milan** (every 2 hours, 5.5 hours, change in Verona, seat reservation required), **Venice** (2/day direct, more with changes in Verona, 5 hours). There are also night trains to **Vienna** (it's a short night, though), **Milan,** and **Rome.** Train info: tel. 051-717 (to get an operator, dial 2, then 2), www.oebb.at.

For directions to Hall by bus or train, see "Getting to Hall," later.

ROUTE TIPS FOR DRIVERS

From Innsbruck to Reutte: Head west (direction Bregenz/Switzerland) and leave the freeway at Telfs, where signs direct you to Reutte (a 1.5-hour drive).

From Innsbruck to Switzerland: Head west on the autobahn. (If you're coming directly from Innsbruck's ski jump, go down into town along the huge cemetery and follow blue *A-12/Garmisch/Arlberg* signs). The 8-mile-long Arlberg tunnel saves you 30 minutes on your way to Switzerland, but costs you lots of scenery and €10 (Swiss francs and credit cards accepted). For a joyride and to save a few bucks, skip the tunnel, exit at St. Anton, and go via Stuben.

After the speedy Arlberg tunnel, you're 30 minutes from Switzerland. Bludenz, with its characteristic medieval quarter, makes a good rest stop. Pass Feldkirch (and another long tunnel) and exit the autobahn at Rankweil/Feldkirch Nord, following signs for *Altstätten* and *Meiningen (CH)*. Crossing the baby Rhine River, you've left Austria.

Over Brenner Pass into Italy's Dolomites: A short swing into Italy is fast and easy from Innsbruck (45-minute drive, easy border crossing). To get to Italy, take the A-13/E-45 expressway, which heads across the great Europa Bridge over Brenner Pass. It costs €9.50, but in 30 minutes you'll be at the border. (Note: Traffic can be heavy on summer weekends.)

Once in Italy (which has pay-as-you-go tollbooths—take a ticket and keep it handy), you can drop in at a variety of sights that line up along the expressway: At the colorful market town of Vipiteno/Sterzing, you can see (perched on a little hill just west of the road) the tourable Reifenstein Castle. Just beyond is Brixen (and the nearby Kloster Neustift monastery complex). Finally, about an hour from where you crossed the border, you reach Bolzano (Bozen)—the main city of the Dolomites (for details on each of these places, see the Italian Dolomites chapter).

Near Innsbruck: Hall

Hall—a rich salt-mining and silver-minting center back when Innsbruck was just a humble bridge town on the Inn River—is an easy jaunt from Innsbruck by car, bus, train, or bike. It's worth ▲ and a few hours for its attractive old town and main square.

Founded in 1303, Hall's name is derived from the Celtic word for "salt." Miners leached natural salt deposits out of a mine six miles away, then piped the brine into town to be distilled. (You can still see the yellow former distillery across the street from the TI.) But the salt deposits became exhausted in 1967, and today, Hall is best known as a tidy, upscale town, enjoyable for some boutique shopping and a lazy cobbled stroll. The main square hosts a brisk farmers market on Saturday mornings, but the town closes down tight for its afternoon siesta and sleeps on Sunday.

GETTING TO HALL

Trains and buses make the short run from Innsbruck Hauptbahnhof to Hall frequently. The **train** is a bit more scenic (4/hour, 9 minutes plus 10-minute walk from Hall station into town—head up Bahnhofstrasse and turn right at Pfannhausstrasse). **Bus #504** leaves from platform A and goes through industrial suburbs before dropping you right in Hall's town center (4/hour, 2/hour on Sun, 25 minutes, covered by Innsbruck Card). Don't take bus #D, which is slow and stops on the far side of Hall's old town.

Drivers approaching on the autobahn should take the Hall-Mitte exit; to park, cross the big bridge over the river to find the small P5 lot on the right (3-hour maximum), or continue straight through the intersection and turn left to the underground P2 parking garage. When returning to Innsbruck, take the autobahn to the Innsbruck Ost exit and follow the signs to *Zentrum*, then *Kongresshaus* (see "Arrival in Innsbruck," earlier, for parking tips).

Hall and Innsbruck are connected by a pleasant **bike path** along the Inn River—a comfortable 30-minute pedal will get you there.

Orientation to Hall

Little Hall (pop. 14,000) is compact and easy to explore. You can walk from one end of its old town to the other in about 10 minutes.

Tourist Information: Hall's helpful TI has a good town map (Mon-Fri 9:00-18:00, Sat until 13:00, closed Sun, near bus stop at Unterer Stadtplatz 19, tel. 05223/455-440, www.hall-wattens.at).

Helpful Hints: Consider enjoying the valley on two wheels. The riverside bike path (7 miles from Hall to Volders) is a treat. Rent bikes at **Die Bike-Box** (€14/half-day, €18/day, electric bikes-€22/day, Mon-Fri 9:00-14:00 & 15:00-18:00, Sat until 12:00, closed Sun, Unterer Stadtplatz 10, 05223/55944, www.diebikebox. com).

Sights in Hall

Hall Old Town Walk

Unlike Innsbruck, Hall was not damaged or destroyed by WWII bombs—leaving it perfectly preserved. You can see sights in the old town in about 30 leisurely minutes— or allow more time to linger inside the church or visit the Mint Museum.

Begin at the base of Langer Graben, along the ring road at the south end of town, near the bus stop from Innsbruck. A few steps up from the ring road—surrounded by cobbles and tight lanes—enter a tiny square with a **fountain** honoring Archduke Sigmund of Habsburg (1427-1496), the local ruler who helped reform the currency system and founded the town's silver mine.

Head gradually uphill toward the main square along **Langer Graben,** for centuries the market town's primary shopping street. Signs over the doors identify each business: bookstore, dish seller, and so on. As you stroll, tune into all the little details. For example, at the Riepenhausen bookstore (at #1), notice the whimsical figures flanking the door: Little Red Riding Hood on the left, and the Big Bad Wolf on the right.

Emerge into the **Main Square** (Oberer Stadtplatz). Just behind the fountain is the recommended bakery Der Bäcker Ruetz. To the left, the big white building with red-and-white shutters is the **Town Hall** (Rathaus). The engraved plaques on the upper floor of the Rathaus Café show symbols of Austria and the Habsburgs (on the left, red and white stripes and a proud peacock) and local symbols of Tirol (on the right, eagle feathers and a shield with a red eagle). Wealthy as Hall became, the town still answered to the Habsburgs—to whom they sent every tenth barrel of salt. In the niche over the café's door is a statue that once stood on a pillar on the main square, representing Hall's status as a "city"—with privileges to host a market, build bridges, and levy tolls. On the left, over the gate into the Town Hall courtyard, is a mosaic shield celebrating *Der Stadt Hall:* two lions protecting a salt barrel. (Locals are nicknamed *Salzkufen*—"salt barrels.")

Walk just past the Town Hall, hook left, and head into the side door of **St. Nicholas Parish Church** (Pfarrkirche St. Nikolaus). This much-appended Gothic church is decorated Baroque. It's dedicated to the patron saint of sailors—in honor of the riverboat crews that kept trade flowing along the Inn River. Immediately to the left as you enter the church is a gated chapel crammed with relics. The knight Florian Waldauf—a friend of Innsbruck's Maximilian I—built this chapel in 1501 to thank God after the two of them survived a harrowing storm at sea, and filled it with more than 2,000 relics (see the gilded cases on the left wall). During Hall's big semiannual markets, visitors could touch these relics to heal their ailments. Gradually Hall's market evolved from a pilgrimage for shoppers into a literal pilgrimage. Before you leave the church, stand in the middle of the nave and note the offset altar. Centuries of additions have left the church crooked as it expanded uphill.

Exiting the church through the same side door, notice the **old tombs** under the canopy (ahead and to the right). These were relocated here after the unsanitary practice of burying the dead in the city center was banned. The second tomb down, dating from 1502, shows a grotesquely realistic, half-decomposed body. This is a classic example of *memento mori:* Essentially, don't get too cocky in life, because eventually we all wind up as worm food.

To visit a sight many tourists miss, hook right around the back end of the church (with the old tombs on your left). You'll pass a covered staircase (which leads back down to the main shopping street), and then—on your left—a boxy little stone chapel with pointed Gothic windows. Even if the door is closed, let yourself in to **St. Magdalen's Chapel** (St. Magdalenenkapelle). The deceased were brought here to be mourned, in a holy place near the church, after the cemetery was closed. The chapel is richly decorated by Hall's wealthy residents, who were eager to facilitate their passage to heaven. The centerpiece is a wood-carved altar from a small church in the Halltal—where simple miners lived and worked—dedicated to St. Barbara, the patron saint of miners. The wall behind the altar commemorates locals who died fighting in World Wars I and II. On the right wall is a gorgeously restored 15th-century *Last Judgment* fresco.

Our walk is done. You can use the covered staircase you just passed to return to the main shopping street.

Hall Mint Museum and Mint Tower (Münze Hall und Münzerturm)

Hall began minting coins in the 15th century, and along with its lucrative salt-mining industry, minting became a hallmark of Hall.

The centerpiece of the museum is a functioning replica of a 16th-century minting press—powered by water and made of wood.

The 150-foot-tall, 14th-century Mint Tower—both a fire watchtower and a castle fortification—is a town landmark. For great views from its top, climb 185 steps... or 202 steps, if you go medieval and take the narrow original stairs.

Cost and Hours: Museum—€8, includes excellent audioguide, tower—€5.50, €11.50 combo-ticket for both; Tue-Sun 10:00-17:00, closed Mon; closed Sun-Mon off-season, closed mid-Jan-March; in Hasegg Castle, between the old town and the TI; www.muenze-hall.at.

Sleeping and Eating in Hall

$$ Gasthof Badl is a big, comfortable, friendly riverside place with 26 rooms run by Sonja and her family, with help from Ella, their enormous, easygoing dog. It's my sentimental favorite for its convenience (right off the Hall-Mitte freeway exit, but a short and scenic walk from Hall's old town), peaceful setting, big breakfast, and warm welcome (family rooms, elevator, laundry service, Innbrücke 4, tel. 05223/56784, www.badl.at, info@badl.at). Their **$$ restaurant** serves excellent dinners in a cozy, friendly, pub-like dining room (closed Sun, limited hours in winter).

In town, **$ Der Bäcker Ruetz** has good, filling sandwiches—along with pretzels, rolls, and pastries (daily, Sparkassengasse 1).

BAVARIAN ALPS

In this picturesque corner of the Alps, you'll find a timeless land of fairy-tale castles, painted buildings shared by cows and farmers, and locals who still dress in dirndls and lederhosen and yodel when they're happy.

This area (1.5 hours northwest of Innsbruck) straddles the border between Bavaria (part of Germany) and Tirol (part of Austria). On the German side, you can tour "Mad" King Ludwig II's ornate Neuschwanstein Castle, Europe's most spectacular. Stop by the Wieskirche, a lavishly decorated Baroque church, and browse through Oberammergau, Germany's woodcarving  capital and home of the famous Passion Play (next performed in 2020). A smaller yet still-impressive Ludwig castle (Linderhof), an important monastery (Ettal), and the highest point in Germany (Zugspitze) round out southern Bavaria's top attractions.

Just over the border in Austria, you can explore the ruined Ehrenberg Castle and scream down a mountain at one of the area's many luge runs. In this chapter, I'll first cover the German side (with the most sights), then the Austrian side around Reutte.

CHOOSING A HOME BASE

My hotel recommendations in this chapter cluster in three areas: Füssen and Oberammergau (in Germany), and Reutte (in Austria). When selecting a home base, consider these factors:

Füssen offers the easiest access to the region's biggest attraction—the "King's Castles" (Neuschwanstein and Hohen-schwangau)—and is the handiest base for train travelers. The town itself is a mix of real-world and cutesy-cobbled, and has some of the glitziest hotels in the area (as well as more affordable options).

Oberammergau is the best-known, most touristy, and cutest town of the bunch. World-famous for its once-per-decade Passion Play, it's much sleepier the other nine years. It's a long bus ride or a 45-minute drive from Oberammergau to the King's Castles. Three lesser yet worthwhile sights are close by: Ettal Monastery, Linderhof Castle, and the German lift to the Zugspitze.

Reutte is the least appealing town and is less practical for train travelers, but the villages around it are home to some of the region's coziest, most pleasant rural accommodations—making it a particularly good option for drivers. Reutte butts up against the ruined Ehrenberg Castle. The King's Castles, Linderhof, and the Austrian approach to the Zugspitze are all within a 30-minute drive.

For specifics on public transit logistics from each town, see "By Public Transportation," later.

PLANNING YOUR TIME AND GETTING AROUND THE BAVARIAN ALPS

While Germans and Austrians vacation here for a week at a time, the typical speedy American traveler will find two days' worth of sightseeing. With a car and more time, you could enjoy three or four days, but a three-night, two-day stay is sufficient. If the weather's good, be sure to ride a lift to an alpine peak.

By Car

This region is best by car, and all the sights are within an easy 60-mile loop from Füssen or Reutte. Even if you're doing the rest of your trip by train, consider renting a car for your time here (for local rental offices, see page 411).

Here's a good plan for a one-day circular drive from **Reutte** (from **Füssen,** you can start about 30 minutes later):

7:00	Breakfast
7:30	Depart hotel
8:00	Arrive at the King's Castles to pick up tickets for the two castles (Neuschwanstein and Hohenschwangau)
9:30	Tour Hohenschwangau
11:30	Tour Neuschwanstein
13:30	Drive to Oberammergau (with a 15-minute stop at the Wieskirche), and spend an hour there browsing the carving shops and grabbing a quick lunch
15:30	Drive to Ettal Monastery for a half-hour stop
16:30	Tour Linderhof Castle
18:30	Drive along the scenic Plansee lake

19:30   Back at hotel
20:00   Dinner

Off-season (mid-Oct–March), start your day an hour later, since Neuschwanstein and Hohenschwangau tours don't depart until 10:00; and skip Linderhof, which closes at 16:30.

The next morning, you could stroll through Reutte, hike to the Ehrenberg ruins and the pedestrian bridge, and ride a mountain luge on your way to your next destination.

If you're based in **Oberammergau** instead, get an early start and hit Neuschwanstein and Hohenschwangau first. If the weather's good, hike to the top of Ehrenberg Castle (in Reutte). Drive along the Plansee and tour Linderhof and Ettal Monastery on your way back home.

By Public Transportation

Where you stay determines which sights you can see most easily. Train travelers use **Füssen** as a base and bus or bike the three miles to the King's Castles and the Tegelberg luge or cable car. Staying in **Oberammergau** gives you easy access to Linderhof and Ettal Monastery, and you can day-trip to the top of the Zugspitze via Garmisch. **Reutte** is the least convenient base if you're carless, but travelers staying there can easily bike or hike to the Ehrenberg ruins and can reach Neuschwanstein by bus (via Füssen) or bike (1.5 hours); if you stay at the recommended Gutshof zum Schluxen hotel (between Reutte and Füssen, in Pinswang, Austria) it's an easy 1.5-hour hike through the woods to Neuschwanstein—a fun opportunity to cross the border on foot.

Visiting sights farther from your home base by local bus requires planning. The Deutsche Bahn (German Railway) website (www.bahn.com) and DB Navigator app are helpful tools when planning your journey, on both sides of the border. (Schedules are also available in German at www.rvo-bus.de.) Those staying in **Füssen** can day-trip by bus to Reutte and the Ehrenberg ruins (but you'll have to taxi back to the train station to catch the bus back to Füssen), to the Wieskirche, or, with some planning, to Oberammergau. From **Oberammergau,** you can reach Neuschwanstein and Füssen by bus if you plan ahead. From **Reutte,** you can take the train to Ehrwald to reach the Zugspitze from the Austrian side, but side trips to Oberammergau and Linderhof are impractical.

If you'll be taking a lot of trains in Bavaria (for example, day-tripping to Munich), consider the **Regional Day Ticket for Bavaria,** also known as a Bayern-Ticket: It covers buses and slower regional trains throughout Bavaria for up to five people at a very low price (€25/day for the first person plus €6 for each additional person).

BAVARIAN ALPS

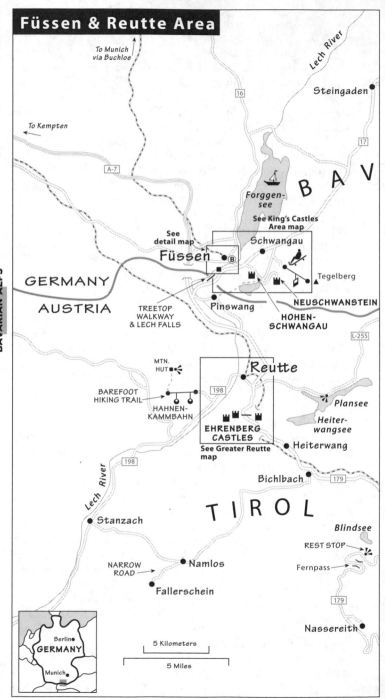

Füssen & Reutte Area

To Munich via Buchloe

Lech River

Steingaden

16

17

To Kempten

A-7

Forggen-see

B A V

See King's Castles Area map

See detail map

Füssen   B

Schwangau

Tegelberg

GERMANY

AUSTRIA

Pinswang

TREETOP WALKWAY & LECH FALLS

NEUSCHWANSTEIN

HOHEN-SCHWANGAU

L-255

MTN. HUT

Reutte

BAREFOOT HIKING TRAIL

198

Plansee

HAHNEN-KAMMBAHN

EHRENBERG CASTLES

Heiter-wangsee

See Greater Reutte map

Heiterwang

Bichlbach

179

198

Lech River

T I R O L

Stanzach

Blindsee

REST STOP

NARROW ROAD

Namlos

Fernpass

Fallerschein

179

Nassereith

GERMANY

Berlin

Munich

5 Kilometers

5 Miles

By Bike

This is great biking country. Some hotels loan bikes to guests, and shops in Reutte and Füssen rent bikes for €10-15 per day. The ride from Füssen or Reutte to Neuschwanstein and the Tegelberg luge (1.5 hours) is a breeze. Simply joyriding in the meadows that stretch out from Neuschwanstein is unforgettable. For a bit more adventure, consider a ride around the Forggensee (about 3 hours; see "Activities near Füssen," later) or the Hopfensee (1-2 hours). The Füssen TI has a map with a multitude of biking tours.

By Tour

Without a car, **House LA**'s full-day tour of Neuschwanstein, Hohenschwangau, Linderhof, and Oberammergau from Füssen can be a time-efficient option (€90/person—price includes Neuschwanstein and Linderhof admission but not Hohenschwangau, mobile 0170-624-8610, www.fussen-info.com). They also offer private, half-day, and bike tours; book at least two days in advance; tours depart from House LA at 9:00—see listing in "Sleeping in Füssen," later.

HELPFUL HINTS

Welcome to Germany: Most of the destinations in this chapter (except for the Reutte area and the Austrian side of the Zugspitze) are in a different country. If calling from an Austrian phone number to a German one, dial 00-49 and then the number (omitting the initial zero). To call from a German phone to an Austrian one, dial 00-43 and then the number (again, omitting the initial zero); see page 564 for dialing instructions.

Sightseeing Pass: The Bavarian Palace Department offers a 14-day ticket (called *Mehrtagesticket*) that covers admission to Neuschwanstein (but not Hohenschwangau) and Linderhof, as well as many other castles not described in this book (including ones in Munich, Nürnberg, and Würzburg). If your travels will take you deeper into Germany, this might be worth considering (one-person pass—€24, family/partner version for up to two adults plus children—€44, www.schloesser.bayern.de).

Visiting Churches: To immerse yourself in traditional southern German culture, consider attending a church service. Road signs for *Heilige Messe* (holy Mass) often indicate the day and time for Mass; otherwise look for a schedule posted at the church. Services are usually on Saturday *(Sa.)* evening or Sunday *(So.)* morning.

Füssen, Germany

Dramatically situated under a renovated castle on the lively Lech River, Füssen (FEW-sehn) has been a strategic stop since ancient times. Its main street was once part of the Via Claudia Augusta, the Roman road across the Alps. Going north, early travelers could follow the Lech River downstream to the Danube and then cross over to the Main and Rhine valleys—a route now known to modern travelers as the "Romantic Road." Today, while Füssen is overrun by tourists in the summer, few venture to the back streets...which is where you'll find the real charm. Apart from my self-guided walk and the Füssen Heritage Museum, there's little to do here—but it's a fine base for visiting the King's Castles and other surrounding attractions.

Orientation to Füssen

Füssen's roughly circular old town huddles around its castle and monastery, along the Lech River. The train station, TI, and many shops are at the north end of town, and my recommended hotels and eateries are within easy walking distance. Roads spin off in all directions (to Neuschwanstein, to Austria, and to numerous lakes). Halfway between Füssen and the German border (as you drive, or a nice woodsy walk from town) is Lech Falls, a thunderous waterfall (with a handy WC).

TOURIST INFORMATION

The TI is in the center of town (July-mid-Sept Mon-Fri 9:00-18:00, Sat 9:30-13:30, Sun until 12:30; off-season Mon-Fri 9:00-17:00, Sat 9:30-13:30, closed Sun; 3 blocks from station at Kaiser-Maximilian-Platz 1, tel. 08362/93850, www.fuessen.de).

BAVARIAN ALPS

BAVARIAN ALPS

Bavarian Craftsmanship

The scenes you'll see painted on the sides of houses in Bavaria are called *Lüftlmalerei.* The term came from the name of the house ("Zum Lüftl") owned by a man from Oberammergau who pioneered the practice in the 18th century. As the paintings became popular during the Counter-Reformation Baroque age, themes tended to involve Christian symbols, saints, and stories (such as scenes from the life of Jesus),

to reinforce the Catholic Church's authority in the region. Some scenes also depicted an important historical event that took place in that house or town.

Especially in the northern part of this region (for example,

in Rothenburg), you'll see *Fach-werkhäuser*—half-timbered houses. A timber frame outlines the wall, which was traditionally filled in with a mixture of wicker and clay. These are most often found inside fortified cities that were once

strong and semi-independent (such as Rothenberg, Nürnberg, and Dinkelsbühl). Farther south, you'll see sturdy, white-walled masonry houses with woodwork on the upper stories and an overhanging roof. The interiors of many Bavarian homes and hotels have elaborate wooden paneling and furniture, often beautifully carved or made from special sweet-smelling wood.

ARRIVAL IN FÜSSEN

By Train: The train station is three blocks from the center of town and the TI. Buses to Neuschwanstein, Reutte, and elsewhere leave from a parking lot next to the station.

By Car: Füssen is known for its traffic jams, and you can't drive into the old town. The most convenient lots (follow signs) are the underground P-5 (near the TI, €13/day) and the aboveground P-3 (off Kemptener Strasse, €12/day).

HELPFUL HINTS

Hotel Card: Be sure to ask your hotel for a **Füssen Card,** which gives you free use of public transit in the immediate region (including the bus to Neuschwanstein and Wieskirche), as well as €1-2 discounts at many attractions: Neuschwanstein, Hohenschwangau, Museum of the Bavarian Kings, Forggensee boat trip, Füssen Heritage Museum, Tegelberg cable car, Royal Crystal Baths, and Hahnenkammbahn cable car near Reutte. Some accommodations won't tell you about the card unless you request it. You may be asked for a €3-5 deposit; be sure to return the card before you leave town. After the hotel activates the card, it can take an hour or two before it works at sights and on buses.

Wi-Fi: Füssen Card holders can access free Wi-Fi hotspots at the TI, Markthalle, and other places in town; look for orange Wi-Fi signs and enter the number on your card to log on.

Convenience Store: For a catchall convenience and drugstore, **Müller** is on the west side of the old town (Mon-Fri 8:30-19:00, Sat until 18:00, closed Sun, Kemptener Strasse 1).

Bike Rental: Ski Sport Luggi outfits sightseers with good bikes and tips on two-wheeled fun in the area (prices per 24 hours: €10—city bike, €15—mountain bike, €25—electric bike; Mon-Fri 9:00-12:00 & 14:00-18:00, Sat until 13:00, Sun until 12:00 or by reservation; shorter hours off-season, call ahead to reserve, ID required, Luitpoldstrasse 11, tel. 08362/505-9155, mobile 0151-2700-0930, www.ski-sport-luggi.de). For a strenuous but enjoyable 20-mile loop trip, see "Activities near Füssen," later.

Taxi: Call 08362/6222 for taxi service to Neuschwanstein Castle (€11), Tegelberg cable car (€14), and other places.

Car Rental: Hertz Rental Car is an easy taxi ride from the center. Andreas speaks English well and Valbona does her best with help from the Google Translate app (Mon-Fri 8:00-12:00 & 14:00-18:00, Sat 8:00-12:00, Sun and holidays by appointment, Füssener Strasse 112, tel. 08362/986-580, www.hertz.de).

Local Guide: Silvia Skelac, an American born to German parents, moved to Europe two decades ago. She is available as a guide—for private tours, hard-to-reach sights, mountain hikes, and alpine herb walks—and as a ski instructor (€80/half-day, €160/full day, up to 4 people, includes transportation in Silvia's SUV, Austrian mobile 0664-978-7488, info@crossroads-services.com).

BAVARIAN ALPS

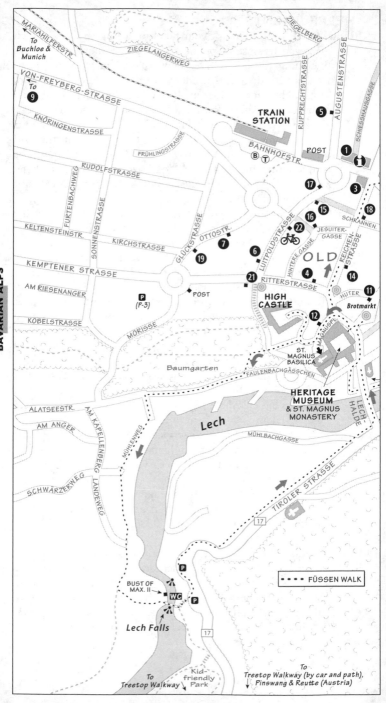

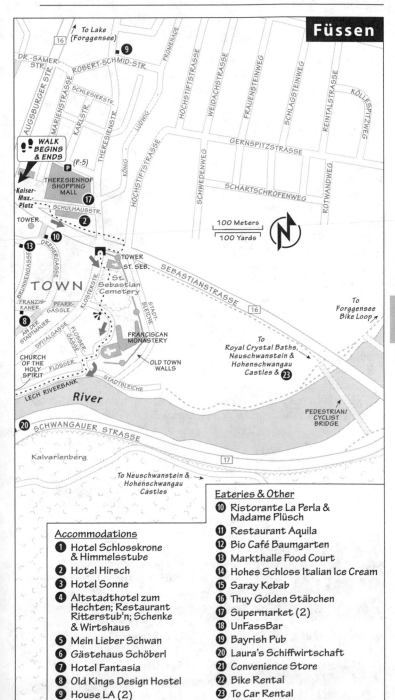

BAVARIAN ALPS

Füssen

WALK BEGINS & ENDS

100 Meters
100 Yards

Accommodations

❶ Hotel Schlosskrone & Himmelsstube
❷ Hotel Hirsch
❸ Hotel Sonne
❹ Altstadthotel zum Hechten; Restaurant Ritterstub'n; Schenke & Wirtshaus
❺ Mein Lieber Schwan
❻ Gästehaus Schöberl
❼ Hotel Fantasia
❽ Old Kings Design Hostel
❾ House LA (2)

Eateries & Other

❿ Ristorante La Perla & Madame Plüsch
⓫ Restaurant Aquila
⓬ Bio Café Baumgarten
⓭ Markthalle Food Court
⓮ Hohes Schloss Italian Ice Cream
⓯ Saray Kebab
⓰ Thuy Golden Stäbchen
⓱ Supermarket (2)
⓲ UnFassBar
⓳ Bayrish Pub
⓴ Laura's Schiffwirtschaft
㉑ Convenience Store
㉒ Bike Rental
㉓ To Car Rental

Füssen Walk

For most, Füssen is just a home base for visiting Ludwig's famous castles. But the town has a rich history and hides some evocative corners, as you'll see when you follow this self-guided orientation walk. This 45-minute stroll is designed to get you out of the cutesy old cobbled core where most tourists spend their time. Throughout the town, "City Tour" information plaques explain points of interest in English (in more detail than I've provided).

• *Begin at the square in front of the TI, three blocks from the train station.*

Kaiser-Maximilian-Platz: The entertaining "Seven Stones" fountain on this square, by sculptor Christian Tobin, was built in 1995 to celebrate Füssen's 700th birthday. The stones symbolize community, groups of people gathering, conviviality... each is different, with "heads" nodding and talking. It's granite on granite. The moving heads are not connected and nod only with waterpower. It's frozen in winter but is a popular and splashy play zone for kids on hot summer days.

• *Walk along the pedestrian street toward the glass building. To your right, you'll soon see...*

Hotel Hirsch and Medieval Towers: Recent renovations have restored some of the original Art Nouveau flavor to Hotel Hirsch,

which opened in 1904. In those days, aristocratic tourists came here to appreciate the castles and natural wonders of the Alps. Across the busy street stands one of two surviving towers from Füssen's medieval town wall (c. 1502), and next to it is a passageway into the old town.

• *Walk along the busy street and cross at the second light to another tower. Head to the information plaque and archway where a small street called Klosterstrasse emerges through a surviving piece of the old town wall. Step through the smaller pedestrian archway, walk along Klosterstrasse for a few yards, and turn left through the gate into the...*

Historic Cemetery of St. Sebastian (Alter Friedhof): This peaceful oasis of Füssen history, established in the 16th century, fills a corner between the town wall and the Franciscan monastery.

It's technically full, and only members of great and venerable Füssen families (who already own plots here) can join those who are buried (free, daily 8:00-19:00, off-season until 17:00).

Immediately inside the gate and on the right is the tomb of Domenico Quaglio, who, in 1835, painted the Romantic scenes decorating the walls of Hohenschwangau Castle. Across the cemetery, on the old city wall (beyond the church), is the World War I memorial, listing all the names of men from this small town killed in that devastating conflict (along with each one's rank and place of death). A bit to the right, also along the old wall, is a statue of the hand of God holding a fetus—a place to remember babies who died before being born. And in the corner, farther to the right, is a gated area with the simple wooden crosses of Franciscans who lived just over the wall in the monastery. Strolling the rest of the grounds, note the fine tomb art from many ages collected here, and the loving care this community gives its cemetery.

• *Exit on the far side, just past the dead Franciscans. Turn left just outside the gate and walk toward the picket fence across the street.*

Town View from Franciscan Monastery (Franziskanerkloster): Enjoy a fine view over the medieval town with an alpine backdrop. In the distance, you'll see the dome and clock tower of the Church of St. Magnus and the aptly named High Castle (the former summer residence of the Bishops of Augsburg), where this walk ends. The tall, skinny smokestack (c. 1886) is a reminder that when Ludwig built Neuschwanstein the textile industry (linen and flax) was very big here. Retrace your steps and follow the wall of the Franciscan Monastery, which still has big responsibilities but only a handful of monks in residence.

• *Go around the corner and down the stairway. At the bottom, turn left through the medieval "Bleachers' Gate" (marked 5½, under the mural of St. George slaying the dragon) to the...*

Lech Riverbank: This low end of town, the flood zone, was the home of those whose work depended on the river—bleachers, rafters, and fishermen. In its heyday, the Lech River was an expressway to Augsburg (about 70 miles to the north). Around the year 1500, the rafters established the first professional guild in Füssen. Cargo from Italy passed here en route to big German cities farther north. Rafters would assemble rafts and pile them high with wine, olive oil, and other goods—or with people needing a lift. If the water was high, they could float all the way to Augsburg in as little as one day. There they'd disassemble their raft and sell off the lumber along with the goods they'd carried, then make their way home to raft again. Today you'll see no modern-day rafters here, as there's a hydroelectric plant just downstream.

• *Walk upstream a bit, appreciating the river's milky color (from mountain rocks, pulverized to a sediment over the long journey from the Alps), and turn right to head inland immediately after crossing under the bridge.*

Church of the Holy Spirit, Bread Market, and Lutemakers: Climbing uphill, you pass the colorful Church of the Holy Spirit (Heilig-Geist-Spitalkirche) on the right. As this was the church of the rafters, their patron, St. Christopher (with the Baby Jesus on his shoulder), is prominent on the facade. Today it's the church of Füssen's old folks' home (it's adjacent—notice the easy-access skyway). Step inside to take in the details packed into this tiny space, from the carved sides of the pews to the trompe l'oeil dome ceiling. Notice also the painting of a raft disaster on the Lech River—once a common fate of those in the dangerous rafting trade.

Farther up the hill on the right is Bread Market Square (Brotmarkt), with a fountain honoring a famous 16th-century lutemaking family, the Tieffenbruckers. In its day, Füssen (surrounded by forests) was a huge center of violin- and lutemaking, with about 200 workshops. Today only three survive.

• *Backtrack and go through the archway into the courtyard of the former...*

St. Magnus Monastery (Kloster St. Mang): From 1717 until secularization in 1802, this Benedictine monastery was the power center of town. Today the courtyard is popular for concerts, and the building houses the City Hall and the Füssen Heritage Museum.

Füssen Heritage Museum: This is Füssen's one must-see sight, spanning a thousand years of the town's history, with industrial artifacts, medieval cloisters, and Baroque halls (€6, €7 combo-ticket includes High Castle painting gallery and tower; Tue-Sun 11:00-17:00, closed Mon; shorter hours and closed Mon-Thu Nov-March; tel. 08362/903-146, www.museum.fuessen.de).

Pick up the loaner English translations and follow the signs to the St. Anna Chapel, with its famous *Dance of Death.* This was painted shortly after a plague devastated the community in 1590. It shows 20 social classes, each dancing with the Grim Reaper—starting with the pope and the emperor. The words above say, essentially, "You can say yes or you can say no, but you must ultimately dance with death." Leaving the chapel, you walk over the metal lid of the crypt. Upstairs, exhibits illustrate Füssen's important trades: ropemaking, rafting, and violin- and lutemaking (with a complete workshop)—but the building itself outshines these creaky displays. Among the exquisitely decorated Baroque rooms are an ornate imperial ballroom and a two-tiered oval library displaying cupid statues and frescoes dating from 1719, with an opening to the refectory below.

• *Leaving the courtyard, hook left around the old monastery and go slightly uphill to the square tower. This marks...*

St. Magnus Basilica (Basilika St. Mang): St. Mang (or Magnus) is Füssen's favorite saint. In the eighth century, he worked miracles all over the area with his holy rod. For centuries, pilgrims came to this medieval basilica from far and wide to enjoy art depicting the great works of St. Magnus. Then, in the 18th century, the basilica got a Baroque facelift. Above the altar dangles a glass cross containing the saint's relics (including that holy stick). At the rear of the church is a chapel bright with primary colors that honors a much more modern saint—Franz Seelos (1819-1867), the local boy who went to America (Pittsburgh and New Orleans) and lived such a righteous life that in 2000 he was beatified by Pope John Paul II.

• *From the church, find the grassy knolls and the trail ahead of you, and walk uphill toward the castle entrance.*

High Castle (Hohes Schloss): This castle, long the summer residence of the Bishop of Augsburg, houses a painting gallery (the

upper floor is labeled in English) and a tower with a view over the town and lake (€6, €7 combo-ticket includes Füssen Heritage Museum, same hours as museum). The courtyard (with handy WCs under the sundial, just before the tower climb) is worth even a few minutes to admire the striking perspective tricks painted onto its flat walls.

• *Exit the castle wall, and follow the call of the Lech River through the ivy-covered archway to the right. It's a 15-minute walk from here to the falls.*

Baumgarten and Lech Falls: As you explore the castle garden, notice the impressive walls that kept the High Castle safe from pesky invaders. Wander toward the Lech River and follow the signs (away from town and into a quaint neighborhood) that point you toward Lech Falls—it's just beyond the tall, skinny smokestack you saw earlier.

Cross the bridge to enjoy a bit of impressive natural beauty

BAVARIAN ALPS

tucked away just outside town. Some say that the name "Füssen" is derived from the Latin word for gorge. Royals and tourists alike have enjoyed this gorge for centuries. Imagine "Mad" King Ludwig coming here with his family to enjoy a special tea arranged on top of the gorge. High above looms a bust of his father (Maximilian II); down below, the interesting rock formations bulge and twist above the roaring water.

• *The Treetop Walkway (described later) is just a 10-minute walk ahead on Tiroler Strasse. Otherwise, from here you can walk downhill to return to town, enjoying a backside view of St. Magnus Monastery where it borders the Lech River. Take a left at the bridge and head back uphill to find the city's main drag (once the Roman Via Claudia and now Reichenstrasse), which leads from a grand statue of St. Magnus past lots of shops, cafés, and strolling people to Kaiser-Maximilian-Platz and the TI...where you began.*

Activities near Füssen

The following sights lie within a few miles of Füssen. All can be reached by car, bike, or foot. See the "King's Castles Area" map, later in this chapter, for locations.

▲Royal Crystal Baths (Königliche Kristall-Therme)

This pool/sauna complex just outside Füssen is the perfect way to relax on a rainy day or to cool off on a hot one. The main part of the complex (downstairs), called the *Therme*, contains two heated indoor pools and a café; outside you'll find a shallow kiddie pool, a lap pool, a heated *Kristallbad* with massage jets and a whirlpool, and a salty mineral bath. The extensive saunas upstairs are well worth the few extra euros, if you're OK with nudity. (Swimsuits are required in the downstairs pools but *verboten* in the upstairs saunas.) Pool and sauna rules are posted in German, but don't worry—just follow the locals' lead.

To enter the baths, first choose the length of your visit and your focus (big outdoor pool only, all ground-floor pools but not the saunas, or the whole enchilada—a flier explains all the prices in English). You'll get a wristband and a credit card-sized ticket with a bar code. Insert that ticket into the entry gate, note your entry time, and keep your ticket—you'll need it to get out. Enter through the changing stalls—where you'll change into your bathing suit (use the clever lever at knee level to lock the door). Then choose a storage locker (€1 coin deposit). When it's time to leave, reinsert your ticket in the gate—if you've gone over the time limit, feed extra euros into the machine.

Cost and Hours: Baths only—€14.50/2 hours, €19/4 hours, €24/all day; saunas—about €6 extra, towel rental—€3, bathrobe rental—€5, bathing suits sold but not rented; daily 9:00-22:00, Fri-Sat until 23:00; nude swimming everywhere Tue and Fri after 19:00; tel. 08362/819-630, www.kristalltherme-schwangau.de.

Getting There: From Füssen, drive, take the bus (#73 or #78, ask driver for best stop), bike, or walk (30 minutes) across the river, turn left toward Schwangau, and then, about a mile later, turn left at signs for *Kristall-Therme*. It's at Am Ehberg 16. If biking from Füssen, it's easy to see the castle, enjoy the spa, and then roll back into town (about an hour of pedaling altogether).

Bike or Boat Around the Forggensee

On a beautiful day, nothing beats a **bike ride** around the bright-turquoise Forggensee, a nearby lake. This 20-mile loop is exclusively on bike paths (give it a half-day; it's tight to squeeze it into the afternoon after a morning of castle visits, but possible with an early start). Locals swear that going clockwise is less work, but either way has a couple of strenuous uphill parts (total elevation gain of about 600 feet). Still, the amazing views of the surrounding Alps will distract you from your churning legs—so this is still a great way to spend the afternoon. Rent a bike (ideally a 21-speed), pack a picnic lunch, and figure about a three-hour round-trip. From Füssen, follow *Festspielhaus* signs; once you reach the theater, follow *Forggensee Rundweg* signs.

You can also take a **boat ride** on the Forggensee, leaving either from the Füssen "harbor" *(Bootshafen)* or the theater *(Festspielhaus),* a 20- to 30-minute walk north of town (€9/50-minute cruise, 5/day; €13/2-hour cruise, 3/day; runs daily June-mid-Oct, no boats off-season, tel. 08362/921-363, www.stadt-fuessen.de). Unless it's very crowded in the summer, you can bring your bike onto the boat and get off across the lake—shortening the total loop.

Treetop Walkway (Baumkronenweg Ziegelwies)

This elevated wooden "treetop path" lets you stroll for a third of a mile, high in the trees on a graceful yet sturdy suspension-bridge-like structure 60 feet in the air. The walkway crosses the Austria-Germany border and offers views of the surrounding mountains and the "wild" alpine Lech River, which can be a smooth glacier-blue mirror one day and a muddy torrent the next.  Located east of Füssen, just past Lech Falls on the road to Reutte, the walkway can be accessed at either end. The Austrian end (closer to Reutte) has a large parking lot and a tiny ticket booth. At the

German end (closer to Füssen) there is a nature center and café, and parking is scarce. Stairs (kids can take the slide) lead down to a riverside trail that loops about a mile through a kid-friendly park, with a log raft to cross a little creek, a wonky little bridge, and a sandy stream great for wading. Those with more energy to burn can try the slightly longer mountain loop, accessed by a tunnel under the road.

Cost and Hours: €5, free for kids 15 and under, daily 10:00-17:00, April and Nov until 16:00, closed Dec-March and in bad weather, Tiroler Strasse 10, tel. 08362/938-7550, www. baumkronenweg.eu.

Sleeping in Füssen

Convenient Füssen is just three miles from Ludwig's castles and offers a cobbled, riverside retreat. My recommended accommodations are within a few handy blocks of the train station and the town center. Parking is easy, and some hotels also have their own lot or garage. Many hotels give a 5-10 percent discount for two-night stays—always ask—and prices drop by 10-20 percent off-season. Competition is fierce, so shop around. Remember to ask your hotelier for a Füssen Card (see page 411).

To call Füssen from Austria, dial 00-49 and then the number (minus the initial zero).

BIG, FANCY HOTELS IN THE CENTER OF TOWN

$$$ Hotel Schlosskrone is formal, with 62 rooms in two wings and all the amenities you need to pamper yourself after a long castle visit. It also runs two restaurants and a fine pastry shop (some rooms with balconies, family rooms, air-con, elevator, free sauna and fitness center, spa, playroom, pay parking, Prinzregentenplatz 2, tel. 08362/930-180, www.schlosskrone.de, rezeption@schlosskrone. de, Norbert Schöll and family).

$$$ Hotel Hirsch is a well-maintained, family-run, 71-room, old-style hotel that takes pride in tradition. Most of their standard rooms are cozy with modern bathrooms, and their rooms with historical and landscape themes are a fun splurge (family rooms, elevator, nice rooftop terrace, free parking, Kaiser-Maximilian-Platz 7, tel. 08362/93980, www.hotelfuessen.de, info@hotelhirsch.de, sibling-owners Harold and Eva).

$$$ Hotel Sonne takes pride in its decorating (some would say overdecorating). From eclectic to classic, its 50 rooms are a convenient home base for a night or two (some rooms with balconies, family rooms, air-con in some rooms, elevator, free laundry machine, free sauna and fitness center, pay parking, kitty-corner from TI at Prinzregentenplatz 1, on GPS you may need to enter

Reichenstrasse 37, tel. 08362/9080, www.hotel-sonne.de, info@
hotel-sonne.de).

SMALLER, MIDPRICED HOTELS AND PENSIONS

$$ Altstadthotel zum Hechten offers 35 rooms (some with balco-
nies) in a friendly, family-run hotel with bright, comfortable rooms
and a borderline-kitschy breakfast room. It's a good value, with
a few fun extras including a travel-resource/game room, borrow-
able hiking gear, and a recommended restaurant (two buildings,
family rooms, elevator, pay parking, situated right under Füssen
Castle in the old-town pedestrian zone at Ritterstrasse 6, on GPS
you may need to enter Hinteregasse 2, tel. 08362/91600, www.
hotel-hechten.com, info@hotel-hechten.com, Pfeiffer and Tramp
families).

$$ Mein Lieber Schwan, a block from the train station, is run
by Herr Bletschacher, a hometown boy who's proud of his accom-
modations' personality and charm. He offers four superbly outfitted
apartments, each with a double bed, sofa bed, kitchen, and antique
furnishings (cash or PayPal only, no breakfast, free parking, laundry facilities, garden, Augustenstrasse 3, tel. 08362/509-980, www.
meinlieberschwan.de, fewo@meinlieberschwan.de). Herr Bletschacher also has two slightly larger apartments at Klosterstrasse 10.

$ Gästehaus Schöberl, run by Pia and her husband Georg
(who co-manages Altstadthotel zum Hechten), makes you feel like
you're staying with friends. Its six bright and spacious rooms are
a great value and set on a quiet street just off the main drag. One
room is in the owners' house, and the rest are in the building next
door (cash only, family room, free parking, closed in Nov, Luitpoldstrasse 14—check-in at #16 around back, tel. 08362/922-411,
www.schoeberl-fuessen.de, info@schoeberl-fuessen.de).

$ Hotel Fantasia, the little sister of Hotel Sonne, has 16 trendy
rooms adorned with violet paint and lots of pictures of King Ludwig that might make the nuns who once lived here blush. The price
is right, but the reception is often unmanned (breakfast extra, family rooms, pay parking, peaceful garden, trampoline, Ottostrasse 1,
tel. 08362/9080, www.hotel-fantasia.de, info@hotel-fantasia.de).

BUDGET BEDS

¢ Old Kings Design Hostel shoehorns two dorm rooms and three
private doubles into an old townhouse that doesn't resemble a typical hostel. While the quarters are tight (all rooms share bathrooms),
the central location, creative decor, and reasonable prices are enticing (bike rental, reception open daily 7:00-11:00 & 16:00-21:00,
buried deep in the pedestrian zone at Franziskanergasse 2, tel.
08362/883-4090, www.oldkingshostel.com, info@oldkingshostel.
com).

BAVARIAN ALPS

¢ **House LA,** run by energetic mason Lahdo Algül and hard-working Aga, has two branches. The backpacker house has 11 basic, clean dorm rooms at rock-bottom prices about a 10-minute walk from the station (private room available, free parking, Wachsbleiche 2). A second building has five family apartments with kitchen and bath (RS%, breakfast extra, free parking, 6-minute walk back along tracks from station to von Freybergstrasse 26; contact info for both: tel. 08362/607-366, mobile 0170-624-8610, www.housela.de, info@housela.de). Both locations rent bikes and have laundry facilities.

Eating in Füssen

$$ **Restaurant Ritterstub'n** offers delicious, reasonably priced German grub plus salads, veggie plates, and a fun kids' menu. They have three eating zones: modern decor in front, traditional Bavarian in back, and a courtyard. Ask about their €19 three-course fixed-price dinners. Their single-trip salad buffet is a great value—pile it high, as you're charged by the plate size. Demure Gabi serves while her husband Claus cooks (cheap lunch specials, Tue-Sun 11:30-14:00 & 17:30-21:30, closed Mon, Ritterstrasse 4, tel. 08362/7759).

$$ **Schenke & Wirtshaus** (inside the recommended Altstadthotel zum Hechten) dishes up hearty, traditional Bavarian dishes from goulash to pork knuckle in a classic interior. Their specialty is pike *(Hecht)* pulled from the Lech River, served with a tasty fresh-herb sauce (daily 11:00-21:00, Ritterstrasse 6, tel. 08362/91600).

$$$ **Ristorante La Perla** is an Italian restaurant run with pride by Michael and his family. Sit either in the classic rosy interior, at streetside tables on a quiet old town lane, or in the hidden courtyard out back (cheaper pizzas and pastas, daily 11:00-22:00, Nov-Jan closed 14:30-17:30 and all day Mon, Drehergasse 44, tel. 08362/7155).

$$$ The **Himmelsstube** is the restaurant inside Hotel Schlosskrone, right on Füssen's main traffic circle. It offers a weekday lunch buffet and live Bavarian zither music most Fridays and Saturdays during dinner. Choose between a traditional dining room and a pastel winter garden (daily 11:30-14:30 & 18:00-22:00, Prinzregentenplatz 2, tel. 08362/930-180, www.schlosskrone.de).

$$ **Restaurant Aquila** serves modern German and Italian-influenced dishes and serious salads in a simple indoor setting, but I prefer the outdoor tables on delightful Brotmarkt square (Wed-Mon 11:30-21:00, closed Tue, reservations smart, Brotmarkt 9, tel. 08362/6253, www.aquila-fuessen.de).

$$$ **Madame Plüsch,** old-school and elegant, serves tasty Bavarian dishes (fish, pork, beef, and veggie options), prepared and

seasoned with care. Dine in a cozy interior or at tables on the square (Thu-Mon 11:30-15:00 & 17:00-23:00, Wed 17:00-23:00, closed Tue, reservations recommended, Drehergasse 48, tel. 08362/938-0949, www.madame-pluesch.de).

$ Bio Café Baumgarten is a tiny healthy oasis near the St. Magnus Basilica tower, with tables inside and out on the square. Its organic fare includes breakfast, smoothies, salads, and sweet and savory crêpes, plus homemade cakes (daily 9:00-18:00, Magnusplatz 6, tel. 08362/989-9750).

Food Court: The fun **$ Markthalle** offers a wide selection of reasonably priced, wurst-free food. Located in a former warehouse from 1483, it's now home to a fishmonger, deli counters, a fruit stand, a bakery, and a wine bar. Buy your food from one of the vendors, park yourself at any one of the tables, then look up and admire the Renaissance ceiling (Mon-Fri 8:00-18:30, Sat until 15:00, closed Sun, corner of Schrannengasse and Brunnengasse).

Brewpub near the Castles: If you have a car, consider heading to **Schloss Brauhaus,** in the village of Schwangau, for local brew and an unbeatable view (described on page 437).

Gelato: Hohes Schloss Italian Ice Cream is a popular *gelateria* on the main drag with a huge menu of decadent sundaes and an inviting people-watching perch (Reichenstrasse 14).

Cheap Eats: $ Saray Kebab is the town's favorite Middle Eastern takeaway joint (Mon-Sat 11:00-23:00, closed Sun, Luitpoldstrasse 1, tel. 08362/2847). **$ Thuy Golden Stäbchen** serves a mix of Vietnamese, Chinese, and Thai food on a deserted back street with outdoor tables and a castle view (Tue-Sun 10:00-22:00, closed Mon, Hinteregasse 29, tel. 08362/939-7714).

Picnic Supplies: Bakeries and butcher shops *(Metzger)* abound and frequently have ready-made sandwiches. For groceries, try the discount **Netto** supermarket, at the roundabout across from Hotel Schlosskrone, or the midrange **REWE** in the Theresienhof shopping complex (both supermarkets open Mon-Sat 7:00-20:00, closed Sun).

Nightlife: At the **UnFassBar,** on Füssen's main drag, locals crowd at streetside tables or inside the cozy interior for drinks and small bites (Wed-Sat 10:00-22:00, closed Sun-Tue, Reichenstrasse 32, tel. 08362/929-6688). **Bayrish Pub** is popular for soccer viewing, live music, and conviviality (Tue-Fri 17:30-late, Sat from 14:30, closed Sun-Mon, Ottostrasse 7, tel. 08362/930-7444). **Laura's Schiffwirtschaft,** just across the river, attracts a younger crowd with live music, a foosball table, and basic bar food. The early-evening river views are exceptional (Wed-Sat 17:00-24:00, closed Sun-Tue, tel. 08362/924-3370).

BAVARIAN ALPS

Füssen Connections

BY BUS AND TRAIN

Bus schedules from Füssen can be very confusing. The website www.bahn.com is good for figuring out your options for a particular day and route. The DB Navigator app is also useful for planning your journey.

From Füssen to: Neuschwanstein (bus #73 or #78, departs from train station, most continue to Tegelberg cable-car station after castles, at least hourly, 10 minutes, €2.30 one way, buses #9606 and #9651 also make the trip); **Wieskirche** (bus #73, #9606, or #9651; 2-6 buses/day, 45-60 minutes); **Oberammergau** (bus #9606, 1-3/day, 1.5 hours, bus sometimes starts as #73 and changes number to #9606 en route—confirm with driver that bus is bound for Oberammergau); **Reutte** (bus #74 in Germany, changes number to #4258 in Austria, Mon-Fri 7/day, Sat-Sun 6/day, last bus 19:00, 30-50 minutes, €4.50 one-way); **Zugspitze** (possible as day trip via bus #74 to Reutte, then train to Ehrwald for Austrian ascent or Garmisch, allow up to 3.5 hours total to reach the top); **Munich** (hourly trains, 2 hours, half with easy transfer in Buchloe); **Innsbruck** (fastest via bus #4258/#74 to Reutte, then train from Reutte to Innsbruck via Garmisch, every 2 hours, 2.5 hours; otherwise via Munich); **Salzburg** (roughly hourly, 4 hours on fast trains, 5 hours on slow trains—included with Regional Day Ticket for Bavaria, transfer in Munich and sometimes in Kaufbeuren or Buchloe); **Rothenburg ob der Tauber** (hourly trains, 5-6 hours, look for connections with only 3 transfers—often in Augsburg, Treuchtlingen, and Steinach); **Frankfurt** (hourly trains, 5-6 hours, 1-2 changes). Train info: www.bahn.com.

The Best of the Bavarian Alps

Within a short drive of Füssen and Reutte, you'll find some of the most enjoyable—and most tourist-filled—sights in Germany. The otherworldly "King's Castles" of Neuschwanstein and Hohenschwangau capture romantics' imaginations, the ornately decorated Wieskirche puts the faithful in a heavenly mood, and the little town of Oberammergau overwhelms visitors with cuteness. Yet another impressive castle (Linderhof), another fancy church (Ettal), and a sky-high viewpoint (the Zugspitze) round out this region's top attractions.

The King's Castles: Neuschwanstein and Hohenschwangau

The most popular tourist destinations in southern Bavaria are the two "King's Castles" (Königsschlösser) near Füssen. The older Hohenschwangau, King Ludwig's boyhood home, is less famous but more historic. The more dramatic Neuschwanstein, which inspired Walt Disney, is the one everyone visits. I recommend visiting both and hiking above Neuschwanstein to Mary's Bridge. Reservations are a magic wand that smooth out your visit. With fairy-tale turrets built by a fairy-tale king in a fairy-tale alpine setting, these castles are understandably a huge hit.

GETTING THERE

If arriving by **car,** note that road signs in the region refer to the sight as *Königsschlösser.* There's plenty of parking (all lots—€6). The first lots require more walking. The most convenient lot, by the lake (#4, *Parkplatz am Alpsee*), is up the small road past the souvenir shops and ticket center.

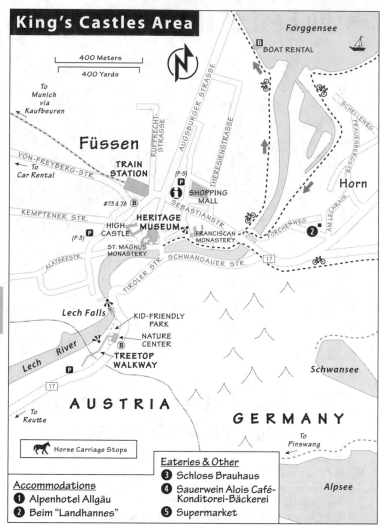

King's Castles Area

Forggensee

400 Meters
400 Yards

To
Munich
via
Kaufbeuren

Füssen

**TRAIN
STATION**

← To
Car Rental

VON-FREYBERG-STR.

(P-5)

AUGSBURGER STRASSE

RUPPRECHT-STRASSE

THERESIENSTRASSE

SCHELLIEWEG

FRAUENBERGSTR.

B BOAT RENTAL

Horn

SHOPPING
MALL

SEBASTIANSTR.

KEMPTENER STR.

#73 & 78 **B**

**HIGH
CASTLE**

**HERITAGE
MUSEUM**

(P-3)

**ST. MAGNUS
MONASTERY**

ALATSEESTR.

**FRANCISCAN
MONASTERY**

FORCHENWEG

AM LECHRAIN

2

TIROLER STR.

SCHWANGAUER STR.

17

Lech Falls

KID-FRIENDLY
PARK

NATURE
CENTER

B

**TREETOP
WALKWAY**

Lech River

Lech

P

17

Schwansee

AUSTRIA

To
Reutte

GERMANY

To
Pinswang

🐎 Horse Carriage Stops

Alpsee

Eateries & Other
3 Schloss Brauhaus
4 Sauerwein Alois Café-
    Konditorei-Bäckerei
5 Supermarket

Accommodations
1 Alpenhotel Allgäu
2 Beim "Landhannes"

BAVARIAN ALPS

From **Füssen,** those without cars can catch **bus** #73 or #78 (at least hourly, generally departs Füssen's train station at :05 past the hour, extra buses often run when crowded, €2.30 each way, 10 minutes; a few departures of #9606 and #9651 also make this trip). A Regional Day Ticket for Bavaria (see "Planning Your Time and Getting Around the Bavarian Alps," earlier) or the Füssen Card available from your hotel (see page 411) let you ride for free. You can also take a **taxi** (€11 one-way), ride a rental **bike** (3 level miles), or—if you're in a pinch—**walk** (less than an hour). The bus drops you at the tourist office (note return times so you aren't stuck waiting); it's a one-minute walk from there to the ticket office. When

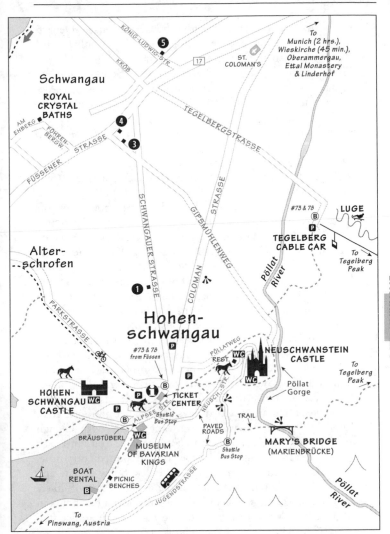

returning, note that buses #73 and #78 pointing left (with your back to the TI) are headed to Füssen, while the same numbers pointing right are going elsewhere.

From **Reutte,** take the bus to the Füssen train station (#4258, number changes to #74 in Germany, Mon-Fri 8/day, Sat-Sun 6/day). Once in Füssen, hop on bus #73 or #78 to the castles (see earlier).

ORIENTATION TO THE KING'S CASTLES

Cost: Timed-entry tickets for Neuschwanstein and Hohen-schwangau cost €13 apiece. A "Königsticket" combo-ticket for both castles costs €25—the Bavarian Palace Department's 14-day ticket may be a better deal if you're only touring Neuschwanstein but seeing other Bavarian sights (see "Helpful Hints" at the beginning of this chapter). A "Schwanenticket," which also covers the Museum of the Bavarian Kings—described later—costs €31.50. Children under age 18 (accompanied by an adult) get in free.

Hours and Entry Times: The ticket center, located at street level between the two castles, is open daily (7:30-17:00, mid-Oct-March 8:30-15:30). The first castle tour of the day departs at 9:00 (10:00 in off-season); the last tour departs at 17:00 (15:30 in off-season).

Tickets, whether reserved in advance or bought on the spot, come with admission times. If you miss your appointed tour time, you can't get in. To tour both castles, you must do Hohenschwangau first (logical, since this gives a better introduction to King Ludwig's short life). You'll get two entry times: Hohenschwangau and then, two hours later, Neuschwanstein. If you're planning to hike up to Mary's Bridge prior to your Neuschwanstein tour, allow plenty of time: There's often a line to get onto the bridge for that famous view.

Information: Tel. 08362/930-830, www.hohenschwangau.de.

Reservations: It's just plain smart to reserve ahead, particularly for holidays and weekends during peak season (June-Oct—especially July-Aug) when slots can book up several days in advance. Reservations cost €1.80 per person per castle and must be made online at least two days in advance (no later than 15:00 local time, www.hohenschwangau.de). With enough notice, a few hotels can book tickets for you. You must pick up reserved tickets an hour before your appointed entry time, as it takes a while to get up to the castles. Show up late and they may have given your slot to someone else (but will likely help you book a new reservation). If you know a few hours in advance that you're running late and can call the office (tel. 08362/930-830), they'll likely rebook you.

If you're staying in Reutte and depending on buses for transportation, make your reservation for midday (noon or later) to give yourself ample time to arrive at Neuschwanstein.

Note that you need a reservation even with the Bavarian Palace Department's 14-day ticket (covers Neuschwanstein only, described earlier). Reserve online; your credit card will be charged only for the booking fee.

Without a Reservation: A percentage of castle tickets are set aside for in-person purchase, so if reservations for your day of choice are sold out online, you can still get a ticket if you arrive early. Because day-trippers from Munich tend to take the morning train—with a bus connection arriving at the castles by about 11:15—if you need to buy a ticket on the spot, arrive by 11:00 to beat the crowd. During August, the busiest month, tickets for English tours can run out by around noon.

Arrival: Make the **ticket center** your first stop. If you have a reservation, stand in the short line for picking up tickets. If you don't have a reservation...welcome to the very long line. Arrive by 7:30 in summer, and you'll likely be touring around 9:00.

Getting Up to the Castles: From the ticket booth, Hohenschwangau is an easy 10-minute **walk** up the paved path past the bus parking (for a quicker ascent zigzag up to the big yellow castle using the ramp/stairs behind Hotel Müller). Neuschwanstein is a moderately steep, 30-minute hike in the other direction (also well signed—the most direct and least steep approach begins near the Bräustüberl restaurant).

To minimize hiking to Neuschwanstein, you can take a shuttle bus or a horse-drawn carriage. Neither option gets you to the castle doorstep. The **shuttle bus** departs about every 20 minutes from the parking lot just below Hohenschwangau and drops you off near Mary's Bridge (Marienbrücke), leaving you a steep, 10-minute downhill walk to the castle—so be sure to see the view from Mary's Bridge *before* hiking down (€2.50 uphill, €1.50 downhill, €3 round-trip). **Horse-drawn carriages,** which leave from in front of Hotel Müller, are slower than walking and stop below Neuschwanstein, leaving you a five-minute uphill hike (€6 up, €3 down). Carriages also run to Hohenschwangau (€4.50 up, €2 down).

Be warned that both buses and carriages can have long lines at peak times—especially if it's raining. You might wait up to 45 minutes, making it slower than walking. If you're cutting it close to your appointed time, you may need to hoof it. Note that buses don't run in snowy or icy conditions, which can happen even in spring.

With time, here's the most economical and least strenuous plan: Ride the bus to Mary's Bridge for the view, hike down to Neuschwanstein, and then catch the horse carriage from below the castle down to the parking lot (round-trip cost: €5.50). If you're on a tight schedule, consider taking the bus back down, as carriages can be unpredictable.

Entry Procedure: At each castle, tourists jumble in the courtyard, waiting for their ticket number to light up on the board. When it does, power through the mob and go to the turnstile. Warning: You must use your ticket while your number is still on the board. If you space out, you'll miss your entry window.

Renovations: Neuschwanstein is undergoing restoration work, so you may encounter scaffolding, and some furnishings may

"Mad" King Ludwig (1845-1886)

A tragic figure, Ludwig II (a.k.a. "Mad" King Ludwig) ruled Bavaria for 22 years until his death in 1886 at the age of 40. Bavaria was weak. Politically, Ludwig's reality was to "rule" as either a pawn of Prussia or a pawn of Austria. Rather than deal with politics in Bavaria's capital, Munich, Ludwig frittered away most of his time at his family's hunting palace, Hohenschwangau. He spent much of his adult life con-

structing his fanciful Neuschwanstein Castle—like a kid builds a tree house—on a neighboring hill upon the scant ruins of a medieval castle. Here and in his other projects (such as Linderhof Castle and the never-built Falkenstein Castle), even as he strove to evoke medieval grandeur, he embraced the state-of-the-art technology of the Industrial Age in which he lived. Neuschwanstein had electricity, running water, and a telephone (but no Wi-Fi).

Ludwig was a true romantic living in a Romantic age. His best friends were artists, poets, and composers such as Richard Wagner. His palaces are wallpapered with misty medieval themes—especially those from Wagnerian operas.

Although Ludwig spent 17 years building Neuschwanstein, he lived in it only 172 days. Soon after he moved in (and before his vision for the castle was completed), Ludwig was declared mentally unfit to rule Bavaria and taken away. Two days after this eviction, Ludwig was found dead in a lake. To this day, people debate whether the king was murdered or committed suicide.

have protective coverings when you visit (photos in rooms show the space without the coverings).

Services: A TI (run by helpful Thomas), bus stop, ATM, pay WC, lockers, and post machine cluster around the main intersection a couple hundred yards before you get to the ticket office (TI open daily 10:00-17:30, Nov-March Sat-Sun until 16:00, closed Mon-Fri, tel. 08362/81980, www.schwangau. de). While the tiny bathrooms inside the castles themselves are free, you'll pay to use the WCs elsewhere.

Wi-Fi: You can get an hour of free Wi-Fi at the TI and other hotspots near the castles. Look for signs with the orange logo.

Best Views: In the morning, the light comes in just above the mountains—making your initial view of Neuschwanstein hazy and disappointing (though views from the ticket center up to Hohenschwangau are nice). Later in the day, the sun drops down into the pasture, lighting up Neuschwanstein magnificently. Regardless of time of day, the best accessible Neuschwanstein view is from Mary's Bridge (or, for the bold, from the little bluff just above it)—a 10-minute hike from the castle. (Many of the postcards and posters you'll see are based on photos taken high in the hills, best left to avid hikers.)

Eating at the Castles: I prefer to bring a packed lunch. The park by the Alpsee (the nearby lake) is ideal for a picnic, although you're not allowed to sit on the grass—only on the benches (or eat out on the lake in one of the old-fashioned rowboats—see "After Your Castle Visit," next). The restaurants in the "village" at the foot of Europe's Disney castle are mediocre and overpriced, serving endless droves of hungry, shop-happy tourists. You can find decent German fare at the snack stand across from the TI or next to Hotel Alpenstuben (between the TI and ticket center). Up near Neuschwanstein itself (near the horse carriage drop-off) is a cluster of overpriced eateries, and inside the castle is a café with remarkable views, solid sustenance, and unremarkable coffee.

If you have a car or a bike, see "Eating Near the King's Castles," later, for better options.

After Your Castle Visit: If you follow my advice, you could be done with your castle tours in the early afternoon. With a car, you could try to squeeze in a nearby sight (such as Linderhof Castle, Ehrenberg Castle ruins, Highline 179 suspension footbridge, or Wieskirche). To stick closer by, here are some ideas: The hike from Neuschwanstein up to **Mary's Bridge** is easy and rewarding; the hike back down to the valley through the **Pöllat Gorge** is also highly recommended (may be closed). When the sun is shining, rent a **pedal boat** or **rowboat** for a scenic float around the **Alpsee,** the lake below Hohenschwangau. With a **bike,** you could pedal through the mostly flat countryside that spreads out in front of Neuschwanstein (perhaps partway around the Forggensee). And nearby—an easy drive or bus ride away—the Tegelberg area has both a high-mountain **cable car** and a fun **luge** ride. All of these options are described later. Yet another option is to walk all the way around the Alpsee (about 1.5 hours, clockwise is less strenuous, some steps). And for some relaxation, the **Royal Crystal Baths** in the town of Schwangau are ideal (described earlier).

SIGHTS AT THE KING'S CASTLES

The two castles complement each other perfectly. But if you have to choose one, Neuschwanstein's wow factor—inside and out—is undeniable.

BAVARIAN ALPS

▲▲▲Hohenschwangau Castle

Standing quietly below Neuschwanstein, the big, yellow Hohenschwangau Castle is where Ludwig spent his summers as a young boy. Originally built in the 12th century, it was ruined by Napoleon. Ludwig's father, King Maximilian II, rebuilt it in 1830. Hohenschwangau (hohen-SHVAHN-gow, loosely translated as "High Swanland") was used by the royal family as a summer hunting lodge until 1912. The Wittelsbach family

(which ruled Bavaria for nearly seven centuries) still owns the place (and lived in the annex—today's shop—until the 1970s).

The interior decor (mostly Neo-Gothic, like the castle itself) is harmonious, cohesive, and original—all done in 1835, with paintings inspired by Romantic themes. As you tour the castle, imagine how the paintings must have inspired young Ludwig. For 17 years, he lived here at his dad's place and followed the construction of his dream castle across the way—you'll see the telescope still set up and directed at Neuschwanstein.

The excellent 30-minute tour gives a better glimpse of Ludwig's life than the more visited and famous Neuschwanstein Castle tour. Tours here are smaller (35 people rather than 60) and more relaxed. You'll explore rooms on two floors—the queen's rooms, and then, upstairs, the king's. (Conveniently, their bedrooms were connected by a secret passage.) You'll see photos and busts of Ludwig and his little brother, Otto; some Turkish-style flourishes (to please the king, who had been impressed after a visit to the Orient); countless swans—try to find them (honoring the Knights of Schwangau, whose legacy the Wittelsbachs inherited); over-the-top gifts the Wittelsbachs received from their adoring subjects; and paintings of VIGs (very important Germans, including Martin Luther—who may or may not have visited here—and an infant Charlemagne).

One of the most impressive rooms is the Banquet Hall (also known as the Hall of Heroes); one vivid wall mural depicts a savage, yet bloodless, fifth-century barbarian battle. Just as the castle itself had running water and electricity despite its historic appearance (both were installed in the 1900s under King Luitpold, Ludwig's uncle), its Romantic decor presents a sanitized version of the medieval past, glossing over inconvenient details. You'll also see Ludwig's bedroom, which he inherited from his father. He kept most of the decor (including the nude nymphs frolicking over his bed) but painted the ceiling black and installed transparent stars that could be lit from the floor above to create the illusion of a night sky.

After the tour is over, wind through the castle gardens and imagine Ludwig frolicking here with his sights set on the hill far in the distance.

▲▲▲Neuschwanstein Castle

Imagine "Mad" King Ludwig as a boy, climbing the hills above his dad's castle, Hohenschwangau, dreaming up the ultimate

fairy-tale castle. Inheriting the throne at the young age of 18, he had the power to make his dream concrete and stucco. Neuschwanstein (noy-SH-VAHN-shtine, roughly "New Swanstone") was designed first by a theater-set designer...then by an architect. While it was built upon the ruins of an old castle and looks medieval, Neuschwanstein is modern iron-and-brick construction with a sandstone veneer—only about as old as the Eiffel Tower. It feels like something you'd see at a home show for 19th-century royalty. Built from 1869 to 1886, it's the epitome of the Romanticism popular in 19th-century Europe. Construction stopped with Ludwig's death (only a third of the interior was finished), and within six weeks, tourists were paying to go through it.

During World War II, the castle took on a sinister role. The Nazis used Neuschwanstein as one of their primary secret store-houses for stolen art. After the war, Allied authorities spent a year sorting through and redistributing the art, which filled 49 rail cars from this one location alone. It was the only time the unfinished rooms were put to use.

Today, guides herd groups of 60 through the castle, giving an interesting—yet often unenthusiastic and rushed—30-minute tour. (While you're waiting for your tour time to pop up on the board, climb the stairs to the upper courtyard to see more of the exterior, which isn't covered on your tour.) Once inside, you'll go up and down more than 300 steps (keep an eye out for a spiral stair-case column that becomes a palm tree), visiting 15 lavish rooms with their original furnishings and fanciful wall paintings—mostly based on Wagnerian opera themes. While renovations are under way, furnishings may be covered up, but the opulence of the build-ing itself delivers plenty of drama.

Ludwig's extravagant throne room, modeled in a Neo-Byzan-tine style to emphasize his royal status, celebrates six valiant Chris-

BAVARIAN ALPS

tian kings (whose mantle Ludwig clearly believed he had donned) under a huge gilded-bronze, crown-like chandelier. The exquisite two-million-stone mosaic floor is a visual encyclopedia of animals and plants. While you're standing on a replica, original segments ring the perimeter. The most memorable stop may be the king's gilded-lily bedroom, with his elaborately carved canopy bed (with a forest of Gothic church spires on top), washstand (filled with water piped in from the Alps), and personal chapel. After passing through Ludwig's living room and a faux grotto, you'll climb to the fourth floor for the grand finale: the Singers' Hall, an ornately decorated space filled with murals depicting the story of Parzival, the legendary medieval knight with whom Ludwig identified.

After the tour, weave through the crowded gift shop and past the WCs and café to see the 13-minute video (runs continuously, English subtitles). This uses historical drawings and modern digital modeling to tell the story of how the castle was built, and illustrates all the unfinished parts of Ludwig's vision (more prickly towers, a central chapel, a fancy view terrace, an ornate bathhouse, and more). Finally, you'll see a digital model of Falkenstein—a whimsical, over-the-top, never-built castle that makes Neuschwanstein look stubby. Falkenstein occupied Ludwig's fantasies the year he died.

Then head downstairs to the kitchen (state-of-the-art for this high-tech king in its day), where you'll see a room lined with fascinating drawings of the castle plans (described in English), as well as a large castle model.

SIGHTS NEAR THE CASTLES

The first three listings are right at the castles, while the cable car and luge are a few miles away.

▲▲Mary's Bridge (Marienbrücke)

Before or after the Neuschwanstein tour, climb up to Mary's Bridge (named for Ludwig's mom) to marvel at Ludwig's castle, just as Ludwig did. Jockey with a United Nations of tourists for the best angle—there's usually a line just to get onto the structure. This bridge was quite an engineering accomplishment 100 years ago. (Access to the bridge is closed in bad winter weather, but many travelers walk around the barriers to get there—at their own risk, of course.)

For an even more glorious castle view, the frisky can hike even higher: After crossing the bridge, you'll see very rough, steep, unofficial trails crisscrossing the hillside on your left. If you're willing to ignore the *Lebensgefahr* (risk of death) signs, you can scamper up to the bluff just over the bridge.

The trail connecting Neuschwanstein to Mary's Bridge is also scenic, with views back on Neuschwanstein's facade in one direction, and classic views of Hohenschwangau—perched on its little hill between lakes, with cut-glass peaks on the horizon—in the other.

▲Pöllat Gorge (Pöllatschlucht)

If it's open, the river gorge that slices into the rock just behind Neuschwanstein's lofty perch is a more interesting and scenic—and less crowded—alternative to shuffling back down the main road. While it takes an extra 15 minutes or so, it's well worth it. You'll find the trailhead just above the Neuschwanstein exit, on the path toward Mary's Bridge (look for *Pöllatschlucht* signs; trail closed in winter and sometimes impassable due to rockslides).

You'll begin by walking down a steep, well-maintained set of concrete stairs, with Germany's finest castle looming through the trees. Then you'll pop out along the river, passing a little beach (with neatly stacked stones) offering a view up at the grand waterfall that gushes beneath Mary's Bridge. From here, follow the river as it goes over several smaller waterfalls—and stroll for a while along steel walkways and railings that make this slippery area safer. After passing an old wooden channel used to harness the power of all that water, you'll hit level ground; turn left and walk through a pleasantly untouristy residential settlement back toward the TI.

Museum of the Bavarian Kings (Museum der Bayerischen Könige)

About a five-minute walk from the castles' ticket center, in a former grand hotel on the shore of the Alpsee, this modern, well-presented exhibit documents the history of the Wittelsbachs, Bavaria's former royal family. On display are plenty of family portraits and busts, as well as treasures including Ludwig II's outlandish royal robe and elaborately decorated fairy-tale sword, and the impressive dining set given as a golden-anniversary present to his cousin Ludwig III and his wife, the last reigning Wittelsbachs. After losing the throne, the family spoke out against the Nazis, and some were sent to concentration camps as a result. A free audioguide lends some context to the family's history, albeit in more detail than you'll probably want. The museum is worthwhile only if you're captivated by this clan and have time to kill. (But trying to squeeze it between your two castle visits is rushing it—especially if you like to linger.)

Cost and Hours: €11, includes audioguide; combo-ticket with Hohenschwangau or Neuschwanstein—€22, with both castles—€31.50; daily April-Sept 9:00-19:00, Oct-March 10:00-

18:00; no reservations required, mandatory lockers, Alpseestrasse 27, tel. 08362/887-250, www.hohenschwangau.de.

▲Tegelberg Cable Car (Tegelbergbahn)

Just north of Neuschwanstein is a fun play zone around the mighty Tegelberg cable car, a scenic ride to the mountain's 5,500-foot summit. At the top on a clear day, you get great views of the Alps and Bavaria and the vicarious thrill of watching hang gliders and paragliders leap into airborne ecstasy. Weather permitting, scores of adventurous Germans line up and leap from the launch ramp at the top of the lift. With someone leaving every two

or three minutes, it's great for spectators. Thrill seekers with exceptional social skills may talk themselves into a tandem ride with a paraglider. From the top of Tegelberg, it's a steep and demanding 2.5-hour hike down to Ludwig's castle. (Avoid the treacherous trail directly below the cable car.) Around the cable car's valley station, you'll find a playground, a cheery eatery, the stubby remains of an ancient Roman villa, and a summer luge ride (described next).

Cost and Hours: €20.60 round-trip, €13.30 one-way; first ascent daily at 9:00; last descent April-Oct at 17:00, mid-Dec-March at 16:00, closed Nov-mid-Dec; 4/hour, 5-minute ride to the top, in bad weather call first to confirm, tel. 08362/98360, www.tegelbergbahn.de.

Getting There: From the castles, most #73 and #78 buses from Füssen continue to the Tegelbergbahn valley station (5-minute ride). It's a 30-minute walk or 10-minute bike ride from the castles.

▲Tegelberg Luge

Next to the cable car's valley station is a summer luge course *(Sommerrodelbahn)*. A summer luge is like a bobsled on wheels (for more details, see "Luge Lesson" on page 467). This course's stainless steel track is heated, so it's often dry and open even when drizzly weather shuts down the concrete luges. A funky cable system pulls riders (in their sleds) to the top without a ski lift. It's not as long, fast, or scenic as Austria's Biberwier luge (described on page 468), but it's handy, harder to get hurt on, and half the price.

Cost and Hours: €3.90/ride, shareable 6-ride card—€16.30; hours typically April-Sept daily 10:00-17:00 depending on weather; call first to confirm, waits can be long in good weather, no children under age 3, ages 3-8 may ride with an adult, tel. 08362/98360, www.tegelbergbahn.de.

SLEEPING NEAR THE KING'S CASTLES

Though best for drivers, both of these places are a quick taxi ride from the Füssen train station and also close to bus stops. In return for paying the Schwangau hotel tax, you get a card with the same benefits as the Füssen Card (see page 411).

$$ Alpenhotel Allgäu is a small, family-run hotel with 18 decent rooms in a bucolic setting perched just below Ludwig's dream castle. It's a 15-minute walk from the castle ticket office and a nice place to frolic when the crowds depart (most rooms with balconies or porches—some with castle views; family rooms, elevator, free parking, just before tennis courts at Schwangauer Strasse 37 in the town of Schwangau—don't let your GPS take you to Schwangauer Strasse 37 in Füssen, tel. 08362/81152, www.alpenhotel-allgaeu. de, info@alpenhotel-allgaeu.de, Frau Reiss).

$ Beim "Landhannes," a 200-year-old working organic dairy farm run by Conny Schön, is a great value for drivers and a unique experience for all. They rent three creaky but sunny rooms and five apartments with kitchenettes, and keep flowers on the balconies, big bells and antlers in the halls, and cows in the yard (cash only, free parking, nearby bike rental, in the village of Horn on the Füssen side of Schwangau—see the "King's Castles Area" map, 100 yards in front of Hotel Kleiner König down a tiny lane through the meadow, Am Lechrain 22, tel. 08362/8349, www.landhannes.de, info@landhannes.de).

EATING NEAR THE KING'S CASTLES

For quick, functional eateries in the immediate castle area, see "Orientation to the King's Castles," earlier.

If you have a car and want to eat at a good-value, nontouristy place with stunning castle views, consider **$$ Schloss Brauhaus,** a sprawling microbrewery restaurant in the village of Schwangau, about 1.5 miles from the castles. They brew five types of beer (dark, light, wheat, and two seasonal brews) and serve classic German fare with limited but hearty vegetarian options. Choose between the woody-industrial interior—with big copper vats and a miniature bowling alley (€8/hour)—and the outdoor *Biergarten,* with minigolf (€5.50, €3/child) and views of Neuschwanstein (food served Mon-Thu 14:00-21:00, Fri-Sun from 11:00; beer served until 23:00; Gipsmühlweg 5 in Schwangau—coming from Füssen, watch for signs on the main street, Füssener Strasse, see the "King's Castles Area" map; tel. 08362/926-4680, www.schlossbrauhaus. de).

Also in Schwangau, try **Sauerwein Alois Café-Konditorei-Bäckerei** for huge, fresh, and cheap sandwiches. They also have tempting pastries (Mon-Fri 6:00-18:00, Sat until 17:00, Sun 13:00-18:00 but no sandwiches, Füssener Strasse 15, tel. 08362/8220).

Farther down the road is a **REWE** supermarket, handy for picnic items, hearty sandwiches, hot deli foods, and build-your-own salads (daily 7:00-20:00, König-Ludwig Strasse 2, tel. 08362/98270).

Wieskirche

Germany's greatest Rococo-style church, this "Church in the Meadow"—worth ▲▲—looks as brilliant now as the day it floated down from heaven. Overripe with decoration but bright and bursting with beauty, this church is a divine droplet, a curly curlicue, the final flowering of the Baroque movement.

GETTING THERE

By **car,** the Wieskirche is a 30-minute drive north of Neuschwanstein or Füssen. Head north, turn right at Steingaden, and follow the brown signs to pay parking. With careful attention to schedules, you can day-trip here from Füssen by **bus** (#73, #9606, or #9651; 2-6/day, 45-60 minutes), but it's a long round-trip for a church that most see in 10-15 minutes.

ORIENTATION TO WIESKIRCHE

Cost and Hours: Donation requested, daily 8:00-20:00, Nov-March until 17:00. The interior is closed to sightseers during services: Sun 8:00-13:00; Tue, Wed, and Sat 10:00-12:00; and Fri 17:00-20:00.

Information: Tel. 08862/932-930, www.wieskirche.de.

Services: Trinket shops, snack stands (one sells freshly made doughnuts—look for *Wieskücherl* sign), and a WC clog the parking area in front of the church; take a commune-with-nature-and-smell-the-farm detour back through the meadow to the parking lot.

VISITING THE CHURCH

This pilgrimage church is built around the much-venerated statue of a scourged (or whipped) Christ, which supposedly wept in 1738. The carving—too graphic to be accepted by that generation's Church—was the focus of worship in a peasant's barn. Miraculously, it shed tears—empathizing with all those who suffer. Pilgrims came from all around. A tiny and humble chapel was built to house the statue in 1739. (You can see it where the lane to the church leaves the parking lot.) Bigger and bigger crowds came.

Two of Bavaria's top Rococo architects, the Zimmermann brothers (Johann Baptist and Dominikus), were commissioned to build the Wieskirche that stands here today.

Follow the theological sweep from the altar to the ceiling: Jesus whipped, chained, and then killed (notice the pelican above

the altar—recalling a pre-Christian story of a bird that opened its breast to feed its young with its own blood); the painting of Baby Jesus posed as if on the cross; the golden sacrificial lamb; and finally, high on the ceiling, the resurrected Christ before the Last Judgment. This is the most positive depiction of the Last Judgment around. Jesus, rather than sitting on the throne to judge, rides high on a rainbow—a symbol of forgiveness—giving any sinner the feeling that there is still time to repent, with plenty of mercy on hand. In the back, above the pipe organ, notice the closed door to paradise, and at the opposite end (above the main altar), the empty throne—waiting for Judgment Day.

Above the doors flanking the altar are murky glass cases with 18th-century handkerchiefs. People wept, came here, were healed, and no longer needed their hankies. Walk through either of these doors and up an aisle flanking the high altar to see votives—requests and thanks to God (for happy, healthy babies, and healing for sick loved ones). Notice how the kneelers are positioned so that worshippers can meditate on scenes of biblical miracles painted high on the ceiling and visible through the ornate scalloped frames. A priest here once told me that faith, architecture, light, and music all combine to create the harmony of the Wieskirche.

Two paintings flank the door at the rear of the church. The one on the right shows the ceremonial parade in 1749 when the white-clad monks of Steingaden carried the carved statue of Christ from the tiny church to its new big one. The second painting (on the left), from 1757, is a votive from one of the Zimmermann brothers, the artists and architects who built this church. He is giving thanks for the successful construction of the new church.

ROUTE TIPS FOR DRIVERS

Driving from Wieskirche to Oberammergau: Cross the **Echelsbacher Bridge,** which arches 230 feet over the Pöllat Gorge. Thoughtful drivers let their passengers walk across to enjoy the views, then meet them at the other side. Notice the painting of the traditional village woodcarver (who used to walk from town to town with his art on his back) on the first big house on the Oberammergau side. It holds the Almdorf Ammertal shop, with a huge selection of overpriced carvings and commission-hungry tour guides.

Oberammergau

The Shirley Temple of Bavarian villages, and exploited to the hilt by the tourist trade, Oberammergau wears too much makeup. During

its famous Passion Play (every 10 years, next in 2020), the crush is unbearable—and the prices at the hotels and restaurants can be as well. The village has about 1,200 beds for the 5,000 playgo-ers coming daily. But the rest of the time, Oberammergau—while hardly "undiscovered"—is a pleasant, and at times even sleepy, Bavarian village.

If you're passing through, Oberammergau is a ▲ sight—worth a wander among the half-timbered, frescoed *Lüftlmalerei* houses (see sidebar on page 410). It's also a relatively convenient home base for visiting Linderhof Castle, Ettal Monastery, and the Zugspi-tze (via Garmisch). A smaller (and less conveniently located) al-ternative to Füssen and Reutte, it's worth considering for drivers who want to linger in the area. A day trip to Neuschwanstein from Oberammergau is manageable if you have a car, but train travelers do better to stay in Füssen.

GETTING TO OBERAMMERGAU

From Füssen, you can take the **bus** (#9606, 1-3/day, 1.5 hours, bus may start as #73 and change to #9606 en route—confirm with driver that bus is going to Oberammergau). **Drivers** can get here from Reutte in less than 30 minutes via the pretty Plansee lake.

Orientation to Oberammergau

This village of about 5,000 feels even smaller, thanks to its remote location. The downtown core, huddled around the onion-domed church, is compact and invites strolling; all of my recommended sights, hotels, and restaurants are within about a 10-minute walk of each other. While the town's name sounds like a mouthful, it's based on the name of the local river (the Ammer) and means, roughly, "Upper Ammerland."

Tourist Information: The helpful, well-organized TI provides

Oberammergau

To Munich

ROTTSTRASSE

SCHMÄDIG.

OBERLANDSTR.

DEUTINGERSTR.

IN DER FURCH

PASSION PLAY THEATER

BUS & TRAIN STATION

PASSIONSWIESE

THEATER STR.

OBERAMMERGAU MUSEUM

BAHNHOFSTRASSE

DORFSTR.

ST.-LUKAS-STR.

To Unterammergau, Wieskirche & ⑩

WELFENG.

FREIKORP.

EUGEN-

To Laber Bergbahn (lift), WellenBerg (pool) & ⑧

FRANZÖSENG.

To Wieskirche, Kolbensattel (chairlift) & Alpine Coaster

Ammer

⑨

VERLEGER

DEDLERSTR.

③

④ ⑧

DAISEN

①

②

⑦

PAPST

PILATUS HOUSE

STR.

DORFSTR.

CHURCH

TIROLER

⑥

HANSEL & GRETEL HOUSE

KÖNIG-LUDWIG-STR.

KOFELAU WEG

River

LITTLE RED RIDING HOOD HOUSE

⑤

MALENSTEINWEG

ETALER STR.

N

200 Meters

200 Yards

To Ettal, Linderhof, Reutte, Garmisch & Munich

Accommodations

① Hotel Fux
② Mammhofer Suite & Breakfast
③ Gasthof zur Rose
④ Gästehaus Magold
⑤ Youth Hostel

Eateries & Other

⑥ Ammergauer Maxbräu
⑦ El Puente
⑧ To Café Hochenleitner
⑨ Eis Café Paradiso
⑩ To Sommerrodelbahn Steckenberg (Summer Luge)

English information on area hikes and will store your bags for free during opening hours (Mon-Fri 9:00-18:00, Sat-Sun until 13:00; closed Sun mid-Sept-mid-June, also closed Sat Nov-Dec; Eugen-Papst-Strasse 9A, tel. 08822/922-740, www.oberammergau.de).

Arrival in Oberammergau: If you're **driving,** you'll find that there are two exits from the main road into Oberammergau—at the north and south ends. Either way, make your way to the free lot between the TI and the river. While there's ample street parking in town, most is time limited and/or requires payment—be sure to read signs carefully. Hotels and sights are well signed in the town.

Helpful Hints: Travelers staying in the Oberammergau area are entitled to a Gäste-Karte—be sure to ask your hotel for one. The TI has a sheet explaining the card's benefits, such as free travel on mountain lifts and local buses (including Garmisch, Linderhof, Füssen, and Ettal Monastery) and free admission to the Oberammergau Museum, Passion Play Theater, and WellenBerg swimming pool.

Woodcarving in Oberammergau

The Ammergau region is relatively poor, with no appreciable industry and no agriculture, save for some dairy farming. What they *do* have is wood. Carving religious and secular themes became a lucrative way for the locals to make some money, especially when confined to the house during the long, cold winter. And with a major pilgrimage site—Ettal Monastery—just down the road, there was a built-in consumer base eager to buy hand-carved crucifixes and other souvenirs. Carvers from Oberammergau peddled their wares across Europe, carrying them on their backs (on distinctive wooden backpack-racks called *Kraxe*) as far away as Rome.

Today, the Oberammergau Carving School (founded in 1887) is a famous institution that takes only 20 students per year out of 450 applicants. Their graduates do important restoration work throughout Europe. For example, much of the work on Dresden's Frauenkirche was done by these artists.

Sights in Oberammergau

BAVARIAN ALPS

▲Local Arts and Crafts

The town's best sight is its woodcarving shops *(Holzschnitzerei)*. Browse through these small art galleries filled with very expensive whittled works. The beautifully frescoed **Pilatus House** at Ludwig-Thoma-Strasse 10 has an open workshop where you can watch woodcarvers and painters at work on summer afternoons (free, late May-mid-Oct Tue-Sun 13:00-17:00, closed Mon and off-season, open weekends in Dec, tel. 08822/949-511). Upstairs in the Pilatus House is a small exhibit of "reverse glass" paintings *(verre églomisé)* that's worth a quick glance.

▲Oberammergau Museum

This museum showcases local woodcarving, with good English explanations. The ground floor has a small exhibit of nativity scenes *(Krippe*—mostly made of wood, but some of paper or wax). In the back, find the small theater, where you can watch an interesting film in English about the 2010 Passion Play. Upstairs is a much more extensive collection of the wood carvings that helped put Oberammergau on the map, including a room of old woodcarving tools, plus a small exhibit on Roman archaeological finds in the region. Your ticket also lets you into the lobby of the Passion Play Theater, described next.

Cost and Hours: €3.50; €6 combo-ticket includes museum and theater lobby; Easter-Oct and Dec-mid-Jan Tue-Sun 10:00-17:00, closed Mon and off-season; Dorfstrasse 8, tel. 08822/94136, www.oberammergaumuseum.de.

Passion Play Theater (Festspielhaus)

Back in 1633, in the midst of the bloody Thirty Years' War and with horrifying plagues devastating entire cities, the people of Oberammergau promised God that if they were spared from extinction, they'd "perform a play depicting the suffering, death, and resurrection of our Lord Jesus Christ" every decade thereafter. The town survived, and as it heads into its 42nd decade, the peo-

ple of Oberammergau are still making good on the deal. For 100 days every 10 years, about half of the town's population (a cast of 2,000) are involved in the production of this extravagant five-hour Passion Play—telling the story of Jesus' entry into Jerusalem, the Crucifixion, and the Resurrection.

If you're not visiting during the Passion Play performances, you'll have to settle for reading the book, seeing Nicodemus tool around town in his VW, or taking a quick look at the theater, a block from the center of town.

Visiting the Theater: The theater lobby hosts a modest exhibit on the history of the performances. A long wall of photographs of past performers shows the many generations of Oberammergauers who have participated in this tradition. Climb the stairs and peek into the theater itself, which has an unusual indoor/outdoor design and a real-life alpine backdrop.

To learn more, take a 45-minute guided tour of the theater, organized by the museum (€3.50, €6 combo-ticket with Oberammergau Museum, €8 with guided tour; tours run Easter-Oct only, Tue-Sun at 11:00 in English, additional tour times in German; theater open same hours as museum, tel. 08822/94136, www. oberammergaumuseum.de).

Oberammergau Church

The town church is typical Bavarian Baroque but a poor cousin of the one at Wieskirche not too far from here. Being in a woodcarving center, it's only logical that all the statues are made of wood and then stuccoed and gilded to look like marble or gold. Saints Peter and Paul flank the altar, where the central painting can be raised to reveal a small stage decorated to celebrate special times during the church calendar. In the central dome, a touching painting shows Peter and Paul bidding each other farewell (with the city of Rome as a backdrop) on the day of their execution—the same day, in the year AD 67. On the left, Peter is crucified upside-down. On the

BAVARIAN ALPS

Passion Play 2020

Anticipation is high for the once-a-decade experience encompassing spirituality and entertainment: Oberammergau's Passion Play. Its 2020 run is from May 16 through October 4. Tickets are so in demand that bookings went on sale more than two years before its opening day.

Throughout the run, the tiny village expects some 450,000 visitors—about half from outside Germany. Performances are five hours long and take place five days a week. The play begins in the afternoon, pauses for a three-hour dinner break, and lets out late in the evening (mid-May–mid-Aug 14:30-22:30, from mid-Aug 13:30-21:30). While this experience is a big investment in money, time, and energy, those who've seen it say it's unforgettably moving and well worth it.

Tickets are easiest to obtain in a one- or two-night package deal that includes hotel, ticket, dinner, shuttle, and a book (€324-1,000+, tel. 08822/949-8857, www.passionsspiele-oberammergau.de). Travelers will most likely have difficulty booking hotel rooms on their own during the Passion Play performance dates (though apartment rentals or pensions are still sometimes possible).

right, Paul is beheaded with a sword. On your way out look for the wooden cross once used in the Passion Play (open daily 8:00-19:30).

Wander through the lovingly maintained **graveyard,** noticing the wide variety in headstones. A towering stone WWI memorial at the gate has an imposing look and sternly worded celebrations of the "heroes" of that war. But around the other side, below it on the outer fence, find the newer glass panel that modifies the sentiment: "We honor and remember the victims of the violence that our land gave the world."

Lüftlmalerei Painted Houses

Wealthy merchants, farmers, and artisans had their houses painted using a special fresco technique called *Lüftlmalerei* that still sets Oberammergau apart today (see sidebar). The motifs are mostly biblical scenes and famous fairy-tale characters. While you'll see plenty of these houses, locals recommend the "Little Red Riding Hood" and "Hansel and Gretel" houses on Ettaler Strasse, the main drag into town (see "Oberammergau" map). If you want to see more, ask the TI for a map.

NEAR OBERAMMERGAU

These attractions are a long walk from town but easy to reach by car or bike.

Mountain Lifts, Luges, and More

Laber Bergbahn, a gondola that lifts you up to fine views, is at the east end of town. For an easy hike take the lift up and walk down in about 2.5 hours (www.laber-bergbahn.de).

Kolbensattel, across town to the west, is a family-friendly park with a chairlift, a mountain playground, a high-ropes course, and a speedy 1.5-mile-long **Alpine Coaster** (similar to a luge, closed off-season; €7.50 each for chairlift or coaster, €11.50 coaster combo-ticket with lift, €26 combo-ticket for coaster, ropes course, and lift, daily April-Nov 10:00-17:00 in good weather, tel. 08822/4760, www.kolbensattel.de). From the top, you can hike along the ridge to a series of mountain huts: In about 1.5 hours, you'll reach Pürschling; two hours later is Brunnenkopf (from which you could hike down to Linderhof Castle). Get tips and maps from the TI before doing these hikes.

WellenBerg Swimming Pool

Near the Laber Bergbahn lift and a 25-minute walk from town is this sprawling complex of indoor and outdoor pools and saunas (€8/3 hours, €12/day, €4.50 extra for sauna, daily 10:00-21:00, Himmelreich 52, tel. 08822/92360, www.wellenberg-oberammergau.de).

Sommerrodelbahn Steckenberg

The next town over, Unterammergau, hosts a stainless steel summer luge track that's faster than the Tegelberg luge but not nearly as wicked as the one in Biberwier. This one has double seats (allowing a parent to accompany kids) and two sticks—one for each hand; be careful of your elbows. Unlike other luges, children under age three are allowed, and you only pay one fare when a parent and child ride together.

Cost and Hours: €3.50/ride, €15/6 rides; May-late Oct Mon-Fri 13:00-17:00, Sat-Sun 10:00-18:00, closed off-season and when wet; Liftweg 1 in Unterammergau, clearly marked and easy 2.5-mile bike ride to Unterammergau along Bahnhofstrasse/Rottenbucherstrasse, take the first left when entering Unterammergau, tel. 08822/4027, www.steckenberg.de.

Sleeping in Oberammergau

Accommodations in Oberammergau tend to be affordable (compared to Füssen or Reutte) and friendly. All offer free parking. I've ranked these based on summer prices (generally May-Oct).

$$ Hotel Fux—quiet, romantic, and well run—rents 10 large rooms and six apartments decorated in the Bavarian *Landhaus* style (free sauna, indoor playground, Mannagasse 2a, tel. 08822/93093, www.hotel-in-oberammergau.de, info@firmafux.de).

$$ Mammhofer Suite & Breakfast, run by friendly Josef,

offers nine contemporary-Bavarian rooms (mostly suites and most with views) in a quiet, residential neighborhood just across the street from the town center (Daisenbergerstrasse 10, tel. 08822/923-753, www.mammhofer.com, stay@mammhofer.com).

$ Gasthof zur Rose is big and centrally located, with 19 mostly small but comfortable rooms run by the friendly Frank family. At the reception desk, look at the several decades' worth of photos showing the family performing in the Passion Play (family rooms, Dedlerstrasse 9, tel. 08822/4706, www.rose-oberammergau.de, info@rose-oberammergau.de).

$ Gästehaus Magold, homey and family-friendly, has three bright and spacious rooms and two apartments—twice as nice as the cheap hotel rooms in town, and for much less (cash only, immediately behind Gasthof zur Rose at Kleppergasse 1, tel. 08822/4340, www.gaestehaus-magold.de, info@gaestehaus-magold.de, hardworking Christine).

¢ Oberammergau Youth Hostel, on the river, is just a short walk from the center (family rooms, reception open 8:00-10:00 & 17:00-19:00, closed mid-Nov-Dec, Malensteinweg 10, tel. 08822/4114, www.oberammergau.jugendherberge.de, oberammergau@jugendherberge.de).

Eating in Oberammergau

$$$ Ammergauer Maxbräu, in the Hotel Maximilian on the edge of downtown, serves high-quality, thoughtfully presented Bavarian fare with a modern, international twist. The rustic-yet-mod interior—with big copper vats where they brew their own beer—is cozy on a rainy day. And in nice weather, locals fill the beer garden out front (daily 11:00-22:00, right behind the church, Ettaler Strasse 5, tel. 08822/948-740, www.maximilian-oberammergau.de).

$$ Gasthof zur Rose, a couple of blocks off the main drag, serves reasonably priced Bavarian food in its dining room and at a few outdoor tables (Tue-Sun 11:30-14:00 & 17:30-21:00, closed Mon, Dedlerstrasse 9, tel. 08822/4706, www.rose-oberammergau.de).

$$ El Puente may vex Mexican-food purists, but it's the most hopping place in town, with margaritas and cocktails attracting young locals and tourists alike. Come not for the burritos and enchiladas but for the bustling energy (pricier steaks, Mon-Sat 18:00-23:30, closed Sun, Daisenbergerstrasse 3, tel. 08822/945-777).

$ Café Hochenleitner, just a few minutes from the center, is quiet with nice outdoor seating and run by a family whose young son is winning awards for his creative confections (Tue-Sun 12:00-18:00, closed Mon, Faistenmantlgasse 7, tel. 08822/1312).

Dessert: Eis Café Paradiso serves up good gelato along the main street. In nice weather, Germans sunbathe with their big €5 sundaes on the generous patio out front (daily 9:00-23:00 in summer, Dorfstrasse 4, tel. 08822/6279).

Oberammergau Connections

From Oberammergau to: Linderhof Castle (bus #9622, 5-6/day Mon-Fri, 4/day Sat-Sun, 30 minutes; many of these also stop at **Ettal Monastery**), **Hohenschwangau** (for Neuschwanstein) and **Füssen** (bus #9606, 3-4/day, 1.5 hours, some transfer or change number to #73 at Echelsbacher Brücke), **Garmisch** (bus #9606, nearly hourly, better frequency in morning, 40 minutes; possible by train with transfer in Murnau, 1.5 hours; from Garmisch, you can ascend the **Zugspitze**), **Munich** (nearly hourly trains, 2 hours, change in Murnau). Train info: www.bahn.com.

Linderhof Castle

This homiest of "Mad" King Ludwig's castles is a small, comfortably exquisite mini Versailles— good enough for a minor god, and worth ▲▲. Set in the woods 15 minutes from Oberammergau and surrounded by fountains and sculpted, Italian-style gardens, it's the only palace I've toured that actually had me feeling envious.

GETTING THERE

Without a car, getting to (and back from) Linderhof is a royal headache, unless you're staying in Oberammergau. Buses from Oberammergau take 30 minutes (#9622, 5-6/day Mon-Fri, 4/day Sat-Sun). If you're driving, pay to park near the ticket office. If driving from Reutte, take the scenic Plansee route.

ORIENTATION TO LINDERHOF CASTLE

Cost: €8.50, €7.50 in winter
Hours: Daily April-mid-Oct 9:00-18:00, mid-Oct-March 10:00-16:30. Outlying buildings are closed mid-Oct-mid-April.
Information: Tel. 08822/92030, www.linderhof.de.
Crowd-Beating Tips: July and August crowds can mean an hour's wait between when you buy your ticket and when you start your tour. It's most crowded in the late morning. During this

BAVARIAN ALPS

period, you're wise to arrive after 15:00. Any other time of year, your wait to tour the palace should be brief. If you do wind up with time to kill, consider it a blessing—the gardens are fun to explore, and some of the smaller buildings can be seen quickly while you're waiting for your appointment.

Sightseeing Tips and Procedure: The complex sits isolated in natural splendor. Plan for lots of walking and a two-hour stop to fully enjoy this royal park. Bring rain gear in iffy weather. Your ticket comes with an entry time to tour the palace, which is a 10-minute walk from the ticket office. At the palace entrance, wait in line at the turnstile listed on your ticket (A through D) to take the required 30-minute English tour. Afterward, explore the rest of the park (grotto closed through 2021) and the other royal buildings dotting the king's playground if you like. You can eat lunch at a **$$** café across from the ticket office.

Renovations: Expect cranes and construction equipment on the grounds while the grotto behind the palace undergoes restoration.

VISITING THE CASTLE

The main attraction here is the **palace** itself. While Neuschwanstein is Neo-Gothic—romanticizing the medieval glory days of Bavaria—Linderhof is Baroque and Rococo, the frilly, overly ornamented styles more associated with Louis XIV, the "Sun King" of France. And, while Neuschwanstein is full of swans, here you'll see fleur-de-lis (the symbol of French royalty) and multiple portraits of Louis XIV, Louis XV, Madame Pompadour, and other pre-Revolutionary French elites. Though they lived a century apart, Ludwig and Louis were spiritual contemporaries: Both clung to the notion of absolute monarchy, despite the realities of the changing world around them. Capping the palace roofline is one of Ludwig's favorite symbols: Atlas, with the weight of the world literally on his shoulders. Oh, those poor, overburdened, misunderstood absolute monarchs!

Ludwig was king for 22 of his 40 years. He lived much of his last eight years here—the only one of his castles that was finished in his lifetime. Frustrated by the limits of being a "constitutional monarch," he retreated to Linderhof, inhabiting a private fantasy world where extravagant castles glorified his otherwise weakened kingship. You'll notice that the castle is small—designed for a single occupant. Ludwig, who never married or had children, lived here as a royal hermit.

The castle tour includes 10 rooms on the upper floor. (The downstairs, where the servants lived and worked, now houses the gift shop.) You'll see room after room exquisitely carved with Rococo curlicues, wrapped in gold leaf. Up above, the ceiling paintings have 3-D legs sticking out of the frame. Clearly inspired by Versailles, Linderhof even has its own (much smaller) hall of mirrors—decorated with over a hundred Nymphenburg porcelain vases and a priceless ivory chandelier. The bedroom features an oversized crystal chandelier, delicate Meissen porcelain flowers framing the mirrors, and a literally king-size bed—a two-story canopy affair draped in blue velvet. Perhaps the most poignant sight, a sad commentary on Ludwig's tragically solitary lifestyle, is his dinner table—preset with dishes and food—which could rise from the kitchen below into his dining room so he could eat alone.

(Examine the incredibly delicate flowers in the Meissen porcelain centerpiece.)

The palace is flanked on both sides with grand, terraced **fountains** (peopled by gleaming golden gods) that erupt at the top and bottom of each hour. If you're waiting for your palace tour to begin, hike up to the top of the terrace for a fine view.

Ludwig's **grotto,** behind the palace, is currently undergoing restoration work. Inspired by Wagner's *Tannhäuser* opera, this artificial cave (300 feet long and 70 feet tall) is actually a performance space. Its rocky walls are made of cement poured over an iron frame. (While Ludwig exalted the distant past, he took full advantage of then-cutting-edge technology to bring his fantasies to life.) The grotto provided a private theater for the reclusive king

to enjoy his beloved Wagnerian operas—he was usually the sole member of the audience. The grotto features a waterfall, fake stalactites, and a swan boat floating on an artificial lake (which could be heated for swimming). Brick ovens hidden in the walls could be used to heat the huge space. The first electricity in Bavaria was generated here, to change the colors of the stage lights and to power Ludwig's fountain and wave machine.

Other Sights at Linderhof: Several other smaller buildings are scattered around the grounds; look for posted maps and directional signs to track them down. Most interesting are the **Moroccan House** and **Moorish Kiosk.** With over-the-top decor seemingly designed by a sultan's decorator on acid, these allowed Ludwig to "travel" to exotic lands without leaving the comfort of

BAVARIAN ALPS

Bavaria. (The Moorish Kiosk is more interesting; look for its gild-ed dome in the woods beyond the grotto.) At the far edge of the property is **Hunding's Hut,** inspired by Wagner's *The Valkyrie*—a rustic-cottage stage-set with a fake ash tree inside it. And closer to the entrance—along the path between the ticket booth and the palace—is the **King's Cottage,** used for special exhibitions (often with an extra charge).

Ettal Monastery

In 1328, the Holy Roman Emperor was returning from Rome with what was considered a miraculous statue of Mary and Jesus. He was

in political and financial trouble, so to please God, he founded a monastery with this statue as its centerpiece. The monastery, located here because it was suit-ably off the beaten path, became important as a place of pilgrim-age, and today Ettal is on one of the most traveled tourist routes in Bavaria. Stopping here (free and easy for drivers) offers a convenient peek at a splendid Baroque church, worth ▲. Restaurants across the road serve lunch.

GETTING THERE

Ettal Monastery dominates the village of Ettal—you can't miss it. Ettal is a few minutes' **drive** (or a delightful **bike** ride) from Oberammergau. Just park (€1/4 hours in larger lots; free in small, crowded lot near the *Klosterladen,* alongside the building) and wan-der in. Some Oberammergau-to-Linderhof **buses** stop here (see "Oberammergau Connections," earlier).

ORIENTATION TO ETTAL MONASTERY

Cost and Hours: The church is free and open daily 8:00-19:45 in summer, until 18:00 off-season. It's best not to visit during Mass (usually Sun at 9:30 and 11:00). If you're moved to make a donation, you can drop a coin in one of the old-fashioned collection boxes.

Information: Tel. 08822/740, www.kloster-ettal.de.

VISITING THE MONASTERY

As you enter the more than 1,000-square-foot **courtyard,** imag-ine the 14th-century Benedictine abbey, an independent religious community. It produced everything it needed right here. In the late Middle Ages, abbeys like this had jurisdiction over the legal system, administration, and taxation of their district. Since then, the monastery has had its ups and downs. Secularized during the French Revolution and Napoleonic age, the Benedictines' property was confiscated by the state and sold. Religious life

returned a century later. Today the abbey survives, with 50 or 60 monks. It remains a self-contained community, with living quarters for the monks, workshops, and guests' quarters. Along with their religious responsibilities, the brothers make their famous liqueur, brew beer, run a hotel, and educate 380 students in their private high school. The monks' wares are for sale at two shops (look for the *Klosterladen* by the courtyard or the *Kloster-Markt* across the street).

After entering the outer door, notice the **tympanum** over the inner door dating from 1350. It shows the founding couple, Emperor Louis the Bavarian and his wife Margaret, directing our attention to the crucified Lord and inviting us to enter the church contemplatively.

Stepping inside, the light draws our eyes to the **dome** (it's a double-shell design, 230 feet high) rather than to the high altar. Illusions—with the dome opening right to the sky—merge heaven and earth. The dome fresco shows hundreds of Benedictines worshipping the Holy Trinity...the glory of the Benedictine Order. This is classic "south-German Baroque."

Statues of the **saints** on the altars are either engaged in a holy conversation with each other or singing the praises of God. Gilded curlicues seem to create constant movement, with cherubs adding to the energy. Side altars and confessionals seem to grow out of the architectural structure; its decorations and furnishings become part of an organic whole. Imagine how 18th-century farmers and woodcutters, who never traveled, would step in here on Sunday and be inspired to praise their God.

The origin of the monastery is shown over the **choir arch** directly above the altar: An angel wearing the robe of a Benedictine monk presents the emperor with a marble Madonna and commissions him to found this monastery. (In reality, the statue was made in Pisa, circa 1300, and given to the emperor in Italy.)

Dwarfed by all the magnificence and framed by a monumental tabernacle is that tiny, most precious statue of the abbey—the miraculous **statue of Mary and the Baby Jesus.**

Nearby: The fragrant **demonstration dairy** (*Schaukäserei*)

20 + C + M + B + 19

All over Germany (and much of Catholic Europe), you'll likely see written on doorways a mysterious message: "20 + C + M + B + 19." This is marked in chalk on Epiphany (Jan 6), the Christian holiday celebrating the arrival of the Magi to adore the newborn Baby Jesus. In addition to being the initials of the three wise men (Caspar, Melchior, and Balthazar), the letters also stand for the Latin phrase *Christus mansionem*

benedicat—"May Christ bless the house." The numbers represent the year (20+19), and the little crosses remind all who enter that the house has been blessed in this year. Epiphany is a bigger deal in Catholic Europe than in the US. The holiday includes gift-giving, feasting, and caroling door to door—often collecting for a charity organization. Those who donate get their doors chalked up in thanks, and these marks are left on the door through the year.

about a five-minute walk behind the monastery is worth a quick look. The farmhouse displays all the steps in the production line, starting with the cows themselves (next to the house), to the factory staff hard at work, and through to the end products, which you can sample in the shop (try the beer cheese). Better yet, enjoy a snack on the deck while listening to the sweet music/incessant clanging of cowbells (free; daily 10:00-17:00, off-season closed Mon; best cheese-making action 10:00-11:00; Mandlweg 1, tel. 08822/923-926, www.schaukaeserei-ettal.de). To walk there from the monastery's exit, take a left and go through the passageway; take another left when you get to the road, then yet another left at the first street (you'll see it up the road, directly behind the abbey).

Zugspitze

The tallest point in Germany, worth ▲▲ in clear weather, is also a border crossing. Lifts from both Austria and Germany meet at the 9,700-foot summit of the Zugspitze (TSOOG-shpit-seh). You can straddle the border between two great nations while enjoying an incredible view. Restaurants, shops, and telescopes await you at the summit.

BAVARIAN ALPS

SUMMITING THE ZUGSPITZE

German Approach: There are several ways to ascend from this side, but they all cost the same (€56 round-trip, less in winter, tel. 08821/7970, www. zugspitze.de).

If relying on public transit, first head to Garmisch (for details on getting there from Füssen, see "Füssen Connections," earlier; from Oberammergau, see "Oberammergau Connections," earlier). From there, ride a train to Eibsee (30 minutes, hourly departures daily 8:15-14:15), at which point you have a choice. You can walk across the parking lot and zip up to the top in a cable car (10 minutes, daily 8:30-16:45, departs at least every 30 minutes; in busy times departs every 10 minutes, but since each car fits only 35—which the electronic board suspensefully counts down as each passenger goes through the turnstile—you may have to wait to board). Or you can transfer to a cogwheel train (45 minutes to the top, departs hourly—coordinated with Garmisch train; once up top, transfer from the train to a short cable car for the quick, 3-minute ascent to the summit).

Drivers can go straight to Eibsee (about 10 minutes beyond Garmisch—head through town following signs for *Fernpass/Reutte,* and watch for the Zugspitze turnoff on the left); once there, you have the same cable car vs. cog railway choice described above. (Even though they're not taking the train from Garmisch, drivers pay the same—€56 round-trip, plus another €4 for parking.)

You can choose how you want to go up and down at the spur of the moment: both ways by cable car, both by cog train, or mix and match. Although the train ride takes longer, many travelers enjoy the more involved cog railway experience—at least one way. The disadvantage of the train is that more than half of the trip is through dark tunnels deep in the mountains; aside from a few fleeting glimpses of the Eibsee sparkling below, it's not very scenic.

Arriving at the top, you'll want to head up to the third floor (elevators recommended, given the high altitude)—follow signs for *Gipfel* (summit).

To get back down to Eibsee, keep in mind that the last cable car departs the summit at 16:45, and the last cogwheel train at 16:30. On busy days, you may have to reserve a return time once you reach the top—if it's crowded, look for signs and prebook your return to avoid getting stuck up top longer than you want. In general, allow plenty of time for afternoon descents: If bad weather hits in the late afternoon, cable cars can be delayed at the summit, causing tourists to miss their train connection from Eibsee back to Garmisch.

Hikers can enjoy the easy six-mile walk around the lovely Eibsee (start 5 minutes downhill from cable-car station).

Austrian Approach: The Tiroler Zugspitzbahn ascent is less crowded and cheaper than the Bavarian one. Make your way to the village of Ehrwald (drivers follow signs for *Tiroler Zugspitzbahn;* free parking). Departing from above Ehrwald, a lift zips you to the top in 10 minutes (€45 round-trip, departures in each direction at :00, :20, and :40 past the hour, daily 8:40-16:40 except closed during bad weather May-June and Oct-Nov, last ascent at

16:00, Austrian tel. 05673/2309, www.zugspitze.at). While those without a car will find the German ascent from Garmisch easier, the Austrian ascent is also doable. It's a 30-minute train trip from Reutte to Ehrwald (train runs every 2 hours); then either hop the bus from the Ehrwald train station to the lift (departures nearly hourly), or pay about €10 for the five-minute taxi ride from the train station.

VISITING THE SUMMIT

Whether you've ascended from the Austrian or German side, you're high enough now to enjoy a little tour of the summit. The two terraces—Bavarian and Tirolean—are connected by a narrow walkway, which was the border station before Germany and Austria opened their borders. The Austrian (Tirolean) side was higher until the Germans blew its top off in World War II to make a flak tower, so let's start there.

Tirolean Terrace: Before you stretches the Zugspitzplatt glacier. Is it melting? A reflector once stood here to slow it from shrinking during summer months. Many ski lifts fan out here, as if reaching for a ridge that defines the border between Germany and Austria. The circular metal building is the top of the cog railway line that the Germans cut through the mountains in 1931. Just above that, find a small square building—the *Hochzeitskapelle* (wedding chapel) consecrated in 1981 by Cardinal Joseph Ratzinger (a.k.a. the retired Pope Benedict XVI).

Both Germany and Austria use this rocky pinnacle for communication purposes. The square box on the Tirolean Terrace provides the Innsbruck airport with air traffic control, and a tower nearby is for the German *Katastrophenfunk* (civil defense network).

This highest point in Germany (there are many higher points in Austria) was first climbed in 1820. The Austrians built a cable car that nearly reached the summit in 1926. (You can see it just over the ridge on the Austrian side—look for the ghostly, abandoned concrete station.) In 1964, the final leg, a new lift, was built connecting that 1926 station to the actual summit, where you stand now. Before then, people needed to hike the last 650 feet to the top. Today's lift carries half a million people up to the Zugspitze every year. The Austrian station, which is much nicer than the German station, has a fine little museum—free with Austrian ticket, €4 if you came up from Germany—that shows three interesting videos (6-minute 3-D mountain show, 30-minute making-of-the-lift documentary, and 45-minute look at the nature, sport, and culture of the region).

Looking up the valley from the Tirolean Terrace, you can see the towns of Ehrwald and Lermoos in the distance, and the valley that leads to Reutte. Looking farther clockwise, you'll see the Eibsee below. Hell's Valley, stretching to the right of the Eibsee, seems to merit its name.

Bavarian Terrace: The narrow passage connecting the two terraces used to be a big deal—you'd show your passport here at the little blue house and shift from Austrian schillings to German marks. Notice the regional pride here: no German or Austrian national banners, but regional ones instead—*Freistaat Bayern* (Bavaria) and *Land Tirol.*

The German side features a golden cross marking the summit...the highest point in Germany. A priest and his friends hauled it up in 1851. The historic original was shot up by American soldiers using it for target practice in the late 1940s, so what you see today is a modern replacement. In the summer, it's easy to "summit" the Zugspitze, as there are steps and handholds all the way to the top. Or you can just stay behind and feed the birds. The yellow-beaked ravens get chummy with those who share a little pretzel or bread. Below the terrace, notice the restaurant that claims—irrefutably— to be the "highest *Biergarten* in Deutschland."

The oldest building up here is the first mountaineers' hut, built in 1897 and entwined with mighty cables that cinch it down. In 1985, observers clocked 200-mph winds up here—those cables were necessary. Step inside the restaurant to enjoy museum-like photos and paintings on the wall (including a look at the team who hiked up with the golden cross in 1851).

Near the waiting area for the cable cars and cogwheel train is a little museum (in German only) that's worth a look if you have some time to kill before heading back down. If you're going down on the German side, remember you must choose between the cable car (look for the *Eibsee* signs) or cog railway (look for *Talfahrt/De-*

BAVARIAN ALPS

scent, with a picture of a train; you'll board a smaller cable car for the quick trip to the train station).

Reutte, Austria

Reutte (ROY-teh, with a guttural *r*), a relaxed Austrian town of 6,000, is a 20-minute drive across the border from Füssen. While overlooked by the international tourist crowd, it's popular with Germans and Austrians for its climate. Doctors recommend its "grade 1" air.

Although its setting—surrounded by alpine peaks—is striking, the town itself is pretty unexceptional. But that's the point. I enjoy Reutte for the opportunity it offers to simply be in a real community. As an example of how the town is committed to its character, real estate can be sold only to those using it as a primary residence. (Many formerly vibrant alpine towns made a pile of money but lost their sense of community by becoming resorts. They allowed wealthy foreigners—who just drop in for a week or two a year—to buy up all the land, and are now shuttered up and dead most of the time.)

Reutte has one claim to fame among Americans: As Nazi Germany was falling in 1945, Hitler's top rocket scientist, Werner von Braun, joined the Americans (rather than the Russians) in Reutte. You could say that the American space program began here.

Reutte isn't featured in any other American guidebook. Its charms are subtle. It was never rich or important. Its castle is ruined, its buildings have painted-on "carvings," its churches are full, its men yodel for each other on birthdays, and its energy is spent soaking its Austrian and German guests in *Gemütlichkeit* (cozy conviviality). Most guests stay for a week, so the town's attractions are more time-consuming than thrilling.

Some travelers tell me this town is over-Reutte-d. Füssen's

tidy pedestrian core and glitzy hotels make it an easier home base. But in my view, Reutte's two big trump cards are its fine country-side accommodations (the farther from the town center, the more rustic, authentic, and relaxing) and its proximity to one of my favorite ruined castles, Ehrenberg. Since you need a car to take best advantage of these pluses (as well as to reach the King's Castles quickly), Reutte is a good place for drivers to spend the night.

Orientation to Reutte

Reutte feels spread out, because it's really a web of several villages that fill a basin hemmed in by mountains and cut through by the Lech River. Drivers find its tangle of crisscrossing roads bewildering at first; know where you're going and follow signs to stay on track (see the "Greater Reutte" map).

Reutte proper, near the train station, has a one-street downtown where you'll find the TI, museum, and a couple of hotels and eateries. The area's real charm lies in the abutting hamlets, and that's where my favorite hotels and restaurants are located: **Breitenwang,** flowing directly from Reutte to the east, marked by its pointy steeple; **Ehenbichl,** a farming village cuddled up against the mountains to the south; **Höfen,** squeezed between an airstrip and a cable-car station, just across the river from Ehenbichl; and remote **Pinswang,** stranded in a forgotten valley halfway to Germany, just over the mountain from Neuschwanstein. Watching over it all to the south are the **Ehrenberg Castle** ruins—viewable from just about everywhere and evocatively floodlit at night—two miles out of town on the main Innsbruck road.

TOURIST INFORMATION

Reutte's TI is a block from the train station (Mon-Fri 8:00-18:00, Sat 9:00-12:30 & 13:00-18:00, off-season Mon-Fri 8:00-17:00, Sat 10:00-14:00, closed Sun year-round, Untermarkt 34, tel. 05672/62336, www.reutte.com). Go over your sightseeing plans, ask about a Tirolean folk evening performance (summer only), and pick up city and biking/hiking maps, bus schedules, the *Griass Enk* twice-yearly events schedule (in German and English), a free town info booklet (with a good self-guided walk), and a brochure explaining the Aktiv-Card (available at hotels; described later, under "Helpful Hints").

ARRIVAL IN REUTTE

By Car: From the expressway, always take the south *(Süd)* exit into town (even if you pass the *Nord* exit first). For parking in town, blue lines denote pay-and-display spots. There are a few spaces just outside the TI that are free for up to 30 minutes—handy for stopping by with a few questions en route to your out-of-town hotel. For longer stays, there's a free lot (P-1) just past the train station on Mühler Strasse (about a 10-minute walk from the town center and TI).

By Train or Bus: When traveling by train make sure to get off at Reutte Bahnhof, not Reutte Schulzentrum. From the tidy little train/bus station (no baggage storage, usually unstaffed), exit straight ahead and walk three minutes straight up Bahnhofstrasse. After the park on your left, you'll see the TI.

HELPFUL HINTS

Hotel Card: Guests staying in the Reutte area (and, therefore, paying the local hotel tax) are entitled to an **Aktiv-Card**—be sure to ask your hotel for one. The TI has a brochure explaining the card's benefits, including free travel on some local buses, low-cost taxi service on most routes in high season, free admission to the recommended museum below Ehrenberg Castle, 50 percent off the Alpentherme bath complex, plus free days and discounts on many outdoor activities.

Laundry: There's no launderette, but a couple of recommended hotels let nonguests use their laundry services: **Hotel Maximilian** (wash, dry, and fold) and **Alpenhotel Ernberg** (self-service).

Bike Rental: Try **Sport 2000 Paulweber** (city bike-€20/day, mountain bike-€25/day, electric bike-€30-35/day, Mon-Fri 8:30-12:00 & 14:00-18:00, Sat 8:30-12:00, closed Sun, Allgäuer Strasse 15, tel. 05672/62232), or check at the Hotel Maximilian.

Taxi: Inexpensive taxi service is available to hotel guests with an Aktiv-Card (described earlier). Those without a card can call **Reutte Taxi** (tel. 0699-1050-4949).

Sights in and near Reutte

▲▲EHRENBERG CASTLE ENSEMBLE

If Neuschwanstein was the medieval castle dream, Ehrenberg *(Festungsensemble Ehrenberg)* is the medieval castle reality. Once the largest fortification in Tirol, its brooding ruins lie about two miles outside Reutte. What's here is actually an "ensemble" of four castles, built to defend against the Bavarians and to bottle up the strategic Via Claudia trade route, which cut through the Alps as it connected Italy and Germany. Half-forgotten and overgrown only a decade ago, they've been transformed into a fine attraction with hiking paths, a museum, guesthouse, and a recent addition: a 1,200-foot pedestrian suspension bridge. The European Union helped fund the project because it promotes the heritage of a multinational region—Tirol—rather than a country.

In Roman times, the Via Claudia—the road below Ehrenberg—was the main route between northern Italy (Verona) and southern Germany (Augsburg), and was broad enough for wheeled traffic. Historians estimate that in medieval times, about 10,000 tons of precious salt passed through this valley each year, so it's no wonder the locals built this complex of fortresses and castles to control traffic and levy tolls on all who passed.

The complex has four parts: the old toll buildings on the valley floor, where you park (the Klause); the oldest castle, on the hilltop directly above (Ehrenberg); a mightier castle on a higher peak of the same hill (Schlosskopf); and a smaller fortification across the valley (Fort Claudia). All four were once a single complex connected by walls. Signs posted throughout the site help orient visitors and explain some background on the region's history, geology, flora, and fauna, and colorful, fun boards relate local folktales.

Cost and Hours: The castle ruins themselves are free and always open, but the museum and suspension bridge charge admission (for details, see individual listings).

Information and Services: A helpful information desk has maps of trails leading up to the castle. Take advantage of the WC stop before you begin your ascent.

Getting There: The castles are on the road to Lermoos and Innsbruck, just five minutes by **car** from Reutte (parking-€4/day). It's a pleasant but steep 30-minute **walk** or a short **bike** ride from town; bikers can use the *Radwanderweg* along the Lech River (the TI has a good map).

Local **bus** #4250 runs sporadically from Reutte's main train station to Ehrenberg (5-8/day Mon-Sat, 1-3/day Sun, 10 minutes, €2.90; see www.vvt.at for schedules—the stop name is "Ehrenberger Klause"). However, no buses run directly *back* to Reutte from the castle. If you aren't driving, a taxi is your only option here (see "Helpful Hints," earlier).

▲Ehrenberg Museum

While there are no real artifacts here, the clever, kid-friendly museum is hands-on and well described in English. The focus is on castles, knights, and medieval warcraft. Some of the exhibits trace the fictional journey of a knight named Heinrich to Jerusalem in

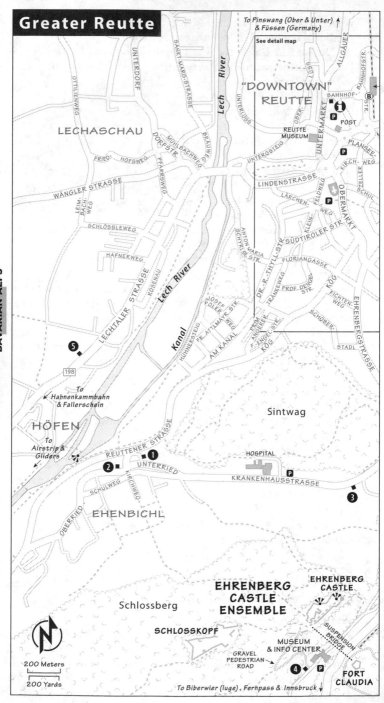

Greater Reutte

To Pinswang (Ober & Unter)
& Füssen (Germany)

See detail map

"DOWNTOWN" REUTTE

LECHASCHAU

Lech River

REUTTE MUSEUM

POST

BAVARIAN ALPS

WÄNGLER STRASSE

SCHLÖSSLEWEG

HAFNERWEG

Lech River

LINDENSTRASSE

OBERMARKT

Kanal

5

198

To Hahnenkammbahn & Fallerschein

HÖFEN

To Airstrip & Gliders

Sintwag

HOSPITAL

2   1

UNTERRIED

REUTTENER STRASSE

KRANKENHAUSSTRASSE

3

EHENBICHL

Schlossberg

EHRENBERG CASTLE ENSEMBLE

EHRENBERG CASTLE

SCHLOSSKOPF

SUSPENSION BRIDGE

MUSEUM & INFO CENTER

GRAVEL PEDESTRIAN ROAD

4

FORT CLAUDIA

N

200 Meters
200 Yards

To Biberwier (luge), Fernpass & Innsbruck

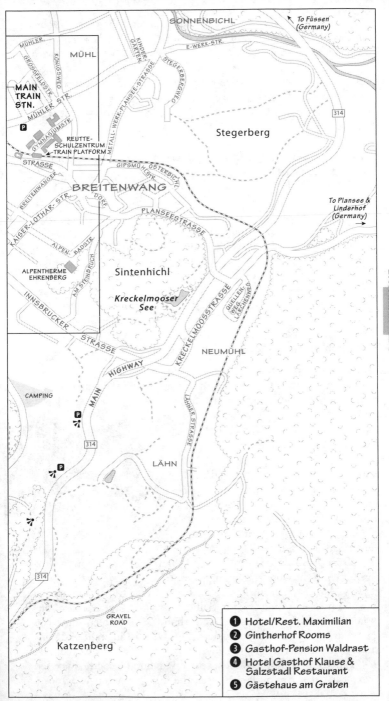

BAVARIAN ALPS

the late 1300s. You can try on a set of armor (and then weigh yourself), see the limited vision knights had to put up with when wearing helmets, learn about everyday medieval life, empathize with victims of the plague, join a Crusade, and pretend to play soccer with gigantic stone balls once tossed by a catapult. In the armory section, you can heft replica weapons from the period. Several videos and soundtracks spring to life if you press a button (select *E* for English).

A smaller exhibit (with separate entry fee) focuses on the still-wild Lech River and how it affects everything around it, from industry (rafting trade) to flora and fauna.

Cost and Hours: Museum—€8, nature exhibit—€5.50, combo-ticket for both—€10.80, daily 9:00-17:00, Dec-April 10:00-16:00, closed Nov, last entry one hour before closing, tel. 05672/62007, www.ehrenberg.at.

Eating: The **$$ Salzstadl** ("salt barn"), next to the museum, once held valuable salt being transported along the Via Claudia. Now it's a refreshingly authentic restaurant serving typical Tirolean meals and snacks *(Brotzeiten)*, as well as the local brew—Lechweg-Bier (lots of outdoor seating, salad bar; daily 11:30-22:30, hot food served until 20:00; tel. 05672/62213, www.gasthof-klause.com). This also serves as the reception for the hotel next door (see "At the Ehrenberg Ruins" under "Sleeping in and near Reutte," later).

▲▲Ehrenberg Ruins

Ehrenberg, a romantic 13th-century ruin, provides a super opportunity to let your imagination off its leash. Hike up 30 minutes from the parking lot in the valley for a great view from your own private ruins. The trail is well marked and has well-groomed gravel, but it's quite steep, and once you reach the castle itself, you'll want good shoes to scramble over the uneven stairs. The castle is always open.

➔ Self-Guided Tour: From the parking lot, follow yellow signs up into the woods, tracking *Ruine Ehrenberg* or *Bergruine Ehrenberg*. At the top of the first switchback, notice the option to turn left and hike 45 minutes up to Schlosskopf, the higher castle (described next; this is an easier ascent than the very steep route you can take from closer to Ehrenberg). But we'll head right and continue up the path through the lower entrance bastion of Ehrenberg.

Emerging from the woods, you'll pop out at a saddle between two steep hills. As you face Reutte, the hill on the left is Schlosskopf (notice the steeper ascent here to reach the top), and to the right is Ehrenberg. Ehrenberg is the older of the two, built around 1290. Thirteenth-century castles were designed to stand boastfully tall. Later, with the advent of gunpowder, castles dug in. (Notice the 18th-century ramparts around the castle.)

Now continue twisting up the path to Ehrenberg Castle. As you approach its outer gate, look for the small **door** to the left. It's the night entrance (tight and awkward, and therefore safer against a surprise attack). But we'll head through the **main gate**—actually, two of them. Castles were designed with layered defenses—outer bastion down below, outer gate here, inner gate deeper within—which allowed step-by-step retreat, giving defenders time to regroup and fight back against invading forces.

After you pass through the outer gate, but before climbing to the top of the castle, follow the path around to the right to a big, grassy courtyard with commanding views and a fat, restored **turret.** This stored gunpowder and held a big cannon that enjoyed a clear view of the valley below. In medieval times, all the trees approaching the castle were cleared to keep an unobstructed view.

Look out over the valley. The pointy spire marks the village of **Breitenwang,** which was the site of a Roman camp in AD 46. In 1489, after a bridge was built across the Lech River at Reutte (marked by the onion-domed church with the yellow tower), Reutte was made a market town and eclipsed Breitenwang in importance. Any gliders circling? They launch from just over the river in Höfen.

For centuries, this castle was the seat of government—ruling an area called the "judgment of Ehrenberg" (roughly the same as today's "district of Reutte"). When the emperor came by, he stayed here. In 1604, the ruler moved downtown into more comfortable quarters, and the castle was no longer a palace.

Now climb to the top of Ehrenberg Castle. Take the high ground. There was no water supply here—just kegs of wine, beer, and a cistern to collect rain. Up at the top, appreciate how strategic this lofty position is—with commanding views over Reutte and its broad valley, as well as the narrow side-valley where the pedestrian bridge looms over the highway down below. But also notice that you're sandwiched between two higher hilltops: Schlosskopf in one direction and Falkenberg (across the narrow valley) in the other. In the days before gunpowder, those higher positions offered no real threat. But in the age of cannonballs, Ehrenberg was suddenly very vulnerable...and very obsolete.

Still, Ehrenberg repelled 16,000 Swedish soldiers in the defense of Catholicism in 1632. But once Schlosskopf was fortified a few decades later, Ehrenberg's days were numbered, and its end was not glorious. In the 1780s, a local businessman bought the castle in order to sell off its parts. Later, in the late 19th century, when vagabonds moved in, the roof was removed to make squatting miserable. With the roof gone, deterioration quickened, leaving only this evocative shell and a whiff of history.

Scramble around the ruined walls a bit—nocking imaginary arrows—and head back down through the main gate, returning to the valley the way you came. If you have more energy and castle curiosity, you could try conquering the next castle over: Schlosskopf.

▲Schlosskopf

When Bavarian troops captured Ehrenberg in 1703, the Tiroleans climbed up to the bluff above it to rain cannonballs down on their former fortress. In 1740, a mighty new castle—designed to defend against modern artillery—was built on this sky-high strategic location: Schlosskopf ("Castle Head"). But it too fell into ruin, and by the end of the 20th century, the castle was completely overgrown with trees—you literally couldn't see it from Reutte. But today the trees have been shaved away, and the castle has been excavated. In 2008, the Castle Ensemble project, led by local architect Armin Walch, opened the site with English descriptions and view platforms. One spot gives spectacular views of the strategic valley. The other looks down on the older Ehrenberg Castle ruins, illustrating the strategic problems presented with the advent of the cannon.

Getting There: There are two routes to Schlosskopf, both steep and time-consuming. The steeper of the two (about 30 minutes straight up) starts at the little saddle of land between the two castles (described earlier). The second, which curls around the back of the hill, is less steep but takes longer (45-60 minutes); this one begins from partway down the gravel switchbacks between Ehrenberg and the valley floor—just watch for *Schlosskopf* signs.

Highline 179 Suspension Footbridge

At more than 1,200 feet long, this suspended pedestrian bridge hangs more than 300 feet above the valley floor, connecting Ehrenberg with the previously difficult-to-reach Fort Claudia across the valley. It was the vision of architect and local trailblazer Armin Walch, who helped restore the Ehrenberg ruins and wanted to do something to draw attention to the region. Designed by Swiss engineers and paid for by private investors, the bridge was erected in just six months. With your ticket, the turnstile lets you in, then you walk to the far side where you're welcome to leave the bridge and enjoy the viewpoint. With the

same ticket, you can walk back across the bridge to your starting point.

I'm not much into adventure sports, but for me, this wobbly ramble is a thrill. If you look down, directly beneath you is the Via Claudia, which in Roman times was the main route between Italy and Germany. Now this bridge is at the foot of all these great castles, allowing travelers a fun way to reach them—if you like a little adventure.

Cost and Hours: €8 round-trip, better to purchase ticket at the complex's information desk (at parking lot level, credit cards accepted) in case the cash-only machines at the top aren't working, children's tickets available only at information desk; daily 8:00-22:00, open rain or shine unless too windy, tel. 05672/62336, www.highline179.com.

IN REUTTE TOWN
Reutte Museum (Museum Grünes Haus)

Reutte's cute city museum offers a quick look at the local folk culture and the story of the castles. There are exhibits on Ehrenberg and the Via Claudia, local painters, and more—ask to borrow the English translations.

Cost and Hours: €3; Tue-Sat 13:00-17:00, closed Sun-Mon; shorter hours and closed Sun-Tue off-season; closed Easter-end of April and Nov-early Dec; in the green building with trompe l'oeil columns and window trim at Untermarkt 25, around corner from Hotel Goldener Hirsch, tel. 05672/72304, www.museum-reutte.at.

▲▲Tirolean Folk Evening

Ask the TI or your hotel if there's a Tirolean folk evening scheduled. During the summer (July-Sept), nearby towns (such as Höfen on Tue) occasionally put on an evening of yodeling, slap dancing, and Tirolean frolic. These are generally free and worth the short drive. Off-season, you'll have to do your own yodeling. Free open-air concerts *(Platzkonzerte)* are held in Reutte and the surrounding communities in the summer. For listings of these and other local events, pick up a copy of the *Griass Enk* entertainment listings at the TI.

Alpentherme Ehrenberg

This extensive swimming pool and sauna complex, a 15-minute walk from downtown Reutte, is a tempting retreat. The Badewelt section features two indoor pools and a big outdoor saltwater pool, and two indoor waterslides. The all-nude Saunaparadies section (no kids under age 16) consists of three indoor saunas, three freestanding outdoor saunas, and a big outdoor swimming pool. You'll be given a wristband that lets you access your locker and buy snacks on credit without needing a key or cash. Those staying in the Reutte area get a 50 percent discount with an Aktiv-Card (see "Helpful Hints," earlier); it's a nice way to relax after hiking around castles all day.

Cost and Hours: Pools only—€10.50/2 hours, €12.50/4 hours, €14.50/day; sauna and pools—€21/3 hours, €27/day; towel rental—€3, robe rental—€5, swimsuits sold but not rented; daily 10:00-21:00, sauna until 22:00, closes for one week every May; Thermenstrasse 10, tel. 05672/72222, www.alpentherme-ehrenberg.at.

ACROSS THE RIVER, IN HÖFEN

Just over the Lech River are two very different ways to reach high-altitude views. To get here from Reutte, head up Lindenstrasse (where the cobbled Obermarkt ends), cross the bridge, and turn left down Lechtaler Strasse; as you enter the village of Höfen, you'll see the cable car to your right and the airstrip to your left.

▲Scenic Flights

For a major thrill on a sunny day, drop by the tiny airport in Höfen, where small single-prop planes and gliders take passengers on scenic flights (April-Oct). Al-

though I've listed contact information below, your best bet is to show up at the airstrip on a good-weather afternoon and ask around. Prop planes can buzz the Zugspitze and Ludwig's castles and give you a bird's-eye peek at the Ehrenberg ruins (tel. 05672/632-0729 or mobile 0664-221-2233, www.flugsportverein-reutte.at). The prop planes and gliders are based out of two different restaurants that face the airstrip. From the main road, watch for the big building marked *Flugplatz* down below.

Hahnenkammbahn

This mountain lift swoops you in small, enclosed cars high above the tree line to an attractive panoramic restaurant and starting point for several hikes. In the alpine flower park, special paths lead you past countless varieties of local flora. Unique to this lift is a barefoot hiking trail *(Barfusswanderweg)*, designed to be walked without shoes—no joke.

Cost and Hours: €13.50 one-way, €19 round-trip, runs June-Oct daily 9:00-16:30, also in good weather late May and early Nov, flowers best in late July, base station across the river in Höfen, tel. 05672/62420, www.reuttener-seilbahnen.at.

Luge Lesson

Taking a wild ride on a summer luge (pronounced "loozh") is a quintessential alpine experience. In German, it's called a *Sommer-rodelbahn* ("summer toboggan run"). To try one of Europe's great accessible thrills, take the lift up to the top of a mountain, grab a wheeled sled-like go-cart, and scream back down the mountainside on a banked course. Then take the lift back up and start all over again.

Luge courses are highly weather dependent and can close at the slightest hint of rain. If the weather's questionable, call ahead to confirm that your preferred luge is open. Stainless steel courses are more likely than concrete ones to stay open in drizzly weather.

Operating the sled is simple: Push the stick forward to go faster, pull back to apply brakes. Even a novice can go very, very fast. Most are cautious on their first run, speed demons on their second...and bruised and bloody on their third. A woman once showed me her travel journal illustrated with her husband's dried five-inch-long luge scab. He had disobeyed the only essential rule of luging: Keep both hands on your stick. To avoid a bumper-to-bumper traffic jam, let the person in front of you get as far ahead as possible before you start. You'll emerge from the course with a windblown hairdo and a smile-creased face.

Key Luge Terms

Lenkstange	lever
drücken / schneller fahren	push / go faster
ziehen / bremsen	pull / brake
Schürfwunde	scrape
Schorf	scab

NEAR REUTTE
Sights Along the Lech River
The Lech River begins high in the Alps and meanders 75 miles (including right past Reutte) on its way to the Lechfall, where it becomes navigable, near Füssen. This stretch of the Lech River Valley (Lechtal) has been developed as a popular hiking trail, called the **Lechweg,** divided into 15 stages *(Strecken)*; part of the area has also

been designated as a nature park. A variety of glossy brochures—mostly in German and available at local TIs and hotels—explain the importance of the Lech to local culture and outline some enticing hikes.

Within the pristine Tiroler Lech Nature Park, a little outside Reutte, is an impressive wooden **lookout tower** from which you can observe the vibrant bird life in the wetlands along the Lech River (110 species of birds nest here). Look for *Vogelerlebnispfad* signs as you're driving through the village of Pflach (on the road between Reutte and Füssen; www.naturpark-tiroler-lech.at).

▲▲Biberwier Luge Course

Near Lermoos, on the road between Reutte and Innsbruck, you'll find the Biberwier *Sommerrodelbahn*. At 4,250 feet, it's the longest summer luge in Tirol. The drawbacks are its brief season, short hours, and a proclivity for shutting down sporadically—even at the slightest bit of rain. This is clearly the most exciting (and dangerous) of the region's luge rides. Keep your knees and elbows in tight, keep both hands on the stick, and watch your speed on corners. Every day some hotshot leaves a big chunk of skin on the course—a painful souvenir that lasts a very long time.

If you don't have a car, this is not worth the trouble; consider the luge near Neuschwanstein instead (see "Tegelberg Luge" on page 436). The ugly cube-shaped building marring the countryside near the luge course is a hotel for outdoor adventure enthusiasts. You can ride your mountain bike right into your room, or skip the elevator by using its indoor climbing wall.

Cost and Hours: €7.80/ride, cheaper with multiride tickets; daily mid-May-early Oct 8:30-17:00, stays open later July-Aug, closed off-season; tel. 05673/2323, www.bergbahnen-langes.at.

Getting There: It's 20 minutes from Reutte on the main road toward Innsbruck; Biberwier is the first exit after a long tunnel.

▲Fallerschein

Easy for drivers and a special treat for those who may have been Kit Carson in a previous life, this extremely remote log cabin village, south of Reutte, is a 4,000-foot-high flower-speckled world of serene slopes and cowbells. Thunderstorms roll down the valley like it's God's bowling alley, but the pint-size church on the high ground, blissfully simple in a land of Baroque, seems to promise that this huddle of houses will survive, and the river and breeze will just keep flowing. The couples sitting on benches are mostly Austrian vacationers who've rented cabins here. Some of them, appreciating the remoteness of Fallerschein, are having affairs.

Getting There: From Reutte, it's a 45-minute drive. Take road 198 to Stanzach (passing Weissenbach am Lech, then Forchach), then turn left toward Namlos. Follow the L-21 Berwang road for about five miles to a parking lot. From there, it's a two-mile walk down a drivable but technically closed one-lane road. Those driving in do so at their own risk.

Sleeping in Fallerschein: ¢ **Michl's Fallerscheiner Stube** is a family-friendly mountain-hut restaurant with a low-ceilinged attic space that has basic dorm beds for up to 17 sleepy hikers. The accommodations aren't fancy, but if you're looking for remote, this is it (May-Oct only, wildlife viewing deck, reservations best made by phone, mobile 0676-727-9681, www.alpe-fallerschein.com, michael@alpe-fallerschein.com, Knitel family).

Sleeping in and near Reutte

While it's not impossible by public transport, staying here makes most sense for those with a car. Reutte is popular with Austrians and Germans, who visit year after year for one- or two-week vacations. Prices stay fairly even throughout the year. Remember to ask for the Aktiv-Card (see page 458). My recommendations all have free parking and a great breakfast.

Most of my listings are in the "villages" around Reutte (such as Breitenwang, Ehenbichl, and Höfen), which basically feel like the suburbs. For even more options, ask the Reutte TI for their list of private homes that rent out rooms. These average about €30 per person per night in a room with breakfast and facilities down the hall.

IN CENTRAL REUTTE

$ Hotel "Das Beck" offers 16 simple, sunny rooms (most with balconies) filling a modern building in the heart of town close to the train station. This is the most practical option for those coming by train or bus. It's a great value, and guests are personally taken care of by Hans, Inge, Tamara, and Manuela. Their small café offers tasty snacks and specializes in Austrian and Mediterranean wines. Expect good conversation, overseen by Hans (family rooms, Untermarkt 11, tel. 05672/62522, www.hotel-das-beck.at, info@hotel-das-beck.at).

IN BREITENWANG

Now basically a part of Reutte, the older and quieter village of Breitenwang has good *Zimmer* and a fine bakery. It's a 20-minute walk from the Reutte train station: From the post office, follow Planseestrasse past the onion-dome church to the pointy straight-dome church near the two hotels. The Hosp family—as well as some others renting private rooms—have places along Kaiser-Lothar-Strasse, the first right past this church. Reutte's Alpentherme indoor pool complex, 50 percent off with your Aktiv-Card, is just around the block.

If staying in Breitenwang and traveling by train, take advantage of the tiny Reutte-Schulzentrum station, just a five-minute walk from these listings. All trains on the Garmisch-Reutte line stop here, but only on demand—which means you have to let the conductor know in advance where you want to get off. To board at Reutte-Schulzentrum, stand on the platform and flag the train down; you'll be able to buy a ticket from the conductor with no penalty.

$$ Alpenhotel Ernberg's 26 comfortable rooms, with wooden accents and colorful terraces, are run with great care by friendly and hardworking Hermann, who combines alpine elegance with modern touches. Nestle in for some serious coziness among the carved-wood eating nooks, tiled stoves, and family-friendly backyard (RS%, family rooms, self-service laundry, popular restaurant, bar, Planseestrasse 50, tel. 05672/71912, www.ernberg.at, info@ernberg.at).

$$ Moserhof Hotel has 40 traditional rooms with alpine accents and balconies plus an elegant dining room and sitting areas throughout (elevator, restaurant, sauna and whirlpool, Planseestrasse 44, tel. 05672/62020, www.hotel-moserhof.at, info@hotel-moserhof.at, Hosp family).

IN EHENBICHL, NEAR THE EHRENBERG RUINS

These listings are a bit farther from central Reutte, a couple of miles upriver in the village of Ehenbichl. From central Reutte, go south on Obermarkt and turn right on Kög, which becomes Reuttener Strasse, following signs to *Ehenbichl*. These places are inconvenient by public transit (you'll need to brave infrequent local buses; see www.vvt.at for schedules). For taxi service, ask your hotelier. For locations, see the "Greater Reutte" map, earlier.

$$ Hotel Maximilian offers 32 rooms and a fine restaurant (evenings only, closed Wed). Friendly Gabi, Monika, and the rest of the Koch family proudly leave no detail unattended and keep guests entertained with table tennis, a pool table, play areas for children (indoors and out), a piano, and a sauna (family rooms, some view rooms, elevator, laundry service, hotel closed late Oct-mid-Dec, Reuttener Strasse 1 in Ehenbichl—don't let your GPS take you to Reuttener Strasse in Pflach, tel. 05672/62585, www.maxihotel.com, info@hotelmaximilian.at). They rent cars to guests only (€0.72/km, automatic transmission) and bikes to anyone (guests—€5/half-day, €8/day; nonguests—€6/half-day, €12/day).

$ Gintherhof is a working dairy farm that provides its guests with fresh milk, butter, and homemade jam. Kind, hardworking Annelies Paulweber offers a warm welcome, geranium-covered

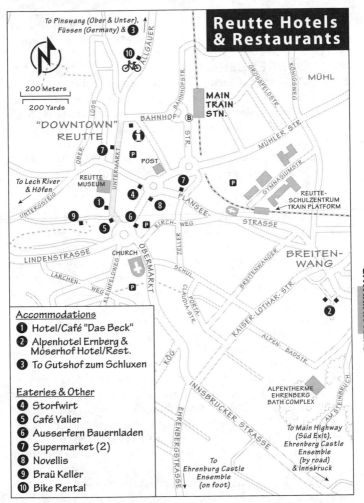

Reutte Hotels & Restaurants

To Pinswang (Ober & Unter), Füssen (Germany) & ③

MÜHL

200 Meters
200 Yards

MAIN TRAIN STN.

"DOWNTOWN" REUTTE

To Lech River & Höfen

REUTTE MUSEUM

POST

BAHNHOF

REUTTE-SCHULZENTRUM TRAIN PLATFORM

PLANSEE-STRASSE

BREITEN-WANG

LINDENSTRASSE

CHURCH

OBERMARKT

ALPENTHERME EHRENBERG BATH COMPLEX

To Main Highway (Süd Exit), Ehrenberg Castle Ensemble (by road) & Innsbruck

INNSBRUCKER STRASSE

To Ehrenburg Castle Ensemble (on foot)

EHRENBERGSTRASSE

BAVARIAN ALPS

Accommodations
① Hotel/Café "Das Beck"
② Alpenhotel Ernberg & Moserhof Hotel/Rest.
③ To Gutshof zum Schluxen

Eateries & Other
④ Storfwirt
⑤ Café Valier
⑥ Ausserfern Bauernladen
⑦ Supermarket (2)
⑧ Novellis
⑨ Braü Keller
⑩ Bike Rental

balconies, four cozy rooms, and one apartment (with kitchenette), all complete with free hiking gear and a Madonna in every corner (cash only, Unterried 7, just up the road behind Hotel Maximilian, tel. 05672/67697, www.gintherhof.com, info@gintherhof.com).

$ Gasthof-Pension Waldrast is run by the Huter family and their dog, Picasso. Built in 1928, the place feels hauntingly quiet and has no restaurant, but it's inexpensive and offers 10 pleasant, spacious rooms with generous sitting areas, castle-view balconies, and traditional Austrian furnishings. It's also within easy walking distance of the Ehrenberg Castle ruins. Friendly Gerd restored a nearly 500-year-old mill and will happily show it to interested guests (cash only, family rooms, Krankenhausstrasse 16, tel. 05672/62443, www.waldrasttirol.com, info@waldrasttirol.com).

AT THE EHRENBERG RUINS
$$ Hotel Gasthof Klause, just below the Ehrenberg ruins and next to the castle museum, rents 12 surprisingly sleek and modern rooms with balconies, as well as 15 apartments (some with kitchenettes). You'll need a car to get anywhere besides Ehrenberg. Reception is in the Salzstadl restaurant just across the street (family rooms, tel. 05672/62213, www.ehrenberg.at, gasthof-klause@ehrenberg.at, see the "Greater Reutte" map, earlier).

ACROSS THE RIVER, IN HÖFEN
$$ Gästehaus am Graben, with 13 rooms, is a good value less than two miles from Reutte, with fine castle views and family rooms sleeping four to six (closed April, Nov, and last three weeks in Jan; from downtown Reutte, cross bridge and follow main road left along river, or take bus #4268 to the Graben stop; Graben 1—see the "Greater Reutte" map, earlier, tel. 05672/626-440, www.hoefen.at, info@hoefen.at, Reyman family).

IN PINSWANG
The village of Pinswang is closer to Füssen (and Ludwig's castles), but still in Austria. While this hotel works best for drivers, about half of the departures of yellow post bus #4258/#74, which runs between the Reutte and Füssen train stations, stop here (3-4/day, get off at Pinswang Gemeindeamt stop, verify details with hotel or at www.postbus.at, or use www.bahn.com and plug in "Pinswang Gemeindeamt" to find a workable train-bus connection).

$$ Gutshof zum Schluxen gets the "Remote Old Hotel in an Idyllic Setting" award. This family-friendly farm, with 24 rooms and a playground, offers rustic elegance and lots of wooden accents. Its picturesque meadow setting will turn you into a dandelion-picker, and its proximity to Neuschwanstein will turn you into a hiker—the castle is about an hour's walk away (family room, some rooms with balconies, laundry service, free loaner bikes for Rick Steves readers, restaurant closed Mon-Tue, between Reutte and Füssen in village of Pinswang, tel. 05677/53217, www.schluxen.at, info@schluxen.at, Mathias).

To reach Neuschwanstein from this hotel by foot or bike, follow the dirt road up the hill behind the hotel. When the road forks at the top of the hill, go right (downhill), cross the Austria-Germany border (marked by a sign and deserted hut), and follow the narrow, paved path to the castles. It's a 1- to 1.5-hour hike or a great circular bike trip (allow 30 minutes; cyclists can return to Schluxen from the castles on a different 30-minute bike route via Füssen).

Eating in Reutte

The nicer restaurants in Reutte are all in hotels. **$$$ Alpenhotel Ernberg,** the **$$$ Moserhof Hotel,** and **$$$ Hotel Maximilian** (evenings only) all have fine restaurants. On weekdays, Alpenhotel Ernberg serves good three-course lunches for €11.

$ Storfwirt is ideal for a quick and cheap weekday lunch. This rustic cafeteria in downtown Reutte serves some 300 happy eaters every day (salad bar, daily soup-and-main-course specials, always something for vegetarians). Their adjacent **deli** is a great place to shop for a Tirolean picnic; choose from the local meats, cheeses, and prepared salads in the glass case, pick up a schnitzel with potato salad, or ask them to make you a sandwich to order. You can take your food away or eat at informal tables (Storfwirt and deli both open Mon-Fri 11:00-14:00, closed Sat-Sun; next door to the big Müller pharmacy at Schrettergasse 15, tel. 05672/62640, www. storfwirt.at, helpful manager Rainer).

$ Café Valier, perfect for coffee and cake, is a local mainstay that has been run by the same family for five generations (Mon-Sat 7:00-18:00, closed Sun, Untermarkt 5, tel. 05672/62462).

Picnic Supplies: Along Mühler Strasse, near the intersection with Untermarkt, is the **Ausserfern Bauernladen** (farmer's shop), where local farmers sell their own products. You can buy picnic fixings (cheeses, spreads, and yummy *Heuwürstchen* sausages cooked in hay), or ask them to make you a rustic sandwich to eat at one of the tables (Wed-Fri 9:00-18:00, Sat until 12:00, closed Sun-Tue, Obermarkt 3, mobile 0676-575-4588). **Eurospar** has groceries and a handy deli section with salads, sandwiches, and hot meals (Mon-Fri 7:15-19:30, Sat until 18:00, Sun until 11:00; Mühler Strasse 20). **Billa** supermarket also has picnic supplies (across from TI at Untermarkt 33, Mon-Fri 7:15-19:30, Sat until 18:00, closed Sun).

Nightlife: **$ Novellis** is the most happening joint in town, with live music on Fridays and Saturdays. Its salads, burgers, and wraps offer a nice escape from typical Bavarian food (Mon-Fri 9:00-24:00, Sat from 10:00, closed Sun; Mühler Strasse 12, tel. 05672/64612). **Braü Keller,** behind Hotel "Das Beck," offers a classier lounge with a nice drink menu and small bites (Thu-Sat 17:00-24:00, closed Sun-Wed, Untermarkt 7a). A strip of bars, dance clubs, and Italian restaurants lines Lindenstrasse.

Reutte Connections

BY PUBLIC TRANSPORTATION

From Reutte by Train to: Ehrwald (at base of Zugspitze lift, every 2 hours, 30 minutes), **Garmisch** (same train, every 2 hours, 1 hour), **Innsbruck** (every 2 hours, 2.5 hours, transfer in Garmisch),

Munich (hourly, about 3 hours, some with 1 transfer), **Salzburg** (every 2 hours, 5 hours, transfer in Garmisch and Munich). Austrian train info: Tel. 051-717 (to get an operator, dial 2, then 2), www.oebb.at; German train info: www.bahn.com.

By Bus to: Füssen (#4258—but known as #74 in Germany, 6-7/day, last bus at 18:05, 30-50 minutes, €4.50 one-way, buses depart from train station, pay driver).

ROUTE TIPS FOR DRIVERS

From downtown Reutte, *Fernpass* signs lead you out to the main Innsbruck road, which is also the best way to reach the Ehrenberg ruins. To reach the Ehrenberg Castle ruins, the Biberwier luge, the Zugspitze (either the Austrian ascent at Ehrwald or the German ascent at Garmisch), or Innsbruck, turn right for the on-ramp (marked *Fernpass* and *Innsbruck*) to highway 179. But if you're headed for Germany via the scenic Plansee, Linderhof Castle, Ettal Monastery, or Oberammergau, continue straight (bypassing the highway on-ramp).

BAVARIAN ALPS

THE DOLOMITES

Bolzano • Castelrotto • Alpe di Suisi

The Italian Dolomites offer some of the best mountain thrills in Europe. The city of Bolzano—about 75 miles south of Innsbruck, over Austria's border with Italy—is the gateway to the Dolomites, blending Austrian tidiness with an Italian love for life. And the village of Castelrotto is a good home base for your exploration of Alpe di Siusi (Seiser Alm), Europe's largest alpine meadow. Dolomite, a sedimentary rock similar to limestone, gives these mountains their distinctive shape and color. The bold, light-gray cliffs and spires flecked with snow, above green, flower-speckled meadows and beneath a blue sky, offer a powerful and memorable mountain experience.

A hard-fought history has left the region bicultural, with an emphasis on the German. In the mountains and closer to the border, most locals speak German first, and some wish they were still part of Austria. In the Middle Ages, as part of the Holy Roman Empire, the region faced north. Later, it was firmly in the Austrian Habsburg realm. By losing World War I, Austria's South Tirol became Italy's Alto Adige. Mussolini did what he could to Italianize the region, including giving each town an Italian name and building a severely fascist-style new town in Bolzano. But even as recently as the 1990s, secessionist groups agitated violently for more autonomy—with some success (see sidebar).

The government has wooed locals with economic breaks, which have made this one of Italy's richest areas (as local prices attest), and today all signs and literature in the province of Alto Adige/Südtirol are in both languages. Some include a third language, Ladin—an ancient Romance language still spoken in a few traditional areas. (I have listed both the Italian and German, so the confusion caused by this guidebook will match that experienced in your travels.)

The Dolomites

DOLOMITES

The Dolomites are well developed, and the region's most famous destinations suffer from après-ski fever. But in spite of all the glamorous resorts and busy construction cranes, the regional color survives in a warm, blue-aproned, ruddy-faced, felt-hat-with-feathers way. There's yogurt and yodeling for breakfast. Culturally, as much as geographically, the area is reminiscent of Austria. In fact, the Austrian region of Tirol is named for a village that is now part of Italy.

PLANNING YOUR TIME

One night in the Dolomites will give you a feel for the South Tirol's alpine culture. But it's best to stay at least two nights so you have at least one full day to hike. Pretty Castelrotto is the best base for hiking in the spectacular Alpe di Siusi alpine meadow, but Italian-flavored Bolzano, down in the valley, is also in easy reach of the high-mountain lifts.

From either town, plan an early start up to Compatsch, the gateway to the high Alpe di Siusi meadow. Tenderfeet stroll and ride the lifts from there. For serious mountain thrills, do an all-day hike. And for an unforgettable memory, spend a night in a mountain hut. With a second day, do more hiking or spend time in Bolzano, where you can stroll the old town and visit Ötzi the Iceman at the excellent archaeology museum (best to get tickets in advance). Always check local transportation timetables before you set out.

Hiking season is mid-June through mid-October. The region is particularly crowded, booming, and blooming from mid-July through mid-September (but once you're out on the trails, you'll leave the crowds behind). It's packed with Italian vacationers in August. Spring is usually dead, with lifts shut down, huts closed, and the most exciting trails still under snow. Many hotels and restaurants close in April and November. By mid-May, most businesses reopen, some lifts start running (check dates at www.seiseralm.it), and—if you luck into good weather—a few rewarding hikes are already possible. Ski season (Dec-Easter) is busiest—and most expensive—of all.

Bolzano

Willkommen to the Italian Tirol! If Bolzano ("Bozen" in German) weren't so sunny, you could be in Innsbruck. This enjoyable old city is the most convenient gateway to the Dolomites, especially if you're relying on public transportation. It's just the place to take a Tirolean stroll.

Bolzano feels like a happy castaway between the Germanic and Italian worlds. The people are warm and friendly, but organized. One person greets you in Italian, the next in German. But everyone can agree the city has a special verve, with lively shopping arcades, a bustling food-and-flower market, and a tidy main square with a backdrop of colorful churches and wooded foothills.

The town has only one museum worth entering, but it's world class, offering the chance to see Ötzi the Iceman—a 5,300-year-old Tirolean found frozen on a mountaintop—in the (shriveled, leathery) flesh. Beyond that, Bolzano is made for strolling, relaxing, and hiking in the nearby hills—and works well as a home base for venturing deeper into the mountains (though Castelrotto is closer to the high-mountain lifts).

Orientation to Bolzano

Virtually everything I mention in Bolzano (pop. 105,000) is in the compact and strollable old town, which radiates out from the main square, Piazza Walther/Waltherplatz. Those curious about fascist architecture can head 10 minutes west of the center to see Mussolini's "New Bolzano" development. And many enticing hikes into the foothills that cradle Bolzano begin from your hotel's doorstep.

TOURIST INFORMATION

Bolzano's TI, just down the street from the train station, is helpful (Mon-Fri 9:00-19:00, Sat 9:30-18:00, may open Sun May-Sept 10:00-15:00, otherwise closed Sun, Via Alto Adige/Südtiroler Strasse 60, www.bolzano-bozen.it).

Discount Card: Consider buying the **Museummobil Card,** which covers most museums in the South Tirol (including the archaeology museum, with its famous Iceman), plus trains, buses, the Funivia del Renon/Rittner Seilbahn cable car to Oberbozen, and more (€30/3 days, available at local TIs and the train station baggage storage office, www.mobilcard.info). It'll pay for itself only if you're very busy (for example, if you visit the Iceman, ride the Renon cable car, and take the bus round-trip from Bolzano to Castelrotto). The **Mobilcard** is a transit-only version that covers trains, buses, and lifts (€15/1 day, €23/3 days, sold at TIs and transit offices, www.mobilcard.info).

Walking Tours: The TI offers a guided town walking tour in English on Saturdays in season (€6, March-Oct at 11:00, departs from TI).

ARRIVAL IN BOLZANO

By Train: There are two train stations for Bolzano—you want *Bolzano,* not *Bolzano Süd.* WCs are in the underground passage by track 1, and luggage storage is just upstairs (see "Helpful Hints," later). To reach the **TI,** exit the station, turn left, and walk two blocks. To get **downtown,** jog left up the tree-lined Viale della Stazione/Bahnhofsallee, and walk past the bus station (on your left) two blocks to Piazza Walther/Waltherplatz and the start of my self-guided walk.

By Car: Be careful driving in Bolzano—keep an eye out for ZTL zones (marked with a red circle), where you'll be automatically ticketed. The most convenient parking lot for a short visit is the P3 garage, right under the main square (€2.50/hour, cheaper overnight; to find it, make your way to the train station, then drive up Viale della Stazione/Bahnhofsallee, watching for the *P3/Piazza Walther* entrance on your right). For longer stays or to save a few euros, try P8 (Parking Centro/Mitte), just south of the ring road and west of the train station—about a 10-minute walk from the main square (€1.50/hour, cheaper overnight, enter from Via Josef Mayr Nusser).

Ich bin ein Italiener

With the exception of Bolzano, where Italian has become the primary language, you'll hear mostly German in Dolomite vil-

lages. Overall, seven in ten Italians living in the South Tirol speak German as their mother tongue. Many are fair-skinned and blue-eyed and prefer dumplings and strudel to pasta and gelato. Most have a working knowledge of Italian, but they watch German-language TV, read newspapers *auf Deutsch,* listen to jaunty oompah music, and live in Tirolean-looking villages.

At the end of World War I, the region was ceded by Austria (loser) to Italy (winner). Mussolini suppressed the Germanic cultural elements as part of his propaganda campaign to praise all things Italian. Many German speakers hoped that Hitler would "liberate" them from Italy, but Hitler's close alliance with Mussolini prevented that from happening. Instead, in June of 1939, residents were given six months to make a hard choice: Move north to the Fatherland and become German citizens, or stay in their homeland *(Heimat)* under Italian rule. The vast majority (212,000, or 85 percent) decided to leave, but with the outbreak of World War II, only 75,000 actually moved.

After the war, German speakers were again disappointed when the Allies refused to grant them autonomy or the chance to become Austrian citizens. Instead, the victors decided to stick with the prewar arrangement. The region rebuilt and the two linguistic groups patched things up, but for the remainder of the 20th century, German speakers were continually outvoted by the Italian-speaking majority in the regional government (comprising two provinces, Italian-speaking Trentino and German-speaking Alto Adige/Südtirol).

German speakers lobbied the national government for more control on the provincial (not regional) level, even turning to demonstrations and violence. Over the years, Rome has slowly and grudgingly granted increased local control. The country's 2001 constitution gave Alto Adige/Südtirol a large measure of autonomy—similar to Sicily and Sardinia—though it's still officially tied to Trentino. Roads, water, electricity, communications, and schools are all under local control, including the Free University of Bozen-Bolzano, founded in 1998.

A good way to sum it all up: In many ways, the people of the Dolomites feel a closer bond with their Austrian ancestors than with their countrymen to the south. But when Italy plays Austria in a big soccer match, who do locals root for? Italy.

Bolzano

To Maretsch & Runkelstein Castles

CORSO DELLA LIBERTA

Piazza della Vittoria

VICTORY MONUMENT

To ⑰

Petrarcha Park

PONTE TALVERA

Talvera River

VIA DEI VANGA

SOUTH TIROL MUSEUM OF ARCHAEOLOGY (ÖTZI THE ICEMAN)

VIA ROGGIA

⑮

VIA MUSEO

⑱ WALK ENDS

NEW BOLZANO

VIA PETER MAYR

VIALE VENEZIA

VIA SAN QUIRINO

MUSEO CIVICO

VIA CASSA DI RISPARMIO

EUROPA GALLERY

VIA LEONARDO DA VINCI

Piazza delle Erbe

⑩ ⑫

VIA

⑬

Piazza Sernesi

VIA DELLA MOSTRA

⑲

VIA ROSMINI

FREE UNIVERSITY OF BOLZANO

VIA OSPEDALE

⑥

Piazza Domenicani

VIA D.

POST

DOMINICAN CHURCH

VIA CAPPUCCINI

CHIESA DEI CAPPUCCINI

Bike Path

Isarco/Eisack

Accommodations
- ❶ Parkhotel Laurin
- ❷ Hotel Greif
- ❸ Stadt Hotel Città
- ❹ Hotel Figl
- ❺ Hotel Feichter
- ❻ Kolpinghaus Bozen
- ❼ Youth Hostel Bolzano

Eateries & Other
- ❽ Weisses Rössl
- ❾ Ca' de Bezzi/Gasthaus Batzenhäusl
- ❿ Hopfen & Company
- ⓫ Paulaner Stuben
- ⓬ Humus
- ⓭ Enoteca Il Baccaro
- ⓮ Dai Carretai
- ⓯ Drago D'Oro
- ⓰ Gul
- ⓱ To Officina del Gelo Avalon
- ⓲ Despar Supermarkets (3)
- ⓳ Launderette
- ⓴ Bike Rental

DOLOMITES

HELPFUL HINTS

Welcome to Italy: If calling from an Austrian phone number to an Italian one, dial 00-39 and then the number (including the initial zero). To call from an Italian phone to an Austrian one, dial 00-43 and then the number (omitting the initial zero); see page 564 for dialing instructions.

Sleepy Sundays: This small, culturally conservative city is really dead on Sunday (young locals add, "and during the rest of the week, too").

Markets: Piazza Erbe/Obstplatz hosts an ancient and still-thriving open-air produce market (Mon-Sat all day, closed Sun). Wash your produce in the handy drinking fountain in the middle of the market. Another market (offering more variety, not just food) runs Saturday mornings on Piazza della Vittoria.

Baggage Storage: You can store bags at **Base Camp Dolomites,** at the train station by track 1 (daily 8:30-18:30, tel. 0471-971-733, Matteo and Lukas).

Laundry: Ecomatic is at Via Rosmini/Rosministrasse 39, southwest of the South Tirol Museum of Archaeology (daily 7:00-

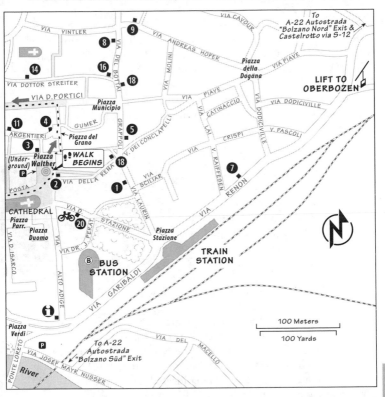

22:30, doors lock automatically at closing time, mobile 340-220-2323).

Bike Rental: The city has a well-developed bike-trail system and cheap, city-subsidized rental bikes (€2/6 hours, €5/6-24 hours, €10 refundable deposit, ID required, Mon-Sat 7:30-19:50, closed Sun and Nov-March, just off Piazza Walther/Waltherplatz on the road to the station, tel. 0471-997-578). For a higher-quality mountain bike or electric bike, try Base Camp Dolomites at the station (see "Baggage Storage," earlier).

Bolzano Walk

This brief self-guided walk will help you get your bearings in central Bolzano.

• *Start the walk in...*

Piazza Walther/Waltherplatz: The statue in the center honors the square's namesake, Walther von der Vogelweide, a 12th-century politically incorrect German poet who courageously stood up to the pope in favor of the Holy Roman (German) Emperor. Walther's spunk against a far bigger power represents the Germanic pride of this region. The statue is made of marble quarried in the village of Laas, north of Bolzano. (The US chose this same marble for the 86,000 crosses and Stars of David needed to mark the WWII dead buried at Normandy and other battlefields across Europe.)

When not hosting Bolzano's Christmas market, flower market (May Day), or Speck Fest (a spring ham festival), Piazza Walther/Waltherplatz is simply the town's living room. And locals care about it. It was the site of Italy's first McDonald's, which, in the early 1990s, became the first McDonald's to be shut down by locals protesting American fast food. Today the square is home to trendy cafés such as Café Walther, where (outside of meal times) you're welcome to nurse a

"Venetian" *spritz* or a pricier cocktail as long as you like.

• *Cross the street to the big church.*

The Cathedral: The cathedral's glazed-tile roof is typical of the Germanic world—a reminder that from the sixth century until 1919, when Italy said *benvenuti* to the Südtirol, German was the region's official language. The church was flattened in World War II (a common consequence of being located near a train station in 20th-century Europe).

Walk around to the right, to the Romanesque Lion's Gate (at the far end), and step inside. The place feels Teutonic, rather than Italian, with a mostly Gothic interior that's broken at the front by an impressive Baroque tabernacle. Partway down the nave, the sandstone pulpit (c. 1500)—with its reliefs of the four Church fathers whose presence gave credibility to sermons preached here—is reminiscent of Vienna's St. Stephen's Cathedral. Most of the art is by Bavarian artists.

• *Leaving the church, return to Piazza Walther/Waltherplatz and cross it diagonally, heading up the street to the right of the big Sparkasse bank building. Follow this for one block, to...*

Piazza del Grano/Kornplatz: Nine hundred years ago, this was Bolzano's main square. The building to your right was the bishop's castle. The traditional food stand selling *Vollkornbrot* (dense, whole-grain bread) and pretzels is another reminder of German heritage. At the top of the square, look for the flower bed with a big, chunky rock. A bronze relief embedded in the rock shows Bolzano's street plan in the 12th century: a one-street arcaded town huddled within a fortified wall.

• *Jog right and continue straight ahead into the original medieval town, passing a* wurstel *(frankfurter) stand on your left. You'll pop out in the middle of...*

Via dei Portici/Laubengasse: This was the only street in 12th-century Bolzano. Step into the center (dodging bikes). Looking east and west, you see the width of the original town.

Turn left and stroll a bit, watching on the right for the frescoed, pointed arches of the old City Hall—the street's only Gothic building (at #30). No-tice that the other buildings, with uniform round arches, are all basically the same: Each had a storm cellar, cows out back, a ground-level shop, and living quarters upstairs. Bay windows were designed for maximum light—just right for clerks keeping track of accounts and for women doing their weaving. The arcades *(Lauben)*, typical of Tirol, sheltered merchants and their goods from both snow and sun. Narrow side passages lead to neighboring streets.

A bit farther along on the left, the only balcony marks the street's lone Baroque building—once the mercantile center (with a fine worth-a-look courtyard), now a skippable museum.

• *Continue to the end of the street, where you'll find a bustling market.*

Piazza Erbe/Obstplatz: This square hosts an open-air produce market, liveliest in the morning (closed Sun). The historic market fountain gives Bolzano its only hint of the sea—a 17th-century statue of Neptune. Stroll around and see what's in season. All the breads, strudel, and hams *schmecken sehr gut.*

• *From the market, Via Museo/Museumstrasse (called Butcher Street until the 19th century, when a museum opened) leads straight ahead to Frozen Fritz.*

Sights in Bolzano

▲▲▲South Tirol Museum of Archaeology (Museo Archeologico dell'Alto Adige/Südtiroler Archäologiemuseum)

This excellent museum, which illuminates the prehistory of the region, boasts a unique attraction: the actual corpse of Ötzi the Iceman, who spent more than five millennia stuck in a glacier. With Ötzi as the centerpiece, the museum takes you on an intriguing journey through time, recounting the evolution of humanity—from the Paleolithic era to the Roman period and finally to the

Middle Ages—in vivid detail. The interactive exhibit offers informative displays and models, and video demonstrations of Ötzi's extraction and his personal effects. Everything's well described in English (skip the €4 audioguide).

Cost and Hours: €9, €37.50 guided tour for up to 15 people (must reserve ahead), Tue-Sun 10:00-18:00, closed Mon except July-Aug and Dec, near the river at Via Museo/Museumstrasse 43, tel. 0471-320-100, www.iceman.it.

Crowd-Beating Tips: Capacity is limited, and ticket-buying lines can be long. It's busiest on rainy days in July and August. To skip the line, it's smart to buy tickets online (same price as at site, must purchase at least one day in advance, exchangeable if your schedule changes). Show your emailed receipt or confirmation code for admission.

Background: Ötzi's frozen body was discovered high in the mountains on the Italian/Austrian border by a German couple in 1991. Police initially believed the corpse was a lost hiker, and Ötzi was chopped roughly out of the glacier, damaging his left side. But upon discovering his pre-Bronze Age hatchet, officials realized what they had found: a 5,300-year-old, nearly perfectly preserved man with clothing and gear in excellent condition for his age. Austria and Italy squabbled briefly over who would get him, but surveys showed that he was located 100 yards inside Italian territory. Tooth enamel studies have now shown that he did grow up on the Italian side. An Austrian journalist dubbed him Ötzi, after the Ötztal valley, where he was discovered.

Visiting the Museum: The permanent exhibit is smartly displayed on three floors (plus temporary exhibits on the top floor). First you'll learn about Ötzi's discovery, excavation, and preservation. Upstairs, you'll walk through displays of his incredibly well-preserved and fascinating clothing and gear, including a finely stitched two-color coat, his goathide loincloth, a fancy hat, shoes, a well-crafted hatchet, 14 arrows, a longbow, a dagger, and shreds of his rucksack (which held fire-making gadgets and a tree fungus used as a primitive antibiotic). And finally, you'll peek into a heavily fortified room to see Ötzi himself—still kept carefully frozen.

One floor up, exhibits focus on the Copper Age. The discovery of Ötzi helped researchers realize that the use of copper occurred in this region more than a millennium earlier than previously thought. There's also a complete medical workup of Ötzi, including an interactive flatscreen where you can zoom in on different parts of his body to see the layers of skin, muscle, and bone. And you'll learn how researchers have used modern forensic science techniques to better understand who Ötzi was and how he died. (Think of it as a very, very, very cold case.)

From all of this, scientists have formed a complete picture of the Iceman: In his mid-40s at the time of his death, Ötzi was 5 feet, 3 inches tall, with brown hair and brown eyes. He weighed about 110 pounds, was lactose-intolerant, ate too much animal fat, and likely had trouble with his knees. And they've even determined the cause of death: an arrowhead buried in Ötzi's left shoulder. At the end of the exhibit, you'll see an eerily lifelike reconstruction of how Ötzi may have looked when he was alive. If you're interested in learning more about Ötzi, *National Geographic* and the public-television program *Nova* have covered the evolving story.

Dominican Church (Chiesa dei Domenicani/Dominikanerkirche)

Art lovers can drop by this otherwise stark and sterile 13th-century church to see its Chapel of St. John (San Giovanni/St. Johannes; chapel is through the archway and on the right), frescoed in the 14th century by the Giotto School.

Cost and Hours: Free, €0.50 coin lights dim interior, Mon-Sat 7:00-19:00, Sun 12:00-18:00, on Piazza Domenicani, two blocks west of Piazza Walther/Waltherplatz.

Lift to Oberbozen and Renon/Ritten

The **Funivia del Renon/Rittner Seilbahn** cable car whisks you over the hills from Bolzano to the touristy resort village of Oberbozen on the high plateau of Renon/Ritten, where Sigmund Freud and his wife once celebrated their wedding anniversary. The reasonably priced, 12-minute ride itself is the main attraction, offering views of the town, surrounding mountains, made-for-yodeling farmsteads, and 18-wheelers downshifting along the expressway from Austria. While the cable car is fun, it's no replacement for a trip to Castelrotto and Alpe di Siusi. But if you're here offseason and unable to go any higher, this lift gives you a taste of the Alpine wonderland that lies above the valley floor.

Cost and Hours: €10 round-trip, cash only, validate tickets in blue box; departures year-round Mon-Sat 6:30-22:45, Sun 7:10-22:45; leaves every 4 minutes—reduced to every 12 minutes after 21:00; closes for maintenance for a week in March and Nov; for info call regional transport hotline at tel. 840-000-471 or visit www.sii.bz.it.

Getting There: The cable car's valley station is a five-block walk east from the Bolzano train station along Via Renon/Rittner Strasse or from Piazza Municipio/Rathausplatz in the old center.

At the Top: Oberbozen (elevation 4,000 feet) is mostly a collection of resort hotels. From Oberbozen, a narrow-gauge train makes the 16-minute trip to **Klobenstein,** a larger and slightly less touristy village at 3,800 feet (€3.50 one-way, €6 round-trip, €15 round-trip for both cable car and train, daily departures every 30 minutes—reduced to hourly early and late). The local TI has branches in both villages (www.ritten.com). In Oberbozen, the TI is in the train station building, just steps from the lift station (Mon-Fri 9:00-12:30 & 15:00-18:00, Sat 9:00-12:30, closed Sun in summer, shorter hours off-season, tel. 0471-345-245). The Klobenstein TI is a five-minute walk from the train station (Mon-Fri 8:30-18:00, Sat 8:30-12:00, closed Sun, tel. 0471-356-100).

The lift station and TIs have brochures suggesting short walks. More interesting than Oberbozen itself (though not a must-see) are the nearby **"earth pyramids"**—Bryce Canyon-like pinnacles that rise out of the ridge, created by eroding glacial debris dumped at the end of the last ice age. Some of these are visible from the Oberbozen cable car, but are challenging to hike to; an easier-to-reach area is a 15-minute walk from Klobenstein. Another walk is the **Freud-promenade,** a fairly level, 1.5-hour stroll between Oberbozen and Klobenstein (you can take the train back).

New Bolzano (Nuova Bolzano)

Just across the river from the Museum of Archaeology, the fascist-style **Victory Monument** (Monumento alla Vittoria) glistens in white Zandobbio marble. It marks the beginning of the "new" city built by the fascist government in the 1920s to Italianize the otherwise Germanic-looking city. Indeed, you won't hear much German spoken in the shops and bars along the colonnaded Corso della Libertà—it feels a world away from the old town. A visit to New Bolzano comes with a delightful stroll over the river and the inviting, parklike Talvera promenade (described later).

In the basement of the arch-like structure, you'll find a small but informative exhibit about the history of the monument itself, the Italianization of the South Tirol, and the effort of the local people to keep their language, culture, and traditions alive. History and architecture buffs will appreciate a quick stop here (monument always viewable, exhibit free and open March-Sept Tue-Sun 11:00-13:00 & 14:00-17:00, Thu 15:00-21:00, shorter hours off-season, closed Mon year-round, good information in English, www.monumenttovictory.com).

The grand plans for this part of the city were never fully realized. But several blocks of buildings were constructed in a repetitive Modernist design, following the idea of imperial monumentalism trumpeting the dawn of a new era in Italy. Most of the structures were intended to house state institutions and highly desirable apartments for state employees. (A few blocks south on Piazza Tribunale, you can still find the somewhat faded image of Mussolini waving from one of the buildings.)

While visiting this neighborhood, consider a stop at **Officina del Gelo Avalon,** a gourmet, organic gelato shop tucked under the arches of Corso della Libertà. Try the pistachio or one of the half-dozen flavors of chocolate (Wed-Mon 13:00-21:30, shorter hours off-season, closed Tue and in winter, Corso della Libertà 44, tel. 0471-260-434).

Runkelstein Castle (Castel Roncolo/Schloss Runkelstein)

This 13th-century "illustrated manor" perches above the river just north of downtown. Inside is an impressively large collection of secular medieval frescoes, with scenes from the everyday lives of knights and ladies. To get here, walk the promenade along the Talvera River (30 minutes from downtown; see "Bolzano Walks," next).

Cost and Hours: €8, Tue-Sun 10:00-18:00, closed Mon, 1.5 miles north of Ponte Talvera on Kaiser-Franz-Josef Weg, tel. 0471-329-808, www.runkelstein.info.

Bolzano Walks

Pick up the clearly marked map at the TI for scenic, accessible strolls that provide a different perspective on the region. One popular option is the easy, shaded **Talvera promenade** just west of the Museum of Archaeology, following the river embankment north. This route has great people-watching in the summer, with views of vineyards and Maretsch Castle (Castello Mareccio/Burg Maretsch) to the right. In about 30 minutes, you'll reach the Bridge of St. Antonio, where you can cross and follow the river for another 15 minutes to the impressive **Runkelstein Castle** (described previously).

To extend your hike, go back to the Bridge of St. Antonio and head up the hill about 45 minutes for the **St. Oswald** walk. This route takes you to the church of Santa Magdalena (with its 14th-century frescoes), offering great views back to the city.

Sleeping in Bolzano

All the places listed here are in the city center, within walking distance of the train and bus stations. Bolzano has no real high or low season. Most hotels have the same rates all year, but they're most likely to make deals in March and November.

$$$$ Parkhotel Laurin is a fancy Old World hotel near the train station, with 100 tastefully decorated rooms, marble bathrooms, a chic dining room and terrace, a swimming pool (summer only), an extensive and luxurious garden, and attentive staff. Frescoes throughout the grand lobby and atmospheric bar depict the legend of King Laurin (air-con, elevator, pay parking, Via Laurin/Laurinstrasse 4, tel. 0471-311-000, www.laurin.it, info@laurin.it).

$$$$ Hotel Greif, a luxury boutique hotel, is right on Piazza Walther/Waltherplatz. Each of the 33 individually designed rooms makes you feel like you're in a modern-art installation (its website gives a room-by-room tour). It's not exactly "cozy," but it is striking, and a stay here comes with one of my favorite breakfasts in Italy (family rooms, air-con, elevator, pay parking at P3/Parking Walther under main square—enter hotel directly from level 1 of the garage, Via della Rena/Raingasse 28, tel. 0471-318-000, www.greif.it, info@greif.it).

$$$ Stadt Hotel Città, a venerable old hotel with 99 modern, straightforward rooms, is ideally situated on Piazza Walther/Waltherplatz. The hotel's café spills out onto the piazza, offering a prime spot for people-watching (family rooms, air-con, elevator, pay parking at P3/Parking Walther under main square—enter hotel directly from level 1 of the garage, Piazza Walther/Waltherplatz 21, tel. 0471-975-221, www.hotelcitta.info, info@hotelcitta.info, Francesco and Hannelore, plus son Fabio and daughter Sandra). This place is an especially good value if you spend an afternoon in their free-for-guests Wellness Center (generally open mid-Sept-June Mon-Sat 16:00-21:30, closed Sun and in summer; Turkish bath, whirlpool, Finnish sauna, biosauna, massage by appointment)—a fine way to unwind.

$$$ Hotel Figl, warmly run by Anton and Helga Mayr, has 23 comfy, bright, good-value rooms. It's situated over a popular-with-locals café on a pedestrian square located a block from Piazza Walther/Waltherplatz (breakfast extra, air-con, elevator, pay parking at P3/Parking Walther under main square—take the escalator to the square and walk a couple of minutes, Piazza del Grano/Kornplatz 9, tel. 0471-978-412, www.figl.net, info@figl.net, include a phone number if you email).

$$ Hotel Feichter is an inexpensive, well-kept, family-run place with simple but sufficient amenities in a great location. Some of the 34 rooms share a communal terrace overlooking the rooftops of Bolzano. Papà Walter, Mamma Hedwig, Hannes, Irene, and Wolfi Feichter have run this homey hotel since 1969 (family rooms, fans, pay parking, 18 steps up to reception and elevator from entrance, ground-floor café serves lunches Mon-Fri 11:30-14:00; from station, walk up Via Laurin/Laurinstrasse, which becomes Via Grappoli/Weintraubengasse—hotel is on the right at #15; tel. 0471-978-768, www.hotelfeichter.it, info@hotelfeichter.it).

$$ Kolpinghaus Bozen, modern, clean, and church-run, has 34 rooms with two twin beds (placed head to toe) and 71 air-conditioned single rooms with all the comforts. Though institutional, it's a good deal...and makes me feel thankful (elevator, pay laundry, pay parking, 4 blocks from Piazza Walther/Waltherplatz near Piazza Domenicani at Largo A. Kolping/Adolph-Kolping-Strasse 3, tel. 0471-308-400, www.kolpingbozen.it, info@kolpingbozen.it). The line of people out front at lunchtime consists mainly of office workers waiting for the cafeteria to open (generally Mon-Fri 11:45-14:00, Sat 12:00-13:30, closed Sun).

¢ Youth Hostel Bolzano is the most comfortable and inviting hostel that I've seen in Italy. It has 17 four-bed rooms (each with two bunk beds and a full bathroom; fifth bed possible) and 10 delightful singles with bath. The bright, clean, modern rooms make it feel like a dorm in a fancy university. With no age limit, easy online reservations, and family discounts, this is a utopian hostel (elevator, pay laundry, 9:00 checkout, 100 yards to the right as you leave the train station at Via Renon/Rittner Strasse 23; tel. 0471-300-865, www.ostello.bz, bolzano@ostello.bz).

Eating in Bolzano

All my recommendations are in the center of the old town. Prices are consistent (you can generally get a good plate of meat and veggies for €10). While nearly every local-style place serves a mix of German/Tirolean and Italian fare, I favor eating Tirolean here in Bozen. Many restaurants have no cover charge but put a basket of bread on the table; as in Austria, if you eat the bread, you'll be charged a small amount. Bolzano's restaurants tend to stay open all day, but at a few places the kitchen closes in the afternoon with only snacks available.

$$ Weisses Rössl ("White Horse") offers an affordable mix of pasta and Tirolean food with meat, fish, and fine vegetarian options. Located in a traditional woody setting, it's good for dining indoors among savvy locals (Mon-Fri 11:00-24:00, Sat 10:00-15:00, closed Sun, 2 blocks north of Piazza Municipio at Via Bottai/Bindergasse 6, tel. 0471-973-267).

$$ Ca' de Bezzi/Gasthaus Batzenhäusl is historic. It's Bolzano's oldest inn, with two Teutonic-feeling upper floors; by contrast, the patio and back room are refreshingly modern and untouristy. They make their own breads, pastas, and beer, and serve traditional Tirolean fare—stick-to-your-ribs grub (daily 12:00-15:00 & 18:00-24:00, one of the rare places open on Sun, Via Andreas Hofer/Andreas-Hofer-Strasse 30, tel. 0471-050-950).

$$ Hopfen and Company fills an 800-year-old house with happy eaters, drinkers, and the beer lover's favorite aroma: hops *(Hopfen)*. A tavern since the 1600s, it's a stylish, fresh microbrewery today. This high-energy, boisterous place is packed with locals who come for its homemade beer, delicious Tirolean food, and reasonable prices (great salads, limited menu outside of mealtimes, daily 9:30-24:00, Piazza Erbe/Obstplatz 17, tel. 0471-300-788).

$$ Paulaner Stuben is a restaurant-pizzeria-*Bierstube* serving good food (more Italian than German) and a favorite Bavarian beer. It has good outside seating and a take-me-to-Germany interior (Mon-Sat 11:00-24:00, closed Sun, Via Argentieri/Silbergasse 16—or use back entrance at Via dei Portici/Laubengasse 51, tel. 0471-980-407).

$$ Humus is a trendy eatery packed with locals enjoying a hearty mix of Italian and Middle Eastern dishes. With an emphasis on organic food, this place feels fresh, lively, and inviting (Mon-Fri 8:00-20:00, Sat until 16:00, closed Sun, Silbergasse/Via Argentieri 16D, tel. 0471-971-961).

Drinks and Light Food: $ Enoteca Il Baccaro, a nondescript hole-in-the-wall wine bar, is an intriguing spot for a glass of wine and bar snacks amid locals. Wines available by the glass are listed on the blackboard (Mon-Fri 8:00-14:00 & 17:00-21:00, Sat 8:00-14:00, closed Sun, located a half-block east of Hopfen and Company on a hidden alley off Via Argentieri/Silbergasse 17, look for *vino* or *wein* sign next to fountain on south side of street and enter courtyard, tel. 0471-971-421). **$ Dai Carretai** is a popular *cicchetti* bar where locals meet after work over a glass of wine—the crowd spills out onto the street. Browse the array of toothpick snacks at the counter, or order a bruschetta from the menu (also serves hot lunches, Mon-Fri 7:00-14:00 & 16:30-21:00, Sat 7:00-14:00, closed Sun, Via Dr. Streiter/Dr.-Streiter-Gasse 20b, tel. 0471-970-558).

International Food: $ Drago D'Oro is a good and affordable Chinese restaurant in the old town (Mon 11:30-15:00, Tue-Sun 11:30-15:00 & 18:00-23:00, Via Roggia/Rauschertorgasse 7a, tel. 0471-977-621). **$$ Gul** has Indian-Pakistani standards (Mon-Sat 12:00-14:30 & 18:00-23:00, closed Sun, at Via Dr. Streiter/Dr.-Streiter-Gasse 2, tel. 0471-970-518). Both are takeout-friendly, as are several small pizzerias in the same area.

Picnics: Assemble the ingredients at the **Piazza Erbe/Obstplatz** market and dine in the park along the Talvera River (the green area with benches past the museum). Or visit one of the three **Despar supermarkets:** The largest is at the end of the Galleria Greif arcade (enter arcade from Piazza Walther/Waltherplatz by Hotel Greif and walk to far end—the supermarket is downstairs; Mon-Sat 8:30-19:30, closed Sun). Smaller branches are on Piazza Erbe/Obstplatz and at Via Bottai/Bindergasse 29 (both open Mon-Sat 8:30-19:30, closed Sun).

Bolzano Connections

Most trains from Bolzano are operated by Trenitalia (departures marked *R* or *RV* on schedules; ticket windows open daily 6:00-21:00, www.trenitalia.com). But some long-distance trains on the Innsbruck-Bolzano-Verona line are run by the German or Austrian railways—DB/ÖBB for short (trains marked *Eurocity, EC,* or *Trenord*). With your back to the Trenitalia ticket counter, the DB *Reisebüro* ticket office is located near the left exit (open Mon-Fri 8:00-19:00, Sat 8:00-15:00, closed Sun; www.oebb.at). Because the German and Italian systems don't cooperate very well, it's best to book tickets through the company that's running your specific departure.

From Bolzano by Train to: **Milan** (about hourly, 4 hours, change in Verona), **Venice** (about hourly, 3.5 hours, change in Verona), **Florence** (every 1-2 hours, 5 hours, change in Verona and/or Bologna), **Innsbruck** (1/hour, 2.5 hours, some regional connections change in Brennero), **Vienna** (4/day, 7 hours, change in Innsbruck), **Salzburg** (7/day, 5 hours, change in Innsbruck or Rosenheim), **Munich** (called "Monaco" in Italy, 5/day direct, 4 hours).

By Bus: Bus #170 connects Bolzano with the **cable car to Compatsch** (putting you at the gateway to all the Alpe di Siusi hikes in about an hour) and the town of **Castelrotto** (direction: Castelrotto, 2/hour Mon-Sat, hourly on Sun, last departure Mon-Sat at 20:10, Sun at 19:10, free schedule at bus station, €4 each way, buy tickets from driver, toll tel. 840-000-471, www.sii.bz.it).

The bus leaves from Bolzano's bus station (one block west of train station) and then winds high into the mountains. For Alpe di Suisi, ask the driver to let you off near the cable-car station (Seiser Alm Bahn/Cabinovia Alpe di Siusi, 40 minutes from Bolzano), then ascend to Compatsch (for more on Alpe di Siusi, see page 504). Otherwise, stay on the bus another 10 minutes to reach the center of Castelrotto.

Castelrotto

Castelrotto (altitude: 3,475 feet) is the ideal home base for a day of hiking at Alpe di Siusi/Seiser Alm. Relax on the traffic-free main square, surrounded by a mountain backdrop and a thousand years of history, with an oversized (and hyperactive) bell tower above you. You'll feel almost lost in another world. (Stay two nights.) Easy bus and cable-car connections bring you up to the trails at Alpe di Siusi and down to Bolzano.

With a population of around 2,000, Castelrotto is a combination of real town, ski resort, and administrative center for surrounding villages. Tourism has become increasingly important here; locals remind visitors that farming—which occupied most of the population in the 1960s—is minimal nowadays. Castelrotto's good lodging and services help make your stay trouble-free. Though I've used the town's Italian name, life here goes on almost entirely in German, and locals call their town Kastelruth. (Fewer than 5 percent of Castelrotto's residents are native Italian speakers.)

Orientation to Castelrotto

TOURIST INFORMATION

The helpful TI is on the main square at Piazza Kraus 2 (Mon-Sat 8:30-12:00 & 15:00-18:00, closed afternoons April and Nov, closed Sun except June-Aug 10:00-12:00, tel. 0471-706-333, www.seiseralm.it). If you plan to hike, pick up the TI's free *Living the Dolomites* pictorial hiking map, which includes estimated walking times and trail numbers. For longer hikes, 1:25,000 maps are about €5.

Transit Deals: If you're sleeping anywhere in the Castelrotto/Alpe di Siusi area (but not in Bolzano), ask your hotel for a free **Alpe di Siusi Live Card.** It covers local buses between Castelrotto and places like Bolzano and the base of the Alpe di Siusi cable car. It doesn't cover anything above the cable-car base (at Seis/Siusi). You'll only get the card if you ask...so ask.

The TI sells a **Combi-Card,** which covers some cable cars and buses; if you're making a few trips up to (and around) Alpe di Siusi, this will likely pay for itself (€39/any 3 days in a 7-day validity period, €52/7 days).

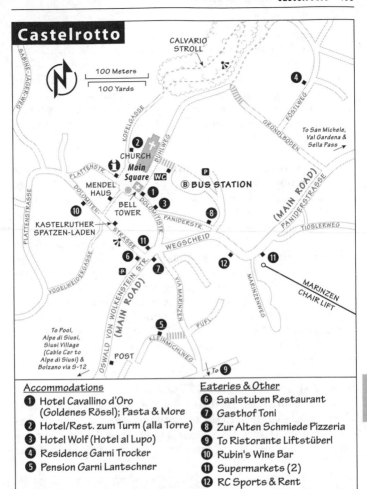

Castelrotto

CALVARIO STROLL

100 Meters
100 Yards

SABINE-JÄGERWEG

KOFELGASSE

4

FÖSTWEG

GRÖNDLBÖDEN

To San Michele,
Val Gardena &
Sella Pass

BÜHLWEG

2
CHURCH

1
Main
Square
WC

P

B BUS STATION

PLATTENSTR.

MENDEL
HAUS

DOLOMITEN

1
3

PANIDERSTR.

(MAIN ROAD)
PANIDERSTRASSE

BELL
TOWER

8

TIOSLERWEG

KASTELRUTHER
SPATZEN-LADEN

PLATTENSTRASSE

STRASSE

11

WEGSCHEID

10

6

7

VOGELWEIDERGASSE

P

VIA MARINZEN

12

MARINZENWEG

11

MARINZEN
CHAIR LIFT

OSWALD VON WOLKENSTEIN STR.
(MAIN ROAD)

5

PUFL

To Pool,
Alpe di Siusi,
Siusi Village
(Cable Car to
Alpe di Siusi) &
Bolzano via S-12

KLEINMICHLWEG

POST

To **9**

Accommodations
1 Hotel Cavallino d'Oro
(Goldenes Rössl); Pasta & More
2 Hotel/Rest. zum Turm (alla Torre)
3 Hotel Wolf (Hotel al Lupo)
4 Residence Garni Trocker
5 Pension Garni Lantschner

Eateries & Other
6 Saalstuben Restaurant
7 Gasthof Toni
8 Zur Alten Schmiede Pizzeria
9 To Ristorante Liftstüberl
10 Rubin's Wine Bar
11 Supermarkets (2)
12 RC Sports & Rent

DOLOMITES

HELPFUL HINTS

Annual Events: The Oswald-von-Wolkenstein Riding Tournament, held the first or second weekend of June, features medieval-style equestrian tournament games, followed by a feast. The town also holds religious processions with locals dressed in traditional costumes, usually on the Sunday after Corpus Christi (June 23 in 2019); on the feast day of the village protectors, Sts. Peter and Paul (June 29—often celebrated on the nearest Sunday instead); and on the local Thanksgiving (first Sun in Oct). In mid-October, the town is packed for the Kastelruther Spatzenfest, a concert weekend for the local musical heartthrobs, the Kastelruther Spatzen.

Spring and Fall Closures: The periods between ski season and hiking season (April-mid-May and Nov) are quiet, with lifts closed for maintenance and most hotels and restaurants shuttered (this is when locals take their own vacations).

Sightseeing Schedule: Shops in Castelrotto close from 12:00 to 15:00—a good time for a long lunch, a hike in the hills...or a siesta. In summer, there's usually a free band concert on Thursday evenings and a small farmers' market on the square on Friday mornings.

Launderette: There's none in the area.

Recreation: A heated outdoor **swimming pool** with alpine views and nearby tennis courts is in the hamlet of Telfen, between Castelrotto and Seis/Siusi (mid-May-mid-Sept 9:00-21:00, tel. 0471-705-090). You can **rent a horse** at Unter-Lanzinerhof in Telfen (tel. 339-868-6868, www.reiterhof-oberlanzin.com, Karin speaks some English). For more excitement, tandem **paragliding** flights—you and the pilot—depart from Alpe di Siusi and land either there or in Castelrotto (tel. 335-603-6400, www.tandem-paragliding.com, Ruben and Kurt). You can rent **skis and snowboards** at both the bottom and top stations of the Alpe di Siusi lift, or at RC Sports and Rent in Castelrotto (Nov-Easter, near the Marinzen lift at Via Panider/Paniderstrasse 10, tel. 0471-711-079, Robert—mobile 339-293-9725).

ARRIVAL IN CASTELROTTO

The **bus station** *(Bushof)* is 100 yards below the town's main square. It's unstaffed, but there's a shelter with timetables and a ticket machine (cash only). Free WCs are in a building at the tip of the bus loop. Take the stairs (by the tiny elevator) to get to the main square and TI.

Drivers can park in one of the two underground parking lots: One is near the bus station, and the other is on Wolkensteinstrasse, next to the recommended Saalstuben Restaurant (€1.70/hour, €10/day, cash only). Each of the recommended hotels also has free parking (ask for details when you book).

Coming from Innsbruck and points north, exit (earlier than you would expect) at *Chiusa/Klausen* and continue five miles toward Bolzano along the secondary road (SS-12) before crossing the river at Ponte Gardena/Waidbruck and following signs for *Castelrotto*.

Castelrotto Walk

Castelrotto is a great place to sleep but has only a little sightseeing of its own—the surrounding mountains and hikes are the attractions here. This quick self-guided walk will get you oriented and trace the town's history.

• *Start in the...*

Main Square (Piazza Kraus): This square is named for the noble family who ruled the town from 1550 to 1800. Their palace, now the City Hall and TI, overlooks the square and sports the Kraus family coat of arms.

Castelrotto puts its square to use. A farmers' market takes place here on Friday mornings in the summer (June-Oct), and a clothing market fills the square most Thursday mornings. Before and after Sunday Mass, the square is crowded with villagers and farmers (who fill the church) dressed in traditional clothing. The main Mass (Sat at 20:00 and Sun at 10:00) is in German. In July and August, when Italian tourists visit, another Mass takes place in Italian (at 11:30).

• *A landmark in the square is the...*

Bell Tower: At 250 feet, the freestanding bell tower dominates the town. It was once attached to a church, which burned down in 1753. While the bell tower was quickly rebuilt, the gutted church was torn down, and the church you see today was constructed farther back, enlarging the square.

When you feel the pride that the locals have in their tower—which symbolizes their town—you'll better understand why Italy has been called "the land of a thousand bell towers." The bells of Castelrotto, which are a big part of the town experience, ring on the hour from 6:00 until 22:00. While sleepy tourists may wonder why the bells clang so very early in the morning, locals who grew up with the chimes find them comforting. The beloved bells mark the hours, summon people to work and to Mass, announce festivals, and warn when storms threaten. In the days when people used to believe that thunder was the devil approaching, the bells called everyone to pray. (Townspeople thought the bells' sound cleared the clouds.) Bells ring big at 7:00, noon, and 19:00. The biggest of the eight bells (7,500 pounds) peals only on special days. When the bells ring at 15:00 on Friday, it commemorates Christ's sacrifice at the supposed hour of his death—a little bit of Good Friday every Friday. The colorful poles in front of the church (yellow-and-white for the Vatican, red-and-white for Tirol) fly flags on festival days. The towering May Pole, a Bavarian tradition, was a gift from Castelrotto's sister city in Bavaria.

• *Also on the square is the...*

Church: Before entering, notice the plaque on the exterior. This commemorative inscription honors the tiny community's WWI dead—*Fraktion Dorf* means from the village itself, and the other sections list soldiers from the surrounding hamlets. Stepping into the church, you're surrounded by harmonious art from about 1850. The church is dedicated to Sts. Peter and Paul, and the paintings that flank the high altar show how each was martyred (crucifixion and beheading). The pews (and smart matching confessionals) are carved of walnut wood.

• *Back outside, belly up to the...*

Fountain: Opposite the church, Castelrotto's fountain dates from 1884. St. Florian, the protector against fires, keeps an eye on it today as he did when villagers (and their horses) first came here for a drink of water.

• *With your back to the church and the fountain on your left, walk a half-block down the lane to see the finely frescoed...*

Mendel Haus: This house, with its traditional facade, contains a woodcarving shop. Its frescoes (from 1886) include many symbol-

ic figures, as well as an emblem of a carpenter above the door—a relic from the days when images, rather than address numbers, identified the house. Notice St. Florian again; this time, he's pouring water on a small painting of this very house engulfed in flames. Inside Mendel Haus are fine carvings, a reminder that this region—especially nearby Val Gardena—is famous for its woodwork. You'll also see many witches, folk figures that date back to when this area was the Salem of this corner of Europe. Women who didn't fit society's mold—including midwives, healers, and redheads—were sometimes burned as witches.

• *Continue downhill to the left of Mendel Haus, then before the underpass, climb the stairs on your right. At the top of the stairs, turn left on Dolomitenstrasse. In 50 yards, on the left at #21, is a shop dedicated to Castelrotto's big hometown heroes.*

Kastelruther Spatzen-Laden: The ABBA of the Alps, the folk-singing group Kastelruther Spatzen (literally "sparrows") is a gang of local boys who put Castelrotto on the map in the 1980s. They have a huge following here and throughout the German-

The Dramatic Dolomites

The Dolomites have been called the most beautiful mountains on earth, and certainly they are among the most dramatic.

They differ from the rest of the Alps because of their dominant rock type, dolomite, which forms sheer vertical walls of white, gray, and pink that rise abruptly from green valleys and meadows. Many parts of the mountains (including Alpe di Siusi) have been turned into regional or national parks, where development is restricted. Still, rail lines, roads, and innumerable lifts make this group of mountains very accessible.

Once dubbed the "Pale Mountains" or the "Venetian Alps," this mountain range was named after French mineralogist Dolomieu, who in the late 1700s first described the rock type responsible for the region's light-colored bluffs and peaks.

These sedimentary rocks (similar to limestone) were formed in warm tropical seas during the Triassic Period (about 250 million years ago). The marine sediments, along with the fossilized remains of coral reefs and other animals, were buried, hardened, and later scooped upward along with the rest of the Alps by the tectonic-plate action of Africa slowly smashing into Europe. Today, marine fossils are found atop the region's highest peaks, including the skyscraping, nearly 11,000-feet-high Marmolada.

During World War I, the front line between the Italian and Austro-Hungarian forces ran through these mountains, and many paths were cut into the range for military use. Today mountaineers can still follow networks of metal rungs, cables, and ladders (called *via ferrata*). One famous wartime trail is the "Strada delle Gallerie," near Rovereto, which passes through 52 tunnels *(gallerie)*.

A paradise for hikers and climbers in summer, the Dolomites are even better known as a popular skiing destination. The 1956 Olympics in Cortina d'Ampezzo put the region on the map. A popular winter activity for intrepid skiers is the "Sella Ronda"—circling the Sella massif using a system of lifts and 28 miles of ski runs.

Whether you experience the Dolomites with your hand on a walking stick, a ski pole, or an *aperitivo* while mountain-gazing from a café, it's easy to enjoy this spectacular region.

speaking world. Though he's now in his 50s, the lead singer, Norbert Rier, is a Germanic heartthrob on par with Tom Jones. You'll see his face on ads all over town—in the recommended Saalstuben Restaurant, suggesting what to order for dessert, or in the Co-op supermarket, reminding you to drink lots of Tirolean milk. The group's feel-good folk-pop style—an alpine version of German *Schlager* music—is popular with the kind of conservative, working-class Germans who like to vacation in the South Tirol. (Younger, more progressive Germans cringe at this stuff, with its nationalistic overtones.) At a big festival in Castelrotto on the second weekend in October, the band puts on a hometown concert, filling this place with fans from as far away as the Alsace, Switzerland, and the Netherlands. They also hold an open-air concert here in June and a Christmas concert.

Browse the store, which is part souvenir shop and part insignia and apparel outlet. Downstairs is a sprawling, folksy museum slathered with gifts, awards, and gold records. The group has won 13 Echo Awards..."more than Robbie Williams." Watch the continuously playing video (€2 museum, entry refunded with €5 purchase in the shop, Mon-Sat 9:00-12:00 & 14:00-18:00, closed Sun).

• *Leaving the shop, cross the street for a...*

Fine Mountain View of the Schlern: This bold limestone peak—so typical of the Dolomites—is a symbol of the Südtirol. Witches are said to live there, and many locals climb it yearly (it's actually an easy—if long—walk up the back side).

Look left—the street points to a ridge in the distance. That's Puflatsch (a high meadow with a popular trail called the Trail of the Witches—see "Activites in Alpe di Siusi" later).

• *Continue up the hill 50 yards, cross left at the crosswalk, pass the little parking lot square, and find two stones marking the top of a cobbled pedestrian lane that leads downhill back into town. Look up at the top of the bell tower. Ahead stands the elegant...*

Hotel Wolf Facade: This was painted by the same artist who did the Mendel Haus. St. Florian is still pouring water on burning houses and locals are busy enjoying the local wine.

As you head left, uphill back to the town square, enjoy windows filled with traditional Südtirol formal wear—delightful dirndls. You'll pass an old hotel, which, by the looks of its street sign, must be called The Golden Horse (*Cavallino d'Oro* or *Goldenes Rössl*). Ahead of you is the inviting sound of a refreshing drink from the town fountain.

• *Our walk is over. Ahead (through a white arch just left of the TI) are two big pictorial maps showing the region in summer and in ski season, as well as a modern café with ice cream and a nice terrace under a tree.*

The arch to the right of the TI leads up to Calvario (Calvary Hill) for a fine little loop walk, described next.

Sights in Castelrotto

Calvario Stroll

For an easy stroll to Castelrotto's finest postcard views—the giant bell tower with a dramatic alpine backdrop—take a 15-minute

mini hike around the town's hill, Calvario (Calvary). Originally, this was the site of the ancient Roman fortress, and later the fortified home of the medieval lord. One lane circles the hill while another spirals to the top past seven little chapels, each depicting a scene from Christ's Passion and culminating in the Crucifixion. Facing the TI, take the road under the arch to the right, and then follow signs to *Kofelrunde* (to go around the hill) or *Kalvarienberg* (to get directly to the top). The light is best late in the day, and the stroll is also great after dark—romantically lit and under the stars. (The lead singer of Kastelruther Spatzen enjoyed his first kiss right here.) For a longer walk back into town, take the Friedensweg (Peace Trail) from the top of the hill. This 30-minute forest walk is decorated with peace-themed artwork by local elementary students.

Marinzen Lift

The little Marinzen chairlift trundles you up above town in two-person seats to the Marinzenhütte café (at 4,875 feet), which has

a playground and animal park for kids (open when the cable car runs). The views from the top are nothing special, but several hikes leave from here— and as you ride back down, you'll enjoy pleasant panoramas over Castelrotto. (Alternatively, it's a scenic

one-hour hike back down.) While the chairlift doesn't compare with going up to Alpe di Siusi, it's still a nice activity. Catch it right in town, up the lane behind the Co-op/Konsum-Market.

Cost and Hours: €7.50 one-way up, €6.50 one-way down, €10.50 round-trip, daily mid-May-mid-Oct 9:00-17:00, slow-and-scenic 22 minutes each way, closed off-season and rainy mornings, tel. 0471-707-160, www.marinzen.com.

DOLOMITES

NEAR CASTELROTTO
Pflegerhof Herb Farm

On a narrow country road a little outside the nearby town of Seis/Siusi, you'll find an organic farm that grows dozens of varieties of herbs. Walk among the scent-filled, fully labeled beds and browse the wide variety of herbal products in the shop. To reach the farm from Castelrotto, drive through Seis/Siusi, pass the turnoff for the cable car on your left, and after about a half-mile, turn right following *St. Oswald* and *Pflegerhof* signs.

Cost and Hours: Free, Mon-Sat 10:00-18:00, Sept-March until 17:00, closed Sun year-round, St. Oswald 24, tel. 0471-706-771, www.pflegerhof.com.

Nightlife in and near Castelrotto

The recommended **Zur Alten Schmiede Pizzeria** in Castelrotto is a fun spot that's open late. **Rubin's,** next door to the Hotel Schgaguler in Castelrotto (tel. 0471-712-502), and **Sasso's,** on Schlernstrasse in the nearby town of Seis/Siusi (tel. 0471-708-068), are trendy wine bars. A popular hangout for the younger crowd in Seis/Siusi is **Santners** (the only dance club in the area). It's at the Seiser Alm Bahn cable-car station (tel. 0471-727-913). If you're here on the weekend, the "Nightliner" shuttle bus can bring you home in the wee hours (Fri-Sat roughly hourly 20:40-2:40, schedules at www.silbernagl.it; €2.50/ride, €4/all-night pass).

Sleeping in and near Castelrotto

Castelrotto has the largest selection of accommodations and is the only truly convenient option for those traveling in this region by public transport. If you've come to hike at Alpe di Siusi, you could also stay in one of the hotels there (in or around Compatsch)—I've listed two less expensive options—or even in a mountain hut.

Dozens of farmhouses in the area also offer accommodations, usually practical only if you have a car. (There's a full list on the TI website.) Some are working farms; others have been converted to tourist accommodations. I've listed a few that are willing to accept guests for one or two nights (the typical American stay). German and Italian tourists—who make up the bulk of the area's business—are more likely to stay for a week and to rent apartments with a kitchen but with no breakfast or daily cleaning service—which can save a great deal of money, especially for families.

Rates skyrocket during July, August, and around Christmas. Accommodations often close in November and from April to mid-May. I've assigned categories based on the price of a double room in June or September.

If sleeping in this area, you're entitled to an **Alpe di Siusi Live Card**—a free pass for many local buses (described earlier, under "Tourist Information"). Be sure to ask your hotelier for one.

IN CASTELROTTO VILLAGE

These listings are within 300 yards of the bus station. The first three are in the traffic-free area of the old town; hotel guests are allowed to drive in to park. All have free parking.

$$$ Hotel Cavallino d'Oro (in German, **Goldenes Rössl**), right on the main square, is plush and welcoming, with the best Tirolean character in town. Run by helpful Stefan and Susanne, the entire place is dappled with artistic, woodsy touches—painted doors, carved wood, and canopy beds in many rooms—and historical photos. If you love antiques by candlelight, this nearly 700-year-old hotel is the place for you (elevator, free self-service laundry, open all year, Piazza Kraus 1, tel. 0471-706-337, www.cavallino.it, info@cavallino.it). Stefan converted his wine cellar into a Roman steam bath and Finnish sauna (free for guests, great after a hike, can book an hour for exclusive use)—complete with heated tile seats, massage rooms, a solarium for tanning, and tropical plants.

$$ Hotel zum Turm (in Italian, **Albergo alla Torre**) is comfortable, cozy, and warmly run by Gabi and Günther. The 15 rooms are woody and modern. If you're staying at least three nights, the €12/person half-board option is a great value (family rooms, elevator, free passes for Marinzen chairlift, closed April and Nov, Kofelgasse 8, tel. 0471-706-349, www.zumturm.com, info@zumturm.com). From Castelrotto's main square, walk (or drive) through the upper of the two archways.

$$ Hotel Wolf (in Italian, **al Lupo**) is pure Tirolean, with all the comforts in 23 neat-as-a-pin rooms, most with balconies (elevator, coin-op laundry, closed April-late May and Nov-mid-Dec, a block below main square at Wolkensteinstrasse 5, tel. 0471-706-332, www.hotelwolf.it, info@hotelwolf.it, Malknecht family).

$ Residence Garni Trocker is run by the Moser family, who rent 11 great rooms in a place that's bomb-shelter solid yet warm-wood cozy. While the family is shy and less welcoming than others listed here, their compound is beautifully laid out—with a café-bar (a popular, often-smoky local hangout), garden, sauna, steam bath, roof deck with Jacuzzi, and coin-op laundry (family rooms, apartments available, elevator, closed Nov, Föstlweg 3, tel. 0471-705-200, www.residencetrocker.com, garni@residencetrocker.com, Stefan). If arriving on Sunday (the family's day off), be sure to let them know in advance what time you'll arrive.

$ Pension Garni Lantschner is family-run and a good budget value. Its 10 rooms—on the two upper floors of a large traditional house—are a little smaller, simpler, and older than at my other listings, but all are comfortable and have balconies with views (Klein-michlweg 8, tel. 0471-706-025, www.garni-lantschner.com, info@garni-lantschner.com).

FARM STAYS NEAR CASTELROTTO

Dozens of working farms around Castelrotto take in visitors, mostly in apartments with a kitchen and a minimum stay of five to seven nights (the TI has a complete list). A few farms also accept guests for short stays—even one night—and serve breakfast. Expect rustic doubles with bath for about €60. Staying in these places is practical only if you have a car. Consider the following (all $): **Goldrainerhof** (a 10-minute uphill trudge from Castelrotto, Tioslerweg 10, tel. 0471-706-100, www.goldrainerhof.com); **Tonderhof** (a fruit farm in a dramatic hillside setting along the road down to Waidbruck/Ponte Gardena, Tisens 25, tel. 0741-706-733, www.tonderhof.com) and their neighbor, **Schiedhof** (Tisens 23, mobile 345-583-7278, www.schiedhof.it); and **Formsunhof** (along the road up to Alpe di Siusi, before the checkpoint, St. Valentin 12, tel. 0471-706-015, www.formsunhof.com).

IN ALPE DI SIUSI/SEISER ALM, NEAR THE HIKING TRAILS

There are more than two dozen hotels in Alpe di Siusi, most in Compatsch (where the cable car from Seis/Siusi arrives) but some farther into the park. Most are quite expensive, four- and five-star affairs, with doubles costing around €200 in July and August. The two hotels listed here cost less—because Compatsch and the park entrance are a 10- to 15-minute uphill walk away. These are only practical for drivers. Half-board is wise here, as there's nowhere else to eat dinner (except other hotels). Serious hikers should consider staying at the park's high-altitude mountain huts (mentioned under "Activities in Alpe di Siusi," later).

$$ Hotel Seelaus, with 25 rooms, is a friendly, mellow, family-run, creekside place with an Austrian feel (family rooms, hearty €15 dinners, free wellness area with sauna, hydro-massage, and minipool; Wi-Fi in common areas only, closed mid-April-mid-May and mid-Oct-early Dec, Compatschweg 8, tel. 0471-727-954, www.hotelseelaus.it, info@hotelseelaus.it, Roberto). Roberto offers free rides from the bus or cable-car station, and affordable transfers to/from Bolzano—arrange in advance.

$$ Hotel Schmung is along the road and has fine, recently renovated rooms. During the day, the Seiser Alm Bahn cable cars float through the air just outside the front balconies (dinner available, free sauna, closed April-May and Nov-mid-Dec, Compatsch 12, tel. 0471-727-943, www.schmung.com, info@schmung.com).

Eating in Castelrotto

$$$ Saalstuben Restaurant serves a selection of hearty and tasty Austrian-Italian dishes indoors or on their terrace, including big salads, vegetarian plates, lots of grilled meats, and Tirolean classics. Their dessert specialty is *Kaiserschmarrn*, a favorite of Austrian Emperor Franz Josef. This eggy pancake with jam is plenty big for two (dressy indoors, Fri-Wed 11:30-14:00 & 17:30-21:00, closed Thu, Wolkensteinstrasse 12, tel. 0471-707-394, www.saalstuben. com).

$$$ Hotel zum Turm tries hard to up the culinary bar in town, focusing on locally sourced ingredients and serving good, meaty fare, including venison. You can sit in the humdrum breakfast room, the cozy and very traditional *Stube,* or out on the back terrace (salad bar, Thu-Tue 12:00-14:00 & 18:00-20:45, closed Wed, closed April-mid-May and Nov, tel. 0471-706-349, www. zumturm.com).

$$ Gasthof Toni, along the main road at the town's main intersection, pleases hungry locals with huge €15 two-course meals served at both lunch and dinner (pick one pasta and one meat course, includes side salad). It's cozy inside but the outdoor tables are just off a noisy street. They also have good pizza (Mon-Sat 12:00-14:00 & 17:00-21:00, pizza until 23:00, closed Sun, Wolkensteinstrasse 15, tel. 0471-706-306).

$$ Zur Alten Schmiede Pizzeria is a great place to enjoy an evening drinking Forst, the local beer, and playing darts. They offer a wide range of nothing-fancy grub—pizzas, pastas, meaty dishes, and wurst meals (Tue-Sun 12:00-14:00 & 17:30-21:00, pizza until 23:00, closed Mon, outdoor seating, near bus station entrance at Paniderstrasse 7, tel. 0471-707-390).

$ Pasta & More, right on the main square, is where Martin dishes up lasagna, vegetable strudel, pastas, and other simple meals—either packed to go or served at a few indoor tables or a couple delightful tables on the square (Mon-Sat 9:00-14:00 & 17:00-19:00, closed Sun, Piazza Kraus 5, tel. 0471-711-085).

Ristorante Liftstüberl is a good bet if you'd like to eat in nature rather than in town. It's a charming local favorite offering good traditional dishes with a classic woody interior and picnic benches with mountain views. Find it in a meadow about a half-mile hike south of town (closed Sun, Via Marinzen 35, tel. 0471-706-804).

Picnics: Castelrotto has several supermarkets. **Eurospar** is the handiest, at the town's main intersection, and has the longest hours (Mon-Sat 8:00-19:30, closed Sun, on Wolkensteinstrasse). The **Co-op/Konsum-Market** has the best selection of locally produced food, and a hardware section where you can pick up a bell for your cow—no joke (Mon-Sat 7:30-12:30 & 15:00-19:00, closed Sun, Paniderstrasse 24).

Castelrotto Connections

From Castelrotto by Bus to: Bolzano (#170, 2/hour Mon-Sat, hourly Sun, 50 minutes, last departure around 19:00; if you're connecting to a train in Bolzano, hop off at the train station—otherwise stay on for the bus station, which is slightly closer to the main square). From Bolzano, you can easily connect to **Innsbruck, Munich, Venice,** and beyond. Get bus schedules at the TI, toll tel. 840-000-471, or check www.sii.bz.it or www.silbernagl.it. For connections to **Alpe di Siusi/Seiser Alm,** see "Getting There," later.

Alpe di Siusi

This grassy mountain plateau above the village of Seis/Siusi (the next over from Castelrotto) is the largest high meadow—and summer pastureland—in the Alps. It's a premier hiking and skiing area, and also home to hundreds of cows every summer. Undulating rather than flat, broken by rushing streams, and dappled with shapely evergreens, what makes Alpe di Siusi (Seiser Alm in German) really spectacular are the views of the surrounding  Dolomite peaks. Well-kept huts, trails, and lifts make hiking here a joy. It's family-friendly, with lots of playgrounds. Being here on a sunny summer day comes with the ambience of a day at the beach.

The cows munching away in this vast pasture all summer after a winter huddled in Castelrotto produce two million gallons of milk annually, much of which is sent to Bolzano to make cheese. After tourism, dairy is the leading industry here.

To enjoy Alpe di Siusi, you'll need a full day and decent weather. Arrive in Compatsch (the main entry point) as early as you can, then hike (or bike) as much as you please. Plan a picnic, or lunch at a high mountain hut, and aim to wrap up the day in midafternoon—many upper lifts close at 17:00, and thunderclouds tend to gather even on days that start out sunny.

The hiking season runs roughly from mid-June through mid-October (though if the weather's good, you can hit some of the trails as early as mid-May). The trails are pretty dead in April, early May, and November. For a fragrant festival of wildflowers suited to growing at 6,000 feet, come in June.

With additional time, you can explore more of the park or overnight in one of the mountain huts as a base for more remote and challenging hikes. You're more than a mile high here, so take it easy and give yourself frequent breaks to catch your breath.

Get to know the park's mountains by sight. The jagged peaks called **Langkofel** (Sasso Lungo, "Long Stone") and **Plattkofel** (Sasso Piatto, "Flat Stone") together form an "M" at the far end of Alpe di Siusi—providing a storybook Dolomite backdrop. The dark, eerie saddle between them fires the imagination. To the right, and closer to Compatsch, the long, flat ridge called the **Schlern** (Sciliar in Italian) ends in spooky crags that boldly stare into the summer haze. The Schlern, looking like a devilish *Winged Victory,* gave ancient peoples enough willies to spawn legends of supernatural forces. The Schlern witch, today's tourist-brochure mascot, was the cause of many a broom-riding medieval townswoman's fiery death.

Compatsch provides great views of the Schlern, but only a peek-a-boo glimpse of Langkofel and Plattkofel. For better views, gain some altitude on a lift, or hop the bus (or hike) toward **Saltria,** at the far end of Alpe di Suisi. (Because Saltria sits down in a valley, the views are even better from the road just above it, near the hut called Rauchhütte.)

GETTING THERE

By Car: The winding, six-mile road up to Compatsch starts between Castelrotto and Seis/Siusi (at San Valentino). To keep the meadow serene, it's closed to cars during the day (9:00-17:00), unless you're staying in one of the hotels in the park. (The road is unblocked, but you'll likely be stopped by roving traffic monitors—be ready to show your hotel reservation confirmation.) But if you're an early riser, there's no reason not to drive up if you can arrive at the checkpoint before 9:00. (You can drive back down at any time.) Compatsch has a huge parking lot (€16/day—the same price as one round-trip cable-car ticket, so groups of at least two save by driving).

From Bolzano or Castelrotto to the Seiser Alm Bahn Cable Car at Seis/Siusi: Regular buses from Bolzano and Castelrotto link to the bottom of the cable car that whisks visitors from Seis/Siusi to Alpe di Siusi (described next). Buses #3 and #4 run from Castelrotto (4/hour July-Aug in morning and afternoon peak times, otherwise 2/hour; 10 minutes, €1.50, use machine, if no machine pay driver). These buses stop directly at the cable-car station. Some buses, including #170 from Bolzano (see page 491), stop

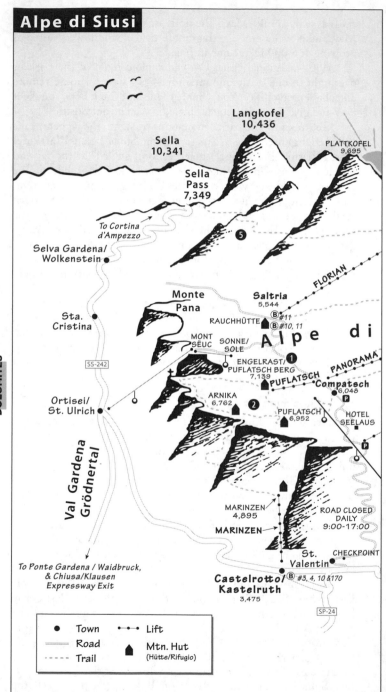

Alpe di Siusi

DOLOMITES

Langkofel 10,436

Sella 10,341

PLATTKOFEL 9,695

Sella Pass 7,349

To Cortina d'Ampezzo

Selva Gardena/ Wolkenstein

FLORIAN

Monte Pana

Saltria 5,544

Sta. Cristina

RAUCHHÜTTE

Ⓑ #11
Ⓑ #10, 11

Alpe di

MONT SËUC

SONNE/ SOLE

Ⓞ

SS-242

ENGELRAST/ PUFLATSCH BERG 7,139

PUFLATSCH

PANORAMA

Compatsch 6,048

Ⓟ

ARNIKA 6,762

Ⓞ

Ortisei/ St. Ulrich

PUFLATSCH 6,952

HOTEL SEELAUS

Ⓟ

Val Gardena Grödnertal

MARINZEN 4,895

MARINZEN

ROAD CLOSED DAILY 9:00-17:00

CHECKPOINT

To Ponte Gardena / Waidbruck, & Chiusa/Klausen Expressway Exit

St. Valentin

Castelrotto/ Kastelruth 3,475

Ⓑ #3, 4, 10 & 170

SP-24

Town	Lift
Road	Mtn. Hut (Hütte/Rifugio)
Trail	

Note: This 3-D view looks southeast & is not to scale. Elevations in feet

Marmolada
10,965

PLATTKOFEL
7,544

4

ZALLINGER
6,683

DIALER
KIRCHL
7,037

WILLIAMS
6,890

3

MAHLKNECHT
6,739

Tierser Alpl
8,006

S i u s i

PANORAMA
6,600

SALTNER
DAIRY FARM
"TSCHAPIT"
6,004

SCHLERNHAUS
7,544

Mt. Pez
8,400

SPITZBÜHL
6,348

6

Schlern

SPITZBÜHL

SEISERALM BAHN
(CANOVA)

#3, 4 &170 **B** Siusi /Seis
3,287

To Bolzano Nord
Expressway Exit

DOLOMITES

1 Compatsch to Saltria Walk
2 "Trail of the Witches"
3 Panorama to Zallingerhütte Hike
4 High Route to Zallingerhütte
5 Loop Around Langkofel & Plattkofel
6 Summit Hike of Schlern

at the turnoff just below the cable-car station—a steep five-minute hike up.

By Cable Car from Seis/Siusi: A cable car (the Seiser Alm Bahn; in Italian, Cabinovia Alpe di Siusi) runs hikers and skiers up to Compatsch (mid-May-early Nov daily 8:00-18:00, mid-June-mid-Sept until 19:00, closed most of Nov and mid-April–mid-May, runs continuously during open hours, 15-minute ride to the top, €11 one-way, €17 round-trip, tel. 0471-704-270, www.seiseralmbahn.it). You can reach the valley station either by car (free outdoor parking; garage parking-€3/day) or by bus (see earlier). The lower cable-car station is a slick mini shopping mall, with lots of outdoor outfitters and a tempting local-products store.

By Bus from Castelrotto: "Express" bus #10 runs from Castelrotto all the way to Compatsch. This is practical but costs the same as the more dramatic and memorable—and environmentally friendly—cable car (8 buses/day mid-June-mid-Oct, 20 minutes, fewer mid-May-mid-June and late Oct, www.silbernagl.it). Note that the Siusi Live Card does not cover buses that go above Seis/Suisi.

GETTING AROUND ALPE DI SIUSI

Shuttle Buses: The plateau is essentially car-free, except for guests staying at a few hotels inside the park. The #11 shuttle bus takes visitors to and from key points along the tiny road between Compatsch—the gateway to Alpe di Siusi—and Saltria, at the foot of the postcard-dramatic Sasso peaks and the base of the Florian lift (2-3/hour mid-June-mid-Oct, fewer mid-May-mid-June and in late Oct, runs about 8:40-18:40—check local schedules, 15 minutes from Compatsch to Saltria, €2, buy ticket at vending machines at the station or pay driver, www.silbernagl.it). At the end of the day, buses back from Saltria can be jam-packed. Bus #14 serves hotels in the meadow but isn't helpful for points in this chapter.

Cable Cars and Chair Lifts: Four upper lifts (marked on maps) are worth the €6-10 per ride to get you into the higher and more scenic hiking areas expeditiously (or back to the shuttle buses quickly). Keep in mind that the upper lifts stop running fairly early (typically at about 17:00; the Seiser Alm Bahn cable car from Compatsch down into the valley runs until 18:00 most of the year—and until 19:00 in high-season). Check schedules and plan your day accordingly.

Orientation to Compatsch Village

Compatsch (about 6,000 feet), at the entrance to Alpe di Siusi, isn't quite a "village," but a collection of hotels and services for visitors to the plateau. Most services cluster around the parking lot (including the TI, ATMs, restaurants, bike rental, small grocery store, and shops). The upper station of the Seiser Alm Bahn cable car, a five-minute walk away, also has WCs and a few shops and eateries.

Make a point to stop by the **TI,** which sells maps and has the latest on snow conditions and trail openings. If considering a demanding hike, review your plan here (Mon-Fri 8:15-12:30, Sat until 12:00, closed Sun, tel. 0471-727-904, www.seiseralm.it).

HELPFUL HINTS

Bike Rental: Two shops offer standard, performance, and electric bikes, along with helmets, maps, and trail advice, and have similar prices (standard bike—€12/1 hour, €25-29/day; performance or electric bike—€43/day). **Sporthaus Fill** is by the cable-car station (tel. 0471-729-063, www.sporthausfill.com) and **Sport Hans** is across from the parking lot (tel. 0471-727-824, www.sporthans.com, Hans and son Samuel). There's a world of tiny paved and gravel lanes to pedal. Pick up their suggested routes and consider the ones I describe later. Rentable baby buggies are popular for those hiking with toddlers.

Groceries: Onkel Eugen's, a tiny store across from the parking lot, has necessities (open early-June-mid-Oct and Dec-Easter 8:00-16:00).

Horse-Drawn Carriage Rides: These are available next to the TI (May-Oct 9:00-16:00, €30-40/half-hour, €80-115 to Saltria, price depends on size of carriage).

Activities in Alpe di Siusi

HIKING

Easy meadow walks abound in Alpe di Siusi, giving novice hikers classic Dolomite views from baby-stroller trails. Experienced hikers should consider the tougher, more exciting treks. Before attempting a hike, call or stop by the TI to confirm lift schedules and check your understanding of the time and skills required. As always, when hiking in the mountains, assume weather can change quickly, and pack

accordingly. Meadow walks, for flower lovers and strollers, are pretty—but for advanced hikers, they can be boring. Chairlifts are springboards for more dramatic and demanding hikes. Upper lifts generally close at 17:00.

DOLOMITES

Trails are very well marked, and the brightly painted numbers are keyed into local maps. Signs also display the next mountain hut along the trail, which serve as helpful navigational landmarks. (When asked for directions, most locals will know the trail by the huts it connects rather than its number.) For simple hikes, you can basically string together three or four names off the free pictorial map. For anything more serious, invest in a good 1:25,000 map from the TI (about €5). Huts (*Hütte* in German, *rifugi* in Italian) offer food and, often, beds. The Alpe di Siusi website (www. seiseralm.it) has more information (click on "Summer," then "Hiking," then "Hiking Trails").

Shoulder-Season Strategies: The Seiser Alm Bahn cable car up to Compatsch starts running in mid-May, but upper lifts begin operating a few weeks later; there's a similar gap at the end of the season (mid-Oct–early Nov). But even during these shoulder seasons, Alpe di Siusi can still be worth visiting (and busy with hikers) in good weather. Many of the hikes listed here are doable without a lift—but only if you're willing to hike to the trailhead (most realistic for the "Trail of the Witches"). Get local advice about snow levels and which hikes are possible. The simplest option is to hike trail #30 or ride bus #11 along the valley floor between Compatsch and Saltria, enjoying the views along the way.

Hiking Club: If you're headed up into the mountains, the Alpenverein Südtirol, a local hiking club, provides good, free trail maps for the whole region on its website (www.trekking.suedtirol. info).

Easy Hikes
Along the Main Road to Saltria

Bus #11 connects Compatsch to Saltria (at the far end of Alpe di Siusi, tucked under Langkofel and Plattkofel) in about 15 minutes—zipping past some impressive scenery en route. For a very easy, mostly level walk, follow this same route by foot, in about 50 minutes (using trail #30, which parallels the route). The last stretch—into Saltria—is steeply downhill and has less impressive views; consider going only as far as **Rauchhütte** (a charming old hut serving good food, spectacular views, closed Wed), located where the road starts to switchback down. Bus #11 stops at various points along this route (including Rauchhütte and Ritschhütte)—making it easy to do as much or as little of this by foot as you like. (Saltria is not a good destination on its own: It's a steep walk below Rauchhütte and has hotels, trail heads, and a bus stop, but no shops.)

The "Trail of the Witches"

This two-hour loop trail—past the legendary stone "witches' benches" *(Hexenbänke)*—is popular with first-time visitors and can be crowded in peak season. You'll enjoy ever-changing views as you get a handy 360-degree panorama of the peaks and valleys that ring Alpe di Siusi. It's mostly downhill all the way around, with a few brief uphill stretches.

First, ride the €6 cable car from Compatsch up to Puflatsch Berg (6,952 feet). A two-minute walk above the lift, an engraved map at the Engelrast ("Angel's Rest") observation point identifies the surrounding mountains. The counterclockwise hike follows *PU/Puflatsch* signs around the rim of the Puflatsch plateau. First you'll have Langkofel and Plattkofel on your right. Eventually you'll hit a little cross overlooking the valley village of St. Ulrich (far below in Val Gardena), then hook left and trace the dramatic rim of the valley. Soon tiny Castelrotto pops into view, you'll pass Arnikahütte (with a café), and finally you'll head back toward the Schlern. Near the end of the loop, you can either hike steeply back up to the Engelrast/Puflatsch Berg cable-car station, or—better and easier—keep going downhill all the way into Compatsch, with fine valley views the entire time.

Note: If you're here when the upper lifts aren't running (or even in the early evening, assuming you're staying in Compatsch or have a car for returning to the valley after the main lift stops running), this is your most realistic and rewarding option. But be ready for a very steep 30-minute uphill hike to the Puflatsch Berg cable-car station to begin the hike.

Moderate Hikes
Panorama to Zallingerhütte

This walk on well-marked trails is a great introduction to Alpe di Siusi. While it starts and ends at about the same altitude, it includes plenty of ups and downs. It comes with fine vistas, changes of scenery (meadows, woods, and high valleys), fun stops along the way, and lifts up and down on each end. Though signs rate it at three hours without stops, allow five or six hours (including the lift from Compatsch, lift down to Saltria, and bus back to Compatsch) so you'll have time to dawdle, yodel, and eat.

Start by riding the €6 lift from Compatsch to Panorama (6,600 feet). From Panorama, follow trail #2 across the meadow to the paved road and then join trail #7. You'll pass the rustic Edlweishütte (snacks only), and the Almrosenhütte (hot food); after about 1.5 hours total you'll reach the Mahlknechthütte (6,739 feet, hot food). From here, you'll cross two streams (one on stepping stones, another by bridge). After the bridge, you can take an uphill scenic detour off trail #7 (20 minutes) to climb briefly to the highest point of the walk, a small wooden church (Dialer Kirchl, 7,037 feet) that makes a good picnic spot. Continuing on trail #7, you'll go gently downhill through woods for another hour and a quarter to Zallingerhütte (6,683 feet). From here it's a 10-minute climb to Williamshütte (6,890 feet, full restaurant), where you catch the €10 Florian lift to Saltria and the shuttle-bus stop (return to Compatsch on bus #11).

For shorter versions, you can ride either lift up, stroll around, and hike or ride the lift back down.

Note: Local hikers often skip the Compatsch-Panorama lift, as you need to hike five minutes down from Compatsch just to catch it, and it's only a brisk 20-30 minute climb from Compatsch to the top of the Panorama lift.

High Route to Zallingerhütte

For a more thrilling, demanding version of the previous hike—longer by two hours—branch off at the wooden church (Dialer Kirchl) following trail #4B and then the high #4 ridge trail, with commanding views both left and right, to Plattkofelhütte (7,544 feet). Then descend steeply to Zallingerhütte and Williamshütte (6,890 feet). No special experience or gear is needed for this trail, and it richly rewards those who take it.

Consider these tips: The hut on the ridge serves excellent lunches (Schutzhaus Plattkofelhütte/Rifugio Sasso Piatto, tel. 0462-601-721). You could do an abbreviated version of this hike by side-tripping from the wooden church a half-hour to the ridge for the view, then returning to trail #7 to continue the lower walk to Zallingerhütte. Serious hikers can hike a steep and satisfying hour from the Plattkofelhütte to the peak of Plattkofel/Sasso Piatto.

Loop Around Langkofel and Plattkofel

Another dramatic but medium-difficulty hike is the 10-mile, six-hour circular walk around the dramatic Langkofel and Plattkofel peaks, partly on what's called the Friedrich August (Federico Augusto) trail. The trail can be narrow (vertigo-inducing) and has sections of loose rocks; good shoes are essential, as is a proper map. Get details and advice from the TI before you start. To reach this trail, ride the bus from Compatsch to Saltria, take the €10 Florian chairlift to Williamshütte, and walk 10 minutes to the Zallingerhütte (one of several possible starting points). On the far side, at Sellajoch Haus, you can ride a lift high up to the ¢ Toni-Demetz-Hütte (8,790 feet, food and simple beds, www.tonidemetz.it) and back down again. (A path from this hut actually crosses the saddle between the Langkofel and Plattkofel, but it's often icy and impassable without technical equipment—even in summer.)

Consider overnighting at the 15-room $$$ Zallingerhütte before this walk—you're allowed to drive to the hut if staying there (dorms and private rooms, tel. 0471-727-947, www.zallinger.com, info@zallinger.com).

Challenging Hikes
Summit Hike of Schlern

For a serious 12-mile (six-hour) hike—with a possible overnight in a traditional mountain refuge (generally open mid-June-Sept)—consider hiking to the summit of Schlern (Sciliar). This route is popular with hardy hikers; some call it the best hike in the region.

Start at the €6 Spitzbühl chairlift, a 20-minute walk below Compatsch (5,659 feet, free parking, Castelrotto-Compatsch bus stops here), which brings you up to 6,348 feet. Trail #5 takes you through a high meadow, down to the Saltner dairy farm (6,004 feet—you want the Saltner dairy farm at Tschapit, not the one near Zallingerhütte), across a stream, and steeply up the Schlern mountain. About three hours into your hike, you'll meet trail #1 and walk across the rocky tabletop plateau of Schlern to the **Schlernhaus** mountain "hut," really a simple restaurant and 120-bed hostel (7,544 feet, called Rifugio Bolzano in Italian). From this dramatic setting, you can enjoy a meal and get a great view of the Rosengarten range. Hike 20 more minutes up the nearby peak (Monte Pez, 8,400 feet), where you'll find a lofty meadow, cows in the summer, and the region's ultimate 360-degree alpine panorama. Unless you're staying overnight, hike back the way you came.

Overnight Option: To do the Schlern summit hike as an overnight, either sleep at the ¢ **Schlernhaus** (bunks and private rooms, cash only, open early June-mid-Oct, no hot water, summer-only tel. 0471-612-024, off-season tel. 0471-724-094, can reserve by email before hut opens in June, www.schlernhaus.it, info@schlernhaus.it) or walk two hours farther along the Schlern to the hut at ¢ **Tierser Alpl,** at 8,006 feet (bunks and private rooms, open late May-late Oct, tel. 0471-727-958 or 0471-707-460, mobile 333-654-6865, www.tierseralpl.com, info@tierseralpl.com). From Tierser Alpl, you can descend to Saltria or Compatsch by any of several different scenic routes.

TRAIL RUNNING

The Running Park Seiser Alm includes 46 miles of signed running trails in the meadow. The clean air and high mountain altitude attract many international runners/masochists. During a one-day,

DOLOMITES

scenic half-marathon on the first Sunday of July, they invite the public to run with them...or at least try. Contact the Compatsch TI for trail info and maps, or go to www.seiseralm.it and click on "Summer," then "Running."

BIKING

Bikes are easy to rent (including electric ones—see "Helpful Hints," earlier), welcome on many lifts for free or a small fee, and permitted on many of the trails and lanes in Alpe di Siusi. The Compatsch TI has a good information flier that lists the best routes. You can also go to www.seiseralm.it and click on "Summer," then "Bike," then "MTB Trails." Get local advice to confirm difficulty levels and your plan before starting any ride; the TI hands out helpful bike-route cards. Those with a bike don't need to worry as much about lifts shutting down early.

For a fairly easy, 2.5-hour ride that gives you the same scenic thrills as the "**Panorama to Zallingerhütte**" hike recommended earlier, try this: Start from Compatsch (6,048 feet), bike or ride the lift to Panorama (6,600 feet), and take road #7, which runs generally uphill to Goldknopf and then follows a series of hills and dips to Mahlknechthütte (6,739 feet). Then take road #8 downhill to Saltria (5,544 feet) and back to Compatsch (6,048 feet). About 60 percent is paved and 40 percent is gravel lanes.

More Sights in the Dolomites

▲▲Short Dolomite Loop Drive

You could spend a day from Bolzano or Castelrotto driving a loop over the scenic Sella Pass (Sellajoch, Passo di Sella)—it's about 70 miles on windy roads, so allow four hours. Going clockwise, you drive first through a long valley, the Grödner Tal/Val Gardena, which is famous for its skiing and hiking resorts, traditional Ladin culture (notice the trilingual road signs), and wood-carvers (the woodcarving company ANRI is from the town of

St. Cristina). You'll pass through the large town of St. Ulrich (with the base station of a different cable car up to Alpe di Siusi—used for more challenging hikes). Within an hour, you'll reach Sella Pass (7,349 feet). After a series of tight hairpin turns a half-mile or so over the pass, you'll see some benches and cars. Pull over and watch the rock climbers. Over the pass is the town of Canazei, with nice ambience and altitude (4,642 feet). From Canazei, lifts (mid-June-late Sept daily 8:30-12:30 & 13:45-17:20) take you to Col dei Rossi Belvedere, where you can hike the Bindelweg trail past Rifugio Belvedere along an easy but breathtaking ridge to Rifugio Viel del Pan (check with the Canazei TI for lift info: tel. 0462-609-500, www.fassa.com). This three-hour round-trip hike has views of the highest mountain in the Dolomites—the Marmolada—and the Dolo-mighty Sella range. Leaving Canazei, you can either follow very twisty roads (via St. Zyprian and Tiers) back to Castelrotto, or take the easier and slightly faster route via Welschnofen and Birchabruck back to Bolzano and the main valley highway.

Brixen (Bressanone)

This charming small city (pop. 20,000), on the highway between Bolzano and Innsbruck, is a worthwhile pit stop (park at garage P2 and take the pedestrian underpass into the old town; the main square is a 5-minute stroll away). With an illustrious history of powerful bishops—and a sleepy present—Brixen feels like a charming, mini Bolzano with a bit more Germanic character. It has a sprawling, traffic-free old town; a big main square with two stately churches (connected by a fine cloister); arcaded shopping streets; and plenty of al fresco cafés and restaurants. Explore the lanes beyond the main square to find a beautiful waterside walking and biking path.

Near Brixen: More impressive than any sight in Brixen itself, the **Kloster Neustift** (Abbazia di Novacella)—just two miles north—is an Augustinian monastery complex that's open to the public. The centerpiece is a basilica with the region's most glorious Bavarian-style Baroque interior—slathered with decadent white and pink stucco, frilly curlicues, twisty columns, and pudgy winged babies everywhere. While a quick stroll through the grounds and a look at the church interior is plenty satisfying, you can also take a guided tour or try the monk-made wines in the *enoteca* (tel. 0472-836-189, www.kloster-neustift.it).

▲Reifenstein Castle (Castel Tasso)

Reifenstein Castle, with one of my favorite castle interiors in Eu-

rope, is just off the highway at the town of Sterzing/Vipiteno. While easy for drivers, it's not worth the trouble for those without wheels—it's unique and interesting but only open for a few non-English tours a day. The castle

DOLOMITES

is privately owned and has not been developed for tourism (no gift shop, no café). Its layout and decor have changed little since the 15th century, when it passed into the hands of the Teutonic Knights. Since 1813, a branch of the noble Thurn and Taxis family has owned the castle. The current heads of the family (an elderly brother and sister) live in Innsbruck, and have chosen to keep the castle just as it was when they spent summer vacations here in the 1940s as children. On your tour, you'll see most of the building, including bedrooms with original wall paneling and decorations, a real dungeon, wooden boxes knights slept in, and a medieval kitchen with a roof that is black with centuries of soot.

Cost and Hours: €7, open early April-Oct; tours Sun-Fri at 10:30, 14:00, and 15:00, late July-early Sept also at 16:00, closed Sat; show up punctually at these times at drawbridge, ideally call ahead to confirm tour, minimum of four people needed for tour to run—but if fewer people show up you can pay the extra admission prices, mobile 339-264-3752 (call between 8:00-10:30, 11:30-14:00, or 17:00-20:00), visit www.sterzing.com, click "Culture," and then "Castles." Frau Steiner, the castle guide and caretaker, can do one-hour private tours in English by appointment for a reasonable price.

Getting There: By car, the castle is about 45 minutes from Bolzano, Castelrotto, and Innsbruck. Exit the Innsbruck-Bolzano expressway at Sterzing/Vipiteno (just on the Italian side of the Brenner Pass and Austrian/Italian border), and carefully follow brown *Reifenstein* signs. Park at the base of the castle's rock and hike up the castle drive (10 minutes). Of the two castles here, Reifenstein is the one to the west of the expressway.

AUSTRIA: PAST & PRESENT

Timeline of Austrian History

Romans and Barbarians
c. AD 1
The Romans occupy and defend previously Celtic lands as far northeast as the Danube River, including the strategically critical north-south Brenner Pass through the Alps. Their settlement in Vienna, called Vindobona, was centered on the site of today's cathedral.

c. 500
Lombard "barbarians"—following on the heels of the Vandals and Huns—drive the last Romans out, claiming this prime location as their own.

Holy Roman Empire and the Rise of the Habsburgs
c. 800
Charlemagne designates Austria—as one boundary of his European empire—the "Eastern Realm," or *Österreich*. Charlemagne is crowned Holy Roman Emperor, a title Austria's rulers would later claim for themselves. Vienna (now called "Wenia") develops further as a thriving trade city.

1147
Vienna's St. Stephen's Cathedral is begun in the Romanesque style (still seen today in the facade). The church would take more than 300 years to complete.

1273
An Austrian noble from the Habsburg family (Rudolf I) is elected

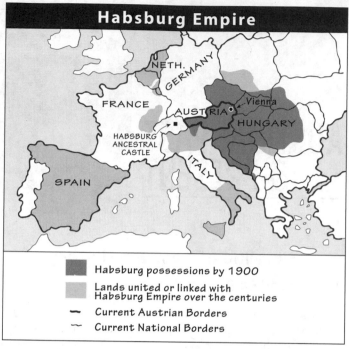

Habsburg Empire

NETH.
GERMANY
FRANCE
AUSTRIA   Vienna
HABSBURG   HUNGARY
ANCESTRAL
CASTLE
ITALY
SPAIN

- **Habsburg possessions by 1900**
- **Lands united or linked with Habsburg Empire over the centuries**
- **Current Austrian Borders**
- **Current National Borders**

Holy Roman Emperor, ruling Austria, Germany, and northern Italy. From 1438 until 1806, every emperor but one is a Habsburg. The Habsburgs arrange strategic marriages for their children with other prominent royalty around Europe, gaining power through international connections.

c. 1450

Vienna flourishes under Holy Roman Emperor Frederick III, considered the "father" of Vienna for turning the small village into a royal town with a cosmopolitan feel. Frederick makes the city his capital, and the Hofburg his home. St. Stephen's soaring 450-foot spire is completed (1433), the north tower is begun (1450), and the church is given a bishopric (1469), becoming a cathedral. Frederick's impressive tomb stands in the cathedral today.

1493

Maximilian I is crowned emperor. His marriage to Mary of Burgundy weds two kingdoms together, and their grandson, Charles V, inherits a vast empire. The combined lands instantly make the Habsburg Empire a major player in European politics. In 1498, Maximilian establishes the Vienna Boys' Choir to sing for him at Mass.

Wars and Turbulence

1519

Charles V (r. 1519-1556) is the most powerful man in Europe, ruling Austria, Germany, the Low Countries, parts of Italy, and Spain (with its New World possessions). Charles is responsible for trying to solve the problems of all those lands, including battling Ottomans in Vienna and Lutherans in Germany. While many lands north of the Danube turn Protestant, Austria remains Catholic.

1522

Charles V gives Austria (and the Ottoman problem) to his little brother, Ferdinand, who, four years later, marries into the Bohemian and Hungarian crowns.

1529

Ottoman invaders from today's Turkey besiege Vienna, beginning almost two centuries of battles between Austria and the Ottoman Empire. In the course of the wars, Austria gains possession of Hungary and much of Eastern Europe.

1533

Vienna—with 50,000 inhabitants and a long history as the major city of the region—becomes the official capital of the Habsburg Empire.

1556

Charles V retires from the throne to enter a monastery, leaving his kingdom to his son (King Philip II of Spain), and the crown of Holy Roman Emperor to his brother, Ferdinand I of Austria. From now on, Austria's rulers would concentrate on ruling their eastern empire, which includes part or all of present-day Austria, Hungary, the Czech Republic, Slovakia, Romania, Slovenia, Croatia, Bosnia-Herzegovina, Serbia, northern Italy (Venice), and, later, parts of Poland and Ukraine.

1648

The Thirty Years' War—a bitter struggle between Catholic and Protestant forces—finally comes to an end, leaving the Holy Roman Empire an empire in name only. Its figurehead emperor oversees a scattered group of German-speaking people, mainly in Austria and (what is now) Germany.

1679

A disastrous bubonic plague kills 75,000 Viennese (remembered today by the plague monument on the Graben).

1683

Almost 200,000 Muslims from Ottoman Turkey surround the city of Vienna once again. The Ottomans are driven off, leaving behind

Habsburg Family Tree

RUDOLF IV (1339-1365)	As the first Habsburg emperor actually born in Austria, he established Vienna as the ruling capital. For the next six centuries, his descendants would rule Austria—many with the title "Emperor."

Two ↓ *Generations*

MAXIMILIAN I (1459-1519)	By war and marriage, extended realm in all directions—making the Habsburgs a major European power.

One ↓ *Generation*

CHARLES V (1500-1558)	Ruled as the most powerful man in Europe, when Habsburg Empire reached its pinnacle, stretching from Bohemia to Bolivia.

Five ↓ *Generations*

MARIA THERESA (& FRANZ I) (1717-1780)	Defended Austria against France. Had 16 children, most of whom she married off to Europe's royalty, including Marie-Antoinette, who became Mrs. Louis XVI, the (last) Queen of France.

↓ *Son*

JOSEF II (1741-1790)	Enlightened ruler abolished serfdom and brought about other democratic reforms. Patron of Mozart.

↓ *Nephew*

FRANZ II (1768-1835)	Demoted from HRE to Emperor of Austria after being defeated by (future son-in-law) Napoleon.

One ↓ *Generation*

FRANZ JOSEF (& SISI) (1830-1916)	The last Habsburg with any real power, his long reign saw the decline of his out-of-date empire.

Great- ↓ *Nephew*   *Nephew* ↘

KARL I (& ZITA) (1887-1922)	**FRANZ FERDINAND** (1863-1914)
At the tail end of his ancestors' dynasty, ruled for two wartime years before renouncing political power.	Heir to the throne—until his assassination in 1914, which sparked World War I and the end of Habsburgs' rule...and Europe as they knew it.

bags of coffee that help fuel a beverage craze around Europe. Vienna's first coffeehouse opens.

1672-1714
Three wars with Louis XIV of France (including the War of the Spanish Succession) drain Austria. Meanwhile, the Habsburgs put down the Hungarian War of Independence (1703-1711), led by Transylvanian prince Ferenc Rákóczi.

1735
The Spanish Riding School is built at the Hofburg in Vienna.

1740
Maria Theresa (r. 1740-1780) ascends to the throne. She eventually has 16 children and still finds time to fight two wars in 25 years, defending her right to rule. Adored by her subjects for her down-to-earth personality, she brings Austria international prestige by marrying her daughters to Europe's royalty. Under Maria Theresa, Schönbrunn Palace reaches its peak of luxury.

1781
Maria Theresa's son Josef II, who frees the serfs and takes piano lessons from Mozart, staves off the tide of democratic revolution, and rules Austria as an "enlightened despot."

1791
Mozart's comic opera *The Magic Flute* debuts. Vienna is the world capital of classical music, home to Haydn (1732-1809), Mozart (1756-1791), and Beethoven (1770-1827). Mozart was married in St. Stephen's Cathedral, and, after his death, his Requiem Mass is played there.

1792
When the French queen, the Habsburg Marie-Antoinette, is imprisoned and (later) beheaded by revolutionaries in Paris, her nephew, Austria's Emperor Franz II, seeks revenge, beginning two decades of wars between revolutionary France and monarchist Austria.

The Austrian Empire
1805
Napoleon defeats Austria at Austerlitz, his greatest triumph over the forces of monarchy. Napoleon occupies Vienna, moves into Schönbrunn Palace, and forces Holy Roman Emperor Franz II to hand over the Imperial Crown (1806), ending a thousand years of empire. Napoleon even marries Franz II's daughter, Marie-Louise.

1814-15
After Napoleon is defeated, an Austrian, Chancellor Metternich,

heads the Congress of Vienna—reinstalling kings and nobles recently deposed by Napoleon. Metternich's politics sets the tone for Vienna's conservative, bourgeois-dominated society.

Early 1800s

Throughout the Habsburgs' central and eastern European holdings, a gradual cultural revival takes place. Natives of Habsburg lands such as Hungary, the Czech Republic, Slovakia, and Slovenia enjoy a renewed appreciation for their unique, traditional, non-Austrian culture and language—setting the stage for a rocky century.

1832

Franz Sacher invents Vienna's signature dessert, the Sacher torte.

1848

Emperor Franz Josef (emperor of Austria, but not the "Holy Roman Emperor") rules for the next 68 years, maintaining white-gloved tradition while overseeing great change—Austria's decline as an empire and entrance into the modern industrial world. During his first year on the throne, another wave of revolution sweeps Europe, endangering many of his holdings.

1849

Almost 100,000 Austrians attend the funeral of violinist Johann Strauss, responsible for the dance craze called the waltz. His son, Johann Strauss II (1825-1899), takes the baton of the Strauss Orchestra and waltzes on.

c. 1850

Austria flourishes in a Golden Age that lasts throughout the latter half of the 19th century. Vienna is the epicenter of European culture: fine music, exquisite art, coffee and chocolates, dress-up balls, enlightened city planning, and cutting-edge science.

1854

Franz Josef marries the beautiful/neurotic Elisabeth ("Sisi"), and they settle into their lavish home in the Hofburg's Imperial Apartments.

1857

Vienna—population 450,000—is bursting at the seams. The city embarks on a massive urban renewal project. The old city wall is torn down and turned into a wide, circular boulevard called the Ringstrasse, lined with grand buildings including the Opera, City Hall, and twin Kunsthistorisches and Natural History Museums. The buildings are state-of-the-art, but decorated in styles that echo the past: Neoclassical, Neo-Gothic, and so on. Vienna's incredible transformation is overseen by Emperor Franz Josef, Mayor Karl Lueger, and chief architect Otto Wagner.

1866
Prussia provokes war and defeats Austria, effectively freezing Austria out of any involvement in a modern German nation.

The Austro-Hungarian Empire
1867
"The Blue Danube," a waltz by Johann Strauss II, debuts. But Austria—while at its cultural peak—is beginning its slow political decline. To better suppress the huge Slavic population in its sprawling empire, and facing a low-morale moment after the war with Prussia, Austria gives partial control over its territories to Hungary. This creates the "Dual Monarchy" of the Austro-Hungarian Empire. In a symbolic compromise, Franz Josef, "emperor" of Austria, is crowned "king" of Hungary (the origin of the royal boast "K+K"—*kaiserlich und königlich,* imperial and royal).

1869
The Vienna Opera House opens. Vienna in the late 19th century is home to composers Johannes Brahms, Richard Strauss, and Gustav Mahler.

1897
The Secession building opens in Vienna, displaying works by an exciting young generation of artists who vow to "secede" from academic art tradition.

1898
The horse-drawn trams on Vienna's Ringstrasse give way to electric-powered streetcars.

1899
Viennese psychiatrist Sigmund Freud publishes *The Interpretation of Dreams,* launching psychoanalysis and the 20th-century obsession with repressed sexual desires, the unconscious mind, and couches.

A New Century and the Fall of the Empire
c. 1900
As the century turns, Vienna is the globe's fifth-largest city (population 2.2 million)—bigger than it is today. It's balanced on the cusp between traditional Old World elegance and subversive modern trends. Stalin and Trotsky are rattling around. Women are smoking, riding bikes, and demanding the right to vote. In 1900, Adolf Loos builds his controversial, minimalist Loos House across from the old-school Hofburg.

1907

Gustav Klimt's painting *The Kiss*—sensual, daring, semi-abstract, and slightly decadent—epitomizes the Viennese *Jugendstil* (Art Nouveau) movement.

1908

A young aspiring artist named Adolf Hitler is rejected by Vienna's Academy of Fine Arts for the second time—one of many rejections and frustrations that will lead him to embrace his violent, anti-Semitic worldview.

1914

Austria fires the opening shots of World War I to avenge the assassination of its heir to the throne, Archduke Franz Ferdinand.

1919

After its defeat in World War I, the Austro-Hungarian Empire is divided into separate democratic nations, with Austria assigned the small, landlocked borders that it has today.

Rise of Fascism and World War II

1927

Riots in the streets of Vienna between liberals and fascists leave dozens dead and hundreds wounded; they show the deep rift in Austrian society. By the time the global Great Depression reaches Austria, the country is a powder keg of extreme ideologies.

1932

Mirroring events in Germany, a totalitarian government (headed by Engelbert Dollfuss) replaces a weak democracy floundering in economic depression.

1938

Led by Austrian-born Chancellor Adolf Hitler, Nazi Germany—using the threat of force and riding a surge of Germanic nationalism—annexes Austria in the *Anschluss,* and leads it into World War II. Hitler returns to Vienna in triumph, stands on the New Palace balcony at the Hofburg (now the World Museum Vienna), and addresses his adoring throngs.

1939-45

During World War II, Austria is part of Nazi Germany and suffers the consequences. Of Vienna's 200,000 Jews, about a third die in death camps. Nearly 100,000 Jews, criminals, and political dissidents die at Mauthausen Concentration Camp, just up the Danube from Vienna.

1943

The first Allied bombs strike Vienna. Over the next two years, half of the historic center is destroyed in Allied air raids. St. Stephen's Cathedral catches fire, collapsing the wooden roof. Many of the city's top art treasures are safely stowed away in cellars and salt mines.

1945

As the war ends, Vienna is liberated by Soviet troops. The city is in ruins. Like Germany, a defeated Austria is divided by the victors into occupied zones, but the country's occupation is short-lived.

Postwar Era and Beyond
1949

The movie *The Third Man* premieres, showing Vienna as a shady, espionage-laced city caught between Cold War superpowers. It's a hit in Britain and the US, but a flop in Austria, a nation not keen to see its recently mighty capital portrayed as an occupied city in ruins.

1952

In Vienna, a new St. Stephen's cathedral roof, rebuilt with local donations, is dedicated.

1955

Modern Austria (with Vienna as its capital) is born as a neutral nation, with the blessing of the international community. The treaty is signed at Belvedere Palace.

1961

President Kennedy meets Soviet Premier Khrushchev in Vienna for peace talks. As neutral territory between East and West, Austria is a natural choice for summits between the Cold War superpowers. Vienna also becomes home to several UN organizations. The OPEC nations make Vienna its seat in 1965.

1974-78

The Graben is pedestrianized, signaling Vienna's determination to modernize while preserving its historic core, and the subway system (U-Bahn) opens its first line (U-1).

1990s

Austria absorbs tens of thousands of war refugees during the breakup of Yugoslavia.

1995

Austria joins the European Union.

Austria Leans to the Right

In the vast sea of liberal Europe, Austria has long been an island of conservatism. And over the past two decades, Austria has inched even further to the right. Austria's right-wing Freedom Party (FPÖ), with a slogan of "Austria First" (Österreich Zuerst), has emerged from the political fringes to become as strong as the country's traditional center-left and center-right parties. The Freedom Party campaigns on a platform of strong nationalist patriotism, a populist appeal to blue-collar workers, and warnings about the dangers of unchecked immigration—particularly the rise in Islamic immigrants. They're big on the concept of Heimat—a love of Austria's homegrown folk roots and values, the cultural identity that binds the nation together. Unlike some extremist parties, the Freedom Party is led by well-educated, articulate men and women in business suits. However, their message also attracts support from neofascists, and opponents call them "wolves in sheep's clothing."

In May 2016, the Freedom Party supported Norbert Hofer for the largely ceremonial role of federal president. He won nearly half the popular vote, but lost (barely) to the Green Party candidate, Alexander Van der Bellen. The Freedom Party demanded a do-over election, held in December 2016. In that vote, Van der Bellen's margin increased tenfold, dealing the Freedom Party what at the time seemed like a clear, if mostly symbolic, defeat. But in 2017, 31-year-old Sebastian Kurz, then the chairman of the conservative Austrian People's Party (ÖVP), was named Austria's youngest-ever chancellor and immediately formed a coalition with the Freedom Party, a move protested by thousands in strongly liberal Vienna. It remains to be seen if Austria will continue to lean right, like governments in Hungary and Poland have in recent years, or if it will become the bridge between western and eastern European Union countries, as Kurz claims it will be.

The 21st Century
2000

The European Union places sanctions on Austria (lifted a few months later) when the far-right Freedom Party—campaigning under the slogan Überfremdung ("Too many foreigners")—gains seats in Austria's parliament. Two years later, the party does poorly in elections.

2003

Vienna's first Starbucks boldly opens—directly across from one of the city's oldest, best-loved coffee shops. Gott in Himmel!

2008

In September, Austria's revived far-right parties win 29 percent of the popular vote. A month later, their leader Jörg Haider is killed in a car crash.

2010
Vienna is named the most livable city in the world by the Mercer Quality of Life survey, citing the city's affordability, cultural vivacity, safety, and excellent public transit. The city retains its No. 1 spot for the next eight years…and counting.

2015
Hundreds of thousands of African and Middle Eastern refugees and immigrants pour through Austria—the first Western European nation encountered by many migrants. In August, the world is horrified when 71 migrants are found suffocated in the back of a smuggler's truck. Austrian politics heat up—and relations with Hungary are strained—by questions of border control and immigration policy.

2016
In May, Freedom Party candidate and anti-immigration hardliner Norbert Hofer comes within 15,000 votes of winning the Austrian presidency (a role more ceremonial than the chancellor's, but symbolically important).

2017
Just after midnight on January 1, more than 50 million people around the world welcome the New Year by watching a broadcast of the Vienna Philharmonic playing a waltz by Strauss.

Today
You arrive in Austria and make your own history.

Notable Austrians

Charles V (1500-1558)
Through a series of marriages and unexpected deaths, Charles V inherited not only the Habsburg properties in Austria, but also the Netherlands and the Spanish Empire, including its colonies in the Americas. He said that he ruled an empire "upon which the sun never sets" (a phrase the British stole for their own dominions in the 19th century). But even the most powerful ruler on earth couldn't stop the spread of Protestantism. Charles' vision of a unified, Catholic, European empire was thwarted by Martin Luther, German Protestant princes, and their allies, the French.

Maria Theresa (1717-1780)
The first and only female head of the Habsburg dynasty, Maria Theresa consolidated the power of the throne but also reformed

Austria by banning torture, funding schools and universities, and allowing some religious freedom for Protestants. Her changes, and those of her son, Josef II, allowed Austria to withstand the upheavals of the French Revolution. Her apartments at Vienna's Schönbrunn Palace are tourable today (see the Schönbrunn Palace Tour chapter; for more on the empress, see page 45).

Marie-Antoinette (1755-1793)

The youngest daughter of Maria Theresa, Marie-Antoinette's marriage to the heir to the French throne was supposed to cement the alliance between France and Austria. But she was not popular; even before the revolution, pamphleteers called her hopelessly stupid, accusing her of adultery, sexual deviance, and treason. During the Reign of Terror, she lost her head to the guillotine, inspiring countless romantic novels and two Hollywood movies.

Wolfgang Amadeus Mozart (1756-1791)

The ultimate child prodigy, Mozart started composing when he was five and performed for Empress Maria Theresa when he was eight. A giant of classical music, he wrote masterpieces in every genre he touched—operas, symphonies, chamber music, piano sonatas, and string quartets. Fans flock to visit his childhood homes in Salzburg (see "Sights in Salzburg" in the Salzburg chapter).

Johann Strauss II (1825-1899)

Vienna was the hometown of many great composers, such as Josef Haydn and Franz Schubert, but Johann Strauss II (the Younger) best captured its spirit. "The Waltz King" helped popularize this musical genre in the 19th century and wrote the most famous waltz of all, "The Blue Danube," as well as the operetta *Die Fledermaus*. These musical achievements came despite the objections of his father—also a famous composer—who wanted his son to be a banker.

Franz Josef (1831-1916)

At the age of 18, Franz Josef became emperor—beginning a 68-year reign surpassed in European history only by France's Louis XIV and a Liechtenstein prince. Franz Josef, a staunch conservative but a terrible general, presided over—and likely contributed to—the decline of the Austro-Hungarian Empire. His family life was similarly troubled; his estranged wife, "Sisi," was assassinated by an Italian anarchist, and his only son, Crown Prince Rudolf, committed suicide (or did he?) in the arms of a mistress. The end of the Habsburg dynasty came two years after Franz Josef's death. His Hofburg Imperial Apartments in Vienna are open to the public (see page 126; for more on the emperor, see page 135).

PAST & PRESENT

Sigmund Freud (1856-1939)

The Austrian physician and psychoanalyst revolutionized the study of human behavior. According to Freud, repressed desires—sexual desires in particular—explained why humans behave the way we do. Although he was a world figure of immense influence, the Nazis despised his Jewish roots and burned his books. After they took over Austria in 1938, Freud left for London, where he died a year later. His office in Vienna has been turned into the Sigmund Freud Museum (see page 75).

Gustav Klimt (1862-1918)

Erotic, symbolic, Byzantine, radical—the turn-of-the-century paintings of Gustav Klimt shook Viennese society. A leader of the Vienna Secession movement, Klimt was criticized at one point for "pornographic" art—years before the gold-wrapped lovers of *The Kiss* became an art school icon. His portrait *The Golden Adele* set a record when American billionaire Ronald Lauder bought it in 2006 for $135 million—at that time the most expensive painting ever sold. Klimt's art is displayed in museums throughout Vienna; *The Kiss*, for example, is in the Belvedere Palace (for more on the artist, see page 71).

Franz Ferdinand (1863-1914)

No one expected Archduke Franz Ferdinand to be the heir to the Habsburg dynasty. But when Crown Prince Rudolf killed himself in 1889 and Franz Ferdinand's father died in 1896, the young archduke suddenly became the hope of the Habsburgs. As inspector general of the army, he was invited to Sarajevo to review Austrian troops. On June 28, 1914, after his chauffeur took a wrong turn on the city's streets, Franz Ferdinand and his wife were assassinated by a Serbian nationalist, triggering World War I and the eventual end of the centuries-old dynasty.

Adolf Loos (1870-1933)

The man who said "decoration is a crime" was one of the most influential architects of the modern era. Born in what is now the Czech Republic, he trained in Germany and even spent three years tramping around America as a dishwasher and a mason. But it was in Vienna where he made his name. Excessive ornamentation was criminal, he declared, because it wasted labor and materials; the modern era deserved stripped-down facades. Examples of Loos' architecture—a bookstore, bar, and even WCs—are in downtown Vienna (see page 92).

Ferdinand Porsche (1875-1951)

This Austrian automotive engineer is best known as the father of the Volkswagen Beetle. Hitler demanded that Germany build a cheap "people's car," so Porsche began working on his world-famous design in 1934. Three years later, Hitler gave him one of Germany's highest awards. This automotive genius is also known for launching (with the help of his son) the Porsche sports car. But he was a century too soon with another one of his inventions: the world's first electric/gasoline hybrid car, the Mixte, created in 1901 in Vienna.

Adolf Hitler (1889-1945)

The future dictator—directly responsible for the deaths of more than 43 million people during World War II—was born in Braunau am Inn, north of Salzburg. After dropping out of high school at age 16, he spent eight years in prewar Vienna trying to make his way as an artist. (He was rejected twice by Vienna's Academy of Fine Arts.) Although Hitler served in the German army during World War I, he didn't become a German citizen until 1932, just one year before becoming the nation's chancellor and der Führer.

Maria von Trapp (1905-1987)

An orphan by age seven, Maria Augusta Kitschier was raised in Tirol by an anti-Catholic socialist. When she mistakenly attended a religious lecture (she had thought it would be a Bach concert), she was so moved that she became a staunch Catholic. Her memoir of life as a novice at a Salzburg convent and later as governess for the Von Trapp family was the basis for *The Sound of Music* (see page 274). The movie (and play) remain a major draw for Salzburg, with its many S.O.M. sights and tours.

Billy Wilder (1906-2002)

Born in Austria, Hollywood legend Billy Wilder won Oscars for directing *The Lost Weekend* and *The Apartment*. He also wrote and/or directed such Hollywood classics as *Some Like It Hot*, *The Seven Year Itch*, *Ball of Fire*, *Sunset Boulevard*, *Stalag 17*, *Sabrina*, and the dark and brooding *Double Indemnity*. He lost his mother in the Holocaust and was often bitter about his native country. "The Austrians are brilliant people," he once said. "They made the world believe that Hitler was a German and Beethoven an Austrian."

Otto Preminger (1906-1986)

Like Wilder, Otto Preminger grew up in Vienna's Jewish community. His success in Viennese theater eventually led to Hollywood, where Preminger hit the big time directing the 1944 mystery *Laura*. Twice nominated for a best-director Oscar (for *Laura* and *The Cardinal*), Preminger made films that challenged Hollywood taboos of the time, such as rape *(Anatomy of a Murder)*, drug addiction *(The Man with the Golden Arm)*, and homosexuality *(Advise and Consent)*.

Arnold Schwarzenegger (b. 1947)

Born in a village near Graz, Arnold Schwarzenegger was obsessed with bodybuilding even as a teenager. After winning international bodybuilding contests, Schwarzenegger got his big break as Conan the Barbarian, a role that spawned a string of blockbuster action movies, including the *Terminator* series. In 2003, Ah-nold switched careers and was elected the Republican governor of California; the "Governator" was reelected to a second term in 2006. After leaving office in 2011, news broke that Schwarzenegger had fathered a son more than 14 years earlier with the family housekeeper—prompting his wife, Maria Shriver, to file for divorce.

Felix Baumgartner (b. 1969)

After learning to parachute in the Austrian military, daredevil sky-diver Felix Baumgartner, who was born in Salzburg, has made a career of high-profile, wildly dangerous jumps off buildings, bridges, and mountains. All of Austria (and millions around the world) watched on October 14, 2012, when he plummeted 24 miles to earth in a heart-stopping supersonic jump from a helium-balloon capsule. Baumgartner simultaneously set three world records: highest-altitude manned balloon flight (24 miles up), highest-altitude parachute jump (128,100 feet), and greatest free-fall velocity (834 mph).

For more on Austrian history, consider Europe 101: History and Art for the Traveler, *written by Rick Steves and Gene Openshaw (available at www.ricksteves.com).*

PAST & PRESENT

PRACTICALITIES

This chapter covers the practical skills of European travel: how to get tourist information, pay for things, sightsee efficiently, find good-value accommodations, eat affordably but well, use technology wisely, and get between destinations smoothly. For more information on these topics, see www.ricksteves.com/travel-tips.

Tourist Information

Austria's national tourist office **in the US** can be a wealth of information. They have itinerary ideas and information on festivals, hiking, wine country, and more. Call 212/944-6880 or visit www.austria.info. The iAustria Travel Guide app is also handy for tips on sightseeing, hiking, transportation, and more.

In Austria, a good first stop is generally the tourist information office (abbreviated **TI** in this book). Throughout Austria, you'll find TIs are usually well-organized and have English-speaking staff. TIs are in business to help you enjoy spending money in their town, but even so, I still make a point to swing by to confirm sightseeing plans, pick up a city map, and get information on public transit, walking tours, special events, and nightlife. Anticipating a harried front-line staffer, prepare a list of questions and a proposed plan to double-check. Some TIs have information on the entire country or at least the region, so try to pick up maps and printed information for destinations you'll be visiting later in your trip.

Travel Tips

Emergency and Medical Help: For any emergency service—ambulance, police, or fire—call **112** from a mobile phone or landline. Operators, who in most countries speak English, will deal with your request or route you to the right emergency service. If you get sick, do as the locals do and go to a pharmacist for advice. Or ask at your hotel for help—they'll know the nearest medical and emergency services.

Theft or Loss: To replace a passport, you'll need to go in person to an embassy (see next). If your credit and debit cards disappear, cancel and replace them (see "Damage Control for Lost Cards," later). File a police report, either on the spot or within a day or two; you'll need it to submit an insurance claim for lost or stolen rail passes or travel gear, and it can help with replacing your passport or credit and debit cards. For more information, see www.ricksteves.com/help.

US Embassy in Vienna: Boltzmanngasse 16, tel. 01/313-390; consular services at Parkring 12a, 4th floor, U: Stephansplatz or Stubentor, daily 8:00-11:30, tel. 01/313-397-535, http://at.usembassy.gov, consulatevienna@state.gov.

Canadian Embassy in Vienna: Laurenzerberg 2, 3rd floor, U: Schwedenplatz, Mon-Fri 8:30-12:30, tel. 01/531-383-000, after-hours emergencies call collect Canadian tel. 613/996-8885, www.austria.gc.ca, vienn@international.gc.ca.

Time Zones: Austria, like most of continental Europe, is generally six/nine hours ahead of the East/West Coasts of the US. The exceptions are the beginning and end of Daylight Saving Time: Europe "springs forward" the last Sunday in March (two weeks after most of North America), and "falls back" the last Sunday in October (one week before North America). For a handy time converter, use the world clock app on your mobile phone or download one (see www.timeanddate.com).

Business Hours: In Austria, most shops are open from about 9:00 until 18:00-20:00 on weekdays, but close earlier on Saturday (as early as 12:00 in towns and as late as 18:00 in cities), and are almost always closed on Sunday. Most banks in Vienna are open weekdays roughly from 8:00 until 15:00, but elsewhere in Austria, banks often close for lunch. Many museums and sights are closed

PRACTICALITIES

on Monday. Catholic regions, including Germany's Bavaria and Italy's South Tirol, shut down during religious holidays.

Sundays have the same pros and cons as they do for travelers in the US: Sightseeing attractions are generally open, while shops and banks are closed, public transportation options are fewer, and there's no rush hour. Friday and Saturday evenings are lively; Sunday evenings are quiet.

Watt's Up? Europe's electrical system is 220 volts, instead of North America's 110 volts. Most newer electronics (such as laptops, battery chargers, and hair dryers) convert automatically, so you won't need a converter, but you will need an adapter plug with two round prongs, sold inexpensively at travel stores in the US. Italy only accepts plugs with slimmer prongs: Don't buy an adapter with the thicker ("Schuko" style) prongs—it won't work. Avoid bringing older appliances that don't automatically convert voltage; instead, buy a cheap replacement in Europe.

Discounts: Discounts for sights are generally not listed in this book. However, seniors (age 60 and over), youths under 19, and students or teachers with proper identification cards (www.isic.org) can get discounts at many sights. Always ask. Some discounts are available only to European citizens.

Online Translation Tips: Google's Chrome browser instantly translates websites; Translate.google.com is also handy. The Google Translate app converts spoken or typed English into most European languages (and vice versa) and can also translate text it "reads" with your phone's camera.

Money

Here's my basic strategy for using money in Europe:
- Upon arrival, head for a cash machine (ATM) at the airport and withdraw some local currency, using a debit card with low international transaction fees.
- Pay for most purchases with your choice of cash or a credit card. You'll save money by minimizing your credit and debit card exchange fees. The trend is for bigger expenses to be paid by credit card, but cash is still the standby for small purchases and tips.
- Keep your cards and cash safe in a money belt.

PLASTIC VERSUS CASH

Although credit cards are widely accepted in Europe, cash is sometimes the only way to pay for cheap food, taxis, tips, and local guides. Some businesses (especially smaller ones, such as B&Bs and mom-and-pop cafés and shops) may charge you extra for using

---

Exchange Rate

1 euro (€) = about $1.20

To convert prices in euros to dollars, add about 20 percent: €20=about $24, €50=about $60. (Check www.oanda.com for the latest exchange rates.) Just like the dollar, one euro (€) is broken down into 100 cents. Coins range from €0.01 to €2, and bills from €5 to €200 (bills over €50 are rarely used; €500 bills are being phased out).

---

a credit card—or might not accept credit cards at all. Having cash on hand helps you out of a jam if your card randomly doesn't work.

I use my credit card to book and pay for hotel reservations, to buy advance tickets for events or sights, and to cover most other expenses. It can also be smart to use plastic near the end of your trip, to avoid another visit to the ATM.

WHAT TO BRING

I pack the following and keep it all safe in my money belt.

Debit Card: Use this at ATMs to withdraw local cash.

Credit Card: Handy for bigger purchases (at hotels, shops, restaurants, travel agencies, car-rental agencies, and so on), payment machines, and ordering online.

Backup Card: Some travelers carry a third card (debit or credit; ideally from a different bank), in case one gets lost, demagnetized, eaten by a temperamental machine, or simply doesn't work.

A Stash of Cash: I always carry $100-200 as a cash backup. A stash of cash comes in handy for emergencies, such as if your ATM card stops working.

What NOT to Bring: Resist the urge to buy euros before your trip or you'll pay the price in bad stateside exchange rates. Wait until you arrive to withdraw money. I've yet to see a European airport that didn't have plenty of ATMs.

BEFORE YOU GO

Use this pre-trip checklist.

Know your cards. Debit cards from any major US bank will work in any standard European bank's ATM (ideally, use a debit card with a Visa or MasterCard logo). As for credit cards, Visa and MasterCard are universal, American Express is less common, and Discover is unknown in Europe.

Know your PIN. Make sure you know the numeric, four-digit PIN for all of your cards, both debit and credit. Request it if you don't have one and allow time to receive the information by mail.

All credit and debit cards now have chips that authenticate

and secure transactions. Europeans insert their chip cards into the payment machine slot, then enter a PIN. American cards should work in most transactions without a PIN—but may not work at self-service machines at train stations, toll booths, gas pumps, or parking lots. I've been inconvenienced a few times by self-service payment machines in Europe that wouldn't accept my card, but it's never caused me serious trouble.

If you're concerned, a few banks offer a chip-and-PIN card that works in almost all payment machines, including those from Andrews Federal Credit Union (www.andrewsfcu.org) and the State Department Federal Credit Union (www.sdfcu.org).

Report your travel dates. Let your bank know that you'll be using your debit and credit cards in Europe, and when and where you're headed.

Adjust your ATM withdrawal limit. Find out how much you can take out daily and ask for a higher daily withdrawal limit if you want to get more cash at once. Note that European ATMs will withdraw funds only from checking accounts; you're unlikely to have access to your savings account.

Ask about fees. For any purchase or withdrawal made with a card, you may be charged a currency conversion fee (1-3 percent) and/or a Visa or MasterCard international transaction fee (1 percent). If you're getting a bad deal, consider getting a new debit or credit card. Reputable no-fee cards include those from Capital One, as well as Charles Schwab debit cards. Most credit unions and some airline loyalty cards have low-to-no international transaction fees.

IN EUROPE
Using Cash Machines

European cash machines have English-language instructions and work just like they do at home—except they spit out local currency instead of dollars, calculated at the day's standard bank-to-bank rate.

In most places, ATMs are easy to locate—in Austria ask for a *Geldautomat*. When possible, withdraw cash from a bank-run ATM located just outside that bank. Ideally use it during the bank's opening hours so if your card is munched by the machine, you can go inside for help.

If your debit card doesn't work, try a lower amount—your request may have exceeded your withdrawal limit or the ATM's limit. If you still have a problem, try a different ATM or come back later—your bank's network may be temporarily down.

Avoid "independent" ATMs, such as Travelex, Euronet, Moneybox, Cardpoint, and Cashzone. These have high fees, can be less secure than a bank ATM, and may try to trick users with "dynamic currency conversion" (see below).

Exchanging Cash

Avoid exchanging money in Europe; it's a big rip-off. In a pinch you can always find exchange desks at major train stations or airports—convenient but with crummy rates. Anything over 5 percent for a transaction is piracy. Banks generally do not exchange money unless you have an account with them.

Using Credit Cards

US cards no longer require a signature for verification, but don't be surprised if a European card reader generates a receipt for you to sign. Some card readers will accept your card as is; others may prompt you to enter your PIN (so it's important to know the code for each of your cards). If a cashier is present, you should have no problems.

At self-service payment machines (transit-ticket kiosks, parking, etc.), results are mixed, as US cards may not work in unattended transactions. If your card won't work, look for a cashier who can process your card manually—or pay in cash.

Drivers Beware: Be aware of potential problems using a US credit card to fill up at an unattended gas station, enter a parking garage, or exit a toll road. Carry cash and be prepared to move on to the next gas station if necessary. When approaching a toll plaza, use the "cash" lane.

Dynamic Currency Conversion

If merchants offer to convert your purchase price into dollars (called dynamic currency conversion, or DCC), refuse this "service." You'll pay extra for the expensive convenience of seeing your charge in dollars. If an ATM offers to "lock in" or "guarantee" your conversion rate, choose "proceed without conversion." Other prompts might state, "You can be charged in dollars: Press YES for dollars, NO for euros." Always choose the local currency.

Security Tips

Pickpockets target tourists. Keep your cash, credit cards, and passport secure in your money belt, and carry only a day's spending money in your front pocket or wallet.

Before inserting your card into an ATM, inspect the front. If anything looks crooked, loose, or damaged, it could be a sign of a card-skimming device. When entering your PIN, carefully block other people's view of the keypad.

Don't use a debit card for purchases. Because a debit card pulls funds directly from your bank account, potential charges incurred

PRACTICALITIES

by a thief will stay on your account while the fraudulent use is investigated by your bank.

While traveling, to access your accounts online, be sure to use a secure connection (see the "Tips on Internet Security" sidebar, on page 566).

Damage Control for Lost Cards

If you lose your credit or debit card, report the loss immediately to the respective global customer-assistance centers. Call these 24-hour US numbers collect: Visa (tel. 303/967-1096), MasterCard (tel. 636/722-7111), and American Express (tel. 336/393-1111). In Austria, to make a collect call to the US, dial 0800-200-288. Press zero or stay on the line for an English-speaking operator. In Germany, dial 0800-225-5288; in Italy, dial 800-172-4444. European toll-free numbers can be found at the websites for Visa and MasterCard.

You'll need to provide the primary cardholder's identification-verification details (such as birth date, mother's maiden name, or Social Security number). You can generally receive a temporary card within two or three business days in Europe (see www.ricksteves.com/help for more).

If you report your loss within two days, you typically won't be responsible for any unauthorized transactions on your account, although many banks charge a liability fee of $50.

TIPPING

Tipping in Austria isn't as automatic and generous as it is in the US. For special service, tips are appreciated, but not expected. As in the US, the proper amount depends on your resources, tipping philosophy, and the circumstances, but some general guidelines apply.

Restaurants: You don't need to tip if you order your food at a counter. Restaurants that have wait staff generally include a service charge in the bill, but it's common to tip by rounding up (about 5-10 percent). For more on tipping in restaurants, see page 553.

Taxis: For a typical ride, round up your fare a bit (for instance, if the fare is €4.50, pay €5). If the cabbie hauls your bags and zips you to the airport to help you catch your flight, you might want to toss in a little more. But if you feel like you're being driven in circles or otherwise ripped off, skip the tip.

Services: In general, if someone in the tourism or service industry does a super job for you, a small tip of a euro or two is appropriate...but not required. If you're not sure whether (or how much) to tip, ask a local for advice.

GETTING A VAT REFUND

Wrapped into the purchase price of your Austrian souvenirs is a Value-Added Tax (VAT) of 20 percent. You're entitled to get most of that tax back if you purchase more than €75.01 (about $90) worth of goods at a store that participates in the VAT-refund scheme. Typically, you must ring up the minimum at a single retailer—you can't add up your purchases from various shops to reach the required amount.

Getting your refund is usually straightforward and, if you buy a substantial amount of souvenirs, well worth the hassle. (Note that if the store ships the goods to your US home, VAT is not assessed on your purchase.)

Get the paperwork. Have the merchant completely fill out the necessary refund document. You'll have to present your passport. Get the paperwork done before you leave the store to ensure you'll have everything you need (including your original sales receipt).

Get your stamp at the border or airport. Process your VAT document at your last stop in the European Union (such as at the airport) with the customs agent who deals with VAT refunds. Arrive an additional hour before you need to check in for your flight to allow time to find the local customs office—and wait. Some customs desks are positioned before airport security; confirm the location before going through security.

It's best to keep your purchases in your carry-on. If they're not allowed as carry-on (such as knives), pack them in your checked bags and alert the check-in agent. You'll be sent (with your tagged bag) to a customs desk outside security; someone will examine your bag, stamp your paperwork, and put your bag on the belt. You're not supposed to use your purchased goods before you leave. If you show up at customs wearing your new dirndl, officials might look the other way—or deny you a refund.

Collect your refund. You can claim your VAT refund from refund companies, such as Global Blue or Planet, with offices at major airports, ports, or border crossings (either before or after security, probably strategically located near a duty-free shop). These services (which extract a 4 percent fee) can refund your money in cash immediately or credit your card (within two billing cycles). Otherwise, you'll need to mail the stamped refund documents to the address given by the shop where you made your purchase.

CUSTOMS FOR AMERICAN SHOPPERS

You are allowed to take home $800 worth of items per person duty-free, once every 31 days. Many processed and packaged foods are allowed, including vacuum-packed cheeses, dried herbs, jams, baked goods, candy, chocolate, oil, vinegar, mustard, and honey. Fresh fruits and vegetables and most meats are not allowed, with exceptions for some canned items. As for alcohol, you can bring in one liter duty-free (it can be packed securely in your checked luggage, along with any other liquid-containing items).

To bring alcohol (or liquid-packed foods) in your carry-on bag on your flight home, buy it at a duty-free shop at the airport. You'll increase your odds of getting it onto a connecting flight if it's packaged in a "STEB"—a secure, tamper-evident bag. But stay away from liquids in opaque, ceramic, or metallic containers, which usually cannot be successfully screened (STEB or no STEB).

For details on allowable goods, customs rules, and duty rates, visit http://help.cbp.gov.

Sightseeing

Sightseeing can be hard work. Use these tips to make your visits to Austria's finest sights meaningful, fun, efficient, and painless.

MAPS AND NAVIGATION TOOLS

A good map is essential for efficient navigation while sightseeing. The maps in this book are concise and simple, designed to help you locate recommended destinations, sights, and local TIs, where you can pick up more in-depth maps.

You can also use a mapping app on your mobile device. Be aware that pulling up maps or turn-by-turn walking directions on the fly requires an internet connection: To use this feature, it's smart to get an international data plan. With Google Maps or City Maps 2Go, it's possible to download a map while online, then go offline and navigate without incurring data-roaming charges, though you can't search for an address or get real-time walking directions. A handful of other apps—including Apple Maps, Off-Maps, and Navfree—also allow you to use maps offline.

PLAN AHEAD

Set up an itinerary that allows you to fit in all your must-see sights. For a one-stop look at opening hours in Vienna and Salzburg, see the "At a Glance" sidebars in the Sights in Vienna and Salzburg & the Salzkammergut chapters. Most sights keep stable hours, but you can easily confirm the latest by checking with the TI or visiting museum websites.

Don't put off visiting a must-see sight—you never know when a place will close unexpectedly for a holiday, strike, or restoration. Given how precious your vacation time is, I recommend getting reservations for any must-see sight that offers them (see page 5). Many museums are closed or have reduced hours at least a few days a year, especially on holidays such as Christmas, New Year's, and Labor Day (May 1). A list of holidays is in the appendix; check online for possible museum closures during your trip. In summer, some sights may stay open late; in the off-season, hours may be shorter.

Going at the right time helps avoid crowds. This book offers tips on the best times to see specific sights, such as Schönbrunn Palace in Vienna and Neuschwanstein Castle in Bavaria. Try visiting popular sights very early or very late. Evening visits (when possible) are usually peaceful, with fewer crowds.

If you plan to hire a local guide, reserve ahead by email. Popular guides can get booked up.

Study up. To get the most out of the self-guided tours and sight descriptions in this book, read them before you visit. Schönbrunn Palace is much more fascinating if you've polished your knowledge of the Habsburg dynasty in advance.

AT SIGHTS

Here's what you can typically expect:

Entering: Be warned that you may not be allowed to enter if you arrive less than 30 to 60 minutes before closing time. And guards start ushering people out well before the actual closing time, so don't save the best for last.

Many sights have a security check. Allow extra time for these lines. Some sights require you to check daypacks and coats. (If you'd rather not check your daypack, try carrying it tucked under your arm like a purse as you enter.)

At churches—which often offer interesting art (usually free) and a cool, welcome seat—a modest dress code (no bare shoulders or shorts) is encouraged, though rarely enforced.

Photography: If the museum's photo policy isn't clearly posted, ask a guard. Generally, taking photos without a flash or tripod is allowed. Some sights ban selfie sticks; others ban photos altogether.

Temporary Exhibits: Museums may show special exhibits in addition to their permanent collection. Some exhibits are included in the entry price, while others come at an extra cost (which you may have to pay even if you don't want to see the exhibit).

Expect Changes: Artwork can be on tour, on loan, out sick, or shifted at the whim of the curator. Pick up a floor plan as you enter, and ask museum staff if you can't find a particular item.

Audioguides and Apps: Many sights rent audioguides, which generally offer useful recorded descriptions in English (about €3-6; often included with admission). Many audioguides have a standard output jack, so if you bring your own earbuds, you can often enjoy better sound. To save money, bring a Y-jack and share one audioguide with your travel partner. Museums and sights often offer free apps that you can download to your mobile device (check their

PRACTICALITIES

websites). And, I've produced free, downloadable audio tours of the major sights in Vienna and Salzburg; look for the 🎧 in this book. For more on my audio tours, see the Introduction chapter.

Services: Important sights usually have a reasonably priced on-site café or cafeteria (handy places to rejuvenate during a long visit). The WCs at sights are free and generally clean.

Before Leaving: At the gift shop, scan the postcard rack or thumb through a guidebook to be sure that you haven't overlooked something that you'd like to see.

Every sight or museum offers more than what is covered in this book. Use the information in this book as an introduction—not the final word.

Sleeping

While accommodations in Austria are fairly expensive, they are normally very comfortable and usually include a hearty breakfast (typically an all-you-can-eat buffet). Choose from hotels; smaller, cheaper hotels and bed-and-breakfasts (called *Gasthof, Gasthaus,* or *Pension*); rooms in private homes (advertised with a *Zimmer Frei* sign); and hostels *(Jugendherberge).*

Extensive and opinionated listings of good-value rooms are a major feature of this book's Sleeping sections. Rather than list accommodations scattered throughout a town, I choose hotels in my favorite neighborhoods that are convenient to your sightseeing.

My recommendations run the gamut, from dorm beds to fancy rooms with all of the comforts. I like places that are clean, central, relatively quiet at night, reasonably priced, friendly, small enough to have a hands-on owner and stable staff, and run with a respect for Austrian traditions. I'm more impressed by a handy location and fun-loving philosophy than flat-screen TVs and a fancy gym. Most of my recommendations fall short of perfection. But if I can find a place with most of these features, it's a keeper.

Book your accommodations as soon as your itinerary is set, especially if you want to stay at one of my top listings or if you'll be traveling during busy times. See the appendix for a list of major holidays and festivals in Austria.

Some people make reservations as they travel, calling ahead a few days to a week before their arrival. It's best to call hotels at about 9:00 or 10:00, when the receptionist knows which rooms will be available. Some apps—such as HotelTonight—specialize in last-minute rooms, often at business-class hotels in big cities. If you encounter a language barrier, ask the fluent receptionist at your current hotel to call for you.

Sleep Code

Hotels in this book are categorized according to the average price of a standard double room with breakfast in high season.

$$$$	**Splurge:** Most rooms over €170
$$$	**Expensive:** €130-170
$$	**Moderate:** €90-130
$	**Budget:** €50-90
¢	**Backpacker: Under** €50
RS%	**Rick Steves discount**

Unless otherwise noted, credit cards are accepted, hotel staff speak basic English, and free Wi-Fi is available. Comparison-shop by checking prices at several hotels (on each hotel's own website, on a booking site, or by email). For the best deal, *book directly with the hotel.* Ask for a discount if paying in cash; if the listing includes **RS%**, request a Rick Steves discount.

RATES AND DEALS

I've categorized my recommended accommodations based on price, indicated with a dollar-sign rating (see sidebar). The price ranges suggest an estimated cost for a one-night stay in a standard double room with a private toilet and shower in high season, include breakfast, and assume you're booking directly with the hotel (not through a booking site, which extracts a commission). Room prices can fluctuate significantly with demand and amenities (size, views, room class, and so on), but relative price categories remain constant. Taxes, which can vary from place to place, are generally insignificant (a dollar or two per person, per night).

Room rates are especially volatile at larger hotels that use "dynamic pricing" to set rates. Prices can skyrocket during festivals and conventions, while business hotels can have deep discounts on weekends when demand plummets. Of the many hotels I recommend, it's difficult to say which will be the best value on a given day—until you do your homework.

Booking Direct: Once your dates are set, compare prices at several hotels. You can do this by checking Hotels.com, Booking.com, and hotel websites. To get the best deal, contact family-run hotels directly by phone or email. When you go direct, the owner avoids the commission paid to booking sites, thereby leaving enough wiggle room to offer you a discount, a nicer room, or a free breakfast (if it's not already included). If you prefer to book online or are considering a hotel chain, it's to your advantage to use the hotel's website.

Getting a Discount: Some hotels extend a discount to those who pay cash or stay longer than three nights. And some accommodations offer a special discount for Rick Steves readers, indi-

PRACTICALITIES

Making Hotel Reservations

Reserve your rooms as soon as you've pinned down your travel dates. For busy national holidays, it's wise to reserve far in advance (see page 581).

Requesting a Reservation: For family-run hotels, it's generally cheaper to book your room directly via email or a phone call. For business-class hotels, or if you'd rather book online, reserve directly through the hotel's official website (not a booking website). For complicated requests, send an email. Almost all of my recommended hotels take reservations in English.

Here's what the hotelier wants to know:

- Type(s) of rooms you want and size of your party
- Number of nights you'll stay
- Your arrival and departure dates, written European-style as day/month/ year (15/06/20 or 15 June 2020); include the total number of nights
- Special requests (en suite bathroom, cheapest room, twin beds vs. double bed, quiet room)
- Applicable discounts (such as a Rick Steves reader discount, cash discount, or promotional rate)

Confirming a Reservation: Most places will request a credit-card number to hold your room. If you're using an online reservation form, look for the *https* or a lock icon at the top of your browser. If you book direct, you can email, call, or fax this information.

Canceling a Reservation: If you must cancel, it's courteous—and smart—to do so with as much notice as possible, especially for

cated in this guidebook by the abbreviation **"RS%."** Discounts vary: Ask for details when you reserve. Generally, to qualify for this discount, you must book direct (not through a booking site), mention this book when you reserve, show this book upon arrival, and sometimes pay cash or stay a certain number of nights. In some cases, you may need to enter a discount code (which I've provided in the listing) in the booking form on the hotel's website. Rick Steves discounts apply to readers with either print or digital books. Understandably, discounts do not apply to promotional rates.

TYPES OF ACCOMMODATIONS
Hotels

In this book, the price for a double room in a hotel ranges from about €45 (very simple, toilet and shower down the hall) to €200-plus (maximum plumbing and more). Prices are higher in big cities and heavily touristed cities, and lower off the beaten path.

Some hotels can add an extra bed (for a small charge) to turn a double into a triple; some offer larger rooms for four or more people

From: rick@ricksteves.com
Sent: Today
To: info@hotelcentral.com
Subject: Reservation request for 19-22 July

Dear Hotel Central,

I would like to stay at your hotel. Please let me know if you have a room available and the price for:
• 2 people
• Double bed and en suite bathroom in a quiet room
• Arriving 19 July, departing 22 July (3 nights)

Thank you!
Rick Steves

smaller family-run places. Cancellation policies can be strict; read the fine print before you book. Many discount deals require pre-payment, with no cancellation refunds.

Reconfirming a Reservation: Always call or email to reconfirm your room reservation a few days in advance. For B&Bs or very small hotels, I call again on my day of arrival to tell my host what time to expect me (especially important if arriving late—after 17:00).

Phoning: For tips on calling hotels overseas, see page 564.

(I call these "family rooms" in the listings). If there's space for an extra cot, they'll cram it in for you. In general, a triple room is cheaper than the cost of a double and a single. Three or four people can economize by requesting one big room.

Room prices depend on the season and the day of the week, but peak times vary from one town to the next. In Vienna, hotels are at their priciest from May or June all the way through October; rates are also high around New Year's Eve. In Salzburg, rates always rise significantly during the music festival (mid-July-Aug), during the four weeks leading up to Christmas, and usually around Easter. High season in Füssen and Reutte is June-September. Rates rise in the Dolomites in July, August, and around Christmas.

Arrival and Check-In: Hotels and B&Bs are sometimes located on the higher floors of a multipurpose building with a secured door. In that case, look for your hotel's name on the buttons by the main entrance. When you ring the bell, you'll be buzzed in.

Hotel elevators are becoming more common, though some older buildings still lack them. You may have to climb a flight of

Using Online Services to Your Advantage

From booking services to user reviews, online businesses are playing a greater role in travelers' planning than ever before. Take advantage of their pluses—and be wise to their downsides.

Booking Sites

Hotel booking websites, including Priceline's Booking.com and Expedia's Hotels.com, offer one-stop shopping for hotels. While convenient for travelers, they present a real problem for small, independent, family-run hotels. Without a presence on these sites, these hotels become almost invisible. But to be listed, a hotel must pay a sizeable commission...and promise that its own website won't undercut the price on the booking-service site.

Here's the work-around: Use the big sites to research what's out there, then book directly with the hotel by email or phone, in which case hotel owners are free to give you whatever price they like. Ask for a room without the commission markup (or ask for a free breakfast if not included, or a free upgrade). If you do book online, be sure to use the hotel's website. The price will likely be the same as via a booking site, but your money goes to the hotel, not agency commissions.

As a savvy consumer, remember: When you book with an online booking service, you're adding a middleman who takes roughly 20 percent. To support small, family-run hotels whose world is more difficult than ever, book direct.

Short-Term Rental Sites

Rental juggernaut Airbnb (along with other short-term rental sites) allows travelers to rent rooms and apartments directly from locals, often providing more value than a cookie-cutter hotel. Airbnb fans appreciate feeling part of a real neighborhood and getting into a daily routine as "temporary Europeans." Depending on the host, Airbnb can provide an opportunity to get to know a local person, while keeping the money spent on your accommo-

stairs to reach the elevator (if so, you can ask the front desk for help carrying your bags up). When you're inside an elevator, press "E" if you want to descend to the "ground floor" *(Erdgeschoss)*. Elevators are typically very small—pack light, or you may need to send your bags up without you.

The EU requires that hotels collect your name, nationality, and ID number. When you check in, the receptionist will normally ask for your passport and may keep it for anywhere from a couple of minutes to a couple of hours. (If not comfortable leaving your passport at the desk for a long time, ask when you can pick it up. Or if you packed a color photocopy of your passport, you can generally show that rather than your original.)

If you're arriving in the morning, your room probably won't

dations in the community.

Critics view Airbnb as a threat to "traditional Europe," saying it creates unfair, unqualified competition for established guesthouse owners. In some places, the lucrative Airbnb market has forced traditional guesthouses out of business and is driving property values out of range for locals. Some cities have cracked down, requiring owners to occupy rental properties part of the year (and staging disruptive "inspections" that inconvenience guests).

As a lover of Europe, I share the worry of those who see residents nudged aside by tourists. But as an advocate for travelers, I appreciate the value and cultural intimacy Airbnb provides.

User Reviews

User-generated review sites and apps such as Yelp and TripAdvisor can give you a consensus of opinions about everything from hotels and restaurants to sights and nightlife. If you scan reviews of a restaurant or hotel and see several complaints about noise or a rotten location, you've gained insight that can help in your decision-making.

But as a guidebook writer, my sense is that there is a big difference between the uncurated information on a review site and the vetted listings in a guidebook. A user-generated review is based on the limited experience of one person, who stayed at just one hotel in a given city and ate at a few restaurants there. A guidebook is the work of a trained researcher who forms a well-developed basis for comparison by visiting many restaurants and hotels year after year.

Both types of information have their place, and in many ways, they're complementary. If something is well reviewed in a guidebook and it also gets good online reviews, it's likely a winner.

be ready. Check your bag safely at the hotel and dive right into sightseeing.

In Your Room: Most hotel rooms have a TV, telephone, and free Wi-Fi (although in old buildings with thick walls, the Wi-Fi signal might be available only in the lobby). Simpler places rarely have a room phone.

More pillows and blankets are usually in the closet or available on request. Towels and linens aren't always replaced every day, so hang your towel up to dry.

Air-conditioning is rare, but if you're here during a heat spell, ask to borrow a fan. Learn how the windows work: You'll often find the windows tipped open from the top to air out the room, with the window handle pointing up. To close the window, push it in and rotate the handle so it points down. The third handle position is horizontal, which lets you swing the entire window open.

Most hotels have gone completely nonsmoking. Some hotels have nonsmoking rooms or floors—let them know your preference when you book.

Breakfast and Meals: Most Austrian hotels and pensions include breakfast in the room price.

Checking Out: While it's customary to pay for your room upon departure, it can be a good idea to settle your bill the day before, when you're not in a hurry and while the manager's in.

Hotelier Help: Hoteliers can be a good source of advice. Most know their city well, and can assist you with everything from public transit and airport connections to finding a good restaurant, the nearest launderette, or a late-night pharmacy.

Hotel Hassles: Even at the best places, mechanical breakdowns occur: Sinks leak, hot water turns cold, toilets may gurgle or smell, or the Wi-Fi goes out. Report your concerns clearly and calmly at the front desk.

If you find that night noise is a problem (if, for instance, your room is over a nightclub), ask for a quieter room in the back or on an upper floor. To guard against theft in your room, keep valuables out of sight. Some rooms come with a safe, and other hotels have safes at the front desk. I've never bothered using one and in a lifetime of travel, I've never had anything stolen from my room.

For more complicated problems, don't expect instant results. Above all, keep a positive attitude. Remember, you're on vacation. If your hotel is a disappointment, spend more time out enjoying the place you came to see.

Guesthouses

Guesthouses—the Austrian equivalent to B&Bs—are small, warm, family-run accommodations. Known as *Pensionen, Gasthäuser,* or *Gasthöfe* in German, they are very common in areas popular with travelers (such as Austria's Tirol, Salzkammergut Lake District, and Salzburg; northern Italy's Dolomites; and Germany's Bavaria). Compared to hotels, a guesthouse gives you double the cultural intimacy for half the price. While you may lose some of the conveniences of a hotel—such as in-room phones, frequent bed-sheet changes, and the ease of paying with a credit card—I happily make the trade-off for the lower rates and personal touches.

Guesthouses range in size, with anywhere from 3 to 10 rooms (sometimes more). Many serve up a hearty breakfast. The smallest establishments are private homes with rooms *(Privatzimmer)* rented out to travelers for as little as €20 per person. In general, you can expect rooms in guesthouses to be clean, comfortable, and simple, though usually homey.

Rooms can run the gamut. Some are suite-like, with multiple rooms, separate entrances, and private baths. Others are spare bedrooms in family homes, with no in-room plumbing (but you have access to the bathroom and shower in the home).

Austrians depend heavily on expensive imported fuel and are very aware of their energy use. You'll endear yourself to your hosts if you turn off lights when you leave and avoid excessively long showers.

Finding and booking a guesthouse is no different than reserving a hotel. Even most smaller places are listed on hotel-booking websites—but a direct booking is especially appreciated at mom-and-pop places, and will likely net you a better price. Private rooms are also available through Airbnb-type services (described below). If you haven't booked ahead, when you arrive at your destination, look for signs that say *Zimmer frei* (green), which means rooms are available; *Zimmer belegt* (orange) means no vacancy. TIs often have a list of guesthouses; use the list to book rooms yourself to avoid having the TI take a cut from you and your host.

Short-Term Rentals

A short-term rental—whether an apartment, house, or room in a local's home—is an increasingly popular alternative, especially if you plan to settle in one location for several nights. For stays longer than a few days, you can usually find a rental that's comparable to—and cheaper than—a hotel room with similar amenities. Plus, you'll get a behind-the-scenes peek into how locals live.

Many places require a minimum stay and have strict cancellation policies. And you're generally on your own: There's no hotel reception desk, breakfast, or daily cleaning service.

Finding Accommodations: Aggregator websites such as Airbnb.com, Flipkey.com, Booking.com, and the HomeAway family of sites (HomeAway, VRBO, and VacationRentals) let you browse properties and correspond directly with European property owners or managers. If you prefer to work from a curated list of accommodations, consider using a rental agency such as Interhomeusa.com or Rentavilla.com. Agency-represented apartments cost more, but this route often offers more help and safeguards than booking direct.

Before you commit, be clear on the location. I like to virtually "explore" the neighborhood using the Street View feature on Google Maps. Also consider the proximity to public transportation and how well-connected it is with the rest of the city. Ask about amenities (elevator, air-conditioning, laundry, Wi-Fi, parking, etc.). Reviews from previous guests can help identify trouble spots.

Think about the kind of experience you want: Just a key and an affordable bed...or a chance to get to know a local? There are typi-

PRACTICALITIES

cally two kinds of hosts: those who want minimal interaction with their guests, and hosts who are friendly and may want to interact with you. Read the promotional text and online reviews to help shape your decision.

Confirming and Paying: Many places require you to pay the entire balance before your trip. It's easiest and safest to pay through the site where you found the listing. Be wary of owners who want to take your transaction offline; this gives you no recourse if things go awry. Never agree to wire money (a key indicator of a fraudulent transaction).

Apartments or Houses: If you're staying somewhere for four or more nights, it's worth considering an apartment or rental house (shorter stays aren't worth the hassle of arranging key pickup, buying groceries, etc.). Apartment or house rentals can be especially cost-effective for groups and families. European apartments, like hotel rooms, tend to be small by US standards. But they often come with laundry machines and small, equipped kitchens, making it easier and cheaper to dine in.

In rural areas, you can find reasonably priced vacation rentals *(Ferienwohnungen)*, ideal for families and small groups who want to explore a region. This kind of arrangement is very popular with Austrian vacationers. You usually get a suite of two or three rooms with a kitchen. Owners discourage short stays and usually require a minimum rental period (3-5 days), and sometimes a deposit.

Rooms in Private Homes: Renting a room in someone's home is a good option for those traveling alone, as you're more likely to find true single rooms—with just one single bed, and a price to match. These can range from air-mattress-in-living-room basic to plush-B&B-suite posh. Some places allow you to book for a single night; if staying for several nights, you can buy groceries just as you would in a rental house. While you can't expect your host to also be your tour guide—or even to provide you with much info— some may be interested in getting to know the travelers who come through their home.

Other Options: Swapping homes with a local works for people with an appealing place to offer (don't assume where you live is not interesting to Europeans). A good place to start is HomeExchange. To sleep for free, Couchsurfing.com is a vagabond's alternative to Airbnb. It lists millions of outgoing members, who host fellow "surfers" in their homes.

Hostels

A hostel *(Jugendherberge)* provides cheap beds where you sleep alongside strangers for about €25 per night. Travelers of any age are welcome if they don't mind dorm-style accommodations and meeting other travelers. Most hostels offer kitchen facilities, guest computers, Wi-Fi, and a self-service laundry. Hostels almost always provide bedding, but the towel's up to you (though you can usually rent one for a small fee). Family and private rooms are often available.

Independent hostels tend to be easygoing, colorful, and informal (no membership required; www.hostelworld.

com). You may pay slightly less by booking directly with the hostel. **Official hostels** are part of Hostelling International (HI) and share an online booking site (www.hihostels.com). HI hostels typically require that you be a member or else pay a bit more per night.

Eating

Traditional Austrian cuisine is heavy and hearty, and borrows much from the cuisines of neighboring Hungary, Bohemia (western Czech Republic), and Germany. Food here is tasty and inexpensive, but can get monotonous if you fall into a schnitzel-filled rut. Be adventurous. If you need variety, you'll find that all but the smallest towns have restaurants serving non-Austrian cuisine.

I look for restaurants that are convenient to your hotel and sightseeing. When restaurant hunting, choose a spot filled with locals, not the place with the big neon signs boasting, "We Speak English and Accept Credit Cards." Venturing even a block or two off the main drag leads to higher-quality food for a better price.

RESTAURANT PRICING

I've categorized my recommended eateries based on the average price of a typical main course, indicated with a dollar-sign rating (see sidebar). Obviously, expensive specialties, fine wine, appetizers, and dessert can significantly increase your final bill.

The categories also indicate the overall personality of a place:

Budget eateries include street food, takeaway, order-at-the-counter shops, basic cafeterias, and bakeries selling sandwiches.

Moderate eateries are nice (but not fancy) sit-down restaurants, ideal for a straightforward, fill-the-tank meal. Most of my listings fall in this category—great for getting a good taste of the local cuisine.

Pricier eateries are a notch up, with more attention paid to the setting, presentation, and (often inventive) cuisine.

Splurge eateries are dress-up-for-a-special-occasion swanky—

Restaurant Code

Eateries in this book are categorized according to the average cost of a typical main course. Drinks, desserts, and splurge items can raise the price considerably.

$$$$ **Splurge:** Most main courses over €20
$$$ **Pricier:** €15-20
$$ **Moderate:** €10-15
$ **Budget:** Under €10

In Austria, a wurst stand or other takeout spot is **$**; a beer hall, *Biergarten,* or basic sit-down eatery is **$$**; a casual but more upscale restaurant is **$$$**; and a swanky splurge is **$$$$**.

typically with an elegant setting, polished service, intricate cuisine, and an expansive (and expensive) wine list.

BREAKFAST

Most Austrian hotels and pensions include breakfast in the room price and pride themselves on laying out an attractive buffet spread. Even if you're not a big breakfast eater, take advantage of the buffet to fortify yourself for a day of sightseeing. Expect sliced bread, rolls, pastries, cereal, yogurt (both plain and with fruit), cold cuts, cheese, and fruit. You'll always find coffee, tea, and some sort of *Saft* (juice). Along with orange, apple, and grapefruit, multivitamin juice is popular. This sweet, smooth blend of various fruits is less acidic than a citrus juice. A bottle of mineral water is standing by to mix with any juice to turn it into a *G'spritzter.*

For breakfast, most Austrians prefer a sandwich with cold cuts and/or a bowl of *Müsli* (an oat cereal like granola, but less sweet), sometimes mixed with corn flakes. Instead of pouring milk over cereal, most Austrians begin with a dollop of yogurt (or *Quark*—sweet curds that resemble yogurt), then sprinkle the cereal on top. If it's not sweet enough, drizzle on some *Honig* (honey). *Bircher Müsli* is a healthy mix of oats, nuts, yogurt, and fruit. To make a local-style sandwich for breakfast, layer *Aufschnitt* (cold cuts), *Schinken* (ham), *Streichwurst* (meat spread, most often *Leberwurst*—liver spread), and *Käse* (cheese) on a slice of bread or a roll.

If a buffet has eggs, they're most likely soft-boiled *(weichgekochte Eier).* To eat it as the Austrians do, set the egg in its stand, gently break the shell around its perimeter, remove the top half of the shell, salt it, and eat it as if from a tiny bowl. Hard-boiled eggs *(hartgekochte Eier)* are often served with rémoulade (similar to tartar sauce). Occasionally a buffet will have *Rühreier* (scrambled eggs) or *Spiegeleier* (fried eggs—literally "mirror eggs"—typically sunny-side up).

PRACTICALITIES

In some hotels, a small garbage can is set on the table for you to dispose of trash as you eat.

LUNCH AND DINNER

Austrians eat lunch and dinner about when we do, though they tend to eat a bigger lunch and smaller dinner.

Most restaurants tack a menu onto their door for browsers and have an English menu inside. In summer, look for a place with outdoor seating so you can join the locals. Once you're seated, take your time—only a rude waiter will rush you. Good service is relaxed (slow to an American).

Traditional restaurants aren't your only option. In Vienna, balmy evenings drive people into the hills to enjoy wine gardens *(Heurigen)* surrounded by fields of grapevines (see page 189). Hotels often serve fine food. A *Gaststätte* is a simple, less-expensive restaurant.

Or try a *Beisl* (BYE-zul), the Viennese word for a pub that serves food. There's one in every neighborhood, filled with poetry teachers and their students, couples loving without touching, housewives on their way home from cello lessons, and waiters who enjoy serving hearty food and drinks at an affordable price. Ask your hotel to recommend a good *Beisl*. (Beware: Because of Austria's lax smoking laws, pubs may be smoky, but most have outdoor seating.) For most travelers, a visit to one of Vienna's grand cafés is a must; see page 186 for details.

Though Austrians are typically health-conscious, many starchy, high-fat, high-calorie traditional foods remain staples on restaurant menus. As a new generation takes over their grandparents' restaurants and inns, however, it's becoming easier to find lighter versions of the meaty standards—and organic ingredients are getting more popular. Order house specials whenever possible. (For a rundown of common dishes, see "Austrian Cuisine," later.)

Most restaurants offer a *"Menü"*—a fixed-price meal—at lunchtime on weekdays (typically around €10 for a main course plus soup or salad). For smaller portions, order from the *kleine Hunger* (small hunger) section of the menu.

Take note: You might be charged for bread you've eaten from the basket on the table; have the waiter take it away if you don't want it. To wish others "Happy eating!" offer a cheery *"Guten Appetit!"* When you want the bill, say, *"Rechnung* (REHKH-noong), *bitte."*

Tipping: At Austrian restaurants that have a wait staff, a service charge is generally included in the bill, although it's common to round up after a good meal (usually 5-10 percent; for an €18.50 meal, pay €20). Rather than leaving coins behind on the table (considered slightly rude), Austrians usually pay directly: When

PRACTICALITIES

> ## Smoke Free? We'll See.
>
> While much of Europe, including Italy, France, and many German states, now enforces strict smoking bans, Austrian restaurants remain a haven for cigarette smokers. Although smoking is prohibited in public places in Austria, restaurants and cafés are exempt from most existing regulations.
>
> A 2015 law mandated that smoking be completely banned in all restaurants and bars by 2018, but recent elections have stalled any permanent changes. For now, expect the possibility of some smoke in any restaurant.

the server comes by with the bill, simply hand over paper money, stating the total you'd like to pay. For example, if paying for a €10 meal with a €20 bill, while handing your money to the server, say "Eleven, please" (or *"Elf, bitte"* if you've got your German numbers down). The server will keep a €1 tip and give you €9 in change. Or just hand over the rounded-up amount and say *"Danke,"* signaling that you don't want any change.

Lately, many restaurants—especially those in well-touristed areas—have added a "Tip is not included" line, in English, to the bottom of the bill. This is misleading, as the prices on any menu in Austria *do* include service. I wouldn't tip one cent more at a restaurant that includes this note on the bill. (Supposedly the trend's been prompted by an influx of tourists from cultures where it's not customary to round up...though I've seen servers circle the "tip not included" line before presenting the bill to Americans, who are known to overtip.) Many locals are rebelling by tipping far less generously at eateries using this approach.

Budget Tips

In Austria, you're never far from a *Würstelstand,* which sells inexpensive sausages (for common types of wurst, see "Best of the Wurst," later). Most bakeries and supermarkets sell cheap sandwiches; look for *Leberkäsesemmel* (similar to a bologna sandwich) as well as *Schnitzelsemmel* (schnitzel sandwich). Supermarkets have prepared foods that are good for picnics. *Stehcafés* (food counters) usually offer open-face finger sandwiches *(belegte Brote)* with a wide array of toppings. For a quick, cheap bite, have a deli make you a *Wurstsemmel*—a basic sausage sandwich. Other budget eateries include department-store cafeterias, *Schnellimbiss* (fast-food) stands, and university cafeterias *(Mensas).*

Ethnic Food

Ethnic restaurants provide a welcome break from Austrian fare.

It's easy to find Italian restaurants and pizzerias. Otherwise, most foreign cuisine is newly arrived with recent immigrants. Asian and Turkish food is a good value, and there are also Middle Eastern fast-food options. *Döner kebab* kiosks are especially popular. Originally from Turkey, *döner kebab* (shaved meat and vegetables served in pita bread) has become a classic takeout meal for locals.

AUSTRIAN CUISINE

Much "Austrian" cooking is actually a mix of influences and flavors—the legacy of a crumbled empire, which included Hungary and Bohemia (where Austrian cuisine gets its goulash and dumplings).

Specialties

Traditional Austrian dishes tend to be meat-heavy (although fish is very popular and generally good in this landlocked country). The classic Austrian dish—and a stand-by on menus—is Wiener schnitzel (a veal cutlet that's been pounded flat, breaded, and fried). Pork schnitzel, which is cheaper, is also common. Austrian *Gulasch,* a meat stew, is a favorite comfort food. Sausage (Wurst) is also a staple.

Chicken *(Huhn)* is usually served grilled or breaded and baked. Pork *(Schwein)* comes in many forms. Beef appears in goulash, as schnitzel, and in the Viennese *Tafelspitz.* Wild game *(Wildbret* or *Wild),* such as *Reh* and *Hirsch* (venison) or *Gams* (chamois or wild goat), is usually served in fall in meat sauces with pasta or as an entrée.

Here are a few other specialties to look out for:

Eintopf: Hearty stew with lots of vegetables, potatoes, and meat combined in "one pot."

Fleischlaberln or *Faschierte Laibchen:* Fried ground-meat patties.

Geräucherte Schweinelende: Pork loin that is first smoked, then boiled.

Geschnetzeltes: Strips of veal or chicken braised in a rich sauce and served with noodles.

Gulasch: Thick, meaty stew spiced with onion and paprika.

Krautrouladen: Cabbage rolls stuffed with minced meat.

Kümmelbraten: Crispy roast pork with caraway.

Leberkäse: Finely ground corned beef, pork, bacon, and onions that's baked as a loaf (like a bologna sausage).

Leberknödel: Liver dumplings.

Marend: Platter of cured meats and hard cheeses (Tirol); called *Brettljause* in the rest of Austria.

Naturschnitzel: Variation of Wiener schnitzel without the breading; served with rice and sauce.

Rouladen or ***Rindsrouladen:*** Strip of beef rolled up with bacon, onion, and pickles, then braised.

Schlachtplatte or ***Schlachtschüssel:*** "Butcher's plate"—usually blood sausage, *Leberwurst*, and other meat over hot sauerkraut.

Schopfbraten: Oven-roasted pork shoulder with gravy.

Schweinsbraten: Roasted pork served with dumplings and sauerkraut.

Selchkarree: Salted, slightly smoked pork.

Speckpalatschinken: Large, savory crêpe with bacon.

Stelze: Roasted pork knuckle, usually garnished with potatoes.

Tafelspitz: Boiled beef, served with vegetables.

Best of the Wurst

Sausage (Wurst) is a staple here. Most restaurants offer it (often as the cheapest thing on the menu), but it's more commonly eaten at a takeout stand *(Würstelstand)*. Options go far beyond the hometown hot dog, and most are pork-based. Generally, the darker the weenie, the spicier it is.

Sausages can be boiled or grilled. The generic term *Bratwurst* simply means "grilled sausage." *Brühwurst* is boiled. While some types of wurst can be found all over, others are unique to a particular area.

At sausage stands, wurst usually comes in or with a roll (*Semmel*—not your typical hot-dog bun). You might be given the choice of a slice of bread *(Brot)*, a pretzel *(Breze)*, or in restaurants, potato salad.

Sauces and sides include *Senf* (mustard; ask for *süss*—sweet, or *scharf*—spicy), ketchup or curry-ketchup (*Currysauce*—curry-infused ketchup), *Kraut* (sauerkraut), and sometimes horseradish (called *Kren* in Austria and southern Germany).

When surveying your options, these terms may help:

Berner-Würstel: Filled with cheese and wrapped with bacon.

Blutwurst or ***Blunzn:*** Blood sausage.

Bosna: Spicy sausage with onions and sometimes curry.

Burenwurst or ***Burenheidl:*** Pork sausage similar to what we'd call "kielbasa."

Debreziner: Boiled, thin, and spicy, with paprika.

Frankfurter: A skinny, pink, boiled sausage—the ancestor of our hot dog (also called *Sacherwürstel*).

Käsekrainer: Boiled, with melted cheese inside.

Knackwurst: Similar to American knockwurst (called *Salzburger* in western Austria).

Waldviertler: Smoked sausage, served with mustard and horseradish.

Weisswurst: Boiled white sausage—peel off the casing before you eat it, served with sweet mustard and a pretzel (found mostly in Bavaria). If it's *frisch* (fresh), you're supposed to "eat it before the noon bell tolls."

Soups, Starches, and Sides

Austrians are fond of soup. Lunch specials at restaurants often include soup and a main course. Dumplings in soup are common (such as *Speckknödel*); *Frittatensuppe* is another favorite (both described below). For a meal-sized salad, order a *Salatteller*.

Eiernockerl: Little egg noodles (like *Spätzle*); often served with melted cheese and fried onions as a stand-alone meal.

Erdapfel: Potato.

Frittatensuppe ("pancake soup"): Beef broth garnished with thin strips of crêpe.

Geröstete Knödel: Roasted dumplings.

Rotkraut: Sweetish red-cabbage sauerkraut.

Schinkenfleckerl: Ham and noodle casserole.

Spargel: Big, white or green asparagus in season in May and June.

Speckknödel: Dumplings with ham or bacon mixed into the dough, often served in broth.

Schlutzkrapfen: Spinach-stuffed ravioli (Tirol).

Pastries and Sweets

Make sure to visit a bakery *(Bäckerei)* or pastry shop *(Konditorei)* to browse the selection of fresh pastries *(Feingebäck)* and cakes. Strudel is everywhere, but the selection goes well beyond the familiar *Apfelstrudel*. Cakes, pastries, and pies are often loaded with fresh fruits, raisins, nuts, and/or *Mohn* (poppy-seed filling).

Buchteln: Sweet pull-apart yeast buns, traditionally filled with jam or topped with baked fruit; called *Rohrnudeln* in Bavaria.

Esterhazytorte: Layer cake of liqueur-flavored buttercream and almond or hazelnut dough, topped with white icing and elegant chocolate designs.

Germknödel: Steamed dumplings filled with plum jam (a cousin of the German *Dampfnudeln*).

Kaiserschmarrn: Thick, fluffy, caramelized crêpe that's pulled apart into pieces; usually prepared with fruit compote, raisins, and/or nuts and topped with powdered sugar (the name is a pun, meaning "Emperor's nonsense").

Kardinalschnitte ("Cardinal's slice"): Layers of cream, spongey meringue, and often jam, made to resemble the pope's robes.

Kipferl: Crescent-shaped yeast roll; sweet versions like *Vanillekipferl* are dusted with vanilla sugar and typical at Christmas.

Krapfen: Doughnut filled with jam or cream, particularly popular for *Faschingsdienstag* (Fat Tuesday).

Malakov Torte: Layer cake made from whipped cream and ladyfingers, with sliced almonds on top.

Mohnzelten: Savory pastry filled with sweet poppy-seed paste, popular on the border of Austria and the Czech Republic.

Mozartkugeln: Confectionary balls of marzipan, hazelnut, and cream, covered in chocolate (see sidebar later).

Palatschinken: Thin, rolled-up crêpes, either sweet (filled with jams, jellies, Nutella) or savory (filled with *Speck*, spinach).

Prügeltorte or *Baumkuchen:* Spit-roasted cylindrical cake made over an open fire.

Punschkrapfen ("Punch cake"): Cake squares layered with jam and soaked in rum, topped with a pink rum icing.

Sachertorte: Vienna's famous chocolate cake—dense and layered with apricot jam.

Salzburger Nockerl: Soufflé shaped like mountain peaks and dusted with powdered sugar (like snow), often served with raspberry sauce.

Topfenstrudel: Wafer-thin strudel filled with sweet cheese and raisins.

Zwetschkenfleck ("Plum patch"): Similar to *Apfelstrudel*, but with plums.

Beverages

For most visitors, it's not only the rich pastries that provide the fondest memories of Austrian cuisine, but the coffee, wine, and beer as well. Menus typically list drink sizes by the deciliter (dl, a tenth of a liter): 2 deciliters is a small glass, and 4 or 5 deciliters is a larger one. For beer sizes, see "Beer", later.

Water, Juice, and Soft Drinks

Tap water *(Leitungswasser)* is sometimes served for a nominal fee (about €0.50), but waiters would prefer that you buy *Mineralwasser* (*mit/ohne Gas*—with/without carbonation). Half-liter mineral-water bottles are available everywhere for about €1. (I refill my water bottle with tap water.)

Popular soft drinks include *Apfelsaft gespritzt* (apple juice with sparkling water), *Spezi* (Coke and orange soda), and the über-Austrian *Almdudler* (a thirst-quenching soda similar to ginger ale). In cafés, look for *Himbeersoda* (raspberry soda) and the refreshing *Holunder gespritzt* (elderberry juice mixed with sparkling water).

Coffee

As in Italy and France, coffee drinks in Austria are espresso-based. *Kaffee* means coffee and *Milch* is milk; *Obers* is cream, while *Schlagobers* is whipped cream. Here are some Austrian coffee terms: Use them elsewhere, and you'll probably get a funny look (some are unique just to Vienna).

Mozart Balls (Mozartkugeln)

The Mozart ball is a chocolate confection with a marzipan, hazelnut, and pistachio-cream center that's become practically a symbol of Austria. Mozart balls make fun gifts and souvenirs, but aren't all created equal. For the absolutely most authentic, handmade Mozart balls (perfectly round and made of just pistachio and chocolate), visit one of the Fürst confectionery shops in Salzburg, which invented the Mozart ball in 1890 (there's one at Getreidegasse 47).

Most Mozart balls today are made by machine. The flat-bottomed ones are made by Reber with pure cocoa butter and milk powder, and cost correspondingly more (at least €3 per 100 grams). Mirabell produces perfectly round balls using cheaper palm oil (€1.50 per 100 grams). You'll see a few off-brands, too, with prices as low as €1 per 100 grams. Supermarkets have the lowest prices. You'll pay more to buy the treats in a decorative box than in a plastic sack.

Schwarzer or *Mokka:* Straight, black espresso; order it *kleiner* (small) or *grosser* (big).

Verlängeter ("lengthened"): Espresso with water, like an Americano.

Brauner: With a little milk.

Schale Gold ("golden cup"): With a little cream (Vienna).

Melange: Like a cappuccino.

Franziskaner: A *Melange* with whipped cream rather than foamed milk, often topped with chocolate flakes.

Kapuziner: Strong coffee with a dollop of sweetened cream.

Verkehrt ("incorrect") or *Milchkaffee:* Two-thirds milk and one-third coffee (Vienna).

Einspänner ("buggy"): With lots and lots of whipped cream, served in a glass with a handle. (It was the drink of horse-and-buggy drivers, who only had one hand free.)

Fiaker ("horse-and-buggy driver"): Black, served with a *sliwowitz* (plum schnapps) or rum (Vienna).

(Wiener) Eiskaffee: Coffee with ice cream.

Maria Theresia: Coffee with orange liqueur.

Wine

Austria specializes in fine boutique wines that are generally not exported and therefore not well-known. Locals order white or red Austrian wines expecting quality equal to French and Italian wines. When in Austria, I go for the better local wines; they're well worth the cost (generally about €4 per small glass). The wine (65

PRACTICALITIES

percent white) from the Danube River Valley and eastern Austria is particularly good.

Try *Grüner Veltliner* if you like a dry white wine. Among red wines, locals favor *Blauer Zweigelt* and *Blaufräkisch*. *Traubenmost* is a heavenly grape juice—alcohol-free but on the verge of wine. *Most* is the same thing, but lightly alcoholic (can also be an apple cider). *Sturm* is "new wine," stronger than *Most,* available only in autumn, and central to the *Heuriger* phenomenon (described on page 189). In fall, try the red "new" wine, *roter Sturm;* it's so fruity that locals say "Eat up!" when toasting with it. Another specialty is the rosé *Schilcher Sturm.*

You can order wine by the glass in two sizes: the *Viertel* (quarter-liter, 8 oz) or *Achtel* (eighth-liter, 4 oz). To ask for a glass of white wine, say *"Ein Achtel Weisswein, bitte."*

Rotwein: Red wine.

Weisswein: White wine.

Gespritzter Wein or **gespritzte Weisse:** Spritzer made with equal portions of white wine and sparkling water; for less wine and more water, ask for a *Sommerspritzer.*

Sekt: Sparkling wine.

Süss: Sweet.

Trocken: Dry.

Halbtrocken: Medium.

Beer

While better known for its wine than its beer, Austria offers plenty of fun for beer drinkers. Each region is proud of its local breweries—in Vienna, try Ottakringer; in Salzburg, look for Stiegl and Augustiner Bräu; and in Tirol, check out Frastanzer and Fohrenburger. Lager (called *Märzen* here) is popular, as are *Pils* (barley-based), *Weissbier* (yeasty and wheat-based), and *Bock* (hoppy seasonal ale). Dark beer *(Dunkles)* is not common in Austria, but easy to find if you make a foray into Bavaria. Designated drivers can try Ottakringer's delicious nonalcoholic beer, called "Null Komma Josef." *Malzbier* is the malted soft drink that children learn on. *Radler* is beer and lemon soda.

At stores, half-liter bottles of beer require a deposit (*Pfand;* usually €0.15 or €0.25—listed in small print on the shelf's price label), which is refunded if you return the bottle for recycling. You can generally return bottles to any supermarket, provided the bottle is a type they sell. Some stores have vending machine-like bottle-return stations that issue a coupon after you insert your bottles (redeem when you pay for your groceries). If you don't want to bother getting your deposit back but do care about recycling, set the bottle on top of or right next to any trash can, whether on the street or in your hotel room. Chances are someone will collect it for the extra cash.

Here are some terms for ordering beer:

Ein Pfiff: Fifth-liter (about 7 oz).
Ein Seidel: Third-liter (10 oz).
Ein Krügerl: Half-liter (17 oz).
Eine Mass: A whole liter (about a quart).
Flaschenbier: Bottled.
Vom Fass: On tap.

Staying Connected

One of the most common questions I hear from travelers is, "How can I stay connected in Europe?" The short answer is this: more easily and cheaply than you might think.

The simplest solution is to bring your own device—mobile phone, tablet, or laptop—and use it just as you would at home (following the tips below, such as getting an international plan or connecting to free Wi-Fi whenever possible). Another option is to buy a European SIM card for your US mobile phone. Or you can use European landlines and computers to connect. Each of these options is described next, and more details are at www.ricksteves.com/phoning. For a very practical one-hour lecture covering tech issues for travelers, see www.ricksteves.com/mobile-travel-skills.

USING A MOBILE PHONE IN EUROPE

Here are some budget tips and options.

Sign up for an international plan. To stay connected at a lower cost, sign up for an international service plan through your carrier. Most providers offer a simple bundle that includes calling, messaging, and data. Your normal plan may already include international coverage (T-Mobile's does).

Before your trip, call your provider or check online to confirm that your phone will work in Europe, and research your provider's international rates. Activate the plan a day or two before you leave, then remember to cancel it when your trip's over.

Use free Wi-Fi whenever possible. Unless you have an un-limited-data plan, you're best off saving most of your online tasks for Wi-Fi. You can access the internet, send texts, and even make voice calls over Wi-Fi.

Most accommodations in Europe offer free Wi-Fi, but some—especially expensive hotels—charge a fee. Many cafés (including Starbucks and McDonald's) have free hotspots for customers; look for signs offering it and ask for the Wi-Fi password when you buy something. You'll also often find Wi-Fi at TIs, city squares, major

PRACTICALITIES

Hurdling the Language Barrier

Austrians speak German (though with a distinctly Austrian flair that differs a bit across regional dialects). Most young and/or well-educated Austrians—especially those in larger towns and the tourist trade—speak at least some English. Still, you'll get more smiles by using German pleasantries (see the "German Survival Phrases for Austria" in the appendix). In smaller towns, the language barrier is higher.

German—like English, Dutch, Danish, Swedish, and Norwegian—is a Germanic language, making it easier on most American ears than Romance languages (such as Italian and French). These tips will help you pronounce German words:

The letter *w* is always pronounced as *v* (e.g., the word for "wonderful" is *wunderbar,* pronounced VOON-der-bar). The vowel combinations *ie* and *ei* are pronounced like the English name of the second letter—so *ie* sounds like a long *e* (as in *hier* and *Bier,* the German words for "here" and "beer"), while *ei* sounds like a long *i* (as in *nein* and *Stein,* the German words for "no" and "stone"). The vowel combination *au* is pronounced "ow" (as in *Frau*). The vowel combinations *eu* and *äu* are pronounced "oy" (as in *neu, Deutsch,* and *Bräu,* the words for "new," "German," and "brew"). To pronounce *ö* and *ü,* purse your lips when you say the vowel; *ä* is pronounced the same as *e* in "men." (In written German, these can be depicted as the vowel followed by an *e—oe, ue,* and *ae,* respectively.) The letter *Eszett (ß)* represents *ss.* Writ-

museums, public-transit hubs, airports, and aboard trains and buses.

Minimize the use of your cellular network. Even with an international data plan, wait until you're on Wi-Fi to Skype, download apps, stream videos, or do other megabyte-greedy tasks. Using a navigation app such as Google Maps over a cellular network can take lots of data, so do this sparingly or use it offline.

Limit automatic updates. By default, your device constantly checks for a data connection and updates apps. It's smart to disable these features so your apps will only update when you're on Wi-Fi. Also change your device's email settings from "auto-retrieve" to "manual" (or from "push" to "fetch").

When you need to get online but can't find Wi-Fi, simply turn on your cellular network just long enough for the task at hand. When you're done, avoid further charges by manually turning off data roaming or cellular data (either works) in your device's Settings menu. Another way to make sure you're not accidentally using data roaming is to put your device in "airplane" mode (which also disables phone calls and texts), and then turn your Wi-Fi back on as needed.

ten German capitalizes all nouns.

Regional dialects aside, the language spoken by Austrians isn't all that different from the *Deutsch* spoken by Germans—but those small differences are a big deal to Austrians. The most important one is how you say "hello": Austrians will greet you (and each other) with a *Grüss Gott,* or perhaps *Servus*—but never with the German *Guten Tag,* a phrase that sounds oddly uptight to Austrians (and as foreign as being wished a "G'day" in the US). Instead, stick to *Grüss Gott* ("May God greet you"), or a simple *Grüss,* for "hello." You'll get the correct pronunciation after the first volley—listen and copy.

You're likely to run into a few other Austrian German words on your trip, such as *Jänner* and *Feber* for January and February (rather than the German *Januar* and *Februar*). Tacking an *-l* or *-erl* on the end of a word makes it a diminutive form—like adding "-ette" or "-ie" to an English word.

Austrians appreciate any effort on your part to speak German—even if it's just *ein Bissl* (a little bit)—and if you already speak some German, they'll understand you just fine. Give it your best shot.

For more tips on hurdling the language barrier, consider the *Rick Steves German Phrase Book* (available at www.ricksteves. com).

Use Wi-Fi calling and messaging apps. Skype, WhatsApp, FaceTime, and Google Hangouts are great for making free or low-cost calls or sending texts over Wi-Fi. With an app installed on your phone, tablet, or laptop, you can log on to a Wi-Fi network and contact friends or family members who use the same service. If you buy credit in advance, with some of these services you can call or send a text anywhere for just pennies per minute.

Some apps, such as Apple's iMessage, will use the cellular network if Wi-Fi isn't available: To avoid this possibility, turn off the "Send as SMS" feature.

USING A EUROPEAN SIM CARD IN A MOBILE PHONE

With a European SIM card, you get a European mobile number and access to cheaper rates than you'll get through your US carrier. This option works best for those who want to make a lot of local calls, need a local phone number, or want faster connection speeds than their US carrier provides. It's simple: You buy a SIM card in Europe to replace the SIM card in your "unlocked" US phone or

How to Dial

International Calls

Whether phoning from a US landline or mobile phone, or from a number in another European country, here's how to make an international call. I've used one of my recommended Vienna hotels as an example (tel. 01/534-050).

Initial Zero: Drop the initial zero from international phone numbers—except when calling Italy.

Mobile Tip: If using a mobile phone, the "+" sign can replace the international access code (for a "+" sign, press and hold "0").

US/Canada to Europe

Dial 011 (US/Canada international access code), country code (43 for Austria), and phone number.

▶ To call the Vienna hotel from home, dial 011-43-1/534-050.

Country to Country Within Europe

Dial 00 (Europe international access code), country code, and phone number.

▶ To call the Vienna hotel from Germany, dial 00-43-1/534-050.

Europe to the US/Canada

Dial 00, country code (1 for US/Canada), and phone number.

▶ To call from Europe to my office in Edmonds, Washington, dial 00-1-425-771-8303.

Domestic Calls

To call within Austria (from one Austrian landline or mobile phone to another), simply dial the phone number, including the initial 0 if there is one.

▶ To call the Vienna hotel from Salzburg, dial 01/534-050.

More Dialing Tips

Austrian Phone Numbers: In Austria, phone numbers can have

tablet (check with your carrier about unlocking it) or buy a basic cell phone in Europe.

SIM cards are sold at department-store electronics counters, newsstands, and vending machines. If you need help setting it up, buy one at a mobile-phone shop (you may need to show your passport). Costing about $5-10, SIM cards usually include prepaid calling credit, with no contract and no commitment. Expect to pay $20-40 more for a SIM card with a gigabyte of data.

There are no roaming charges for EU citizens using a domestic SIM card in other EU countries. Theoretically, providers don't have to offer Americans this "roam-like-at-home" pricing, but most do.

varying lengths. For instance, a hotel might have a seven-digit phone number and an eight-digit fax number.

Toll-Free Calls: International rates apply to US toll-free numbers dialed from the Austria—they're not free.

More Phoning Help: See www.howtocallabroad.com.

European Country Codes		Ireland & N. Ireland	353 / 44
Austria	43	Italy	39
Belgium	32	Latvia	371
Bosnia-Herzegovina	387	Montenegro	382
Croatia	385	Morocco	212
Czech Republic	420	Netherlands	31
Denmark	45	Norway	47
Estonia	372	Poland	48
Finland	358	Portugal	351
France	33	Russia	7
Germany	49	Slovakia	421
Gibraltar	350	Slovenia	386
Great Britain	44	Spain	34
Greece	30	Sweden	46
Hungary	36	Switzerland	41
Iceland	354	Turkey	90

To be sure, buy your SIM card at a mobile-phone shop and ask if non-EU citizens also have roam-like-at-home pricing.

When you run out of credit, you can top your SIM card up at newsstands, tobacco shops, mobile-phone stores, or many other businesses (look for your SIM card's logo in the window), or possibly online.

WITHOUT A MOBILE PHONE

It's possible to travel in Europe without a mobile device. You can make calls from your hotel and check email or browse websites using public computers.

Most **hotels** charge a fee for placing calls—ask for the rates

PRACTICALITIES

Tips on Internet Security

Make sure that your device is running the latest version of its operating system, security software, and apps. Next, ensure that your device and key programs (like email) are password- or passcode-protected. On the road, use only secure, password-protected Wi-Fi hotspots. Ask the hotel or café staff for the specific name of their Wi-Fi network, and make sure you log on to that exact one.

If you must access your financial info online, use a banking app rather than accessing your account via a browser. A cellular connection is more secure than Wi-Fi. Avoid logging onto personal finance sites on a public computer.

Never share your credit-card number (or any other sensitive information) online unless you know that the site is secure. A secure site displays a little padlock icon, and the URL begins with *https* (instead of the usual *http*).

before you dial. You can use a prepaid international phone card (usually available at newsstands, tobacco shops, and train stations) to call out from your hotel. Dial the toll-free access number, enter the card's PIN code, then dial the number.

You'll only see **public pay phones** in a few post offices and train stations. Most don't take coins but instead require insertable phone cards, which you can buy at a newsstand, convenience store, or post office. Except for emergencies, they're not worth the hassle.

Most hotels have **public computers** in their lobby for guests to use; otherwise you may find them at public libraries (ask your hotelier or the TI for the nearest location). On a European keyboard, use the "Alt Gr" key to the right of the space bar to insert the extra symbol that appears on some keys. On German-language keyboards, to type an @ symbol, press the "Alt Gr" key and the key that shows the @ symbol. If you can't locate a special character (such as @), simply copy it from a Web page and paste it into your email message.

MAIL

You can mail one package per day to yourself worth up to $200 duty-free from Europe to the US (mark it "personal purchases"). If you're sending a gift to someone, mark it "unsolicited gift." For details, visit www.cbp.gov, select "Travel," and search for "Know Before You Go." The Austrian postal service works fine, but for quick transatlantic delivery (in either direction), consider services such as DHL (www.dhl.com).

Transportation

Figuring out how to get around in Europe is one of your biggest trip decisions. Cars work well for two or more traveling together (especially families with small kids), those packing heavy, and those delving into the countryside. Trains and buses are best for solo travelers, blitz tourists, city-to-city travelers, and those who want to leave the driving to others. Smart travelers can use short-hop flights within Europe to creatively connect the dots on their itineraries. Just be aware of the potential downside of each option: A car is an expensive headache in any major city; with trains and buses you're at the mercy of a timetable; and flying entails a trek to and from a usually distant airport.

If your itinerary mixes cities and countryside, my advice is to connect cities by train and to explore rural areas by rental car. Arrange to pick up your car in the last big city you'll visit, then use it to lace together small towns and explore the countryside. For more detailed information on transportation throughout Europe, see www.ricksteves.com/transportation.

TRAINS

Austrian trains—most operated by Austrian Railways (a.k.a. Österreichische Bundesbahn, or ÖBB)—are generally speedy and fairly punctual, with synchronized connections; all are nonsmoking. They cover cities well, but some frustrating schedules make a few out-of-the-way recommendations not worth the time and trouble for the less determined (www.oebb.at).

Types of Trains

Austrian Railways' several classes of trains differ substantially in speed, comfort, and price. Its newest, fastest, and reddest train, the Railjet, streaks between Budapest, Vienna, Munich (or Innsbruck), and Zürich. Red regional trains (labeled R and REX on schedules) are the slowest—the milk-run R trains stop at every small station—but cost much less. Midlevel, usually white IC and EC trains are air-conditioned, but are older than the Railjets and German ICE trains (and don't always have outlets for your laptop).

The private Westbahn company (www.westbahn.at) runs blue-and-white express trains about as fast as the Railjet between Vienna and Salzburg. Germany's Deutsche Bahn trains run into Austria and Italy's Dolomites (www.bahn.com).

Schedules

Schedules change by season, weekday, and weekends. Verify Austrian Railways times listed in this book at www.oebb.at (with full price information), www.bahn.com (Germany's excellent Europe-

Public Transportation in Austria

wide timetable site, without most prices but easier to navigate), or ÖBB's "Scotty" app (schedules, maps, and route planning for all transportation in Austria).

At staffed train stations, attendants will print out a step-by-step itinerary for you, free of charge. Schedules are also posted at stations. The trackside machines marked *Fahrkarten* show prices but do not give schedule information.

If you're changing trains en route and have a tight connection, note the numbers of the platforms (*Bahnsteig* or *Gleis*) where you will arrive and depart (listed on itineraries). This will save you precious time hunting for your connecting train.

To reach Austria's train information number from anywhere in the country, dial toll tel. 051-717 (to get an operator, dial 2, then 2) and ask for an English speaker.

Rail Passes

The easy-to-use Eurail Austria pass can be a good value if you're making several train journeys within Austria. If you're also traveling beyond Austria, consider the Eurail Global Pass, covering most of Europe. If you buy two separate passes for neighboring countries, note that you'll use a travel day on each when crossing the border.

Your Austria rail pass covers certain extras, such as discounts on Danube boats. Flexipass holders should note that fully covered ("free") trips start the use of a travel day, while discounted trips do not. Seat reservations are not required on daytime trains except in the ritzy Railjet business compartment. Optional seat reservations in first or second class cost €3 extra.

Two other passes, which are independent of the Eurail brand, are worth considering. The European East Pass covers nearly all trains in Austria, Czech Republic, Slovakia, and Hungary (cheaper than the Eurail Global Pass, kids pay half-price, not valid on Westbahn trains in Austria and a few private trains in the Czech

Rail Pass or Point-to-Point Tickets?

Will you be better off buying a rail pass or point-to-point tickets? It pays to know your options and choose what's best for your itinerary.

Rail Passes

A Eurail Austria Pass lets you travel by train in Austria for three to eight days (consecutively or not) within a one-month period. Austria is also covered (along with most of Europe) by the classic Eurail Global Pass. Discounted rates are offered for seniors (age 60 and up) and youths (ages 12-27). Up to two kids (ages 4-11) can travel free with each adult-rate pass (but not with senior rates). All rail passes offer a choice of first or second class for all ages.

Austria is also a key element in two independent regional passes: the European East Pass and the Central European Triangle Pass. Rail passes are best purchased outside Europe (through travel agents or Rick Steves' Europe). For more on rail passes, including current prices, go to RickSteves.com/rail.

Point-to-Point Tickets

For short trips, individual point-to-point tickets may save you money over a pass. Use this map to add up approximate pay-as-you-go fares for your itinerary, and compare that to the price of a rail pass. Keep in mind that significant discounts on point-to-point tickets may be available with advance purchase.

Map shows approximate costs, in USD, for one-way, second-class tickets on faster trains.

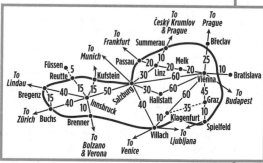

Republic). Another option, the Central Europe Triangle Pass, covers three train trips in a circle of either Vienna-Budapest-Prague or Vienna-Salzburg-Prague. If these routes fit your trip, then this pass saves you money over point-to-point tickets.

For more detailed advice on figuring out the smartest rail pass options for your trip, visit RickSteves.com/rail.

Point-to-Point Tickets

Ticket fares are shown in the "Rail Passes and Train Travel in Austria" sidebar, and at www.oebb.at. Bikes cost an extra 10 percent on top of your train fare (also requires €3 advance reservation for long-distance trains).

Buying Tickets: Major Austrian stations have a handy *Reisezentrum* (travel center) where you can ask questions and buy tickets. Many smaller stations are unstaffed, with tickets sold only from machines (marked *Fahrkarten*, "tickets"). You can pay with bills, coins, or credit cards. Boarding a local train without a ticket can earn you a hefty fine if you could have bought a ticket at the station where you boarded.

It's worth knowing about a few special ticket deals that can save you some money:

Daypass: Austrian Railways' **Einfach-Raus-Ticket** ("Just Get Outta Here" ticket) is a cheap way for couples and small groups to travel. It's valid only on slower regional trains: R, REX, S-Bahn, RSB, ER, and EZ (€34 for 2 people, €4 for each additional person up to 5 total, €9 extra with bikes—no matter how many, covers whole day of travel except not valid Mon-Fri before 9:00, cannot be used by solo travelers).

Discount Card: Many Austrians have a **Vorteils** card, which knocks 50 percent off all rail fares. The adult version (€99, valid one year) isn't worth it for most travelers, but the **youth** version (under 26 only, €19) and **senior** version (age 64 and above, €29) pay for themselves with just one trip from Vienna to Innsbruck. The **family** version (€19 per parent) is also a great deal—parents get the 50 percent discount, and with each parent, up to 2 kids ages 6-14 go free (normally they'd pay half the adult fare). To get a Vorteils card, go to any station ticket counter; you'll get a temporary card on the spot that's valid for two months (the permanent card will be sent to your address back home).

Advance-Purchase Discounts: If you book online at www.oebb.at at least three days in advance, Austrian Railways offers **"SparSchiene"** fares that can be as low as €9 domestically and €19 internationally. Availability is limited, and these tickets lock you into a departure time.

Bavaria Deal: For a whole day of travel on local trains in Bavaria, such as from Salzburg to Munich and Füssen, consider the **Regional Day Ticket for Bavaria**—a.k.a. Bayern-Ticket (€25/day for the first person plus €6 for each additional person).

BUSES

While long-distance buses don't offer as extensive a network as trains, they do cover the most popular cities for travelers (including nearly all the destinations recommended in this book), often with a direct connection. In Austria, the bus can be the best—and sometimes only—way to reach mountainous areas.

Bus tickets are sold on board, at kiosks at some bus terminals, or online. Because the cheapest fares often sell out, it's best to book online as soon as you're sure of your plans. The main bus operators to check out are Postbus (www.postbus.at), Westbus (www.westbus.at), and Flixbus (www.flixbus.com).

Though not as comfortable as trains, each company's buses are surprisingly well-outfitted and make for a more pleasant ride than your average Greyhound trip. Most offer free Wi-Fi and WCs.

TAXIS AND RIDE-BOOKING SERVICES

Most European taxis are reliable and cheap. In many cities, two people can travel short distances by cab for little more than the cost of bus or subway tickets. If you like ride-booking services such as Uber, their apps usually work in Europe just like they do in the US: Request a car on your mobile phone (connected to Wi-Fi or data), and the fare is automatically charged to your credit card.

RENTING A CAR

It's cheaper to arrange most car rentals from the US, so research and compare rates before you go.

Most of the major US rental agencies (including Avis, Budget, Enterprise, Hertz, and Thrifty) have offices throughout Europe. Also consider the two major Europe-based agencies, Europcar and Sixt. Consolidators such as Auto Europe/Kemwel (www.autoeurope.com—or the sometimes cheaper www.autoeurope.eu) compare rates at several companies to get you the best deal.

Wherever you book, always read the fine print. Ask about add-on charges—such as one-way drop-off fees, airport surcharges, or mandatory insurance policies—that aren't included in the "total price."

Rental Costs and Considerations

Figure on paying roughly $250 for a one-week rental for a basic compact car. Allow extra for supplemental insurance, fuel, tolls, and parking. To save money on fuel, request a diesel car.

Manual vs. Automatic: Almost all rental cars in Europe are manual by default—and cars with a stick shift are generally cheaper. If you need an automatic, request one in advance. When selecting a car, don't be tempted by a larger model, as it won't be as maneuverable on narrow, winding roads or when squeezing into tight parking lots.

Age Restrictions: Some rental companies impose minimum and maximum age limits. Young drivers (25 and under) and seniors (69 and up) should check the rental policies and rules section of car-rental websites. If you're considered too young or too old, look into leasing (covered later), which has less stringent age restrictions.

Choosing Pick-up/Drop-off Locations: Always check the hours of the locations you choose: Many rental offices close from midday Saturday until Monday morning and, in smaller towns, at lunchtime. When selecting an office, plug the address into a mapping website to confirm the location. A downtown site is generally cheaper—and might seem more convenient than the airport. But pedestrianized and one-way streets can make navigation tricky when returning a car at a big-city office or urban train station. Wherever you select, get precise details on the location and allow ample time to find it.

Have the Right License: If you're renting a car in Austria, bring your driver's license. You're also technically required to have an International Driving Permit—an official translation of your license (sold at your local AAA office for $20 plus the cost of two passport-type photos; see www.aaa.com). While that's the letter of the law, I generally rent cars without having this permit. How this is enforced varies from country to country: Get advice from your car-rental company.

Crossing Borders in a Rental Car: Be aware that international trips—say, picking up in Vienna and dropping off in Munich—can be expensive if the rental company assesses a drop-off fee for crossing a border.

Always tell your car-rental company up front exactly which countries you'll be entering. Some companies levy extra insurance fees for trips taken in certain countries with certain cars (such as BMWs, Mercedes, and convertibles). Double-check with your rental agent that you have all the documentation you need before you drive off (especially if you're crossing borders into non-Schengen countries, such as Croatia, where you might need to present proof of insurance).

Picking Up Your Car: Before driving off in your rental car, check it thoroughly and make sure any damage is noted on your rental agreement. Rental agencies in Europe are very strict when it comes to charging for even minor damage, so be sure to mark everything. Find out how your car's gearshift, lights, turn signals, wipers, radio, and fuel cap function, and know what kind of fuel the car takes (diesel vs. unleaded). When you return the car, make sure the agent verifies its condition with you. Some drivers take pictures of the returned vehicle as proof of its condition.

Car Insurance Options

When you rent a car in Europe, the price typically includes liability insurance, which covers harm to other cars or motorists—but not the rental car itself. To limit your financial risk in case of damage to the rental, choose one of these options: Buy a Collision Damage Waiver (CDW) with a low or zero deductible from the car-rental

Driving in Austria

Note: Your times may vary based on traffic, construction, and road conditions.

GERMANY

To Prague
240m · 4h

To Rothenburg
150m · 2h

20 Kilometers
20 Miles

m = miles
h = hours

Munich

80m · 1.25h
Salzburg

80m · 1.25h

70m · 1.5h

100m · 1.5h

Füssen

15m
.5h

Berchtesgaden

12m
.25h

Reutte

Lake Constance

60m · 1.25h

110m · 2h

Hall

140m · 3.5h

180m · 3.5h

Innsbruck

25m
.5h

Brenner Pass

220m · 3.5h

To Zürich

150m · 2.5h

SWITZERLAND

ITALY

To Verona

---

company (roughly 30-40 percent extra), get coverage through your credit card (free, but more complicated), or get collision insurance as part of a larger travel-insurance policy.

Basic **CDW** costs $10-30 a day and typically comes with a $1,000-2,000 deductible, reducing but not eliminating your financial responsibility. When you pick up the car, you'll be offered the chance to "buy down" the deductible to zero (for an additional $10-30/day; this is often called "super CDW" or "zero-deductible coverage").

If you opt for **credit-card coverage,** you must decline all coverage offered by the car-rental company—which means they can place a hold on your card for up to the full value of the car. In case of damage, it can be time-consuming to resolve the charges. Before relying on this option, quiz your card company about how it works.

If you're already purchasing a **travel-insurance policy** for your trip, adding collision coverage can be an economical option. For example, Travel Guard (www.travelguard.com) sells affordable renter's collision insurance as an add-on to its other policies; it's valid everywhere in Europe except the Republic of Ireland, and

some Italian car-rental companies refuse to honor it, as it doesn't cover you in case of theft.

For more on car-rental insurance, see www.ricksteves.com/cdw.

Leasing

For trips of three weeks or more, consider leasing (which automatically includes zero-deductible collision and theft insurance). By technically buying and then selling back the car, you save money on taxes and insurance. Leasing provides you a brand-new car with unlimited mileage and a 24-hour emergency assistance program. You can lease for as little as 21 days to as long as five and a half months. Car leases must be arranged from the US. One of several companies offering affordable lease packages is Auto Europe.

Navigation Options

If you'll be navigating using your phone or a GPS unit from home, remember to bring a car charger and device mount.

Your Mobile Phone: The mapping app on your phone works

PRACTICALITIES

fine for navigation in Europe, but for real-time turn-by-turn directions and traffic updates, you'll need mobile data access. And driving all day can burn through a lot of very expensive data.

The economical work-around is to use map apps that work offline. By downloading in advance from Google Maps, Apple Maps, Here WeGo, or Navmii, you can still have turn-by-turn voice directions and maps that recalibrate even though they're offline.

You must download your maps before you go offline—and it's smart to select large regions. Then turn off your data connection so you're not charged for roaming. Call up the map, enter your destination, and you're on your way. Even if you don't have your data roaming, this option is great for navigating in areas with poor connectivity.

GPS Devices: If you want the convenience of a dedicated GPS unit, consider renting one with your car ($10-30/day). These units offer real-time turn-by-turn directions and traffic without the data requirements of an app. The unit may come loaded only with maps for its home country; if you need additional maps, ask. Also make sure your device's language is set to English before you drive off.

A less expensive option is to bring a GPS device from home. Be sure to buy and install the European maps you'll need before your trip.

Maps and Atlases: Even when navigating primarily with a mobile app or GPS, I always make it a point to have a paper map. It's invaluable for getting the big picture, understanding alternate routes, and filling in when my phone runs out of juice. The free maps you get from your car-rental company usually don't have enough detail. It's smart to buy a better map before you go, or pick one up at a European gas station, bookshop, newsstand, or tourist shop.

Driving

Road Rules: Be aware of typical European road rules; for example, many countries require headlights to be turned on at all times, and nearly all forbid handheld mobile-phone use. In Austria, you're required to use low-beam headlights when driving in urban areas. Austria also requires an "emergency corridor" during traffic jams on expressways and toll roads—follow what other drivers are doing and stay out of the cleared lane.

In Europe, you're not allowed to turn right on a red light, unless there is a sign or signal specifically authorizing it, and on expressways it's illegal to pass drivers on the right. Ask your car-rental company about these rules, or check the "International Travel" section of the US State Department website (www.travel.state.gov, search for your country in the "Country Information" box, then

STOP AND LEARN THESE ROAD SIGNS

Speed Limit (km/hr) — Yield — No Passing — End of No Passing Zone

One Way — Intersection — Main Road — Expressway

Danger — No Entry — Cars Prohibited — All Vehicles Prohibited

No Through Road — Restrictions No Longer Apply — Yield to Oncoming Traffic — No Stopping

Parking — No Parking — Customs or Toll Road — Peace

click on "Travel and Transportation").

Tolls: Austria charges drivers to use their major roads. You'll need a *Vignette* sticker stuck to the inside of your rental car's windshield (buy at the border crossing, big gas stations near borders, or a rental-car agency; www.asfinag.at). The cost is €9 for 10 days, or €26 for two months. Not having one earns you a stiff fine. Place it on your windshield exactly as shown on the back of the sticker, and keep the lower tear-off portion—it's your receipt.

Fuel: Unleaded gasoline *(Benzin)* comes in regular (91 octane) and "Euro-Super" (95 octane). If you're also driving in Germany, pumps marked "E10" or "Super E10" mean the gas contains 10 percent ethanol—make sure your rental can run on this mix. You don't have to worry about learning the German word for diesel—it's the same word as in English. Your US credit and debit cards may not work at self-service gas pumps. Pay the attendant or be sure to carry sufficient cash in euros.

Navigation: Use good local maps and study them before each drive. Learn which exits you need to look out for, which major cities you'll travel toward, where the ruined castles lurk, and so on. Ring roads go around a city. Learn the universal road signs (explained in charts in most road atlases and at service stations). To get to the center of a city, follow signs for *Zentrum* or *Stadtmitte*. When navigating, you'll see *nord, süd, ost,* and *west*.

Autobahn: Every long drive between my recommended destinations is via the autobahn (super-freeway) and *Schnellstrassen* (expressway) system, and nearly every scenic backcountry drive is paved and comfortable.

The shortest distance between any two points is the autobahn. Blue signs direct you to the autobahn, and in Austria, unlike in Germany, the autobahn has a speed limit (130 km/hour, unless otherwise signed). Learn the signs: *Dreieck* ("three corners") means a Y in the road; *Autobahnkreuz* is a freeway interchange. While all

PRACTICALITIES

roads seem to lead to the little town of Ausfahrt, that's the German word for exit. Exits are spaced about every 20 miles and often have a gas station, restaurant, a minimarket, and sometimes a tourist information desk. Exits and intersections refer to the next major city or the nearest small town. Peruse the map and anticipate which town names to look out for.

Parking: To park on the street, pick up a plastic or cardboard clock (*Parkscheibe*, available free at gas stations, police stations, and *Tabak* shops). Display your arrival time on the clock and put it on the dashboard, so parking attendants can see you've been there less than the posted maximum stay (blue lines indicate 90-minute zones on Austrian streets). Your US credit and debit cards may not work at automated parking garages—bring cash.

Theft: Thieves easily recognize rental cars and assume they are filled with a tourist's gear. Be sure all your valuables are out of sight and locked in the trunk, or even better, with you or in your room.

FLIGHTS

To compare flight costs and times, begin with a travel search engine: Kayak.com is the top site for flights to and within Europe, easy-to-use Google Flights has price alerts, and Skyscanner.com includes many inexpensive flights within Europe.

Flights to Europe: Start looking for international flights about four to six months before your trip, especially for peak-season travel. Depending on your itinerary, it can be efficient and no more expensive to fly into one city and out of another. If your flight requires a connection in Europe, see my hints on navigating Europe's top hub airports at www.ricksteves.com/hub-airports.

Flights within Europe: Flying between European cities has become surprisingly affordable. Before buying a long-distance train or bus ticket, first check the cost of a flight on one of Europe's airlines, whether a major carrier or a no-frills outfit like EasyJet and Ryanair.

Be aware of the potential drawbacks of flying with a discount airline: nonrefundable and nonchangeable tickets, minimal customer service, time-consuming treks to secondary airports, and stingy baggage allowances (also an issue on major airlines). To avoid unpleasant surprises, read the small print about the costs for "extras" such as reserving a seat, checking a bag, or checking in and printing a boarding pass.

Flying to the US and Canada: Because security is extra tight for flights to the US, be sure to give yourself plenty of time at the airport. It's also important to charge your electronic devices before you board because security checks may require you to turn them on (see www.tsa.gov for the latest rules).

Resources from Rick Steves

Begin Your Trip at RickSteves.com

My mobile-friendly **website** is *the* place to explore Europe in preparation for your trip. You'll find thousands of fun articles, videos, and radio interviews; a wealth of money-saving tips for planning your dream trip; travel news dispatches; a video library of my travel talks; my travel blog; my latest guidebook updates (www.ricksteves.com/update); and my free Rick Steves Audio Europe app. You can also follow me on Facebook and Twitter.

Our **Travel Forum** is a well-groomed collection of message boards where our travel-savvy community answers questions and shares their personal travel experiences—and our well-traveled staff chimes in when they can be helpful (www.ricksteves.com/forums).

Our **online Travel Store** offers bags and accessories that I've designed to help you travel smarter and lighter. These include my popular carry-on bags (which I live out of four months a year), money belts, totes, toiletries kits, adapters, guidebooks, and planning maps (www.ricksteves.com/shop).

Our website can also help you find the perfect **rail pass** fit for your itinerary and your budget, with easy, one-stop shopping for rail passes, seat reservations, and point-to-point tickets (www.ricksteves.com/rail).

Rick Steves' Tours, Guidebooks, TV Shows, and More

Small Group Tours: Want to travel with greater efficiency and less stress? We offer more than 40 itineraries reaching the best destinations in this book...and beyond. Each year about 25,000 travelers join us on about 1,000 Rick Steves bus tours. You'll enjoy great guides and a fun bunch of travel partners (with small groups of 24 to 28 travelers). You'll find European adventures to fit every vacation length. For all the details, and to get our tour catalog, visit www.ricksteves.com/tour or call us at 425/608-4217.

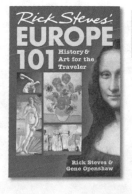

Books: *Rick Steves Vienna, Salzburg & Tirol* is just one of many books in my series on European travel, which includes country and city guidebooks, Snapshots (excerpted chapters from bigger guides), Pocket guides (full-color little books on big cities), "Best Of" guidebooks (condensed, full-color country guides), and my budget-travel skills handbook, *Rick Steves Europe Through the Back Door*. A more complete list of my titles—including phrase books, cruising guides, and more—appears near the end of this book.

TV Shows and Travel Talks: My public television series, *Rick Steves' Europe,* covers Europe from top to bottom with over 100 half-hour episodes—and we're working on new shows every year (watch full episodes on my website for free). Or to raise your travel I.Q., check out the video versions of our popular classes (covering most European countries as well as travel skills, packing smart, cruising, tech for travelers, European art, and travel as a political act—www.ricksteves.com/travel-talks).

Radio: My weekly public radio show, *Travel with Rick Steves,* features interviews with travel experts from around the world. It airs on 400 public radio stations across the US, or you can hear it as a podcast. A complete archive of programs is available at www.ricksteves.com/radio.

Audio Tours on My Free App: I've produced dozens of free, self-guided audio tours of some of the top sights in Europe. For those tours and other audio content get my free Rick Steves Audio Europe app, an extensive online library organized by destination. For more on my app, see the Introduction chapter.

APPENDIX

Holidays and Festivals

This list includes selected festivals in major cities, plus national holidays observed throughout Austria. Vienna and Salzburg have music festivals nearly every month, and many sights and banks close on national holidays—keep this in mind when planning your itinerary. Before planning a trip around a festival, verify the dates with the festival's website, TI sites (www.austria.info), or my "Upcoming Holidays and Festivals in Austria" web page (www.ricksteves.com/europe/austria/festivals).

Jan-Feb	Vienna Ball Season (2,000 hours of dancing, www.wien.info, search on "Balls"); Mozart Week (daily performances), Salzburg
Jan-Feb	Fasnacht (carnival season, balls, parades), western Austria
Week before Easter	Osterfestspiele Salzburg and OsterKlang Wien (Easter music festivals), Salzburg and Vienna
Easter & Easter Monday	Ostersonntag & Ostermontag (April 21-22 in 2019, April 12-13 in 2020)

May-June	Vienna Festival of Arts and Music (www.festwochen.at)
May 1	May Day with maypole dances, throughout Austria
Ascension	Christi Himmelfahrt (May 30 in 2019, May 21 in 2020)
Pentecost Monday	Pfingstmontag (June 10 in 2019, June 1 in 2020)
Corpus Christi	Fronleichnam (June 23 in 2019, June 14 in 2020)
Late June	Danube Island Music Festival (three days of free music), Vienna
Late June	Midsummer Eve celebrations, throughout Austria
Mid-July-Aug	Salzburg Festival (www.salzburgerfestspiele.at)
Aug 15	Assumption (Mariä Himmelfahrt), parts of Austria
Sept 24	St. Rupert's Day (Ruperti-Kirtag; parade and fireworks), Salzburg
Mid-Sept-early Oct	Wiener Wiesn-Fest (Oktoberfest celebrations in the Prater), Vienna; also fall beer festivals, throughout Austria and Bavaria
Mid-Oct	Salzburg Kulturtage (series of affordable concerts)
Oct 26	Austrian National Day (Nationalfeiertag)
Nov 1	All Saints' Day (Allerheiligen)
Nov 11	St. Martin's Day celebrations, Austria and Bavaria
Late Nov-Dec	Christmas markets across Austria and Bavaria
Dec	Perchtenlaufen (winter processions), Alpine regions
Dec 6	St. Nicholas Day (Nikolaustag, parades), throughout Austria
Dec 8	Feast of the Immaculate Conception (Mariä Empfängnis)
Dec 24	Christmas Eve (Heilige Abend), when Austrians celebrate Christmas
Dec 25	Christmas
Dec 26	St. Stephen's Day (Stefanitag)

Dec 31	New Year's Eve (Silvester, a.k.a. Alt-jahrstag; fireworks), throughout Austria, particularly Vienna

Books and Films

To learn more about Austria past and present, check out a few of these books and films.

Nonfiction

The Age of Insight (Eric R. Kandel, 2012). Kandel beautifully tells how the Vienna School of Medicine inspired pioneers in science, medicine, and art.

The Austrians: A Thousand-Year Odyssey (Gordon Brook-Shepherd, 2003). This overview of Austrian history focuses on Austria's political history in the 19th and 20th centuries.

Beethoven: The Music and the Life (Lewis Lockwood, 2005). This biography weaves together the musician's life in Vienna and his contributions to Viennese culture.

Fin-de-Siècle Vienna: Politics and Culture (Carl E. Schorske, 1981). This is a comprehensive analysis of the birth of modern art and thought through the work of Klimt, Freud, and other Viennese luminaries.

The Habsburgs: The History of a Dynasty (Benjamin Curtis, 2013). This in-depth but never dry volume brings the Habsburgs to life.

The Hare with the Amber Eyes: A Family's Century of Art and Loss (Edmund de Waal, 2010). De Waal insightfully recounts the rise and fall of his storied family, whose Vienna home, the Palais Ephrussi on the Ringstrasse, was confiscated by the Nazis in the *Anschluss*.

Hitler's Vienna: A Dictator's Apprenticeship (Brigitte Hamann, 1999). This book paints a disturbing portrait of the young Hitler's formative years in Vienna.

A Nervous Splendor and *Thunder at Twilight* (Frederic Morton, 1979 and 1983). In these companion volumes, Morton tells the story of the Austro-Hungarian Empire's last years.

The Spell of the Vienna Woods: Inspiration and Influence from Beethoven to Kafka (Paul Hofmann, 1994). Personal anecdotes, tourist information, and stories about artists who found inspiration in Vienna are blended in this history.

The Story of the Trapp Family Singers (Maria von Trapp, 2001). Maria tells the extraordinary story behind the famous singing family.

Wittgenstein's Vienna (Allan Janik and Stephen Toulmin, 1973).

APPENDIX

Janik follows the philosopher Ludwig Wittgenstein as he crafts his ideas in his native city of Vienna.

World of Yesterday (Stefan Zweig, 1942). Zweig recalls living through Vienna's golden days, World War I, and the Hitler years.

Fiction

Airs Above the Ground (Mary Stewart, 1965). A woman goes to Vienna in search of her missing husband in this classic featuring Lipizzaner stallions and the Austrian Alps.

Brother of Sleep (Robert Schneider, 1992). In an Austrian mountain village in the early 19th century, a musical prodigy goes unappreciated by the locals.

A Death in Vienna (Daniel Silva, 2004). A bombing in Vienna leads to a shocking series of discoveries dating back to World War II in this fast-paced thriller.

Embers (Sándor Márai, 1942). Two military friends become reacquainted in cobblestoned, gaslit Vienna just before the empire's glory begins to fade.

The Empty Mirror (J. Sydney Jones, 2009). This mystery connects historic Vienna and famous Austrian figures.

The Exiles Return (Elizabeth de Waal, 2013). Three exiles return to Vienna in the years after World War II, variously seeking change, fortune, and a return to a lost way of life.

Henry James' Midnight Song (Carol de Chellis Hill, 1993). A cast of famous historical characters is caught up in a series of mysterious deaths in fin-de-siècle Vienna.

The Painted Kiss (Elizabeth Hickey, 2005). In the lush elegance of turn-of-the-century Vienna, a relationship develops between painter Gustav Klimt and his pupil Emilie Flöge, who posed for Klimt's *The Kiss*.

The Piano Teacher (Elfriede Jelinek, 1983). Austrian feminist Jelinek, who won the 2004 Nobel Prize in Literature, tells of a troubled piano teacher who upends the lives of her students. The book was made into a 2001 film.

The Radetzky March (Joseph Roth, 1932). This classic novel follows four generations of an aristocratic family during the decline and fall of the Habsburgs.

The Seven-Per-Cent Solution (Nicholas Meyer, 1974). Sherlock Holmes travels to Vienna to meet with Sigmund Freud and gets involved in a case.

When Nietzsche Wept (Irvin D. Yalom, 1992). Set in the 19th century, this novel tells a fascinating story of the birth of psychoanalysis.

Films

Amadeus (1984). Mozart's life is told from the perspective of his fellow composer Antonio Salieri, who recounts Mozart's unmatched gift and unorthodox character.

Before Sunrise (1995). Ethan Hawke sightsees, talks, romances, and talks some more with Julie Delpy as they spend one night in Vienna.

A Dangerous Method (2011). Michael Fassbender and Viggo Mortensen play opposite each other in this film about the tumultuous relationship between Sigmund Freud and Carl Jung.

The Illusionist (2006). A magician in circa-1900 Vienna uses his abilities to gain the love of a woman engaged to the crown prince.

Immortal Beloved (1994). Beethoven's assistant tries to unravel the mystery suggested by the composer's real-life letters to an "immortal beloved" in this biopic starring Gary Oldman.

Letter from an Unknown Woman (1948). A concert pianist receives a letter from a mysterious woman as he prepares to flee Vienna to avoid a duel.

Mahler (1974). Flashbacks and dreams tell the story of Austrian composer Gustav Mahler.

Mayerling (1968). Omar Sharif portrays the Habsburg heir Archduke Rudolf, whose suicide played a pivotal role in Austrian history.

Miracle of the White Stallions (1963). The Lipizzaner stallions are the stars in this true story of their liberation by General Patton after World War II.

Museum Hours (2012). A museum steward and a Canadian tourist bond over famous works of art and wander through the streets of Vienna.

The Sound of Music (1965). The beloved musical, about a nun-turned-governess in Salzburg on the eve of World War II, helped turn Julie Andrews into a star.

The Third Man (1949). Filled with noir foreboding, this celebrated film, starring Orson Welles, was shot in bombed-out Vienna after World War II.

Sissi (1955). The first in a trilogy, this movie shares the story of beloved princess Elizabeth "Sissi" of Austria.

Conversions and Climate

Numbers and Stumblers

- Europeans write a few of their numbers differently than we do. 1 = 1, 4 = 4, 7 = 7.
- In Europe, dates appear as day/month/year, so Christmas 2020 is 25/12/20.
- Commas are decimal points and decimals are commas. A dol-

lar and a half is $1,50, one thousand is 1.000, and there are 5.280 feet in a mile.

- When counting with fingers, start with your thumb. If you hold up your first finger to request one item, you'll probably get two.
- What Americans call the second floor of a building is the first floor in Europe.
- On escalators and moving sidewalks, Europeans keep the left "lane" open for passing. Keep to the right.

Metric Conversions

A **kilogram** equals 1,000 grams (about 2.2 pounds). One hundred **grams** (a common unit at markets) is about a quarter-pound. One liter is about a quart, or almost four to a gallon.

A **kilometer** is six-tenths of a mile. To convert kilometers to miles, cut the kilometers in half and add back 10 percent of the original (120 km: 60 + 12 = 72 miles). One **meter** is 39 inches—just over a yard.

1 foot = 0.3 meter	1 square yard = 0.8 square meter
1 yard = 0.9 meter	1 square mile = 2.6 square kilometers
1 mile = 1.6 kilometers	1 ounce = 28 grams
1 centimeter = 0.4 inch	1 quart = 0.95 liter
1 meter = 39.4 inches	1 kilogram = 2.2 pounds
1 kilometer = 0.62 mile	32°F = 0°C

Clothing Sizes

When shopping for clothing, use these US-to-European comparisons as general guidelines (but note that no conversion is perfect).

Women: For pants and dresses, add 30 in Austria (US 10 = Austrian 40). For blouses and sweaters, add 8 for most of Europe (US 32 = European 40). For shoes, add 30-31 (US 7 = European 37/38).

Men: For shirts, multiply by 2 and add about 8 (US 15 = European 38). For jackets and suits, add 10. For shoes, add 32-34.

Children: Clothing is sized by height—in centimeters (2.5 inches = 1 cm), so a US size 8 roughly equates to 132-140. For shoes up to size 13, add 16-18, and for sizes 1 and up, add 30-32.

Vienna's Climate

First line, average daily high; second line, average daily low; third line, average days with rain. For more detailed weather statistics for destinations in this book (as well as the rest of the world), check www.wunderground.com.

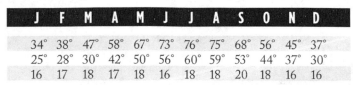

J	F	M	A	M	J	J	A	S	O	N	D
34°	38°	47°	58°	67°	73°	76°	75°	68°	56°	45°	37°
25°	28°	30°	42°	50°	56°	60°	59°	53°	44°	37°	30°
16	17	18	17	18	16	18	18	20	18	16	16

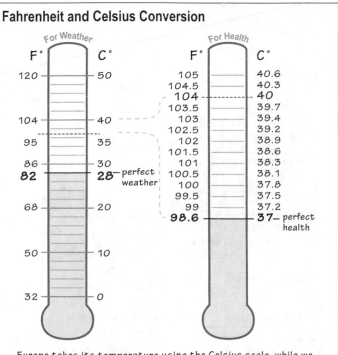

Fahrenheit and Celsius Conversion

Europe takes its temperature using the Celsius scale, while we opt for Fahrenheit. For a rough conversion from Celsius to Fahrenheit, double the number and add 30. For weather, remember that 28°C is 82°F—perfect. For health, 37°C is just right. At a launderette, 30°C is cold, 40°C is warm (usually the default setting), 60°C is hot, and 95°C is boiling. Your air-conditioner should be set at about 20°C.

Packing Checklist

Whether you're traveling for five days or five weeks, you won't need more than this. Pack light to enjoy the sweet freedom of true mobility.

Clothing

- ☐ 5 shirts: long- & short-sleeve
- ☐ 2 pairs pants (or skirts/capris)
- ☐ 1 pair shorts
- ☐ 5 pairs underwear & socks
- ☐ 1 pair walking shoes
- ☐ Sweater or warm layer
- ☐ Rainproof jacket with hood
- ☐ Tie, scarf, belt, and/or hat
- ☐ Swimsuit
- ☐ Sleepwear/loungewear

Money

- ☐ Debit card(s)
- ☐ Credit card(s)
- ☐ Hard cash (US $100-200)
- ☐ Money belt

Documents

- ☐ Passport
- ☐ Tickets & confirmations: flights, hotels, trains, rail pass, car rental, sight entries
- ☐ Driver's license
- ☐ Student ID, hostel card, etc.
- ☐ Photocopies of important documents
- ☐ Insurance details
- ☐ Guidebooks & maps

Toiletries Kit

- ☐ Basics: soap, shampoo, toothbrush, toothpaste, floss, deodorant, sunscreen, brush/comb, etc.
- ☐ Medicines & vitamins
- ☐ First-aid kit
- ☐ Glasses/contacts/sunglasses
- ☐ Sewing kit
- ☐ Packet of tissues (for WC)
- ☐ Earplugs

Electronics

- ☐ Mobile phone
- ☐ Camera & related gear
- ☐ Tablet/ebook reader/laptop
- ☐ Headphones/earbuds
- ☐ Chargers & batteries
- ☐ Phone car charger & mount (or GPS device)
- ☐ Plug adapters

Miscellaneous

- ☐ Daypack
- ☐ Sealable plastic baggies
- ☐ Laundry supplies: soap, laundry bag, clothesline, spot remover
- ☐ Small umbrella
- ☐ Travel alarm/watch
- ☐ Notepad & pen
- ☐ Journal

Optional Extras

- ☐ Second pair of shoes (flip-flops, sandals, tennis shoes, boots)
- ☐ Travel hairdryer
- ☐ Picnic supplies
- ☐ Water bottle
- ☐ Fold-up tote bag
- ☐ Small flashlight
- ☐ Mini binoculars
- ☐ Small towel or washcloth
- ☐ Inflatable pillow/neck rest
- ☐ Tiny lock
- ☐ Address list (to mail postcards)
- ☐ Extra passport photos

German Survival Phrases for Austria

When using the phonetics, pronounce ī sounds like the long i in "light." Bolded syllables are stressed.

English	German	Pronunciation
Good day.	Grüss Gott.	**grews** gote
Do you speak English?	Sprechen Sie Englisch?	**shprehkh**-ehn zee **ehgn**-lish
Yes. / No.	Ja. / Nein.	yah / nīn
I (don't) understand.	Ich verstehe (nicht).	ikh fehr-**shtay**-heh (nikht)
Please.	Bitte.	**bit**-teh
Thank you.	Danke.	**dahng**-keh
I'm sorry.	Es tut mir leid.	ehs toot meer līt
Excuse me.	Entschuldigung.	ehnt-**shool**-dig-oong
(No) problem.	(Kein) Problem.	(kīn) proh-**blaym**
(Very) good.	(Sehr) gut.	(zehr) goot
Goodbye.	Auf Wiedersehen.	owf **vee**-der-zayn
one / two	eins / zwei	īns / tsvī
three / four	drei / vier	drī / feer
five / six	fünf / sechs	fewnf / zehkhs
seven / eight	sieben / acht	**zee**-behn / ahkht
nine / ten	neun / zehn	noyn / tsayn
How much is it?	Wieviel kostet das?	**vee**-feel **kohs**-teht dahs
Write it?	Schreiben?	**shrī**-behn
Is it free?	Ist es umsonst?	ist ehs oom-**zohnst**
Included?	Inklusive?	in-kloo-**zee**-veh
Where can I buy / find...?	Wo kann ich kaufen / finden...?	voh kahn ikh **kow**-fehn / **fin**-dehn
I'd like / We'd like...	Ich hätte gern / Wir hätten gern...	ikh **heh**-teh gehrn / veer **heh**-tehn gehrn
...a room.	...ein Zimmer.	īn **tsim**-mer
...a ticket to ___.	...eine Fahrkarte nach ___.	ī-neh **far**-kar-teh nahkh
Is it possible?	Ist es möglich?	ist ehs **mur**-glikh
Where is...?	Wo ist...?	voh ist
...the train station	...der Bahnhof	dehr **bahn**-hohf
...the bus station	...der Busbahnhof	dehr **boos**-bahn-hohf
...the tourist information office	...das Touristen-informations-büro	dahs too-**ris**-tehn-in-for-maht-see-**ohns**-**bew**-roh
...the toilet	...die Toilette	dee toh-**leh**-teh
men	Herren	**hehr**-rehn
women	Damen	**dah**-mehn
left / right	links / rechts	links / **rehkhts**
straight	geradeaus	geh-**rah**-deh-**ows**
What time does this open / close?	Um wieviel Uhr wird hier geöffnet / geschlossen?	oom **vee**-feel oor veerd heer geh-**urf**-neht / geh-**shloh**-sehn
At what time?	Um wieviel Uhr?	oom **vee**-feel oor
Just a moment.	Moment.	moh-**mehnt**
now / soon / later	jetzt / bald / später	yehtst / bahld / **shpay**-ter
today / tomorrow	heute / morgen	**hoy**-teh / **mor**-gehn

In a German/Austrian Restaurant

English	German	Pronunciation
I'd like / We'd like...	Ich hätte gern / Wir hätten gern...	ikh **heh**-teh gehrn / veer **heh**-tehn gehrn
...a reservation for...	...eine Reservierung für...	**ī**-neh reh-zer-**feer**-oong fewr
...a table for one / two.	...einen Tisch für eine Person / zwei Personen.	**ī**-nehn tish fewr **ī**-neh pehr-zohn / tsvī pehr-zohnehn
Non-smoking.	Nichtraucher.	**nikht**-rowkh-er
Is this seat free?	Ist hier frei?	ist heer frī
Menu (in English), please.	Speisekarte (auf Englisch), bitte.	**shpī**-zeh-kar-teh (owf **ehng**-lish) **bit**-teh
service (not) included	Trinkgeld (nicht) inklusive	**trink**-gehlt (nikht) in-kloo-**zee**-veh
cover charge	Eintritt	**īn**-trit
to go	zum Mitnehmen	tsoom **mit**-nay-mehn
with / without	mit / ohne	mit / **oh**-neh
and / or	und / oder	oont / **oh**-der
menu (of the day)	(Tages-) Karte	(**tah**-gehs-) **kar**-teh
set meal for tourists	Touristenmenü	too-**ris**-tehn-meh-**new**
specialty of the house	Spezialität des Hauses	shpayt-see-ah-lee-**tayt** dehs **how**-zehs
appetizers	Vorspeise	**for**-shpī-zeh
bread / cheese	Brot / Käse	broht / **kay**-zeh
sandwich	Sandwich	**zahnd**-vich
soup	Suppe	**zup**-peh
salad	Salat	zah-**laht**
meat	Fleisch	flīsh
poultry	Geflügel	geh-**flew**-gehl
fish	Fisch	fish
seafood	Meeresfrüchte	**meh**-rehs-**frewkh**-teh
fruit	Obst	ohpst
vegetables	Gemüse	geh-**mew**-zeh
dessert	Nachspeise	**nahkh**-shpī-zeh
mineral water	Mineralwasser	min-eh-**rahl**-vah-ser
tap water	Leitungswasser	**lī**-toongs-vah-ser
milk	Milch	milkh
(orange) juice	(Orangen-) Saft	(oh-**rahn**-zhehn-) zahft
coffee / tea	Kaffee / Tee	kah-**fay** / tay
wine	Wein	vīn
red / white	rot / weiß	roht / vīs
glass / bottle	Glas / Flasche	glahs / **flah**-sheh
beer	Bier	beer
Cheers!	Prost!	prohst
More. / Another.	Mehr. / Noch eins.	mehr / nohkh īns
The same.	Das gleiche.	dahs **glīkh**-eh
Bill, please.	Rechnung, bitte.	**rehkh**-noong **bit**-teh
tip	Trinkgeld	**trink**-gehlt
Delicious!	Lecker!	**lehk**-er

APPENDIX

For more user-friendly German phrases, check out *Rick Steves' German Phrase Book and Dictionary* or *Rick Steves' French, Italian & German Phrase Book.*

INDEX

INDEX

INDEX

MAP INDEX

Explore Europe

At ricksteves.com you can browse through thousands of articles, videos, photos and radio interviews, plus find a wealth of money-saving travel tips for planning your dream trip. And with our mobile-friendly website, you can easily access all this great travel information anywhere you go.

TV Shows

Preview the places you'll visit by watching entire half-hour episodes of Rick Steves' Europe (choose from all 100 shows) on-demand, for free.

ricksteves.com

Radio Interviews

Enjoy ready access to Rick's vast library of radio interviews covering travel

tips and cultural insights that relate specifically to your Europe travel plans.

Travel Forums

Learn, ask, share! Our online community of savvy travelers is a great resource

for first-time travelers to Europe, as well as seasoned pros. You'll find forums on each country, plus travel tips and restaurant/hotel reviews. You can even ask one of our well-traveled staff to chime in with an opinion.

Travel News

Subscribe to our free Travel News e-newsletter, and get monthly updates from Rick on what's happening in Europe.

Audio Europe™

Rick Steves has

Experience maximum Europe

Save time and energy

This guidebook is your independent-travel toolkit. But for all it delivers, it's still up to you to devote the time and energy it takes to manage the preparation and logistics that are essential for a happy trip. If that's a hassle, there's a solution.

Rick Steves Tours

A Rick Steves tour takes you to Europe's most interesting places with great

great tours, too!

with minimum stress

guides and small groups of 28 or less. We follow Rick's favorite itineraries, ride in comfy buses, stay in family-run hotels, and bring you intimately close to the Europe you've traveled so far to see. Most importantly, we take away the logistical headaches so you can focus on the fun.

travelers—nearly half of them repeat customers—along with us on four dozen different itineraries, from Ireland to Italy to Athens. Is a Rick Steves tour the right fit for your travel dreams? Find out at ricksteves.com, where you can also request Rick's latest tour catalog. Europe is best experienced with happy travel partners. We hope you can join us.

Join the fun

This year we'll take thousands of free-spirited

A Guide for Every Trip

BEST OF GUIDES

Full-color guides in an easy-to-scan format. Focused on top sights and experiences in the most popular European destinations

Best of England
Best of Europe
Best of France
Best of Germany
Best of Ireland
Best of Italy
Best of Scotland
Best of Spain

COMPREHENSIVE GUIDES

City, country, and regional guides printed on Bible-thin paper. Packed with detailed coverage for a multi-week trip exploring iconic sights and venturing off the beaten path

Amsterdam & the Netherlands
Barcelona
Belgium: Bruges, Brussels, Antwerp & Ghent
Berlin
Budapest
Croatia & Slovenia
Eastern Europe
England
Florence & Tuscany
France
Germany
Great Britain
Greece: Athens & the Peloponnese
Iceland
Ireland
Istanbul
Italy
London
Paris
Portugal
Prague & the Czech Republic
Provence & the French Riviera
Rome
Scandinavia
Scotland
Sicily
Spain
Switzerland
Venice
Vienna, Salzburg & Tirol

HE BEST OF ROME

me, Italy's capital, is studded with
...an remnants and floodlit-fountain
...res. From the Vatican to the Colos-
..., with crazy traffic in between, Rome
...nderful, huge, and exhausting. The
...ds, the heat, and the weighty history

of the Eternal City where Caesars walked
can make tourists wilt. Recharge by taking siestas, gelato breaks, and after-dark
walks, strolling from one atmospheric
square to another in the refreshing evening air.

Rick Steves books are available from your favorite bookseller.
Many guides are available as ebooks.

POCKET GUIDES
Compact color guides for shorter trips

Amsterdam

Athens

Barcelona

Florence

Italy's Cinque Terre

London

Munich & Salzburg

Paris

Prague

Rome

Venice

Vienna

SNAPSHOT GUIDES
Focused single-destination coverage

Basque Country: Spain & France

Copenhagen & the Best of Denmark

Dublin

Dubrovnik

Edinburgh

Hill Towns of Central Italy

Krakow, Warsaw & Gdansk

Lisbon

Loire Valley

Madrid & Toledo

Milan & the Italian Lakes District

Naples & the Amalfi Coast

Nice & the French Riviera

Normandy

Northern Ireland

Norway

Reykjavík

Rothenburg & the Rhine

Sevilla, Granada & Southern Spain

St. Petersburg, Helsinki & Tallinn

Stockholm

CRUISE PORTS GUIDES
Reference for cruise ports of call

Mediterranean Cruise Ports

Scandinavian & Northern European
 Cruise Ports

Complete your library with...

TRAVEL SKILLS & CULTURE
*Study up on travel skills and gain
insight on history and culture*

Europe 101

Europe Through the Back Door

European Christmas

European Easter

European Festivals

Postcards from Europe

Travel as a Political Act

PHRASE BOOKS & DICTIONARIES

French

French, Italian & German

German

Italian

Portuguese

Spanish

PLANNING MAPS

Britain, Ireland & London

Europe

France & Paris

Germany, Austria & Switzerland

Iceland

Ireland

Italy

Spain & Portugal

Credits

RESEARCHERS
For help with this edition, Rick relied on...

Cameron Hewitt

Born in Denver and raised in central Ohio, Cameron settled in Seattle in 2000. Ever since, he has spent three months each year in Europe, contributing to guidebooks, tours, radio and television shows, and other media for Rick Steves' Europe, where he serves as content manager. Cameron married his high school sweetheart (and favorite travel partner), Shawna, and enjoys taking pictures, trying new restaurants, and planning his next trip.

Carrie Shepherd

After a childhood spent traipsing around New England, Carrie's college semester in London spurred her to explore and travel as much as her budget and employers allow. She's spent her career writing and editing arts and entertainment content, and now works as a guidebook editor and researcher for Rick Steves' Europe.

Cary Walker

Cary discovered international travel during college and has been feeding her wanderlust ever since. A former teacher, she believes that Europe is the best classroom for those who travel with an open mind and an adventurous spirit. When not researching guidebooks or leading Rick Steves' Europe tours, she resides in Dallas where she enjoys helping her friends plan their next European adventure.

CONTRIBUTOR

Gene Openshaw

 Gene has co-authored a dozen *Rick Steves* books, specializing in writing walks and tours of Europe's cities, museums, and cultural sights. He also contributes to Rick's public television series, produces tours for Rick Steves Audio Europe, and is a regular guest on Rick's public radio show. Outside of the travel world, Gene has co-authored *The Seattle Joke Book.* As a composer, Gene has written a full-length opera called *Matter,* a violin sonata, and dozens of songs. He lives near Seattle with his daughter, enjoys giving presentations on art and history, and roots for the Mariners in good times and bad.

ACKNOWLEDGMENTS

Rick and his staff extend sincere thanks to tour guides Ursula Klaus, Wolfgang Höfler, Lisa Zeiler, and Martin Sloboda for their help with this book.

PHOTO CREDITS

Front Cover: Hofburg Complex, Vienna © Francesco Iacobelli/AWL-Images Ltd., Getty Images

Title Page: Mozart at the Schönbrunn Palace © Dominic Arizona Bonuccelli

Public Domain via Wikimedia Commons: 294, 295, 306, 430

Additional Photography: Dominic Arizona Bonuccelli, Lisa Friend, Cameron Hewitt, David C. Hoerlein, Sandra Hundacker, Gene Openshaw, Rick Steves, Gretchen Strauch, Laura Van Deventer, Ian Watson. Photos are used by permission and are the property of the original copyright owners.

Avalon Travel
Hachette Book Group
1700 Fourth Street
Berkeley, CA 94710

Printed in Canada by Friesens.
Sixth Edition. First printing May 2019.

ISBN 978-1-64171-107-4

For the latest on Rick's talks, guidebooks, tours, public television series, and public radio show, contact Rick Steves' Europe, 130 Fourth Avenue North, Edmonds, WA 98020, tel. 425/771-8303, www.ricksteves.com, rick@ricksteves.com.

Rick Steves' Europe
Managing Editor: Jennifer Madison Davis
Assistant Managing Editor: Cathy Lu
Special Publications Manager: Risa Laib
Editors: Glenn Eriksen, Julie Fanselow, Tom Griffin, Suzanne Kotz, Rosie Leutzinger, Jessica Shaw, Carrie Shepherd
Editorial & Production Assistant: Megan Simms
Editorial Intern: Christina Ausley
Researchers: Cameron Hewitt, Carrie Shepherd, Cary Walker
Graphic Content Director: Sandra Hundacker
Maps & Graphics: David C. Hoerlein, Lauren Mills, Mary Rostad
Digital Asset Coordinator: Orin Dubrow

Avalon Travel
Senior Editor and Series Manager: Madhu Prasher
Editors: Jamie Andrade, Sierra Machado
Copy Editor: Maggie Ryan
Proofreader: Lisa Theobald
Indexer: Stephen Callahan
Production: Ravina Schneider
Cover Design: Kimberly Glyder Design
Maps & Graphics: Kat Bennett, Mike Morgenfeld

Let's Keep on Travelin'

Your trip doesn't need to end.

Follow Rick on social media!